Mathematical economics

Modern economics

Series editor: David W. Pearce

Basic econometrics
M. S. Common

Theory of the firm
M. A. Crew

The political economy of Marx
M. C. Howard and J. E. King

Environmental economics
D. W. Pearce

Microeconomics
R. Rees and H. Gravelle

Macroeconomics
A. J. Westaway and T. G. Weyman-Jones

Mathematical economics
J. E. Woods

Development economics
S. Ghatak

Economics of public transport
C. A. Nash

Economics of the labour market
D. Bosworth and P. Dawkins

Monetary economics
G. Dennis

Social economics
K. Lee and P. Mackie

Welfare economics
P. Jackson and D. T. Ulph

Mathematical economics

J E Woods

Longman
LONDON and NEW YORK

Longman Group Limited London

Associated companies, branches and representatives throughout the world

Published in the United States of America by Longman Inc., New York

First published 1978

Library of Congress Cataloging in Publication Data

Woods J. E.
Mathematical economics.
(Modern economics)
1. Economics, Mathematical. 2. Interindustry economics. I. Title.
HB135.W64 330'.01'51 77-1660
ISBN 0-582-44675-9 pbk.

Printed in Great Britain by
Richard Clay (The Chaucer Press), Ltd, Bungay, Suffolk

Contents

Preface

This book is aimed at second- and third-year undergraduates who have had some mathematical training (in linear algebra and calculus). I have tried to make the book as self-contained as possible. To this end, most of the mathematical theory required for economic analysis is derived somewhere in the book (in either the text or the exercises), with a few notable exceptions: Brouwer's Fixed-Point Theorem (Lemma A1 in the appendix to Chapter 2), the fundamental existence theorem on the solution of a system of differential equations (Theorem 2 of Chapter 4), Lyapunov's stability theorems (Theorems 17 and 18 of Chapter 4), the implicit function theorem (Theorem 7 of Chapter 6) and the Kuhn–Tucker Theorem (see 4.2 of 8.10§). The exercises form an integral part of the book. Some will, hopefully, test the reader's understanding of the (economic) theory developed in the text. Others will invite the reader to extend that theory. Finally, as mentioned above, some exercises are used to derive purely mathematical results.

Let me conclude with a brief explanation of the notation used in this book. I have tried to follow the convention of denoting scalars by lower-case greek letters, vectors by lower-case roman letters and matrices by upper-case roman letters. Of course, there are exceptions: for example, $\boldsymbol{\omega}$ (in Theorem 36 of Chapter 2) and $\boldsymbol{\lambda}$ in 8.10 are vectors. The typical element of the matrix A is denoted by a_{ij}; x_i is the typical component of the vector x. $\mathbf{1}$ denotes the vector with each component equal to unity; $\mathbf{0}$ is the zero vector and [0] the zero matrix. Occasionally, subscripts are attached to a vector or matrix to indicate the order of the vector or matrix (i.e. the number of components in the vector or elements in the matrix). Finally, a word on the representation of inequalities. $\alpha \geqslant \beta$ means α is greater than or equal to β; $x \geqq y$ means $x_i \geqslant y_i$ for all i; $x \geqslant y$ means $x_i \geqslant y_i$ for all i and $x_i \neq y_i$ for at least one i (i.e. $x \geqslant y$ means $x \geqq y$ and $x \neq y$); $x > y$ means $x_i > y_i$ for all i.

Acknowledgements

I would like to thank David Pearce for his invitation to contribute to the *Modern Economics Series*. His advice and encouragement throughout the preparation of this book has been greatly appreciated.

I am grateful to Ian Bradley of the Department of Economics, University of Leicester, for taking the time and trouble to read a draft of the book and send me his comments. Let it be clear that I claim responsibility for all errors, obscurities, etc.

I would also like to thank the editorial staff of Longman Group and the printers for their excellent work.

My greatest debt is to my wife, Anne. Without her support over a long period of time, I would not have been able to write the book. All I can do is to offer this book to her and to our children.

Finally, I take the occasion of the publication of my first (and possibly last) book to express publicly my gratitude to my parents for the considerable sacrifices they made for my benefit.

J. E. Woods
November 1976

We are grateful to Piero Sraffa for permission to reproduce extracts from his book *Production of Commodities by Means of Commodities* published by Cambridge University Press.

To Anne, Patrick Daniel and Andrew

1

Introduction

1. It will be only too evident to anyone who has read the Contents that this book is not an encyclopaedia of mathematical economics. Nor, I assert, is it a series of discussions of unrelated topics in economics. On the contrary, I have tried to present a set of connected ideas.

I wish to emphasise two types of relationships—on the one hand, those between the economic models studied, and on the other hand, those between the economic models and the mathematical theory used in their analysis.

2. Let us consider first the relations between the economic models.

2.1. We begin in Chapter 2 with the analysis of the static input–output model, which is probably the simplest type of production model. (This model is also used in Chapter 3 but for the different purpose of analysing the relation between wages, profits and prices under competition, a topic not considered in Chapter 2.)

At various stages in the book, we relax assumptions on which this model is based. For example, in §2.7, we relax the assumption that each sector has only one technique of production available; in §4.2.12 and §5.2, we introduce time lags; in §5.3, we allow the existence of capital goods (under restrictive assumptions); a proper treatment of capital goods requires the recognition of joint production, which is done in Chapter 7; and the linearity assumptions are relaxed in §6.2. So, it can be seen that the development of the analysis of production systems is one of the themes of this book.

Parallel to this, we have the analysis of a static linear expenditure system in §2.5, dynamic linear systems in §5.1 and §5.4 and a non-linear system in §6.3. The introduction of time lags and non-linearities into the multi-sector expenditure systems is analogous to their introduction into the production systems. There are two further points to be made about these production and expenditure systems. First of all, each yields an intuitively appealing matrix multiplier concept; this is, perhaps, not surprising when it is realised that the systems have similar mathematical representations, but what we are discussing here is the economic interpretation (in terms of a multiplier). Secondly, a synthesis of the production and expenditure systems can be achieved; a linear model is derived and analysed in §5.4, a non-linear model in §6.4.

2.2. An alternative synthesis of production and consumption behaviour is discussed in Chapter 8—a simple general equilibrium model is derived. Many of the models discussed earlier in the book may be regarded as special cases of the general equilibrium system; we think here of the Leontief (static input–output) model of Chapter 2, the non-linear input–output model of §6.2 and the von Neumann model of Chapter 7, all of which are primarily production systems, and the multi-country trade model of §5.1 which is an expenditure model. Similar questions are asked about the simpler models as are asked about the general model: for example, given the specification of the technology, we ask if the model can support an equilibrium (i.e. a situation in which there is no excess demand for any commodity); if the equilibrium is unique; how the equilibrium is affected by changes in tastes (i.e. comparative statics analysis); and if the equilibrium is stable. Indeed, there is an intimate connection between the last three questions, for it is only with regard to unique stable equilibria that comparative statics analysis makes sense; so conditions which guarantee a unique stable equilibrium will usually yield definite comparative statics results. So, in Chapter 8, we find the gross substitutability condition recurring in the analysis of stability, uniqueness and comparative statics; the conditions that guarantee unique non-negative solutions to the linear and non-linear static input–output models also guarantee definite comparative statics results.

3. As regards the relation between the economics and the mathematics, there are two points to be made. In **3.1**, we discuss the recurrence of similar mathematical conditions in the solution of similar economic models; and in **3.2**, we illustrate how some mathematical conditions arise naturally in economic analysis.

3.1. Just as we solve the static linear input–output model in §2.1 by the Hawkins–Simon theorem, so in §6.2.1 we solve the static non-linear input–output model by means of a generalised Hawkins–Simon theorem. Similarly, while the Perron–Frobenius theorem may be used to solve the static input–output model in §2.3, the solution of a dynamic non-linear model in §6.3 requires a generalised (i.e. non-linear) Perron–Frobenius theorem. This very point about the Perron–Frobenius theorems could be repeated with respect to the integrated production-expenditure models of §§5.4.2–5.4.4 and §6.3.2; the Frobenius root of a certain matrix (i.e. a linear mapping) provides a limit to the rate of growth in the linear model in Chapter 5, while the Frobenius root of a non-linear mapping plays the same role in providing a limit to growth in the non-linear model in Chapter 6. This discussion establishes parallels between economic models on the one hand and mathematical theorems on the other. This particular point is further illustrated by the use of P-matrices in discussing uniqueness questions, whether it is in the general equilibrium models (§8.4 and §6.2.2), or a non-linear input–output model (§6.2.1) or even a linear input–output model (§2.1).

3.2. There is a more natural relation to be observed in §8.2 in the analysis of existence of general equilibrium—that between a fixed point of a continuous mapping and an economic equilibrium; prices respond in a continuous way to excess demands; a fixed point is a culmination of the process to find a price vector corresponding to which there is no excess demand for any commodity. Likewise we may see that the diagonal dominance conditions of §2.2 arise naturally in the analysis of productive input–output systems; if we say that a system is productive (i.e. the system can satisfy more than inter-industry requirements), we are, in effect, stating the diagonal dominance conditions. If we change the units of measurement so that the gross output of each commodity is one, then the input–output coefficients are in fact the inter-industry flows. The statement that the system is productive implies that each row sum of the input–output matrix A is less than 1 (see §2.6); from the work in §2.4.5, this implies that the Frobenius root of A is less than 1. So two of the three conditions for solving the input–output model can be seen to arise naturally.

4. A final word is in order on the role of mathematics in the book. It is intended that the book be self-contained as far as possible—this explains the presence, for example, of the matrix theory in Chapter 2, the theory of differential and difference equations in Chapter 4, the theory on linear inequalities in Chapter 6 and the theory of convex sets in Chapter 7. It is also intended that most of the theory, both economic and mathematical, should be rigorously proved. Some propositions have less economic content than others and it may seem that, in their derivation, our main concern is with the mathematics; examples of this may be the relative stability theorems of Chapters 5 and 6. Proof of relative stability for a model may not imply very much; however, absence of relative stability will generally indicate that the solution of a model becomes meaningless (i.e. an essentially non-negative variable becomes negative). Accordingly, the relative stability test may be useful in deciding which models are to be rejected, rather than those which are to be accepted; other conditions, requiring more tests, might be demanded of an economic model before its acceptance.

2

Input-output and matrix theory

This chapter has the dual purpose of analysing the simplest input–output model and developing much of the mathematics (principally matrix theory) that will be required in this book. In §§2.1, 2.2 and 2.3, we are concerned with the problem of solving the model, i.e. finding conditions under which, given a non-negative vector of final demands, there is a corresponding non-negative vector of gross outputs. In §2.6, we examine the effect of a change in the final demand for only one commodity (say the k-th) on the gross output of each commodity, in the context of an indecomposable technology (which means roughly that each commodity is required either directly or indirectly in the production of every commodity); we are able to conclude that the gross output of each commodity will increase, that the largest percentage increase in gross output will be achieved by commodity k and that this percentage will be less than or equal to the percentage increase in the final demand for k. A characteristic of the simplest input–output model is that there is only one technique of production for each commodity; it is natural to enquire into the effects of relaxing this assumption—this is done in §2.7. The main result—the non-substitution theorem—may surprise some readers.

It may be thought that the problem of solving the simplest input–output model is particularly difficult, given that §§2.1, 2.2 and 2.3.3 are devoted to it. Let fears be allayed. One of the main reasons for opening the book with this input–output model is that it permits the introduction, in a very natural way, of a number of mathematical concepts that are useful not only in this chapter but also throughout the book. Our very first result in §2.1 is the Hawkins–Simon theorem, which states that the input–output model has a non-negative solution if and only if each principal minor of a certain matrix ($I-A$, I being the identity matrix, A the matrix of input–output coefficients) is positive; in short, $I-A$ is a P-matrix. Now conditions involving the signs of principal minors are notoriously difficult to interpret. Compare this with the transparent interpretation of the second necessary and sufficient condition for the solution of the input–output model which is outlined in §2.2 (see Exercises §2.2, Q13). We are talking here of our second mathematical concept—a quasi-dominant diagonal matrix.

Our third concept is that of a semi-positive matrix, each element of which is non-negative, at least one being positive; an example of such a matrix, as we shall see, is the matrix of input–output coefficients, A. Semi-positive matrices have a number of interesting properties, summarised in the Perron–Frobenius theorems of §§2.3.1 and 2.3.2—it is by no means evident that a semi-positive matrix has a non-negative characteristic root (called the Frobenius root) of greatest absolute value, with a corresponding semi-positive characteristic vector. Some unity is provided in the text by our derivation of these (Perron–Frobenius) theorems for we use the P-matrix concept and the Hawkins–Simon theorem mentioned above.(1)* In §2.3.3, we prove that a (third) necessary and sufficient condition for the solution of the input–output model is that the Frobenius root of A should be less than 1.

The importance of these three mathematical concepts is clearly demonstrated—each provides us with a necessary and sufficient condition for solution of the input–output model. Their applicability does not remain with the input–output model; for example, much uniqueness theory seems to rest on P-matrices (see §6.1.2); quasi-dominant diagonal matrices arise naturally under economic hypotheses in stability analysis (see §8.6.1); the Frobenius root and the corresponding characteristic vector provide us with a non-negative solution to some dynamic systems (for application to a linear system, see §5.3, a non-linear system see §6.3.1.). The concepts need modification before being applied to models other than input–output. In so far as this requires development of matrix theory, this theory is presented in this chapter. For example, the material on P-matrices outlined in §2.4.1 and §2.4.2 is used directly in §5.1 and §6.1; in §2.2, we summarise most of the theory of quasi-dominant diagonal matrices that will be required throughout the book; extensions of the Perron–Frobenius theory for dynamic analysis are make in §§2.3.5, 2.4.3 and 2.4.4.

§2.1 The Hawkins–Simon Theorem

Our starting point is the study of the simplest type of input–output model, the defining characteristics of which are:

(i) no joint production; each sector or industry produces one and only one commodity; thus, there is a 1–1 correspondence between sectors and commodities and we talk of the two interchangeably;

(ii) only one technique of production for each sector; the production function is of the fixed coefficients variety—to produce one unit of commodity j, sector j requires a_{ij} units of commodity i; $i,j=1,\ldots,n$;

(iii) no production lag;

* Superior numerals in (parentheses) refer to the Notes at the end of the Chapter.

(iv) no capital goods; the model does not allow for the existence of commodities which enter production repeatedly in more than one period, but contains only those commodities which cease to exist once used in the production process;
(v) no foreign trade;
(vi) no government activity.
Given these assumptions and the following notation:

x_i = gross output of sector i
x_{ij} = amount of commodity i used as input by sector j
$a_{ij} = x_{ij}/x_j$
c_i = final demand for commodity i $\quad i,j = 1, \ldots, n$

we can write the basic balance equation for each sector as:

$$x_i = \sum_{j=1}^{n} x_{ij} + c_i \qquad i = 1, \ldots, n \quad \text{or}$$

$$x_i = \sum_{j=1}^{n} a_{ij}x_j + c_i \quad \text{or}$$

$$x = Ax + c \quad \text{where} \quad A = [a_{ij}], \qquad i,j = 1, \ldots, n.$$

The coefficients relating to the production process in the j-th sector are contained in the j-th column of A. $(a_{1j}, \ldots, a_{nj})'$ is the activity vector for the j-th sector, describing the technique of production employed there. Defining $B = I - A$, we have:

$$Bx = c \qquad \cdots [1]$$

We now consider the following question: given $c \geqslant \mathbf{0}$, can we find $x \geqslant \mathbf{0}$ satisfying eqn [1]? That this question is non-trivial is illustrated by the following example:

$$A = \begin{bmatrix} \frac{1}{2} & \frac{1}{2} \\ \frac{2}{3} & \frac{1}{2} \end{bmatrix}, \qquad c = \begin{bmatrix} \frac{1}{2} \\ \frac{1}{2} \end{bmatrix}.$$

Given A and c, the solution to eqn [1] is $x = (-6 \quad -7)'$ which is not meaningful.

Hawkins and Simon considered precisely this question under the following restrictions:

(i) $b_{ii} > 0$; $b_{ij} < 0$, $i \neq j$; $i, j = 1, \ldots, n$;
(ii) $c > \mathbf{0}$.

They argued that the restriction (i) did "not involve any essential loss of generality because of the continuity of these equations with respect to variations of these coefficients".[(2)]

We now state and prove a generalised Hawkins–Simon theorem due to Nikaido.[(3)] This theorem is of interest in its own right for it provides a set of necessary and sufficient conditions for $x \geqslant \mathbf{0}$, given $c \geqslant \mathbf{0}$; it also plays the role of a fundamental lemma in the proof of the Perron–Frobenius theorem on semi-positive matrices.

Theorem 1: Consider $Bx = c$, where $b_{ij} \leqslant 0$, for all $i \neq j$. The following conditions are equivalent:

(i) Given $c > \mathbf{0}$, $x \geqslant \mathbf{0}$;
(ii) Given $c \geqq \mathbf{0}$, $x \geqq \mathbf{0}$;
(iii) The upper left-hand principal minors of B are positive;
(iv) B is a P-matrix (i.e. all principal minors of B are positive).

Proof: The proof is divided into four parts (**i–iv**). In the first three, we demonstrate the equivalence of (i)–(iii); in the fourth, we demonstrate the equivalence of (iv) to (i)–(iii).

(**i**). We prove that (i) implies (iii). We shall employ the method of mathematical induction.
Let $p(k)$ be some statement depending on the positive integer k. In this instance, let $p(k)$ be the following: "(i) implies (iii) is true for a system of order k."
$p(1)$ is valid, for the system of order 1 is just $b_{11}x_1 = c_1$. If (i) is satisfied (i.e. $x_1 \geqslant 0$ for some $c_1 > 0$), it follows that (iii) is satisfied (i.e. $b_{11} > 0$).
Now assume that $p(n-1)$ is valid and we shall show that $p(n)$ follows. This means that we are assuming that (i) holds for a system of order n and that $p(n-1)$ is valid.
By (i), eqn [1] has a solution $x \geqslant \mathbf{0}$ for some $c > \mathbf{0}$. Consider the first equation of [1]:

$$b_{11}x_1 - c_1 - \sum_{j=2}^{n} b_{1j}x_j \qquad \cdots [2]$$

The right-hand side is positive as $c_1 > 0$, $b_{1j} \leqslant 0$, $x_j \geqslant 0$, for all $j = 2, \ldots, n$. So $b_{11}x_1 > 0$. As $x_1 > 0$, we have $b_{11} > 0$. Applying elementary row operations to eqn [1], we obtain:

$$\begin{aligned} b_{11}x_1 + b_{12}x_2 + \cdots + b_{1n}x_n &= c_1 \\ b'_{22}x_2 + \cdots + b'_{2n}x_n &= c'_2 \\ \cdot \qquad \cdot \qquad &\cdot \\ \cdot \qquad \cdot \qquad &\cdot \\ \cdot \qquad \cdot \qquad &\cdot \\ b'_{n2}x_2 + \cdots + b'_{nn}x_n &= c'_n \end{aligned} \qquad \cdots [3]$$

In fact eqn [3] is obtained by adding $-b_{i1}/b_{11}$ times the first equation in [1] to the i-th equation in [1]. Let us now consider the signs of the coefficients b'_{ij}, $i, j = 2, \ldots, n$ and c'_i, $i = 2, \ldots, n$ in eqn [3].

$$b'_{ij} = b_{ij} - \frac{b_{i1}}{b_{11}} \cdot b_{1j}; \qquad c'_i = c_i - \frac{b_{i1}}{b_{11}} \cdot c_1 \qquad i, j = 2, \ldots, n. \qquad \cdots [4]$$

Given the sign conditions on b_{ij}, for all $i \neq j$, c_i and $b_{11} > 0$, we obtain: $b'_{ij} < 0$, for all $i \neq j$; $c'_i > 0$.
So the system of equations (extracted from eqn [3]):

$$\begin{bmatrix} b'_{22} & \cdots & b'_{n2} \\ \cdot & & \cdot \\ \cdot & & \cdot \\ \cdot & & \cdot \\ b'_{n2} & \cdots & b'_{nn} \end{bmatrix} \begin{bmatrix} x_2 \\ \cdot \\ \cdot \\ \cdot \\ x_n \end{bmatrix} = \begin{bmatrix} c'_2 \\ \cdot \\ \cdot \\ \cdot \\ c'_n \end{bmatrix} \qquad \cdots [5]$$

satisfies the sign conditions $b'_{ij} \leqslant 0$, for all $i \neq j$, and has a non-negative solution for a particular $(c'_2, \ldots, c'_n)'$. By the induction hypothesis, the matrix in eqn [5] has positive upper left-hand principal minors, i.e.

$$\det \begin{bmatrix} b'_{22} & \cdots & b'_{2k} \\ \cdot & & \cdot \\ \cdot & & \cdot \\ \cdot & & \cdot \\ b'_{k2} & \cdots & b'_{kk} \end{bmatrix} > 0 \qquad k = 2, \ldots, n$$

$$\text{Now } \det \begin{bmatrix} b_{11} & \cdots & b_{1k} \\ \cdot & & \cdot \\ \cdot & & \cdot \\ \cdot & & \cdot \\ b_{k1} & \cdots & b_{kk} \end{bmatrix} = \det \begin{bmatrix} b_{11} & b_{12} & \cdots & b_{1k} \\ 0 & b'_{22} & \cdots & b'_{2k} \\ \cdot & \cdot & & \cdot \\ \cdot & \cdot & & \cdot \\ \cdot & \cdot & & \cdot \\ 0 & b'_{k2} & \cdots & b'_{kk} \end{bmatrix}$$

$$= b_{11} \cdot \det \begin{bmatrix} b'_{22} & \cdots & b'_{2k} \\ \cdot & & \cdot \\ \cdot & & \cdot \\ \cdot & & \cdot \\ b'_{k2} & \cdots & b'_{kk} \end{bmatrix} \qquad \cdots [6]$$

Hence B satisfies (iii), as required.

(ii). We now prove that (iii) implies (ii). Again we use the method of induction. Let $p(k)$ be the following statement: "(iii) implies (ii) is true for a system of order k."
$p(1)$ is valid; when $k = 1$, we have $b_{11}x_1 = c_1$; if (iii) is satisfied ($b_{11} > 0$), then (ii) follows ($x_1 \geqslant 0$, for any $c_1 \geqslant 0$). Assume $p(n-1)$ is valid: we shall show that $p(n)$ follows. This means that we are assuming that (iii) holds for a system of order n and that $p(n-1)$ is valid.
By (iii), $b_{11} > 0$. So we can use elementary operations as above to transform eqn [1] into eqn [3]. Now consider eqn [5], in which the matrix satisfies the sign conditions $b'_{ij} \leqslant 0$, for all $i \neq j$. The matrix in eqn [5] satisfies (iii), as can be seen from eqn [6]. From eqn [4], $c'_i \geqslant 0$, $i = 2, \ldots, n$, for any $c_j \geqslant 0$, $j =$

$1, \ldots, n$. By the induction hypothesis, eqn [5] has a non-negative solution $(x_2, \ldots, x_n)'$ for any $(c_2', \ldots, c_n')' \geqslant \mathbf{0}$.

From eqn [2], $x_1 = (1/b_{11})\left(c_1 - \sum_{j=2}^{n} b_{1j}x_j\right) \geqslant 0$.

So, we have a non-negative solution for eqn [3] when $(c_1, c_2', \ldots, c_n')' \geqslant \mathbf{0}$. Hence eqn [1] satisfies condition (ii), as required.

(iii). To prove that (ii) implies (i) it is necessary to show only that if $c > \mathbf{0}$, then $x \neq \mathbf{0}$, which is trivial.

(iv). It is obvious that (iv) implies (iii). So, to complete the proof of the theorem, we have to show that one of (i)–(iii) implies (iv). In fact, we prove that (ii) implies (iv). Assume that (ii) is satisfied. Let S be a permutation matrix.

From eqn [1], we have: $SBx = SBS^{-1}Sx = Sc$ or

$$SBS^{-1}y = d \qquad y = Sx, \qquad d = Sc.$$

By this device, any principal sub-matrix of B can be transformed into an upper left-hand principal sub-matrix of SBS^{-1}. Note that if B satisfies the sign conditions—that all off-diagonal elements are non-positive—then so does SBS^{-1}.

Also, if $c \geqslant \mathbf{0}$, $d \geqslant \mathbf{0}$.

Conditions (ii) and (iii) are equivalent. So assuming (ii) is satisfied for eqn [1], it will be satisfied for $SBS^{-1}y = d$, where S is an arbitrary permutation matrix. Then SBS^{-1} satisfies condition (iii). As this is true for an arbitrary permutation matrix, it follows that all principal minors of B are positive. This completes the proof of the (generalised) Hawkins–Simon theorem.

At this stage, we can conveniently introduce the concept of indecomposability.

Definition 1: The square matrix A is *decomposable* if there exists a permutation matrix P such that

$$P^{-1}AP = \begin{bmatrix} A^{11} & A^{12} \\ 0 & A^{22} \end{bmatrix}$$

where A^{11} and A^{22} are square sub-matrices, not necessarily of the same order, and 0 denotes a zero sub-matrix.

The square matrix A is *indecomposable* if it is not decomposable.

The concept of decomposability has an intuitive economic interpretation which can be illustrated easily in the context of an input–output model. Let I be the set of indices relating to the rows and columns of A^{11}, J the set of indices relating to A^{22}. If A is decomposable, then no commodity indexed by an element of J enters the production of a commodity indexed by an element of I. The commodities in I are, in a sense, produced independently of those in J; however, the production of commodities in J depends on inputs of commodities in I.

A refinement of the decomposability concept is that of complete decomposability. In this case, $A^{12}=0$. In effect, we have two independent sub-economies.

We now derive an intuitively evident result for indecomposable matrices.

Theorem 2: Consider $Bx=c$, where $b_{ij} \leqslant 0$, for all $i \neq j$. Let A be an indecomposable P-matrix. Then, given $c \geqslant \mathbf{0}$, $x > \mathbf{0}$.

Proof: If A is indecomposable, so is B.
Let $I=\{k : x_k=0\}$; $J=\{k : x_k>0\}$.
Consider the r-th components of $Bx=c$, where $r \in I$:

$$\sum_{j \neq r} b_{rj}x_j = c_r \quad \text{as} \quad b_{rr}x_r = 0 \text{ by assumption.}$$

If $c_r>0$, we have an immediate contradiction as the left-hand side is non-positive, while the right-hand side is positive. If $c_r=0$, we have:

$$\sum_{j \in I} b_{rj}x_j + \sum_{j \in J} b_{rj}x_j = 0 \quad \text{or} \quad \sum_{j \in J} b_{rj}x_j = 0.$$

As $x_j>0$, for all $j \in J$, it follows that $b_{rj}=0$, for all $r \in I$, $j \in J$. This is just the definition that B is decomposable. So, again we have a contradiction. As we have derived a contradiction in each of the two possible cases, it follows that $x_j \neq 0$, for all j.

We might now refer back to the original Hawkins–Simon theorem.[3] Hawkins and Simon considered the case where $A>[0]$. Trivially, A is indecomposable. So far, we have merely stated the definition of an indecomposable matrix without deriving necessary and/or sufficient conditions for its existence. This will be rectified below.

Now, having taken a brief look at the quantity equations of the input–output model, we take a briefer look at the price equations. The pricing theory for the Leontief model states that the price of a commodity equals its unit cost of production. Let:
p_i = price of commodity i;
v_i = value added per unit of output of commodity i.
Then:

$$p_j = \sum_{i=1}^{n} p_i a_{ij} + v_j$$

or

$$p' = p'A + v'$$

or

$$B'p = v \qquad \ldots[7]$$

It can immediately be observed that the off-diagonal elements of B' are non-positive. So Theorem 1 provides with a set of equivalent conditions for a meaningful solution to eqn [7].

Theorem 3: Consider $B'p = v$, where $b_{ij} \leqslant 0$, for all $i \neq j$. The following conditions are equivalent:

(i) Given $v > \mathbf{0}$, $p \geqslant \mathbf{0}$;
(ii) Given $v \geqq \mathbf{0}$, $p \geqq \mathbf{0}$;
(iii) The upper left-hand principal minors of B' are positive;
(iv) B' is a P-matrix.

As B is a P-matrix iff B' is a P-matrix, the following theorem is evident:

Theorem 4: $Bx = c$ has a meaningful solution iff $B'p = v$ has a meaningful solution.

§2.2 Quasi-dominant diagonal matrices

In the previous section, we introduced a simple input–output model and derived necessary and sufficient conditions for a meaningful solution in terms of the signs of the principal minors of a matrix. Here, we shall develop an alternative (but equivalent) condition using the concepts of diagonal dominance. These ideas of diagonal dominance will prove useful in the analysis of models other than input–output. For this reason, we now present all the results on dominant diagonal matrices that will be relevant throughout the book and not only to input–output.

Note that in §2.1 the square matrix A was semi-positive. Here, unless otherwise stated, no restrictions are placed on the signs of the elements of A.

Definition 2: The square matrix A has a *dominant diagonal in the original sense* (abbreviated to d.d.) if

$$|a_{jj}| > \sum_{\substack{i=1 \\ i \neq j}}^{n} |a_{ij}| = Q_j \qquad j = 1, \ldots, n$$

where $|a_{ij}|$ denotes the modulus of a_{ij}.

Our definition is in terms of column sums, as will be all further definitions and theorems. Equally, we could have provided a definition in terms of row sums, i.e. A has a d.d. if

$$|a_{ii}| > \sum_{\substack{j=1 \\ j \neq 1}}^{n} |a_{ij}| = P_i \qquad i = 1, \ldots, n$$

A basic result is the following:

Theorem 5: If A has a d.d., then it is non-singular.

Proof: By contradiction.

Assume that A is singular. Then there exists $x \neq \mathbf{0}$ such that $x'A = \mathbf{0}'$. Let $|x_k| = \max_i |x_i|$. Consider the k-th equation of $x'A = \mathbf{0}'$:

$$\sum_{i=1}^{n} x_i a_{ik} = 0$$

or

$$-x_k a_{kk} = \sum_{\substack{i=1 \\ i \neq k}}^{n} x_i a_{ik}$$

Taking absolute values, we have:

$$|x_k|\,|a_{kk}| \leqslant \sum_{i \neq k} |x_i|\,|a_{ik}|$$

Dividing through by $|x_k| > 0$, we obtain:

$$|a_{kk}| \leqslant \sum_{i \neq k} \frac{|x_i|}{|x_k|} |a_{ik}| \leqslant \sum_{i \neq k} |a_{ik}| = Q_k$$

This contradicts the hypothesis that A has a d.d. Hence A is non-singular.

We can now derive:

Theorem 6 (Gersgorin): Each root of A lies in at least one of the circles: $|z - a_{jj}| \leqslant Q_j$, $j = 1, \ldots, n$ and in at least one of the circles: $|z - a_{ii}| \leqslant P_i$, $i = 1, \ldots, n$

Proof: Let λ be a root of A. Then $\det(\lambda I - A) = 0$.
If $|\lambda - a_{jj}| > Q_j$, for all j, we have:

$$|\lambda \delta_{jj} - a_{jj}| > \sum_{i \neq j} |a_{ij}| = \sum_{i \neq j} |\lambda \delta_{ij} - a_{ij}|$$

Where δ_{ij} is the Kronecker delta i.e. $\delta_{ij} = 0$ if $i \neq j$, $\delta_{ij} = 1$ if $i = j$.
So $(\lambda I - A)$ has a d.d. By Theorem 5, $(\lambda I - A)$ is non-singular.
This contradicts the fact that λ is a root of A.
Hence $|\lambda - a_{jj}| \leqslant Q_j$, some j.
The second part of the theorem can be derived by employing the definition of a d.d. matrix in terms of row sums.
Our proof follows Taussky (1949). An alternative proof is given in Brauer (1946).

Gersgorin's theorem enables us to derive the following result on a sub-class of d.d. matrices.

Theorem 7: If A has a d.d. that is negative, the real part of each root of A is negative.

Proof: Let A have a d.d. that is negative. Assume that $\mathrm{Re}(\lambda) \geqslant 0$, where λ is a root of A.
Then

$$|a_{jj} - \lambda| = |a_{jj} - \lambda\delta_{jj}| \geqslant |a_{jj}| > \sum_{i \neq j} |a_{ij}|$$

$$= \sum_{i \neq j} |a_{ij} - \lambda\delta_{ij}|$$

i.e.

$$|\lambda - a_{jj}| = |a_{jj} - \lambda| > Q_j.$$

This contradicts Gersgorin's theorem. The result follows

Theorems analogous to this under more general diagonal dominance hypotheses will be derived below and will prove useful in stability analysis. Let us now combine the two concepts of indecomposability and diagonal dominance to obtain:

Theorem 8 (Taussky): Let A be indecomposable. If $|a_{jj}| \geqslant Q_j$, for all j, with at least one strict inequality, then A is non-singular.

Proof: Let $|a_{ss}| > Q_s$. Assume that A is singular; then there exists $x \neq \mathbf{0}$ such that $x'A = \mathbf{0}'$. Then (as in Theorem 5):

$$-x_s a_{ss} = \sum_{i \neq s} x_i a_{is}$$

or taking absolute values:

$$|x_s|\,|a_{ss}| \leqslant \sum_{i \neq s} |x_i|\,|a_{is}|$$

If $|x_i| = |x_j|$, $i, j = 1, \ldots, n$, then we have:

$$|a_{ss}| \leqslant \sum_{i \neq s} |a_{is}| = Q_s$$

which is a contradiction.

So $|x_i| \neq |x_j|$, some i, j. Let $|x_k| = \max_i |x_i|$.
Let $J = \{j : |x_j| = |x_k|\}$. Considering the k-th equation of $x'A = \mathbf{0}'$, we have on taking absolute values:

$$|x_k|\,|a_{kk}| \leqslant \sum_{i \neq k} |x_i|\,|a_{ik}|$$

Dividing through by $|x_k| > 0$, we have:

$$|a_{kk}| \leqslant \sum_{i \neq k} \frac{|x_i|}{|x_k|} |a_{ik}|$$

or

$$|a_{kk}| \leqslant \sum_{\substack{i \neq k \\ i \in J}} |a_{ik}| + \sum_{i \notin J} \frac{|x_i|}{|x_k|} |a_{ik}|$$

If $|a_{ik}| \neq 0$, for some $i \notin J$, then as $|x_i| < |x_k|$ for this i, we must have:

$$|a_{kk}| < \sum_{\substack{i \neq k \\ i \in J}} |a_{ik}| + \sum_{i \notin J} |a_{ik}| = Q_k$$

This contradicts the hypothesis $|a_{jj}| \geqslant Q_j$, for all j.
So $|a_{ik}| = 0$, for all $i \notin J$. In fact, $a_{ik} = 0$, for all $i \notin J$, $k \in J$.
But this is just the definition that A is decomposable. This contradicts indecomposability of A. So our assumption that A is singular is false and the result follows.

Theorems 5–8 are basic theorems on d.d. matrices and will be used to derive further results. First, a generalisation of the d.d. concept.

Definition 3: The square matrix A has a *dominant diagonal in the extended sense* (D.D.) if there exist $d_i > 0$, $i = 1, \ldots, n$, such that:

$$d_j |a_{jj}| > \sum_{i \neq j} d_i |a_{ij}|$$

It is fairly clear to see that if A has a D.D., then $B = DA$ has a d.d., where $D = [d_i \delta_{ij}]$.

Theorem 9: If the square matrix A has a D.D., it is non-singular.

Proof: If A has a D.D., then $B = DA$ has a d.d. B is non-singular by Theorem 5. D is non-singular as $d_i > 0$, for all i. So A is non-singular.

Analogous to Theorem 8, we have:

Theorem 10: If A is indecomposable and there exist $d_i > 0$, $i = 1, \ldots, n$, such that $d_j |a_{jj}| \geqslant \sum_{i \neq j} d_i |a_{ij}|$, for all j, with at least one strict inequality, then A is non-singular.

Proof: It is evident that $B = DA$ satisfies the hypotheses of Theorem 8 and hence is non-singular. Then A is non-singular.

The most general d.d. concept is due to McKenzie.

Definition 4: The square matrix A has a *quasi-dominant diagonal* (q.d.d.) if:

(i) when A is indecomposable, there exist $d_i > 0$, $i = 1, \ldots, n$, such that $d_j |a_{jj}| \geqslant \sum_{i \neq j} d_i |a_{ij}|$, for all j, with at least one strict inequality;

(ii) when A is decomposable (i.e. $a_{ij}=0,\ i\in I,\ j\in J$, where $I\cup J=N=\{1,\ldots,n\}$, $I\cap J=\emptyset$), there exist $d_i>0,\ i=1,\ldots,n$, such that $d_j\,|a_{jj}|\geqslant \sum_{i\neq j} d_i\,|a_{ij}|$, for all j, with at least one strict inequality for $j\in J$.

Not surprisingly, our next result is a non-singularity theorem.

Theorem 11: If A has a q.d.d., A is non-singular.

Proof: (i) When A is indecomposable, the proof is the same as the proof of Theorem 10.

(ii) Let A be decomposable. As non-singularity is preserved under a similarity transformation, consider

$$P^{-1}AP=\begin{bmatrix} A^{11} & A^{12} \\ 0 & A^{22} \end{bmatrix}=\begin{bmatrix} F & G \\ 0 & H \end{bmatrix}$$

where P is a permutation matrix and where the rows and columns of $A^{11}=F$ are indexed by elements of J, the rows and columns of $A^{22}=H$ by elements of I.

By definition, $d_j\,|f_{jj}|\geqslant \sum_{i\neq j} d_i\,|f_{ij}|$, for all $j\in J$, with at least one strict inequality.
Then by Theorem 10, F is non-singular.
Now consider the columns of $P^{-1}AP$ indexed by elements of I. We have two cases to consider.
First, let $G\neq[0]$. Then, we have from Definition 4:

$$d_j\,|h_{jj}|\geqslant \sum_{\substack{i\neq j\\ i\in I}} d_i\,|h_{ij}|+\sum_{i\in J} d_i\,|g_{ij}| \quad \text{for all} \quad j\in I$$

Let $g_{rk}\neq 0$ for some $r\in J,\ k\in I$. Then we have:

$$d_k\,|h_{kk}|>\sum_{\substack{i\neq j\\ i\in I}} d_i\,|h_{ik}|$$

Combining these last two inequalities, we have the following:

$$d_j\,|h_{jj}|\geqslant \sum_{\substack{i\neq j\\ i\in I}} d_i\,|h_{ij}|, \quad \text{for all} \quad j\in I,$$

with at least one strict inequality. Then by Theorem 10, H is non-singular. Non-singularity of H and F implies non-singularity of $P^{-1}AP$ and thus of A.
The second case to consider is when $G=[0]$. Then by the definition, H is non-singular in exactly the same way as F is. Again, non-singularity of H and F implies non-singularity of A.

Analogous to Theorem 7, we have:

Theorem 12 (McKenzie): If A has a q.d.d. that is negative, the real part of each root of A is negative.

Proof: Assume $\mathrm{Re}(\lambda) \geqslant 0$, where λ is a root of A. Then

$$|a_{jj} - \lambda| \geqslant |a_{jj}|.$$

Hence,

$$d_j\ |a_{jj} = \lambda\delta_{jj}| \geqslant d_j\ |a_{jj}|.$$

As A has a q.d.d., then

$$d_j\ |a_{jj}| \geqslant \sum_{i \neq j} d_i\ |a_{ij}|, \quad \text{for all} \quad j,$$

with at least one strict inequality.
Combining these inequalities, we obtain:

$$d_j\ |a_{jj} - \lambda\delta_{jj}| \geqslant \sum_{i \neq j} d_i\ |a_{ij} - \lambda\delta_{ij}|, \quad \text{for all} \quad j,$$

with at least one strict inequality. Hence $(A - \lambda I)$ has a q.d.d. and is non-singular by Theorem 11. This contradicts the fact that λ is a root of A. So $\mathrm{Re}(\lambda) < 0$.

This theorem will enable us to derive local stability of exchange equilibrium under Walras' law. If the q.d.d. concept involving row sums is used, then the theorem corresponding to Theorem 12 enables us to derive local stability under zero homogeneity of excess demand functions.

We have strayed some distance from the simple input–output model, our justification being to present all the relevant results of dominant diagonal matrices in one section. We now show how the q.d.d. concept can be employed to solve the input–output model.

Theorem 13 (McKenzie): Let B be a square matrix with $b_{ii} > 0$, for all i, and $b_{ij} \leqslant 0$, for all $i \neq j$. Then $Bx = c$ has a unique solution $x \geqq \mathbf{0}$, given $c \geqq \mathbf{0}$, iff B has a q.d.d.

Proof:

Sufficiency: Assume that B has a q.d.d. Then B is non-singular by Theorem 11. $Bx = c$ thus has a unique solution $x = B^{-1}c$. If $c = \mathbf{0}$, $x = \mathbf{0}$. Let $N = \{1, \ldots, n\}$. Let $J = \{j : x_j < 0\} \subseteq N$. $x_j \geqslant 0$, for $j \notin J$.
Consider the i-th equation of $Bx = c$, where $i \in J$:

$$\sum_{j \notin J} b_{ij}x_j + \sum_{j \in J} b_{ij}x_j = c_i \geqslant 0$$

Multiplying by $d_i > 0$ and summing over $i \in J$, we have:

$$\sum_{i \in J} \sum_{j \notin J} d_i b_{ij} x_j + \sum_{i \in J} \sum_{j \in J} d_i b_{ij} x_j = \sum_{i \in J} d_i c_i \geqslant 0 \qquad \cdots [1]$$

Consider the first term on the left-hand side:
for $i \in J$, $j \notin J$, $b_{ij} \leqslant 0$; $x_j \geqslant 0$ for $j \notin J$; $d_i > 0$, for all i.
So this first term is non-positive.
Now consider the second term:

$$\sum_{i \in J} \sum_{j \in J} d_i b_{ij} x_j = \sum_{j \in J} \left[\sum_{i \in J} d_i b_{ij} \right] x_j$$

In particular, consider $\sum_{i \in J} d_i b_{ij}$.

By Definition 4 and given the sign conditions on the elements of B, we have:

$$d_j b_{jj} \geqslant -\sum_{i \neq j} d_i b_{ij}$$

with at least one strict inequality, or

$$\sum_{i \in J} d_i b_{ij} + \sum_{i \notin J} d_i b_{ij} \geqslant 0$$

with at least one strict inequality.

We assert that $\sum_{i \in J} d_i b_{ij} > 0$ for some $j \in J$. To derive this, assume that

$$\sum_{i \in J} d_i b_{ij} = 0, \quad \text{for all} \quad j \in J.$$

This implies that

$$\sum_{i \notin J} d_i b_{ij} \geqslant 0, \quad \text{for all} \quad j \in J.$$

As $d_i > 0$, for all i, and given that $b_{ij} \leqslant 0$, for all $i \neq j$, this implies that $b_{ij} = 0$, $i \notin J$, $j \in J$. B is then decomposable.
From Definition 4 (ii), we have:

$$\sum_{i \in J} d_i b_{ij} \geqslant 0$$

with at least one strict inequality. So

$$\sum_{i \in J} d_i b_{ij} > 0$$

for some $j \in J$ as required.
As $x_j < 0$, for all $j \in J$, we have:

$$\sum_{j \in J} \left(\sum_{i \in J} d_i b_{ij} \right) x_j < 0$$

So the left-hand side of eqn [1] is negative, while the right-hand side is non-negative. This contradiction implies that $J = \emptyset$. Hence, if $c \geqslant \mathbf{0}$, $x \geqslant \mathbf{0}$.
Necessity: Assume that $Bx = c \geqq \mathbf{0}$ has a unique solution $x \geqq \mathbf{0}$.
Let $c = \mathbf{0}$. If $Bx = \mathbf{0}$, then $B(\alpha x) = \mathbf{0}$. If the solution is unique, then $x = \mathbf{0}$.
Consider $Bx = c > \mathbf{0}$. Let $x \geqslant \mathbf{0}$ but $x \not> \mathbf{0}$. Let $x_k = 0$. Then considering the k-th equation of $Bx = c$, we have:

$$\sum_{j=1}^{n} b_{kj}x_j = c_k > 0$$

or

$$\sum_{\substack{j=1 \\ j \neq k}}^{n} b_{kj}x_j = c_k > 0$$

as $x_k = 0$.
Now the left-hand side of this equation is non-positive as $b_{kj} \leqslant 0$, for all $k \neq j$, $x_j \geqslant 0$. The resulting contradiction implies that $x > \mathbf{0}$.
So $Bx > \mathbf{0}$ implies $x > \mathbf{0}$. Transposing, $x'B' > \mathbf{0}'$ which is the condition that B' has a q.d.d. Now if B' has a q.d.d., by the first part of the theorem $B'z = f > \mathbf{0}$ has a unique solution $z > \mathbf{0}$. i.e. $B'z > \mathbf{0}$. Transposing, we have $z'B > \mathbf{0}'$, i.e. B has a q.d.d.

We can combine Theorems 1 and 13 to obtain:

Theorem 14: Let B be a square matrix with $b_{ii} > 0$, for all i, $b_{ij} \leqslant 0$, for all $i \neq j$. Then B is a P-matrix iff B has a q.d.d.

If $B = I - A$ has a q.d.d., then a positive price vector permits a semi-positive value-added vector. If B has a q.d.d. then by Theorem 14, B is a P-matrix which implies that B' is a P-matrix, so that B' has a q.d.d. by Theorem 14 again. This is merely a restatement of Theorem 4. Then a positive gross output vector permits a semi-positive net output vector.

We have so far considered two alternative approaches to the solution of the input–output model. In the next section, we shall consider a third—in terms of the roots of the input–output matrix A. The fundamental result will be the Perron–Frobenius theorem, which we shall derive by use of the Hawkins–Simon theorem.

§2.3 Perron–Frobenius theorems

§2.3.1 *The Perron–Frobenius theorem for semi-positive matrices*

Our aim is to derive the following:

Theorem 15: Let $A \geqslant [0]$ be a square matrix. There exists a non-negative root of A, denoted by $\lambda^*(A)$, and a corresponding semi-positive characteristic vector.

The proof will be based on the following lemmata:

Lemma 1: Let B be a square matrix such that $b_{ij} \leqslant 0$, $i \neq j$. Then $B^{-1} \geqslant [0]$ iff B is a P-matrix.

Proof:

Necessity: Consider $Bx = c \geqslant \mathbf{0}$. Then $x = B^{-1}c \geqslant \mathbf{0}$. This is just condition (i) of Theorem 1. Conditions (i) and (iv) are equivalent. Hence, B is a P-matrix.

Sufficiency: Again using the equivalence of (i) and (iv) of Theorem 1, we have $x = B^{-1}c \geqslant \mathbf{0}$ for any $c \geqslant \mathbf{0}$. Put $c = \mathrm{e}^i$, where e^i is the i-th unit vector. i.e. $\mathrm{e}^i = [\delta_{ij}]$, $j = 1, \ldots, n$. Hence $(B^{-1})^i \geqslant \mathbf{0}$, for all i, where $(B^{-1})^i$ denotes the i-th column of B^{-1}. So $B^{-1} \geqslant [0]$.

Definition 5: Let $A \geqslant [0]$. Define $H(A) = \{\alpha : (\alpha I - A)^{-1} \geqslant [0]\}$.

$H(A)$ is just the set of scalars α such that $\alpha I - A$ satisfies the generalised Hawkins–Simon theorem. We now derive some properties of this set.

Lemma 2: $H(A) \neq \emptyset$.

Proof: Let $x = \mathbf{1}$. For sufficiently large α, say $\alpha > \max_i \sum_j a_{ij}$, we have $\alpha x > Ax$ or $(\alpha I - A)x > \mathbf{0}$. Condition (ii) of Theorem 1 is thus satisfied. So, for this α, $(\alpha I - A)$ is a P-matrix and $(\alpha I - A)^{-1} \geqslant [0]$ by Lemma 1. Hence, $H(A) \neq \emptyset$.

Lemma 3: If $\alpha \in H(A)$, $\beta \in H(A)$ for all $\beta \geqslant \alpha$.

Proof: Given $(\alpha I - A)x \geqslant \mathbf{0}$, $\beta \geqslant \alpha$ implies $(\beta I - A)x \geqslant \mathbf{0}$. So, by condition (i) of Theorem 1, $(\beta I - A)$ is a P-matrix and $(\beta I - A)^{-1} \geqslant [0]$ by Lemma 1. Hence $\beta \in H(A)$.

Lemma 4: If $\alpha \in H(A)$, $\alpha > 0$.

Proof: Assume $\alpha \leqslant 0$. Let $c > \mathbf{0}$. Then from Definition 5, Lemma 1 and condition (ii) of Theorem 1, we have: $(\alpha I - A)x = c > \mathbf{0}$ has a solution $x \geqslant \mathbf{0}$. For $\alpha \leqslant 0$, we have an immediate contradiction.

From Lemmata 2–4, we conclude that there is a non-negative lower limit, but no upper limit, on α for $(\alpha I - A)^{-1} \geqslant [0]$.

Definition 6: Let $\lambda^*(A) = \inf\{\alpha : \alpha \in H(A)\}$. $\lambda^*(A) \geqslant 0$.

Immediately, we can derive:

Lemma 5: $\lambda^*(A) \notin H(A)$.

Proof: Assume $\lambda^*(A) \in H(A)$. Then there exists $x \geqslant \mathbf{0}$ such that $(\lambda^*(A)I - A)x > \mathbf{0}$ from condition (ii) of Theorem 1. For the same x, there exists $\gamma < \lambda^*(A)$ such that $(\gamma I - A)x \geqslant \mathbf{0}$. This implies that $\gamma \in H(A)$. This contradicts the definition of $\lambda^*(A)$ and the result follows.

Definition 7: Let $c > \mathbf{0}$. For $\alpha \in H(A)$, let $y(\alpha) = (\alpha I - A)^{-1}c$.

Lemma 6: Let $\alpha, \beta \in H(A)$, $\beta > \alpha$. Then $y(\alpha) \geqslant y(\beta)$.

Proof: $(\beta I - A)y(\beta) = c$; $(\alpha I - A)y(\alpha) = c$.
Subtracting:

$$\alpha y(\alpha) - Ay(\alpha) - \beta y(\beta) + Ay(\beta) = \mathbf{0}$$

or

$$(\alpha I - A)(y(\alpha) - y(\beta)) = (\beta - \alpha)y(\beta)$$

So

$$y(\alpha) - y(\beta) = (\beta - \alpha)(\alpha I - A)^{-1}y(\beta) \geqslant \mathbf{0}$$

Hence $y(\alpha) \geqslant y(\beta)$, as required.

Definition 8: Let $\{\alpha_\nu\}$ be a decreasing sequence of scalars in $H(A)$ such that $\lim_{\nu\to\infty} \alpha_\nu = \lambda^*(A)$.

Let $\{y(\alpha_\nu)\}$ be a corresponding sequence of vectors as in Definition 7.
Let

$$s(\nu) = \sum_{i=1}^{n} y_i(\alpha_\nu).$$

We now derive properties of the sequences $\{y(\alpha_\nu)\}$ and $\{s(\nu)\}$.

Lemma 7: (i) $\{y(\alpha_\nu)\}$ is an increasing sequence of vectors; (ii) $\{s(\nu)\}$ is an increasing sequence and $\lim_{\nu\to\infty} s(\nu) = +\infty$.

Proof: (i) This follows from Lemma 6.
(ii) By Definition 8 and (i) above, $\{s(\nu)\}$ is an increasing sequence. Assume that it is bounded from above. Then as $y(\alpha_\nu) \geqslant \mathbf{0}$, $y_i(\alpha_\nu)$ is bounded from above and tends towards $\bar{y}_i \geqslant 0$. So $\lim_{\nu\to\infty} y(\alpha_\nu) = \bar{y} \geqslant \mathbf{0}$.

Consider $(\alpha_\nu I - A)y(\alpha_\nu) = c$. As $\nu \to \infty$, we have:

$$(\lambda^*(A)I - A)\bar{y} = c, \qquad c > \mathbf{0}, \qquad \bar{y} \geqslant \mathbf{0}.$$

This implies that $\lambda^*(A) \in H(A)$, which contradicts Lemma 5. The result follows.

Definition 9: Let $x(\nu) = y(\alpha_\nu)/s(\nu)$. $x(\nu) \in S = \left\{z \geqslant \mathbf{0}\colon \sum_{i=1}^{n} z_i = 1\right\}$.

We are now in a position to prove Theorem 15.

Proof of Theorem 15: S is a closed and bounded set. Without loss of generality, assume that $\{x(\nu)\}$ converges to some $x \in S$.
Consider

$$(\alpha_\nu I - A)y(\alpha_\nu) = c$$

Dividing by $s(\nu)$, we have:

$$(\alpha_\nu I - A)x(\nu) = c/s(\nu)$$

As $\nu \to \infty$, $\alpha_\nu \to \lambda^*(A)$ and $c/s(\nu) \to \mathbf{0}$, for $s(\nu)$ increases without bound by Lemma 7 (ii). Then in the limit, we have:

$$(\lambda^*(A)I - A)x = \mathbf{0}; \qquad x \geqslant \mathbf{0}$$

or

$$Ax = \lambda^*(A)x; \qquad \lambda^*(A) \geqslant 0, \qquad x \geqslant \mathbf{0}.$$

An alternative proof, based on Brouwer's fixed point theorem, will be provided in the Appendix.

We now derive some properties of $\lambda^*(A)$.

Theorem 16: If, for $y \geqslant \mathbf{0}$, $Ay \geqq \mu y$, then $\lambda^*(A) \geqslant \mu$.

Proof: Assume $\mu > \lambda^*(A)$. Then $(\mu I - A)^{-1} \geqslant [0]$, by the structure of $H(A)$.
$\mathbf{0} \geqq (\mu I - A)y$. Pre-multiplying by $(\mu I - A)^{-1} \geqslant [0]$, we have $\mathbf{0} \geqq y$. This contradiction yields the desired result.

Theorem 17: If, for $y > \mathbf{0}$, $Ay \leqq \mu y$, then $\lambda^*(A) \leqslant \mu$.

Proof: A and A' have the same roots. So by Theorem 15, there exists $x \geqslant \mathbf{0}$ such that:

$$A'x = \lambda^*(A)x \quad \text{or} \quad x'A = \lambda^*(A)x'.$$

Post-multiplying by $y > \mathbf{0}$ yields:

$$x'Ay = \lambda^*(A)x'y \leqslant \mu x'y.$$

As $x'y > 0$, we have $\lambda^*(A) \leqslant \mu$.

Theorem 18: If, for $y \geqslant \mathbf{0}$, $Ay < \mu y$, then $\lambda^*(A) < \mu$.

Theorem 19: If, for $y \geqslant \mathbf{0}$, $Ay > \mu y$, then $\lambda^*(A) > \mu$.

The proofs of these two theorems are similar to those of Theorems 16 and 17.

Theorem 20: $\lambda^*(A) \geqslant |\lambda_i(A)|$, where $\lambda_i(A)$ denotes any root of A other than $\lambda^*(A)$.

Proof: Let $\lambda_i(A) = \lambda$ and $Az = \lambda z$.
That is

$$\lambda z_r = \sum_{j=1}^{n} a_{rj} z_j, \qquad r = 1, \ldots, n.$$

Taking absolute values, we have:

$$|\lambda|\,|z_r| \leqslant \sum_j |a_{rj}|\,|z_j| = \sum_j a_{rj}|z_j|$$

Let $|z_j| = y_j$, $j = 1, \ldots, n$. Then $y \geqslant \mathbf{0}$. So, we have:

$|\lambda| y \leqq Ay$ for $y \geqslant \mathbf{0}$.

From Theorem 16, we have $\lambda^*(A) \geqslant |\div| = |\lambda_i(A)|$.

Theorem 21: If $A \geqslant B \geqq [0]$, then $\lambda^*(A) \geqslant \lambda^*(B)$.

Proof: It suffices to show that $H(A) \subseteq H(B)$. If $\alpha \in H(A)$, then there exists $x \geqslant \mathbf{0}$ such that $\alpha x \geqslant Ax$. As $A \geqslant B \geqq [0]$, it follows that $\alpha x \geqslant Bx$ or $(\alpha I - B)x \geqslant \mathbf{0}$. So $\alpha \in H(B)$. Hence, $\lambda^*(A) = \inf_{\alpha \in H(A)} \alpha \geqslant \inf_{\alpha \in H(B)} \alpha = \lambda^*(B)$.

Theorem 22: $\lambda^*(A) \geqslant \lambda^*(C)$, where C is any principal sub-matrix of A.

Proof: Let $B = \begin{bmatrix} C & 0 \\ 0 & 0 \end{bmatrix}$ which has been obtained from A by replacing appropriate rows and columns of A by zeros and then applying a similarity transformation (viz. a permutation). $\lambda^*(B) = \lambda^*(C)$, trivially. $\lambda^*(A) \geqslant \lambda^*(B)$ by Theorem 21 and the result follows.

This completes our analysis of the roots of arbitrary semi-positive matrices; we shall now examine special classes of semi-positive matrices—namely, indecomposable, primitive and stochastic matrices.

§2.3.2 *Indecomposable matrices*

Some of Theorems 15–22 can be strengthened under the assumption that A is indecomposable. In particular, the Frobenius root, $\lambda^*(A)$, is positive, as is the associated characteristic vector.

Our first result provides us with a necessary and sufficient condition for decomposability of a matrix; this is itself useful, but it also serves as a lemma to Theorem 24.

Theorem 23: $A \geqslant [0]$ is decomposable iff $Ax \leqslant \mu x$, $\mu \geqslant 0$, $x \geqslant \mathbf{0}$ but $x \not> \mathbf{0}$.

Proof:

Necessity:

Let $B = P^{-1}AP = \begin{bmatrix} A^{11} & A^{12} \\ 0 & A^{22} \end{bmatrix}$.

By Theorem 15, $A^{11}y^1 = \lambda^*(A^{11})y^1$, $\lambda^*(A^{11}) \geqslant 0$, $y^1 \geqslant \mathbf{0}$.

So $\begin{bmatrix} A^{11} & A^{12} \\ 0 & A^{22} \end{bmatrix} \begin{bmatrix} y^1 \\ \mathbf{0} \end{bmatrix} = \lambda^*(A^{11}) \begin{bmatrix} y^1 \\ \mathbf{0} \end{bmatrix}$

or $P^{-1}APz = \mu z$ where $z = (y^1 \quad \mathbf{0})'$, $\mu = \lambda^*(A^{11})$. Let $Pz = x$. $x \geq \mathbf{0}$ but $x \not> \mathbf{0}$ as P is a permutation matrix.
Hence $Ax = \mu x$ or
$Ax \leqslant \mu x$ as required.

Sufficiency: Let $I = \{i : x_i = 0\}$, $J = \{j : x_j > 0\}$.
Consider $Ax \leqslant \mu x$, where $\mu \geq 0$, $x \geq \mathbf{0}$ but $x \not> \mathbf{0}$. For $i \in I$, we have:

$$\sum_{j=1}^{n} a_{ij} x_j \leqslant \mu x_i = 0$$

or

$$\sum_{j \in J} a_{ij} x_j \leqslant 0$$

As $a_{ij} \geq 0$, for all i, j, and $x_j > 0$, for all $j \in J$, it follows that $a_{ij} = 0$, for all $i \in I$, $j \in J$. This is just the definition that A is decomposable.

We can now strengthen the results of Theorem 15 in the indecomposable case:

Theorem 24: If $A \geq [0]$ is indecomposable, then $\lambda^*(A) > 0$ and the corresponding characteristic vector is positive.

Proof: Consider $Ax = \lambda^*(A)x$. $\lambda^*(A) \geq 0$, $x \geq \mathbf{0}$ by Theorem 15. As A is indecomposable, we conclude immediately from Theorem 23 that $x > \mathbf{0}$ (if $x \geq \mathbf{0}$ but $x \not> \mathbf{0}$, then A would be decomposable).
$\lambda^*(A) \geq 0$. Assume $\lambda^*(A) = 0$. Then we have:

$$\sum_{j=1}^{n} a_{ij} x_j = 0 \quad \text{for all} \quad i$$

As $x_j > 0$, for all j, we have $a_{ij} = 0$, for all i, j. This trivially contradicts $A \geq [0]$. Hence $\lambda^*(A) > 0$.

Theorem 21 can be strengthened to:

Theorem 25: If A is indecomposable and $A \geq B \geqq [0]$, then $\lambda^*(A) > \lambda^*(B)$.

Proof: Let $C = \frac{1}{2}(A + B)$, which is indecomposable. Let $Cz = \lambda^*(C)z$, $\lambda^*(C) > 0$, $z > \mathbf{0}$ by Theorem 24. As $A \geq C$,

$$Az \geq Cz = \lambda^*(C)z \qquad \cdots [1]$$

Let

$$y'A = \lambda^*(A)y' \qquad \cdots [2]$$

$\lambda^*(A) > 0$, $y > \mathbf{0}$ by Theorem 24. Pre-multiplying eqn [1] by y' yields:

$$y'Az > y'Cz = \lambda^*(C)y'z$$

Now $y'Az = \lambda^*(A)y'z$ from eqn [2]. Hence:

$$\lambda^*(A)y'z > \lambda^*(C)y'z.$$

As $y'z > 0$, we have $\lambda^*(A) > \lambda^*(C)$.
By Theorem 21, $\lambda^*(C) \geqslant \lambda^*(B)$ and the result follows.

Theorem 26: All principal minors, except the determinant, of $(\lambda^*(A)I - A)$ are positive.

Proof: Let $B = \begin{bmatrix} C & 0 \\ 0 & 0 \end{bmatrix}$ as in Theorem 22.
$A \geqslant B$ implies $\lambda^*(A) > \lambda^*(B) = \lambda^*(C)$ by Theorem 25. So $\lambda^*(A) \in H(C)$ which implies that $(\lambda^*(A)I - C)$ is a P-matrix. This is true for all non-trivial principal sub-matrices of A; the result follows.

With the help of this theorem, we are able to derive:

Theorem 27: $\lambda^*(A)$ is a simple root of A.

Proof: $f'_A(\lambda) = \sum_{i=1}^{n} \det(\lambda I - A^{ii})$.

For $\lambda = \lambda^*(A)$, $\det(\lambda I - A^{ii}) > 0$, for all i, by Theorem 26. If $\lambda^*(A)$ were repeated, then $f'_A(\lambda^*(A)) = 0$. As this is not so, the result follows.

Having derived a result on the Frobenius root of a semi-positive indecomposable matrix, we now derive a result on the corresponding characteristic vector.

Theorem 28: Let $A \geqslant [0]$ be indecomposable and let $Ax = \lambda^*(A)x$. x is the only possible positive characteristic vector of A.

Proof: The proof can be derived by use of the following result on arbitrary matrices which we state as a separate lemma.

Lemma 8: Let λ and μ be distinct roots of the arbitrary square matrix A. Let $Ax = \lambda x$, $y'A = \mu y'$. Then $x'y = 0$.

Proof: Pre-multiplying $Ax = \lambda x$ by y', post-multiplying $y'A = \mu y'$ by x, we obtain:

$$y'Ax = \lambda y'x$$

$$y'Ax = \mu y'x$$

Subtracting and noting that $\lambda \neq \mu$, we obtain $x'y = 0$.

We now return to the proof of the theorem.
First of all, note that $\lambda^*(A)$ is a simple root. As the geometric multiplicity of a root is less than or equal to its algebraic multiplicity, it follows that there is only one characteristic vector associated with $\lambda^*(A)$—this vector is positive by Theorem 24.
Let $y'A = \lambda^*(A)y'$, $y > \mathbf{0}$. Let $Ax^i = \lambda_i(A)x^i$, where $\lambda_i(A)$ denotes any root of A other than the Frobenius root, $\lambda^*(A)$. By Lemma 8 $x^{i\prime}y = 0$, for all i. As $y > \mathbf{0}$, it follows that no x^i could be positive (or even semi-positive). The result follows.

In the next section, we show how the theory developed here can be used in the study of the static input–output model.

§2.3.3 *The Perron–Frobenius theorem and input–output*

Let us consider again the static model:

$$x = Ax + c, \quad \text{or} \quad (I - A)x = c \qquad \cdots [1]$$

We have already developed necessary and sufficient conditions for the solution of this model in terms of the signs of the principal minors of $(I-A)$ and in terms of $(I-A)$ having a q.d.d. We now develop conditions in terms of the roots of A.

It is evident that a meaningful solution can be obtained to eqn [1] iff $(I-A)^{-1} \geqslant [0]$, which will be true iff $1 \in H(A)$. We formalise this as:

Theorem 29: Let $A \geqslant [0]$. The equation $(I-A)x = c$ has a solution $x \geqslant \mathbf{0}$ for $c \geqslant \mathbf{0}$ iff $1 > \lambda^*(A)$.

So our three sets of necessary and sufficient conditions for the existence of meaningful solutions to eqn [1] are:
(i) $I - A$ is a P-matrix.
(ii) $I - A$ has a q.d.d.
(iii) $1 > \lambda^*(A)$.
The equivalence of (i) and (iii) yields the following theorem due to Metzler (1945):

Theorem 30: Let $A \geqslant [0]$. Then $|\lambda_i(A)| < 1$ iff $I - A$ is a P-matrix.

Likewise, we can use the equivalence of (ii) and (iii) to derive another necessary and sufficient condition for $|\lambda_i(A)| < 1$. (See Exercises §2.2,Q5.)

Conditions (i)–(iii) are not easy to apply. Easily calculable sufficient conditions will be derived below.

We now use the Perron–Frobenius theorem to derive two results on the price system:

$$p' = p'A + v \qquad \cdots [2]$$

Theorem 31: There exists a price vector p which supports a uniform average value-added ratio.

Proof: Let

$$v_j = \beta_j \sum_{i=1}^{n} p_i a_{ij} \qquad j = 1, \ldots, n$$

where β_j is the ratio of value added to cost of production in the j-th sector. Let $\beta_j = \beta$, for all j. So $v = \beta A'p$. Substituting in eqn [2], we have:

$$p' = p'A + \beta p'A = (1+\beta)p'A$$

or

$$p'A = \lambda p' \quad \text{where} \quad \lambda = 1/(1+\beta) \qquad \cdots [3]$$

Eqn [3] has a solution $\lambda = \lambda^*(A) > 0$, $p \geqslant \mathbf{0}$.

$\beta = 1/\lambda^*(A) - 1$. If $\lambda^*(A) < 1$, $\beta > 0$.

So, if the model is workable (i.e. $\lambda^*(A) < 1$), the required price vector exists.

Theorem 32: There exists a price vector which supports a uniform profit rate.

Proof: We decompose the value-added vector thus:

$v = q + wl$ or $v_j = q_j + wl_j$, $j = 1, \ldots, n$

where

$q_j =$ profit per unit of output of good j

$l_j =$ unit labour coefficient in the j-th sector

$w =$ uniform wage rate

Let

$$q_j = \gamma_j\left(\sum_{i=1}^{n} p_i a_{ij} + wl_j\right)$$

or

$q' = \gamma(p'A + wl)$ assuming $\gamma_j = \gamma$, for all j.

Substituting in eqn [2], we have:

$$\begin{aligned} p' &= p'A + v' = p'A + q' + wl' \\ &= p'A + \gamma(p'A + wl') + wl' \\ &= (1+\gamma)(p'A + wl') \end{aligned}$$

or

$p'(\alpha I - A) = wl'$ $\alpha = 1/(1+\gamma)$

Now $p \geqslant \mathbf{0}$ for $wl \geqslant \mathbf{0}$ iff $(\alpha I - A)^{-1} \geqslant [0]$, which is true iff $\alpha > \lambda^*(A)$, i.e. iff $1/(1+\gamma) > \lambda^*(A)$ or

$1/\lambda^*(\mathrm{A}) - 1 > \gamma$

For $\gamma > 0$, we require $\lambda^*(A) < 1$.
Again, as in the previous theorem, if the model is workable, the required price vector exists.

§2.3.4 *Stochastic matrices*

Stochastic matrices arise particularly in probability theory; we shall be employing then in an examination of exchange equilibrium models.

Definition 10: Let $P \geqslant [0]$. P is *stochastic* iff

$$\sum_{j=1}^{n} p_{ij} = 1 \quad \text{for all} \quad i = 1, \ldots, n$$

(An equivalent definition could be given in terms of column sums.)

Theorem 33: $P \geqslant [0]$ is stochastic iff it has a root 1 with a corresponding (right) characteristic vector $\mathbf{1}$.

Proof: The proof is straightforward and is left as an exercise.

In fact, 1 is the Frobenius root of P—this will be demonstrated below when we discuss bounds for roots.

It is perhaps worth mentioning here that no assumption of decomposability/indecomposability is made about P. Yet we have been able to show that it has a positive characteristic vector (associated with the Frobenius root). So, let us emphasise that a decomposable matrix may have a positive characteristic vector associated with its Frobenius root, an indecomposable matrix will always have such a positive vector.

Theorem 34: Let $A \geqslant [0]$, with $Ax = \lambda^*(A)x$. If $\lambda^*(A) > 0$, $x > \mathbf{0}$, then $(\lambda^*(A))^{-1}X^{-1}AX = P$, where P is a stochastic matrix and $X = [x_i\delta_{ij}]$.

Proof: The (i, j)-th element of $(\lambda^*(A))^{-1}X^{-1}AX$ is

$$p_{ij} = \frac{1}{\lambda^*(A)} \cdot \frac{a_{ij}x_j}{x_i}$$

then

$$\sum_{j=1}^{n} p_{ij} = \frac{1}{\lambda^*(A)x_i} \sum_{j=1}^{n} a_{ij}x_j$$

$$= 1 \quad \text{as} \quad \sum_{j=1}^{n} a_{ij}x_j = \lambda^*(A)x_i$$

Hence P is stochastic.

Alternatively, under the hypotheses of Theorem 34, we have $X^{-1}AX = \lambda^*(A)P$. Then each row sum of $X^{-1}AX$ is equal to $\lambda^*(A)$.

Definition 11: Let $M \geqslant [0]$. If $\sum_{j=1}^{n} m_{ij} = \alpha$, for all i, then M is a *generalised stochastic* matrix. Evidently, M/α is a stochastic matrix.

Theorem 34 is valid in particular for indecomposable matrices. It is possible to derive properties of semi-positive indecomposable matrices by considering instead the stochastic and generalised stochastic matrices of Theorem 34 and Definition 11 (in fact, we do this in Theorem 36 below).

§2.3.5 *Primitive matrices*

The theory developed in §2.3.1 and §2.3.2 is sufficient for the analysis of static (input–output) models. In the study of dynamic models, it is essential to know if the indecomposable matrix A has a root equal in absolute value to the Frobenius root. Immediately, we state:

Definition 12: Let $A \geqslant [0]$ be indecomposable. A is primitive if $\lambda^*(A) > |\lambda_i(A)|$ where $\lambda_i(A)$ denotes any root of A other than the Frobenius root.
A is *imprimitive* if there exists at least one root $\lambda_i(A)$ such that $\lambda^*(A) = |\lambda_i(A)|$.

An example of a primitive matrix is given in the following:

Theorem 35: Let $A > [0]$. Then $\lambda^*(A) > |\lambda_i(A)|$.

Proof: By Theorem 20, $\lambda^*(A) \geqslant |\lambda_i(A)|$.
Assume $\lambda^*(A) = |\lambda_j(A)| = |\lambda|$ for some root $\lambda = \lambda_j(A)$. Let $Az = \lambda z$.
Consider $A(\delta) = A - \delta I$, where $\delta > 0$ is chosen such that $A(\delta) > [0]$. The roots of $A(\delta)$ are given by $\lambda_i(A) - \delta$, $i = 1, \ldots, n$, the Frobenius root being $\lambda^*(A) - \delta$. We consider separately the cases where λ is real and where λ is complex.
Assume λ is real. As $\lambda^*(A)$ is a simple root, by Theorem 27, it follows that $\lambda = -\lambda^*(A)$.
Then

$$\begin{aligned} |\lambda - \delta| &= |-\lambda^*(A) - \delta| \\ &= \lambda^*(A) + \delta > \lambda^*(A) - \delta \end{aligned}$$

This is a contradiction as $\lambda^*(A) - \delta \geqslant |\lambda_i(A) - \delta|$, for all roots of $A(\delta)$ by Theorem 20.
Now assume that λ is complex, say $\lambda = \alpha + i\beta$.
Then

$$\begin{aligned} |\lambda - \delta| &= |\alpha + i\beta - \delta| \\ &= (\alpha^2 + \beta^2 + \delta^2 - 2\alpha\delta)^{\frac{1}{2}} \qquad \cdots [1] \end{aligned}$$

$$\begin{aligned} |\lambda^*(A) - \delta| &= |\lambda^*(A) - \delta| \\ &= (\lambda^*(A)^2 + \delta^2 - 2\lambda^*(A))^{\frac{1}{2}} \qquad \cdots [2] \end{aligned}$$

Now compare the right-hand sides of eqns [1] and [2].
$\alpha^2 + \beta^2 = \lambda^*(A)^2$ by the hypothesis $|\lambda| = \lambda^*(A)$. δ^2 is common to both.

$$2\lambda^*(A)\delta > 2\alpha\delta \quad \text{as} \quad \lambda^*(A) > \alpha.$$

So the right-hand side of eqn [1] is greater than the right-hand side of eqn [2]. Hence $|\lambda - \delta| > \lambda^*(A) - \delta$.
This again contradicts the property that $\lambda^*(A) - \delta$ has the largest absolute value of any root of $A(\delta)$.
Hence, $\lambda^*(A) > |\lambda_i(A)|$, as required.

The following theorem provides us with a necessary and sufficient condition for imprimitivity of a matrix.

Theorem 36: Let $A \geqslant [0]$ be indecomposable. A is imprimitive iff there exists a permutation matrix P such that:

$$B = P^{-1}AP = \begin{bmatrix} 0 & A_{12} & 0 & \cdots & 0 & 0 \\ 0 & 0 & A_{23} & \cdots & 0 & 0 \\ \cdot & & \cdot & & & \cdot \\ \cdot & & & \cdot & & \cdot \\ \cdot & & & & \cdot & \cdot \\ 0 & 0 & 0 & \cdots & 0 & A_{k-1,k} \\ A_{k1} & 0 & 0 & \cdots & 0 & 0 \end{bmatrix}$$

where the i-th zero on the main diagonal denotes a zero square matrix of order n_i, $i = 1, \ldots, k$. (The matrix $A_{i,i+1}$ is of order $n_i \times n_{i+1}$, with the convention that $k+1$ is read as 1). $n_1 + n_2 + \cdots + n_k = n$.

Proof:

Sufficiency: Assume that $P^{-1}AP$ is as written above.
Let $By = \lambda^*(B)y$, where $\lambda^*(B) = \lambda^*(A) > 0$, $y > \mathbf{0}$.
Let $D = [y_i\delta_{ij}]$, $i, j = 1, \ldots, n$.
By Theorem 34, $C = D^{-1}BD$ is a generalised stochastic matrix with each row sum equal to $\lambda^*(A)$.

$$D^{-1}BD = \begin{bmatrix} 0 & B_{12} & 0 & \cdots & 0 & 0 \\ 0 & 0 & B_{23} & \cdots & 0 & 0 \\ \cdot & & \cdot & & & \cdot \\ \cdot & & & \cdot & & \cdot \\ \cdot & & & & \cdot & \cdot \\ 0 & 0 & 0 & \cdots & 0 & B_{k-1,k} \\ B_{k1} & 0 & 0 & \cdots & 0 & 0 \end{bmatrix}$$

$Cx = \lambda^*(C)x$, where $\lambda^*(C) = \lambda^*(B) = \lambda^*(A)$, $x = \mathbf{1}$.

We shall prove that $Cz = \lambda z$, where $\lambda = \lambda^*(A)\omega$, where $\omega = \exp(2\pi i/k)$, $i = 0, 1, \ldots, k-1$; i.e. ω is any k-th root of unity. The case $i = 0$ has already been dealt with. We shall actually prove more than is stated in the theorem for we shall derive the number of roots equal to $\lambda^*(A)$ in absolute value.

Let $z = (\mathbf{1} \quad \boldsymbol{\omega}^1 \quad \boldsymbol{\omega}^2 \quad \cdots \quad \boldsymbol{\omega}^{k-1})'$

where $\mathbf{1}$ has n_1 components, $\boldsymbol{\omega}^h$ has n_{h+1} components each equal to ω^h, $h = 1, \ldots, k-1$.

Now, consider

$$Cz = D^{-1}BDz = \begin{bmatrix} B_{12}\boldsymbol{\omega}^1 \\ B_{23}\boldsymbol{\omega}^2 \\ \cdot \\ \cdot \\ \cdot \\ B_{k-1,k}\boldsymbol{\omega}^{k-1} \\ B_{k1}\mathbf{1} \end{bmatrix} \qquad \cdots [1]$$

Now $B_{h,h+1}\boldsymbol{\omega}^h = \omega^h B_{h,h+1}\mathbf{1} = \omega^h\lambda^*(A)\mathbf{1} = \lambda^*(A)\boldsymbol{\omega}^h$. So on substituting in eqn [1], we obtain:

$$Cz = \lambda^*(A)\begin{bmatrix} \boldsymbol{\omega}^1 \\ \boldsymbol{\omega}^2 \\ \cdot \\ \cdot \\ \cdot \\ \boldsymbol{\omega}^{k-1} \\ \mathbf{1} \end{bmatrix} = \lambda^*(A)\omega \begin{bmatrix} \mathbf{1} \\ \boldsymbol{\omega}^1 \\ \boldsymbol{\omega}^2 \\ \cdot \\ \cdot \\ \cdot \\ \boldsymbol{\omega}^{k-1} \end{bmatrix} = \lambda^*(A)\omega z$$

Hence $\lambda^*(A)\omega$ is a root of C and hence of A.
As $|\lambda^*(A)\omega| = \lambda^*(A)$, for any k-th root of unity, it follows that A is imprimitive.

Necessity: Assume that A is imprimitive. Let $Ax = \lambda^*(A)x$, $\lambda^*(A) > 0$, $x > \mathbf{0}$ by indecomposability of A. Let $D = [x_i\delta_{ij}]$. Then $M = D^{-1}AD$ is a generalised stochastic matrix with each row sum equal to $\lambda^*(A)$. If A is imprimitive, then so is M. M will have a root $\lambda^*(A)\eta$, $\eta = \exp(i\theta)$.

Consider $Mz = \lambda^*(A)\eta z$. Without loss of generality, let $|z_1| = \max_j |z_j|$ and suppose

$|z_1| = |z_2| = \cdots = |z_r|$.

Consider $\lambda^*(A)\eta z_h = \sum_{j=1}^{n} m_{hj}z_j \qquad h = 1, \ldots, r$

Taking absolute values, we have:

$$|\lambda^*(A)\eta||z_h| = \lambda^*(A)|z_h| \leq \sum_{j=1}^{n} |m_{hj}||z_j| = \sum_{j=1}^{n} m_{hj}|z_j|$$
$$\leq |z_1| \sum_{j=1}^{n} m_{hj} = |z_1|\lambda^*(A) \qquad h = 1, \ldots, r$$

as M is a generalised stochastic matrix.
So, we have:

$$\lambda^*(A)|z_h| = \sum_{j=1}^{n} m_{hj}|z_j| \qquad h = 1, \ldots, r$$

Assume $r < n$. Then:

$$\lambda^*(A)|z_h| = \sum_{j=1}^{r} m_{hj}|z_j| + \sum_{j=r+1}^{n} m_{hj}|z_j|$$

It is evident that this equation will be satisfied only if $m_{hj} = 0$, $h = 1, \ldots, r$, $j = r+1, \ldots, n$. This implies that M is decomposable. Hence A is decomposable. This contradiction implies that $|z_1| = |z_2| = \cdots = |z_n|$.

Consider

$$\lambda^*(A)\eta z_u = \sum_{j=1}^{n} m_{uj}z_j \qquad u=1,\ldots,n$$

For each u, the arguments of all non-zero $m_{uj}z_j$ are equal; in fact, they are equal to the argument of $\lambda^*(A)\eta z_u$.

$$\begin{aligned}\arg(m_{uj}z_j) &= \arg(\lambda^*(A)\eta z_u) = \arg(\eta z_u)\\ &= \theta + \arg(z_u) \quad \text{where} \quad m_{uj} > 0. \qquad \cdots [2]\end{aligned}$$

Without loss of generality, put $z_1 = 1$.
Then as all components have the same absolute value, we have

$$z_u = \exp(i\theta s) \qquad u=1,\ldots,n$$

At least one element of the first column of M, say m_{l1}, is non-zero. Put $z_1 = \exp(i(k-1)\theta)$. From eqn [2]:

$$\arg(m_{l1}z_1) = \theta + \arg(z_1) = \theta + (k-1)\theta = k\theta$$

Hence $1 = \exp(ik\theta)$. z_u is then a k-th root of unity. Apply a permutation to $Mz = \lambda^*(A)\eta z$ such that $P^{-1}z$ can be written as:
$y = P^{-1}z = (\mathbf{1} \quad \boldsymbol{\omega}^1 \quad \boldsymbol{\omega}^2 \quad \cdots \quad \boldsymbol{\omega}^{k-1})'$, as in the first part of the theorem. Let $C = P^{-1}MP$.
Let

$$y_l = \omega^t, \qquad l = n_t + 1, \ldots, n_{t+1}.$$

For these l and for all j such that $y_j \neq \omega^{t+1}$, we must have $c_{lj} = 0$. Hence C is of the form:

$$\begin{bmatrix} 0 & C_{12} & 0 & \cdots & 0 & 0 \\ 0 & 0 & C_{23} & \cdots & 0 & 0 \\ \cdot & & \cdot & & & \cdot \\ \cdot & & & \cdot & & \cdot \\ \cdot & & & & \cdot & \cdot \\ 0 & 0 & 0 & \cdots & 0 & C_{k-1,k} \\ C_{k1} & 0 & 0 & \cdots & 0 & 0 \end{bmatrix}$$

We have proved that the generalised stochastic matrix M can be reduced to the required form. Given the relation between A and M, it follows that A can likewise be reduced.

This theorem provides us with a characterisation of imprimitive matrices. We now turn our attention to primitive matrices.

Theorem 37: If A is primitive, A^t is primitive for every positive integer t.

Proof: As $\lambda^*(A) > |\lambda_i(A)|$, where $\lambda_i(A)$ denotes any root of A other than the Frobenius root, we have:

$$\lambda^*(A^t) > |\lambda_i(A^t)| \quad (4)$$

So, the Frobenius root of A^t is greater than any other root of A^t in absolute value.
We have to show that A^t is indecomposable.
Suppose that A^k is decomposable. Then, we have:

$$P^{-1}A^kP=\begin{bmatrix} B & C \\ 0 & D \end{bmatrix}$$

where P is a permutation matrix.
$Ax=\lambda^*(A)x$, $\lambda^*(A)>0$, $x>\mathbf{0}$ implies $A^kx=\lambda^*(A^k)x$. So $P^{-1}A^kx=P^{-1}APP^{-1}x=\lambda^*(A^k)P^{-1}x$. Let $P^{-1}x=(z^1 \quad z^2)'>\mathbf{0}$. Then

$$\begin{bmatrix} B & C \\ 0 & D \end{bmatrix}\begin{bmatrix} z^1 \\ z^2 \end{bmatrix}=\lambda^*(A^k)\begin{bmatrix} z^1 \\ z^2 \end{bmatrix}$$

In particular,

$$Dz^2=\lambda^*(A^k)z^2. \qquad \cdots[1]$$

Also, $y'A^k=\lambda^*(A^k)y'$, $y>\mathbf{0}$. Then:
$y'PP^{-1}A^kP=\lambda^*(A^k)y'P$; let $y'P=(w^1 \quad w^2)'>\mathbf{0}$

or

$$(w^1 \quad w^2)'\begin{bmatrix} B & C \\ 0 & D \end{bmatrix}=\lambda^*(A^k)(w^1 \quad w^2)'$$

In particular,

$$w^{1\prime}B=\lambda^*(A^k)w^1 \qquad \cdots[2]$$

So, from eqns [1] and [2], $\lambda^*(A^k)$ is a repeated root of A^k, as it is a root of both B and D.
Hence it is a repeated root of A. As A is primitive, this cannot be so. Hence A^k is not decomposable, for any k.

Theorem 38: Let $A\geqslant[0]$ be indecomposable and let $\sigma>0$. Then $(\sigma I+A)^{n-1}>[0]$.

Proof: We prove that for any $x\geqslant\mathbf{0}$, $(I+A)^{n-1}x>\mathbf{0}$. Putting $x=e^i$, we obtain $((\sigma I+A)^{n-1})^i>\mathbf{0}$. Hence,
$(\sigma I+A)^{n-1}>[0]$.
Define $x^t=(\sigma I+A)^{t-1}x$, for any $x\geqslant\mathbf{0}$.
Then $x^{t+1}=(\sigma I+A)^tx=(\sigma I+A)x^t=\sigma x^t+Ax^t$.
It is evident that x^{t+1} can have a zero component only where x^t has one. Assume that all zero components are preserved, i.e. if $x_i^t=0$, then $x_i^{t+1}=0$. Without loss of generality, let $x^t=(z \quad \mathbf{0})'$, $z>\mathbf{0}$. Then

$$x^{t+1}=\sigma\begin{bmatrix} z \\ \mathbf{0} \end{bmatrix}+\begin{bmatrix} A^{11} & A^{12} \\ A^{21} & A^{22} \end{bmatrix}\begin{bmatrix} z \\ \mathbf{0} \end{bmatrix}=\begin{bmatrix} w \\ \mathbf{0} \end{bmatrix}, \qquad w>\mathbf{0}$$

So, we have:

$$\sigma z + A^{11}z = w$$
$$A^{21}z = \mathbf{0}$$

This second equation implies that $A^{21} = [0]$, i.e. A is decomposable. The contradiction implies that not all zero components are preserved. In fact, each application of $(\sigma I + A)$ to x reduces the number of zero components by at least one.
Hence $(\sigma I + A)^{n-1}x > \mathbf{0}$ for any $x \geqslant \mathbf{0}$.
i.e.
$(\sigma I + A)^{n-1} > [0]$.

Theorem 39: If $A \geqslant [0]$ is indecomposable and $a_{ii} > 0$, for all i, then $A^{n-1} > [0]$.

Proof: Choose σ such that $0 < \sigma < \min_i a_{ii}$.

Let $A = \sigma I + C$, where $c_{ij} = a_{ij}$, for all $i \neq j$; $c_{ii} = a_{ii} - \sigma$; $C \geqslant [0]$. C is indecomposable if A is. Hence by Theorem 38, $(\sigma I + C)^{n-1} > [0]$. Or $A^{n-1} > [0]$ as required.

We now introduce the following notation: let $A^t = [a_{ij}^{(t)}]$.

Theorem 40: Let $A \geqslant [0]$ be indecomposable. For any i, j, there exists $t = t(i, j)$ such that $a_{ij}^{(t)} > 0$.

Proof: We consider separately the cases $i \neq j$ and $i = j$.
First: $i \neq j$. Expanding $(I + A)^{n-1}$ by the binomial theorem:

$$(I+A)^{n-1} = A^{n-1} + (n-1)A^{n-2} + \frac{(n-1)(n-2)A^{n-3}}{2!} + \cdots$$
$$+ \frac{(n-1)(n-2)A^2}{2!} + (n-1)A + I$$

$(I + A)^{n-1} > [0]$ by Theorem 38. Hence, for any i, j $(i \neq j)$, there exists some t such that $a_{ij}^{(t)} > 0$, $1 \leqslant t \leqslant n-1$.

Second: $i = j$. By indecomposability, A cannot have a column of zeros. So, there exists k such that $a_{ki} > 0$.
If $k = i$, $a_{ii}^{(t)} > 0$, for all t, trivially.
If $k \neq i$, $a_{ik}^{(t-1)} > 0$, for some $t-1$, from the first part of the proof.
Then $a_{ii}^{(t)} = \sum_{r=1}^{n} a_{ir}^{(t-1)} a_{ri} \geqslant a_{ik}^{(t-1)} a_{ki} > 0$, as required.

With the aid of Theorems 37–40, we are now in a position to prove:

Theorem 41: Let $A \geqslant [0]$. $A^t > [0]$ for some positive integer t iff A is primitive.

Proof:
Necessity: Suppose $A^t > [0]$. Let the roots of A be
$\lambda^*(A), \lambda_2(A), \ldots, \lambda_n(A)$.

Then the roots of A^t are: $\lambda^*(A)^t, \lambda_2(A)^t, \ldots, \lambda_n(A)^t$. As $A^t > [0]$, $\lambda^*(A)^t > |\lambda_i(A)^t|$ for all $i = 2, \ldots, n$, by Theorem 35. Hence

$$\lambda^*(A) > |\lambda_i(A)|, \qquad i = 2, \ldots, n.$$

We have also to prove that A is indecomposable.
Assume that A is decomposable. Then, for some permutation matrix P, we have:

$$P^{-1}AP = \begin{bmatrix} B & C \\ 0 & D \end{bmatrix}.$$

Hence

$$(P^{-1}AP)^t = P^{-1}A^tP = \begin{bmatrix} B^t & F \\ 0 & D^t \end{bmatrix} \quad \text{for some matrix } F.$$

Then

$$A^t = P\begin{bmatrix} B^t & F \\ 0 & D^t \end{bmatrix}P^{-1} \not> [0].$$

Clearly this contradicts $A^t > [0]$. Hence A is indecomposable. Combining this statement with the earlier one—$\lambda^*(A) > |\lambda_i(A)|$— we conclude that A is a primitive matrix.
Sufficiency: Let A be primitive. Then $\lambda^*(A) > |\lambda_i(A)|$, $i = 2, \ldots, n$. Hence $\lambda^*(A)^t > |\lambda_i(A)^t|$.
As A is indecomposable, we know from Theorem 40 that there exists a positive integer t_1 such that $a_{11}^{(t_1)} > 0$
Define $A_1 = A^{t_1} = [a_{ij}(1)]$ where $a_{11}(1) = a_{11}^{(t_1)}$.
As A is primitive, so is A_1 by Theorem 37. As A_1 is indecomposable, we know from Theorem 40 that there exists a positive integer t_2 such that $a_{22}(1)^{(t_2)} > 0$.
Let $A_2 = A_1^{t_2} = A^{t_1 t_2} = [a_{ij}(2)]$. Note that $a_{11}(2) = a_{11}(1)^{(t_2)} > 0$. We repeat this argument a further $n-2$ times until we obtain a matrix $A_n = A_{n-1}^{t_n} = A^{t_1 t_2 \cdots t_n} = [a_{ij}(n)]$, where

$$a_{nn}(n-1)^{(t_n)} = a_{nn}(n) > 0.$$

By the way in which A_n has been constructed, it is clear that $a_{ii}(n) > 0$, for all $i = 1, \ldots, n$.
So we have a primitive matrix A_n with positive diagonal elements. By Theorem 39, $(A_n)^s > [0]$, for some $s \leqslant n-1$. i.e. $(A^{t_1 t_2 \cdots t_n})^s = A^t > [0]$, as required.

Theorem 39, in conjunction with Theorem 41, provides us with a sufficient condition for primitivity. Our final theorem in this section provides us with a weaker sufficient condition.

Theorem 42: Let $A \geqslant [0]$ be indecomposable. If $a_{ii} > 0$, for at least one i, then A is primitive.

Proof: Without loss of generality, let $a_{11}>0$.
By Theorem 40, $a_{1j}^{t_j}>0$, for some positive integer t_j, $j=2,\ldots,n$.

Let $t_{j1}=\min_{j=2,\ldots,n} t_j$. Then $a_{1,j1}^{t_{j1}}>0$ and in fact

$a_{1,j1}^{(\tau)}>0$, for all $\tau\geq t_{j1}$.

Let t_{j2} be the next largest of the t_j's.
Then $a_{1,j2}^{t_{j2}}>0$ and $a_{1,j2}^{(\tau)}>0$, for all $\tau\geq t_{j2}$.
Continuing in this way, we see that if $t_{jn}=\max_{j=2,\ldots,n} t_j$,

then not only $a_{1,jn}^{(t_{jn})}>0$, but also $a_{1j}^{t_{jn}}>0$, for all $j=1,\ldots,n$.
So the first row of $A^{t_{jn}}=A^s$ is positive.
By an exactly similar argument we can prove that there exists a positive integer r such that the first column of A^r is positive.
Consider A^rA^s. This is a positive matrix. So, $A^t>[0]$, for $t=r+s$. By Theorem 41, A is primitive.

§2.4. Further matrix theory

The concept of a P-matrix, besides being useful in the solution of input–output models and in the derivation of the Perron–Frobenius theorem, finds application in the stability analysis of multiple exchange systems. Hicks's perfect stability conditions are given in terms of the signs (alternately negative and positive) of the principal minors of the Jacobian matrix of excess demand functions, as we shall see below. To relate these stability conditions to the true dynamic stability conditions, we need to be able to characterise the spectrum (i.e. the set of roots) of a P-matrix. We begin this section by analysing the roots of P-matrices. Then we shall consider a sub-class of P-matrices – M-matrices, an example of which is the matrix B in Theorem 1. An M-matrix has non-positive off-diagonal elements and positive principal minors. The theory of M-matrices can be applied to the stability analysis of the gross substitute system. (The Jacobian matrix of excess demand functions has non-negative off-diagonal elements in the gross substitute case, but a simple operation enables us to use M-matrices.) Later in §2.4, we shall be examining matrices which are related to positive matrices. In particular, we shall be considering Morishima matrices, which are similar to positive matrices, and power-positive matrices which, as their name suggests, become positive when raised to a sufficiently large power. Both of these types of matrices are useful in stability analysis later on, as they enable us to derive some results on systems containing complementary commodities. Finally, we shall discuss bounds for roots; in particular, we shall derive sufficient conditions for $(\alpha I-A)^{-1}\geq[0]$, where A is semi-positive. This is of interest in the solution of input–output models and multi-sector expenditure systems. After this review, we now get down to work.

§2.4.1. *P-matrices*

As stated above, our aim is to characterise the spectrum of a P-matrix.

Theorem 43: A is a P-matrix iff each real root of A, as well as of each principal sub-matrix of A, is positive.

Proof: Assume that A is a P-matrix. Consider the characteristic equation of A:

$$f_A(\lambda)=\det(A-\lambda I)=(-\lambda)^n+b_{n-1}(-\lambda)^{n-1}+\cdots+b_1(-\lambda)+b_0=0.$$

It is well known that b_r is equal to the sum of all $(n-r)$-rowed principal minors of A. As A is a P-matrix, $b_r>0$, for all $r=0, 1, \ldots, n-1$.
Assume that A has a zero root. Putting $\lambda=0$, we obtain: $f_A(0)=b_0=0$. But $b_0>0$. So A cannot have a zero root.
Assume that A has a negative real root, say $\lambda=-\beta$, $\beta>0$.
Then

$$f_A(-\beta)=\beta^n+b_{n-1}\beta^{n-1}+\cdots+b_1\beta+b_0=0.$$

But

$$\beta^n>0 \quad\text{and}\quad b_r\beta^r>0, \quad\text{for all}\quad r=0,1,\ldots,n-1.$$

So A cannot have a negative real root. Hence, A can have only positive real roots. Similarly, by considering the characteristic equation of each principal sub-matrix of A, we can prove that the real roots of each principal sub-matrix are positive. The converse is easily proved, given that the determinant of a matrix is equal to the product of its roots.

Definition 13: A is a P_0-matrix iff all principal minors of A are non-negative.

Theorem 44: A is a P_0-matrix iff, for every positive diagonal matrix D, each real root of DA is non-negative.

Proof: Let $N=\{1,\ldots,n\}$. Let $S\subseteq N$; partition N into S and T. Denote by A^{ss} the sub-matrix of A formed by taking those rows and columns numbered by indices in S; by A^{st} the sub-matrix of those rows numbered by indices in S and columns numbered by indices in T; similarly for A^{ts} and A^{tt}.
Now assume that each real root of DA is non-negative and we have to prove that A is a P_0-matrix.
The case of $\det A^{ss}=0$ is trivial and can be dispensed with immediately. We consider the case of $\det A^{ss}\neq 0$.

Define $D(\delta)=\begin{bmatrix} I^{ss} & 0^{st} \\ 0^{ts} & \delta I^{tt}\end{bmatrix}$, $\delta>0$.

Then $D(\delta)A=\begin{bmatrix} A^{ss} & A^{st} \\ \delta A^{ts} & \delta A^{tt}\end{bmatrix}$ and $D(0)A=\begin{bmatrix} A^{ss} & A^{st} \\ 0^{ts} & 0^{tt}\end{bmatrix}$.

So the non-zero roots of $D(0)A$ are the non-zero roots of A^{ss}. Let $0<\propto<\min\limits_{\lambda}[|\lambda(A^{ss})|]$, where $\lambda(A^{ss})$ denotes a root of A^{ss}. Then as δ tends towards zero, some of the roots of $D(\delta)A$ tend towards the roots of A^{ss}, while others tend towards zero—this follows because the roots of $D(\delta)A$ are continuous functions of δ. For δ sufficiently small, those roots approaching the roots of A^{ss} will be greater than α in absolute value—call this set of roots the α-set—while the others will be less than α in absolute value. Now the real roots of $D(\delta)A$ are non-negative for $\delta>0$. Therefore, the product of the roots in the α-set is non-negative for $\delta>0$. As the roots in the α-set approach the roots of A^{ss} (as δ tends to zero), the product of the roots of A^{ss} must be non-negative. But this product equals $\det A^{ss}$. So, for $\det A^{ss}\neq 0$, we have $\det A^{ss}>0$.
It is now evident that A is a P_0-matrix.

The converse is proved in a way similar to Theorem 43.
Assume that A is a P_0-matrix and we have to prove that each real root of DA is non-negative.
Consider the characteristic equation of DA:

$$f_{DA}(\lambda)=(-\lambda)^n+c_{n-1}(-\lambda)^{n-1}+\cdots+c_1(-\lambda)+c_0=0$$

$c_0=\det DA$ and $c_r=$ the sum of all $(n-r)$-rowed principal minors of DA. As A is a P_0-matrix, so is DA. Hence, $c_r\geqslant 0$, with at least one strict inequality, $r=0,1,\ldots,n-1$.
Assume that DA has a negative real root; a contradiction is readily obtained. Hence the real roots of DA are non-negative.

The proof of the final theorem in this section employs a continuity argument similar to that used in Theorem 44.

Theorem 45: Let A be a P-matrix. Then there exists a positive diagonal matrix D such that all roots of DA are positive, real and simple.

Proof: Assume that the result is true for a matrix of order $n-1$ and we shall show that it is true for a matrix of order n.
Let A be a P-matrix. Partition A thus:

$$A=\begin{bmatrix}A^{11} & A^{12}\\ A^{21} & A^{22}\end{bmatrix}$$ where A^{11} is a square matrix of order $n-1$.

By hypothesis, there exists a diagonal matrix of order $n-1$, $D^1=[d_i^1\delta_{ij}]$, $d_i^1>0$, for all $i=1,\ldots,n-1$, such that D^1A^{11} has real, positive, simple roots.
Now define a square matrix of order n:

$$D(\rho)=\begin{bmatrix}D^1 & \mathbf{0}\\ \mathbf{0}' & \rho\end{bmatrix}$$ where $\mathbf{0}$ is of order $n-1$ and $\rho>0$.

Then $$D(\rho)A=\begin{bmatrix}D^1A^{11} & D^1A^{12}\\ \rho A^{21} & \rho A^{22}\end{bmatrix}$$ and $$D(0)A=\begin{bmatrix}D^1A^{11} & D^1A^{12}\\ \mathbf{0}' & \cdot\, 0\end{bmatrix}.$$
So the non-zero roots of $D(0)A$ are just the roots of D^1A^{11} which are positive and simple.

Now the roots of $D(\rho)A$ are continuous functions of ρ. So for sufficiently small $\rho > 0$, the real parts of the roots of $D(\rho)A$ are n distinct real numbers, of which at least $n-1$ are positive. Choosing some appropriate ρ, say $\rho = \bar{\rho}$, we observe that all the roots of $D(\bar{\rho})A$ must be distinct and real (given that the real parts are distinct and that complex roots occur in pairs), with at least $n-1$ of them positive.
Now

$$\det D(\bar{\rho})A = \det D(\bar{\rho}) \cdot \det A.$$

As A is a P-matrix and

$$\det D(\bar{\rho}) = \rho \det D^1 > 0$$

it follows that

$$\det D(\bar{\rho})A > 0.$$

The determinant of a matrix is equal to the product of its roots. We conclude that $D(\bar{\rho})A$ cannot have a non-positive root.
To complete the theorem, it remains only to observe that the case of $n-1=1$ is trivial.

§2.4.2. *N-matrices and M-matrices*

In this section, we shall be examining matrices with non-positive off-diagonal elements.

Definition 14: A is an N-matrix if $a_{ij} \leqslant 0$, for all $i \neq j$. A is an M-matrix if it is an N-matrix and a P-matrix.

An example of an M-matrix is the input–output matrix, $I-A$, of §2.2.

In Theorems 46–51, we shall be examining the following matrix:

$$C = \begin{bmatrix} b_1 & -a_{12} & \cdots & -a_{1n} \\ -a_{21} & b_2 & \cdots & -a_{2n} \\ \cdot & \cdot & \cdot & \cdot \\ \cdot & \cdot & \cdot & \cdot \\ \cdot & \cdot & \cdot & \cdot \\ -a_{n1} & a_{n2} & \cdots & b_n \end{bmatrix} \quad \text{where } a_{ij} \geqslant 0, \text{ for all } i \neq j$$

Theorem 46: Let $b_j \geqslant \sum_{\substack{i=1 \\ i \neq j}}^{n} a_{ij}$, for all j. Then C is a P_0-matrix.

Proof: By Gersgorin's theorem (Theorem 6), each root of C has a non-negative real part. As the determinant is equal to the product of the roots, it follows that $\det C \geqslant 0$.

The same argument can be applied to any principal sub-matrix of C. Hence, C is a P_0-matrix.

Theorem 47 (Ledermann): Under the hypothesis of Theorem 46, all cofactors of C are non-negative.

Proof: Denote the cofactors by C_{ij}.
$C_{ii} \geqslant 0$, from Theorem 46.
Consider C_{ij}, $i \neq j$. Expanding by the j-th row, we have:

$$C_{ij} = \sum_{k \neq j} -a_{jk} C_{ij;jk} = \sum_{k \neq j} a_{jk} C_{jj;ik} \qquad \cdots [1]$$

where $C_{ij;jk}$ are cofactors in C_{ij}.
Assume that the cofactors of order $n-2$ are non-negative.
As $a_{jk} \geqslant 0$, for all $k \neq j$, it follows from eqn [1] that $C_{ij} \geqslant 0$, for all $i \neq j$.
To complete the proof, we need to establish the proposition for a matrix of order 2. Consider

$$\begin{bmatrix} b_1 & -a_{12} \\ -a_{21} & b_2 \end{bmatrix}.$$

The cofactors are b_1, b_2, a_{12}, a_{21}, which are all non-negative.
The theorem is then proved.

It is appropriate to consider now the following theorems due to Mosak and Metzler.

Theorem 48 (Mosak): Let C be a P-matrix and $a_{ij} > 0$, for all $i \neq j$. Then $C_{ij} > 0$.

Proof: Eqn [1] above holds. Assume that the result is true for a matrix of order $n-1$. Then, as in the previous theorem, $C_{jj;ik} > 0$. Hence $C_{ij} > 0$, for all i, j. To complete the proof, the proposition needs to be established for a matrix of order 2 which is trivial.

Theorem 49 (Metzler, 1950): If $b_j > \sum_{i=j} a_{ij}$, for all j, then C is a P-matrix.

Proof: This theorem is really a corollary to Theorem 46.
The same method as employed there, in conjunction with the stronger hypothesis, yields the stronger result.
Metzler has an alternative proof.

Theorem 50 (Metzler, 1950): If $b_j < \sum_{i \neq j} a_{ij}$, for all j, then C is not a P-matrix.

Proof: Let $u_j = b_j - \sum_{i \neq j} a_{ij}$. Adding the last $n-1$ rows to the first row of C, we obtain the following matrix:

$$\begin{bmatrix} u_1 & u_2 & \cdots & u_n \\ -a_{21} & & & \\ -a_{31} & & C^{11} & \\ \cdot & & & \\ \cdot & & & \\ \cdot & & & \\ -a_{n1} & & & \end{bmatrix}$$

where C^{11} is that sub-matrix of C obtained by deleting the first row and column.
Then

$$\begin{aligned} \det C &= u_1 C_{11} + \sum_{j \neq 1} u_j C_{1j} \\ &= u_1 C_{11} + \sum_{\substack{j \neq 1 \\ k \neq 1}} u_j(-a_{k1} C_{1j;k1}) \end{aligned}$$

Assume that C is a P-matrix; then $C_{11} > 0$; $C_{11;kj} \geqslant 0$ by an argument similar to that used in Theorem 48 (if $a_{ij} \geqslant 0$, for all $i \neq j$, we cannot derive $C_{11;kj} > 0$ without further hypotheses).
As $u_j < 0$, for all $j = 1, \ldots, n$, it follows that $\det C < 0$.
Hence, C is not a P-matrix.

Theorem 51 (Metzler, 1951): If $b_j > \sum_{i \neq j} a_{ij}$, for all j, then $C_{jj} \geqslant C_{ij}$, for all $i \neq j$.

Proof: Suppose $C_{kj} = \max_i C_{ij}$, $k \neq j$.

Then considering the product of the j-th row of adj$C$ with the k-th column of C, we obtain:

$$C_{kj} b_k - \sum_{i \neq k} C_{ij} a_{ik} = 0$$

or

$$C_{kj} b_k = \sum_{i \neq k} C_{ij} a_{ik} \qquad \cdots [2]$$

As $b_j > \sum_{i \neq j} a_{ij}$, for all j, and as $C_{kj} = \max C_{ij}$, it follows that the left-hand side of eqn [2] is greater than the right-hand side. The contradiction yields the required result.

The theorems of Mosak and Metzler will be used in the analysis of multi-sector expediture systems below.

Let us now assume that A is an N-matrix with each real root positive—the reason for this asumption will become apparent later. Let $B \geqq A$.

Theorem 52: $A^{-1} \geqslant B^{-1} \geqslant [0]$.

Proof: There exists $\beta > 0$ such that $\bar{B} = I - \beta B \geqslant [0]$.
Then $\bar{A} = I - \beta A \geqslant I - \beta B = \bar{B} \geqslant [0]$. Let $\lambda^*(\bar{A})$ denote the Frobenius root of $\bar{A}$, $\lambda^*(\bar{B})$ the Frobenius root of $\bar{B}$.
Consider $\det(\bar{A} - \lambda^*(\bar{A})I) = \det[(1 - \lambda^*(\bar{A}))I - \beta A] = 0$.
By hypothesis, A has only positive real roots. So $1 - \lambda^*(\bar{A}) > 0$ or $1 > \lambda^*(\bar{A}) > 0$. Hence. $1 \in H(\bar{A})$, which implies $(I - \bar{A})^{-1} \geqslant [0]$, from §2.3.1 above.
Now $(I - \bar{A})^{-1} = (\beta A)^{-1} = \beta^{-1} A^{-1} \geqslant [0]$. So, $A^{-1} \geqslant [0]$.
From Theorem 21, $\lambda^*(\bar{A}) \geqslant \lambda^*(\bar{B})$. Hence, $1 > \lambda^*(\bar{B}) > 0$.
So $1 \in H(\bar{B})$ which implies that $(I - \bar{B})^{-1} \geqslant [0]$. Using the same argument as for A, we conclude that $B^{-1} \geqslant [0]$.
Then $B \geqslant A$ implies $A^{-1} \geqslant B^{-1} \geqslant [0]$.

Theorem 53: Each real root of B is positive.

Proof: Let $\alpha \leqslant 0$. $B \geqslant A$ implies $B - \alpha I \geqslant A$. By the previous theorem, $(B - \alpha I)^{-1}$ exists. Hence α is not a root of B.

Theorem 54: $\det B \geqslant \det A > 0$.

Proof: By induction. Assume that the result is true for matrices of order $n-1$, in particular for A^{nn} and B^{nn}. Now $B \geqslant A$ implies $A^{-1} \geqslant B^{-1} \geqslant [0]$. In particular, $(A^{-1})_{nn} \geqslant (B^{-1})_{nn} \geqslant 0$ or $\det A^{nn}/\det A \geqslant \det B^{nn}/\det B \geqslant 0$. $\det A$ and $\det B$ are both positive as each has only positive real roots. So $\det B \geqslant \det A \cdot \det B^{nn}/\det A^{nn}$. By the induction hypothesis, $\det B^{nn} \geqslant \det A^{nn}$. Hence $\det B \geqslant \det A > 0$.
It remains only to establish the result for $n = 2$.

In the remaining theorems, we assume that A is an N-matrix.

Theorem 55: Let B be an N-matrix with $B \geqslant A$. Then $B^{-1} \geqslant [0]$ iff A is an M-matrix.

Proof: $A^{-1} \geqslant [0]$ iff A is a P-matrix by Lemma 1 above. If A is a P-matrix, it has positive real roots, from Theorem 43.
Then $B^{-1} \geqslant [0]$ by Theorem 52.

Theorem 56: A is an M-matrix iff each real root of A is positive.

Proof: Let $\alpha \leqslant 0$. Then $B = A - \alpha I \geqslant A$. Then B^{-1} exists by the previous theorem and so α cannot be a root of A.

This theorem can be strengthened to:

Theorem 57: A is an M-matrix iff the real part of each root of A is positive.

Proof: We use the previous theorem, proving that each real root of A is positive iff the real part of each root of A is positive.
Assume that each real root of A is positive. Let $\alpha > 0$ such that $\alpha I - A \geq [0]$. Then the Frobenius root of $(\alpha I - A)$, $\lambda^*(\alpha I - A)$, satisfies $\lambda^*(\alpha I - A) \geq |\alpha - \lambda_i(A)|$.
There exists a real root of A, $\bar{\lambda}(A)$, such that $\lambda^*(\alpha I - A) = \alpha - \bar{\lambda}(A)$. By hypothesis, $\bar{\lambda}(A) > 0$. So:

$$\alpha - \text{Re}(\lambda_i(A)) \leq |\alpha - \lambda_i(A)| \leq \lambda^*(\alpha I - A) = \alpha - \bar{\lambda}(A) < \alpha$$

for each root $\lambda_i(A)$. This implies that $\text{Re}(\lambda_i(A)) > 0$.
The converse is obvious.

Theorem 57 is our main result on M-matrices, for which Theorems 52–56 have served as lemmata. Theorem 57 can provide us with a proof of local stability of the gross substitute system.

We conclude this section with a further result on the roots of M-matrices.

Theorem 58: Let A be an M-matrix. There exists a real root of A, $\mu(A)$, such that $\text{Re}(\lambda_i(A)) \geq \mu(A)$, where $\lambda_i(A)$ is any root of A.

Proof: There exists $\alpha > 0$ such that $\alpha I - A \geq [0]$. Let

$$\mu(A) = \alpha - \lambda^*(\alpha I - A) \qquad \cdots [3]$$

where $\lambda^*(\alpha I - A)$ is the Frobenius root of $(\alpha I - A)$. $\mu(A)$ is obviously a real root of A. As A is an M-matrix, $\mu(A) > 0$ by Theorem 56. Let $\lambda_i(A)$ be any root of A. So $\alpha - \lambda_i(A)$ is a root of $(\alpha I - A)$. Now $\alpha - Re(\lambda_i(A)) \leq |\alpha - \lambda_i(A)| \leq \lambda^*(\alpha I - A)$ by Theorem 20; from eqn [3], $\lambda^*(\alpha I - A) = \alpha - \mu(A)$. Hence,

$$\alpha - \text{Re}(\lambda_i(A)) \leq \alpha - \mu(A)$$

or

$$\text{Re}(\lambda_i(A)) \geq \mu(A).$$

§2.4.3. *Morishima matrices*

The analysis of the next class of matrices is motivated by a simple consideration—similar matrices have the same roots. In particular, the Perron–Frobenius theorem (that is, as far as it applies to the roots of a matrix) and its corollaries apply to $P^{-1}AP$, where A is semi-positive and P is any non-singular matrix. We now examine the special class of matrices defined in:

Definition 15: A is a *Morishima* matrix if:
(i) $a_{ii} > 0$, for all i;
(ii) $a_{ij} \neq 0$, for all i, j;
(iii) $\text{sign} a_{ij} = \text{sign} a_{ji}$, for all i, j;
(iv) $\text{sign} a_{ik} = \text{sign} a_{ij} a_{jk}$, $i \neq j \neq k \neq i$.

Theorem 59: The set of conditions (i)–(iv) is equivalent to either of the following sign patterns of A:

$$\begin{bmatrix} + & \cdots & + \\ \vdots & \ddots & \vdots \\ + & \cdots & + \end{bmatrix} \quad \text{or} \quad \begin{bmatrix} + & \cdots & + & - & \cdots & - \\ \vdots & \ddots & \vdots & \vdots & & \vdots \\ + & \cdots & + & - & \cdots & - \\ - & \cdots & - & + & \cdots & - \\ \vdots & & \vdots & \vdots & \ddots & \vdots \\ - & \cdots & - & + & \cdots & + \end{bmatrix}$$

Proof: By induction.
Assume that (i)–(iv) are satisfied for a system of order $n-1$. Let the sign pattern of A^{nn} be

$$\begin{bmatrix} + & \cdots & + \\ \vdots & \ddots & \vdots \\ + & \cdots & + \end{bmatrix}$$

As $\text{sign} a_{ij} a_{jn} = \text{sign} a_{in}$, for all $i = 1, \ldots, n-1$, all the elements a_{in} have the same sign, $i = 1, \ldots, n-1$. As $\text{sign} a_{in} = \text{sign} a_{ni}$ and sign $a_{nn} > 0$, it follows that A has either of the following sign patterns:

$$\begin{bmatrix} + & \cdots & + & + \\ \vdots & \ddots & \vdots & \vdots \\ + & \cdots & + & + \\ + & \cdots & + & + \end{bmatrix} \quad \text{or} \quad \begin{bmatrix} + & \cdots & + & - \\ \vdots & \ddots & \vdots & \vdots \\ + & \cdots & + & - \\ - & \cdots & - & + \end{bmatrix}$$

which are of the required form.
Now let the sign pattern of A^{nn} be:

$$\begin{bmatrix} + & \cdots & + & - & \cdots & - \\ \vdots & \ddots & \vdots & \vdots & & \vdots \\ + & \cdots & + & - & \cdots & - \\ - & \cdots & - & + & \cdots & + \\ \vdots & & \vdots & \vdots & \ddots & \vdots \\ - & \cdots & - & + & \cdots & + \end{bmatrix}$$

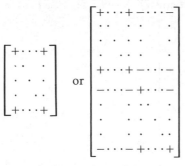

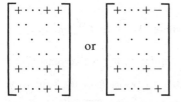

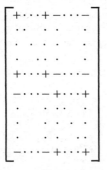

As $\operatorname{sign} a_{ij} a_{jn} = \operatorname{sign} a_{in}$, then $\operatorname{sign} a_{in} = \operatorname{sign} a_{jn}$ if $a_{ij} > 0$, and $(-1) \operatorname{sign} a_{in} = \operatorname{sign} a_{jn}$ if $\operatorname{sign} a_{ij} < 0$.
So A has either of the following sign patterns:

$$\begin{bmatrix} + \cdots + & - \cdots - & - \\ \vdots & \vdots & \vdots \\ + \cdots + & - \cdots - & - \\ - \cdots - & + \cdots + & + \\ \vdots & \vdots & \vdots \\ - \cdots - & + \cdots + & + \\ - \cdots - & + \cdots + & + \end{bmatrix} \quad \text{or} \quad \begin{bmatrix} + \cdots + & - \cdots - & + \\ \vdots & \vdots & \vdots \\ + \cdots + & - \cdots - & + \\ - \cdots - & + \cdots + & - \\ \vdots & \vdots & \vdots \\ - \cdots - & + \cdots + & - \\ + \cdots + & - \cdots - & + \end{bmatrix}$$

As the indices can be taken in any order, the second sign matrix can be reduced to the first by a simultaneous permutation of the rows and columns. So, if the result holds for a system of order $n-1$, it holds for a system of order n. As the result holds for a system of order 2, it follows that the result holds for any n. The converse is obvious.

Definition 16: Given Theorem 59, we can formulate Definition 15 as: A is a Morishima matrix if it can be written in the form:

$$\begin{bmatrix} A^{11} & A^{12} \\ A^{21} & A^{22} \end{bmatrix}$$

$A^{11} > [0]$, $A^{22} > [0]$; $A^{12} < [0]$, $A^{21} < [0]$; where A^{11} and A^{22} are square.

Theorem 60: A Morishima matrix is similar to a positive matrix.

Proof: We need only exhibit the matrix to be used in the similarity transformation.

Let $P = \begin{bmatrix} I & 0 \\ 0 & -I \end{bmatrix}$. Then $P^{-1}AP = \begin{bmatrix} A^{11} & -A^{12} \\ -A^{21} & A^{22} \end{bmatrix} > [0]$.

Theorem 61: A Morishima matrix possesses a real, simple, positive root $\lambda^*(A)$ such that $\lambda^*(A) > |\lambda_i(A)|$ and $\lambda^*(A) > a_{ii}$, for all i.

Proof: The proof follows from Theorems 35 and 60.

Theorem 62: Let A be a Morishima matrix. Let $\alpha > \lambda^*(A)$. Then $G = (\alpha I - A)^{-1}$ is of the form:

$$\begin{bmatrix} G^{11} & G^{12} \\ G^{21} & G^{22} \end{bmatrix} \quad \text{where} \quad G^{11} > [0]; \quad G^{22} > [0]; \quad G^{12} < [0]; \quad G^{21} < [0].$$

Proof: As α is not a root of A, G exists. Pre-multiplying G by P, post-multiplying by P^{-1}, where P is as defined in Theorem 60, we obtain:

$$\begin{aligned} PGP^{+1} &= P(\alpha I - A)P^{-1} \\ &= (\alpha I - \bar{A})^{-1} \quad \text{where} \quad \bar{A} = PAP^{-1} > [0] \\ &= B > [0] \text{ by Exercises §2.3.} \end{aligned}$$

Thus

$$\begin{aligned} G = P^{-1}BP &= \begin{bmatrix} I & 0 \\ 0 & -I \end{bmatrix} \begin{bmatrix} B^{11} & B^{12} \\ B^{21} & B^{22} \end{bmatrix} \begin{bmatrix} I & 0 \\ 0 & -I \end{bmatrix} \\ &= \begin{bmatrix} B^{11} & -B^{12} \\ -B^{21} & B^{22} \end{bmatrix} \end{aligned}$$

Theorem 63: Let A be a Morishima matrix and let $\alpha > \lambda^*(A)$. Then: (i) $\det(\alpha I - A) > 0$;
(ii) the sign of the cofactor of $(\alpha\delta_{ij} - a_{ij})$ is the same as the sign of a_{ij}, for all i, j.

Proof: (i) $\det(\alpha I - A) \neq 0$, as α is not a root of A.

$$\begin{aligned} \det(\alpha I - A) &= \det P \,.\, \det(\alpha I - A) \,.\, \det P^{-1} \\ &= \det P(\alpha I - A)P^{-1} \\ &= \det(\alpha I - \bar{A}) \quad \text{where} \quad \bar{A} = PAP^{-1} > [0]. \\ &> 0 \text{ by the Hawkins–Simon theorem} \end{aligned}$$

(ii) Let $B = (\alpha I - A)$. Let $G = (1/\det B) \cdot \operatorname{adj} B$.
As $\det B > 0$, the result follows by comparing the signs of

$$\begin{bmatrix} A^{11} & A^{12} \\ A^{21} & A^{22} \end{bmatrix} \quad \text{and} \quad \begin{bmatrix} G^{11} & G^{12} \\ G^{21} & G^{22} \end{bmatrix}$$

§2.4.4. *Power-positive matrices*

The analysis of power-positive matrices is motivated by two considerations: firstly, that if $Ax = \lambda x$, then $A^k x = \lambda^k x$; secondly, that the roots of a matrix are continuous functions of the elements of the matrix; so, matrices which have mainly positive elements, but some negative ones which are small absolutely, may be expected to possess some of the properties of positive matrices.

Definition 17: A is *power-positive* if there exists a positive integer k such that $A^k > [0]$.

Theorem 64: Let A be power-positive. Then there exists a real, simple root $\lambda^*(A)$ such that $|\lambda^*(A)| > |\lambda_i(A)|$, with a corresponding positive characteristic vector.

Proof: Let $A^k > [0]$. By Theorem 35, A^k has a greatest positive root. If the roots of A are $\lambda_1, \lambda_2, \ldots, \lambda_n$, then the roots of A^k are $\lambda_1^k, \lambda_2^k, \ldots, \lambda_n^k$.

Let $\lambda_1^k > \max_{i \neq 1} |\lambda_i^k|$, without loss of generality.

Hence, $|\lambda_1| > \max_{i \neq 1} |\lambda_i|$; let $\lambda_1 = \lambda^*(A)$. $\lambda^*(A^k)$ and so $\lambda^*(A)$ are simple roots by Theorem 27.
Consider $A^k x = \lambda^*(A^k)x$. $x > \mathbf{0}$ by Theorem 24.

Note that, under the hypothesis of this theorem, we cannot prove that $\lambda^*(A) > 0$. Our next two theorems will provide us with sufficient conditions for $\lambda^*(A) > 0$.

Theorem 65: Let A be power-positive of odd exponent, i.e. there exists an odd integer k such that $A^k > [0]$. Then A has a positive root of greatest absolute value.

Proof: Let $A^k > [0]$ for k odd. By Theorem 64, that root of A with greatest absolute value is real and equals the k-th root of $\lambda^*(A)^k$, i.e. $\lambda^*(A) > 0$.

Theorem 66: Let A be power-positive. If all the elements of a row or column are non-negative, then $\lambda^*(A) > 0$.

Proof: We derive the result for rows.
If A had a row of zeros, it could not be power-positive.
Assume that all the elements of the i-th row of A are non-negative (in effect, the i-th row is a semi-positive vector). Then

$$\sum_{j=1}^{n} a_{ij} x_i = \lambda^*(A) x_i.$$

$x > \mathbf{0}$, from Theorem 64.
Hence the left-hand side is positive and the result follows.

§2.4.5. *Bounds for roots*

In §2.3.3, we proved that the input–output model has a solution iff $1 > \lambda^*(A)$. As the roots of a matrix are not easy to calculate, we naturally turn now to a discussion of some of the work on deriving bounds for roots in the hope that this will provide us with useful sufficient conditions for $1 > \lambda^*(A)$ say, or more generally, $\alpha > \lambda^*(A)$. This in turn leads us to consider matrix norms.

We begin with two important results on arbitrary square matrices.

Theorem 67: $|\lambda| \leq \min(R, T)$, where λ denotes any root of the matrix A, $R = \max_i R_i$, $T = \max_j T_j$; $R_i = \sum_{j=1}^{n} |a_{ij}|$, $T_j = \sum_{i=1}^{n} |a_{ij}|$.

Proof:
By Gersgorin's theorem (Theorem 6), $|\lambda - a_{ii}| \leqslant P_i$ for some i.

$|\lambda - a_{ii}| \geqslant |\lambda| - |a_{ii}|$.

So

$|\lambda| \leqslant |a_{ii}| + P_i = R_i \leqslant R$.

Likewise, $|\lambda| \leqslant T$.

An alternative proof (due to Barankin) considers the m-th components of $Ax = \lambda x$, where $|x_m| = \max_j |x_j|$. On taking absolute values and dividing by $|x_m|$, we obtain:

$|\lambda| \leqslant R_m \leqslant R$.

By applying the same method to $y'A = \lambda y'$, we obtain $|\lambda| \leqslant T$.

We shall be concerned mainly with deriving bounds for the roots of semi-positive matrices. Before proceeding with this, we have a result which demonstrates the application of such bounds to arbitrary matrices.

Theorem 68: Let C be a complex matrix. Let $A = [|c_{ij}|]$. Then $|\lambda^*(C)| \leqslant \lambda^*(A)$, where $\lambda^*(C)$ is that root of C with greatest absolute value.

Proof: Let $\lambda^*(C)x = Cx$ or $\lambda^*(C)x_i = \sum_{j=1}^{n} c_{ij}x_j$.

Taking absolute values, we have:

$$|\lambda^*(C)|\,|x_i| \leqslant \sum_{j=1}^{n} |c_{ij}|\,|x_j| = \sum_{j=1}^{n} a_{ij}\,|x_j|.$$

Let $|x_i| = y_i$; then $y \geqslant \mathbf{0}$. So, we have:

$$|\lambda^*(C)|y \leqslant Ay \qquad y \geqslant \mathbf{0}.$$

By Theorem 16, $\lambda^*(A) \geqslant |\lambda^*(C)|$.

Theorem 69: Let $A \geqslant [0]$. Using the same definitions as in Theorem 67 and $r = \min_i R_i$, $t = \min_j T_j$, we have the following:

(i) $r \leqslant \lambda^*(A) \leqslant R$;
(ii) $t \leqslant \lambda^*(A) \leqslant T$.

Proof: (i) Let

$$y'\lambda^*(A) = y'A \quad \text{where} \quad y \geqslant \mathbf{0}, \qquad \sum_{i=1}^{n} y_i = 1,$$

or

$$\lambda^*(A)y_j = \sum_{i=1}^{n} y_i a_{ij}$$

Summing over j, we obtain:

$$\sum_{j=1}^{n} \lambda^*(A)y_j = \lambda^*(A) \sum_{j=1}^{n} y_j = \lambda^*(A)$$

$$= \sum_i \sum_j y_i a_{ij} = \sum_i y_i \sum_j a_{ij}$$

i.e.

$$\lambda^*(A) = \sum_i y_i R_i$$

The result then follows, as $\lambda^*(A)$ is a weighted average of the row sums.

(ii) Apply a similar method to the equation $Ax = \lambda^*(A)x$, where $x \geqslant \mathbf{0}$, $\sum_{i=1}^{n} x_i = 1$.

This result can be strengthened to:

Theorem 70: Let A be indecomposable. Then:
(i) $\lambda^*(A) = T$ implies that $\lambda^*(A) = t$;
(ii) $\lambda^*(A) = R$ implies that $\lambda^*(A) = r$.

Proof: (i) From Theorem 69 (ii), we have:

$$\sum_{j=1}^{n} x_j T_j = \lambda^*(A) \sum_{j=1}^{n} x_j$$

or

$$\sum_{j=1}^{n} (\lambda^*(A) - T_j)x_j = 0$$

If $\lambda^*(A) = T$, then $\lambda^*(A) - T_j \geqslant 0$, for all j. But $x_j > 0$, for all j. So, we must have $\lambda^*(A) = T_j$ for all j.

(ii) Similar to (i).

For further work on the bounds of positive and semi-positive indecomposable matrices, the reader might consult the papers of Ledermann, Ostrowski, et al., mentioned in the references.

We now show how our results on bounds can be used to derive sufficient conditions for the solution of the input–output model. For a meaningful solution to the static input–output model

$$x = Ax + c \qquad A \geqslant [0] \qquad \cdots [1]$$

we require $(I - A)^{-1} \geqslant [0]$. From §2.3.3 above, we know that $(I - A)^{-1} \geqslant [0]$ iff $1 > \lambda^*(A)$. In this section, we shall derive easily calculable sufficient conditions for $1 > \lambda^*(A)$. Our input–output model can be considered as a special case of:

$$\alpha x = Ax + c \qquad \cdots [2]$$

We concentrate on deriving a sufficient condition for

$(\alpha I - A)^{-1} \geqslant [0]$.

Theorem 71: Either (i) $\alpha > R_i$, for all i, or (ii) $\alpha > T_j$, for all j, is sufficient for $(\alpha I - A)^{-1} \geqslant [0]$.

Proof: Let $c_i = \alpha - R_i > 0$, $i = 1, \ldots, n$. For this vector $c = (c_1, \ldots, c_n)'$, $x = \mathbf{1}$ solves eqn [2]. $(\alpha I - A)$ is a P-matrix by Theorem 1 and $(\alpha I - A)^{-1} \geqslant [0]$ by Lemma 1. This proves that (i) is sufficient for $(\alpha I - A)^{-1} \geqslant [0]$.
Now let $c_i = \alpha - T_i > 0, i = 1, \ldots, n$. For this c, $y = \mathbf{1}$ solves $y = A'y + c$. Hence, $(\alpha I - A')^{-1} \geqslant [0]$ by Theorem 1 and Lemma 1. But $(\alpha I - A')^{-1} \geqslant [0]$ iff $(\alpha I - A)^{-1} \geqslant [0]$.
So, (ii) is sufficient for $(\alpha I - A)^{-1} \geqslant [0]$.

Returning to eqn [1], we can state that if each row sum or column sum of A is less than 1, $(I - A)^{-1} \geqslant [0]$. To demonstrate that this condition is not necessary, consider the following matrix:

$$A = \begin{bmatrix} \frac{1}{6} & 2 \\ \frac{1}{3} & \frac{1}{6} \end{bmatrix}$$

Neither the row sum nor the column sum condition is satisfied, but

$$(I - A)^{-1} = \begin{bmatrix} 30 & 72 \\ 24 & 30 \end{bmatrix}$$

Theorem 71 can be strengthened to:

Theorem 72: Let A be a semi-positive indecomposable matrix. Either (i) $\alpha \geqslant R_i$, for all i, with at least one strict inequality, or (ii) $\alpha \geqslant T_j$, for all j, with at least one strict inequality, is sufficient for $(\alpha I - A)^{-1} \geqslant [0]$.

Proof: (i) Consider

$$y'A = \lambda^*(A)y', \qquad \lambda^*(A) > 0, \qquad y > \mathbf{0}, \qquad \sum_{i=1}^{n} y_i = 1,$$

or

$$\sum_{i=1}^{n} y_i a_{ij} = \lambda^*(A) y_j.$$

Summing over j:

$$\begin{aligned} \sum_{j=1}^{n} \lambda^*(A) y_j = \lambda^*(A) \sum_{j=1}^{n} y_j &= \lambda^*(A) \\ = \sum_j \sum_i y_i a_{ij} &= \sum_i y_i \sum_j a_{ij} \\ = \sum_i y_i R_i &< \alpha \sum_i y_i < \alpha \end{aligned}$$

So, $\lambda^*(A) < \alpha$, which implies that $(\alpha I - A)^{-1} \geqslant [0]$.

(ii) Apply the same method to the equation $Ax = \lambda^*(A)x$, where $\lambda^*(A) > 0$, $x > \mathbf{0}$, $\sum_{i=1}^{n} x_i = 1$.

We have derived upper and lower bounds for $\lambda^*(A)$ in terms of the row and column sums of A. It is possible to generalise this by introducing the concept of a matrix norm, of which the largest row and column sums are examples. The usefulness of the row and column sum conditions lies in the relative ease of their computation, a comment which applies to many matrix norms.
Note that we now drop any sign restrictions on A.

Definition 18: Let A and B be arbitrary $n \times n$ matrices. The real-valued function $\|A\|$ is a *matrix norm* if:

(i) $\|A\| \geqslant 0$ with $\|A\| = 0$ iff $A = [0]$;
(ii) $\|\alpha A\| = |\alpha| \,.\, \|A\|$;
(iii) $\|A + B\| \leqslant \|A\| + \|B\|$;
(iv) $\|AB\| \leqslant \|A\| \,.\, \|B\|$.

Examples of matrix norms are:

(a) $\max_j \sum_i |a_{ij}|$; (b) $\max_i \sum_j |a_{ij}|$; (c) $\sum_i \sum_j |a_{ij}|$;

(d) $\left(\sum_i \sum_j |a_{ij}|^2\right)^{1/2}$; (e) $n \,.\, \max_{i,j} |a_{ij}|$; (f) $\left(\sum_i \sum_j |a_{ij}|^p\right)^{1/p}$, $1 \leqslant p \leqslant 2$.

The following theorem is fundamental:

Theorem 73: Let $|\lambda_1(A)| = \max_i |\lambda_i(A)|$. Then for any matrix norm, $\|A\| \geqslant |\lambda_1(A)|$.

Proof: Let $Ax = \lambda_1(A)x$. Define $X = [x \quad \mathbf{0} \quad \mathbf{0} \cdots \mathbf{0}]$ to be of order n. Then $AX = \lambda_1(A)X$.
From (ii) and (iv) of Definition 17, we have:

$|\lambda_1(A)| \,.\, \|X\| \leqslant \|A\| \,.\, \|X\|$

As $X \neq [0]$, $\|X\| > 0$. So, dividing by $\|X\|$ yields:

$|\lambda_1(A)| \leqslant \|A\|$ as required.

This result justifies the use of the theory of norms. Another useful result is the following:

Theorem 74: $N(A) = \|P^{-1}AP\|$ is a matrix norm, for any matrix norm $\| \quad \|$ and any non-singular matrix P.

Proof: It is easy to verify (i) and (ii) of Definition 17. Then

$$N(A+B)=\|P^{-1}(A+B)P\|=\|P^{-1}AP+P^{-1}BP\|$$
$$\leqslant\|P^{-1}AP\|+\|P^{-1}BP\| \text{ by (iii)}$$
$$=N(A)+N(B)$$

$$N(AB)=\|P^{-1}ABP\|=\|P^{-1}APP^{-1}BP\|\leqslant\|P^{-1}AP\|\cdot\|P^{-1}BP\|=N(A)\cdot N(B).$$

So $N(A)$ satisfies (i) to (iv) of Definition 18 and is a matrix norm.

§2.5. Stochastic matrices revisited

With the help of some results on bounds for roots, we can complete our discussion of stochastic matrices begun in §2.3.4.

Theorem 75: Let $A\geqslant[0]$ be stochastic. Then 1 is the Frobenius root of A.

Proof: From Theorem 69, we have $r\leqslant\lambda^*(A)\leqslant R$. As $r=R=1$, it follows that $\lambda^*(A)=1$.

We now discuss somc applications of stochastic matriccs. Thc input–output model which we have been considering so far is an open model—the final demand vector, which might be thought of as consumption by households, is exogenous. Now, let households be considered as an industry, supplying labour inputs to other industries, receiving the products of other industries as components of the (subsistence) wage basket. Assume that there are no flows of goods into or out of the economy. We then have:

$$\sum_{j=1}^{n} x_{ij}=x_i \qquad i=1,\ldots,n$$

where households are considered as the n-th industry, say. Using the input–output coefficients, this last equation can be written as:

$$Ax=x$$

A thus has a root equal to 1. It is evident that if we redefine our units of measurement so that the gross output of each sector is equal to one, we obtain:

$$D^{-1}AD\mathbf{1}=\mathbf{1} \quad \text{where} \quad D=[x_i\delta_{ij}], \qquad x_i>0, \text{ for all } i,$$

or

$$M\mathbf{1}=\mathbf{1}$$

where $M=D^{-1}AD$ is a stochastic matrix.
Now let us consider the price equations. As there is no surplus, price is equal to cost of production:

$$p_j=\sum_{i=1}^{n} p_i a_{ij} \qquad j=1,\ldots,n$$

or

$p' = p'A \qquad p \geqslant \mathbf{0}$ by the Frobenius theorem.

We thus have:

Theorem 76: The closed input–output model permits meaningful price and output solutions.

A mathematically similar model is the following. Consider a closed economy of n regions or a world economy of n countries. Income is generated in each region by sales in all regions. Region i spends a constant fraction, a_{ij}, of its income on goods produced in region j. $a_{ij} \geqslant 0$, for all i, j. Assume $\sum_{j=1}^{n} a_{ij} = 1$, for all i. Let y_i represent the income of the i-th region. The j-th region's sales are given by $\sum_{i=1}^{n} y_i a_{ij}$. This is just the j-th region's income. So, we have: $y_j = \sum_{i=1}^{n} y_i a_{ij}$ or $y' = y'A$, where A is stochastic. 1 is the Frobenius root of A, by Theorem 75, corresponding to which there is a semi-positive vector of regional incomes, y. To ensure $y > \mathbf{0}$ would require additional assumptions, the simplest one of which would be $a_{ij} > 0$, for all i, j. Summarising our discussion, we have:

Theorem 77: The static multi-region income model permits a meaningful solution.

We now consider a more general model of exchange. Consider an economy in which there are R individuals, indexed by $j = 1, \ldots, R$, and n commodities available for exchange, indexed by k, $i = 1, \ldots, n$.

At the beginning of each week, each individual is endowed with an initial vector of assets:

$$w^j = (w_1^j, w_2^j, \ldots, w_n^j) \qquad j = 1, \ldots, R$$

which reflects his ownership of commodities prior to trade. Let us choose our units of measurement so that

$$w = \sum_{j=1}^{R} w^j = \mathbf{1}.$$

All individuals meet at the market on Monday to exchange commodities. Each individual's aim is to maximise his utility subject to his budget constraint. The utility function can be written as:

$$u_j = u_j(x_1^j, \ldots, x_n^j) \qquad j = 1, \ldots, R$$

where x_i^j denotes the consumption of the i-th good by the j-th individual.

The j-th individual's income is given by:

$$m_j = \sum_{i=1}^{n} p_i w_i^j \qquad j = 1, \ldots, R$$

obtained under the assumption that he can dispose of his entire vector of assets, given a price vector $p=(p_1, \ldots, p_n)'$. The maximisation process yields for the j-th individual a vector of demands, d^j:

$$d^j(m_j; p) = d^j(p) = (d_1^j(p), \ldots, d_n^j(p))' \qquad j=1, \ldots, R$$

The market demand vector is obtained by summing the individual demand vectors:

$$d(p) = \sum_{j=1}^{R} d^j(p).$$

We are now in a position to define an equilibrium. The price vector $p^* \geqslant \mathbf{0}$ is an equilibrium price vector if $d(p^*) = w$. To obtain some definite results, we need to specify a functional form for u_j. We adopt the Cobb–Douglas function:

$$u_j(x) = x_1^{j a_1^j} \; x_2^{j a_2^j} \; \ldots x_n^{j a_n^j} \qquad j=1, \ldots, R$$

with $a_i^j > 0$, for all i, and $\sum_{i=1}^{n} a_i^j = 1$, for all j.

Each individual has a Cobb–Douglas utility function, but the exponents, a_i^j, differ between individuals, $j=1, \ldots, R$.
The assumption that all exponents are positive is rather strong but it ensures that each commodity is in demand and so all prices are positive.

The j-th consumer's demand vector has as its typical component:

$$d_k^j(p) = a_k^j m_j / p_k \qquad k=1, \ldots, n; \; j=1, \ldots, R \qquad \cdots [1]$$

This is obtained by the method of Lagrange multipliers. The second-order conditions (for a constrained maximum) are satisfied, given the functional form of the u_j. To find the market demand vector, we sum the individual demand vectors. The k-th component of the market demand vector is given by:

$$d_k(p) = \sum_{j=1}^{R} d_k^j(p) = \frac{1}{p_k} \sum_{j=1}^{R} a_k^j m_j$$

$$= \frac{1}{p_k} \sum_{j=1}^{R} a_k^j \sum_{i=1}^{n} p_i w_i^j$$

$$= \frac{1}{p_k} \sum_{i=1}^{n} p_i \sum_{j=1}^{R} a_k^j w_i^j$$

or

$$d_k(p) = \frac{1}{p_k} \sum_{i=1}^{n} p_i b_{ki} \qquad \cdots [2]$$

where $b_{ki} = \sum_{j=1}^{R} a_k^j w_i^j$.

In equilibrium, we have:

$d_k(p^*) = w_k = 1, \quad \text{for all } k.$

Using eqn [2], we have:

$$1 = \frac{1}{p_k^*} \sum_{i=1}^{n} p_i^* b_{ki}$$

or

$$p_k^* = \sum_{i=1}^{n} b_{ki} p_i^*$$

or

$$p^* = Bp^* \qquad B = [b_{ki}] \qquad \cdots [3]$$

So, we now ask if there exists an equilibrium for this economy; that is, does there exist $p^* \geqslant \mathbf{0}$ satisfying eqn [3]. Consider the matrix B, in particular its column sums:

$$\sum_{k=1}^{n} b_{ki} = \sum_{k=1}^{n} \sum_{j=1}^{R} a_k^j w_i^j = \sum_{j=1}^{R} w_i^j \sum_{k=1}^{n} a_k^j$$

Now $\sum_{k=1}^{n} a_k^j = 1$, for all j, by assumption.

So

$$\sum_{k=1}^{n} b_{ki} = \sum_{j=1}^{R} w_i^j = w_i = 1, \; k \text{ for all } i.$$

Each column of B is thus equal to one. B' is then a stochastic matrix and has a Frobenius root 1.
Transposing eqn [3], we have:

$$p^{*\prime} = p^{*\prime} B'$$

B' has a right characteristic vector $\mathbf{1}$ corresponding to the Frobenius root 1. Given our assumption $a_k^j > 0$, for all j, k, it follows that $b_{ki} > 0$, for all k, i. So, B is a positive matrix. From Theorem 24, we know that there exists $p^* > \mathbf{0}$ such that

$$p^{*\prime} = p^{*\prime} B' \quad \text{or} \quad p^* = Bp^*$$

The equilibrium is unique up to scalar multiplication, for p^* is the only possible positive left characteristic vector of B', by Theorem 28.

Summarising our discussion, we have:

Theorem 78: Given Cobb–Douglas utility functions with all exponents positive, the exchange model possesses a unique equilibrium.

We emphasise the limitations of this result. We have proved only that an equilibrium is possible and that it is unique up to scalar multiplication. We have not established a method of convergence to equilibrium.

§2.6. Comparative Statics

If the technology (as represented by the input–output matrix) is decomposable, it is evident that an increase in the final demand for some commodities will have no effect on the gross output of others. For instance, consider:

$$\begin{bmatrix} x^1 \\ x^2 \end{bmatrix} = \begin{bmatrix} A^{11} & A^{12} \\ 0 & A^{22} \end{bmatrix} \begin{bmatrix} x^1 \\ x^2 \end{bmatrix} + \begin{bmatrix} c^1 \\ c^2 \end{bmatrix}$$

Changes in c^1 will not induce changes in x^2, though changes in c^2 induce changes in x^1.

Suppose that the technology is indecomposable and that $(I-A)$ satisfies the Hawkins–Simon conditions (i.e. the model is workable). We can derive a couple of intuitively reasonable results.

Theorem 79: Given an increase in the final demand for good k, all other final demands being held constant:
(i) the output of each commodity will increase;
(ii) the output of commodity k will increase by the largest proportion.

Proof: (i) Let $\bar{c}$, $\bar{x}$ denote the new final demand and gross output vectors respectively, where $\bar{c}_i = c_i$, for all $i \neq k$, $\bar{c}_k = \gamma c_k$, $\gamma > 1$. We have:

$$(I-A)x = c$$

$$(I-A)\bar{x} = \bar{c}$$

Subtracting the first equation from the second, we obtain:

$$(I-A)(\bar{x}-x) = \bar{c} - c = \gamma e^k$$

or

$$\bar{x} - x = (I-A)^{-1}\gamma e^k$$

From Exercises §2.3, $(I-A)^{-1} > [0]$. Hence, $\bar{x} > x$.

(ii) Let $\bar{x}_j = \beta_j x_j$; $\beta_j > 1$, for all j.

Suppose $\beta_r = \max\limits_i \beta_j$, $r \neq k$.

Consider the r-th equation of $(I-A)(\bar{x}-x) = \bar{c} - c$, i.e.

$$\sum_{j-1}^{n} (\delta_{rj} - a_{rj})(\beta_j - 1)x_j = 0$$

or

$$(1-a_{rr})(\beta_r - 1)x_r = \sum_{\substack{j=1 \\ j\neq r}}^{n} a_{rj}(\beta_j - 1)x_j \, .$$

Dividing through by $(\beta_r - 1)$, we obtain:

$$(1-a_{rr})x_r = \sum_{\substack{j=1\\j\neq r}}^{n} a_{rj}\frac{(\beta_j - 1)x_j}{(\beta_r - 1)} < \sum_{\substack{j=1\\j\neq r}}^{n} a_{rj}x_j \qquad \cdots[1]$$

$x > \mathbf{0}$ in an indecomposable system for any $c \geqslant \mathbf{0}$. So eqn [1] contradicts the fact that $I-A$ should have a q.d.d. with the given $x > \mathbf{0}$. This contradiction yields the desired result.

Definition 19: The *elasticity* of gross output of commodity i with respect to the final demand for commodity k is given by: $e_{ik} = (c_k/x_i) \cdot (\Delta x_i/\Delta c_k)$ where $\Delta x_i = \bar{x}_i - x_i$, $\Delta c_k = \bar{c}_k - c_k$.

Theorem 80: Under the same hypotheses as Theorem 79 $e_{ik} \leqslant 1$.

Proof: $$e_{ik} = \frac{c_k \cdot \Delta x_i}{x_i \cdot \Delta c_k} = \frac{c_k(\beta_i - 1)x_i}{x_i(\gamma - 1)c_k} = \frac{\beta_i - 1}{\gamma - 1}$$

Suppose $\beta_i > \gamma$, for all i.

$$x_k = \sum_{j=1}^{n} a_{kj}x_j + c_k \quad \text{for all } k \qquad \cdots[2]$$

Using the definitions of $\bar{x}_j$ and $\bar{c}_k$, we obtain:

$$\frac{\bar{x}_k}{\beta_k} = \sum_{j=1}^{n} a_{kj}\frac{\bar{x}_j}{\beta_j} + \frac{\bar{c}_k}{\gamma} \qquad \cdots[3]$$

Under the new final demand vector, we have:

$$\bar{x}_k = \sum_{j=1}^{n} a_{kj}\bar{x}_j + \bar{c}_k \qquad \cdots[4]$$

As $\beta_k \geqslant \beta_j > \gamma$, for all $j \neq k$, we have $1/\beta_j \geqslant 1/\beta_k$, for all $j \neq k$ and $1/\gamma > 1/\beta_k$. From eqn [4], we must then have:

$$\frac{\bar{x}_k}{\beta_k} < \sum_{j=1}^{n} a_{kj}\frac{\bar{x}_j}{\beta_j} + \frac{\bar{c}_k}{\gamma} \qquad \cdots[5]$$

Equation [5] plainly contradicts eqn [3]. Then $\beta_i \leqslant \gamma$, for all i. Hence $e_{ik} \leqslant 1$, as required.

We have considered the comparative statics effects (on gross output) of a final demand change, let us now consider the comparative statics effects (on prices) of the introduction of taxes and subsidies. It will be advantageous to:

(a) change units of measurement so that $x_i = 1$, for all i;
(b) assume $a_{ii} = 0$ (x_i is measured net of input into its own industry);
(c) assume $c_i > 0$, for all i.

Let us consider the effect of the change in units. From

$$x = Ax + c$$

we have, using $D\mathbf{1}=x$, $D=[x_i\delta_{ij}]$:

$$D\mathbf{1}=AD\mathbf{1}+c$$

or

$$\mathbf{1}=D^{-1}AD\mathbf{1}+D^{-1}c$$

or

$$\mathbf{1}=F\mathbf{1}+w \qquad F=D^{-1}AD, \qquad w=D^{-1}c$$

As $w_i>0$, it follows that $\sum_{j=1}^{n} f_{ij}<1$, for all i.

Suppose without loss of generality that commodity 1 is taxed, while commodity 2 is subsidised. Let τ be the amount of the tax and subsidy. Then the price equations are:

$$p_1=\sum_{i\neq 1} p_i f_{i1}+v_1+\tau$$

$$p_2=\sum_{i\neq 2} p_i f_{i2}+v_2-\tau \qquad \cdots [6]$$

$$p_j=\sum_{i\neq j} p_i f_{ij}+v_j \qquad j=3,\ldots,n$$

Let $G=I-F$.

Differentiating eqn [6] with respect to τ, we obtain:

$$(\mathrm{d}p/\mathrm{d}\tau)'=(\mathrm{d}p/\mathrm{d}\tau)'F+(1,-1,0,\ldots,0)$$

or

$$(\mathrm{d}p/\mathrm{d}\tau)'=(1,-1,0,\ldots,0)G^{-1}$$

Specifically:

$$\mathrm{d}p_1/\mathrm{d}\tau=(G_{11}-G_{12})/\det G$$

$$\mathrm{d}p_2/\mathrm{d}\tau=(G_{21}-G_{22})/\det G$$

$$\mathrm{d}p_i/\mathrm{d}\tau=(G_{i1}-G_{i2})/\det G \qquad i=3,\ldots,n$$

Given the sign conditions on the a_{ij} and hence on the f_{ij}, and given the row-sum condition $\sum_{j=1}^{n} f_{ij}<1$, it follows from Theorem 49 that G is an M-matrix. By Theorem 51, $G_{ii}\geqslant G_{ij}$, for all i, $j\neq i$.

Hence $\mathrm{d}p_1/\mathrm{d}\tau\geqslant 0$, $\mathrm{d}p_2/\mathrm{d}\tau\leqslant 0$, as we would expect. However, nothing conclusive can be said about $\mathrm{d}p_i/\mathrm{d}\tau$, $i=3,\ldots,n$.

Summarising our discussion, we have:

Theorem 81 (Metzler): Consider a workable input–output model. Let a tax be applied to commodity 1, an equal subsidy be applied to commodity

2. The price of commodity 1 cannot fall while the price of commodity 2 cannot rise.

§2.7. Static Efficiency

§2.7.1. *Introduction*

In a productive economy where there is only one technique of production for each sector, the question of efficiency never arises. It is only when there are alternative techniques of production for at least one sector that concepts of efficiency need to be considered. It might be thought that our work so far, which has been based on the assumption of only one technique for each sector, is unduly restrictive. For, it might be hypothesised, an industry with alternative techniques available will in general find it profitable to switch techniques consequent on a change in final demand. The non-substitution theorem (which is the main result in this section) denies this under assumptions of no joint production, only one non-produced factor (usually thought of as homogeneous labour) and others to be stated below. Prior to statement of assumptions and derivation of the theorem, we formalise relevant ideas about technology and efficiency.

There are $n+1$ commodities to be distinguished, with labour the only non-produced commodity being the $(n+1)$-th.

Let y^j = output vector of the j-th sector

w^j = input vector in the j-th sector

l_j = labour input in the j-th sector

where

$$y^j \geqslant \mathbf{0}, \qquad w^j \geqslant \mathbf{0}, \qquad l_j \geqslant 0.$$

In a Leontief economy (i.e. of the type outlined in §2.1), $y^j = [y_i \delta_{ij}]$, where y_j is the gross output of the j-th sector and $w^j = [a_{ij} y_j]$, $i = 1, \ldots, n$, and the a_{ij} are the familiar input–output coefficients.

The information contained in the vectors y^j and w^j and the scalar l_j specify a technique of production for the j-th sector. We describe the technique by the ordered pair $(y^j - w^j, -l_j)$. Outputs are represented by non-negative numbers, inputs by non-positive numbers. Thus $y^j - w^j$ is the vector of net outputs produced by the j-th sector, $-l_j$ is the labour input in the j-th sector.

Let T_j be the set of all techniques available to the j-th sector, i.e. the set of all ordered pairs $(y^j - w^j, -l_j)$, where $y^j = y_j e^j$.

Define:

$$y = \sum_{j=1}^{n} y^j; \qquad w = \sum_{j=1}^{n} w^j; \qquad l = \sum_{j=1}^{n} l_j \qquad \cdots [1]$$

Then $y - w$ is the vector of net outputs produced by the economy, and $-l$ the total labour input used by the economy.

Let

$$T=\{(y-w,\ -l):(y^j-w^j,\ -l_j)\in T_j,\ j=1,\ldots,n\} \qquad \cdots[2]$$

T is thus the technology set for the economy as a whole.

We may now list our assumptions about T_j (and T).

(A1): T_j is convex (i.e. externalities are absent in T_j).
If $(y^j-w^j,\ -l_j)$, $(\bar{y}^j-\bar{w}^j,\ -\bar{l}_j)\in T_j$ and $\alpha_1,\ \alpha_2\geqslant 0$, $\alpha_1+\alpha_2=1$, then $\alpha_1(y^j-w^j,\ -l_j)+\alpha_2(\bar{y}^j-\bar{w}^j,\ -\bar{l}_j)\in T_j$.
We may easily derive that T is convex.
Defining $\bar{y}$, $\bar{w}$ and $\bar{l}$ analogously with y, w and l respectively, we have:
If $(y-w,\ -l)$ and $(\bar{y}-\bar{w},\ -\bar{l})\in T$ and $\alpha_1,\ \alpha_2\geqslant 0$, $\alpha_1+\alpha_2=1$, then $\alpha_1(y-w,\ -l)+\alpha_2(\bar{y}-\bar{w},\ -\bar{l})\in T$.

(A2): T_j is a cone (i.e. there are constant returns to scale). If $(y^j-w^j,\ -l_j)\in T_j$ and $\alpha\geqslant 0$, then $\alpha(y^j-w^j,\ -l_j)\in T_j$.
Evidently, T is a cone.
For if $(y-w,\ -l)\in T$ and $\alpha\geqslant 0$, it follows that $\alpha(y-w,\ -l)\in T$.

(A3): Indispensability of labour.
If $(y^j-w^j,\ -l_j)\in T_j$ and $l_j=0$, then $y^j=\mathbf{0}$.
For the economy as a whole, we have:
If $(y-w,\ -l)\in T$, $l=0$ implies $y=\mathbf{0}$.

(A4); Irreversibility of techniques.
If $(y^j-w^j,\ -l_j)\in T_j$, then $(w^j-y^j,\ l_j)\notin T_j$.
If $(y-w,\ -l)\in T$, then $(w-y,\ l)\notin T$.
The existence of an unproduced factor (labour), indispensable for techniques operated at non-zero levels, is sufficient to ensure that assumption (A4) is satisfied.

(A5): T_j is closed.
The limit of any convergent sequence of possible techniques is also possible.

To motivate consideration of efficiency concepts, we mention that nothing so far stated has ruled out a technique $(y_j-w_j,\ -l_j)\in T_j$ where $w^j\geqslant y^j$, or for the economy as a whole $(y-w,\ -l)\in T$ where $w\geqslant y$. We would be justified in using the terminology "unproductive" to describe such techniques. So, let us restrict ourselves to productive subsets of the technology sets.

Definition 20: The *productive subset* of T_j, denoted by P_j, is defined by:

$$P_j=\{(y^j-w^j,-l_j):y^j\geqq w^j,\ (y^j-w^j,-l_j)\in T_j\}\quad j=1,\ldots,n.$$

P, the productive subset of T, is defined by:

$$P=\{(y-w,-l):y\geqq w,\ (y-w,-l)\in T\}.$$

Further refinements would seem to be suggested by the following example. Let $(y-w,-l)$, $(\bar{y}-w,-l)\in P$, $y\geqslant\bar{y}$. Both techniques are in the productive subset of T, yet the first is obviously a more productive, or efficient, technique than the second. So, we have:

Definition 21: Let $(y-w,\ -l)$, $(\bar{y}-\bar{w},\ -\bar{l})\in P$. $(y-w,\ -l)$ is *more efficient* than $(\bar{y}-\bar{w},\ -\bar{l})$ if $(y-w,\ -l)\geqslant(\bar{y}-\bar{w},\ -\bar{l})$..

Definition 22: Let $(y-w, -l)\in P$. Then $(y-w, -l)$ is *efficient* if there does not exist a more efficient technique in P.

Definition 23: Let $E(P)$ denote the set of all efficient techniques in P.

Our first result in this section provides us with a relation between efficiency and profit maximisation.

Theorem 82: Let $p>\mathbf{0}$. If $(y^*-w^*,\ -l^*)$ maximises $(p\quad 1)'(y-w,\ -l)$, then $(y^*-w^*,\ -l^*)$ is efficient.

Proof: Suppose that the technique is not efficient. Then there exists a technique $(\bar{y}-\bar{w}, -\bar{l})$ such that

$(\bar{y}-\bar{w}, -\bar{l})\geqslant(y^*-w^*, -l^*)$.

Pre-multiplying by $(p\quad 1)'>\mathbf{0}'$, we have:

$(p\quad 1)'(\bar{y}-\bar{w}, -\bar{l})>(p\quad 1)'(y^*-w^*, -l^*)$

which plainly contradicts profit maximisation.

§2.7.2. *The non-substitution theorem*

The aim of the non-substitution theorem is to characterise the set $E(P)$. We shall derive the theorem by using properties of M-matrices.

Given a non-negative net output vector, c, and a labour supply, $\tilde{l}$, let us write:

$P(c, -\tilde{l})=\{(y-w, -l): y-w\geqq c, -l\geqslant-\tilde{l}, (y-w, -l)\in T\}$.

We assert that $P(c, -\bar{l})$ is a non-empty, compact set (see Exercises §2.7). Then we may derive:

Theorem 83: $(p\quad 1)'(y-w, -l)$ attains its maximum at $(\bar{y}-\bar{w}, -\bar{l})$ on $P(c, -\tilde{l})$. Furthermore, $(\bar{y}-\bar{w}, -\bar{l})$ is efficient in P.

Proof: As a continuous function attains its maximum on a compact set, there will be a profit maximising technique $(\bar{y}-\bar{w}, -\bar{l})$ satisfying the final demand vector c, within the labour constraint $\tilde{l}$. By the previous theorem, this technique will be efficient.
As a corollary, we have:

Theorem 84: $\alpha(\bar{y}-\bar{w}, -\bar{l})$ is efficient in P, for any $\alpha\geqslant0$.

Proof: Suppose there exists $(y-w, -l)\in P$ such that:

$$y-w\geqq\alpha(\bar{y}-\bar{w}), -l\geqslant-\alpha\bar{l} \qquad \cdots[3]$$

Suppose $\alpha > 0$. Then:

$(y-w)/\alpha \geqq \bar{y}-\bar{w}, \ -l/\alpha \geqslant -\bar{l}$.

$((y-w)/\alpha, \ -l/\alpha) \in P$ by assumption (A2). As $(\bar{y}-\bar{w}, \ -\bar{l})$ is efficient, it follows that equalities hold in eqn [3].

Now suppose $\alpha = 0$. Then we have from eqn [3]:

$$y - w \geqq \mathbf{0}, \qquad -l \geqslant 0.$$

But $l \geqslant 0$. Hence $l = 0$. Hence $l_j = 0$, for all j. Hence, $y^i = \mathbf{0}$ for all j, by (A3). So $y = \mathbf{0}$.

Then, from the inequality above, $-w \geqq \mathbf{0}$. but $w \geqq \mathbf{0}$. So $w = \mathbf{0}$.

Again, equalities hold in eqn [3].

So, we have demonstrated efficiency in the two cases $\alpha > 0$ and $\alpha = 0$.

We now come to our main result:

Theorem 85: Suppose that the technology permits a positive net output vector. Then under assumptions (A1)–(A5), no joint production and only one non-produced factor, there exist techniques $(y^{j*} - w^{j*}, \ -1) \in T_j$, $j = 1, \ldots, n$, such that any technique in $E(P)$ can be written as: $\sum_{j=1}^{n} \alpha_j (y^{j*} - w^{j*}, \ -1)$, $\alpha_j \geqslant 0$, for all j.

Proof: Let c be the final demand vector. Let $y - w = c > \mathbf{0}$. By Theorem 83, $P(c, -\bar{l})$ contains an efficient process $(\bar{y} - \bar{w}, -\bar{l})$. First of all, let us apply Theorem 84 to normalise this process.

So, we have as an efficient process $(\bar{\bar{y}} - \bar{\bar{w}}, \ -1)$, $\alpha = 1/\bar{l}$.

This may be decomposed thus:

$$\bar{\bar{y}} = \sum_j \bar{\bar{y}}^j, \qquad \bar{\bar{w}} = \sum_j \bar{\bar{w}}^j, \qquad 1 = \sum_j \bar{\bar{l}}_j, \qquad \bar{\bar{l}}_j > 0 \quad \text{for all } j.$$

the technique employed by the j-th sector being $(\bar{\bar{y}}^j - \bar{\bar{w}}^j, \ -\bar{\bar{l}}_j)$. Each of these sectoral techniques may in turn be normalised to a technique involving unit labour input. So, again by Theorem 84, we have as the j-th sector's technique $(y^{j*} - w^{j*}, \ -1)$, $j = 1, \ldots, n$, obtained by dividing by $\bar{\bar{l}}_j$.

This set of techniques, it will be remembered, is efficient. Define $B = [b_{ij}]$ by $b_{ij} = \bar{\bar{y}}^j_i - \bar{\bar{w}}^j_i$. Evidently, $b_{ij} \leqslant 0$, for all $i \neq j$.

Let $a = (\bar{\bar{l}}_1, \ldots, \bar{\bar{l}}_n)' > \mathbf{0}$. From the definitions, we have:

$$Ba = \bar{\bar{y}} - \bar{\bar{w}} = c/\bar{l} > \mathbf{0}.$$

As $a > \mathbf{0}$, it follows by the Hawkins–Simon theorem and Lemma 1 of §2.3 that $B^{-1} \geqslant [0]$.

We are required to prove that $E(P)$ can be written as

$$\{(Bd, \ -\mathbf{1}'d) : d \geqq \mathbf{0}\}.$$

Given any non-negative final demand vector $y - w$, we have:

$$Bb = y - w \qquad b \geqq \mathbf{0} \text{ by the Hawkins–Simon theorem.}$$

So $(y-w, -\mathbf{1}'b) \in P$, i.e. it is feasible. It remains to demonstrate efficiency.
So suppose $(y-w, -l) \in E(P)$.
By efficiency, $-l \geqslant -\mathbf{1}'b$. Let $\mathbf{1}'b = 1$ without loss of generality.
We wish to derive equality; so suppose $-l > -\mathbf{1}'b$.
As $Ba > \mathbf{0}$, there exists $\mu < 0$ such that:

$$c(\mu) = (1-\mu)Ba + \mu Bb > \mathbf{0}$$
$$= B[(1-\mu)a + \mu b]$$

or

$$(1-\mu)a + \mu b = B^{-1}c(\mu) > \mathbf{0}.$$

$$\mathbf{1}'[(1-\mu)a + \mu b] = (1-\mu)\mathbf{1}'a + \mu\mathbf{1}'b = 1, \quad \text{as} \quad \mathbf{1}'a = 1.$$

So $(c(\mu), -1) \in P$.

Now define $\gamma = -\mu/(1-\mu)$. $1 > \gamma > 0$.
Consider the following convex combination of processes:

$$(1-\gamma)(c(\mu), -1) + \gamma(Bb, -l) = (c(\mu) - \gamma c(\mu) + \gamma Bb, -1 + \gamma - \gamma l)$$

After elementary manipulation, we obtain:

$$c(\mu) - \gamma c(\mu) + \gamma Bb = Ba.$$

Also, $1 - \gamma + \gamma l < 1$, given $l < \mathbf{1}'b = 1$.
So the process $(Ba, -1 + \gamma - \gamma l)$ is more efficient than $(Ba, -1)$.
This is a contradiction. Hence $l = \mathbf{1}'b$.
To complete the proof, we now demonstrate that $(Bd, -\mathbf{1}'d) \in E(P)$ for any $d \geqslant \mathbf{0}$.
By Theorem 83, $P(Bd, -\mathbf{1}'d)$ contains an efficient process $(y-w, -l)$, which may be written as $(Bb, -\mathbf{1}'b)$.
So $Bb \geqq Bd$, $-\mathbf{1}'b \geqslant -\mathbf{1}'d$.
As $B^{-1} \geqslant [0]$, the first inequality implies $b \geqq d$. Therefore, $\mathbf{1}'b \geqslant \mathbf{1}'d$. Combining this with the second inequality, we have $b = d$, as required.
This completes the proof.

The non-substitution theorem provides us with theoretical justification for concentrating on the Leontief model, even when there are alternative techniques available to each sector (in §2.1, we defined the Leontief model as one having, *inter alia*, only one technique of production for each sector). For if we choose a set of techniques (one for each sector) that is efficient for a given final demand vector, it will be efficient for any final demand vector.

§2.8. Review

By a stretch of the imagination, the input–output model analysed in this chapter can be considered as a very simple type of general equilibrium model that will be discussed in Chapter 8. In the input–output model, production conditions are particularly closely specified (no joint production, fixed coefficients, only one technique for each sector, etc.), while no restrictions are placed on consumption behaviour—we take as given a non-negative final demand vector. However, the questions that we have discussed in this chapter are similar to those to be raised in Chapter 8—existence and uniqueness of equilibrium and comparative statics.

Given the specification of the model, the question of existence resolves itself into the non-negative solution of the equation $Bx = c$, $c \geqslant \mathbf{0}$. We derived three equivalent sets of necessary and sufficient conditions for existence of equilibrium. The first one to be derived—B is a P-matrix—is similar to the condition derived in §§6.1.2 and 8.4.1 for uniqueness of general equilibrium. So the P-matrix condition (or either of the other two equivalent sets of conditions) automatically yields uniqueness.

When it comes to comparative statics, there is an even closer analogy between the results derived here for input–output systems and those to be derived in §8.9 for gross substitute systems. Compare Theorem 79 above with Theorem 43 of §8.9.2, each of which may be described as stating the three Hicksian laws of comparative statics. It should be emphasised that in doing comparative statics analysis, we are not analysing a process through time; rather we compare two different equilibria, one obtained from the other as a result of some parameter change.

Appendix to Chapter 2: Alternative proofs of the Perron-Frobenius theorem

Appendix 2.1: Arbitrary semi-positive matrices

Our results in this and the following Section are based on Brouwer's fixed point theorem, which we state as:

Lemma A.1: Let f be a continuous point-to-point mapping from a compact, convex set S to itself. Then f has a fixed point, i.e. there exists $x^* \in S$ such that $f(x^*) = x^*$.

Let $S = \left\{ x \geqslant \mathbf{0} : \sum_{i=1}^{n} x_i = 1 \right\}$.

Theorem A.1: Let $A \geqslant [0]$. A has a non-negative root, $\lambda^*(A)$, and a corresponding semi-positive characteristic vector.

Proof: Consider the following mapping $f : S \to R^n$ defined by

$$f_i(x) = \left(x_i + \sum_{j=1}^{n} a_{ij} x_j \right) \Big/ \left(1 + \sum_i \sum_j a_{ij} x_j \right)$$

$\sum_{i=1}^{n} f_i(x) = 1$. So, $f : S \to S$. f is continuous.

Then by Lemma A.1, there exists $x^* \in S$ such that $f(x^*) = x^*$. Hence

$$(1+\mathbf{1}'Ax^*)x^* = x^* + Ax^*$$
$$Ax^* = (\mathbf{1}'Ax^*)x^*$$

Let $\lambda^*(A) = \mathbf{1}'Ax^* \geqslant 0$. So, we have the desired result.

Appendix 2.2: Indecomposable matrices

We begin with the following result on indecomposable matrices:

Lemma A.2: Let $x \geqslant \mathbf{0}$. Then $Ax \geqslant \mathbf{0}$.

Proof: $Ax \geqq \mathbf{0}$. Suppose $Ax = \mathbf{0}$. A must then have a column of zeros, which contradicts indecomposability.

We now state and prove the Perron–Frobenius theorem for semi-positive indecomposable matrices:

Theorem A.2: Let $A \geqslant [0]$ be indecomposable. Then A has a positive root, $\lambda^*(A)$, and a corresponding positive characteristic vector.

Proof: Consider the mapping $f: S \rightarrow R^n$ defined by:

$$f_i(x) = \left(\sum_{j=1}^{n} a_{ij}x_j\right) \Big/ \left(\sum_i \sum_j a_{ij}x_j\right)$$

$\sum_{i=1}^{n} f_i(x) = 1$. So, $f: S \rightarrow S$. f is continuous.
By Lemma A.1, there exists $x^* \in S$ such that $f(x^*) = x^*$.

Hence $(\mathbf{1}'Ax^*)x^* = Ax^*$.

By Lemma A.2, $Ax^* \geqslant \mathbf{0}$ and so $\mathbf{1}'Ax^* > 0$. Put $\lambda^*(A) = \mathbf{1}'Ax^* > 0$. Suppose $x^* \not> \mathbf{0}$. Consider the equation:

$$Ax^* = \lambda^*(A)x^*$$

or

$$PAP^{-1}Px^* = \lambda^*(A)Px^* \quad \text{where} \quad Px^* = \begin{bmatrix} \tilde{x} \\ \mathbf{0} \end{bmatrix}, \qquad \tilde{x} > \mathbf{0},$$

or

$$\begin{bmatrix} A^{11} & A^{12} \\ A^{21} & A^{22} \end{bmatrix} \begin{bmatrix} \tilde{x} \\ \mathbf{0} \end{bmatrix} = \lambda^*(A) \begin{bmatrix} \tilde{x} \\ \mathbf{0} \end{bmatrix}$$

So, $A^{21}\tilde{x} = \mathbf{0}$. As $\tilde{x} > \mathbf{0}$, it follows that $A^{21} = [0]$. This contradicts indecomposability of A. Hence, $x^* > \mathbf{0}$.

We state the main properties of the Frobenius root as the following:

Theorem A.3: Under the same hypotheses as Theorem A.2:

(i) $\lambda^*(A) \geqslant |\lambda_i(A)|$;
(ii) if $B \geqslant A$, $\lambda^*(B) > \lambda^*(A)$;

(iii) $\lambda^*(A)$ is a simple root;
(iv) $(\alpha I-A)^{-1}>[0]$ iff $\alpha>\lambda^*(A)$;
(v) $(\alpha I-A)$ is a P-matrix iff $\alpha>\lambda^*(A)$.

Proof: Consult the paper by Debreu and Herstein.

Appendix 2.3: A further proof

We now derive a third proof in the indecomposable case; we then indicate how this result can be applied to the decomposable case.

We begin with the following:

Lemma A.3: Let $A\geqslant[0]$ be indecomposable. Then $(I+A)^{n-1}>[0]$.

Proof: The proof follows immediately from Theorem 38 by putting $\sigma=1$.

Definition A.1: Let $x\geqslant\mathbf{0}$. Define $\lambda(x)=\min\limits_{x_i\neq 0}\dfrac{(Ax)_i}{x_i}$.

We can derive the following properties of $\lambda(x)$:

Lemma A.4: (i) $\lambda(x)\geqslant 0$;
(ii) $\lambda(x)x\leqslant Ax$;
(iii) $\lambda(x)=\max\{\alpha:\alpha x\leqslant Ax\}$;
(iv) $\lambda(\beta x)=\lambda(x)$, for all $\beta>0$.

Definition A.2: Define $\lambda^*(A)=\sup\limits_{x\in R}\lambda(x)$, where R denotes the set of semi-positive vectors. Given Lemma A.4 (iv), we are justified in restricting attention to those x in the set $S=\left\{x\geqslant\mathbf{0}:\sum\limits_{i=1}^{n}x_i=1\right\}$. We redefine $\lambda^*(A)$ thus:

Let $x\in S$. Define $\lambda^*(A)=\sup\limits_{x\in S}\lambda(x)$.

S is a compact set. If $\lambda(x)$ were a continuous function, we could state that it attains its bounds on S. However, $\lambda(x)$ is not continuous, as the following example (due to Schneider) illustrates:

Let $A=\begin{bmatrix}0&1&0\\0&0&2\\1&0&2\end{bmatrix}$. For $x^1=(0,0,1)$, we have $\lambda(x^1)=2$.

For all $x=(\varepsilon,\varepsilon,1-2\varepsilon)$, $0<\varepsilon\leqslant\frac{1}{4}$, we have $\lambda(x)=1$.

Problems arise when components of x are zero. To circumvent this, consider the set $T=\{y:y=(I+A)^{n-1}x,\ x\in S\}$. By Lemma A.3, if $y\in T$, then $y>\mathbf{0}$. T is a compact set. $\lambda(y)$ is continuous on T and hence attains its bounds there.

Lemma A.5: $\lambda^*(A)=\max\limits_{y\in T}\lambda(y)$.

Proof: Let $x \in S$, with the corresponding $y \in T$.

$$\begin{aligned}\lambda(x)y &= \lambda(x)(I+A)^{n-1}x \\ &= (I+A)^{n-1}\lambda(x)x \\ &\leqslant (I+A)^{n-1}Ax \quad \text{as} \quad \lambda(x)x \leqslant Ax \\ &= A(I+A)^{n-1}x \\ &= Ay\end{aligned}$$

So, we have: $\lambda(x)y \leqslant Ay$ for every $y \in T$.
As $\lambda(y) = \max\{\alpha : \alpha y \leqslant Ay\}$, it follows that $\lambda(x) \leqslant \lambda(y)$. Hence:

$$\lambda^*(A) = \sup_{x \in S} \lambda(x) \leqslant \max_{y \in T} \lambda(y) \qquad \cdots [1]$$

As T is a subset of R, it follows that:

$$\max_{y \in T} \lambda(y) \leqslant \sup_{x \in R} \lambda(x) \qquad \cdots [2]$$

But

$$\sup_{x \in R} \lambda(x) = \sup_{x \in S} \lambda(x)$$

Hence:

$$\max_{y \in T} \lambda(y) \leqslant \sup_{x \in S} \lambda(x) = \lambda^*(A) \qquad \cdots [3]$$

Combining eqns [1] and [3], we have:

$$\lambda^*(A) = \max_{y \in T} \lambda(y)$$

We can now derive:

Theorem A.4: $\lambda^*(A)$ is positive and is a root of A, with a corresponding positive characteristic vector.

Proof: We first prove that $\lambda^*(A)$ is positive.

Let $y = \mathbf{1}$. Then $\lambda(y) = \min_j \sum_j a_{ij} > 0$; for, if $\sum_j a_{ij} = 0$, for some i, A would be decomposable.
We now prove that $\lambda^*(A)$ is a root of A.
Suppose $x \in S$ satisfies:

$$\lambda^*(A)x \leqslant Ax \quad \text{or} \quad Ax - \lambda^*(A)x \geqslant \mathbf{0} \qquad \cdots [4]$$

Let $y = (I+A)^{n-1}x > \mathbf{0}$, by Lemma A.3.
Pre-multiplying eqn [4] by $(I+A)^{n-1} > [0]$, we have:

$$(I+A)^{n-1}(A - \lambda^*(A)I)x > \mathbf{0}$$

or

$$A(I+A)^{n-1}x-\lambda^*(A)(I+A)^{n-1}x>\mathbf{0}$$

or

$$Ay-\lambda^*(A)y>\mathbf{0}.$$

This implies that $\lambda^*(A)<\lambda(y)$. This contradicts the definition of $\lambda^*(A)$. Hence:

$$Ax=\lambda^*(A)x.$$

Now $y=(I+A)^{n-1}x=(1+\lambda^*(A))^{n-1}x$.
As $y>\mathbf{0}$, $\lambda^*(A)>0$, it follows that $x>\mathbf{0}$.

Theorem A.5: $\lambda^*(A)\geqslant|\lambda_i(A)|$.

Proof: Let $\lambda_i(A)=\lambda$. Consider $\lambda x=Ax$. Taking absolute values, we have: $|\lambda||x|\leqslant A|x|$. Where $|x|$ is the vector with $|x_i|$ as its i-th component. Hence: $|\lambda|\leqslant\lambda(|x|)\leqslant\lambda^*(A)$, as required.

We discuss briefly the application of our results in this Section to the decomposable case.
Let A be decomposable. Then for some permutation matrix P, we have:

$$P^{-1}AP=\begin{bmatrix}A^{11} & A^{12}\\ 0 & A^{22}\end{bmatrix}$$

where A^{11} and A^{22} are indecomposable.
Consider the equation:

$$\begin{bmatrix}A^{11} & A^{12}\\ 0 & A^{22}\end{bmatrix}\begin{bmatrix}x^1\\ x^2\end{bmatrix}=\lambda\begin{bmatrix}x^1\\ x^2\end{bmatrix}$$

The roots of A are evidently the roots of A^{11} plus the roots of A^{22}.
We have a number of cases to consider:

(a) – where A^{11} and A^{22} are both semi-positive indecomposable

(a.1) Let $\lambda=\lambda^*(A^{11})>\lambda^*(A^{22})$.

$$A^{22}x^2=\lambda^*(A^{22})x^2 \quad \text{implies} \quad x^2=\mathbf{0}.$$

$$A^{11}x^1+A^{12}x^2=\lambda^*(A^{11})x^1$$

or

$$A^{11}x^1=\lambda^*(A^{11})x^1 \quad \text{which implies} \quad x^1>\mathbf{0}.$$

So, in this case, we have $\lambda=\lambda^*(A)>0$, $x\geqslant\mathbf{0}$.

(a.2) Let $\lambda=\lambda^*(A^{22})>\lambda^*(A^{11})$

$$A^{22}x^2=\lambda^*(A^{22})x^2 \quad \text{implies} \quad x^2>\mathbf{0}.$$

$$A^{11}x^1+A^{12}x^2=\lambda^*(A^{22})x^1$$

or

$$(\lambda^*(A^{22})I-A^{11})x^1=A^{12}x^2.$$

By Theorem A.3 (iv), $(\lambda^*(A^{22})I - A^{11})^{-1} > [0]$.
Hence, $x^1 \geqslant \mathbf{0}$.
So, in this case, we have $\lambda = \lambda^*(A^{22}) > 0$, $x \geqslant \mathbf{0}$.

(a.3) Let $\lambda = \lambda^*(A^{11}) = \lambda^*(A^{22})$.
Again $x^2 > \mathbf{0}$.

$$A^{11}x^1 + A^{12}x^2 = \lambda x^1 \quad \text{or} \quad (\lambda I - A^{11})x^1 = A^{12}x^2.$$

$(\lambda I - A)$ is singular. Perform elementary row operations, denoted by the matrix E:

$$E(\lambda I - A^{11})x^1 = EA^{12}x^2$$

so that the first row of the matrix $E(\lambda I - A^{11})$ consists of zeros, and the first component of $EA^{12}x^2$ is zero:

$$\left[\begin{array}{c|ccc} 0 & 0 & \cdots & 0 \\ -a_{21} & & & \\ \cdot & & & \\ \cdot & & \lambda I_{n-1} - B & \\ \cdot & & & \\ -a_{n1} & & & \end{array}\right] \begin{bmatrix} w_1 \\ w^2 \end{bmatrix} = \begin{bmatrix} 0 \\ c^2 \end{bmatrix}$$

where B denotes that sub-matrix of A^{11} obtained by deleting its first row and column, c^2 denotes the last $n-1$ components of $EA^{12}x^2$, w_1 denotes the first component of x^1 and w^2 the last $n-1$.
Rewriting the equation, we have:

$$(\lambda I_{n-1} - B)w^2 = c^2 + w_1 a^1$$

where $a^1 = (a_{21}, a_{31}, \ldots, a_{n1}) \geqslant \mathbf{0}$.
By Theorem A.3 (ii) and (iv), $(\lambda I_{n-1} - B)^{-1} > [0]$.
Putting $w_1 \geqslant 0$, we obtain $w^2 \geqslant \mathbf{0}$, i.e. $x^1 \geqslant \mathbf{0}$.
Hence, in this case, we have $\lambda = \lambda^*(A^{11}) = \lambda^*(A^{22}) > \mathbf{0}$, $x \geqslant \mathbf{0}$.

(b) – where one of A^{11} and A^{22} is indecomposable.
In fact, this case has been considered above in (a.1) and (a.2).

(c) – where both A^{11} and A^{22} are zero.
Then all roots of A are zero.
We have: $A^{12}x^2 = \mathbf{0}$, a solution of which is $x^2 = \mathbf{0}$.
As there are no restrictions on x^1, we can choose $x^1 > \mathbf{0}$.
So, in this case, we have $\lambda^*(A) = 0$, $x \geqslant \mathbf{0}$.

Exercises

§2.1

1. Let $A \geqslant [0]$ be decomposable. Prove that A^k is also decomposable, for any positive integer k.

2. Let $A \geqslant [0]$ be decomposable. Is A^k decomposable for all positive integers k?

3. Let $A \geqslant [0]$ be decomposable. Let $x \geqslant \mathbf{0}$. Prove that $Ax \geqslant \mathbf{0}$.

§2.2

1. What is the relation between row and column q.d.d.?

2. If A has a D.D. that is negative, prove that $\text{Re}(\lambda(A)) < 0$.

3. If A has a q.d.d., prove that A has a D.D.

4. Let $a_{ij} \geqslant 0$, for all $i \neq j$. Prove that $\text{Re}(\lambda(A)) < 0$ iff A has a negative D.D. (McKenzie)

5. Let $A \geqslant [0]$. Prove that $|\lambda(A)| < 1$ iff $I - A$ has a positive D.D. (McKenzie)

6. Let $a_{ii} \geqslant 0$, for all i; $a_{ij} \leqslant 0$, for all $i \neq j$. Assume that $a_{kk} \geqslant \sum_{i \neq k} |a_{ik}|$, for all k. Prove that A is singular iff $\sum_{i=1}^{n} a_{ik} = 0$. (Taussky)

7. Let $a_{ij} \leqslant 0$, for all $i \neq j$. Suppose there exist $d_i > 0$ such that $\sum_i d_i a_{ij} \geqslant 0$, for all j. Prove that A is non-singular iff it has a q.d.d. with these d_i. (McKenzie)

8. Let A be an arbitrary square matrix. Define $C = [c_{ij}]$ by the equation $c_{ij} = |a_{ij}|$, for all i, j. C is the diagonal form of A. Prove that A has a D.D. iff C is a P-matrix. (McKenzie)

9. Let $a_{kk} > \sum_{i \neq k} |a_{ik}|$, for all k.
   (i) Prove that $\det A > 0$.
   (ii) Prove that $\text{Re}(\lambda(A)) > 0$.
   (iii) Is A a P-matrix?

10. Let A have a d.d. Let $\alpha = \min_k \{|a_{kk}| - \sum_{i \neq k} |a_{ik}|\}$.

    Prove that $|\det A| \geqslant \alpha^n$.

11. Let A have a d.d. Let $\alpha_k = |a_{kk}| - \sum_{i \neq k} |a_{ik}|$.

    Prove that $\det A \geqslant \prod_{i=1}^{n} \alpha_i$.

12. Prove that if there exist $d_i > 0$, for all i, such that

    $$d_j\, |a_{jj}| \leqslant \sum_{j \neq i} d_i\, |a_{ij}| \quad \text{for all} \quad j,$$

    then A does not have a q.d.d.

13. Prove that if A has a positive q.d.d., then A is a P-matrix.

14. Suppose that the matrix $B = I - A$ has a q.d.d. in the row sense. Then by Q3 above, it has a D.D., i.e.

$$x_i(1-a_{ii}) > \sum_{j \neq i} a_{ij}x_j \quad \text{for all} \quad i = 1, \ldots, n$$

Interpret this condition in terms of the productiveness of the economy.

§2.3

1. Let $A \geqslant [0]$ be indecomposable.
   (i) Prove that $\lambda^*(A) > a_{ii}$, for all i.
   (ii) Prove that $\min_i \sum_{j=1}^{n} a_{ij} \leqslant \lambda^*(A) \leqslant \max_i \sum_{j=1}^{n} a_{ij}$.
   (iii) Prove that $(\alpha I - A)^{-1} > [0]$ iff $\alpha > \lambda^*(A)$.

2. Let $a_{ij} \leqslant 0$, for all $i \neq j$. Prove the equivalence of the following statements:
   (i) $A^{-1} \geqslant [0]$;
   (ii) A is a P-matrix;
   (iii) A has a d.d.

3. Let $a_{ij} \geqslant 0$, for all $i \neq j$. Prove that:
   (i) A has a root, $\phi(A)$, such that $\phi(A) \geqslant \text{Re}(\lambda(A))$;
   (ii) there exists $x \geqslant \mathbf{0}$ such that $Ax = \phi(A)x$;
   (iii) if $b_{ij} \geqslant 0$, for all $i \neq j$, and $B \geqslant A$, then $\phi(B) \geqslant \phi(A)$;
   (iv) $\phi(A) \geqslant 0$ iff there exists $x \geqslant \mathbf{0}$ such that $Ax \geqslant \mathbf{0}$.

4. Let A be a generalised stochastic matrix with row sum α. Let $\lambda \neq \alpha$ be a root of A. Let $y'A = \lambda y'$. Prove that $\sum_{i=1}^{n} y_i = 0$.

5. Let A be a stochastic matrix. Let $a_{kk} = \min_i a_{ii}$. Prove that all roots lie in the circle (i.e. inside or on the boundary of the circle) $|z - a_{kk}| \leqslant 1 - a_{kk}$.

6. Let $a_{ij} \geqslant 0$, for all $i \neq j$ and suppose that there exist $d_i > 0$, for all i, such that $\sum_{j=1}^{n} a_{ij}d_j \leqslant 0$. Prove that $\text{Re}(\lambda(A)) \leqslant 0$. If $\sum_{j=1}^{n} a_{ij}d_j < 0$, for all i, prove that $\text{Re}(\lambda(A)) < 0$.

7. Let $A \geqslant [0]$ be indecomposable.
   (i) Let $a_{ii} > 0$ for at least one i. Prove that $A^{2n-2} > [0]$.
   (ii) Let $a_{ii} > 0$. Let n_i equal the number of zeros in the ith row and the ith column. Prove that $A^{2n_i+2} > [0]$.

8. Consider the matrix $A \geqslant [0]$ where $a_{i,i+1} \neq 0$, $i = 1, \ldots, n$, (where $n+1$ is read as 1), $a_{ij} = 0$, for all $j \neq i+1$. Prove that A is indecomposable.

9. Consider the series $(1/\alpha)\sum_{\tau=0}^{\infty} A^{\tau}/\alpha^{\tau}$, $\alpha > 0$. Let $(\alpha I - A)^{-1} \geqslant [0]$.

Prove that $(\alpha I - A)^{-1} = (1/\alpha)\sum_{\tau=0}^{\infty} A^{\tau}/\alpha^{\tau}$.

(Hint: Define $B_t = (1/\alpha)\sum_{\tau=0}^{t} A^{\tau}/\alpha^{\tau}$.

(i) Show that

$$(\alpha I - A)B_t = I - (A^{t+1}/\alpha^{t+1}) \qquad \cdots [1]$$

which implies that $(\alpha I - A)B_t \leqslant I$.

(ii) Hence show that $B_t \leqslant (\alpha I - A)^{-1}$ which implies that the sequence of matrices $\{B_t\}$ is bounded from above.

(iii) Show that the sequence $\{B_t\}$ is non-decreasing.

(iv) Parts (ii) and (iii) imply that $(1/\alpha)\sum_{\tau=0}^{\infty} A^{\tau}/\alpha^{\tau}$ converges. Let $\lim_{t\to\infty} B_t = B$.

(v) B_t and B_{t+1} tend to the same limit. Show that $A^{t+1}/\alpha^{t+1} \to [0]$ as $t \to \infty$. Let $t \to \infty$ in eqn [1] and we have $(\alpha I - A)B = I$ or $B = (\alpha I - A)^{-1}$, as required.)

10. If $\alpha > 0$ and $(1/\alpha)\sum_{\tau=0}^{\infty} A^{\tau}/\alpha^{\tau}$ converges, prove that

$$(\alpha I - A)^{-1} = (1/\alpha)\sum_{\tau=0}^{\infty} A^{\tau}/\alpha^{\tau} \geqslant [0].$$

(Hint: Use eqn [1])

11. Discuss the application of matrix multipliers (as outlined in Q9 and Q10) to input–output; in particular, interpret the vectors in the series:

$$\left(\sum_{\tau=0}^{\infty} A^{\tau}\right) f = f + Af + A^2 f + \cdots + A^t f + \cdots.$$

(For a generalisation, see Chapter 5.)

12. How can the results in Q3 above be strengthened if we assume, in addition, that A is indecomposable?

13. Let $A \geqslant [0]$. Suppose that there are k roots of A equal in modulus to the Frobenius root, $\lambda^*(A)$. Prove that there exists a permutation matrix P such that:

$$(P^{-1}AP)^k = P^{-1}A^kP = \begin{bmatrix} A_1 & & & \bigcirc \\ & A_2 & & \\ & & \ddots & \\ \bigcirc & & & A_k \end{bmatrix}$$

where the A_i matrices are square and primitive with Frobenius root $\lambda^*(A)^k$.

§2.4

1. Let A be a P-matrix. Prove that $Ax \leqslant \mathbf{0}$, $x \geqslant \mathbf{0}$ have only the trivial solution $x = \mathbf{0}$.

2. Let A be an M-matrix, B an N-matrix such that $B \geqslant A$. Prove the following:
   (i) B is an M-matrix;
   (ii) $\det B \geqslant \det A > 0$;
   (iii) $A^{-1}B \geqq I$, $BA^{-1} \geqq I$;
   (iv) $B^{-1}A \leqq I$, $AB^{-1} \leqq I$;
   (v) $B^{-1}A$ and AB^{-1} are M-matrices;
   (vi) $\lambda^*(A^{-1}B) = [1 - \lambda^*(I - B^{-1}A)]^{-1}$;
   (vii) $\nu^* = \max_i[\lambda_i(I - B^{-1}A)] < 1$, where $\nu^* = \lambda^*(I - B^{-1}A)$;
   (viii) $\mu(B) \geqslant \mu(A)$.

3. Let A be power-positive, with $\lambda^*(A)$ the root of greatest absolute value. Prove that $\lambda^*(A)$ lies between the largest and smallest row sums of A.

4. If $A^2 > [0]$ and $a_{ij}a_{ji} \geqslant 0$, for all i, j, prove that $|\lambda^*(A)| > |a_{ii}|$, for all i.

5. Let $c_i > 0$, $i = 1, \ldots, n$. Let $K = \max_r K_r$, where

$$K_r = \sum_{j=1}^{n} |a_{rj}| \, c_j / c_r.$$

   Prove that $|\lambda(A)| \leqslant K$.

6. Let A be an arbitrary $n \times n$ matrix. Suppose A has n distinct roots.
   (i) Prove that the vectors associated with the distinct roots are linearly independent.
   (ii) Prove that A is similar to a diagonal matrix.

7. Let A be symmetric. Prove that A is orthogonally similar to a diagonal matrix.

8. Prove that any square matrix is unitarily similar to a triangular matrix.

9. Prove that for any matrix norm $\|\ \|$:

$$\|I\| \geqslant 1; \qquad \|A^n\| \geqslant \|A\|^n; \qquad \|A^{-1}\| \geqslant 1/\|A\|.$$

10. (i) Prove that $\left\{\sum_{i,j} |a_{ij}|^2\right\}^{\frac{1}{2}}$ is a matrix norm.

   (ii) Prove that $n \cdot \max_{i,j} |a_{ij}|$ is a matrix norm.

11. Prove that, for any matrix A:

$$\left\{\sum_{i,j} |a_{ij}|^2\right\}^{\frac{1}{2}} \leqslant n \,.\, \max_{i,j} |a_{ij}|$$

12. Derive the following result (due to Jacobi):

$$A_{ii}A_{jk} - A_{ji}A_{ik} = \det A \,.\, A_{ii;jk}.$$

Questions 13–23 deal with the theory of *quadratic forms.*
A real polynomial

$$f = f(x_1, \ldots, x_n) = \sum_{i,j=1}^{n} a_{ij}x_ix_j$$

is a quadratic form in $x_1, \ldots, x_n$.
We may rewrite any given quadratic form f as $f = x'Ax$, where $A' = A$ (the coefficient of x_ix_j in f is clearly $a_{ij} + a_{ji}$, $i \neq j$; without loss of generality, we may take $a_{ij} = a_{ji}$). On the other hand, we may construct quadratic forms using non-symmetric matrices, for, given any real $n \times n$ matrix A, there is nothing to stop us considering the function $x'Ax$. However, symmetry is a very powerful assumption, as the following theory indicates.

13. Let $f = x'Ax$, $g = y'By$, where A and B are orthogonally similar, i.e. there exists an orthogonal matrix T such that $T'AT = B$. Let $S(f)$ and $S(g)$ be the sets of values assumed by f and g respectively, as x and y take on all values. Prove that $S(f) = S(g)$.

14. Using Q7 above, prove that there exists an orthogonal transformation which transforms $f = x'Ax$ into $g = y'Dy$, $D = [\lambda_i(A)\delta_{ij}]$.

15. (a) f is positive (negative) definite iff $f > (<) 0$ for all $x \neq \mathbf{0}$. Prove that f is positive (negative) definite iff $\lambda_i > (<) 0$, for all i.
(b) f is positive (negative) semi-definite iff $f \geqslant (\leqslant) 0$ for all $x \neq \mathbf{0}$. Prove that f is positive (negative) semi-definite iff $\lambda_i \geqslant (\leqslant) 0$, for all i.
(c) f is indefinite iff $f > 0$ for some x, $f < 0$ for other x. Prove that f is indefinite iff $\lambda_i > 0$, for some i, $\lambda_j < 0$, for some j.

16. The symmetric matrix A is positive (negative) definite iff $x'Ax > (<) 0$ for all $x \neq \mathbf{0}$. Prove that A is positive definite iff there exists a positive definite matrix C such that $A = C'C$.

17. Prove that if $f = x'Ax$ is positive definite, $\det A > 0$.

18. Prove that $f = x'Ax$ is positive definite iff A is a P-matrix.
Hint: *Necessity*: Let $M \subseteq N = \{1, \ldots, n\}$. $M \neq \emptyset$.
For $i \in M$, let $x_i \neq 0$; for $j \neq M$, $x_j = 0$.
Then $x'Ax = \bar{x}'\bar{A}\bar{x}$, $\bar{A} = [a_{rs}]$, $\bar{x} = [x_r]$, r, $s \in M$.
As $f > 0$ for all $x \neq \mathbf{0}$, $\bar{x}'\bar{A}\bar{x} > 0$. By Q17, $\det\bar{A} > 0$. As $\bar{A}$ is an

arbitrary principal sub-matrix of A, it follows that all principal minors of A are positive, i.e. A is a P-matrix.

Sufficiency: We require the standard result that the roots of a symmetric matrix are real. By Theorem 43, the real roots of the P-matrix A are positive. Then, as A is symmetric, all its roots are positive. Then by Q15(a), $f = x'Ax > 0$ for all $x \neq \mathbf{0}$, as required.

19. (a) Let A be any real matrix (not necessarily square). Prove that $A'A$ is positive definite or positive semi-definite.
(b) Let $\{x^1, \ldots, x^k\}$ be a set of vectors. Stack the vectors to form the matrix X. Prove that the set is linearly independent (linearly dependent) iff $\det X'X > (=) 0$.

20. Prove that A is positive definite iff:
(a) A^{-1} is positive definite;
(b) A^t is positive definite, for any positive integer t.

21. Prove that $f = x'Ax$ is negative definite iff A is an $(N-P)$-matrix.(5)

22. Prove that $f = x'Ax$ is positive (negative) semi-definite iff A is a P_0 (an $(N-P)_0$) matrix.

23. Let A be any real $n \times n$ matrix. $h = x'Ax$ is quasi-positive (negative) definite iff $x'Ax > (<) 0$, for all $x \neq \mathbf{0}$. A is quasi-positive (negative) definite iff $h = x'Ax$ is quasi-positive (negative) definite.
(a) Prove that a quasi-positive definite matrix is a P-matrix.
Hint: Prove that the real part of any root of A is positive; the result follows.
Consider

$$Ax = \lambda x, \qquad \lambda = \alpha + i\beta, \qquad x = y + iz.$$

Then

$$x^{c\prime} Ax = \lambda x^{c\prime} x, \qquad x^c = y - iz.$$

Evaluating this equation and equating real parts, we have:

$$y'Ay + z'Az = \alpha(y'y + z'z)$$

$y'Ay > 0$ if $y \neq \mathbf{0}$; $z'Az > 0$ if $z \neq \mathbf{0}$. As y and z are not simultaneously $\mathbf{0}$, it follows that the left-hand side and the bracketed term on the right-hand side are positive. Hence $\alpha > 0$. Then $\det A > 0$.
Follow the method used in the *Necessity* part of Q18 to prove that the real part of each root of any principal sub-matrix of A is positive, i.e. each principal minor of A is positive.
(b) Prove that if A is quasi-negative definite, it is stable (i.e. the real part of each root of A is negative).

Applicability to stability analysis is a feature common to the theory of quadratic forms and the theory of norms. There is some discussion in the text of matrix norms; here, we concentrate mainly on *vector norms.* Let x and y be n-dimensional vectors. The real-valued function $\nu(x)$ is a vector norm if:

(a) $\nu(x) \geqslant 0$ with $\nu(x) = 0$ iff $x = \mathbf{0}$;
(b) $\nu(\alpha x) = |\alpha|\, \nu(x)$ for any scalar α;
(c) $\nu(x+y) \leqslant \nu(x) + \nu(y)$.

24. Prove that the following are vector norms:

(i) $\max_i |x_i|$; (ii) $\sum_i |x_i|$; (iii) $\left(\sum_i x_i^2\right)^{\frac{1}{2}}$;

(iv) $\sum_i \alpha_i |x_i|$; (v) $\max_i \alpha_i |x_i|$

(In (iv) and (v), $\alpha_i > 0$ for all i.)

25. Prove that $\nu(x-y) \geqslant |\nu(x) - \nu(y)|$, for any vector norm $\nu(x)$.

26. Prove that $\eta(x) = (x'Ax)^{\frac{1}{2}}$ is a vector norm, if A is a positive definite matrix.

27. Let ν be a vector norm, A a non-singular matrix. Prove that $\rho(x) = \nu(Ax)$ is also a vector norm.

28. (The relation between vector norms and matrix norms)
(a) Let ν be a vector norm. Define the function:

$$f(A) = \max_{x \neq \mathbf{0}} \nu(Ax)/\nu(x)$$

(b) Prove that $f(A) = \max_{\nu(x)=1} \nu(Ax)$.

(Hence, x may be restricted to the unit sphere, Z. As $\mu(x)$ is a continuous function on the compact set Z, it follows that there exists at least one vector, $\bar{x}$, in Z such that: $f(A) = \nu(A\bar{x})$.)

(c) Prove that $f(A) = \max_{x \in Z} \nu(Ax)$ is a matrix norm.

[Hint: (i)–(iii) of Definition 17 follow straightforwardly from the vector norm axioms. To establish (iv), we need the following: Define $w = x/\nu(x)$. Then $\nu(w) = 1$.

$$\nu(Ax) = \nu(\nu(x)Aw) = \nu(x) \cdot \nu(Aw) \leqslant \nu(x) \cdot \max_{y \in Z} \nu(Ay)$$
$$= \nu(x) \cdot f(A).$$

We now derive (iv).

$$f(AB) = \max_{x \in Z} \nu(ABx) = \nu(AB\bar{x}).$$

From the result just established,

$\nu(AB\bar{x}) \leqslant f(A) \, . \, \nu(B\bar{x})$.

Using the same result again,

$\nu(B\bar{x}) \leqslant f(B) \, . \, \nu(\bar{x}) = f(B)$.

Hence, $f(AB) \leqslant f(A) \, . \, f(B)$, as required,]
f is the matrix norm induced by ν.

29. (a) Prove that the matrix norm induced by $\nu(x) = (x'x)^{\frac{1}{2}}$ is $f(A) = (\lambda^*(A'A))^{\frac{1}{2}}$.

(b) Prove that $\nu(x) = \max_i |x_i|$ induces the matrix norm

$$f(A) = \max_i \sum_j |a_{ij}|.$$

(c) Prove that $\nu(x) = \sum_i |x_i|$ induces the matrix norm

$$f(A) = \max_j \sum_i |a_{ij}|.$$

30. Is a stable matrix quasi-negative definite?

31. Consider the following iterative scheme for solving the simple input–output model:

$x^0 = c \geqslant \mathbf{0}$

$x^\tau = Ax^{\tau-1} + c \qquad \tau = 1, 2, \ldots$

Prove that if $\|A\| < 1$, this iterative scheme yields the unique meaningful solution of $x = Ax + c$.
Interpret the x^τ, $\tau = 1,2,\ldots$. (Evans)

32. Let ν be a vector norm, $A \geqslant [0]$. Prove that if there exists $\alpha \in (0, 1)$ such that $\nu(Ax^1 - Ax^2) < \alpha\nu(x^1 - x^2)$, for all x^1, x^2, then $\lambda^*(A) < 1$.

§2.5

1. Consider a very simple closed model in which commodities (numbered $1, \ldots, n-1 = m$) are produced by labour alone. The only possible non-zero elements of the input–output matrix are: a_{in}, a_{ni}, $i = 1, \ldots, m$.
The basic balance equation is: $(I - A)x = \mathbf{0}$.
The price equation is: $p'(I - A) = \mathbf{0}'$.
A necessary condition for a solution (to both systems) is $\det(I - A) = 0$.
Show that $\det(I - A) = 1 - \sum_{i=1}^{m} a_{in}a_{ni}$. Interpret the condition $\sum_{i=1}^{m} a_{in}a_{ni} = 1$. (Examine $a_{in}a_{ni}$, for each i). What if $\sum_{i=1}^{m} a_{in}a_{ni} >$ (or $<$) 1?

2. Now consider a more complex model where consumption goods (numbered $1, \ldots, m$) are produced by labour and a specific capital good, while capital goods (numbered $n+1, \ldots, n+m$) are produced by labour alone. Denote replacement coefficients by $a_{n+j,j}$, new investment coefficients by $a_{n+j,n}$, $j=1, \ldots, m$. The coefficient matrix of order $n+m \times n+m$ can be written as:

$$\begin{bmatrix} \bigcirc & \begin{matrix} a_{1n} \\ \vdots \\ a_{mn} \end{matrix} & \bigcirc \\ a_{n1} \quad \cdots \quad a_{nm} & 0 & a_{n,n+1} \quad \cdots \quad a_{n,n+m} \\ \begin{matrix} a_{n+1,1} & & \bigcirc \\ & \ddots & \\ \bigcirc & & a_{n+m,m} \end{matrix} & \begin{matrix} a_{n+1,n} \\ \vdots \\ a_{n+m,n} \end{matrix} & \bigcirc \end{bmatrix}$$

Show that the condition for a non-trivial solution is:

$$1-\sum_{j=1}^{m} a_{nj}a_{jn} - \sum_{j=1}^{m} a_{n+j,j}a_{n,n+j}a_{jn} - \sum_{j=1}^{m} a_{n,n+j}a_{n+j,n} = 0$$

The price equation can be written as:

$$p'(I-A)+q' = \mathbf{0}'$$

where $p=(p_1, \ldots, p_m, p_n, p_{n+1}, \ldots, p_{n+m})'$, $p_n = w$,

$$q = \pi\left(p_{n+1}, \ldots, p_{n+m}, \sum_{i=1}^{m} p_{n+i}x_i/x_n, 0, \ldots, 0\right)',$$

π being the rate of profit and w the wage rate, A being the matrix given above.
The price equation can be rewritten as:

$$p'(I-\bar{A}) = \mathbf{0}'$$

where $\bar{a}_{nj} = a_{nj}$, $j=1, \ldots, m, n+1, \ldots, n+m$; $\bar{a}_{in} = a_{in}$, $i=1, \ldots, m$; $\bar{a}_{n+i,n} = a_{n+i,n} - \pi a_{in}$, $i=1, \ldots, m$; $\bar{a}_{n+i,i} = a_{n+i,i} + \pi$, $i=1, \ldots, m$; all other a_{ij} are zero.
Prove that $\det(I-\bar{A}) = \det(I-A)$. Hence, the price and output systems have non-trivial solutions simultaneously. Solve the model for:
(a) x_i in terms of x_n; (b) p_i in terms of w and π;

$i=1, \ldots, m, n+1, \ldots, n+m$.

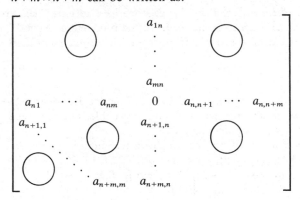

3. Modify the previous model as follows: consumption good i is produced by capital good $n+i$ and labour; capital good $n+i$ is produced by itself and labour.
(A reference for these questions is Pasinetti.)

§2.6

1. Examine the effect of technical change on prices. In particular, prove that, if a technical improvement occurs in the production of good i, the price of good i decreases and the price of each other good does not increase.

§2.7

1. Consider the following generalised Leontief model (i.e. where at least one sector has more than one technique available, but otherwise the assumptions of §2.1 are maintained):
The first sector has available the following techniques:
[(1, −0.2), −0.4], [(1, −0.5), −0.2] and [(1, −0.3), −0.3].
The second sector has [(−0.3, 1), −0.6] and [(−0.6, 1), −0.2]
Which techniques characterise $E(P)$?

2. Answer the same question as Q1 with respect to the following economy:
[(0.9, −0.6), −0.4] and [(0.8, −1), −0.3] are available to the first sector, [(−0.4, 1),−0.6] and [(−0.3, 0.8), −0.5] are available to the second sector.

3. Discuss the validity of the non-substitution theorem if:
(i) there is joint production;
(ii) there is more than one non-produced commodity.

4. Prove that $P(c, \tilde{l})$ is a non-empty, compact set.
Non-emptiness is trivial. Compactness is equivalent to boundedness and closedness.
Boundedness: suppose that the set is unbounded. This implies that there exists a sequence $\{(y(\nu)-w(\nu))-l(\nu)\}$ in the set such that

$$\lim_{\nu\to\infty}\|y(\nu)\|=+\infty.$$

Decompose $(y(\nu)-w(\nu), -1(\nu))$ into sectoral techniques and apply $(A2)$ and (A5) so that $(\bar{y}(\nu)^j-w(\nu)^j, -1(\nu)_j)/\eta(\nu)$ tends to $(z^j-u^j, -m_j)\in T_j$, where $\eta(\nu)=\|y(\nu)\|$.

Then $\lim_{\nu\to\infty}\|y(\nu)\|=+\infty$ implies $m_j=0$ which by (A3) implies that $z^j=\mathbf{0}$.

Therefore $\lim_{\nu\to\infty}\left[\sum_{j=1}^{n} y(\nu)^j\right]\Big/\eta(\nu)=\mathbf{0}$. This is a contradiction for the limit is 1. So the set is bounded. Closedness: This follows by decomposing $(y(\nu)-w(\nu), -l(\nu))$ as above and applying (A5).

Appendix

1. Let $A \geqslant [0]$ be indecomposable. Let $\bar{A}$ denote that sub-matrix of A obtained by deleting, say, the first row and column. Let $\lambda^*(A)$, $\lambda^*(\bar{A})$ denote the largest real root of A, $\bar{A}$ respectively. Let $G = \lambda I - A$, $H = \lambda I - \bar{A}$. Denote cofactors by G_{ij}, H_{ij}.
(a) Prove that $\lambda^*(A) > \lambda^*(\bar{A})$;
(b) Prove that $G_{ij} > 0$ for $\lambda \geqslant \lambda^*(A)$, $i \neq j$.
Hint: Use induction.

Using $G_{1j} = \sum_{i=2}^{n} a_{i1} H_{ij}$ and $G_{i1} = \sum_{j=2}^{n} a_{1j} H_{ij}$, we have:

$$\det(\lambda I - A) = (\lambda - a_{11}) \det H - \sum_{i,j=2}^{n} a_{i1} a_{1j} H_{ij}$$

Then by the induction hypothesis:

$\lambda^*(\bar{A}) > 0$ and $H_{ij} > 0$ for $\lambda > \lambda^*(\bar{A})$, $i \neq j$, imply

$$\det(\lambda^*(\bar{A}) I - A) = -\sum_{i,j=2}^{n} a_{i1} a_{1j} H_{ij} < 0$$

using indecomposability.

As $\det(\lambda I - A) = \prod_{i=1}^{n} (\lambda - \lambda_i) > 0$ for sufficiently large λ, it follows by continuity that there exists $\lambda^*(A) > \lambda^*(\bar{A})$ such that $\det(\lambda^*(A) I - A) = 0$.
By induction: $G_{1j} > 0$, $G_{i1} > 0$, for $\lambda \geqslant \lambda^*(A) > \lambda^*(\bar{A})$, $i, j = 2, \ldots, n$.
Now use Jacobi's theorem (Exercises §2.4, Q12). In terms of G, we have:

$$G_{11} G_{ij} - G_{i1} G_{1j} = \det G \, . \, G_{11;ij}$$

or

$$\det H \, . \, G_{ij} - G_{i1} G_{1j} = \det G \, . \, H_{ij}$$

or

$$G_{ij} = (\det G \, . \, H_{ij} + G_{i1} G_{1j}) / \det H$$

$\det H = \det(\lambda I - \bar{A}) > 0$ for $\lambda > \lambda^*(\bar{A})$; so, all the terms on the right-hand side are positive. Hence, $G_{ij} > 0$, $i \neq j$.
The proof is completed by examining the 2×2 case.

2. Hence, prove that the semi-positive indecomposable matrix A has a positive, simple root $\lambda^*(A)$ and an associated positive characteristic vector.

3. Also, prove that $(\alpha I - A)^{-1} > [0]$ for any $\alpha > \lambda^*(A)$.

4. How can the above results be relaxed if we dispense with the indecomposability assumption?

Notes

1. Alternative proofs of the Perron–Frobenius theorem are provided in the appendix to this chapter for those not too happy with the proof in the text. One proof in the Appendix used Brouwer's fixed point theorem; this proof, in the indecomposable case, is the same as that uses for the generalised (i.e. non-linear) Perron–Frobenius theorem in §6.3.1.

2. Hawkins, D. and H. A. Simon: "Note: Some conditions of macro-economic stability," *Econometrica*, **17** (1949). p. 245.

3. Nikaido, H.: *Introduction to Sets and Mappings in Modern Economics*, North-Holland, 1970. Chapter 1.

4. A note on the representation of characteristic roots. In general, we write down the roots of the matrix A as follows: $\lambda_1(A), \lambda_2(A), \ldots, \lambda_n(A)$; a typical root is written as $\lambda_i(A)$ or sometimes $\lambda(A)$. The notation $\lambda^*(A)$ is reserved for the Frobenius root of the matrix $A \geqq [0]$. $\lambda_i(A^t)$ denotes the i-th root of A^t; $\lambda_i(A)^t$ denotes the i-th root (of A) raised to the power t. It can be proved by induction that, if λ is a root of A, λ^t is a root of A^t; however, it does not follow that, if λ^t is a root of A^t, λ is a root of A.

5. A is an $(N-P)$-matrix if each odd-ordered principal minor of A is negative and each even-ordered principal minor is positive, i.e. if $-A$ is a P-matrix. Likewise, A is an $(N-P)_0$-matrix if $-A$ is a P_0-matrix.

References

§2.1

Chipman, J. S.: "A note on stability, workability and duality in linear economic models", *Metroeconomica*, **6** (1954).

Hawkins, D. & H. A. Simon: "Note: some conditions of macroeconomic stability", *Econometrica*, **17** (1949).

Nikaido, H.: *Introduction to Sets and Mappings in Modern Economics*, North-Holland, 1970, Chapter 1.

For discussions of permutation matrices, consult:
Hohn, F. E.: *Elementary Matrix Algebra*, Collier Macmillan, 3rd edn 1973.

Lancaster, P.: *Theory of Matrices*, Academic Press, 1969.

§2.2

McKenzie, L. W.: "Matrices with dominant diagonals and economic theory" in *Mathematical Methods in the Social Sciences* (K. J. Arrow et al. eds), Stanford UP, 1960.

Taussky, O.: "A recurring theorem on determinants", *American Mathematical Monthly*, **56** (1949).

The following papers might also be consulted:
Brauer, A.: "Lomits for the characteristic roots of a matrix", *Duke Mathematical Journal*, **13** (1946).

Woodbury, M. A.: "Properties of Leontief-type input–output matrices" in *Economic Activity Analysis* (O. Morgenstern, ed.) Wiley, 1954.

Wong, Y. K.: "Inequalities for Minkowski-Leontief matrices" op. cit.

§2.3
§2.3.1
Nikaido, H.: *Introduction to Sets and Mappings in Modern Economics*, North-Holland, 1970.

§2.3.2
Woodbury, M. A.: "Characteristic roots of input–output matrices" in *Economic Activity Analysis* (O. Morgenstern, ed.), Wiley, 1954.

§2.3.3
Metzler, L. A.: "Stability of multiple markets: the Hicks conditions", *Econometrica*, **13** (1945).

§2.3.4
Bellman, R.: *Introduction to Matrix Analysis*, McGraw-Hill, 2nd edn 1970.

Lancaster, P.: *Theory of Matrices*, Academic Press, 1969.

§2.3.5
Brauer, A.: "On the theorems of Perron and Frobenius on non-negative matrices" in *Studies in Mathematical Analysis and Related Topics: Essays in honour of George Polya* (G. Szego et al., eds), Stanford U.P., 1962.

Herstein, I. N.: "Note on primitive matrices", *American Mathematical Monthly*, **61** (1954).

Lancaster, P.: *Theory of Matrices*, Academic Press, 1969.

Solow, R.: "On the structure of linear models", *Econometrica*, **20** (1952).

§2.4
§2.4.2
Ledermann, W.: "On the asymptotic probability distribution for certain Markoff processes", *Proceedings of the Cambridge Philosophical Society*, **46** (1950).

Metzler, L. A.: "A multiple-region theory of income and trade", *Econometrica*, **18** (1950).

Metzler, L. A.: "A multiple-country theory of income transfers", *Journal of Political Economy*, **59** (1951).

Mosak, J.: *General Equilibrium Theory in International Trade,* Cowles Commission Monograph no. 7, 1944.

§2.4.3

Morishima, M.: "On the laws of change of the price system in an economy which contains complementary commodities", *Osaka Economic Papers,* **1** (1952).

§2.4.4

Brauer, A.: "On the characteristic roots of power-positive matrices", *Duke Mathematical Journal,* **28** (1961).

§2.4.5

Barankin, E. W.: "Bounds for the characteristic roots of a matrix", *Bulletin of the American Mathematical Society,* **51** (1945).

Brauer, A.: "Limits for the characteristic roots of a matrix", *Duke Mathematical Journal,* **13** (1946).

Brauer, A.: "Limits for the characteristic roots of a matrix, III", *Duke Mathematical Journal,* **15** (1948).

Brauer, A.: "The theorems of Ledermann and Ostrowski on positive matrices", *Duke Mathematical Journal,* **24** (1957).

Fisher, F. M.: "An alternate proof and extension of Solow's theorem on non-negative square matrices", *Econometrica,* **30** (1962).

Hall, C. A. & T. A. Porsching: "Bounds for the maximal eigenvalue of a non-negative irreducible matrix", *Duke Mathematical Journal,* **36** (1969).

Lancaster, P.: *Theory of Matrices,* Academic Press, 1969.

Ledermann, W.: "Bounds for the greatest latent root of a positive matrix", *Journal of the London Mathematical Society,* **25** (1950).

Ostrowski, A.: "Bounds for the greatest latent root of a positive matrix", *Journal of the London Mathematical Society,* **27** (1952).

Ostrowski, A. & H. Schneider: "Bounds for the maximal characteristic root of a non-negative irreducible matrix", *Duke Mathematic Journal,* **27** (1960).

Solow, R. M.: "On the structure of linear models", *Econometrica,* **20** (1952).

§Exercises

§2.4

Evans, W. D.: "Input output computations" in *The Structural Interdependence of the Economy,* T. Barna, ed. Wiley, 1954.

§2.5

Pasinetti, L. L.: "A new theoretical approach to the problems of economic growth" in *The Economic Approach to Development Planning*, Pontificiae Academiae Scientiarum, Scripta Varia, 28, North-Holland, 1965.

§2.6

Metzler, L. A.: "Taxes and subsidies in Leontief's input–output model", *Quarterly Journal of Economics*, **65** (1951).

Morishima, M.: "On the three Hicksian laws of comparative statics", *Review of Economic Studies*, **27** (1960).

§2.7

Arrow, K. J.: "Alternative proof of the substitution theorem for Leontief models in the general case" in *Activity Analysis of Production and Allocation*, Cowles Foundation Monograph no. 13, Wiley, 1951.

§Appendix

§2.2

Debreu, G. & I. N. Herstein: "Non-negative square matrices", *Econometrica*, **21** (1953).

§2.3

Lancaster, P.: *Theory of Matrices*, Academic Press, 1969.

Schneider, H.: "Note on the fundamental theorem on irreducible non-negative matrices", *Proceedings of the Edinburgh Mathematical Society*, **11** (1958).

3

Two topics in capital theory

In this chapter, we discuss two topics raised by Sraffa in his book *Production of Commodities by Means of Commodities.* The first concerns the construction of an invariable standard of value, i.e. a commodity or basket of commodities the price of which is invariant with respect to changes in the rate of profits and the wage rate. Our method of solving the (Ricardian) problem of finding an invariable standard of value is based on the Perron–Frobenius theorems on indecomposable matrices. The second topic concerns the implications of the reswitching of techniques and related phenomena (reswitching occurs when a technique is most profitable at two distinct values of the rate of profits, with another technique most profitable at an intermediate value of the rate of profits).

In an economy which produces commodities by means of commodities and labour, the price system cannot be determined unless either the rate of profits or the wage rate is given exogenously; if prices are not known, then, in particular, the value of capital is not known, so that the distribution of the surplus (or net product) between wages and profits is indeterminate (profits being distributed in proportion to the value of capital advanced).

This view of distribution contrasts sharply with the neo-classical view which attempts to subsume distribution within the theory of value; the distributive parameters (the "prices" of labour and capital) are supposed to be determined in exactly the same way as the prices of any other commodities. We may distinguish aggregate and dis-aggregate versions of neo-classical distribution theory; it is the former that will be discussed in this chapter, the latter in Chapter 8.

One aggregate version rests on the concept of an aggregate production function which relates output per man to the value of capital per man such that the lower the marginal product of capital, the higher the values of output per man and capital per man. In competitive conditions, under profit maximisation, the rate of profits is determined by the marginal productivity of capital. To explain distribution by marginal productivity, capital has to be a single magnitude, i.e. capital has to be measured in value, not physical, terms. However, the value of a capital good, like that of any other commodity, varies with the wage rate and the rate of profits, which are themselves to be explained by the quantity of capital. So the possibility of a circular argument is evident.

Rehabilitations of the aggregate production function version of neoclassical theory were attempted by Samuelson (with his surrogate production function) and Champernowne (with his chain-index measure of capital). However, both constructions fail in the event of either reswitching or capital-reversing (capital-reversing occurs when there is a switch in techniques from one with a higher value of capital per man to one with a lower value of capital per man as the rate of profits falls; reswitching implies capital-reversing but not vice versa). The assumption employed by Samuelson in his two-sector model to prevent either reswitching or capital-reversing was that, for each technique, the method of production should be identical in both sectors (a technique defines a method of production for each sector). Once this assumption of equal capital–labour ratios is relaxed, it is impossible to construct a surrogate production function (see the four truths of §3.2.1). Champernowne assumed straightforwardly that neither reswitching nor capital-reversing would occur; however, he failed to determine distribution by marginal productivity because he needed an exogenous rate of profits to value the capital stock, which was then inserted into the production function so that the marginal product of capital was equal to the given exogenous value of the rate of profits, i.e. distribution of the net product between wages and profits remain undetermined.

In §3.2.1, we introduce the basic concepts of the wage curve, reswitching of techniques and capital-reversing within the context of a two-sector model. This is generalised to an n-sector model in §3.2.2. Levhari claimed to have proved a non-switching theorem for a (Sraffa) circulating capital model, which is a special case of ours. Levhari's claim is shown to be false.

§3.1. The standard commodity

§3.1.1. *Introduction*

Section 3.1 will form a commentary on certain aspects of Part 1 of Piero Sraffa's *Production of Commodities by Means of Commodities.* Accordingly, this section is best read in conjunction with Sraffa's work (though, not necessarily, vice versa.) We shall refer to sections in Sraffa's book by numbers in square brackets.

Chapter 1, [1]–[3], deals with a subsistence economy. Propositions contained there can be derived straightforwardly using properties of stochastic matrices.

It is in Chapter 2 that Sraffa begins consideration of an economy which generates a surplus. Prior to taking up Sraffa's argument, there are two preliminaries.

The first refers to returns to scale:

"No changes in output and no changes in the proportions in which different means of production are used by an industry are considered, so that no question arises as to the variation or constancy of returns to scale." (p. v.).

The second refers to the treatment of the labour input. At the outset, we shall regard "wages as consisting of the necessary subsistence of the workers and thus entering the system on the same footing as the fuel for the engines or the feed for the cattle." ([8], p. 9) Later it becomes necessary to allow workers a share of the surplus product. Ideally then, the wage should consist of two parts—the fixed part, consisting of the goods necessary for subsistence (which would appear in the means of production), and the variable part, consisting of the share of the surplus. However, following Sraffa, we treat "the whole of the wage as variable. The drawback of this course is that it involves relegating the necessaries of consumption to the limbo of non-basic products." ([8], p. 10)

Our main purpose is to derive Sraffa's standard commodity—this we achieve by applying Frobenius theorems. To facilitate this, we introduce input–output coefficients:

$$a_{ij} = x_{ij}/x_j \qquad i, j = 1, \ldots, n$$

(Sraffa deals with flow matrices $X = [x_{ij}]$.) From Chapter 2 above, we have the following equations:

$$x = Ax + f \qquad \cdots [1]$$

$$p' = p'A + v' \qquad \cdots [2]$$

§3.1.2. *Production with a surplus*

We consider a system which yields a physical surplus, i.e. $Ax \leqslant x$ (or $\mathbf{0} \leqslant f$).

"The surplus (or profit) must be distributed in proportion to the means of production (or capital) advanced in each industry; and such a proportion between two aggregates of heterogeneous goods (in other words, the rate of profits) cannot be determined before we know the prices of the goods. On the other hand, we cannot defer the allotment of the surplus till after the prices are known for ... the prices cannot be determined before knowing the rate of profits. The result is that the distribution of the surplus must be determined through the same mechanism and at the same time as are the prices of commodities." ([4], p. 6)

So putting $v' = rp'A$ in eqn [2], we have:

$$p' = (1+r)p'A$$

or

$$p'A = (1/(1+r))p' \qquad \cdots [3]$$

where r is the uniform rate of profits.

The Frobenius theorem can be applied immediately to eqn [3] to yield a meaningful solution, i.e. $p \geq \mathbf{0}$, $r \geq 0$.

§3.1.3. *Basic commodities*

"One effect of the emergence of a surplus must be noticed. Previously, all commodities ranked equally, each of them being found among both the products and among the means of production; as a result, each, directly or indirectly, entered the production of all the others, and each played a part in the determination of prices. But now there is room for a new class of 'luxury' products which are not used, whether as instruments of production or as articles of subsistence, in the production of others. These products have no part in the determination of the system. Their role is purely passive." ([6])

A basic commodity enters either directly or indirectly into the production of all commodities. We may illustrate this by reference to the following matrix:

$$\begin{array}{cc} I \\ J \end{array} \quad \begin{bmatrix} A^{11} & A^{12} \\ 0 & A^{22} \end{bmatrix} \\ \qquad\quad I \qquad J$$

where A^{11} and A^{22} are indecomposable. The commodities indexed by $i \in I$ are basic; those by $j \in J$ are non-basic.

§3.1.4. *Production with a surplus (continued)*

We now adopt the second interpretation of the wage, as outlined in §3.1.1. We must now represent explicitly the quantity of labour employed in each industry. So, we introduce the vector of labour input coefficients:

$$l = (l_1, \ldots, l_n) \quad \text{where} \quad \sum_{i=1}^{n} l_i = 1$$

Replacing v' by $wl' + rp'A$ in eqn [2], we obtain:

$$p' = (1+r)p'A + wl' \qquad \cdots [4]$$

We may define the national income as:

$$p'(I-A)x = 1 \qquad \cdots [5]$$

Together eqns [4] and [5] constitute a system of $(n+1)$ equations in $(n+2)$ unknowns—n prices, w and r. (Note that the national income becomes the standard in terms of which w and p are expressed.) So the system operates with one degree of freedom. Let us take r as exogenous.

If $r=R\ (=r_{max})=(1-\lambda^*(A))/\lambda^*(A)$, $w=0$. This follows from eqn [4] with $w=0$.

We now consider the case of $w>0$. From eqn [4]:

$$p'[I-(1+r)A]=wl'$$

Then $p\geqslant\mathbf{0}$ for $wl\geqslant\mathbf{0}$ iff $1>(1+r)\lambda^*(A)$, which after manipulation becomes: $R>r$.

So, as long as we choose $r<R$, we are assured of $p\geqslant\mathbf{0}$, $w\geqslant 0$. We may evaluate p and w, corresponding to a given r, thus: let $r=\bar{r}<R$, $w=\bar{w}$. Then

$$\bar{p}'=\bar{w}l'[I-(1+\bar{r})A]^{-1}\geqslant\mathbf{0}'$$

Substituting in eqn [5], we have two possibilities:
(i) $\bar{p}'(I-A)x=1$; in which case, we write $\bar{p}=\tilde{p}$, $\bar{w}=\tilde{w}$.
(ii) $\bar{p}'(I-A)x=\sigma\neq 1$.
Then $(\bar{p}'/\sigma)(I-A)x=1$; write $\tilde{p}=\bar{p}/\sigma$ and $\tilde{w}=\bar{w}/\sigma$ so that

$$\tilde{p}'(I-A)x=1.$$

In the next section, we take up this theme of variations in the distributional parameters, r and w.

§3.1.5. *The effect of variations in r and w*

"The key to the movement of relative prices consequent upon a change in the wage lies in the inequality of the proportions in which labour and means of production are employed in the various industries." ([15])

Given the inequality of proportions in the various industries, prices will, in general, change consequent on a change in w (and r).

"The necessity of having to express the price of one commodity in terms of another which is arbitrarily chosen as standard, complicates the study of the price movements which accompany a change in distribution. It is impossible to tell of any particular price fluctuation whether it arises from the peculiarities of the commodity which is being measured or from those of the measuring standard." ([23])

So, it would be desirable to have "some invariable standard measure of value, which should itself be subject to none of the fluctuations to which the other commodities are exposed."(1)

Suppose that there was an industry which employed labour and means of production in a "critical" proportion, so that, with a fall in wages say, the proceeds of the wage-reduction would equal the payment of profits at the general rate of profits. We then say that the proportion of labour to means of production is "balanced". Suppose also that the means of production (in aggregate) were produced by labour and means of production in the "critical" proportion; and so on, through all "layers" of production relating to means of production, means of production for means of production, etc. In such an industry, the ratio of the value of output to the value of the means of production would be unaffected by distributional changes.

"Of such a (commodity) it is impossible to be possessed."[2]

"A mixture of commodities, however, or a 'composite commodity' would do equally well.... We should, however, not get very far with the attempt to concoct such a mixture before realising that the perfect composite commodity of this type, in which the requirements are filled to the letter, consists of the same commodities (combined in the same proportions) as does the aggregate of its own means of production—in other words, such that both product and means of production are quantities of the self-same composite commodity." ([24])

§3.1.6. *The standard commodity*

It is evident from the last quotation above that we are interested in a system consisting of basic commodities only. This implies that the associated matrix of input–output coefficients is indecomposable (and non-negative). Without loss of generality, let A be this matrix, with l the vector of labour input coefficients.

Consider:

$$x = Ax + f \qquad \cdots [6]$$

where $y = Ax$ is the vector of means of production.

"The fact that in the Standard System the various commodities are produced in the same proportions as they enter the aggregate means of production implies that the rate by which the quantity produced exceeds the quantity used up in production is the same for each of them." ([27])

Hence, $f = \alpha y$, $\alpha > 0$, given the relation between the composite commodity and its means of production. Hence eqn [6] becomes:

$$x = (1+\alpha)Ax$$

or

$$Ax = 1/(1+\alpha)x \qquad \cdots [7]$$

As $A \geqslant [0]$ is indecomposable, there exists $\lambda^*(A) > 0$, $x^* > \mathbf{0}$ satisfying eqn [7], by the Frobenius theorem. We have:

$$\alpha = (1-\lambda^*(A))/\lambda^*(A) - R \qquad \cdots [8]$$

The standard system consists of the set of equations referring to all the basic commodities.

The components of the vector x^* indicate the proportions of the various basic commodities in the standard commodity. The "size" of the standard system is obtained by solving:

$$l'x^* = 1 \qquad \cdots [9]$$

As an illustration, we solve Sraffa's example in [25]. It is evident that:

$$A = \begin{bmatrix} \frac{1}{2} & \frac{1}{9} & \frac{1}{12} \\ \frac{2}{3} & \frac{5}{18} & \frac{1}{12} \\ \frac{1}{3} & \frac{1}{3} & \frac{5}{12} \end{bmatrix}$$

The roots of this matrix are: $\frac{1}{6}, \frac{7}{36}, \frac{5}{6}$.

$\lambda^*(A) = \frac{5}{6}$; hence, from eqn [8], $\alpha = \frac{1}{6}/\frac{5}{6} = \frac{1}{5} = R$, which confirms Sraffa's result in [27].

To find the proportions of the standard commodity, we solve the equation: $Ax = \lambda^*(A)x$. Routine calculations yield $x = \beta(1, \frac{3}{2}, 2)$. x^* is that vector x which satisfies eqn [9].

Now $l' = (\frac{3}{16} \cdot \frac{1}{180}, \frac{5}{16} \cdot \frac{1}{450}, \frac{8}{16} \cdot \frac{1}{180})$

Putting $l'x = 1$ yields $\beta = 240$.

Hence $x^* = (240, 360, 480)$, as in [26]

R (the maximum rate of profits) is the standard ratio, the proportion by which the gross output of the standard system exceeds its aggregate means of production. Hence:

$$f = Ry \qquad \cdots [10]$$

regardless of the distribution between wages and profits.

Now suppose that a fraction, w^*, of the standard net product is allocated to wages ($0 < w^* < 1$), the fraction $(1 - w^*)$ being allocated to profits. Then the rate of profits, r, is given by

$$r = \frac{p'(1 - w^*)Ry}{p'y} = (1 - w^*)R \cdot \frac{p'y}{p'y} = (1 - w^*)R$$

$$r = (1 - w^*)R \qquad \cdots [11]$$

This relation obtains in the standard system, assuming that the wage is measured in terms of the standard commodity. Eqn [11] is in fact a physical relation (i.e. it can be derived without reference to prices at all).

Let q be the vector of commodities comprising profits. Evidently, $q = (1 - w^*)f$, where f is the standard net product. Using eqn [10], we have:

$$q = (1 - w^*)Ry \qquad \cdots [12]$$

As q and y are positive vectors, we have:

$$r\mathbf{1} : \mathbf{1} = (1 - w^*)Ry : y$$

from which eqn [11] follows straightforwardly.

"The rate of profits in the Standard System thus appears as a ratio between quantities of commodities irrespective of their prices." ([29])

"Such a relation is of interest only if it can be shown that its application is not limited to the imaginary Standard System but is capable of being extended to the actual economic system of observation." ([30])

We now extend eqn [11] to the actual, as distinct from the standard system on the assumption that the wage is measured in terms of the standard commodity. With the standard net product as numeraire, we have:

$$p'(I-A)x^*=1 \qquad \cdots [13]$$

From eqn [4]:

$$p'=(1+r)p'A+w^*l' \qquad \cdots [14]$$

We have also from eqns [7] and [8]:

$$Ax^*=(1/(1+R))x^* \qquad \cdots [15]$$

$$l'x^*=l'x=1 \qquad \cdots [16]$$

Post-multiplying eqn [14] by x^*, we have

$$p'x^*=(1+r)p'Ax^*+w^*l'x^*$$

or

$$p'Ax^*+1=p'Ax^*+rp'Ax^*+w^*$$

using eqns [13] and [16], or

$$rp'Ax^*=1-w^* \qquad \cdots [17]$$

Pre-multiplying eqn [15] by p′, we have:

$$p'Ax^*=(1/(1+R))p'x^*$$

or $(1+R)p'Ax^*=1+p'Ax^*$ using eqn [13], or

$$1=Rp'Ax^* \qquad \cdots [18]$$

From eqns [17] and [18], we have:

$$\frac{1-w^*}{r}=\frac{1}{R}$$

or

$$r=(1-w^*)R \quad \text{(i.e. eqn [11])} \qquad \cdots [19]$$

Finally, we establish the uniqueness of the standard system and the standard commodity.

Given indecomposability of A, it follows from Theorem 28 of Chapter 2 that x^* is the only possible semi-positive characteristic vector of A. Uniqueness then follows trivially.

§3.1.7. *Conclusions*

Given *any* system of single-product industries (i.e. no joint production), we may extract those industries producing basic commodities. In this basic, or standard, system, a standard commodity exists; with the standard net product as numeraire, a simple relation exists between the rate of profits and the wage rate which is independent of prices. This relation holds in the original system (from which the standard system was constructed), if the standard net product is maintained as numeraire. This is consistent with the classical view that the determination of distribution is logically prior to and independent of prices.

The results derived above do not depend on assumptions about fixed coefficients, or constant returns to scale, etc. If the input–output coefficients vary between time periods, due to increasing returns or technical change, there will still exist in each time period a (unique) standard system and standard commodity, on the basis of which we may derive the relation between the wage rate and the rate of profits.

§3.2. Reswitching of techniques

§3.2.1. *A two-sector model*

1. Sraffa's "rigorous demonstration of the possibility of . . . 'the double-switching of techniques'" was, according to Dobb, his "most important single contribution to a 'Critique of Economic Theory'."[(3)] Double-switching, or reswitching, occurs when a technique of production is the most profitable at (at least) two distinct values of the rate of profit, with a different technique most profitable at an intermediate value of the rate of profit. The significance of reswitching may be appreciated from what follows.

"The neo-classical tradition, like the Christian, believes that profound truths may be told by way of parable. The neo-classical parables are intended to enlighten believers and non-believers alike concerning the forces which determine the distribution of income between profit-receivers and wage-earners, the patterns of capital accumulation and economic growth over time and the choice of techniques of production associated with these developments. Four truths which, before the revelations of the false and true prophets in the course of the recent debate, were thought to be established were:
(i) an association between lower rates of profits and higher values of capital per man employed;
(ii) an association between lower rates of profits and higher capital–output ratios;
(iii) an association between lower rates of profits and (through investment in more 'mechanised' or 'round-about' methods of production) higher sustainable steady states of consumption per head (up to a maximum);
(iv) that, in competitive conditions, the distribution of income between

profit-receivers and wage-earners can be explained by knowledge of marginal products and factor supplies."[4]

2. We illustrate this by reference to a fixed-coefficients two-sector model.
2.1. A technique of production describes a method of production for each sector, i.e. one method for producing the consumption good by labour and a specific capital good, and one method for producing the specific capital good by labour and itself. We suppose that the capital good has a rate of mortality, δ, independent of age; also, that the rate of profits, r, and the wage rate, w, are uniform. Then, we have the following price equations:

$$\begin{aligned} 1 &= pa_{21}(r+\delta)+wa_{31} \\ p &= pa_{22}(r+\delta)+wa_{32} \end{aligned} \qquad \cdots [1]$$

where p is the price of the capital good (indexed by 2) in terms of the consumption good (assumed to be the numeraire and indexed by 1), and labour is indexed by 3.
From eqn [1]:

$$w=[1-a_{22}(r+\delta)]/[a_{31}+(a_{32}a_{21}-a_{31}a_{22})(r+\delta)] \qquad \cdots [2]$$

we assume: $1>\delta a_{22}$; $a_{21}\neq 0$, $a_{22}\neq 0$; $a_{31}\neq 0$ or $a_{32}\neq 0$. Under these assumptions, we see that when $r=0$, $w=w_{max}=W$; as r rises from 0, w falls continuously from W until when $w=0$, $r=r_{max}=R$.

Equation [2] is the wage-curve. The notion of an "integrated consumption-good industry" can now be introduced with advantage. In such an industry, the proportion, ρ, of the capital goods industry to the consumption goods industry just ensures the replacement of the capital goods consumed in the consumption goods industry. (We require this construct if the net product is to consist of a physical quantity of the consumption good, i.e. if the net product is to be unaffected by relative price changes.)

Consider Figure 1, in which examples of wage-curves are drawn. OW = wage rate when r is zero = net physical output per man (obtained from the technique of production in question) = output to be divided between wages and profits.

Fig. 1. Examples of wage-curves

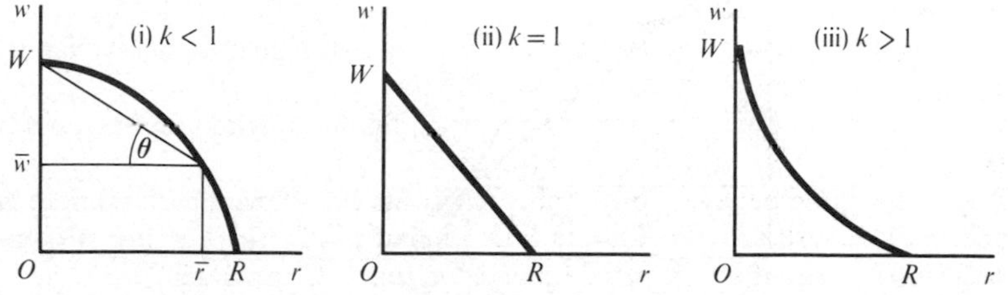

At wage $O\bar{w}$, $\bar{w}W$ measures the amount of consumption paid as profits per man. Then $\tan\theta$ measures the value of capital per man at $r=\bar{r}$.

It can be easily demonstrated that in our model the shape of the wage curve depends on $k=(a_{21}/a_{31})/(a_{22}/a_{32})$.

Exercises

1. Consider Figure 1. Prove that (i) is associated with $k<1$, (ii) with $k=1$, and (iii) with $k>1$.
2. Derive an expression for p from eqn [1]. Prove that $p>0$ if $0\leqslant r\leqslant R$. Prove that if $k<(>)1$, p rises (falls) with r, while if $k=1$, p is constant.
3. Prove that $\rho=a_{21}\delta/(1-a_{22}\delta)$.
4. What happens if we do not assume the existence of the "integrated consumption-good industry"?

(Hint: Suppose that the economy grows at a steady rate g. Let M be the stock of machines per man, m the gross (physical) investment per man and c the level of consumption per man. Then $m=(g+\delta)M$. Dual to the price equations, we have the quantity equations:

$$\begin{aligned} 1 &= a_{32}(g+\delta)M+a_{31}c \\ M &= a_{22}(g+\delta)M+a_{21}c \end{aligned} \qquad \cdots [3]$$

Just as eqn [2] is obtained from eqn [1], so a consumption–growth curve can be obtained from eqn [3]. If we rewrite [2] as $w=f(r)$, prove that the consumption–growth curve is $c=f(g)$. On this, consult the paper by Spaventa, listed in the References.)

2.2 We may repeat the above analysis for different techniques of production. Consider Figure 2. Technique (α) has the straight-line wage-curve, technique (β) the concave wage-curve.

Exercise 5. Which technique is chosen for a given value of r? Let W_σ, R_σ denote the maximum wage rate and rate of profits respectively for technique σ, $\sigma=\alpha$, β. Suppose $R_\alpha>R_\beta$, as in Figure 2. If $R_\beta<r\leqslant R_\alpha$, it is

Fig. 2. Wage-curves for different techniques

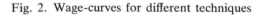

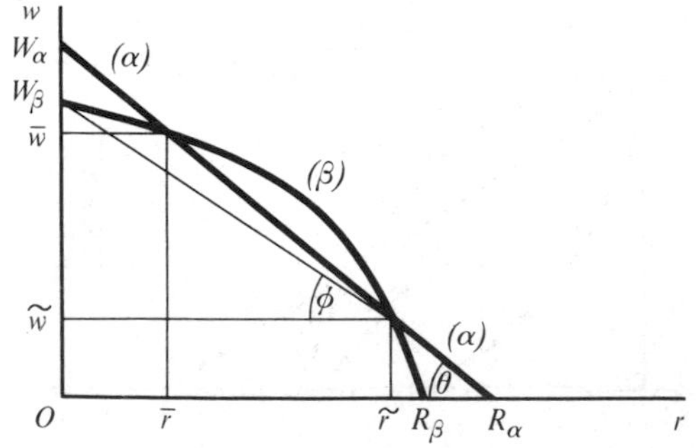

evident that technique (α) will be chosen. So suppose that $r < R_\alpha$ and $r < R_\beta$. Evaluate prices and the wage rate corresponding to the given value of r. Prove that one technique minimises costs regardless of which set of prices, wage rate and rate of profits is used. Hence, given r, that technique yielding the highest w is used. (A similar result is derived below for an n-sector model).

Prove that a switch-point (if there is one), r, w and prices are identical for techniques (α) and (β).

Hence only a technique with part of its wage-curve on the outer envelope (or north-east frontier) will ever be chosen. So, in Figure 2, (α) is chosen for $0 \leqslant r \leqslant \bar{r}$ and $\bar{r} \leqslant r \leqslant R_\alpha$, while ($\beta$) is chosen for $\bar{r} \leqslant r \leqslant \bar{r}$. $\bar{r}$ and $\bar{r}$ are the switch-points.

Consider now Figure 3. Technique (γ) will never be chosen because it is dominated by either (α) or (β) for any feasible value of r, i.e. for $0 \leqslant r \leqslant R_\gamma$, the maximum wage yielded by technique (α) or (β) is greater than that yielded by (γ).

Figure 2 provides us with an illustration of reswitching of techniques. Let us trace its implications. (Incidentally, the value of capital per man is constant for technique (α) and is given by $\tan\theta$; the value of capital per man for technique (β) varies with r.) Suppose r is initially at R_α; technique (α) is most profitable and is chosen. Consider smaller values of r. Around $\tilde{r}$, there will be a switch from technique (α), with net output per man OW_α and value of capital per man $\tan\theta$, to technique (β), with net output per man OW_β and value of capital per man $\tan\phi$. Technique (α) has a higher value of capital per man and a higher capital–output ratio than technique (β) in the neighbourhood of of ($\tilde{r}$, $\tilde{w}$). So, Truths (i) and (ii), mentioned in **1** above, are falsified.

Now let r take on smaller values. Around $\bar{r}$, there will be a switch back from technique (β) to technique (α)—reswitching. This time, it can be seen that higher values of capital per man and higher capital–output ratios are associated with lower values of r.

Fig. 3. Technique (γ) is dominated by (α) and (β)

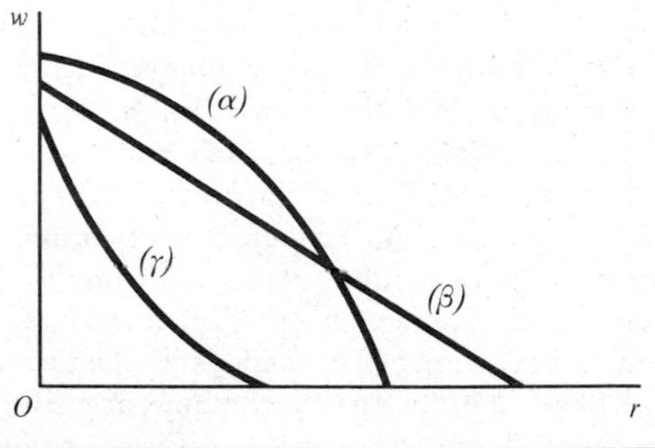

Fig. 4. The relation between consumption per man and the rate of profits (based on Fig. 2)

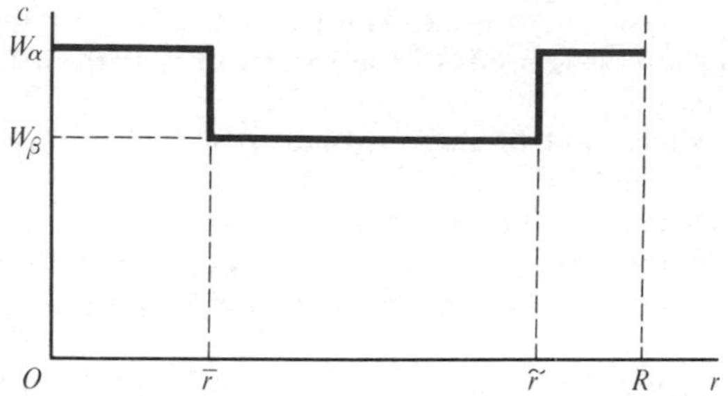

Given our integrated consumption industry construct, we can also discuss Truth (iii). Consider Figure 4. Consumption per man (or, in this case, net output per man) is measured on the vertical axis.
It is evident that Truth (iii) is also falsified. "The reversal of direction of the (r, c) relation was, I must confess, the single most surprising revelation from the reswitching discussion."(5)

2.3. An early reference to the reswitching phenomenon is to be found in Champernowne: "The same physical stock of capital equipment and working capital, producing the same flow of consumption goods, can appear under two equilibrium conditions, differing only in respect to the rate of interest and the rate of real wages, as two different amounts of capital."(6) Champernowne explicitly assumed away reswitching; see, in particular, his assumptions 8 and 9, which are "necessary in order to get neat results . . . intuition suggests that the excluded case is unrealistic, but there is no logical justification for the assumption(s); it is as easy to imagine a world featuring the excluded case as one free of it."(7)

2.4. The analysis so far has been carried out in terms of only two techniques of production. However, once we permit more than two techniques of production, the "paradoxical/perverse/anomalous" behaviour illustrated in **2.2** can arise without reswitching: "capital-reversing" suffices. This latter concept has, in fact, already been introduced. In Figure 2 above, around $(\tilde{r}, \tilde{w})$, there is a switch from the technique with higher output per man and a higher value of capital per man to the technique with lower output per man and lower value of capital per man, as r decreases.

Pasinetti refers to the "unobtrusive postulate" that capital-reversing is assumed away. In conjunction with assumptions of capital malleability and an infinite number of techniques (all ordered according to the "unobtrusive postulate"), this postulate enables us to derive continuity of values of capital per man and net output per man as r changes in the opposite direction. Thus, we have an ordering of techniques according to either value of capital (or net output) per man or the rate of profits at which each technique is most profitable. However, the reswitching debate has conclusively demonstrated that "continuity in variation of techniques, as the rate of profits changes, does not imply continuity in the variation of values of capital goods per man and of net outputs per man."[(8)] This contradicts "the marginal theory interpretation of the rate of profits as a selector of capital intensity, i.e. as 'index of scarcity' of the 'quantity of capital'."[(9)]

Exercises

1. Construct an example (geometrical) to show that capital-reversing can occur without reswitching.
7. Suppose that there are two available techniques, (α) and (β). Prove that if either (i) $R_\alpha > R_\beta$ and $W_\alpha < W_\beta$ or (ii) $R_\alpha < R_\beta$ and $W_\alpha > W_\beta$ there is only one switch-point between the two techniques.
8. Suppose that $k = 1$ for a number of techniques (i.e. each wage-curve is a straight line). It is evident that the reswitching and capital reversing phenomena cannot occur. It is within this context that we discuss Truth (iv).
   Consider Figure 1 (ii). The slope of the straight line RW measures the value of capital per man; as OW measures net output per man, it follows that OR measures the output–capital ratio. Consider Figure 5 below, in which wage curves are drawn for three techniques: verify Truths (i)–(iii) in this context.
   To derive Truth (iv), we proceed as follows. Introduce a continuum of techniques (for each of which $k = 1$) so that each technique is the most profitable at only one rate of profits. We thus have an ordering of techniques according to either decreasing values of capital per man or increasing rates of profits or decreasing capital–output ratios—the ordering is the same no matter which criterion is used. In this case, the

Fig. 5. Wage-curves for different techniques (each with $\kappa = 1$)

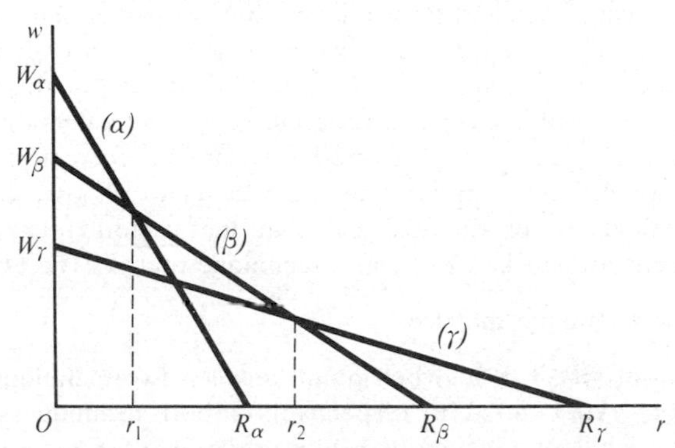

value of capital per man and the capital–output ratio vary continuously in one direction as the rate of profits varies continuously in the other. Hence, we may construct a smooth neo-classical "jelly" production function, $y = f(k)$.

Differentiating $y = rk + w$ (y, k and w each being a quantity of "jelly" per man), we obtain:

$$dy = ydk + kdr + dw$$

Assuming marginal productivity factor pricing, $r = dy/dk$, it follows that:

$$k = -dw/dr.$$

We may write $w = w(r)$ as the equation of the outer envelope (or north-east frontier) of wage curves. Then $-dw/dr$ is the slope of this outer envelope. The elasticity of the envelope at each point is: $(-r/w)dw/dr$. Substituting for $-dw/dr$, we obtain as the elasticity: rk/w. So, we have the distribution of income! Examine the consequences of relaxing the assumption that $k = 1$ for each technique.

§3.2.2. *An n-sector model*

1. We now consider a fixed-coefficients n-sector model in which there is one consumption good, indexed by 1, and m capital goods, indexed by $2, \ldots, n$. We maintain the no joint production assumption.

Denoting the depreciation rate of the j-th capital good by ρ_j, the technical coefficients by $A = [a_{ij}]$, the price vector by p, the rate of profits by r, the wage rate by w, we have in matrix notation:

$$p' = wl' + p'D(r)A \qquad D(r) = [d_i(r)\delta_{ij}],$$

$$d_1(r) = 1,\ d_i(r) = r + \rho_i, \qquad i = 2, \ldots, n,$$

or

$$P' = l' + P'D(r)A \qquad P = p/w \qquad \cdots [1]$$

We shall investigate the conditions under which we can obtain a meaningful solution to eqn [1], i.e. $P \geqslant \mathbf{0}$. First, we have one or two observations. As will be made clear in Chapter 7, our method of dealing with fixed capital evades the specfic problems of fixed capital, i.e. joint production. However, if $\rho_i = 1$, for all $i = 2, \ldots, n$, the model yields the correct treatment of circulating capital. Now suppose that the j-th sector chooses one of its ν_j available methods of production and that the vectors representing the chosen methods are stacked to form a technique matrix. The economy has $\prod_{j=1}^{n} \nu_j$ of these technique matrices.

A rate of profits, $\bar{r}$, is a switch-point between two techniques α and β (represented by $A(\alpha)$ and $A(\beta)$ respectively) if both techniques are equally profitable at $\bar{r}$, while one technique is more profitable for (some) values less than $\bar{r}$, the other for (some) values of r greater than $\bar{r}$. Reswitching occurs if technique α is most profitable at r_1 and r_2, while at least one other technique is most profitable at an intermediate value of r.

Levhari denied the possibility of reswitching in the context of an indecomposable, circulating-capital model. Levhari's non-switching theorem was quickly shown to be false. Before outlining the refutation of the non-switching theorem, we shall discuss the equilibrium price relations. We conclude the chapter with a discussion of the equilibrium quantity relations and the relation between consumption per head and the rate of profits (see Truth (iii) above.)

We begin with an outline of the price relations; we consider the simple case, first of all, where each sector has only one available method of production; the economy has then only one technique matrix.

We are interested in non-negative solutions to eqn [1]. We make the following assumptions:

(A1): each capital good is required directly or indirectly to produce the consumption good; the production of each capital good requires at least one capital good.

(A2): labour is required directly or indirectly to produce each good.

With these assumptions, we can derive:

Theorem 1: If $P > \mathbf{0}$ when $r = 0$, then $(I - D(r)A)^{-1} \geqslant [0]$ iff $r < 1/\lambda^*$, $\lambda^* = \lambda^*[A(I - D(0)A)^{-1}]$.

Proof: Putting $r = 0$, we have:

$$P' = l' + P'D(0)A$$

or

$$P'(I - D(0)A) = l' \qquad \cdots [2]$$

Post-multiplying eqn [2] by $\hat{P}^{-1} = [P_i \delta_{ij}]^{-1}$, we have:

$$\mathbf{1}'\hat{P}[I - D(0)A]\hat{P}^{-1} = l'\hat{P}^{-1}$$

or

$$\mathbf{1}'(I - B) = b'$$

$$\text{where } B = \hat{P}D(0)A\hat{P}^{-1}, \qquad b' = l'\hat{P}^{-1} \geqslant \mathbf{0}'. \qquad \cdots [3]$$

From (A1) and (A2), it follows by Theorems 1 and 29 of Chapter 2 that $\lambda^*(B) < 1$. As $D(0)A$ and B are similar matrices, it follows that $\lambda^*(D(0)A) < 1$. Then $(I - D(0)A)^{-1} \geqslant [0]$.
Now $(I - D(r)A) = [I - \hat{r}A(I - D(0)A)^{-1}](I - D(0)A)$, $\hat{r} = D(r) - D(0)$.
If $(I - D(r)A)^{-1}$ exists, we have:

$$(I - D(r)A)^{-1} = (I - D(0)A)^{-1}[I - \hat{r}A(I - D(0)A)^{-1}]^{-1} \qquad \cdots [4]$$

By the hypothesis of the theorem, it follows that $(I - D(0)A)^{-1} \geqslant [0]$. Then from eqn [4]:

$(I-D(r)A)^{-1} \geqslant [0]$ iff $[I-\hat{r}A(I-D(0)A)^{-1}]^{-1} \geqslant [0]$, which will be true iff $1/r > \lambda^*[A(I-D(0)A)^{-1}]$, by Theorems 1 and 29 and Lemma 1 of Chapter 2. The result follows.

We now introduce:

Definition 1: A given value of r is *feasible* if the solution of eqn [1], corresponding to that value of r, is positive.

In view of Theorem 1, our next result is not altogether surprising.

Theorem 2: r is feasible iff $(I-D(r)A)^{-1} \geqslant [0]$.

Proof:

Sufficiency: We may expand $(I-D(r)A)^{-1}$ as a matrix power series (see Exercises §2.3, Q9):

$$(I-D(r)A)^{-1} = I + D(r)A + [D(r)A]^2 + \cdots$$

Then:

$$P' = l' + l'D(r)A + l'[D(r)A]^2 + \cdots$$

If $l_j > 0$, evidently $P_j > 0$.
If $l_j = 0$, then by (A1) there exists an integer h and index i such that $l_i a_{ij}^{(h)} > 0$, where $A^h = [a_{ij}^{(h)}]$. Hence $P_j > 0$.
So, in either case, $P_j > 0$. Hence, $P > \mathbf{0}$.

Necessity: The proof is the same as the first part of Theorem 1 with 0 replaced by r.

In the next theorem, we examine how P changes with r.

Theorem 3: If r is feasible, then $\mathrm{d}P_i/\mathrm{d}r > 0$, for all i.

Proof: If r is feasible, then:

$$\begin{aligned} P' &= l'(I-D(r)A)^{-1} \\ &= l' + l'D(r)A + l'[D(r)A]^2 + \cdots \end{aligned}$$

Then by (A1) and (A2), $\mathrm{d}P/\mathrm{d}r > \mathbf{0}$ (using an argument similar to that employed in Theorem 2).

Armed with this, we can now construct a wage-curve for the one technique, call it (α). This curve, which graphs $w/p_i = 1/P_i$ against r, is illustrated in Figure 6.
By Theorem 3, we have $\mathrm{d}(w/p_i)/\mathrm{d}r = \mathrm{d}(1/P_i)/\mathrm{d}r < 0$. The sign of the second derivative is ambiguous. So the only restriction on the shape of the curve is that it is downward sloping.
Let us now suppose that alternative techniques are available, say (α), (β),

Fig. 6. Wage-curve for technique (α)

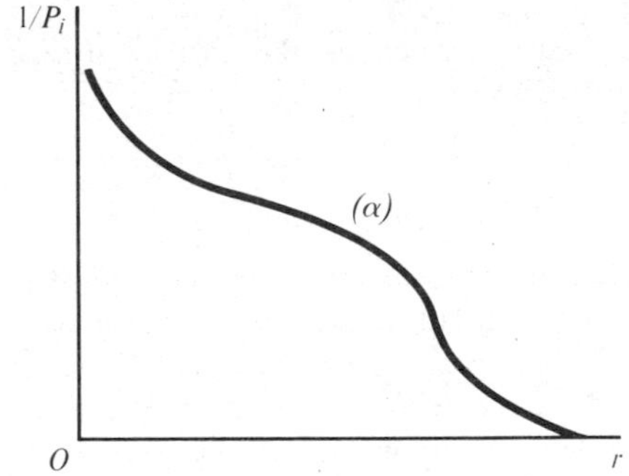

(γ), (δ), (ε), ... The above analysis may be repeated for each technique; in particular, we may construct wage-curves, as in Figure 7.

We now consider the problem of choice of technique in equilibrium. The first point to note is illustrated in Figure 7; if $1/\lambda^*_\beta > 1/\lambda^*_\gamma$, r is feasible for just one technique, (β). So, for r in this interval, there is no problem of choice of technique. Having dealt with this rather trivial case, we now suppose that r is feasible for two techniques, (α) and (β), and our problem is to determine the one to be employed in equilibrium. Suppose $A(\alpha)$ and $A(\beta)$ differ only in the activity vector used by the n-th sector to produce the n-th commodity (i.e. the n-th column of the matrix). As r is feasible for

Fig. 7. Wage-curves for techniques (α), (β), (γ)

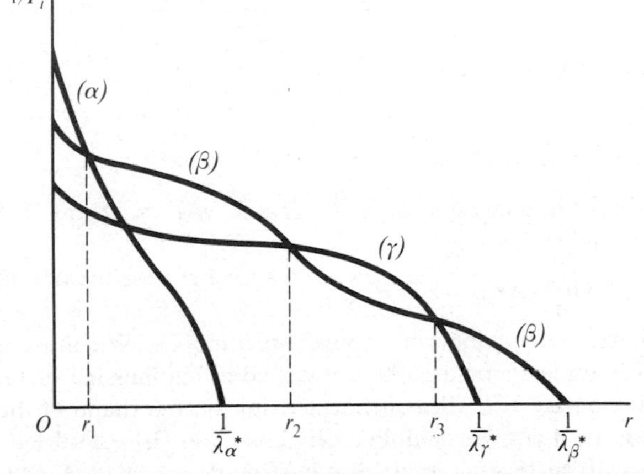

(α), we evaluate the corresponding price vector, $P(\alpha)$:

$$P(\alpha)' = l(\alpha)'(I - D(r)A(\alpha))^{-1}$$

Now use this price vector to calculate the cost of production of the n-th commodity using technique (β). We have:

$$\bar{P}_n(\beta) = l_n(\beta) + \sum_{i=2}^{n} P_i(\alpha)(r + \delta_i)a_{in}(\beta).$$

Suppose $\bar{P}_n(\beta) < P_n(\alpha)$; then, if we use technique (β), it follows from (A1) and (A2) that there will be a fall in the price of the n-th commodity and of any commodity using the n-th commodity either directly or indirectly. Hence, $P(\beta) \leqslant P(\alpha)$. So in the choice between the two techniques, (α) and (β), (β) will be chosen. We now repeat the argument with respect to techniques (β) and (γ), for which r is assumed to be feasible. If $\bar{P}_m(\gamma) < P_m(\beta)$, then by exactly the same argument as above, we have $P(\gamma) \leqslant P(\beta)$, so that (γ) will be chosen in preference to (β). As $P(\gamma) \leqslant P(\alpha)$, it follows that (γ) will be chosen in preference to (α), i.e. we would never encounter intransitivity in the choice of technique matrix, for a given value of r. On the basis of this discussion, we assert:

Theorem 4 (Levhari): Let r be exogenous. Among the set of all techniques for which r is feasible, say $\{(\alpha), (\beta), (\gamma), \ldots, (\kappa), \ldots\}$, there is one, say (κ), that minimises prices in terms of the wage rate (or maximises real wages).

Proof: Suppose technique (κ) is such that using $P(\kappa)$, there is no other activity vector for producing commodity j that yields lower costs. Consider the alternative activity vector, $A(\eta)^j$, the j-th column of the technique matrix $A(\eta)$. By hypothesis:

$$P_j(\kappa) \leqslant l_j(\eta) + P(\kappa)'D(r)A(\eta)^j$$

or

$$P_j(\kappa) - P(\kappa)'D(r)A(\eta)^j \leqslant l_j(\eta)$$

or

$$P(\kappa)'[I - D(r)A(\eta)] \leqq l(\eta)' \qquad \cdots [5]$$

As r is feasible for technique (η), $[I - D(r)A(\eta)]^{-1} \geqslant [0]$, by Theorem 4. Hence eqn [5] becomes:

$$P(\kappa)' \leqq l(\eta)'[I - D(r)A(\eta)]^{-1} = P(\eta)'.$$

So far we have been comparing "pure" techniques. We must now take account of techniques generated by convex combinations of "pure" techniques. Let us compare the prices generated on the one hand by (κ) and on the other hand by a convex combination of (κ) and (η). Let the technology matrix of the mixed technique be $A = \mu A(\kappa) + (1-\mu)A(\eta)$, $\mu \in (0, 1)$, the labour input vector be $l = \mu l(\kappa) + (1-\mu) l(\eta)$, and the price vector be P. We have:

$$P' = l'(I - D(r)A)^{-1}$$

or

$$P'(I - D(r)A) = l' = \mu l(\kappa)' + (1-\mu) l(\eta)' \qquad \cdots [6]$$

Now from the first part of the proof:

$$P(\kappa)'(I - D(r)A(\eta)) \leqslant l(\eta)' \qquad \cdots [7]$$

From eqns [6] and [7]:

$$\begin{aligned} P'(I - D(r)A &\geqslant \mu l(\kappa)' + (1-\mu)P(\kappa)'(I - D(r)A(\eta)) \\ &= \mu P(\kappa)'(I - D(r)A(\kappa)) + (1-\mu)P(\kappa)'(I - D(r)A(\eta)) \\ &= P(\kappa)'(I - D(r)A) \qquad \cdots [8] \end{aligned}$$

From Theorem 21 of Chapter 2, the Frobenius root of A lies between those of $A(\kappa)$ and $A(\eta)$. Hence, if r is feasible for techniques (κ) and (η), it must certainly be feasible for the mixed technique, i.e. $(I - D(r)A)^{-1} \geqslant [0]$. Then, from eqn [8], we have: $P' \geqslant P(\kappa)'$ as required.

This result provides us with a criterion for choice of technique. For example, in Figure 7, (α) is chosen for $r \in [0, r_1]$, (β) for $r \in [r_1, r_2]$ and $r \in [r_3, 1/\lambda^*_\beta)$, (γ) for $r \in [r_2, r_3]$. At the switch points, r_1, r_2 and r_3, two techniques are equally profitable and so either (or a convex combination of the two) could be chosen. Incidentally, Figure 7 illustrates the reswitching phenomenon, for (β) is most profitable over two disconnected intervals of r. Levhari asserted that reswitching could not occur in an indecomposable (Sraffa) circulating capital model. We conclude this section by demonstrating the possibility of reswitching in our model, which includes the circulating capital model as a special case.

Consider the case where (α) and (β) differ with respect to only one activity vector, say the n-th, and $l(\alpha)$ and $l(\beta)$ differ only in their last components.

Suppose that for $r = \tilde{r}$, technique (α) is chosen. Then

$$P(\alpha) \leqslant P(\beta) \quad \text{evaluated at} \quad r = \tilde{r} \qquad \cdots [9]$$

for the other technique (β) for which $\tilde{r}$ is feasible.

$$P(\alpha)' = l(\alpha)' + P(\alpha)'D(r)A(\alpha) \qquad \cdots [10]$$

$$P(\alpha)' \leqslant l(\beta)' + P(\alpha)'D(r)A(\beta) \qquad \cdots [11]$$

as (α) is chosen. From eqns [9]–[11], we have:

$$l(\alpha)' - l(\beta)' + P(\alpha)'D(r)(A(\alpha) - A(\beta)) \leqslant \mathbf{0}' \qquad \cdots [12]$$

Write:

$$P(\alpha)' = l(\alpha)'(I - D(r)A(\alpha))^{-1} \qquad \cdots [13]$$
$$= l(\alpha)' \operatorname{adj}(I - D(r)A(\alpha))/\det(I - D(r)A(\alpha))$$

For a feasible value of r, $\det(I - D(r)A(\alpha)) > 0$ (in fact, $(I - D(r)A(\alpha))$ is an M-matrix).
Define:

$$F(r) = \det(I - D(r)A(\alpha)) \cdot (l(\alpha) - l(\beta))'$$
$$+ l(\alpha)' \operatorname{adj}(I - D(r)A(\alpha)) \, . \, D(r)[A(\alpha) - A(\beta)] \qquad \cdots [14]$$

Evidently:

$$F(\tilde{r}) \leqslant \mathbf{0} \qquad \cdots [15]$$

By construction:

$$F_i(r) = 0, \qquad i = 1, \ldots, m, \quad \text{for all } r; \qquad F_n(\tilde{r}) < 0 \qquad \cdots [16]$$

If $\bar{r}$ is a switching-point between techniques (α) and (β), we must have:

$$F(\bar{r}) = \mathbf{0} \qquad \cdots [17]$$

Given eqn [16], we are interested in the number of solutions of the equation $F_n(r) = 0$ over the set of feasible r's. From eqn [14], $F_i(r)$ is a polynomial of degree n, $i = 1, \ldots, n$, and may thus have up to n roots over the set of feasible r's.
Exercise 9. Generalise this argument to take account of the case where (α) and (β) differ by more than one activity vector.

2. In **2.2** of §3.2.1., we demonstrated the possibility of a reversal of direction of the relation between the level of consumption per man and the rate of profits. We reconsider this relation in the context of our model.

Denote the vector of outputs at (the beginning of) t by $Y(t) = [Y_i(t)]$, $i = 1, \ldots, n$, and the vector of capital stocks available for use during t by $K(t) = [K_i(t)]$ $(K_1(t) = 0)$. Then on the assumption that inputs employed during t yield outputs at the beginning of $t+1$, we have the following equation to describe the stock of the j-th capital good available in $t+1$:

$$K_j(t+1) = Y_j(t+1) + (1 - \rho_j)K_j(t) \qquad \cdots [18]$$

If technique (α) is employed, we have, assuming full employment:

$$A(\alpha)Y(t+1) = K(t) \qquad \cdots [19]$$

$$l(\alpha)'Y(t+1) = L(t) \qquad \cdots [20]$$

Let:

$$C(t) = (Y_1(t), 0, \ldots, 0)' \qquad \cdots [21]$$

Then from eqns [18]–[21], we have:

$$Y(t+1) = A(\alpha)[Y(t+2) - Y(t+1)] + D(0)A(\alpha)Y(t+1) + C(t+1) \qquad \cdots [22]$$

Suppose:

$$L(t+1)=(1+g)L(t) \qquad \cdots [23]$$

Expressing eqn [22] in per capita terms, $y(t+1)=Y(t+1)/L(t)$, we have:

$$y(t+1)=A(\alpha)[(1+g)y(t+2)-y(t+1)]+D(0)A(\alpha)y(t+1)+c(t+1) \qquad \cdots [24]$$

We are interested in steady-state, i.e. $y(t)=y$, for all t. Substituting in eqn [24], we obtain:

$$(I-D(g)A(\alpha))y=c \qquad \cdots [25]$$

This is formally similar to the equilibrium price equation developed above. By Theorem 1, iff $g<1/\lambda^*_\alpha$, $\lambda^*_\alpha=\lambda^*[A(\alpha)(I-D)(0)A(\alpha))^{-1}]$, $(I-D(g)(\alpha))^{-1}\geqslant[0]$ and so a meaningful solution exists. By eqn [20], $l(\alpha)'y=1$, so that y_1 can be calculated from:

$$l(\alpha)'(I-D(g)A(\alpha))^{-1}\begin{bmatrix} y_1 \\ 0 \\ \cdot \\ \cdot \\ \cdot \\ 0 \end{bmatrix}=1 \qquad \cdots [26]$$

(Eqn [26] may be called the consumption-growth curve.)

Suppose that choice of technique is determined by cost minimisation. Suppose that, given g, $y_1(\alpha)\neq y_1(\beta)$. Further, let $\bar{r}$ be a switch-point between (α) and (β), $(\alpha)/(\beta)$ being chosen for a sufficiently small set of values of r less than/greater than $\bar{r}$. Then for all r in this neighbourhood of $\bar{r}$ (except $\bar{r}$ itself) the level of consumption per man is uniquely determined. At $\bar{r}$, (α) or (β) or any convex combination of the two could be chosen; while the level of consumption per man is not uniquely determined at $\bar{r}$, it lies between $y_1(\alpha)$ and $y_1(\beta)$. This is illustrated in Figure 8.
The third possibility, not illustrated, is that, given g, $y_1(\alpha)=y_1(\beta)$; then, reswitching of techniques at $\bar{r}$ does not alter consumption per man.

Fig. 8. (i) $y_1(\alpha)>y_1(\beta)$ (ii) $y_1(\beta)>y_1(\alpha)$

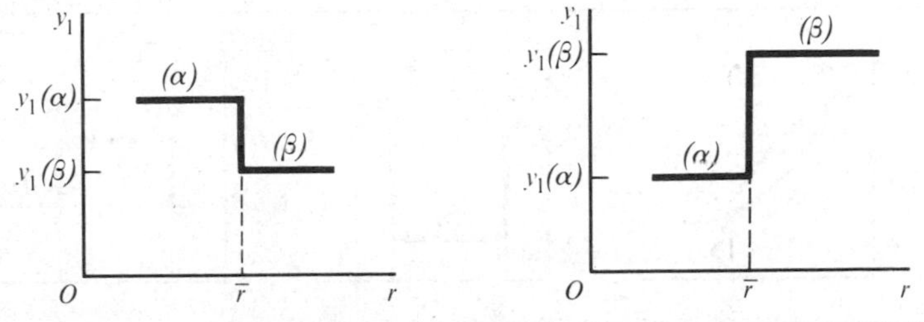

Fig. 9. An example of the relation between consumption per man and the rate of profits

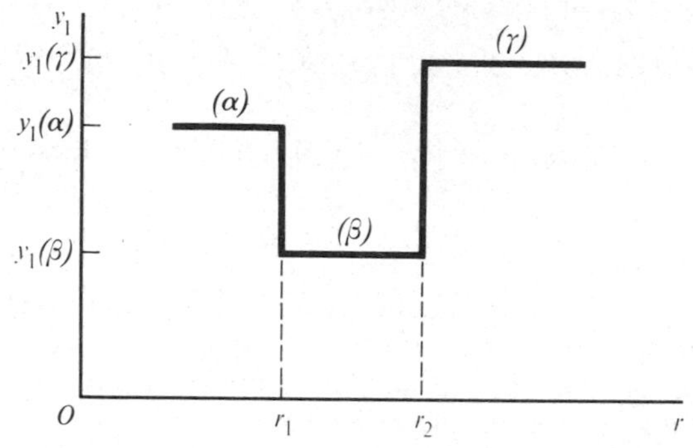

We know that eqn [25] has a meaningful solution iff $g<1/\lambda^*_\alpha$. r is feasible iff $r<.1/\lambda^*_\alpha$. So, if we insist on simultaneous meaningful solutions to the equilibrium price and quantity relations for technique (α), we require both g and r to be less than $1/\lambda^*_\alpha$.

Now suppose that alternative techniques (α), (β), (γ), . . . are available and that $g<1/\lambda^*_\sigma$, $\sigma=\alpha,\ \beta,\ \gamma,\ldots$. The behaviour illustrated in Figure 9 is possible.

The reversal in the direction of consumption per man with changes in r does not necessarily imply the existence of reswitching of techniques, though reswitching suffices to yield the reversal in the direction, as illustrated in Figure 10.

Our concluding result in this chapter is:

Theorem 5: Suppose technique (κ) is employed. Given g, the level of consumption per man is obtained from the wage curve $1/P_1$ by putting $r=g$. In the stationary state (i.e. $g=0$), the level of consumption per man is measured by the intercept of the wage curve on the vertical axis.

Fig. 10. Reswitching and the relation between consumption per man and the rate of profits

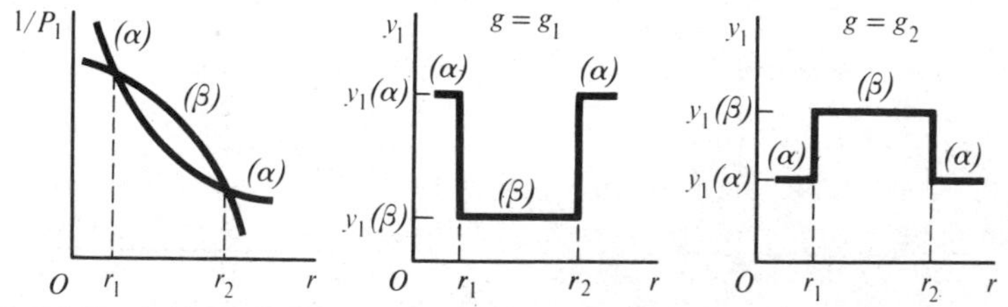

Fig. 11. The effect of a change in the rate of growth on the relation between consumption per man and the rate of profits

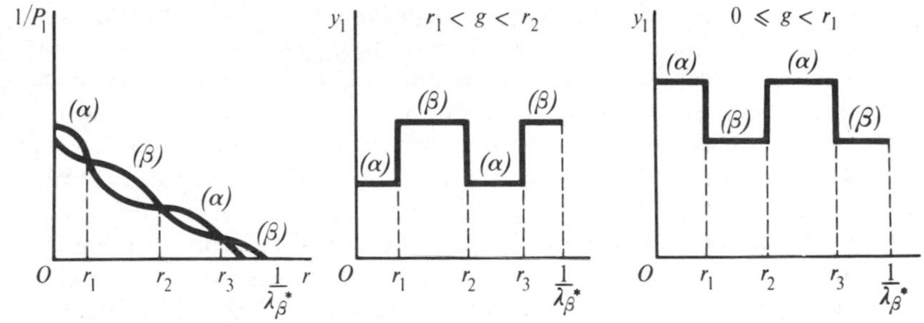

Proof: From eqn [25], $y_1(\kappa) = 1/[l(\kappa)'(I - D(g)A(\kappa))^{-1}]_1$. The price equation for technique (κ) is

$$P(\kappa) = l(\kappa)'(I - D(r)A(\kappa))^{-1}$$

Hence

$$1/P_1(\kappa) = 1/[l(\kappa)'(I - D(r)A(\kappa))^{-1}]_1$$

and the first part of the theorem follows. The second part is trivial. In the stationary state, the analysis of the relation between consumption per man and the rate of profits is considerably simplified.

We conclude this chapter by re-iterating that Figures 8–10 have been constructed on the assumption that g is a given constant. If g changes, the curves would have to be redrawn. It is possible that the relation between $y_1(\alpha)$ and $y_1(\beta)$ for $g = g_1$ would be different from that for $g = g_2$. See Figure 11.

§3.3. Review

"The neo-classical theory of value, production and distribution comes in at least three handy sizes .... The aggregate production function version ... is the simplest and most persuasive version at both the pedagogic and apologetic levels, even if it is not the most respectable or rigorous intellectually." (10) "The other versions are the development of Irving Fisher's theories of the rate of interest in an aggregate, economy-wide setting and the modern model of general equilibrium." (11)

In this review, we shall discuss only the aggregate versions, principally the first; discussion of the third version is appropriately deferred until Chapter 8.

The importance of the aggregate production function concept may be easily explained—it plays a central role in both empirical work and theoretical analysis; with regard to the former, an aggregate production function may be "fitted" with a view to estimating the relative contributions of technical progress and capital accumulation to economic growth; with regard to the latter, production functions are used to explain both the level of (aggregate) output in terms of "labour" and "capital" inputs, and, by use of marginal productivity theory, the distribution of income. (Thus, two "birds" are killed with one "stone".) To do this, capital must be measured in a way that is independent of distribution (and relative prices); for, if the value of capital depends on distribution, how can the production function, which incorporates a measure of capital and *ipso facto* depends on distribution, explain distribution? Champernowne suggested a chain-index method of measuring capital; however, he explicitly assumed the absence of reswitching (and the presence of only two factors of production). An implication of reswitching is that "two physically identical outfits of capital equipment can represent different amounts of 'capital'." (12) Solow argued that "from the point of view of production, two identical plants represent two identical plants." (13)

This must lead us to enquire into the nature of capital. There are (at least) two dimensions of capital that we may distinguish—capital (or physical capital or produced means of production) as an aid to production, and capital (or value capital) as private property yielding income in a private ownership economy.

Solow, like Champernowne, is concerned with the question of the same physical stock of capital appearing at two distinct sets of values of r and w as two different amounts of value capital. This presents obvious difficulties to the economist who is trying to predict the flow of output given factor supplies. So from the point of view of the theory of production, it would seem that Solow's comment is relevant. However, the point is that the production/distribution dichotomy is untenable.(14) This may be clarified as follows:(15)

By definition, we have:

$$y = rk + w \qquad \cdots [1]$$

y being the net national income per man, k the value of capital per man, w the real wage per man, each being measured in terms of a homogeneous consumption good, and r being the rate of profits. Totally differentiating eqn [1], we have:(16)

$$\mathrm{d}y = r\mathrm{d}k + k\mathrm{d}r + \mathrm{d}w \qquad \cdots [2]$$

Evidently, $\mathrm{d}y/\mathrm{d}k \neq r$. This disturbed Champernowne in particular; one of his aims in constructing the chain-index measure of capital was to derive equality between the wage rate and the marginal product of labour, and the rate of profits and the marginal product of capital. Champernowne realised, as noted in paragraph **2.3** of §3.2.1, that his chain-index could not be constructed in the event of reswitching of techniques. He also realised that the presence of capital-reversing would preclude the construction of the chain-index; for he stated in that section of his paper on "Possible anomalies in the two-factor model" that the further assumption needed (in addition to the absence of reswitching, etc.) to obtain a neoclassical production function was that, if two techniques have a switch-point at $(\bar{r}, \bar{w})$, the technique employed for values of r less than $\bar{r}$ would have the higher output per man. Under this assumption, a gradual fall in the rate of profits would entail increases in both output per man and the quantity of capital per man. But although this may fit in well with preconceived notions, there is no logical justification for this assumption.(17)

Champernowne's method of obtaining equality between the rate of profits and the marginal product of capital (and hence of the wage rate and the marginal product of labour) was to differentiate eqn [1] for fixed values of r and w, i.e. $dw = dr = 0$.

The reswitching and capital reversing phenomena, which played such a vital role in the capital controversies of the 1960s, had thus been noted by economists at least one decade earlier. In the preface, Sraffa refers to the central propositions of his book as having taken shape in the late 1920s. Joan Robinson was aware of the capital reversing phenomenon when she wrote *The Accumulation of Capital*, published in 1956; she regarded it "rather unlikely that cases of this kind should be common .... (and) We may therefore take it as a general rule that a higher degree of mechanisation is associated with a higher, not a lower, level of wages in terms of product." (18) Clearly, the implications has not been seen and remained unsuspected. Indeed, Joan Robinson described her analysis of the capital-reversing phenomenon (or "Ruth Cohen Curiosum") as "not of great importance".(19)

Exercises

§3.2

Nos 1–9 are found within text of §3.2.

10. Consider the situation where $A(\alpha)$ and $A(\beta)$ differ only in the last column and $l(\alpha)$ and $l(\beta)$ only in the last component. Let $z = \begin{bmatrix} A(\alpha)^n - A(\beta)^n \\ l_n(\alpha) - l_n(\beta) \end{bmatrix}$. Prove that (α) and (β) do not have a switch-point if: (i) $z = \mathbf{0}$; (ii) $z \geqslant \mathbf{0}$; (iii) $z \leqslant \mathbf{0}$.

11. Let $\bar{r}$ be feasible for techniques (α) and (β). Prove that $P(\alpha) = P(\beta)$, at $r = \bar{r}$, iff $F(\bar{r}) = \mathbf{0}$ [$F(r)$ is defined in eqn [14] of §3.2.2].

12. Consider the following example (due to Pasinetti):
To produce one unit of a commodity, say G, at the end of the current period:
Technique (α) requires 0.8 units of G during the current period and 20 units of labour 8 periods ago;
Technique (β) requires 0.8 units of G and 24 units of labour during the current period and 1 unit of labour 25 periods ago.

(i) Write down the matrices $A(\alpha)$ and $A(\beta)$, the labour input vectors $l(\alpha)$ and $l(\beta)$.

(The problem is one of representing the maturing labour inputs; $A(\alpha)$ and $l(\alpha)$ are of order 9, $A(\beta)$ and $l(\beta)$ of order 26.)

(ii) Evaluate $1/\lambda_\alpha^*$ and $1/\lambda_\beta^*$ (they are equal).

(iii) Write down the price equations and wage curves for the two techniques. Determine the switch-points.

13. Consider the relation between consumption per man, y_1, and the rate of profits, r. Prove that y_1 attains its maximum when $r=g$. Demonstrate that $r=g$ is not necessary for a maximum of y_1.

14. Is reswitching possible in an economy with only one kind of capital good?

15. How should the analysis be modified to take account of the existence of more than one consumption good?

16. "Capital (is) a field unsuitable to the application of the calculus and infinitesimal analysis, and thus of marginal analysis." [20] Discuss.

17. "The question that confronts us is not whether the Cambridge criticism is theoretically valid. It is. Rather the question is an empirical or econometric one: is there sufficient substitutability within the system to establish neo-classical results?" [21] Discuss.

18. "It is, however, a peculiar feature of the set of propositions now published that, although they do not enter into any discussion of the marginal theory of value and distribution, they have never the less been designed to serve as the basis for a critique of that theory." [22] Discuss.

19. "It is the heterogeneity of capital goods (whether fixed or circulating) as well as the time pattern of production which gives rise to the possibility of double-switching." [23] Elucidate.

Notes

1. Ricardo, David: *On the Principles of Political Economy and Taxation*, Sraffa edn, Cambridge U.P., 1951. p. 43.

2. ibid.

3. Dobb, M.: *Theories of Value and Distribution since Adam Smith*, Cambridge U.P., 1973. p. 252.

4. Harcourt, G. C.: *Some Cambridge Controversies in the Theory of Capital*, Cambridge U.P., 1972. p. 122.

5. Samuelson, P. A.: "A summing up", *Quarterly Journal of Economics,* **80** (1966), reprinted in *Capital and Growth* (G. C. Harcourt and N. F. Laing, eds), Penguin, 1971. p. 243.

6. Champernowne, D. G.: "The production function and the theory of capital: a comment", *Review of Economic Studies,* **21** (1953–54); reprinted in Capital and Growth (G. C. Harcourt & N. F. Laing, eds), Penguin, 1971. p. 66.

7. op. cit. pp 76–7.

8. Pasinetti, L. L.: "Switches of technique and the 'rate of return' in capital theory", *Economic Journal,* **79** (1969); reprinted in *Capital and Growth* (G. C. Harcourt & N. F. Laing, eds), Penguin, 1971. pp 280–1.

9. op. cit. p. 283.

10. Harcourt, G. C.: "The Cambridge controversies: the afterglow", in *Contemporary Issues in Economics* (M. Parkin & A. R. Nobay, eds), Manchester U.P., 1975. pp 305–6.

11. ibid. p. 307.

12. Solow, R. M.: "The production function and the theory of capital", *Review of Economic Studies,* **23** (1956). p. 101.

13. ibid.

14. If situations A and B differ in respect of r and w but employ the same technique, we say nonetheless that A and B are distinct economic states; the difference in the distributive parameters implies that there will be a difference in the price vectors, which in turn implies a difference in the values of capital between A and B, i.e. the difference between A and B has economic significance.

15. Consult the following papers:

Bhaduri, A.: "On the significance of recent controversies in capital theory: a Marxian view", *Economic Journal,* **79** (1969).

Bhaduri, A.: "The concept of the marginal productivity of capital and the Wicksell effect", *Oxford Economic Papers,* **18** (1966).

16. That is, assuming that the operation makes sense, for Pasinetti (*Economic Journal,* 1969) has shown that continuous changes in r (and w) do not necessarily yield continuous changes in y and k.

17. The second half of this paragraph has been transcribed more or less from:

Champernowne, D. G.: "The production function and the theory of capital: a comment", *Review of Economic Studies,* **21** (1953); reprinted in G, C. Harcourt & N. F. Laing: *Capital and Growth,* Penguin, 1971. p. 75, with changes in terminology to make it consistent with that used here.

18 Robinson, J.: *The Accumulation of Capital*, (Macmillan, 1956). p. 110.

19. ibid. p. 109.

20. Pasinetti, L. L. op. cit. p. 281.

21. Ferguson, C. E.: *The Neo-Classical Theory of Production and Distribution*, Cambridge U.P., 1969. p. 266.

22. Sraffa P.: *Production of Commodities by Means of Commodities*, Cambridge U.P., 1963. p. vi.

23. Harcourt, G. C.: *Some Cambridge controversies in the Theory of Capital, Cambridge U.P.*, 1972. p. 154.

References

§3.1

Ricardo, D.: *On the Principles of Political Economy and Taxation*, Sraffa edn, Cambridge U.P., 1951.

Sraffa, P.: *Production of Commodities by Means of Commodities*, Cambridge U.P., 1963.

§3.2

The following collections of articles are useful:

Harcourt, G. C. & N. F. Laing (eds.): *Capital and Growth*, Penguin, 1971; in particular, Parts One and Five and Nuti's paper in Part Six

Hunt, E. K. & J. G. Schwartz (eds): *A Critique of Economic Theory*, Penguin, 1972; in particular, Part Three.

"Symposium on Paradoxes in Capital Theory"; *Quarterly Journal of Economics* **80** (4) November 1966). (This symposium includes papers by Pasinetti, Morishima, Garegnani, Samuelson, and Bruno, Burmeister and Shehinski).

§3.2.1

Garegnani, P.: "Heterogeneous capital, the production function and the theory of distribution", *Review of Economic Studies*, **37** (1970).

Spaventa, L.: "Rate of profit, rate of growth and capital intensity in a simple production model", *Oxford Economic Papers*, **22** (1970).

§3.2.2

Bruno, M., Burmeister, E. & E. Sheshinski: "The nature and implications of the reswitching of techniques", *Quarterly Journal of Economics*, **80** (1966).

Levhari, D.: "A non-substitution theorem and the switching of techniques", *Quarterly Journal of Economics*, **79** (1965).

Pasinetti, L. L.: "Changes in the rate of profit and switches in techniques", *Quarterly Journal of Economics*, **80** (1966).

§3.3

In addition to the works mentioned in §§3.1, 3.2 and the notes, the reader might also consult:

Fisher, F. M.: "The existence of aggregate production functions", *Econometrica*, **37** (1969).

4

Matrix difference and differential equations

The aim of this chapter is to survey those aspects of the theory of (linear) difference and differential equations that are potentially applicable in economics. As can be seen from merely reading the contents of this chapter, there is a common structure to the presentation of the theory of difference and differential equations; many theorems in §4.2 have direct analogues in §4.1, as the reader will discover.

Sections 4.1.1–4.1.7 and 4.2.1–4.2.6 are devoted to the general question of obtaining explicit solutions (in terms of characteristic roots) to systems of linear differential and difference equations respectively. The stability conditions are then derived—in the case of a system of differential equations (§4.1.8), the real part of each root must be negative; for difference equations (§4.2.7), the modulus of each root must be less than one. An alternative approach to stability theory is then outlined (in §§4.1.9 and 4.2.8) which does not directly involve the roots of a matrix—this approach, due to Lyapunov, uses the theory of quadratic forms and suggests an extension to the stability theory of non-linear equations, which is taken up in §4.1.10. The stability theory of linear equations will be applied in Chapter 8 to problems of "local" stability, while the theory of non-linear equations is used in the "global" stability analysis of §8.8.

The remaining sections of §§4.1 and 4.2 are devoted to the analysis of a series of problems that arise particularly in economics.

In §§4.1.11 and 4.2.9, we are concerned with the question of non-negativity of the solution of a system of differential (difference) equations. Non-negativity is, after all, a minimal requirement to place on the solution of a system of equations describing, say, the behaviour of prices or outputs.

Sections 4.2.10–4.2.12 are concerned with the effect of different lag structures on the stability of a system of linear difference equations. This work is important because knowledge of the lag structure of economic relationships is uncertain, to say the least; hence the usefulness of a result such as: "No amount of restructuring of lags will make the stable system,

S_1, unstable, or the unstable system, S_2, stable," on the basis of which an economist can cease to worry about the lag structures involved in S_1 and S_2. As an example of the work of these sections, we have the following remarkable result: Consider a first-order difference equation with a non-negative matrix A:

$$x(t+1) = Ax(t) \qquad \cdots [1]$$

Introduce a more complicated lag structure so that $x(t+1)$ depends on the value of x in the previous T periods:

$$x(t+1) = \sum_{\tau=0}^{T-1} A_\tau x(t-\tau) \qquad \cdots [2]$$

Suppose that only the lag structure has been altered, so that the systems have the same "potential," i.e. $A = \sum_{\tau=0}^{t-1} A_\tau$. Then eqn [1] is stable if and only if eqn [2] is stable.

The derivation of this result makes use of the theory of norms discussed in §2.4.5 and of the equivalence of the quasi-dominant diagonal condition on a non-negative matrix to the condition that the Frobenius root is less than 1 (this latter point was established, it will be remembered, in §§2.2 and 2.3 in our analysis of input–output). The work done in these sections will be applied in §5.4.3 below when we consider the effect of the lag structure on an integrated input–output/expenditure model; meanwhile, Exercises §4.2 provide examples in an aggregate model.

The first twelve sections of §4.2 are concerned with forward difference equations; the value of $x(t+1)$ depends on $x(t)$ and possibly previous values of x. This is implied by an expenditure model with lags. However, the introduction of lags into a production model, say input–output, yields not a forward but a backward difference equation, in which $x(t)$ depends on $x(t+1)$ and possibly later values of x. Some of the difficulties involved in the solution of these backward difference equations are discussed in §4.2.13.

§4.1. Differential equations

§4.1.1. *Introduction*

In the first half of this chapter, we shall be studying equations of the form:

$$\frac{dx}{dt} = Ax + f(t) \qquad \cdots [1]$$

$$\frac{dx}{dt} = Ax \qquad \cdots [2]$$

where x, $f(t)$ and dx/dt are vectors with n components and A is an $n \times n$ matrix.

$$f(t) = [f_i(t)], \qquad \frac{dx}{dt} = \left[\frac{dx_i}{dt}\right] \qquad i = 1, \ldots, n$$

The following justifies the general approach that we shall adopt to the solution of eqn [1].

Theorem 1: Let $\bar{x}(t)$ be any solution of eqn [1]. If $\tilde{x}(t)$ is any other solution of eqn [1], $x(t)=\bar{x}(t)-\tilde{x}(t)$ is a solution of eqn [2].

The proof of this is evident. It enables us to state that the most general solution of eqn [1] is obtained by adding to any particular solution of eqn [1] the general solution of eqn [2]. So, if we are faced with the problem of solving eqn [1], first of all, we solve eqn [2] completely and then add some solution of eqn [1].

Sections 4.1.2–4.1.6 are devoted to the derivation of the general solution of eqn [2]. In §4.1.7, we discuss the construction of particular solutions. Sections 4.1.8–4.1.12 are devoted to stability theory.

§4.1.2. *The solution of* $\mathrm{d}x/\mathrm{d}t = Ax$*: basic results*

Our presentation is not completely self-contained. We shall not prove Theorem 2 below—for a proof, the reader is referred to the books listed in the references. Theorem 2 is the basic existence and uniqueness theorem.

Theorem 2: There exists one and only one solution, denoted by $x(t)$, of $\mathrm{d}x/\mathrm{d}t = Ax$ such that $x(t_0)=x^0$, for any $t_0 \in R$, $x^0 \in R^n$.

The value of this theorem is well illustrated in the following:

Theorem 3: The set of all solutions of $\mathrm{d}x/\mathrm{d}t = Ax$ constitutes an n-dimensional vector space.

Proof: Let x^1, x^2 be solutions of $\dfrac{\mathrm{d}x}{\mathrm{d}t} = Ax$. Then:

$$\begin{aligned}\frac{\mathrm{d}}{\mathrm{d}t}(\alpha_1 x^1 + \alpha_2 x^2) &= \alpha_1 \frac{\mathrm{d}x_1}{\mathrm{d}t} + \alpha_2 \frac{\mathrm{d}x_2}{\mathrm{d}t} \\ &= \alpha_1 A x^1 + \alpha_2 A x^2 \\ &= A(\alpha_1 x^1 + \alpha_2 x^2).\end{aligned}$$

i.e. $\alpha_1 x^1 + \alpha_2 x^2$ is a solution of $\dfrac{\mathrm{d}x}{\mathrm{d}t} = Ax$. Hence the set of solutions of $\mathrm{d}x/\mathrm{d}t = Ax$ is a vector space.

We now prove that this vector space is *n-dimensional.*

Let $\{\bar{x}^1, \bar{x}^2, \ldots, \bar{x}^n\}$ be a linearly independent set of vectors, say the set of n unit vectors.

By Theorem 2, there exists a solution of $\mathrm{d}x/\mathrm{d}t = Ax$, denoted by $x^i(t)$, such that $x^i(\bar{t}) = \bar{x}^i$, $i = 1, \ldots, n$, some $\bar{t} \in R$.

It remains to demonstrate that the set of vectors $\{x^1(t), \ldots, x^n(t)\}$ is linearly independent and that any solution of $\mathrm{d}x/\mathrm{d}t = Ax$ can be expressed as a linear combination of these vectors, i.e. that $\{x^1(t), \ldots, x^n(t)\}$ is a basis of the vector space of solutions of $\mathrm{d}x/\mathrm{d}t = Ax$.

First we demonstrate linear independence.

Suppose that the set is linearly dependent. Then, there exist α_i, $i=1, \ldots, n$, not all zero such that:

$$\sum_{i=1}^{n} \alpha_i x^i(t) = \mathbf{0} \quad \text{for all} \quad t \in R$$

In particular, this is true for $t = \bar{t}$. Substituting this value of t, we obtain:

$$\sum_{i=1}^{n} \alpha_i x^i(\bar{t}) = \sum_{i=1}^{n} \alpha_i \bar{x}^i = \mathbf{0}$$

This contradicts the linear independence of the set $\{\bar{x}^1, \ldots, \bar{x}^n\}$. So the set of solutions $\{x^1(t), \ldots, x^n(t)\}$ is linearly independent.
We now demonstrate that any solution can be expressed as a linear combination of the vectors $x^1(t), \ldots, x^n(t)$. Let $x(t)$ be a solution of $\mathrm{d}x/\mathrm{d}t = Ax$ such that $x(\bar{t}) = \bar{x}$. As $\{\bar{x}^1, \ldots, \bar{x}^n\}$ is a basis of R^n, we have:

$$\bar{x} = \sum_{i=1}^{n} \beta_i \bar{x}^i$$

Then $\sum_{i=1}^{n} \beta_i x^i(t)$ is a solution of $\mathrm{d}x/\mathrm{d}t = Ax$ which assumes the value $\bar{x}$ at $t = \bar{t}$.
By Theorem 2, which is an existence and a uniqueness theorem, there can be only one solution which assumes the value $\bar{x}$ at $t = \bar{t}$. Hence

$$x(t) = \sum_{i=1}^{n} \beta_i x^i(t).$$

This theorem is instructive for it tells us that, if we wish to obtain the most general solution of $\mathrm{d}x/\mathrm{d}t = Ax$, we must obtain n linearly independent solutions.

Definition 1: If G is an $n \times n$ matrix the columns of which are n linearly independent solutions of $\mathrm{d}x/\mathrm{d}t = Ax$, then G is called a *fundamental matrix* for $\mathrm{d}x/\mathrm{d}t = Ax$.

It is evident that G satisfies the equation:

$$\frac{\mathrm{d}G}{\mathrm{d}t} = AG$$

Theorem 4: If G is a fundamental matrix for $\mathrm{d}x/\mathrm{d}t = Ax$ and B is a non-singular matrix, then GB is also a fundamental matrix for $\mathrm{d}x/\mathrm{d}t = Ax$. Also, each fundamental matrix for $\mathrm{d}x/\mathrm{d}t = Ax$ is of the type GB, for some non-singular matrix B.

Proof: $\dfrac{\mathrm{d}}{\mathrm{d}t}(GB) = \dfrac{\mathrm{d}G}{\mathrm{d}t} \cdot B = AG \cdot B = A(GB)$.
A fundamental matrix is non-singular, from Definition 1. So, to conclude

that GB is a fundamental matrix, we have to observe that it must be non-singular, given that G and B are. Now let G_1 and G_2 be fundamental matrices. Let $G_2 = G_1 H(t)$. Differentiating with respect to t, we obtain:

$$\frac{dG_2}{dt} = \frac{dG_1}{dt} \cdot H(t) + G_1 \cdot \frac{dH(t)}{dt}$$

or

$$AG_2 = AG_1 H(t) + G_1 \cdot \frac{dH(t)}{dt}$$

or

$$AG_1 H(t) = AG_1 H(t) + G_1 \cdot \frac{dH(t)}{dt}$$

As G_1 is non-singular, this implies that $\dfrac{dH(t)}{dt} = [0]$.

Hence H is a constant matrix. As G_1 and G_2 are non-singular, it follows that H must be non-singular.

We now derive a fundamental matrix for $dx/dt = Ax$. As a preliminary, we need the following:

Definition 2: Let A be an $n \times n$ matrix. The *matrix exponential* of A, denoted by $\exp A$, is defined by the infinite series:

$$\exp A = I + A + \frac{A^2}{2!} + \cdots + \frac{A^m}{m!} + \cdots.$$

Theorem 5: The matrix exponential is convergent for every square matrix.

Proof: Let $\|A\| = \alpha$ be some norm.

Then $\|A^k/k!\| \leqslant \alpha^k/k!$.

$$\|\exp A\| \leqslant \sum_{k=0}^{\infty} \|A^k/k!| = e^{\alpha}$$

Thus the exponential series in A is absolutely convergent and hence is convergent.

We now outline some properties of the matrix exponential.

Theorem 6: (i) $\exp(P^{-1}AP) = P^{-1}(\exp A)P$;
(ii) $\exp(A+B) = (\exp A)(\exp B)$ iff $AB = BA$;
(iii) $\exp A$ is non-singular; $(\exp A)^{-1} = \exp(-A)$.

Proof: (i) The following identities can be easily established:

$$P^{-1}(A+B)P = P^{-1}AP + P^{-1}BP; \; (P^{-1}AP)^k = P^{-1}A^k P.$$

Then

$$P^{-1}\left(\sum_{k=0}^{T} A^k/k!\right)P = \sum_{k=0}^{T} (P^{-1}AP)^k/k!.$$

The result follows by taking limits.

(ii) If $AB = BA$, $(A+B)^m/m! = \sum_{j+k=m} (A^j/j!)(B^k/k!)$

Then

$$\begin{aligned}\exp(A+B) &= \sum_{m=0}^{\infty}\left(\sum_{j+k=m} (A^j/j!)(B^k/k!)\right)\\ &= \left(\sum_{j=0}^{\infty} A^j/j!\right)\left(\sum_{k=0}^{\infty} B^k/k!\right)\\ &= (\exp A)(\exp B).\end{aligned}$$

The converse is obtained straightforwardly by expanding $\exp(A+B)$ and $(\exp A)(\exp B)$ and using the hypothesis.

(iii) A and $-A$ obviously commute. Then putting $B=-A$, we have: $(\exp A)(\exp(-A)) = \exp(A-A) = \exp[0] = I$. The result follows.

Theorem 7: $G = \exp(At)$ is a fundamental matrix for $\mathrm{d}x/\mathrm{d}t = Ax$.

Proof:

$$\begin{aligned}\frac{\mathrm{d}G}{\mathrm{d}t} = \frac{\mathrm{d}}{\mathrm{d}t}(\exp(At)) &= \lim_{h\to 0}\frac{\exp(A(t+h)) - \exp(At)}{h}\\ &= \lim_{h\to 0}\frac{(\exp(At))(\exp(Ah)) - \exp(At)}{h}\\ &= \lim_{h\to 0}\frac{(\exp(At))(\exp(Ah) - I)}{h}\\ &= (\exp(At)).\lim_{h\to 0}\frac{\exp(Ah) - I}{h}\\ &= (\exp(At))A\\ &= A(\exp(At))\end{aligned}$$

as A commutes with each term in the expansion of $\exp(At)$ and hence with $\exp(At)$. From Definition 1, G is the required fundamental matrix.

Let us now refer to Theorem 2, which states that there is a unique solution of $\mathrm{d}x/\mathrm{d}t = Ax$, denoted by $x(t)$, such that $x(t_0) = x^0$.

Theorem 8: $\mathrm{d}x/\mathrm{d}t = Ax$ with $x(t_0) = x^0$ has a unique solution $x(t) = (\exp(A(t-t_0)))x^0$.

Proof: The proof follows immediately from Theorems 2 and 7. Frequently $t_0 = 0$ so that the solution is $x(t) = (\exp At)x^0$.

§4.1.3. *The solution of* dx/dt = Ax: *real distinct roots*

We now begin to develop solutions of $dx/dt = Ax$ in terms of the roots and corresponding characteristic vectors of A. Assume, in this section, that A has n distinct roots. The results that we shall derive here depend only on the distinctness of the roots, not the realness. So, our results apply also to the case of distinct complex roots. As there may be some difficulty in conceptualising solutions involving complex roots and vectors, we defer consideration of them until the next section.

Theorem 9: Let $x(t)$ solve $dx/dt = Ax$. If for $t = t_0$, $Ax^0 = \lambda x^0$, where $x(t_0) = x^0$, then $Ax(t) = \lambda x(t)$, for all t.

Proof: Define $y(t) = dx(t)/dt - \lambda x(t) = Ax(t) - \lambda x(t)$.

$$\begin{aligned} dy(t)/dt &= \frac{d}{dt}(Ax(t) - \lambda x(t)) = A\,dx(t)/dt - \lambda\,dx(t)/dt \\ &= A\,dx(t)/dt - \lambda Ax(t) = A(dx(t)/dt - \lambda x(t)) \\ &= Ay(t). \end{aligned}$$

So $y(t)$ solves $dx/dt = Ax$.
$y(t_0) = Ax^0 - \lambda x^0 = \mathbf{0}$ by the hypothesis.
By Theorem 8, $y(t) = \mathbf{0}$ for all t, i.e. $Ax(t) = \lambda x(t)$.

We might call the $x(t)$ of Theorem 9 a characteristic solution. Our next result provides us with a simple representation of these solutions.

Theorem 10: Corresponding to each root, λ, of A there is a characteristic solution:

$$x(t) = e^{\lambda(t-t_0)}x^0$$

where

$$Ax^0 = \lambda x^0.$$

Proof: Let $Ax^0 = \lambda x^0$. Let $x(t)$ solve $dx/dt = Ax$ such that $x(t_0) = x^0$. From Theorem 9, $dx(t)/dt = Ax(t) = \lambda x(t)$,

i.e.

$$dx_i(t)/dt = \lambda x_i(t) \qquad i = 1, \ldots, n$$

This last equation has solution $x_i(t) = e^{\lambda t}k_i$, where k_i has yet to be determined. At $t = t_0$, $x(t_0) = x^0$; so $x_i^0 = e^{\lambda t_0}k_i$ or $k_i = e^{-\lambda t_0}x_i^0$.
Then

$$x_i(t) = e^{\lambda(t-t_0)}x_i^0$$

or

$$x(t) = e^{\lambda(t-t_0)}x^0$$

We now use the fact that A has n distinct roots to derive:

Theorem 11: Let A have n distinct real roots. The n characteristic solutions form a basis for the space of solutions of $\mathrm{d}x/\mathrm{d}t = Ax$.

Proof: Let $Ax^i = \lambda_i x^i$. As in Theorem 10, let $x^i(t)$ solve $\mathrm{d}x/\mathrm{d}t = Ax$ such that $x^i(t_0) = x^i$. Then we have:

$$x^i(t) = \mathrm{e}^{\lambda(t-t_0)}x^i$$

which is our typical characteristic solution, $i = 1, \ldots, n$.
We have to prove that the set of characteristic solutions forms a basis.
Suppose that the set is linearly dependent. Then there exist α_i, $i = 1, \ldots, n$, not all zero such that:

$$\sum_{i=1}^{n} \alpha_i x^i(t) = \mathbf{0} \quad \text{for all } t$$

Putting $t = t_0$, we have:

$$\sum_{i=1}^{n} \alpha_i x^i - \mathbf{0}$$

This implies that the set of characteristic vectors is linearly dependent. However, the vectors associated with distinct roots are linearly independent. So, if we have n distinct roots, we must have a set of linearly independent characteristic vectors.
This contradiction implies that the n characteristic solutions of $\mathrm{d}x/\mathrm{d}t = Ax$ form a linearly independent set. As the set of solutions of $\mathrm{d}x/\mathrm{d}t = Ax$ is an n-dimensional vector space (from Theorem 3), it follows that the characteristic solutions form a basis for this space.

§4.1.4. *The solution of* $\mathrm{d}x/\mathrm{d}t = Ax$*: complex roots*

In this section, we relax the assumption that A has only real roots; we now permit the existence of complex roots, but we retain the assumption of n distinct roots.
Let $\lambda = \sigma + \mathrm{i}\theta$ be a complex root of A.
Let $Ax = \lambda x$, where $x = w + \mathrm{i}z$, with w, $z \in R^n$.
Then $Ax^c = \lambda^c c^c$, i.e. λ^c is also a root of A.
The characteristic solutions $\mathrm{e}^{\lambda t}x$ and $\mathrm{e}^{\lambda^c t}x^c$ solve $\mathrm{d}x/\mathrm{d}t = Ax$.

$$\mathrm{e}^{\lambda t}x = \mathrm{e}^{\sigma t}[w\cos\theta t - z\sin\theta t] + \mathrm{i}\mathrm{e}^{\sigma t}[z\cos\theta t + w\sin\theta t]$$

$$\mathrm{e}^{\lambda^c t}x^c = \mathrm{e}^{\sigma t}[w\cos\theta t - z\sin\theta t] - \mathrm{i}\mathrm{e}^{\sigma t}[z\cos\theta t + w\sin\theta t]$$

The following are also solutions of $\mathrm{d}x/\mathrm{d}t = Ax$:

$$\mathrm{e}^{\lambda t}x + \mathrm{e}^{\lambda^c t}x^c = 2\mathrm{e}^{\sigma t}[w\cos\theta t - z\sin\theta t]$$

$$\mathrm{e}^{\lambda t}x - \mathrm{e}^{\lambda^c t}x^c = 2\mathrm{i}\mathrm{e}^{\sigma t}[z\cos\theta t + w\sin\theta t]$$

Hence $\frac{1}{2}(\mathrm{e}^{\lambda t}x + \mathrm{e}^{\lambda^c t}x^c) = \mathrm{e}^{\sigma t}(w\cos\theta t - z\sin\theta t)$ and

$\dfrac{1}{2\mathrm{i}}(\mathrm{e}^{\lambda t}x - \mathrm{e}^{\lambda^c t}x^c) = \mathrm{e}^{\sigma t}(z\cos\theta t + w\sin\theta t)$ solve $\mathrm{d}x/\mathrm{d}t = Ax$.

A linear combination of these solutions will also solve $dx/dt = Ax$. Summarising our discussion, we have:

Theorem 12: Suppose A has a complex root $\lambda = \sigma + i\theta$, with a corresponding characteristic vector $x = w + iz$. Then the solution corresponding to the roots λ and λ^c is given by $e^{\sigma t}(\alpha_1 w + \alpha_2 z)\cos\theta t + e^{\sigma t}(\alpha_2 w - \alpha_1 z)\sin\theta t$.

Example: Consider the equation

$$\frac{dx}{dt} = \begin{bmatrix} 3 & 2 \\ -1 & 1 \end{bmatrix} x \quad \text{with} \quad x^0 = x(0) = \begin{bmatrix} 1 \\ 3 \end{bmatrix}$$

The roots of the matrix A are $2 \pm i$. So $\sigma = 2$, $\theta = 1$.
The vector x of Theorem 12 is given by:

$$x = \begin{bmatrix} 1+i \\ -1 \end{bmatrix} = \begin{bmatrix} 1 \\ -1 \end{bmatrix} + i\begin{bmatrix} 1 \\ 0 \end{bmatrix} = w + iz$$

The general solution of $dx/dt = Ax$ is then given by

$$\alpha_1 e^{2t}\left[\begin{bmatrix} \cos t \\ -\cos t \end{bmatrix} - \begin{bmatrix} \sin t \\ 0 \end{bmatrix}\right] + \alpha_2 e^{2t}\left[\begin{bmatrix} \cos t \\ 0 \end{bmatrix} + \begin{bmatrix} \sin t \\ \sin t \end{bmatrix}\right]$$

$$= e^{2t}\begin{bmatrix} \alpha_1 \cos t + \alpha_2 \cos t \\ -\alpha_1 \cos t \end{bmatrix} + e^{2t}\begin{bmatrix} -\alpha_1 \sin t + \alpha_2 \sin t \\ \alpha_2 \sin t \end{bmatrix}$$

Putting $t = 0$, we obtain:

$$\begin{bmatrix} 1 \\ 3 \end{bmatrix} = \begin{bmatrix} \alpha_1 + \alpha_2 \\ -\alpha_1 \end{bmatrix}$$

which implies $\alpha_1 = -3$, $\alpha_2 = 4$.

§4.1.5. *Repeated roots*

The existence of repeated roots presents fundamental difficulties in the construction of characteristic solutions. Consider, for example, the following matrix:

$$A = \begin{bmatrix} 0 & 0 \\ 1 & 0 \end{bmatrix}$$

which has a repeated root 0, but only one characteristic vector, which is of the form $(x_1, 0)$. Thus a more general approach is called for.

It will be convenient if we have the following operator notation available to us in our analysis below:
We shall use $\mathscr{D}$ to denote the differentiation operator, i.e. $\mathscr{D}x = dx/dt$. For $k \geqslant 1$, $\mathscr{D}^k x = d^k x/dt^k$. We shall adopt the convention that $\mathscr{D}^0 x = Ix = x$.
Our differential equation:

$$\frac{dx}{dt} = Ax \qquad \cdots [1]$$

can then be written as

$$\mathscr{D}x = Ax \qquad \cdots [2]$$

By induction, we can easily derive:

$$\mathscr{D}^k x = A^k x \quad \text{for any positive integer } k \qquad \cdots [3]$$

So, if $P(A)$ denotes a matrix polynomial in A with constant coefficients and if x is a solution of eqn [1] (or [2]), we have:

$$P(\mathscr{D})x = P(A)x \qquad \cdots [4]$$

Theorem 13: Let $x(t)$ solve eqn [2]. Suppose that

$$(A - \lambda I)^m x^0 = \mathbf{0} \qquad \cdots [5]$$

Then

$$(A - \lambda I)^m x(t) = \mathbf{0} \quad \text{for all } t \qquad \cdots [6]$$

and

$$(\mathscr{D} - \lambda I)^m x(t) = \mathbf{0} \quad \text{for all } t \qquad \cdots [7]$$

Proof: From eqn [4]:

$$(A - \lambda I)^m x(t) = (\mathscr{D} - \lambda I)^m x(t) \qquad \cdots [8]$$

Define

$$y(t) = (\mathscr{D} - \lambda I)^m x(t) \qquad \cdots [9]$$

Now

$$\begin{aligned} \mathscr{D}(\mathscr{D}^k x(t)) &= \mathscr{D}^k(\mathscr{D}x(t)) = \mathscr{D}^k(Ax(t)) \\ &= A(\mathscr{D}^k x(t)) \qquad \cdots [10] \end{aligned}$$

In general:

$$\mathscr{D}(P(\mathscr{D})x(t)) = A(P(\mathscr{D})x(t)) \qquad \cdots [11]$$

i.e. $P(\mathscr{D})x(t)$ solves eqn [2].
As $y(t)$ can be written in the form $P(\mathscr{D})x(t)$, it follows that $y(t)$ is a solution of eqn [2],
i.e.

$$y(t) = (\exp(A(t - t_0)))y^0 \qquad \cdots [12]$$

Putting $t = t_0$ in eqn [9] yields:

$$\begin{aligned} y^0 = y(t_0) = (\mathscr{D} - \lambda I)^m x^0 &= (A - \lambda I)^m x^0 \quad \text{from eqn [8]} \\ &= \mathbf{0} \quad \text{from eqn [5]} \end{aligned}$$

Substituting for y^0 in eqn [12] we obtain:

$y(t) = \mathbf{0}$ for all t,

i.e.

$(\mathscr{D} - \lambda I)^m x(t) = \mathbf{0}$ for all t

and

$(A - \lambda I)^m x(t) = \mathbf{0}$ for all t, from eqn [8].

Definition 3: Let λ be a root of A of multiplicity m. A *primitive solution*, $x(t)$, associated with λ satisfies the equation:

$$(A - \lambda I)^m x(t) = \mathbf{0} \quad \text{for all } t \qquad \cdots [13]$$

(Note that primitive solutions are unconnected with primitive matrices discussed in Chapter 1.)

Before deriving an explicit form for these primitive solutions, we prove the following:

Lemma 1: If $z_i(t)$ possesses continuous derivatives of all orders up to and including the m-th, we have:

$$(\mathscr{D} - \lambda I)^m e^{\lambda t} z_i(t) = e^{\lambda t} \mathscr{D}^m z_i(t) \qquad \cdots [14]$$

where λ is any constant.

Proof: By induction.
Eqn [14] is trivial for $m = 0$.
Assume eqn [14] is true for $m = k - 1$.
Then

$$(\mathscr{D} - \lambda I)^k e^{\lambda t} z_i(t) = (\mathscr{D} - \lambda I)(\mathscr{D} - \lambda I)^{k-1}(e^{\lambda t} z_i(t))$$
$$= (\mathscr{D} - \lambda I) e^{\lambda t} \mathscr{D}^{k-1} z_i(t)$$

by hypothesis

$$= \mathscr{D}[e^{\lambda t} \mathscr{D}^{k-1} z_i(t)] - \lambda e^{\lambda t} \mathscr{D}^{k-1} z_i(t)$$
$$= \lambda e^{\lambda t} \mathscr{D}^{k-1} z_i(t) + e^{\lambda t} \mathscr{D}^k z_i(t) - \lambda e^{\lambda t} \mathscr{D}^{k-1} z_i(t)$$
$$= e^{\lambda t} \mathscr{D}^k z_i(t)$$

as required.

Theorem 14: Let $x(t)$ be a primitive solution of eqn [2] associated with the root λ of multiplicity m. Then $x(t)$ can be written in the form:

$$x(t) = e^{\lambda t}(p_1(t), \ldots, p_n(t))' \qquad \cdots [15]$$

where $p_i(t)$, $i = 1, \ldots, n$, denotes a polynomial in t of order less than or equal to $m - 1$.

Proof: From Theorem 13, $x(t)$ satisfies eqn [7]:

$$(\mathscr{D} - \lambda I)^m \mathbf{x}(t) = \mathbf{0} \quad \text{for all } t,$$

or

$$(\mathscr{D} - \lambda I)^m x_i(t) = 0 \quad \text{for all } t,\ i = 1, \ldots, n \qquad \cdots [16]$$

Writing $x_i(t) = e^{\lambda t} e^{-\lambda t} x_i(t)$ in [16], we have:

$$\begin{aligned}(\mathscr{D} - \lambda I)^m [e^{\lambda t} e^{-\lambda t} x_i(t)] &= (\mathscr{D} - \lambda I)^m [e^{\lambda t}(e^{-\lambda t} x_i(t))] \\ &= e^{\lambda t} \mathscr{D}^m (e^{-\lambda t} x_i(t)) \quad \text{by Lemma 1} \\ &= 0\end{aligned}$$

Hence:

$$\mathscr{D}^m (e^{-\lambda t} x_i(t)) = 0 \qquad \cdots [17]$$

Integrating, we obtain:

$$e^{-\lambda t} x_i(t) = p_i(t) \qquad i = 1, \ldots, n \qquad \cdots [18]$$

where $p_i(t)$ is a polynomial in t of order less than or equal to $m - 1$. Hence:

$$x_i(t) = e^{\lambda t} p_i(t)$$

or

$$x(t) = e^{\lambda t}(p_1(t), \ldots, p_n(t))' \qquad \cdots [19]$$

as required.

We conclude this section by outlining the method of construction of primitive solutions.

Suppose λ is a root of A of multiplicity m. From Theorem 14 we know the form of the solution. This may alternatively be written as:

$$x(t) = e^{\lambda t}(w^0 + w^1 t + w^2 t^2 + \cdots + w^{m-1} t^{m-1}) \qquad \cdots [20]$$

where w^j, $j = 0, 1, \ldots, m - 1$, is a vector (of scalars).
$x(t)$ solves eqn [1]:

$$dx/dt = Ax$$

Substituting for $x(t)$ on the right-hand and left-hand sides of [1], we obtain:

$$Ax(t) = e^{\lambda t} A(w^0 + w^1 t + \cdots + w^{m-2} t^{m-2} + w^{m-1} t^{m-1}) \qquad \cdots [21]$$

$$\begin{aligned}dx/dt = e^{\lambda t}(&\lambda w^0 + \lambda w^1 t + \cdots + \lambda w^{m-2} t^{m-2} + \lambda w^{m-1} t^{m-1} + \\ &+ w^1 + 2w^2 t + \cdots + (m-1) w^{m-1} t^{m-2})\end{aligned} \qquad \cdots [22]$$

Comparing eqns [21] and [22], we obtain:

$$Aw^{m-1} = \lambda \quad \lambda w^{m-1}$$

$$Aw^{m-2} = \lambda w^{m-2} + (m-1)w^{m-1}$$

$$\vdots$$

$$Aw^{j} = \lambda w^{j} + (j+1)w^{j+1} \qquad \cdots [23]$$

$$\vdots$$

$$Aw^{1} = \lambda w^{1} + 2w^{2}$$

$$Aw^{0} = \lambda w^{0} + w^{1}$$

Let us illustrate the above procedure with the following example:

$$\frac{dx}{dt} = \begin{bmatrix} 1 & 2 & 3 \\ 0 & 1 & 4 \\ 0 & 0 & 1 \end{bmatrix} x \qquad x(0) = \begin{bmatrix} 1 \\ 4 \\ 2 \end{bmatrix}$$

1 is the only root of A, being of multiplicity three. So, from eqn [23] above, we are looking for solutions to:

$$Aw^2 = w^2$$

$$Aw^1 = w^1 + 2w^2$$

$$Aw^0 = w^0 + w^1$$

Straightforward manipulations yield:

$$w^2 = \begin{bmatrix} \alpha \\ 0 \\ 0 \end{bmatrix}; \qquad w^1 = \begin{bmatrix} \beta \\ \alpha \\ 0 \end{bmatrix}; \qquad w^0 = \begin{bmatrix} \gamma \\ \frac{1}{2}(\beta - 3\alpha/4) \\ \alpha/4 \end{bmatrix}$$

$$x(t) = e^t(w^0 + w^1 t + w^2 t^2)$$

Putting $t = 0$ yields $\alpha = 8$, $\beta = 14$, $\gamma = 1$. So the solution is

$$x(t) = e^t \begin{bmatrix} 1 \\ 4 \\ 2 \end{bmatrix} + te^t \begin{bmatrix} 14 \\ 8 \\ 0 \end{bmatrix} + t^2 e^t \begin{bmatrix} 8 \\ 0 \\ 0 \end{bmatrix}$$

§4.1.6. *Reduction of higher-order systems*

Consider the following equation:

$$d^2y/dt^2 + a_1 dy/dt + a_0 y = 0 \qquad \cdots [1]$$

Define new variables thus:

$$x_1 = y; \qquad x_2 = dx_1/dt = dy/dt \qquad \cdots [2]$$

From eqn [1], $dx_2/dt = -a_1 x_2 - a_0 x_1$

Let $x = \begin{bmatrix} x_1 \\ x_2 \end{bmatrix}$. Then eqn [1] can be rewritten as:

$$\frac{dx}{dt} = \begin{bmatrix} \frac{dx_1}{dt} \\ \frac{dx_2}{dt} \end{bmatrix} = \begin{bmatrix} 0 & 1 \\ -a_0 & -a_1 \end{bmatrix} \begin{bmatrix} x_1 \\ x_2 \end{bmatrix} \qquad \cdots [3]$$

Our matrix methods developed above can then be applied to constant-coefficients systems such as eqn [1] above.

Now consider the following equation which is more general than [1]:

$$d^n y/dt^n + a_{n-1} d^{n-1} y/dt^{n-1} + \cdots + a_2 d^2 y/dt^2 + a_1 dy/dt + a_0 y = 0 \qquad \cdots [4]$$

We now define new variables thus:

$x_1 = y$

$x_2 = dx_1/dt = dy/dt$

$x_3 = dx_2/dt = d^2y/dt^2$

.

.

.

$x_j = dx_{j-1}/dt = d^{j-1}y/dt^{j-1}$ $\qquad \cdots [5]$

.

.

.

$x_n = dx_{n-1}/dt = d^{n-1}y/dt^{n-1}$

From eqn [4]:

$dx_n/dt = -a_{n-1}x_n - a_{n-2}x_{n-1} - \ldots - a_1x_2 - a_0x_1$

Define the vector $x = (x_1 \quad x_2 \quad \ldots \quad x_n)'$.

Then eqn [4] can be rewritten as:

$$\frac{dx}{dt} = Ax, \qquad \cdots [6]$$

where

$$A = \begin{bmatrix} 0 & 1 & 0 & \cdots & 0 & 0 \\ 0 & 0 & 1 & \cdots & 0 & 0 \\ \cdot & \cdot & & \cdot & & \cdot \\ \cdot & \cdot & & \cdot & & \cdot \\ \cdot & \cdot & & \cdot & & \cdot \\ 0 & 0 & & \cdots & 0 & 1 \\ -a_0 & -a_1 & & \cdots & -a_{n-2} & -a_{n-1} \end{bmatrix} \qquad \cdots [7]$$

The first $n-1$ equations of eqn [6] are merely definitional, i.e. $dx_j/dt = x_{j+1}$, $j = 1, \ldots, n-1$.

This technique of reducing the order of a system will also prove useful in the analysis of difference equations.

§4.1.7. *Non-homogeneous equations and particular solutions*

Let us now consider the equation:

$$\mathrm{d}x/\mathrm{d}t = Ax + f(t) \quad \cdots [1]$$

Let us look for a solution of the form:

$$x(t) = (\exp(At))g(t) \quad \cdots [2]$$

Differentiating eqn [2], we have:

$$\begin{aligned}\mathrm{d}x(t)/\mathrm{d}t &= A(\exp(At))g(t) + (\exp(At))\mathrm{d}g(t)/\mathrm{d}t \\ &= Ax(t) + (\exp(At))\mathrm{d}g(t)/\mathrm{d}t \quad \cdots [3]\end{aligned}$$

If eqn [2] solves [1], we have on substituting from eqns [2] and [3] into [1]:

$$Ax(t) + f(t) = Ax(t) + (\exp(At))\mathrm{d}g(t)/\mathrm{d}t$$

whence

$$f(t) = (\exp(At))\mathrm{d}g(t)/\mathrm{d}t$$

or

$$\mathrm{d}g(t)/\mathrm{d}t = (\exp(-At))f(t) \quad \cdots [4]$$

Integrating eqn [4], we obtain:

$$g(t) = g^0 + \int_{t_0}^{t} (\exp(-As))f(s)\mathrm{d}s \quad \cdots [5]$$

Then from eqn [2]:

$$x(t) = (\exp(At))\left[g^0 + \int_{t_0}^{t} (\exp(-As))f(s)\mathrm{d}s\right]$$

or

$$x(t) = (\exp(At))g^0 + (\exp(At))\int_{t_0}^{t} (\exp(-As))f(s)\mathrm{d}s \quad \cdots [6]$$

Note that from eqn [2], $g^0 = (\exp(-At_0))x^0$.

Summarising our discussion, we have:

Theorem 15: The equation $\mathrm{d}x/\mathrm{d}t = Ax + f(t)$, with $x(t_0) = x^\circ$, has solution:

$$x(t) = (\exp(A(t-t_0)))x^0 + (\exp(At))\int_{t_0}^{t} (\exp(-As))f(s)\mathrm{d}s \quad \cdots [7]$$

It can be established easily (by differentiation) that eqn [7] indeed solves eqn [1]. We now show that every solution of eqn [1] is of the same form as eqn [7].

Let $y(t)$ be another solution of [1]. Then by Theorem 1, $y(t) - x(t)$ solves the homogeneous equation

$$\mathrm{d}x/\mathrm{d}t = Ax$$

which has the unique solution

$$y(t)-x(t)=(\exp(At))b \quad \text{where} \quad b=(\exp(-At_0))(y^0-x^0)$$

So

$$y(t)=x(t)+(\exp(At))b$$

which is of the same form as eqn [7].

In general, the matrix exponential (in eqn [7]) is not easily calculable. However, in certain circumstances, the matrix exponential can be derived straightforwardly; we mention, for example, the case where A is diagonal; then $\exp(At)=[e^{a_{ii}t}\delta_{ij}]$, i, $j=1,\ldots,n$.

More generally, if A can be diagonalised by a similarity transformation (a sufficient condition for which is that A has n distinct roots), then an explicit solution of eqn [1] can be obtained fairly easily by a transformation of variables. We consider this case in detail.

We have the equation:

$$\mathrm{d}x/\mathrm{d}t=Ax+f(t) \qquad x(0)=x^0$$

If A has n distinct roots, define the matrix X by

$$X=[x^1 \quad x^2 \quad \cdots \quad x^n]$$

where

$$Ax^i=\lambda_i x^i, \qquad i=1,\ldots,n \qquad \cdots[8]$$

Let

$$Xz(t)=x(t) \qquad \cdots[9]$$

Substituting from eqn [9] into eqn [1], we have:

$$X\mathrm{d}z(t)/\mathrm{d}t=AXz(t)+f(t) \qquad z(0)=z^0=X^{-1}x^0$$

or

$$\mathrm{d}z(t)/\mathrm{d}t=X^{-1}AXz(t)+X^{-1}f(t)$$

or

$$\mathrm{d}z(t)/\mathrm{d}t=Dz(t)+h(t) \qquad z^0=X^{-1}x^0 \qquad \cdots[10]$$

where $D=[\lambda_i\delta_{ij}]$, $h(t)=X^{-1}f(t)$.

By Theorem 15, the solution of eqn [10] can be written as:

$$z(t)=(\exp(Dt))z^0+(\exp(Dt))\int_0^t(\exp(-Ds))h(s)\mathrm{d}s \qquad \cdots[11]$$

This solution is, in principle, calculable if $h(s)$ is not too complicated. We then derive $x(t)$ from eqn [9].

Let us now apply this method to the following numerical cxamples.

1. Our equation is

$$\mathrm{d}x/\mathrm{d}t=\begin{bmatrix}3 & 1\\ 1 & 3\end{bmatrix}x+\begin{bmatrix}4\\ 2\end{bmatrix} \qquad x(0)=x^0=\begin{bmatrix}-7\\ 3\end{bmatrix}$$

The matrix A has roots 4 and 2, with a pair of corresponding vectors $(1 \quad 1)'$ and $(-1 \quad 1)'$ respectively.

Then as in eqn [8], we have $X = \begin{bmatrix} 1 & -1 \\ 1 & 1 \end{bmatrix}$; $X^{-1} = \frac{1}{2}\begin{bmatrix} 1 & 1 \\ -1 & 1 \end{bmatrix}$.

Applying the transformation as described in eqn [9], we obtain:

$$\mathrm{d}z/\mathrm{d}t = \begin{bmatrix} 4 & 0 \\ 0 & 2 \end{bmatrix} z + \begin{bmatrix} 3 \\ -1 \end{bmatrix} \qquad z(0) = z^0 = \begin{bmatrix} -2 \\ 5 \end{bmatrix}$$

$$\int_0^t (\exp(-Ds))h(s)\mathrm{d}s = \int_0^t \begin{bmatrix} \mathrm{e}^{-4s} & 0 \\ 0 & \mathrm{e}^{-2s} \end{bmatrix} \begin{bmatrix} 3 \\ -1 \end{bmatrix} \mathrm{d}s$$

$$= \int_0^t \begin{bmatrix} 3\mathrm{e}^{-4s} \\ -\mathrm{e}^{-2s} \end{bmatrix} \mathrm{d}s$$

$$= \begin{bmatrix} -\frac{3}{4}\mathrm{e}^{-4t} + \frac{3}{4} \\ \frac{1}{2}\mathrm{e}^{-2t} - \frac{1}{2} \end{bmatrix}$$

Then as in eqn [11], we have:

$$z(t) = \begin{bmatrix} \mathrm{e}^{4t} & 0 \\ 0 & \mathrm{e}^{2t} \end{bmatrix} \begin{bmatrix} -2 \\ 5 \end{bmatrix} + \begin{bmatrix} \mathrm{e}^{4t} & 0 \\ 0 & \mathrm{e}^{2t} \end{bmatrix} \begin{bmatrix} -\frac{3}{4}\mathrm{e}^{-4t} + \frac{3}{4} \\ \frac{1}{2}\mathrm{e}^{-2t} - \frac{1}{2} \end{bmatrix}$$

$$= \begin{bmatrix} -\frac{5}{4}\mathrm{e}^{4t} \\ -\frac{9}{2}\mathrm{e}^{2t} \end{bmatrix} + \begin{bmatrix} -\frac{3}{4} \\ \frac{1}{2} \end{bmatrix}$$

Transforming back to x variables, we obtain:

$$x(t) = Xz(t) = \begin{bmatrix} -\frac{5}{4} \\ -\frac{5}{4} \end{bmatrix} \mathrm{e}^{4t} + \begin{bmatrix} \frac{9}{2} \\ -\frac{9}{2} \end{bmatrix} \mathrm{e}^{2t} + \begin{bmatrix} -\frac{5}{4} \\ -\frac{1}{4} \end{bmatrix}$$

2. Our equation is

$$\mathrm{d}x/\mathrm{d}t = \begin{bmatrix} 0 & -1 \\ 1 & 0 \end{bmatrix} x + \begin{bmatrix} 0 \\ t \end{bmatrix} \qquad x(0) = x^0 = \begin{bmatrix} 2 \\ -3 \end{bmatrix}$$

$$\exp(At) = \begin{bmatrix} \cos t & -\sin t \\ \sin t & \cos t \end{bmatrix}$$

In this case, there is no need to transform variables. We use eqn [7] with $t_0 = 0$.

$$\int_0^t (\exp(-As))f(s)\mathrm{d}s = \int_0^t \begin{bmatrix} \cos s & \sin s \\ -\sin s & \cos s \end{bmatrix} \begin{bmatrix} 0 \\ s \end{bmatrix} \mathrm{d}s$$

$$= \int_0^t \begin{bmatrix} s\sin s \\ s\cos s \end{bmatrix} \mathrm{d}s$$

$$= \begin{bmatrix} -t\cos t + \sin t \\ t\sin t + \cos t - 1 \end{bmatrix}$$

Evaluating as in eqn [7], we obtain the solution

$$x(t) = \cos t\begin{bmatrix}2\\4\end{bmatrix} + \sin t\begin{bmatrix}4\\2\end{bmatrix} + \begin{bmatrix}-t\\1\end{bmatrix}$$

We now discuss a different approach to the solution of eqn [1]:

$$\mathrm{d}x/\mathrm{d}t = Ax + f(t)$$

The approach is based on *ad hoc* methods (of trial and error), in contrast with the exact analysis outlined above. In certain circumstances, it might be possible to obtain a particular solution quite easily. We illustrate by means of the following cases.

Case A: $f(t) = f$, where f is a constant vector; A is non-singular. As a particular solution, try $\bar{x}(t) = a$, where a is also a constant vector. Substituting in eqn [1], we obtain:

$$\mathbf{0} = Aa + f \quad \text{or} \quad a = -A^{-1}f.$$

Then, from Theorem 1, the most general solution of eqn [1] is given by:

$$x(t) - A^{-1}f$$

where $x(t)$ is the general solution of the homogeneous equation $\mathrm{d}x/\mathrm{d}t = Ax$. As an example, consider the equation:

$$\mathrm{d}x/\mathrm{d}t = \begin{bmatrix}3 & 1\\1 & 3\end{bmatrix}x + \begin{bmatrix}4\\2\end{bmatrix} \qquad x(0) = x^0 = \begin{bmatrix}-7\\3\end{bmatrix}$$

This is Example 1 above.

$$x(t) = \alpha_1 e^{4t}\begin{bmatrix}1\\1\end{bmatrix} + \alpha_2 e^{2t}\begin{bmatrix}-1\\1\end{bmatrix}$$

is the general solution of the homogeneous equation, where α_1 and α_2 depend on the initial conditions.
As a particular solution, try $\bar{x}(t) = a$. Substituting, we have:

$$a = -\tfrac{1}{8}\begin{bmatrix}3 & -1\\-1 & 3\end{bmatrix}\begin{bmatrix}4\\2\end{bmatrix} = \begin{bmatrix}-\frac{5}{4}\\-\frac{1}{4}\end{bmatrix}$$

So

$$x(t) = \alpha_1 e^{4t}\begin{bmatrix}1\\1\end{bmatrix} + \alpha_2 e^{2t}\begin{bmatrix}-1\\1\end{bmatrix} + \begin{bmatrix}-\frac{5}{4}\\-\frac{1}{4}\end{bmatrix}$$

Putting $t = 0$ in this last equation enables us to calculate $\alpha_1 = -\frac{5}{4}$, $\alpha_2 = -\frac{9}{2}$. This confirms the result obtained earlier.

Case B: $f(t) = ft + h$, where f and h are constant vectors; A is non-singular.
We might try as a particular solution $\bar{x}(t) = at + b$.
Substitution in eqn [1] yields the following:

$$a = -A^{-1}f$$

$$b = -A^{-1}(A^{-1}f + h)$$

Case C: $f(t) = e^{\psi t}f$, where ψ is not a root of A and f is a constant vector.

Let $\bar{x}(t) = e^{\psi t}a$, where a is also a constant vector.
Substituting in eqn [1], we obtain:

$$e^{\psi t}a = Ae^{\psi t}a + e^{\psi t}f$$

or

$$(\psi I - A)a = f.$$

As ψ is not a root of A, $(\psi I - A)^{-1}$ exists.
Hence, $a = (\psi I - A)^{-1}f$.

Case D: $f(t) = e^{\psi t}f$, where ψ is a root of A.
Try $\bar{x}(t) = e^{\psi t}(at + b)$, where a and b are constant vectors. Substituting in eqn [1], we obtain:

$$\begin{aligned} \psi a &= Aa \\ \psi b + a &= Ab + f \end{aligned} \qquad \cdots [12]$$

We illustrate this case with the following examples.

1. $\mathrm{d}x/\mathrm{d}t = \begin{bmatrix} 3 & 1 \\ 1 & 3 \end{bmatrix} x + e^{4t} \begin{bmatrix} 1 \\ -1 \end{bmatrix}$

The vector corresponding to the root 4 is of the form $(1 \quad 1)'$. Putting $a = (1 \quad 1)'$ in eqn [12], we obtain:

$$(4I - A)b = \begin{bmatrix} 1 & -1 \\ -1 & 1 \end{bmatrix} b = f - a = \begin{bmatrix} 0 \\ -2 \end{bmatrix}$$

As this equation cannot be solved for b, we try $a = \mathbf{0}$ in eqn [12], which is always a possibility. We then obtain:

$$\begin{bmatrix} 1 & -1 \\ -1 & 1 \end{bmatrix} b = \begin{bmatrix} 1 \\ -1 \end{bmatrix}$$

which can be solved.

2. $\mathrm{d}x/\mathrm{d}t = \begin{bmatrix} 4 & 2 \\ 1 & 3 \end{bmatrix} x + e^{2t} \begin{bmatrix} -1 \\ -2 \end{bmatrix}$

The vector corresponding to the root 2 is of the form $(1 \quad -1)'$. Putting $a = (1 \quad -1)'$ in eqn [12], we have:

$$\begin{bmatrix} -2 & -2 \\ -1 & -1 \end{bmatrix} b = f - a = \begin{bmatrix} -2 \\ -1 \end{bmatrix}$$

which can be solved for b.
Finally, note that Case D takes account of the following:

$$\mathrm{d}x/\mathrm{d}t = Ax + f$$

where f is constant and A is singular.

The trial solution $\bar{x}(t) = at + b$ yields these equations:

$\mathbf{0} = Aa$

$a = Ab + f$

§4.1.8. *Stability theory*

The theory of differential equations finds applications in economics in growth theory and stability theory, *inter alia.* As we shall see later, the dis-equilibrium behaviour of some systems can be described by an equation of the form:

$$\frac{\mathrm{d}x}{\mathrm{d}t} = Ax \qquad \cdots [1]$$

x measures the disturbances from an equilibrium vector, x^e. It is natural to ask if the equilibrium is stable, i.e. does x tend to $\mathbf{0}$ as t tends to infinity.

It seems likely that the work done above on solving eqn [1] in terms of the roots of A will be of more use to us than the work involving the matrix exponential, $\exp(At)$.

Let us consider first the case where A has n distinct roots. Then the solution of eqn [1] can be written as:

$$x(t) = \sum_{i=1}^{n} \alpha_i \mathrm{e}^{\lambda_i t} x^i$$

as in §4.1.3.

$$\|x(t)\| = \left\| \sum_i \alpha_i \mathrm{e}^{\lambda_i t} x^i \right\|$$

$$\leqslant \sum_i \| \alpha_i \mathrm{e}^{\lambda_i t} x^i \|$$

$$= \sum_i |\alpha_i| \cdot |\mathrm{e}^{\lambda_i t}| \cdot \|x^i\|$$

$$= |\alpha_1| \cdot |\mathrm{e}^{\lambda_1 t}| \cdot \|x^1\| + \sum_{i=2}^{n} |\alpha_i| \cdot |\mathrm{e}^{\lambda_i t}| \cdot \|x^i\|$$

where λ_1 is that root of A with largest real part. If the system is to be stable for any initial conditions, it follows that we cannot always have $\alpha_1 = 0$. If $\mathrm{Re}(\lambda_1) > 0$, $|\mathrm{e}^{\lambda_1 t}| \to \infty$ as $t \to \infty$. This contradicts stability. So $\mathrm{Re}(\lambda_1) \leqslant 0$. If $\mathrm{Re}(\lambda_1) = 0$, then $|\alpha_1| \cdot |\mathrm{e}^{\lambda_1 t}| \cdot \|x^1\| = |\alpha_1| \cdot \|x^1\|$ for all t. Again $\|x(t)\|$ does not tend to 0 as t tends to infinity. Hence $\mathrm{Re}(\lambda_i) < 0$. Hence $\mathrm{Re}(\lambda_i) < 0$, for all $i = 1, \ldots, n$. Conversely, if $\mathrm{Re}(\lambda_i) < 0$, for all i, it follows that $\|x(t)\| \to 0$ as $t \to \infty$, i.e. the system is stable.

Let us now formalise our discussion.

Definition 4: The system represented by the equation $\mathrm{d}x/\mathrm{d}t = Ax$ is *stable* iff $\lim_{t\to\infty} x(t) = \mathbf{0}$ for any initial conditions, where $x(t)$ is the solution of $\mathrm{d}x/\mathrm{d}t = Ax$. If the system $\mathrm{d}x/\mathrm{d}t = Ax$ is stable, then A is a stable matrix.

Theorem 16: A is a stable matrix iff the real part of each root of A is negative.

Proof:
Necessity: Suppose A has k distinct roots. Then the solution of $dx/dt = Ax$ can be written in the form:

$$x(t) = \sum_{j=1}^{k} \alpha_j e^{\sigma_j t}[p^j(t)\cos\theta_j t + q^j(t)\sin\theta_j t]$$

where $\lambda_j = \sigma_j + i\theta_j$, $j = 1, \ldots, k$; and $p^j(t)$, $q^j(t)$ denote vectors, each of which has as its typical component a polynomial in t of order $m_j - 1$, where m_j is the multiplicity of λ_j, $j = 1, \ldots, k$.
(If all roots are real, the $\theta_j = 0$ and we have:

$$x(t) = \sum_{j=1}^{k} \alpha_j e^{\sigma_j t} p^j(t))$$

Let λ_1 be that root with largest real part. Then:

$$\begin{aligned}\|x(t)\| \leqslant |\alpha_1| \cdot |e^{\sigma_1 t}| \cdot \|p^1(t)\cos\theta_1 t + q^1(t)\sin\theta_1 t\| + \\ + \sum_{j=2}^{k} |\alpha_j| \cdot |e^{\sigma_j t}| \cdot \|p^j(t)\cos\theta_j t + q^j(t)\sin\theta_j t\| \\ \leqslant |\alpha_1| \cdot |e^{\sigma_1 t}| \cdot (\|p^1(t)\| + \|q^1(t)\|) + \\ + \sum_{j=2}^{k} |\alpha_j| \cdot |e^{\sigma_j t}| \cdot (\|p^j(t)\| + \|q^j(t)\|)\end{aligned}$$

Again if the system is to be stable for any initial conditions, we cannot always have $\alpha_1 = 0$. Stability requires $\sigma_1 < 0$. Conversely, if $\sigma_j < 0$, for all j, $\|x(t)\| \to 0$ as $t \to \infty$.

We now outline alternative proofs of Theorem 16.

Second proof. From Exercises §2.4, Q8, there exists a unitary matrix U such that $U^{-1}AU = B$, where B is an upper triangular matrix with the roots of A along the main diagonal. Let us transform variables by the equation:

$$Uz = x \qquad \cdots [2]$$

Then $dx/dt = U dz/dt$; $Ax = AUz$. So $dx/dt = Ax$, $x(t_0) = x^0$, can be rewritten as:

$$dz/dt = U^{-1}AUz = Bz \qquad z^0 = z(t_0) = U^{-1}x^0 \qquad \cdots [3]$$

Writing out eqn [3] in extensive form, we have:

$$\begin{aligned} dz_1/dt &= b_{11}z_1 + b_{12}z_2 + \cdots + b_{1n}z_n \\ dz_2/dt &= \qquad\quad b_{22}z_2 + \cdots + b_{2n}z_n \\ &\;\;\vdots \\ dz_n/dt &= \qquad\qquad\qquad\quad b_{nn}z_n \end{aligned} \qquad \cdots [4]$$

where $b_{jj} = \lambda_j(A)$, $j = 1, \ldots, n$.
From eqn [2], it follows that $x(t) \rightarrow \mathbf{0}$ iff $z(t) \rightarrow \mathbf{0}$. In other words, the system [1] is stable iff the system [3] is stable. As eqn [3] is in a form more manageable than eqn [1], we operate with [3].
Solving the last equation in [4], we have:

$$z_n = z_n^0 e^{b_{nn}t} \qquad \cdots [5]$$

If eqn [1] is stable, then we obviously have $\text{Re}(b_{nn}) < 0$. We substitute from eqn [5] into the penultimate equation of [4] to obtain:

$$dz_{n-1}/dt = b_{n-1,n-1}z_{n-1} + b_{n-1,n}z_n^0 e^{b_{nn}t} \qquad \cdots [6]$$

If $b_{n-1,n-1} \neq b_{nn}$, eqn [6] has solution:

$$z_{n-1}(t) = z_{n-1}^0 e^{b_{n-1,n-1}t} + (e^{b_{nn}t} - e^{b_{n-1,n-1}t})/\beta \qquad \cdots [7]$$

where

$$\beta = b_{n-1,n}z_n^0/(b_{nn} - b_{n-1,n-1}).$$

If $b_{n-1,n-1} = b_{nn}$, eqn [6] has solution:

$$z_{n-1}(t) = z_{n-1}^0 e^{b_{n-1,n-1}t} + b_{n-1,n}z_n^0 t e^{b_{nn}t} \qquad \cdots [8]$$

In either case, if $z_{n-1}(t) \rightarrow 0$, as $t \rightarrow \infty$, we must have $\text{Re}(b_{n-1,n-1}) < 0$.
We could then substitute for $z_n(t)$ and $z_{n-1}(t)$ in the $(n-2)$-th equation of [4] and show that the stability of eqn [1] implies that $\text{Re}(b_{n-2,n-2}) < 0$.
A more formal proof would be by induction, based on the following:
If $\rho(t) \rightarrow 0$ as $t \rightarrow \infty$, then the solution of

$$dy/dt = \alpha y + \rho(t) \qquad \cdots [9]$$

tends to zero as $t \rightarrow \infty$ iff $\text{Re}(\alpha) < 0$.
The solution of eqn [9] can be written as:

$$y(t) = e^{\alpha t}y^0 + e^{\alpha t}\int_0^t e^{-\alpha t}\rho(\tau)d\tau \qquad \cdots [10]$$

from which the desired result can easily be obtained. Let $\rho(t) = z_n(t)$ from eqn [5] and let $y = z_{n-1}(t)$. Then we obtain $\text{Re}(b_{n-1,n-1}) < 0$.
Then let $\rho(t) = b_{n-2,n-1}z_{n-1}(t) + b_{n-2,n}z_n(t)$, $y = z_{n-2}(t)$, from which we obtain $\text{Re}(b_{n-2,n-2}) < 0$.
Continuing in this way, we obtain the result:

$$\text{Re}(b_{jj}) = \text{Re}(\lambda_j(A)) < 0 \quad \text{for all} \quad j - 1, \ldots, n$$

The converse should by now be evident.

Third proof. This is, in a sense, a modification of the second. If we are willing to use the Jordan normal form, the proof becomes simpler.

Let $T^{-1}AT = J$ where J is the Jordan normal form of A.

$$J = \begin{bmatrix} J_1 & 0 & & & \\ 0 & J_2 & 0 & & \bigcirc \\ & & \ddots & & \\ \bigcirc & & & & J_k \end{bmatrix}$$

where

$$J_j = \begin{bmatrix} \lambda_j & 1 & & & \\ & \lambda_j & 1 & & \bigcirc \\ & & \ddots & \ddots & \\ & & & & 1 \\ \bigcirc & & & & \lambda_j \end{bmatrix}$$

(See Chapter 4 of Lancaster for a derivation of this form.)

§4.1.9. Stability theory: an alternative approach

We now briefly consider a different approach to stability theory from that just outlined—we aim to use quadratic forms to discuss stability questions. Consider the equation:

$$dx/dt = Ax \qquad \cdots [1]$$

and the quadratic form:

$$v = x'Vx \qquad \cdots [2]$$

evaluated at a solution of eqn [1]:
Differentiating eqn [2], we obtain:

$$dv/dt = (dx/dt)'Vx + x'V(dx/dt)$$
$$= x'A'Vx + x'VAx$$

using eqn [1], i.e.

$$dv/dt = x'(A'V + VA)x \qquad \cdots [3]$$

Suppose that we can find a positive definite matrix V such that:

$$A'V + VA = -W \qquad \cdots [4]$$

where W is also positive definite.
Then

$$dv/dt = -x'Wx = -(x'Vx)(x'Wx)/x'Vx$$
$$= -v(x'Wx)/(x'Vx)$$
$$\leqslant -v\lambda_n(W)/\lambda_1(V) \qquad \cdots [5]$$

where $\lambda_n(W)$ is the smallest root of W, $\lambda_1(V)$ the largest root of V; by positive definiteness of V and W, both roots are positive.

Hence, we may rewrite eqn [5] as:

$$dv/dt \leqslant -\beta v \qquad \beta = \lambda_n(W)/\lambda_1(V) > 0 \qquad \cdots [6]$$

So

$$v \leqslant e^{-\beta t} v(0) \qquad \cdots [7]$$

$v \to 0$ as $t \to \infty$. From eqn [2], $v \to 0$ iff $x \to \mathbf{0}$. So $x \to \mathbf{0}$ as $t \to \infty$, i.e. the system described by eqn [1] is stable.

We may also prove that, if A is stable, there exists a positive definite matrix V such that $A'V + VA = -W$, where W is any positive definite matrix. Summarising our discussion, we have:

Theorem 17 (Lyapunov): A is a stable matrix iff there exists a positive definite matrix V such that $A'V + VA = -W$, where W is any positive definite matrix.

For a proof of this theorem, consult Chapter 8 of Lancaster.

In the next section, we consider a similar method of solving non-linear generalisations of eqn [1] above.

§4.1.10. *Lyapunov stability theory: non-linear equations*

Consider the equation:

$$dx/dt = F(x) \qquad \cdots [1]$$

where F is a point-to-point mapping from R^n to R^n. The function which corresponds to the quadratic form in §4.1.9 is given in:

Definition 5: The function $v(x)$ from R^n to R is *positive definite* if, for all x: (i) $dv(x)/dt$ has continuous partial derivatives; (ii) $v(x) > 0$ for all $x \neq \mathbf{0}$; (iii) $v(\mathbf{0}) = 0$.

A *Lyapunov function*, $v(x)$, for eqn [1] is a positive definite function, evaluated at a solution of [1], which satisfies the condition: (iv) $dv(x)/dt < 0$ for all $x \neq \mathbf{0}$.

The basic result, which is a generalisation of Theorem 17, is:

Theorem 18: The system represented by eqn [1] is stable if there exists a Lyapunov function for eqn [1].

For a proof, consult Hahn, or LaSalle and Lefschetz, or Hirsch and Smale.

As an illustration of Theorem 18, consider the system:

$$dx_1/dt = -x_1 + x_2; \qquad dx_2/dt = -x_1 - x_2 - x_3^2 \qquad \cdots [2]$$

Consider the function $v(x) = x'x = x_1^2 + x_2^2$, which is certainly positive definite. We now check to see if it satisfies condition (iv).

$$dv(x)/dt = \sum_{i=1}^{2} (\partial v/\partial x_i)(dx_i/dt) = 2x_1 \cdot dx_1/dt + 2x_2 \cdot dx_2/dt$$

$$= -2x_1^2 - 2x_2^2 - 2x_2^4.$$

$v(x)$ is then a Lyapunov function and so eqn [2] is stable.

For application of this theory, see pp. 325–8 below, for example.

§4.1.11. *Non-negativity in solutions of linear equation*

Our aim is to derive necessary and sufficient conditions for non-negative solutions of systems such as:

$$\frac{\mathrm{d}x}{\mathrm{d}t} = Ax + f(t) \qquad \cdots [1]$$

where $f(t) \geqslant \mathbf{0}$, for all t and $x(0) \geqslant \mathbf{0}$.

Theorem 19: Eqn [1] has a non-negative solution for all t iff there exists $\alpha \geqslant 0$ such that $\alpha I + A \geqslant [0]$.

Proof: From Theorem 15, the solution of eqn [1] is:

$$x(t) = (\exp(At))x(0) + (\exp(At)) \int_0^t (\exp(-As))f(s)\mathrm{d}s \qquad \cdots [2]$$

The proof turns on the following:

Lemma 2: $\exp(At) \geqslant [0]$, for all t, iff there exists $\alpha \geqslant 0$ such that $\alpha I + A \geqslant [0]$.

Proof:
Sufficiency: Suppose there exists $\alpha \geqslant 0$ such that $\alpha I + A \geqslant [0]$.
Now

$$\exp(At) = (\exp(-\alpha It))(\exp(\alpha It))(\exp(At))$$

or

$$\exp(At) = (\exp(-\alpha It))(\exp(\alpha I + A)t) \qquad \cdots [3]$$

As $\alpha I + A \geqslant [0]$ by hypothesis, $\exp(\alpha I + A)t \geqslant [0]$ by the definition of the matrix exponential.
$\exp(-\alpha It) = \mathrm{e}^{-\alpha t}I$, where $\mathrm{e}^{-\alpha t}$ is a scalar exponential.
As $\mathrm{e}^{-\alpha t} > 0$, for all α, it follows that $\exp(-\alpha It) \geqslant [0]$.
Hence, from eqn [3], $\exp(At) \geqslant [0]$.

Necessity: Let $\exp(At) = M$. Suppose $a_{rs} < 0$, $r \neq s$.
For sufficiently small t:

$$M = \exp(At) \simeq I + At = t((1/t)I + A)$$

In particular, $\mathrm{sign}(m_{rs}) = \mathrm{sign}(a_{rs})$.
However, this contradicts the hypothesis that $\exp(At) \geqslant [0]$ for all t. Hence $a_{rs} \geqslant 0$ for all $r \neq s$, as required.

We now take up the proof of the theorem.

Sufficiency: Suppose there exists $\alpha \geqslant 0$ such that $\alpha I + A \geqslant [0]$. Then from eqn [2], we have:

$$x(t) = (\exp(At))x(0) + \int_0^t (\exp(A(t-s)))f(s)\mathrm{d}s$$

By Lemma 2, $\exp(At) \geqslant [0]$ under the hypothesis.
Also, $\exp(A(t-s)) \geqslant [0]$, for all $t \geqslant s$, by the lemma.
As $f(s) \geqslant \mathbf{0}$, for all s, it follows that the solution [2] of eqn [1] is non-negative for all t.

Necessity: Put $f(t) = \mathbf{0}$ for all t.
Then $x(t) = (\exp(At))x(0)$ from eqn [2]. Putting $x(0) = \mathrm{e}^i$, $i = 1, \ldots, n$, we obtain:

$$(\exp(At))^i \geqslant \mathbf{0} \qquad i = 1, \ldots, n$$

where $(\exp(At))^i$ denotes the i-th column of $\exp(At)$.
So, we have: $(\exp(At)) \geqslant [0]$.
Then by Lemma 2, there exists $\alpha \geqslant 0$ such that $\alpha I + A \geqslant [0]$, as required.

Non-negativity is a minimal requirement of some economic systems. As we shall see later, Theorem 19 (and its analogue for difference equations) will find application in the analysis of some dynamic economic systems.

§4.2. Difference equations

§4.2.1. *Introduction and basic results*

There is a close parallel between the analysis of such equations as:

$$x(t+1) = Ax(t) + f(t) \qquad \cdots [1]$$

$$x(t+1) = Ax(t) \qquad \cdots [2]$$

and the analysis of the differential equations [1] and [2] of §4.1.1. This is illustrated in our very first result:

Theorem 20: Let $\bar{x}(t)$ be any solution of eqn [1]. If $\tilde{x}(t)$ is any other solution of eqn [1], $x(t) = \bar{x}(t) - \tilde{x}(t)$ is a solution of eqn [2].

Theorems 2 and 3 can likewise be transferred, with appropriate modification, to the difference equations case. Armed with these analogues of Theorems 2 and 3, we can derive:

Theorem 21: $x(t+1) = Ax(t)$ has unique solution $x(t) = A^{t-t_0}x^0$.

This result can be obtained by straightforward iteration.

In §4.1, having obtained a solution of the homogeneous differential equation $\mathrm{d}x/\mathrm{d}t = Ax$ in terms of the matrix exponential, we proceeded to derive characteristic solutions (involving the roots and characteristic vectors of A). Likewise, here, we turn our attention to deriving characteristic solutions of eqn [2]. As in §4.1, we assume first that the roots are distinct, dealing separately with the real and complex cases, before considering the more complicated solutions required in the event of repeated roots.

Then we shall discuss particular solutions of eqn [1] and we conclude the chapter with a discussion of stability theory of difference equations.

§4.2.2. *Real, distinct roots*

Corresponding to Theorem 9, we have:

Theorem 22: Let $x(t)$ solve $x(t+1)=Ax(t)$. If, for $t=t_0$, $Ax^0=\lambda x^0$, then $Ax(t)=\lambda x(t)$, for all t.

The proof is virtually the same as that of Theorem 9.

We are now in a position to derive a characteristic solution of the homogeneous difference equation.

Theorem 23: Corresponding to each root, λ, of A, there is a characteristic solution $x(t)=\lambda^{t-t_0}x^0$, where $Ax^0=\lambda x^0$.

Proof: Let $Ax^0=\lambda x^0$. Let $x(t)$ solve $x(t+1)=Ax(t)$ such that $x(t_0)=x^0$.
From Theorem 22, $x(t+1)=Ax(t)=\lambda x(t)$,
i.e. $x_i(t+1)=\lambda x_i(t)$, which has solution $x_i(t)=\lambda^{t-t_0}x_i^0$. Hence, $x(t)=\lambda^{t-t_0}x^0$.

With appropriate modification, Theorem 11 carries over to the difference equations case.

§4.2.3. *Complex roots*

We now derive the solutions of the homogeneous equation corresponding to a pair of complex (conjugate) roots.
Let $Ax=\lambda x$, where $\lambda=\sigma+i\theta$, σ, $\theta\in R$, $x=w+iz$, w, $z\in R^n$.
Then $Ax^c=\lambda^c x^c$.
Write $\lambda=\sigma+i\theta=r(\cos\delta+i\sin\delta)$.
Then the characteristic solution $\lambda^t x$ can be written as:

$$\begin{aligned}\lambda^t x &= r^t(\cos\delta+i\sin\delta)^t(w+iz)\\ &= r^t(\cos\delta t+i\sin\delta t)(w+iz) \quad \text{using de Moivre's theorem}\\ &= r^t(w\cos\delta t-z\sin\delta t)+ir^t(z\cos\delta t+w\sin\delta t).\end{aligned}$$

Similarly:

$$\lambda^{ct}x^c=r^t(w\cos\delta t-z\sin\delta t)-ir^t(z\cos\delta t+w\sin\delta t)$$

$$\lambda^t x+\lambda^{ct}x^c=2r^t(w\cos\delta t-z\sin\delta t)$$

and

$$\lambda^t x-\lambda^{ct}x^c=2ir^t(z\cos\delta t+w\sin\delta t)$$

solve $x(t+1)=Ax(t)$.
So $\frac{1}{2}(\lambda^t x+\lambda^{ct}x^c)$ and $(1/2i)(\lambda^t x-\lambda^{ct}x^c)$ solve the homogeneous equation.

Summarising our discussion, we have:

Theorem 24: Suppose A has a complex root $\lambda = \sigma + i\theta$, with a corresponding characteristic vector $x = w + iz$. Then the solution corresponding to the roots λ and λ^c is given by $r^t(\alpha_1 w + \alpha_2 z)\cos\delta t + r^t(\alpha_2 w - \alpha_1 z)\sin\delta t$.

§4.2.4. *Repeated roots*

Let us introduce the following operator notation:
Let $\mathscr{E}x(t) = x(t+1)$; $\Delta x(t) = x(t+1) - x(t) = (\mathscr{E} - I)x(t)$.
So the equation

$$x(t+1) = Ax(t) \qquad \cdots [1]$$

can be rewritten as:

$$\mathscr{E}x(t) = Ax(t) \qquad \cdots [2]$$

As in the differential equations case, we have:

$$\mathscr{E}^k x(t) = A^k x(t) \qquad \cdots [3]$$

for any positive integer k,

$$P(\mathscr{E})x(t) = P(A)x(t) \qquad \cdots [4]$$

where $x(t)$ solves eqn [1] and $P(A)$ is a matrix polynomial in A with constant coefficients.

Our first result in this section is the analogue of Theorem 13:

Theorem 25: Let $x(t)$ solve eqn [2]. Suppose that:

$$(A - \lambda I)^m x^0 = \mathbf{0} \qquad \cdots [5]$$

Then

$$(A - \lambda I)^m x(t) = \mathbf{0} \qquad \cdots [6]$$

for all t and

$$(\mathscr{E} - \lambda I)^m x(t) = \mathbf{0} \qquad \cdots [7]$$

for all t.

Proof:

$$(A - \lambda I)^m x(t) = (\mathscr{E} - \lambda I)^m x(t) \qquad \cdots [8]$$

Let

$$y(t) = (\mathscr{E} - \lambda I)^m x(t) \qquad \cdots [9]$$

We have:

$$\mathscr{E}(\mathscr{E}^k x(t)) = A(\mathscr{E}^k x(t)) \qquad \cdots [10]$$

and more generally

$$\mathscr{E}(P(\mathscr{E})x(t)) = A(P(\mathscr{E})x(t)) \qquad \cdots [11]$$

So, $P(\mathscr{E})x(t)$ solves eqn [2] if $x(t)$ does. As $y(t)$ can be written in this form, we have:

$$y(t) = A^{t-t_0}y^0$$

But $y^0 = \mathscr{E} - \lambda I)^m x^0 = (A - \lambda I)^m x^0 = \mathbf{0}$, from eqn [5].
Hence, $y(t) = \mathbf{0}$ for all t. The result follows.

Definition 6: Let λ be a root of A of multiplicity m. A *primitive solution*, $x(t)$, associated with λ satisfies

$$(A - \lambda I)^m x(t) = \mathbf{0} \qquad \cdots [12]$$

for all t.

Lemma 3: $(\mathscr{E} - \lambda I)^m(\lambda^t x(t)) = \lambda^{t+m}\Delta^m x(t)$ $\qquad \cdots [13]$

Proof: By induction.
Eqn [13] is trivial for $m = 0$.
Assume that it is true for $m = k - 1$. Then:

$$\begin{aligned}(\mathscr{E} - \lambda I)^k(\lambda^t x(t)) &= (\mathscr{E} - \lambda I)((\mathscr{E} - \lambda I)^{k-1}(\lambda^t x(t))) \\ &= (\mathscr{E} - \lambda I)(\lambda^{t+k-1}\Delta^{k-1}x(t))\end{aligned}$$

by the induction hypothesis

$$\begin{aligned}&= \lambda^{t+k}\Delta^k x(t) + \lambda^{t+k}\Delta^{k-1}x(t) \\ &\quad - \lambda^{t+k}\Delta^{k-1}x(t) \quad \text{as} \quad \mathscr{E} = \Delta + I\end{aligned}$$

as required.

We can now derive an explicit form for the primitive solutions.

Theorem 26: Let $x(t)$ be a primitive solution of eqn [2] associated with the root λ of multiplicity m. Then $x(t)$ can be written in the form:

$$x(t) = \lambda^t(p_1(t), p_2(t), \ldots, p_n(t)) \qquad \cdots [14]$$

where $p_j(t)$ denotes a polynomial in t of order less than or equal to $m - 1$, $j = 1, \ldots, n$.

Proof: By Theorem 25, we have (eqn [7]):

$$(\mathscr{E} - \lambda I)^m x(t) = \mathbf{0} \quad \text{for all } t \text{, or}$$

$$(\mathscr{E} - \lambda I)^m x_j(t) = 0 \quad j = 1, \ldots, n \qquad \cdots [15]$$

Writing $x_j(t) = \lambda^t\lambda^{-t}x_j(t)$. we have:

$$(\mathscr{E} - \lambda I)^m(\lambda^t\lambda^{-t}x_j(t)) = 0.$$

By Lemma 3:

$$(\mathscr{E} - \lambda I)^m(\lambda^t y_j(t)) = \lambda^{t+m}\Delta^m y_j(t)$$

where $y_j(t) = \lambda^{-t}x_j(t)$.

So, we have:

$$\lambda^{t+m}\Delta^m y_j(t)=0$$

or

$$\Delta^m y_j(t)=0 \quad j=1,\ldots,n \qquad \cdots[16]$$

Let $q(t)$ be a polynomial in t of order k. It can be shown that:

$$\Delta^m q(t)=\bar{q}(t)$$

where $\bar{q}(t)$ is a polynomial in t of order $k-m$.
So, if $\Delta^m y_j(t)=0$, it follows that $y_j(t)$ is a polynomial in t of order not greater than $m-1$.
So, we have:

$$y_j(t)=\lambda^{-t}x_j(t)=p_j(t) \quad j=1,\ldots,n \qquad \cdots[17]$$

where $p_j(t)$ is a polynomial in t of order less than or equal to $m-1$.

The construction of primitive solutions is analogous to the method outlined in §4.1.5 for differential equations.

§4.2.5. *Reduction of higher-order systems*

Consider the equation:

$$y(t+2)+a_1y(t+1)+a_0y(t)=0 \qquad \cdots[1]$$

Define new variables thus:

$$x_1(t)=y(t)$$

$$x_2(t)=\mathscr{E}x_1(t)=y(t+1) \qquad \cdots[2]$$

Then, from eqn [1],

$$x_2(t)=y(t+2)=-a_1x_2(t)-a_0x_1(t).$$

Let $x(t)=(x_1(t) \quad x_2(t))'$. Then eqn [1] becomes:

$$\mathscr{E}x(t)=\begin{bmatrix}\mathscr{E}x_1(t)\\ \mathscr{E}x_2(t)\end{bmatrix}=\begin{bmatrix}0 & 1\\ -a_0 & -a_1\end{bmatrix}\begin{bmatrix}x_1(t)\\ x_2(t)\end{bmatrix}$$

Likewise, the equation:

$$y(t+n)+a_{n-1}y(t+n-1)+\cdots+a_1y(t+1)+a_0y(t)=0 \qquad \cdots[3]$$

can be reduced to:

$$x(t)=Ax(t) \qquad \cdots[4]$$

by the introduction of new variables, where A has the same form as in §4.1.6, eqn [8].

§4.2.6. *Particular solutions*

Corresponding to eqn [7] of §4.1.7, we obtain by iteration on

$$x(t+1)=Ax(t)+f(t) \qquad \cdots[1]$$

the following:

$$x(t) = A^t x(0) + \sum_{\tau=0}^{t-1} A^\tau f(t-\tau) \qquad \cdots [2]$$

which is a particular solution of eqn [1].

Corresponding to the trial and error solutions discussed in §4.1.7, we have the following:

Case A: $f(t) = f$; $I - A$ is non-singular.
The trial solution $\bar{x}(t) = a$ yields $a = (I-A)^{-1} f$

Case B: $f(t) = ft + h$; $I - A$ is non-singular.
The trial solution $\bar{x}(t) = \psi^t (at + b)$ yields the equations:

$$a = Aa + f$$

$$a + b = Ab + h$$

which can certainly be solved if $(I-A)^{-1}$ exists.

Case C: $f(t) = \psi^t f$, where ψ is not a root of A.
The trial solution $\bar{x}(t) = \psi^t\,(at + b)$ yields the equation

$$\psi a = Aa + f$$

which can be solved as $(\psi I - A)^{-1}$ exists when ψ is not a root of A.

Case D: $f(t) = \psi^t f$, where ψ is a root of A.
The trial solution $\bar{x}(t) = \varphi^t (at + b)$ yields the equations:

$$\psi a = Aa$$

$$\psi a + \psi b = Ab + f$$

§4.2.7. *Stability theory*

Definition 4 can be adapted easily to the difference equations case. Consider now the equation:

$$x(t+1) = Ax(t) \qquad \cdots [1]$$

In the case of real distinct roots, we can write the solution of eqn [1] as:

$$x(t) = \sum_{j=1}^{n} \alpha_j \lambda_j^t x^j \qquad \cdots [2]$$

Let λ_1 be that root with largest absolute value.

$$\|x(t)\| = \left\| \sum_{j=1}^{n} \alpha_j \lambda_j^t x^j \right\|$$

$$\leqslant \sum_{j=1}^{n} |\alpha_j| \cdot |\lambda_j^t| \cdot \|x^j\|$$

$$= \sum_{j=1}^{n} |\alpha_j| \cdot |\lambda_j|^t \cdot \|x^j\| = \sum_{j=1}^{n} \phi(j)$$

$$= \phi(1)\left[1 + \sum_{j=2}^{n} \phi(j)/\phi(1)\right]$$

As $|\lambda_1|>|\lambda_j|$, for all $j=2,\ldots,n$, it follows that $\phi(j)/\phi(1)\to 0$, for all $j=2,\ldots,n$.
Hence, $x(t)\to\phi(1)=|\alpha_1|\,.\,|\lambda_1|^t\,.\,\|x^1\|$.
So, $\|x(t)\|\to 0$ iff $|\lambda_1|<1$.

In the general case, we have as the solution of eqn [1]:

$$x(t)=\sum_{j=1}^{k}\alpha_j r_j^t[p^j(t)\cos\delta_j t+q^j(t)\sin\delta_j t]$$

where k is the number of distinct roots of A.
If $|r_j|<1$, for all j, then $x(t)\to\mathbf{0}$.
Conversely:

$$\|x(t)\|\leqslant F(1)\left[1+\sum_{j=2}^{k}F(j)/F(1)\right]$$

where $F(j)=|\alpha_j|\cdot|r_j|^t\cdot\|p^j(t)+q^j(t)\|$ for all $j=1,2,\ldots,n$.
If $\|x(t)\|\to 0$, it follows that $|r_j|<1$, for all $j=1,2,\ldots,n$.

Summarising our discussion, we have:

Theorem 27: The solution of the equation $x(t+1)=Ax(t)$ is stable iff the modulus of each root of A is less than 1.

§4.2.8. *Lyapunov stability theory*

Our approach follows that of §4.1.9.
Consider the equation:

$$x(t+1)=Ax(t) \qquad \cdots[1]$$

and the quadratic form:

$$v=x'Vx \qquad \cdots[2]$$

evaluated at a solution of eqn [1].

$$\begin{aligned}\Delta v&=v(x(t+1))-v(x(t))\\&=x(t)'A'VAx(t)-x(t)'Vx(t)\quad\text{using eqn [1]}\\&=x(t)'(A'VA-V)x(t)\qquad\cdots[3]\end{aligned}$$

Suppose that there exists a positive definite matrix V such that:

$$A'VA-A=-W \qquad \cdots[4]$$

where W is also positive definite.
Then, in eqn [3], we have:

$$\Delta v=-x(t)'Wx(t)<0 \qquad \cdots[5]$$

from which we can conclude that $v\to 0$, i.e. $x(t)\to\mathbf{0}$.

We formalise our discussion in the following:

Theorem 28: Let W be a positive definite matrix. The modulus of each root of A is less than 1 iff $A'VA - V = -W$ has a positive definite solution V.

For a proof of this theorem consult Hahn.

§4.2.9. *Non-negativity in solutions of linear equations*

Our aim is to derive a set of necessary and sufficient conditions for non-negative solutions of equations such as:

$$x(t+1) = Ax(t) + f(t) \qquad \cdots [1]$$

where $f(t) \geqq \mathbf{0}$ for all t and $x(0) \geqslant \mathbf{0}$.

Our result here is the analogue of Theorem 19 in §4.1.13.

Theorem 29: Eqn [1] has a non-negative solution for all t iff $A^i \geqslant \mathbf{0}$ (where A^i denotes the i-th column of A).

Proof: The solution of eqn [1] is:

$$x(t) = A^t x(0) + \sum_{\tau=0}^{t-1} A^\tau f(t-\tau-1) \qquad \cdots [2]$$

The proof of the theorem turns on the following lemmata:

Lemma 4: $Ax \geqslant \mathbf{0}$ for $x \geqslant \mathbf{0}$ iff $A^i \geqslant \mathbf{0}$ for all $i = 1, \ldots, n$.

Proof:
Sufficiency: Obvious.
Necessity: Putting $x = e^i$, $i = 1, \ldots, n$, yields the desired result.

Lemma 5: $(A^\tau)^i \geqslant \mathbf{0}$, for all i, iff $A^i \geqslant \mathbf{0}$, for all i, for any positive integer τ.

Proof:
Sufficiency: By induction.
$A^\tau = AA^{\tau-1}$. If the result is true for $\tau - 1$ (i.e. $(A^{\tau-1})^i \geqslant \mathbf{0}$, for all i), then it follows immediately for τ by Lemma 4.
Necessity: Trivial; put $\tau = 1$.

We now take up the proof of the theorem.
Sufficiency: If $A^i \geqslant \mathbf{0}$, for all i, then $(A^\tau)^i \geqslant \mathbf{0}$, for all i, for any positive integer τ, by Lemma 5. Then $x(t) \geqslant \mathbf{0}$ in eqn [2].
Necessity: Putting $f(t) = \mathbf{0}$, for all t, in eqn [1], the result follows immediately from Lemmata 4 and 5.

§4.2.10. *Lags and stability under non-negativity*

We begin by analysing the stability of the first-order system:

$$x(t+1) = Ax(t) \qquad A \geqslant [0] \qquad \cdots [1]$$

The results of Chapter 2—in particular, the Frobenius theorems and the results on bounds for roots—are of obvious relevance.

Next, we consider a model related to eqn [1] but with a more complex lag structure, i.e.

$$x(t+1)=\sum_{\tau=0}^{T-1} A_\tau x(t-\tau) \quad A_\tau \geqslant [0], \quad \text{for all} \quad \tau=0,1,\ldots,T-1 \qquad \cdots [2]$$

Eqn [2] can be converted by a transformation of variables into a first-order system:

$$y(t+1)=By(t) \qquad B \geqslant [0] \qquad \cdots [3]$$

where B is a square matrrix of order nT.
Results derived for eqn [1] can be applied to eqn [2].
In the case where $A = \sum_{\tau=0}^{T-1} A_\tau$, we derive the (surprising) result that eqn [1] is stable iff eqn [2] is stable.

In §§4.2.11 and 4.2.12, we extend the analysis of this section. First of all, we relax the non-negativity restrictions on A and A_τ, though we do impose the restriction that the A_τ have basically the same sign pattern. Then, we consider the following generalisation of eqn [1]:

$$Cx(t+1)=Ax(t) \qquad \cdots [4]$$

where C is non-singular.
Under this assumption, we have:

$$x(t+1)=C^{-1}Ax(t) \qquad \cdots [5]$$

which is basically of the same form as eqn [1].
However, the imposition of a lag structure on eqn [5] does not, in general, yield the same results as the imposition of a lag structure on eqn [4], a point to be discussed below.

Our formal analysis begins with eqn [1]:

$$x(t+1)=Ax(t) \qquad A \geqslant [0]$$

where we assume that A is indecomposable.
From Theorem 27, a system such as eqn [1] is stable iff $|\lambda_i(A)|<1$, for all $i=1,\ldots,n$—this holds without reference to the signs of the elements of A.
Given our assumptions on A, we may apply the Frobenius theory of §2.3, in particular Theorem 24.
Let $Ax=\lambda^*(A)x$, $\lambda^*(A)>0$, $x>\mathbf{0}$.
The conditions of Theorem 34 (of Chapter 2) are satisfied.
So, if we define $D=[d_i\delta_{ij}]$, $d_i=x_i>0$, for all $i=1,\ldots,n$, then $D^{-1}AD=\lambda^*(A)Q$, where Q is a stochastic matrix. So, by applying a similarity transformation to A, we obtain a matrix with each row sum equal to $\lambda^*(A)$.

Let us reconsider eqn [1]. Define new variables by the equation

$$x(t)=Dz(t) \qquad \cdots [6]$$

where D is the diagonal matrix just described.

Then eqn [1] becomes:

$$z(t+1)=D^{-1}ADz(t)$$

or

$$z(t+1)=\lambda^*(A)Qz(t). \qquad \cdots [7]$$

We are now in a position to derive:

Theorem 30: Let A be indecomposable. Eqn [1] is stable iff there exists a positive diagonal matrix D such that all row sums of $D^{-1}AD$ are less than or equal to 1, with at least one strict inequality.

Proof:
Sufficiency: As A and $D^{-1}AD$ have the same roots, the hypothesis implies that $1>\lambda^*(A)$, by Theorem 72 (of Chapter 2). Stability follows.
Necessity: If eqn [1] is stable, then $1>\lambda^*(A)$. As $D^{-1}AD=\lambda^*(A)Q$, where Q is stochastic and D is positive diagonal, it follows that all row sums of $D^{-1}AD$ are equal to $\lambda^*(A)<1$.

The following instability theorem can be derived likewise:

Theorem 31: Eqn [1] is unstable iff there exists a positive diagonal matrix D such that all row sums of $D^{-1}AD$ are greater than or equal to 1.

Having analysed the indecomposable case, we now consider the decomposable case. If A is decomposable, there exists a permutation matrix P such that:

$$P^{-1}AP=\begin{bmatrix} A^{11} & A^{12} \\ 0 & A^{22} \end{bmatrix} \qquad \cdots [8]$$

where A^{11} and A^{22} are square.
As eqn [1] can be rewritten as:

$$P^{-1}x(t+1)=P^{-1}APP^{-1}x(t) \qquad \cdots [9]$$

where $P^{-1}x(t)$ is a re-arrangement of $x(t)$, there is no loss of generality in taking A in the form given by the right-hand side of eqn [8]. Let $I(J)$ be the set of indices referring to the rows of $A^{11}(A^{22})$.

We have the following stability result:

Theorem 32: Let A be decomposable. Consider separately the sets I and J. Eqn [1] is stable iff there exists a positive diagonal matrix D such that the i-th row sum of $D^{-1}AD$ is less than or equal to 1, with at least one strict inequality, for all $i\in I$ and for all $i\in J$.

Proof:
Sufficiency: As A^{11} and A^{22} are indecomposable, the hypotheses of the theorem ensure that $\lambda^*(A^{11})<1$, $\lambda^*(A^{22})<1$.
As the set of roots of A is the union of the sets of roots of A^{11} and A^{22}, it follows that $\lambda^*(A)<1$. Hence, eqn [1] is stable.

Necessity: Suppose that eqn [1] is stable.
As A^{11} and A^{22} are indecomposable, there exist positive diagonal matrices D_1 and D_2, stochastic matrices Q_1 and Q_2 such that:

$$D_1^{-1}A^{11}D_1 = \lambda^*(A^{11})Q_1 \qquad \lambda^*(A^{11})<1 \qquad \cdots [10]$$

$$D_2^{-1}A^{22}D_2 = \lambda^*(A^{22})Q_2 \qquad \lambda^*(A^{22})<1 \qquad \cdots [11]$$

Let

$$\bar{D} = \begin{bmatrix} D_1 & 0 \\ 0 & D_2 \end{bmatrix} \qquad \cdots [12]$$

Then

$$\bar{D}^{-1}A\bar{D} = \bar{D}^{-1}\begin{bmatrix} A^{11} & A^{12} \\ 0 & A^{22} \end{bmatrix}\bar{D} = \begin{bmatrix} \lambda^*(A^{11})Q_1 & \bar{D}^{-1}A^{12}\bar{D} \\ 0 & \lambda^*(A^{22})Q_2 \end{bmatrix} \qquad \cdots [13]$$

Let

$$\bar{D}^{-1}A^{12}\bar{D} = \bar{A}^{12} \qquad \cdots [14]$$

Define $\tilde{D}$ by:

$$\tilde{d}_i = d_I, \qquad i \in I; \qquad \tilde{d}_i = d_J, \qquad i \in J \qquad \cdots [15]$$

Then:

$$\tilde{D}^{-1}\bar{D}^{-1}\begin{bmatrix} A^{11} & A^{12} \\ 0 & A^{22} \end{bmatrix}\bar{D}\tilde{D} = \begin{bmatrix} \lambda^*(A^{11})Q_1 & d_I^{-1}d_J\bar{A}^{12} \\ 0 & \lambda^*(A^{22})Q_2 \end{bmatrix} \qquad \cdots [16]$$

Let $D = \bar{D}\tilde{D}$. Then by appropriate choice of d_I, d_J, the i-th row sum of $D^{-1}AD$ is less than or equal to 1, with at least one strict inequality, for all $i \in I$.
From eqns [11] and [16], the row sum condition is satisfied for all $i \in J$.

This completes our analysis of eqn [1].
We now consider the following generalisation of eqn [1]:

$$x(t+1) = \sum_{\tau=0}^{T-1} A_\tau x(t-\tau) \qquad A_\tau \geqslant [0] \quad \text{for all} \quad \tau \qquad \cdots [2]$$

Defining:

$$y_{\tau n+i}(t) = x_i(t-\tau) \qquad i = 1, \ldots, n$$
$$\tau = 0, 1, \ldots, T-1 \qquad \cdots [17]$$

we can rewrite eqn [2] as:

$$y(t+1) = By(t) \qquad \cdots [18]$$

i.e.

$$\begin{bmatrix} x(t+1) \\ x(t) \\ \cdot \\ \cdot \\ \cdot \\ x(t-T+2) \end{bmatrix} = \begin{bmatrix} A_0 & A_1 & \cdots & & A_{T-1} \\ I & 0 & \cdots & & 0 \\ \cdot & \cdot & \cdot & & \cdot \\ \cdot & \cdot & \cdot & & \cdot \\ \cdot & \cdot & \cdot & & \cdot \\ 0 & 0 & \cdots & I & 0 \end{bmatrix} \begin{bmatrix} x(t) \\ x(t-1) \\ \cdot \\ \cdot \\ \cdot \\ x(t-T+1) \end{bmatrix} \qquad \cdots [19]$$

Let us call the first n rows of B non-definitional rows, the last $n(T-1)$ rows definitional rows.

The procedure to be followed in analysing eqn [18] will be similar to that employed on eqn [1] above. First, a preliminary.
Suppose:

$$d_{n\tau+i} = d_i \qquad i=1,\ldots,n; \qquad \tau=0,1,\ldots,T-1 \qquad \cdots [20]$$

Then the diagonal matrix to be used on eqn [18] may be written as:

$$\bar{D} = \begin{bmatrix} D & & & \bigcirc \\ & D & & \\ & & \ddots & \\ \bigcirc & & & D \end{bmatrix} \qquad D = [d_i \delta_{ij}], \quad d_i > 0, \quad \text{for all } i \qquad \cdots [21]$$

Define:

$$y(t) = \bar{D}z(t) \qquad \cdots [22]$$

Then eqn [18] becomes:

$$z(t+1) = \bar{D}^{-1}B\bar{D}z(t) \qquad \cdots [23]$$

To appreciate eqn [20], we may think of eqn [22] (and eqn [6] above) as representing a redefinition of the units of measurement of the y variables. From eqn [17], we see that the vector $y(t)$ is just the stacked vector of $x(\sigma)$ vectors, from $\sigma = t$ to $\sigma = t - T + 1$. In eqns [20] and [22], we apply an identical change in the unit of measurement to the same variable in different time periods—such a change has been described as "consistent" (the implication of this terminology being that, if eqn [20] were not satisfied, the change in units described by eqn [22] would be inconsistent?). However, as Fisher points out, "The use of consistent units is really one of convenience and aesthetics only." (1)

Our first stability result is the analogue of Theorem 30.

Theorem 33: Suppose that B in eqn [18] is indecomposable. Equation [18] is stable iff there exists a set of consistent units such that each non-definitional row sum of $\bar{D}^{-1}B\bar{D}$ is less than or equal to 1, with at least one strict inequality.

Proof: Consider the matrix $\bar{D}^{-1}B\bar{D}$ where $\bar{D}$ is defined in eqn [21]. The advantage of consistent units is that definitional rows (and hence row sums) are unaffected by a consistent units change; evidently, the definitional rows (and hence row sums) are affected by non-consistent units changes.

Sufficiency: Applying a consistent change of units to eqn [18], we obtain:

$$\bar{D}^{-1}B\bar{D}=\begin{bmatrix} D^{-1}A_0D & D^{-1}A_1D & \cdots & D^{-1}A_{T-1}D \\ I & 0 & \cdots & 0 \\ 0 & I & \cdots & 0 \\ \cdot & \cdot & \cdot & \cdot \\ \cdot & \cdot & \cdot & \cdot \\ \cdot & \cdot & \cdot & \cdot \\ 0 & 0 & \cdots I & 0 \end{bmatrix} \qquad \cdots [24]$$

As the matrix is indecomposable, the hypothesis implies that $\lambda^*(B)<1$ by Theorem 30.

Necessity: If:

$$Bx=\lambda^*(B)x, \qquad \cdots [25]$$

we may write:

$$x=\begin{bmatrix} \bar{x}/\lambda^*(B) \\ \bar{x}/\lambda^*(B)^2 \\ \cdot \\ \cdot \\ \cdot \\ \bar{x}/\lambda^*(B)^T \end{bmatrix} \qquad \bar{x}>\mathbf{0}_n \qquad \cdots [26]$$

Let:

$$d_i=\bar{x}_i \qquad i=1,\ldots,n \qquad \cdots [27]$$

Let $\bar{D}$ be the block diagonal matrix with T matrices along the main diagonal, all equal to D, where $D=[d_i\delta_{ij}]$ (as in eqn [21] above).

From eqn [25]:

$$(\bar{D}^{-1}B\bar{D})(\bar{D}^{-1}x)=\lambda^*(B)\bar{D}^{-1}x \qquad \cdots [28]$$

$$(\bar{D}^{-1}B\bar{D})(\bar{D}^{-1}x)=\begin{bmatrix} D^{-1}A_0D & D^{-1}A_1D & \ldots & D^{-1}A_{T-1}D \\ I & 0 & \ldots & 0 \\ \cdot & \cdot & & \cdot \\ \cdot & \cdot & \cdot & \cdot \\ \cdot & \cdot & \cdot & \cdot \\ 0 & 0 & \ldots I & 0 \end{bmatrix}\begin{bmatrix} \mathbf{1}/\lambda^*(B) \\ \mathbf{1}/\lambda^*(B)^2 \\ \cdot \\ \cdot \\ \cdot \\ \mathbf{1}/\lambda^*(B)^T \end{bmatrix} \qquad \cdots [29]$$

$$\lambda^*(B)\bar{D}^{-1}x=\begin{bmatrix} \mathbf{1} \\ \mathbf{1}/\lambda^*(B) \\ \cdot \\ \cdot \\ \cdot \\ \mathbf{1}/\lambda^*(B)^{T-1} \end{bmatrix} \qquad \cdots [30]$$

We need consider only the first n components of the right-hand sides of eqns [29] and [30] (i.e. those associated with the non-definitional rows), from which we obtain:

$$\left[\sum_{\tau=0}^{T-1} \frac{D^{-1}A_\tau D}{\lambda^*(B)^{\tau+1}}\right]\mathbf{1}=\mathbf{1} \qquad \cdots[31]$$

As $\lambda^*(B)<1$, we have from eqn [31]:

$$\left[\sum_{\tau=0}^{T-1} D^{-1}A_\tau D\mathbf{1}\right]<\mathbf{1} \qquad \cdots[32]$$

as required.

We can now compare the stability properties of eqn [2]:

$$x(t+1)=\sum_{\tau=0}^{T-1} A_\tau x(t-\tau) \qquad A_\tau \geqslant [0] \text{ for all } \tau$$

with those of:

$$x(t+1)=\bar{A}x(t) \qquad \cdots[33]$$

where

$$\bar{A}=\sum_{\tau=0}^{T-1} A_\tau \qquad \cdots[34]$$

Equation [2] may be written as:

$$y(t+1)=By(t) \qquad \cdots[18]$$

where B is defined in eqn [19].

Assume that B is indecomposable (from Exercises §2.3, this is true iff A_{T-1} is indecomposable); then $\bar{A}$ is indecomposable. The necessary and sufficient conditions for the stability of eqn [2] (and eqn [18]) are given by Theorem 33, those of eqn [33] by Theorem 30.

If the non-definitional row sums of $\bar{D}^{-1}B\bar{D}$ are less than or equal to 1, with at least one strict inequality, then so are the row sums of $D^{-1}\bar{A}D$. Hence, stability of eqn [2] implies stability of eqn [33].

The converse can be established likewise. So, we have:

Theorem 34: Eqn [2] is stable iff eqn [33] is stable.

§4.2.11. *Lags and stability (continued)*

In this section, we relax the non-negativity assumption on A_τ, but we impose the following restrictions:

if

$\bar{a}_{ij} \neq 0, \quad \text{then} \quad \bar{a}_{ij}a_{ij\tau} \geqslant 0, \quad \text{for all} \quad \tau = 0, \ldots, T-1 \qquad \cdots [1]$

if

$\bar{a}_{ij} = 0, \quad \text{then} \quad a_{ij\tau} = 0, \quad \text{for all} \quad \tau = 0, \ldots, T-1 \qquad \cdots [2]$

where $A_\tau = [a_{ij\tau}]$, $i, j = 1, \ldots, n$.
The A_τ matrices then have the same sign pattern.
Before deriving results, more notation:
Let M be any square matrix. Then $M^* = [|m_{ij}|]$; $M^* \geqslant [0]$.

From Exercises §2.2, we have the following stability criterion (see also Exercises §4.2):

Theorem 35: If $M \geqslant [0]$, $\lambda^*(M) < 1$ iff $I - M$ has a positive D.D. (From Theorems 13 and 29 of Chapter 2, we know that $\lambda^*(M) < 1$ iff $I - M$ has a positive q.d.d. By Exercises §2.2, Q5, $I - M$ has a positive q.d.d. iff it has a positive D.D.)

If M is not non-negative, we have the following weaker result:

Theorem 36: $|\lambda(M)| < 1$ if $I - M^*$ has a positive D.D., $\lambda(M)$ being any root of M.

Proof: If $I - M^*$ has a positive D.D., there exist $d_i > 0$ such that:

$$d_j(1 - |m_{jj}|) > \sum_{\substack{i=1 \\ i \neq j}}^{n} d_i \, |m_{ij}| \qquad \cdots [3]$$

Suppose $|\lambda(M)| \geqslant 1$. Considering $\lambda I - M$, we have:

$$|\lambda(M)\delta_{jj} - m_{jj}| \geqslant |\lambda(M)| - |m_{jj}| \geqslant 1 - |m_{jj}| \qquad \cdots [4]$$

Substituting in eqn [3]:

$$d_j \, |\lambda(M) \, \delta_{jj} - m_{jj}| > \sum_{\substack{i=1 \\ i \neq j}}^{n} d_i \, |\lambda(M) \, \delta_{ij} - m_{ij}| = \sum_{i \neq j} d_i \, |m_{ij}| \qquad \cdots [5]$$

Hence $\lambda(M)I - M$ has a positive D.D. By Theorem 9 of Chapter 2, $\lambda(M)I - M$ is non-singular. So, $\lambda(M)$ is not a root of M.
This contradiction implies that $|\lambda(M)| < 1$.

On the assumption that $\bar{A}^* = \sum_{\tau=0}^{T-1} A^*_\tau$, we have the following:

Theorem 37: Under the hypothesis $\bar{A}^* = \sum_{\tau=0}^{T-1} A^*_\tau$, $I - B^*$ has a positive D.D. iff $I - \bar{A}^*$ has a positive D.D.

Proof:
Necessity: Suppose $I-B^*$ has a positive D.D., i.e. there exists $d'=(d^0\ d^1 \cdots d^{T-1})' > \mathbf{0}'_{nT}$ such that:

$$(d^0\ d^1 \cdots d^{T-1})' \begin{bmatrix} I-A_0^* & -A_1^* & \cdots & & A_{T-1}^* \\ -I & I & 0 & \cdots & 0 \\ \cdot & \cdot & & & \cdot \\ \cdot & \cdot & & & \cdot \\ \cdot & \cdot & & & \cdot \\ 0 & 0 & \cdots & -I & I \end{bmatrix} > \mathbf{0}'_{nT} \qquad \cdots [6]$$

or:

$$d^{\tau\prime} - d^{\tau+1\prime} - d^{0\prime}A_\tau^* > \mathbf{0}'_n \quad \tau = 0, 1, \ldots, T-2 \qquad \cdots [7]$$

$$d^{T-1\prime} - d^{0\prime}A_{T-1}^* > \mathbf{0}'_n \qquad \cdots [8]$$

Summing eqn [7] over $\tau = 0, 1, \ldots, T-2$ and then adding eqn [8], we obtain:

$$d^{0\prime} - d^{0\prime} \sum_{\tau=0}^{T-1} A_\tau^* > \mathbf{0}'_n \qquad \cdots [9]$$

or

$$d^{0\prime}(I - A^*) > \mathbf{0}'_n \qquad \cdots [10]$$

This is just the definition that $(I - A^*)$ has a positive D.D.
Sufficiency: Suppose $(I - \bar{A}^*)$ has a positive D.D., i.e. there exists $d^0 > \mathbf{0}_n$ such that:

$$d^{0\prime}(I - \bar{A}^*) > \mathbf{0}'_n \qquad \cdots [11]$$

We now make the following definitions:

$$e' = d^{0\prime}(I - \bar{A}^*) \qquad (> \mathbf{0}'_n) \qquad \cdots [12]$$

$$e^\tau = e(T-\tau)/(T-1) \qquad \tau = 1, \ldots, T-1 \qquad \cdots [13]$$

$$d^{\tau\prime} = d^{0\prime}\left(\sum_{\sigma=\tau}^{T-1} A_\sigma^*\right) + e^{\tau\prime} \qquad \tau = 1, \ldots, T-1 \qquad \cdots [14]$$

From eqn [14]:

$$d^{\tau\prime} = d^{0\prime}A_\tau^* + d^{0\prime}\left(\sum_{\sigma=\tau+1}^{T-1} A_\sigma^*\right) + e^{\tau+1\prime} + e^{T-1\prime}$$

using eqn [13] i.e.

$$d^{\tau\prime} = d^{0\prime}A_\tau^* + d^{\tau+1\prime} + e^{T-1\prime} \qquad \cdots [15]$$

for $\tau = 0, \ldots, T-2$, using eqn [14].
For $\tau = T-1$, we have:

$$d^{T-1\prime} = d^{0\prime}A_{T-1}^* + \mathring{e}^{T-1\prime} \qquad \cdots [16]$$

Equations [15] and [16] may be rewritten as:

$$d^{\tau\prime} - d^{\tau+1\prime} - d^{0\prime}A^*_\tau > \mathbf{0}_n \qquad \tau = 0, 1, \ldots, T-2 \qquad \cdots [17]$$

$$d^{T-1\prime} - d^{0\prime}A^*_{T-1} > \mathbf{0}_n \qquad \cdots [18]$$

using eqn [13], i.e.

$$d'(I - B^*) > \mathbf{0}_{nT} \qquad \cdots [19]$$

where

$$d = (d^0 \quad d^1 \cdots d^{T-1})' \qquad \cdots [20]$$

So, $(I - B^*)$ has a D.D.; we have now to establish that it has a positive D.D. Consider eqn [6]. It is evident that we have to examine only $I - A^*_0$. As $I - \bar{A}^*$ has a positive D.D. and $\bar{A}^* = \sum_{\tau=0}^{T-1} A^*_\tau \geqslant A^*_o$, it follows that $(I - B^*)$ also has a positive D.D.

This theorem will be useful in analysing the stability properties of models with different lag structures, but with the same potential. However, when compared with the results derived in §4.2.10 (for the non-negative case), the results derived here are not as strong. The reason for this is explained by a comparison of Theorems 35 and 36. From the former, stability and positive diagonal dominance are equivalent concepts under non-negativity; such equivalence does not in general carry over to the case where the matrix is not non-negative, as we see in Theorem 36. There is an obvious exception to this, when the matrix is triangular; this is dealt with in the exercises.

We now use Theorem 37 to compare the stability of:

$$y(t+1) = By(t) \qquad \cdots [21]$$

(i.e., eqn [18] of §4.2.10.)

$$x(t+1) = \bar{A}x(t) \qquad \cdots [22]$$

(i.e., eqn [33] of §4.2.10.)

Theorem 38: Suppose $\bar{A}^* = \sum_{\tau=0}^{T-1} A^*_\tau$.

(i) If $(I - \bar{A}^*)$ has a positive D.D., then eqn [21] is stable.
(ii) If $(I - B^*)$ has a positive D.D., then eqn [22] is stable.

Proof: The proofs follow from Theorems 36 and 37.

Note that in stating the hypotheses, we did not say: "If $(I - \bar{A}^*)$ (or $(I - B^*)$) is stable ...." Stability of $\bar{A}$ (or B) does not imply that $(I - \bar{A}^*)$ (or $(I - B^*)$) has a positive D.D.—this follows from Theorem 36.

§4.2.12. *Lags and stability concluded*

Let us consider a more general structural equation than eqn [1] of

§4.2.10. Our equation is:

$$\bar{C}x(t+1)=\bar{A}x(t) \qquad \bar{A}=\sum_{\tau=0}^{T-1} A_\tau \qquad \cdots [1]$$

(Equation [1] above is really a generalisation of eqn [33] of §4.2.10.) The model with a different lag structure, but the same potential, is given by:

$$\bar{C}x(t+1)=\sum_{\tau=0}^{T-1} A_\tau x(t-\tau) \qquad \cdots [2]$$

or

$$Cy(t+1)=By(t) \qquad \cdots [3]$$

where B is given by eqn [18] of §4.2.10, $y(t)$ by eqn [17], and

$$C=\begin{bmatrix} \bar{C} & & & \\ & I & & \bigcirc \\ & & \ddots & \\ \bigcirc & & & I \end{bmatrix}$$

If $\bar{C}$ is non-singular, we have instead of eqns [1] and [3]:

$$x(t+1)=\bar{C}^{-1}\bar{A}x(t)=\bar{E}x(t) \qquad \cdots [4]$$

$$y(t+1)=C^{-1}By(t)=Fy(t) \qquad \cdots [5]$$

The introduction of lags into eqn [4] yields the equation:

$$y(t+1)=Ey(t) \qquad \cdots [6]$$

where

$$E=\begin{bmatrix} \bar{E}_0 & \bar{E}_1 & \cdots & & \bar{E}_{T-1} \\ I & 0 & \cdots & & 0 \\ \cdot & \cdot & \cdot & & \cdot \\ \cdot & \cdot & \cdot & & \cdot \\ \cdot & \cdot & & \cdot & \cdot \\ 0 & 0 & \cdots & I & 0 \end{bmatrix} \qquad \cdots [7]$$

$$F=\begin{bmatrix} \bar{C}^{-1}A_0 & \bar{C}^{-1}A_1 & \cdots & & \bar{C}^{-1}A_{T-1} \\ I & 0 & \cdots & & 0 \\ \cdot & \cdot & \cdot & & \cdot \\ \cdot & \cdot & \cdot & & \cdot \\ \cdot & \cdot & & \cdot & \cdot \\ 0 & 0 & \cdots & I & 0 \end{bmatrix} \qquad \cdots [8]$$

A comparison of eqns [7] and [8] leads us to conclude that E and F in general do not have the same roots. So, it is not a matter of indifference to impose a lag structure on the original model, such as eqn [1], and on the reduced form of the model, such as eqn [4]. No general results exist here; we have only the following:

Theorem 39: Suppose $B \geqslant [0]$, $\bar{C}^{-1} \geqslant [0]$. Then eqn [4] is stable iff eqn [5] is stable iff eqn [6] is stable.

Proof: Under the hypotheses, $\bar{E} \geqslant [0]$. The result then follows from Theorem 34.

§4.2.13. *Backward difference equations*

So far, the equations examined have been of the form:

$$x(t+1) = Ax(t) + f(t) \qquad \cdots [1]$$

As we shall see in the following chapter, we can give meaning to an equation of the form:

$$x(t) = Ax(t+1) + f(t+1) \qquad \cdots [2]$$

which we call, in contrast to eqn [1], a backward difference equation. We shall be particularly interested in the case where $A \geqslant [0]$ and where the solution is non-negative. Let us suppose that the matrix A is non-singular. Then, eqn [2] becomes:

$$x(t+1) = A^{-1}x(t) + g(t) \qquad g(t) = -A^{-1}f(t+1) \qquad \cdots [3]$$

As A is non-negative, we know that in general A^{-1} cannot be non-negative. From §4.2.9, we know that eqn [3] has a meaningful solution iff $(A^{-1})^i \geqslant \mathbf{0}$, for all i (assuming $g(t) \geqq \mathbf{0}$).
If A is singular, the problem becomes more difficult.
Special methods are required to solve these equations. Some are outlined in this Section, others in §5.2.2 below.

As in the solution of forward difference equations, we can consider separately the homogeneous and non-homogeneous equations. In this section, we consider only the homogeneous equation:

$$x(t) = Ax(t+1) \qquad \cdots [4]$$

Our task is further simplified by the following assumption: $A \geqslant [0]$ is indecomposable.

If we are interested in non-negative solutions, we can immediately derive:

Theorem 40: Let $Ax^* = \lambda^*(A)x^*$. Then the unique balanced solution of eqn [4] is: $u(t) = x^*/\lambda^*(A)^t$.

Proof: By Theorem 28 of Chapter 2, x^* is the only possible non-negative characteristic vector of A. By substituting $u(t)$ in eqn [4], the result follows.

Retaining interest in non-negative solutions, we can strengthen Theorem 40 if we make the further assumption that A is primitive. This is the case which we examine first. Then, we examine the other case—where A is imprimitive.

Theorem 41: If A is primitive, the balanced solution is the only non-trivial solution of eqn [4].

Proof: Iterating eqn [4], we obtain:

$$x(0)=A^t x(t) \qquad \cdots [5]$$

Let

$$p^{*\prime}A=\lambda^*(A)p^{*\prime} \qquad p^*>\mathbf{0} \qquad \cdots [6]$$

Pre-multiplying eqn [5] by $p^{*\prime}$, we have:

$$\begin{aligned} p^{*\prime}x(0) &= (p^{*\prime}A^t)x(t)=(p^{*\prime}\lambda^*(A)^t)x(t) \\ &= p^{*\prime}(\lambda^*(A)^t x(t)) \end{aligned} \qquad \cdots [7]$$

$\lambda^*(A)^t x(t)\geqslant\mathbf{0}$, $p^*>\mathbf{0}$, $x(0)\geqslant\mathbf{0}$. Hence the sequence $\lambda^*(A)^t x(t)$ is bounded. So there is a convergent subsequence $\lambda^*(A)^\tau x(\tau)$ where:

$$\lim_{\tau\to\infty}\lambda^*(A)^\tau x(\tau)=\bar{x} \qquad \cdots [8]$$

From eqn [5]:

$$x(0)=\left[\frac{A}{\lambda^*(A)}\right]^\tau(\lambda^*(A)^\tau x(\tau)) \qquad \cdots [9]$$

Letting $\tau\to\infty$, we have from eqns [8] and [9]:

$$x(0)=L\bar{x}=\sum_{i=1}^{n}L^i\bar{x}_i=L^i\sum_{i=1}^{n}\bar{x}_i \qquad \cdots [10]$$

where

$$L=\lim_{\tau\to\infty}\left[\frac{A}{\lambda^*(A)}\right]^\tau \qquad \cdots [11]$$

From Exercises §2.3, we know that the columns of L are identical (each being a characteristic vector of A corresponding to the root $\lambda^*(A)$). From eqn [10], we see that $x(0)$ is also a characteristic vector corresponding to the root $\lambda^*(A)$. By the same argument, $x(t)$ is also a characteristic vector of A corresponding to $\lambda^*(A)$, for any t—for $x(t)$ could be considered as the initial conditions of the solution starting at t.

So $x(t) = Ax(t+1) = \lambda^*(A)x(t+1)$, where $x(t)$ and $x(t+1)$ are proportional to x^*. Iterating, we have:

$$x(t) = x(0)/\lambda^*(A)^t$$

i.e. $u(t) = x^*/\lambda^*(A)^t$, as required.

We now consider the case where A is imprimitive, with index of imprimitivity k, i.e. there are k roots of A equal in modulus to $\lambda^*(A)$. From Exercises §2.3, we know that there exists a permutation matrix P such that:

$$(P^{-1}AP)^k = P^{-1}A^kP = \begin{bmatrix} A_1 & & & & \\ & A_2 & & & \bigcirc \\ & & \cdot & & \\ & \bigcirc & & \cdot & \\ & & & & \cdot \\ & & & & A_k \end{bmatrix} \qquad \cdots [12]$$

where the A_i matrices are square and primitive with Frobenius root $\lambda^*(A)^k$. (Without loss of generality, P may be equated with I; for, as P is a permutation matrix, its effect on any vector is merely a re-arrangement of its components. Clearly there is nothing lost in assuming that any such re-arrangements have been made.)
Let:

$$A_i w^i = \lambda^*(A_i)w^i \qquad i = 1, \ldots, k$$
$$w^i > \mathbf{0}; \qquad \lambda^*(A_i) = \lambda^*(A)^k, \quad \text{for all} \quad i \qquad \cdots [13]$$

Define:

$$w = \begin{bmatrix} w^1 \\ \cdot \\ \cdot \\ \cdot \\ w^i \\ \cdot \\ \cdot \\ \cdot \\ w^k \end{bmatrix} \qquad \cdots [14]$$

Theorem 42: If A is imprimitive with index $k(\geqslant 2)$, eqn [3] has k linearly independent solutions. Each solution of eqn [3] can be written as a linear combination of these k solutions.

This result is due to Nikaido. We outline the proof of the first part. Let $r(t)$ denote the smallest non-negative remainder obtainable when t is divided by k. Then we may write $t = vk + r(t)$, v a non-negative integer,

$k > r(t) \geqslant 0$. Define the vector:

$$z^s(t) = (1/\lambda^*(A)^t)\begin{bmatrix} \delta_{1,r(s+t)}w^1 \\ \delta_{2,r(s+t)}w^2 \\ \cdot \\ \cdot \\ \cdot \\ \delta_{i,r(s+t)}w^i \\ \cdot \\ \cdot \\ \cdot \\ \delta_{k-1,r(s+t)}w^{k-1} \\ \delta_{0,r(s+t)}w^k \end{bmatrix} \qquad \cdots[15]$$

$\delta_{i,r(s+t)}$ denotes the Kronecker delta (we have written $\delta_{0,r(s+t)}$ instead of $\delta_{k,r(s+t)}$ simply to ensure consistency in the use of the Kronecker delta), $i = 0, 1, \ldots, k-1$. Obviously, $r(s+t)$ takes on the values $0, 1, \ldots, k-1$. The k z-vectors defined in eqn [15] form a linearly independent set. Assuming $P = I$, it is evident from eqns [12] and [13) that w solves:

$$A^k w = \lambda^*(A)^k w \qquad \cdots[16]$$

Hence:

$$Aw = \lambda^*(A)w \qquad \cdots[17]$$

where

$$A = \begin{bmatrix} 0 & A_{12} & 0 & \cdots & 0 \\ 0 & 0 & A_{23} & \cdots & 0 \\ \cdot & \cdot & & \cdot & \cdot \\ \cdot & \cdot & & \cdot & \cdot \\ \cdot & \cdot & & \cdot & \cdot \\ 0 & 0 & 0 & \cdots & A_{k-1,k} \\ A_{k1} & 0 & 0 & \cdots & 0 \end{bmatrix}$$

Writing eqn [17] in extensive form, we can easily see that:

$$Az^s(t+1) = z^s(t) \qquad \cdots[18]$$

We conclude this section by considering the following generalisation of eqn [4]:

$$x(t) = A_T x(t+T) \qquad \cdots[19]$$

where A_T is indecomposable.

Defining

$$y(t)=\begin{bmatrix} x(t) \\ x(t+1) \\ \cdot \\ \cdot \\ \cdot \\ x(t+T-1) \end{bmatrix} \quad \text{and} \quad A=\begin{bmatrix} 0 & 0 & \cdots & 0 & A_T \\ I & 0 & \cdots & 0 & 0 \\ \cdot & \cdot & & & \cdot \\ \cdot & \cdot & \cdot & & \cdot \\ \cdot & \cdot & & & \cdot \\ 0 & 0 & \cdots & I & 0 \end{bmatrix} \qquad \cdots[20]$$

eqn [19] becomes:

$$y(t)=Ay(t+1) \qquad \cdots[21]$$

A is imprimitive. In fact, we know that A^k is a block diagonal matrix, with A_T^k (k of them) on the diagonal. To solve eqn [21], we need to know the index of imprimitivity of A, which is equal to the index of imprimitivity of A^k. If A_T is primitive, then A^K has index k. If A_T has index m, then A^K has index mk.

Exercises

§4.1

1. (*Uniqueness of solution.*) *Consider the scalar equation*:

   $$\mathrm{d}x/\mathrm{d}t = ax \qquad \cdots[1]$$

   which has a solution $x(t)=x^0 e^{at}$, where $x^0=x(0)$.
   We wish to prove that there are no other solutions.
   Consider $u(t)e^{-at}$, where $u(t)$ is any solution of eqn [1].
   Show that $\mathrm{d}(u(t)e^{-at})/\mathrm{d}t=0$, which implies that $u(t)e^{-at}=k$. It is evident that $k=x^0$.

2. Now consider the matrix equation:

   $$\mathrm{d}x/\mathrm{d}t = Ax \qquad x(0)=x^0 \qquad \cdots[2]$$

   By Theorem 7, we know that $(\exp(At))x^0$ solves eqn [2].
   To derive uniqueness, we first let $y(t)=(\exp(-At))x(t)$, where $x(t)$ is any solution of eqn [2].
   Show that $\mathrm{d}y(t)/\mathrm{d}t=\mathbf{0}$, which implies that $y(t)=k$ for all t, where k is now a vector. It is easily seen that $k=x^0$ and uniqueness follows.

3. Evaluate $\exp A$ for the following matrices A:

   (i) $\begin{bmatrix} \alpha & 0 \\ 0 & \beta \end{bmatrix}$; (ii) $\begin{bmatrix} \alpha & 0 \\ \beta & \alpha \end{bmatrix}$; (iii) $\begin{bmatrix} \alpha & 0 \\ 1 & \alpha \end{bmatrix}$; (iv) $\begin{bmatrix} \alpha & -\beta \\ \beta & \alpha \end{bmatrix}$;

   (v) $\begin{bmatrix} 0 & 1 \\ 1 & 0 \end{bmatrix}$; (vi) $\begin{bmatrix} 5 & -6 \\ 3 & -4 \end{bmatrix}$; (vii) $\begin{bmatrix} 0 & 1 & 2 \\ 0 & 0 & 3 \\ 0 & 0 & 0 \end{bmatrix}$.

4. Find 2×2 matrices A and B such that $\exp(A+B)\neq(\exp A)(\exp B)$.

5. If $AB = BA$, prove that $(\exp A)(\exp B) = (\exp B)(\exp A)$ and $(\exp A)B = B(\exp A)$.

6. Find a matrix A such that one solution of $dx/dt = Ax$ is $(e^{2T} - e^{-t}, e^{2t} + 2e^{-t})$.

7. Solve $dx/dt = Ax$, $x(0) = x^0$ in the following cases (A and x^0 given):

(i) $A = \begin{bmatrix} 0 & -1 \\ 1 & 0 \end{bmatrix}$, $x^0 = \begin{bmatrix} 1 \\ 1 \end{bmatrix}$; (ii) $A = \begin{bmatrix} 1 & -2 \\ 2 & 7 \end{bmatrix}$, $x^0 = \begin{bmatrix} 3 \\ -9 \end{bmatrix}$;

(iii) $A = \begin{bmatrix} 0 & -4 \\ 1 & 0 \end{bmatrix}$, $x^0 = \begin{bmatrix} 0 \\ -7 \end{bmatrix}$; (iv) $A = \begin{bmatrix} 0 & -2 \\ 1 & 2 \end{bmatrix}$, $x^0 = \begin{bmatrix} 3 \\ -2 \end{bmatrix}$;

(v) $A = \begin{bmatrix} -1 & 0 \\ 1 & 2 \end{bmatrix}$, $x^0 = \begin{bmatrix} 0 \\ 3 \end{bmatrix}$; (vi) $A = \begin{bmatrix} 2 & 1 \\ 1 & 1 \end{bmatrix}$, $x^0 = \begin{bmatrix} 1 \\ 1 \end{bmatrix}$;

(vii) $A = \begin{bmatrix} 0 & 3 \\ 1 & -2 \end{bmatrix}$, $x^0 = \begin{bmatrix} 3 \\ 0 \end{bmatrix}$.

8. If the 2×2 matrix A has roots $\alpha + i\beta$, prove that there exists a matrix Q such that:

$$Q^{-1}AQ = \begin{bmatrix} \alpha & -\beta \\ \beta & \alpha \end{bmatrix}$$

9. Derive an explicit solution of $dx/dt = Ax$ to take account of repeated complex roots.

10. Solve the equation:

$$\frac{dx}{dt} = \begin{bmatrix} 0 & 1 & 0 & 0 \\ -1 & 0 & 0 & 0 \\ 0 & 0 & 0 & -1 \\ 0 & 0 & 1 & 0 \end{bmatrix} x \qquad x(0) = \begin{bmatrix} 1 \\ -1 \\ 2 \\ 0 \end{bmatrix}$$

11. Solve the equation:

$$\frac{dx}{dt} = \begin{bmatrix} 6 & 2 & 2 \\ -2 & 2 & 0 \\ 0 & 0 & 2 \end{bmatrix} x \qquad x(0) = \begin{bmatrix} 0 \\ 1 \\ 1 \end{bmatrix}$$

12. Solve the equation:

$$\frac{dx}{dt} = \begin{bmatrix} 3 & -1 \\ 1 & 1 \end{bmatrix} x \qquad x(0) = \begin{bmatrix} 3 \\ -1 \end{bmatrix}$$

13. Prove that the characteristic equation of

$$\begin{bmatrix} 0 & 1 & 0 & 0 & \cdots & 0 & 0 \\ 0 & 0 & 1 & 0 & \cdots & 0 & 0 \\ \cdot & \cdot & \cdot & \cdot & \cdot & \cdot & \cdot \\ \cdot & \cdot & \cdot & \cdot & \cdot & \cdot & \cdot \\ \cdot & \cdot & \cdot & \cdot & \cdot & \cdot & \cdot \\ 0 & 0 & 0 & 0 & \cdots & 0 & 1 \\ -a_0 & -a_1 & -a_2 & -a_3 & \cdots & -a_{n-2} & -a_{n-1} \end{bmatrix}$$

is

$$\lambda^n + a_{n-1}\lambda^{n-1} + a_{n-2}\lambda^{n-2} + \cdots + a_2\lambda^2 + a_1\lambda + a_0 = 0.$$

14. Solve the following equations:
   (i) $d^2y/dt^2 + 2dy/dt + y = 0$, $y(0) = 1$, $dy(0)/dt = 2$;
   (ii) $d^2y/dt^2 + y = 0$, $y(0) = 1$, $dy(0)/dt = -1$;
   (iii) $d^2y/dt^2 - 3dy/dt + 2y = 0$, $y(0) = 0$, $dy(0)/dt = -1$.

15. Solve the following equations:
   (i) $d^2y/dt^2 + 3y = 0$;
   (ii) $d^3y/dt^3 - d^2y/dt^2 + 4dy/dt - 4y = 0$.

16. Solve the following equation:

$$\frac{dx}{dt} = \begin{bmatrix} 6 & 2 & 2 \\ -2 & 2 & 0 \\ 0 & 0 & 2 \end{bmatrix} x + e^{4t} \begin{bmatrix} \alpha \\ 0 \\ 0 \end{bmatrix}$$

(See Q11 above.)

17. Solve the following equations:

(i) $$\frac{dx}{dt} = \begin{bmatrix} 0 & 1 \\ -1 & 0 \end{bmatrix} x + \begin{bmatrix} 0 \\ 2 \end{bmatrix};$$

(ii) $$\frac{dx}{dt} = \begin{bmatrix} 0 & 1 \\ -4 & 0 \end{bmatrix} x + \begin{bmatrix} 0 \\ \sin 2t \end{bmatrix};$$

(iii) $$\frac{dx}{dt} = \begin{bmatrix} 3 & 1 \\ 1 & 3 \end{bmatrix} x + e^{3t} \begin{bmatrix} 1 \\ 2 \end{bmatrix}.$$

18. Solve the following equations:
   (i) $d^2y/dt^2 + 4y = \cos 2t$, $y(0) = 0$, $dy(0)/dt = 1$;
   (ii) $d^2y/dt^2 - 4dy/dt + 4y = 2te^{2t}$

19. Prove that Lyapunov's theorem (Theorem 17) is equivalent to the following:
Let X be a real $n \times n$ matrix which is the sum of a negative scalar matrix and a skew-symmetric matrix. Let D be a real diagonal matrix. Then XD is stable iff each diagonal element of D is positive. (Taussky)

20. Consider the system $\mathrm{d}x/\mathrm{d}t = Ax$. Let $v(x) = x'x$. Prove that the system is stable if A is quasi-negative definite.

21. Consider the equation $\mathrm{d}x/\mathrm{d}t = Ax$, where A is singular, indecomposable, and $a_{ij} \geqslant 0$ for all $i \neq j$. Suppose that 0 is the root with largest real part. Discuss stability concepts, such as convergence to a non-negative solution.
(Use Exercises §2.3, Q3 & Q12.)

22. Let A be a Morishima matrix (see §2.4.3). Prove that the following conditions are equivalent:
(a) $A - \alpha I$ is a stable matrix;
(b) $A - \alpha I$ is an $(N-P)$-matrix;
(c) $\alpha > \lambda^*(A)$ ($\lambda^*(A)$ being the Frobenius root of A);
(d) $A - \alpha I$ has a negative q.d.d.

23. Suppose that $a_{ij} \geqslant 0$ for all $i \neq j$. Prove that the solution of $\mathrm{d}x/\mathrm{d}t = Ax + b$ is non-negative for all t, if $b \geqq \mathbf{0}$, $x(0) \geqq \mathbf{0}$.

§4.2

1. The $n \times n$ matrix A is *simple* iff, for each distinct root, the algebraic multiplicity is equal to the geometric multiplicity. Prove that A is simple iff it is similar to a diagonal matrix.
A sufficient condition for A to be simple is that it has n distinct roots.

2. Prove that A is simple iff A' is simple.

3. Let $Ax^i = \lambda_i x^i$, $A'y^i = \lambda_i y^i$, $i = 1, \ldots, n$.
Let $X = [x^1 \;\; x^2 \cdots x^n]$, $Y = [y^1 \;\; y^2 \;\; \cdots \;\; y^n]$.
Prove that, if A is simple, X and Y can be chosen such that

$$Y'X = I \quad \text{and} \quad A = XDY' \qquad D = [\lambda_i \delta_{ij}]$$

4. Define a constituent matrix $G_i = x^i y^{i\prime}$, $i = 1, \ldots, n$.

Prove that $A^t = \sum_{i=1}^{n} \lambda_i^t G_i$, if A is simple.

(A reference for the material in questions 1–4 is Lancaster's book.)

5. Consider the equation:

$$x(t+1) = A'x(t) \qquad \cdots [1]$$

where A' is stochastic with n distinct roots.
Using the results in questions 1–4, find the asymptotic solution of eqn [1].

6. Solve the following equations:

(i) $x(t+1) = \begin{bmatrix} 1 & -1 \\ 0 & 2 \end{bmatrix} x(t) \qquad x(0) = \begin{bmatrix} 1 \\ 3 \end{bmatrix}$

(ii) $x(t+1)=\begin{bmatrix}1 & 4\\ -3 & 2\end{bmatrix}x(t)$

(iii) $x(t+1)=\begin{bmatrix}1 & -1\\ 1 & 3\end{bmatrix}x(t) \qquad x(0)=\begin{bmatrix}-2\\ 0\end{bmatrix}$

7. Solve the following equations:
 (i) $y(t+2)+3y(t+1)-4y(t)=t^2$
 (ii) $y(t+2)+y(t)=\cos t$
 (iii) $y(t+2)-4y(t)=2^t$
 (iv) $y(t+3)+3y(t+2)-y(t+1)-3y(t)=0$

8. Consider the equation:

$$x(t+1)=Ax(t) \quad \text{where} \quad A \geqslant [0] \qquad \cdots [2]$$

Prove that eqn [2] is stable iff $(I-A)$ has a positive dominant diagonal.

9. Define $B=[b_{ij}]$ by $b_{ij}=|a_{ij}|$, $i, j=1,\ldots,n$, where $A=[a_{ij}]$ is any square matrix. If $(I-B)$ has a positive dominant diagonal, prove that the system

$$x(t+1)=Ax(t)$$

is stable.

10. Consider the following systems of equations:

$$dp_i/dt=\sum_{j=1}^{n} a_{ij}p_j \qquad \cdots [3]$$

$$y_i(t+1)=\sum_{j=1}^{n} a_{ij}y_j(t)+y_i(t) \qquad \cdots [4]$$

The coefficients, a_{ij}, which are common to eqns [3] and [4], satisfy the sign conditions: $a_{ii}<0$, for all i; $a_{ij}>0$, for all $i\neq j$; $i, j=1,\ldots,n$. Prove that eqn [3] is stable iff eqn [4] is stable. (Metzler)

11. To see the connection between eqns [1] of §4.1.11 and [4] of §4.2.8, make the substitution $A'=(B+I)^{-1}(B-I)$ in the former.

12. Derive the conditions for stability of $x(t+1)=Ax(t)$:
 (i) on the assumption that A has n distinct roots;
 (ii) by use of a unitary transformation or Jordan normal for form (see Exercise §2.4, Q8 and Theorem 16 above).

13. Consider the following pair of equations:

$$y(t)=\begin{bmatrix}1 & \alpha\\ \beta & \frac{1}{2}\end{bmatrix}y(t-1) \qquad \cdots [1]$$

$$y(t)=\begin{bmatrix}0 & \alpha\\ 0 & \frac{1}{2}\end{bmatrix}y(t-1)+\begin{bmatrix}1 & 0\\ \beta & 0\end{bmatrix}y(t-2) \qquad \cdots [2]$$

Show that, if $-\frac{1}{16}<\alpha\beta<0$, eqn [1] is stable, whereas eqn [2] is unstable.

14. Consider the following (one-way) foreign-trade multiplier models (where $I(t)$ and $X(t)$ are assumed constant):

(i) $Y(t)=C(t)+I(t)+X(t)-M(t)$

$$C(t)=\gamma+\alpha Y(t-1)$$

$$M(t)=\delta+\beta Y(t-1)$$

Derive the matrix difference equation involving $Y(t)$, $M(t)$. Show that, if $1>\alpha>\beta>0$, the model is stable.

(ii) Now let:

$$C(t)=\gamma+\alpha Y(t-2)$$

$$M(t)=\delta+\beta Y(t-3)$$

Derive the matrix difference equation involving $Y(t)$, $M(t)$. Show that, if $\alpha+\beta>1$, the model is unstable.
Note that (i) may be stable, while (ii) is unstable.

15. Consider eqns [1] and [3] of §4.2.12.
Let $\bar{C}=I$ and $\bar{A}$ be triangular.
(i) Prove that, if eqn [1] is stable, eqn [3] is also stable.
(ii) Construct an example to show that the converse is not necessarily true.

16. (Continuation of Q15.) Suppose that $\bar{A}$ and $\bar{C}$ are triangular. Prove that eqn [3] is stable, if eqn [1] is stable.
(A reference for questions 13–16 is Bear, 1966).

17. Let $g(\ )$ be a matrix norm such that $B\geqslant A\geqslant[0]$ implies $g(B)\geqslant g(A)$. Let $f(\ )$ be any matrix norm. Suppose A can be partitioned into square blocks, A^{ij}, $i, j=1,\ldots,m$.
Prove that $h(A)=g[f(A^{ij})]$, $i, j=1,\ldots,m$, is a matrix norm.

18. Consider the system $x(t+1)=Ax(t)+b$. Let $f(A)$ be a matrix norm. Prove that if $f(A)<1$, a unique stable equilibrium exists.
As outlined in Exercises §2.4, the vector norm $v(x)=(x'x)^{\frac{1}{2}}$ induces the matrix norm $f(A)=(\lambda^*(A'A))^{\frac{1}{2}}$. So $(\lambda^*(A'A))^{\frac{1}{2}}<1$ is sufficient for the existence of a unique stable equilibrium. Prove that $(\lambda^*(A'A))^{\frac{1}{2}}<1$ iff $I-A'A$ is positive definite.

19. Consider the structural equation $x(t+1)=Bx(t+1)+Cx(t)+d$, of which the equation in Q18 is the reduced form, i.e. $b=(I-B)^{-1}d$, $A=(I-B)^{-1}C$. Let $f(\ )$ be a matrix norm such that $f(I)=1$. Prove that if $f(B)+f(C)<1$, the structural equation has a unique stable equilibrium.

20. Consider the following generalisation of the equation in Q19: $x(t+1) = A_1x(t)+A_2x(t-1)+\cdots+A_Tx(t-T+1)+b$. Let $f(\ )$ be a matrix norm such that $f(I)=1$. Prove that if $\sum_{\tau=1}^{T} f(A_\tau)<1$, a unique stable equilibrium exists.
[Hint: Rewrite the equation as a first-order matrix equation as in §4.2.10, with matrix A. Replace A by the matrix

$$D^{-1}BD = D^{-1}\begin{bmatrix} f(A_1) & f(A_2) & \cdots & & f(A_T) \\ 1 & 0 & \cdots & & 0 \\ 0 & 1 & \cdots & & 0 \\ \cdot & & \cdot & & \cdot \\ \cdot & & \cdot & & \cdot \\ \cdot & & & \cdot & \cdot \\ 0 & 0 & \cdots & 1 & 0 \end{bmatrix} D$$

$D=[d_i\delta_{ij}]$, $i, j=1,\ldots, T$; $\quad d_1>d_2>\cdots>d_T$.

Then by Q17 and Theorem 74 of Chapter 2, $h(A)=g(D^{-1}BD)$ is also a matrix norm. Let $g(\ )$ be the row sum norm. By choice of d_i, each row sum of $D^{-1}BD$ is less than 1.
Hence $h(A)=g(D^{-1}BD)<1$, which implies $|\lambda_1(A)|<1$ by Theorem 73 of Chapter 2.]

21. Consider the equation:

$$y(t+1)=\alpha_1y(t)+\alpha_2y(t-1)+\cdots+\alpha_Ty(t-T+1)$$

where the y are scalar variables and $\alpha_\tau>0$, for all τ.

Prove that the system is stable iff $\sum_{\tau=1}^{T}\alpha_\tau<1$.

22. Consider the set of matrices $C_1,\ldots, C_T$, where $\sum_{\tau=1}^{T} f(C_\tau)<1$, $f(\ )$ being a matrix norm such that $f(I)=1$.
Prove that the system:

$$x(t+1)=\sum_{\sigma=1}^{s} A_\sigma x(t-\sigma+1)+b$$

is stable, where the A_σ are obtained by summing C_τ such that each C_τ appears in one and only one sum, A_σ.

23. Consider the equation:

$$x(t+1)-x(t)=Ax(t) \quad \text{or} \quad x(t+1)=(A+I)x(t).$$

If $(A+I)$ is a contraction mapping, i.e. $\nu((A+I)x)<\nu(x)$, for all x, for some norm $\nu(\ )$, it is evident that the system is stable. The problem is to find conditions under which $(A+I)$ is a contraction mapping.

(a) Using the norm $\nu(x) = \sum_i \alpha_i |x_i|$, prove that if A has a negative column q.d.d., then $(A+I)$ is a contraction mapping.

(b) Using the norm $\nu(x) = \max \alpha_i |x_i|$, $\alpha_i > 0$ for all i and given, prove that if A has a negative row q.d.d., then $(A+I)$ is a contraction mapping.

(References for questions 17–23 are the articles by Newman and Conlisk.)

24. Consider the equation $x(t+1) = Ax(t)$, where $A \geqslant [0]$. Under which conditions do we obtain convergence to the Frobenius solution? (Hint: Use the theory of primitive matrices, discussed in §2.3.5. Also, see §6.3.1.)

Notes

1. Fisher, F. M.: "Choice of units, column sums and stability in linear dynamic models with non-negative square matrices", *Econometrica*, **33** (1965). p. 449.

References

§4.1

Bellman, R.: *Introduction to Matrix Analysis*, McGraw-Hill, 2nd edn, 1970.

Coddington, E. & N. Levinson: *The Theory of Ordinary Differential Equations*, McGraw-Hill, 1955.

Hahn, W.: *Theory and Applications of Lyapunov's Direct Method*, Prentice-Hall, 1963.

Hirsch, M. W. & S. Smale: *Differential Equations, Dynamical Systems and Linear Algebra*, Academic Press, 1975.

Hurewicz, W.: *Lectures on Ordinary Differential Equations*, M.I.T. Press, 1958.

Lancaster, P.: *Theory of Matrices*, Academic Press, 1969.

LaSalle, J. & S. Lefchetz: *Stability by Lyapunov's Direct Method with Applications*, Academic Press, 1961.

§4.2

Bellman, R.: op. cit.

Hahn, W.: op. cit.

Lancaster, P.: op. cit.

§4.2.10–§4.2.12

Bear, D. V. T.: "The matrix multiplier and distributed lags", *Econometrica*, **31** (1965).

Bear, D. V. T.: "Distributed lags and economic theory", *Review of Economic Studies*, **33** (1966).

Fisher, F. M.: "Choice of units, column sums and stability in linear dynamic systems with non-negative square matrices", *Econometrica*, **33** (1965).

§4.2.13

Nikaido, H.: "Some dynamic phenomena in the Leontief model of reversely-lagged type", *Review of Economic Studies*, **29** (1962).

§*Exercises*

Conlisk, J.: "Quick stability checks and matrix norms", *Economica*, **30** (1973).

Metzler, L. A.: "Stability of multiple markets: the Hicks conditions", *Econometrica*, **13** (1945).

Newman, P.: "Approaches to stability analysis", *Economica*, **28** (1961).

Taussky, O.: "A remark on a theorem of Lyapunov", *Journal of Mathematical Analysis and Applications*, **2** (1961).

5

Dynamic Linear models

In this chapter, we discuss applications of the Frobenius theory (on semi-positive matrices) of Chapter 2 and the theory of difference and differential equations of Chapter 4. The underlying (mathematical) model of §5.1 can be considered as a dynamic generalisation of the static input–output equations of Chapter 2. The basic interpretation placed upon it is that of an expenditure system, not a production system. The model is versatile, permitting us to discuss multi-sector multipliers, a multi-country model of income and trade and (aspects of) the transfer problem. Section 5.1 is thus squarely based on the rather neglected work of Metzler.

Numerous writers have interpreted the model of §5.1 as being a faithful representation of an input–output model with a production lag. Nikaido was the first to demonstrate the error of such an interpretation. Production lags lead to backward, not forward, difference equations. These are dealt with in §5.2.

Section 5.3 is devoted to the dynamic Leontief model. The open model (with proportional growth in autonomous expenditures) has a number of interesting particular solutions; two are discussed in §5.3, one involving a generalisation of the matrix multipliers of §5.1, the other illustrating the limits to growth in terms of the Frobenius root of the matrix of the dynamic Leontief system. We also discuss the dual stability theorem due to Jorgenson.

In §5.4, we attempt to extend to the long-run the expenditure models of §5.1 and a linear production-expenditure model. In particular, we devote our attention to a generalisation of Metzler's multi-country model of income and trade. Complete, general results seem not to be possible, a conclusion suggested by the related work of Brown and Jones.

§5.1. Multiplier models

§5.1.1. *Static or instantaneous multiplier*

We begin by considering a very simple closed economy. We distinguish n sectors. Let

Y_i = income of sector i
F_i = expenditure of sector i
a_{ij} = sector j's marginal propensity to spend on goods
produced by sector i

$i, j = 1, \ldots, n.$
Suppose that the economy is initially in equilbrium and that then there occur autonomous increments in expenditure denoted by the vector $f = (f_1, f_2, \ldots, f_n)'$. Let

$$y_i = Y_i - Y_i^0$$
$$f_i = F_i - F_i^0 \qquad i = 1, \ldots, n$$

where the superscript "0" refers to the equilibrium value of a variable.

Let us assume that there are no lags and all repercussions occur instantaneously. Then we can write the following equation for the change in the income of the i-th sector consequent on the changes in autonomous expenditures:

$$y_i = \sum_{j=1}^{n} a_{ij} y_j + f_i \qquad i = 1, \ldots, n \qquad \cdots [1]$$

or

$$y = Ay + f \quad \text{or} \quad (I - A)y = f \qquad \cdots [2]$$

$A^j = (a_{1j}, a_{2j}, \ldots, a_{nj})$ is the vector of j's marginal propensities to spend.

Normally, $a_{ij} \geq 0$, for all i, j. It is reasonable also to assume that $\sum_{i=1}^{n} a_{ij} \leq 1$, for all j. If $\sum_{i=1}^{n} a_{ij} = 1$ for all j, then the Frobenius root of A is 1, the matrix $(I - A)$ is singular and there is in general no solution of eqn [2]. This corresponds to the single-sector case of an infinite multiplier where the marginal propensity to consume is equal to 1.

If $\sum_{i=1}^{n} a_{ij} < 1$, for all j, we know from Theorem 71 of Chapter 2 that $(I - A)^{-1} \geq [0]$. So, if $f \geq \mathbf{0}$, $y \geq \mathbf{0}$; if $f \leq \mathbf{0}$, $y \leq \mathbf{0}$. If $\sum_{i=1}^{n} a_{ij} \leq 1$, for all j, with at least one strict inequality, and if A is indecomposable, then from Theorem 72 of Chapter 2 we have $(I - A)^{-1} > [0]$. Then, if $f \geq (\leq) \mathbf{0}$, $y > (<) \mathbf{0}$.
In this case, we can have at most $n - 1$ sectors each with a marginal propensity to spend of one, as long as there is one country which has a marginal propensity to spend of less than 1, i.e. as long as there is at least one country which acts as a "sink".

§5.1.2. *Dynamic multiplier*

We now modify the analysis of §5.1.1 by introducing a uniform expenditure lag of one period for all sectors. So eqn [1] of §5.1.1 becomes:

$$y_i(t) = \sum_{i=1}^{n} a_{ij} y_j(t-1) + f_i \qquad i = 1, \ldots, n \qquad \cdots [1]$$

or

$$y(t) = Ay(t-1) + f \qquad \cdots [2]$$

The associated homogeneous equation is:

$$y(t) = Ay(t-1) \qquad \cdots [3]$$

which has solution:

$$y(t) = A^t y(0) \qquad \cdots [4]$$

or

$$y(t) = \sum_{i=1}^{n} \alpha_i \lambda_i^t x^i \quad \text{in the case of } n \text{ distinct roots} \qquad \cdots [5]$$

$$y(t) = \sum_{i=1}^{k} \lambda_i^t p^i(t) \quad \text{in the case of } k < n \text{ distinct roots}$$

where $p^i(t)$ denotes a polynomial in t of order $m_i - 1$, m_i being the multiplicity of the root λ_i. (See §4.2.4.)

If $\sum_{i=1}^{n} a_{ij} < 1$, for all j (or in the indecomposable case, $\sum_{i=1}^{n} a_{ij} \leqslant 1$ with at least one strict inequality), then by Theorem 71 or 72 (see Chapter 2) we can derive $1 > \lambda^*(A)$. Hence the solution, [5], of the homogeneous eqn [3] tends to zero asymptotically, i.e. the system [3] is stable.

Retaining the hypothesis on the column sums, we try as a particular solution $y(t) = y$, a constant vector, for all t. From eqn [2], we have:

$$(I - A)y = f$$

Under the hypothesis, $(I - A)^{-1} \geqslant [0]$ (or $> [0]$ in the indecomposable case).

$$y = (I - A)^{-1} f \qquad \cdots [6]$$

is a particular solution of eqn [2].

The general solution of eqn [2] is then obtained by adding the solution of eqn [3] to the particular solution [6].

So, assuming $\sum_{i=1}^{n} a_{ij} < 1$ for all j, we conclude that $y(t) \to (I - A)^{-1} f$, where $y(t)$ is the general solution of eqn [2]. A similar conclusion follows when the appropriate modification is made in the indecomposable case.

§5.1.3. *A multi-country model of income and trade*

In this section, we maintain basically the same structure as in the two previous sections. However, we re-interpret it in terms of n countries rather than n sectors of a closed economy. For this reason, we state explicit national income equations thus:

$$Y_i = C_i + I_i + X_i - M_i \qquad i = 1, \ldots, n \qquad \cdots [1]$$

where

Y_i = income of country i

C_i = expenditure on consumption goods by country i

I_i = expenditure on investment goods by country i plus government expenditure in country i

X_i = exports of country i

M_i = imports of country i

In our analysis, we shall be restricting ourselves solely to the examination of changes in income and the balance of trade. To simplify our analysis, we make the heroic assumption that all prices, costs and exchange rates are constant. Let us introduce a little more notation:
Let M_{ji} = country i's imports from country j. Then

$$M_i = \sum_{\substack{j=1 \\ j\neq 1}}^{n} M_{ji}$$

Given our assumption on prices, we can consider M_{ji} as a function of Y_i. So, we write:

$$M_i(Y_i) = \sum_{j\neq 1} M_{ji}(Y_i) \qquad \cdots [2]$$

Once the M_{ji} are defined, we have:

$$X_i = \sum_{\substack{j=1 \\ j\neq i}}^{n} M_{ij}(Y_j) \qquad \cdots [3]$$

Let:

$$U_i(Y_i) = C_i(Y_i) + I_i(Y_i) \qquad \cdots [4]$$

= total expenditure of the i-th country on consumption and investment goods.

(We suppose for simplicity that C_i and I_i have an identical import content.)
Then eqn [1] can be rewritten as:

$$Y_i = U_i(Y_i) + \sum_{j\neq i} M_{ij}(Y_j) - \sum_{j\neq i} M_{ji}(Y_i) \qquad i = 1, \ldots, n \qquad \cdots [5]$$

We shall be concerning ourselves, first of all, with income changes. However, there is an obvious relation to be derived from eqn [5] which we may as well mention now.

Let

b_i = country i's balance of trade

$$= X_i - M_i \qquad \cdots [6]$$

$$= Y_i - U_i(Y_i)$$

Suppose that the trading system is initially in equilibrium (we may interpret this to imply that $b_i = 0$, for all i, initially) and that there is then a disturbance so that at least one of the Y_i is no longer at its equilibrium value. To test the stability of the trading system, we must first specify a reaction mechanism. As we are interested in changes in income (or output), let us suppose that each country responds to the dis-equilibrium by adjusting its output in proportion to the difference between demand for its output and supply, i.e.

$$\frac{\mathrm{d}Y_i}{\mathrm{d}t} = k_i\left[U_i(Y_i) + \sum_{j \neq i} M_{ij}(Y_j) - \sum_{i \neq j} M_{ji}(Y_i) - Y_i\right] \qquad \cdots [7]$$

$i = 1, \ldots, n$, and k_i measures the i-th country's speed of response.
To make the model manageable, we linearise eqn [7] by taking a Taylor series around $Y^0 = (Y_1^0, Y_2^0, \ldots, Y_n^0)'$ thus:

$$\frac{\mathrm{d}(Y_i - Y_i^0)}{\mathrm{d}t} = k_i\left[\frac{\mathrm{d}U_i}{\mathrm{d}Y_i} \cdot (Y_i - Y_i^0) + \sum_{j \neq i} \frac{\mathrm{d}M_{ij}}{\mathrm{d}Y_j} \cdot (Y_j - Y_j^o)\right.$$

$$\left. - \sum_{j \neq i} \frac{\mathrm{d}M_{ji}}{\mathrm{d}Y_i} \cdot (Y_i - Y_i^0) - 1(Y_i - Y_i^0)\right] \qquad \cdots [8]$$

Let us now introduce further notation:

$$y_i = Y_i - Y_i^0$$

$$u_i = \mathrm{d}U_i/\mathrm{d}Y_i$$

$$m_{ij} = \mathrm{d}M_{ij}/\mathrm{d}Y_j \qquad \text{for all } i, j \qquad \cdots [9]$$

$$m_i = \sum_{j \neq i} m_{ji}$$

Substituting from [9] into eqn [8], we have:

$$\frac{\mathrm{d}y_i}{\mathrm{d}t} = k_i\left(u_i y_i + \sum_{j \neq i} m_{ij} y_j - m_i y_i - y_i\right) \qquad i = 1, \ldots, n \qquad \cdots [10]$$

Define the following matrices:

$$U = [u_i \delta_{ij}]; \qquad K = [k_i \delta_{ij}]; \qquad i, j = 1, \ldots, n \qquad \cdots [11]$$

$$M = \begin{bmatrix} -m_1 & m_{12} & \cdots & m_{1n} \\ m_{21} & -m_2 & \cdots & m_{2n} \\ \cdot & \cdot & \cdot & \cdot \\ \cdot & \cdot & \cdot & \cdot \\ \cdot & \cdot & \cdot & \cdot \\ m_{n1} & m_{n2} & \cdots & -m_n \end{bmatrix} \qquad \cdots [12]$$

Note that:

$$\mathbf{1}'M = \dot{\mathbf{0}}' \qquad \cdots [13]$$

from the last equation of [9].
Writing eqn [10] in vector-matrix form and using eqns [11] and [12], we have:

$$\frac{\mathrm{d}y}{\mathrm{d}t} = K(U - I + M)y = KBy \qquad \cdots [14]$$

where

$$B = U - I + M.$$

We are now in a position to derive our first result:

Theorem 1: If $\mu_i < 1$, for all i, the system [14] is stable. If $\mu_i > 1$, *for all i*, the system [14] is unstable.

Proof: Consider the matrix $KB = K(U - I + M)$.
Let $d' = \mathbf{1}'K^{-1} > \mathbf{0}'$. Then:

$$d'KB = \mathbf{1}'K^{-1}KB = \mathbf{1}'B = \mathbf{1}'(U - I), \quad \text{as} \quad \mathbf{1}'M = \mathbf{0}' \quad \text{from eqn [13]}$$

It follows immediately that:

(i) if $u_i < 1$, for all i, KB has a negative D.D. By Theorem 12 of Chapter 2, the real part of each root of KB is negative. From Theorem 16 of Chapter 4, it follows that eqn [14] is stable.

(ii) if $u_i > 1$, for all i, KB has a positive D.D. Hence, the real part of each root of KB is positive. By Theorem 16 of Chapter 4, it follows that eqn [14] is unstable.

The proof is now complete.

The familiar modification can be made in the case where M is indecomposable. For stability, we permit $u_i \leqslant 1$, for all i, but we require at least one strict inequality. On the other hand, if $u_i \leqslant 1$, for all i, we have instability. Formal proofs, by use of the q.d.d. concept, are left as an exercise.

Having examined the local stability of the system [5], we now turn our attention to comparative statics. Accordingly, we introduce autonomous expenditures into [5]. Let:

$$Y_i = U_i(Y_i) + \sum_{j \neq i} M_{ij}(Y_j) - \sum_{j \neq i} M_{ji}(Y_i) + A_i \qquad \cdots [15]$$

$$Y_k = U_k(Y_k) + \sum_{j \neq k} M_{kj}(Y_j) - \sum_{j \neq k} M_{jk}(Y_k)$$

We wish to examine the effect of an increase in investment (i.e. autonomous expenditure) in country i on the incomes of all countries.

Differentiating the equations of [15] with respect to A_i, we obtain:

$$\frac{\mathrm{d}Y_i}{\mathrm{d}A_i}=u_i\frac{\mathrm{d}Y_i}{\mathrm{d}A_i}+\sum_{j\neq i} m_{ij}\frac{\mathrm{d}Y_j}{\mathrm{d}A_i}-m_i\frac{\mathrm{d}Y_i}{\mathrm{d}A_i}+1$$
$$\frac{\mathrm{d}Y_k}{\mathrm{d}A_i}=u_k\frac{\mathrm{d}Y_k}{\mathrm{d}A_i}+\sum_{j\neq k} m_{kj}\frac{\mathrm{d}Y_k}{\mathrm{d}A_i}-m_k\frac{\mathrm{d}Y_k}{\mathrm{d}A_i} \qquad \cdots[16]$$

or:

$$(I-U-M)\frac{\mathrm{d}Y}{\mathrm{d}A_i}=e^i \quad \text{or} \quad C\frac{\mathrm{d}Y}{\mathrm{d}A_i}=e^i \qquad \cdots[17]$$

where

$$\frac{\mathrm{d}Y}{\mathrm{d}A_i}=\left(\frac{\mathrm{d}Y_1}{\mathrm{d}A_i},\ldots,\frac{\mathrm{d}Y_n}{\mathrm{d}A_i}\right),$$

e^i is the unit vector with 1 in the i-th place, and $C=(I-U-M)=-B$. Let us maintain the assumption that each country has a marginal propensity to spend of less than 1. The hypotheses of Theorem 49 of Chapter 2 are satisfied. So C is a P-matrix. All cofactors of C are non-negative by Theorem 47 of Chapter 2. From eqn [17]:

$$\frac{\mathrm{d}Y}{\mathrm{d}A_i}=\frac{1}{\det C}(C_{i1}, C_{i2},\ldots, C_{in})'\geqslant\mathbf{0} \qquad \cdots[18]$$

Summarising, we have:

Theorem 2: If each country has a marginal propensity to spend of less than 1, an increase in investment in country i cannot cause a fall in income in country j, for any $i, j=1,\ldots, n$.

Corollary: Under the same hypothesis as Theorem 2, if $m_{ij}>0$ for all $i\neq j$, then an increase in investment in country i causes a rise in income in country j, for any $i, j=1,\ldots, n$.

Proof: We have to establish that all the cofactors of C are positive, given the conditions:
(i) $u_i<1$, for all i;
(*ii*) $m_{ij}>0$, for all $i\neq j$.
The positivity of cofactors follows immediately from Theorem 48 of Chapter 2.

Theorem 3: If $u_i<1$. for all i, then:

$$1/(1-u_i)\geqslant\frac{\mathrm{d}Y_i}{\mathrm{d}A_i}\geqslant 1/(1-u_i+m_i) \qquad \cdots[19]$$

Proof: $1/(1-u_i)$ is the closed-economy multiplier; $1/(1-u_i+m_i)$ is that foreign-trade multiplier which takes account of leakages in the form of imports but ignores the effects of income changes in other countries on the demand for country *i's* exports.

From eqn [18]:

$$dY_i/dA_i = C_{ii}/\det C \qquad \cdots [20]$$

Adding all rows to the i-th row in $\det C$ and then expanding by this row, we obtain:

$$\det C = \sum_{j=1}^{n} (1-u_j)C_{ij} \qquad \cdots [21]$$

As we are operating under the same hypothesis as in Theorem 2, we note that $C_{ii} > 0$ for all i, as C is a P-matrix.

Substituting from eqn [21] into eqn [20] and dividing numerator and denominator by C_{ii}, we obtain:

$$dY_i/dA_i = 1/\left[\sum_{j=1}^{n} (1-u_j)C_{ij}/C_{ii}\right]$$

$$= 1/\left[(1-u_i) + \sum_{\substack{j=1 \\ j\neq i}}^{n} (1-u_j)C_{ij}/C_{ii}\right] \qquad \cdots [22]$$

As in Theorem 2, all cofactors of C are non-negative. Hence:

$$dY_i/dA_i \leqslant 1/(1-u_i) \qquad \cdots [23]$$

To obtain the second inequality in [19], we expand $\det C$ along the i-th column:

$$\det C = (1-u_i+m_i)C_{ii} - \sum_{\substack{k=1 \\ k\neq i}}^{n} m_{ki}C_{ki} \qquad \cdots [24]$$

Substituting in eqn [20], we obtain:

$$dY_i/dA_i = 1/\left[(1-u_i+m_i) - \sum_{\substack{k=1 \\ k\neq i}}^{n} m_{ki}C_{ki}/C_{ii}\right] \qquad \cdots [25]$$

Again as all cofactors of C are non-negative, we have:

$$dY_i/dA_i \geqslant 1/(1-u_i+m_i) \qquad \cdots [26]$$

The result follows from inequalities [23] and [26].

Sufficient conditions for the replacement of weak by strong inequalities in [19] are:

(i) $m_{ij} > 0$, for all $i \neq j$;

(ii) M is indecomposable.

Having examined the effect of changes in autonomous expenditures on the incomes of all countries, we now turn our attention to their effect on balances of trade. From eqns [6] and [15], we have:

$$\begin{aligned} b_i &= Y_i - U_i(Y_i) - A_i \\ b_k &= Y_k - U_k(Y_k) \qquad k \neq i \end{aligned} \qquad \cdots [27]$$

Differentiating with respect to A_i, we obtain:

$$\begin{aligned} \mathrm{d}b_i/\mathrm{d}A_i &= (1-u_i)\mathrm{d}Y_i/\mathrm{d}A_i - 1 \\ \mathrm{d}b_k/\mathrm{d}A_i &= (1-u_k)\mathrm{d}Y_k/\mathrm{d}A_i \qquad k \neq i \end{aligned} \qquad \cdots [28]$$

Let us deal first with the effect on country k. From Theorem 2, $\mathrm{d}Y_k/\mathrm{d}A_i \geqslant 0$. Then $\mathrm{d}b_k/\mathrm{d}A_i \geqslant 0$, given $1 > u_k$.
If $1 > u_k$, for all $k \neq i$, it follows that country i must experience a deterioration in its balance of trade (unless it is completely isolated from all other countries, in which case there is no change).
From inequality [19], $(1-u_i)\mathrm{d}Y_i/\mathrm{d}A_i \leqslant 1$. Summarising, we have:

Theorem 4: Under the same hypothesis as Theorem 3, if there is an increase in autonomous investment in country i:
(i) the i-th country's balance of trade cannot improve;
(ii) the k-th country's balance of trade cannot deteriorate.

Note that wc cannot conclude what happens if $u_k > 1$. We might be tempted to state that as $\mathrm{d}Y_k/\mathrm{d}A_i \geqslant 0$, $u_k > 1$ implies $\mathrm{d}b_k/\mathrm{d}A_i \leqslant 0$. However, if $u_k > 1$, we are unable to determine the sign of $\mathrm{d}Y_k/\mathrm{d}A_i$, our results being dependent on $u_k < 1$. (See Theorems 49 and 50 of Chapter 2 in this regard.) The discussion in the next section is based on the same model as outlined here.

§5.1.4. *The transfer problem*

In this section, we shall examine the effect of an income transfer from one country to another country on the income and balance of trade on each country in the trading system. We operate with the same model as in §5.1.3. Let country i be the donor, country r the receiver. Then our income equations are:

$$\begin{aligned} Y_i &= U_i(Y_i) + \sum_{j \neq i} M_{ij}(Y_j) - M_i(Y_i) - T \\ Y_r &= U_r(Y_r) + \sum_{j \neq r} M_{rj}(Y_j) - M_r(Y_r) + T \\ Y_k &= U_k(Y_k) + \sum_{j \neq k} M_{kj}(Y_j) - M_k(Y_k) \qquad k \neq i, r \end{aligned} \qquad \cdots [1]$$

where T is the amount of the transfer.
Differentiating with respect to T, we obtain:

$$(I - U - M)\frac{\mathrm{d}Y}{\mathrm{d}T} = -e^i + e^r \qquad \cdots [2]$$

or

$$C\frac{\mathrm{d}Y}{\mathrm{d}T}=e^r-e^i$$

where $\mathrm{d}Y/\mathrm{d}T$ is the vector of income derivatives.
Hence:

$$\begin{aligned}\mathrm{d}Y_i/\mathrm{d}T&=(C_{ri}-C_{ii})/\det C\\ \mathrm{d}Y_r/\mathrm{d}T&=(C_{rr}-C_{ir})/\det C\\ \mathrm{d}Y_k/\mathrm{d}T&=(C_{rk}-C_{ri})/\det C \qquad k\neq i, r\end{aligned} \qquad \cdots[3]$$

In the normal case where $u_k<1$, for all k, we know that C is a P-matrix and all cofactors of C are non-negative. Theorem 51 of Chapter 2 provides us with a result on the relation between C_{jj} and C_{js}, for any j, s. By this theorem, we have:

$$\mathrm{d}Y_i/\mathrm{d}T\leqslant 0; \qquad \mathrm{d}Y_r/\mathrm{d}T\geqslant 0 \qquad \cdots[4]$$

$\mathrm{d}Y_k/\mathrm{d}T$ unsigned for $k\neq i, r$

We now turn to the balance of trade:

$$\begin{aligned}b_i&=Y_i-U_i(Y_i)+T\\ b_r&=Y_r-U_r(Y_r)-T\\ b_k&=Y_k-U_k(Y_k)\end{aligned} \qquad \cdots[5]$$

These equations follow from eqns [1] above and eqn [6] of §5.1.3. Differentiation with respect to T yields:

$$\begin{aligned}\mathrm{d}b_i/\mathrm{d}T&=(1-u_i)\mathrm{d}Y_i/\mathrm{d}T+1\\ \mathrm{d}b_r/\mathrm{d}T&=(1-u_r)\mathrm{d}Y_r/\mathrm{d}T-1\\ \mathrm{d}b_k/\mathrm{d}T&=(1-u_k)\mathrm{d}Y_k/\mathrm{d}T\end{aligned} \qquad \cdots[6]$$

Consider the expression for $\mathrm{d}b_i/\mathrm{d}T$:

$$\begin{aligned}\mathrm{d}b_i/\mathrm{d}T&=(1-u_i)\mathrm{d}Y_i/\mathrm{d}T+1\\ &=(1-u_i)\frac{(C_{ri}-C_{ii})}{\det C}+1\\ &=\frac{(1-u_i)C_{ri}}{\det C}-\frac{(1-u_i)C_{ii}}{\det C}+1\end{aligned}$$

From Theorem 3:

$$C_{ii}/\det C\leqslant 1/(1-u_i)$$

Hence. $\mathrm{d}b_i/\mathrm{d}T\geqslant 0$.
As $C_{ii}\geqslant C_{ri}$, it follows that $\mathrm{d}b_i/\mathrm{d}T\leqslant 1$. Combining these inequalities, we have:

$$1\geqslant \mathrm{d}b_i/\mathrm{d}T\geqslant 0 \qquad \cdots[7]$$

Similarly, for db_r/dT:

$$db_r/dT = (1-u_r)dY_r/dT - 1$$
$$= (1-u_r)\frac{(C_{rr}-C_{ir})}{\det C} - 1 \leqslant 0$$

Hence:

$$0 \geqslant db_r/dT \geqslant -1 \qquad \cdots [8]$$

The only conclusion to be drawn about k's balance of trade is that it moves in the same direction as its income.

Summarising, we have:

Theorem 5: If $u_k < 1$ for all k, we have;

(i) $dY_i/dT \leqslant 0$; $1 \geqslant db_i/dT \geqslant 0$;

(ii) $dY_r/dT \geqslant 0$; $0 \geqslant db_r/dT \geqslant -1$;

(iii) dY_k/dT unsigned, but the changes in income and the balance of trade are in the same direction.

§5.2. Input–output with a production lag

§5.2.1. *Introduction*

In Chapter 2, we consistently maintained the assumption of no time lag in production. In §5.1, the introduction of lags into an expenditure model led to a standard forward difference equation, the solution of which was discussed (at length) in Chapter 4. We now introduce lags into the production system—this leads to a backward difference equation. Attempts to integrate production and expenditure systems are dealt with in §5.4, though we revert there to the assumption of no production lag. The problems that are raised by the existence of a production lag should become obvious by the end of this section.

Suppose that output produced during period t becomes available only during period $(t+1)$ to satisfy inter-industry demands and final demands. Suppose that the technology can be represented by an input–output matrix, A. Then we have:

$$x_i(t) = \sum_{j=1}^{n} a_{ij}x_j(t+1) + f_i(t+1) \qquad \cdots [1]$$

or

$$x(t) = Ax(t+1) + f(t+1) \qquad \cdots [2]$$

In §4.2.13, we analysed extensively the homogeneous equation:

$$x(t) = Ax(t+1) \qquad \cdots [3]$$

In §5.2.2, we aim to find conditions for a meaningful solution to eqn [2]. Of interest is the case where $f(t)$ is growing at a constant rate. The result we derive contrasts with the corresponding result in §5.4.1.

§5.2.2. *The non-homogeneous equation*

We begin with:

Lemma 1: $\sum_{v=0}^{\infty} A^v f(v+1)$ converges iff $\sum_{v=0}^{\infty} \lambda^v f(v+1)$ converges, where $\lambda = \lambda^*(A)$.

Proof: As both sums have non-negative terms, convergence is equivalent to boundedness from above. Let $p^{*\prime} A = \lambda p^{*\prime}$. Then

$$p^{*\prime} \sum_{v=0}^{T} A^v f(v+1) = p^{*\prime} \sum_{v=0}^{T} \lambda^v f(v+1), \quad \text{given} \quad p^{*\prime} > \mathbf{0}.$$

Hence the two series of vectors are simultaneously bounded from above.

Theorem 6: Equation [2] has a meaningful solution iff $\sum_{v=0}^{\infty} A^v f(v+1)$ converges.

Proof:
Necessity: Iterating eqn [2], we obtain:

$$x(s-1) = A^{t+1} x(s+t) + \sum_{v=0}^{t} A^v f(v+s) \qquad \cdots [4]$$

Hence,

$$x(s-1) \geqslant \sum_{v=0}^{t} A^v f(v+s), \qquad t = 0, 1, \ldots.$$

Hence $\sum_{v=0}^{t} A^v f(v+s)$ is bounded with respect to t. As the sum has non-negative terms, convergence follows for any s, in particular $s = 1$.

Sufficiency: Suppose $\sum_{v=0}^{\infty} A^v f(v+1)$ converges. First of all, we prove that:

$$\sum_{v=0}^{\infty} A^v f(v+s) \qquad \cdots [5]$$

converges.
As the sum consists of non-negative terms, convergence of the series [5] is equivalent to boundedness from above.
Employing the vector $p^* > \mathbf{0}$ again, we have:

$$p^{*\prime} \sum_{v=0}^{\infty} A^v f(v+s) = p^{*\prime} \lambda^{1-s} \sum_{v=s-1}^{\infty} \lambda^v f(v+1) \qquad \cdots [6]$$

Convergence of the right-hand side of eqn [6] follows from Lemma 1. Hence, we have convergence of [5].

On the basis of this result, we can state that:

$$y(t)=\sum_{v=0}^{\infty} A^v f(v+t+1) \qquad t=0, 1, \ldots \qquad \cdots [7]$$

is well-defined.
Equation [7] also solves eqn [2]. As $u(t)$ (of §4.2.13) solves the homogeneous eqn [3], we can now state that:

$$x(t)=u(t)+y(t) \qquad \cdots [8]$$

solves eqn [2],
i.e. [2] has a solution.
This completes the proof of the theorem.

Let us consider the special case of $f(t)=\alpha^t f$. From Lemma 1 and Theorem 6, we conclude that eqn [2] has a meaningful solution iff $f.\sum_{v=0}^{\infty} \lambda^v \alpha^v$ converges, i.e. iff $\sum_{v=0}^{\infty} (\alpha\lambda)^v$ converges. This will be true iff $\alpha\lambda<1$, i.e. iff $\alpha<1/\lambda$.
$1/\lambda$ is thus an upper limit on the growth rate of the final demand vector.

§5.3. Dynamic Leontief model

§5.3.1. *Introduction*

In §5.2, we generalised the analysis of Chapter 2 by introducing production lags. Here, we revert to our original assumption of no production lags but we allow the existence of capital goods. The other assumptions—no joint production, only one technique of production, no government activity nor foreign trade—are maintained.

We modify assumption (ii) of §2.1 as follows:

(vii) to produce one unit of commodity j, sector j requires a_{ij} units as current input of commodity i, and b_{ij} units as capital input.
Let s_{ij} = stock of commodity i held by sector j

$$b_{ij}=s_{ij}/x_j \quad \text{for all } i, j$$

The basic balance equation for sector i is then:

$$x_i=\sum_{j=1}^{n} x_{ij}+\sum_{j=1}^{n}\frac{\mathrm{d}s_{ij}}{\mathrm{d}t}+f_i$$

$$=\sum_{j=1}^{n} a_{ij}x_j+\sum_{j=1}^{n} b_{ij}\frac{\mathrm{d}x_j}{\mathrm{d}t}+f_i$$

or

$$x=Ax+B\frac{\mathrm{d}x}{\mathrm{d}t}+f \qquad \cdots [1]$$

in continuous time.

In discrete time, we have:

$$x_i(t) = \sum_j x_{ij}(t) + \sum_j (s_{ij}(t+1) - s_{ij}(t)) + f_i(t)$$

$$= \sum_j a_{ij}x_j(t) + \sum_j b_{ij}(x_j(t+1) - x_j(t)) + f_i(t)$$

or

$$x(t) = Ax(t) + B[x(t+1) - x(t)] + f(t) \qquad \cdots [2]$$

Equations [1] and [2] are open models. The corresponding closed models arc obtained by putting $f = \mathbf{0}$ in eqn [1], $f(t) = \mathbf{0}$ in eqn [2].

§5.3.2. *The closed model*

We introduce the following assumption:

(viii) B is non-singular.

The continuous-time model can then be described by:

$$\mathrm{d}x/\mathrm{d}t = B^{-1}(I - A)x = Cx \qquad \cdots [3]$$

The solution of eqn [3] is:

$$x = \sum_{j=1}^{k} \alpha_j \mathrm{e}^{\lambda_j t} p^j(t) \qquad \cdots [4]$$

where $p^j(t)$ is a vector of polynomials in t of order $m_j - 1$, m_j being the multiplicity of the root λ_j, k being the number of distinct roots of C. Further progress can be made by noting that $C^{-1} = (I - A)^{-1}B \geqslant [0]$, and that $\lambda_i(C^{-1}) = \lambda_i(C)^{-1}$.

(In fact, if A is indecomposable, $(I - A)^{-1} > [0]$ and hence $C^{-1} > [0]$.) C^{-1} possesses a Frobenius root, $\lambda^*(C^{-1})$, and an associated vector $x^* > \mathbf{0}$ which is the only non-negative characteristic vector. Then C has a root $\lambda^*(C^{-1})^{-1} = \mu^*(C)$, with the same associated vector x^*. $\mu^*(C)$ does not necessarily have the largest absolute value of the roots of C; hence, it does not necessarily have the largest positive real part. Thus, we are not assured that the Frobenius characteristic solution will dominate eqn [4]; in general, we cannot expect eqn [4] to have a meaningful solution.

We illustrate our discussion with these numerical examples:

1. $A = \begin{bmatrix} \frac{1}{3} & \frac{1}{3} \\ \frac{1}{4} & \frac{1}{2} \end{bmatrix}, \quad B = \begin{bmatrix} 1 & 0 \\ 0 & 1 \end{bmatrix}$

The roots of C^{-1} are $(7 \pm \sqrt{13})/6$.

Here $\mu^*(C) = 6/(7 + \sqrt{13}) < 6/(7 - \sqrt{13}) = \mu_2$.

The Frobenius solution does not dominate eqn [4].

2. $A = \begin{bmatrix} \frac{1}{3} & \frac{1}{3} \\ \frac{1}{4} & \frac{1}{2} \end{bmatrix}, \quad B = \begin{bmatrix} 0 & 1 \\ 1 & 0 \end{bmatrix}$

The roots of C^{-1} are $(7 \pm \sqrt{193})/6$.

Here $\mu^*(C)=6/(7+\surd 193)>6/(7-\surd 193)=\mu_2$.
In this case, the Frobenius solution dominates.

To formalise our ideas, we introduce the following concept:

Definition 1: The unique, positive (Frobenius) solution, $e^{\mu^*(C)t}x^*$ is *globally relatively stable* iff, for every $\varepsilon>0$, there exists $T>0$ such that, for all $t>T$:

$$\left|\frac{x_i(t)}{e^{\mu^*(C)t}x_i^*}-\frac{x_1(t)}{e^{\mu^*(C)t}x_1^*}\right|<\varepsilon$$

where $x(t)=(\exp(Ct)x(0))$ is the general solution of eqn [3].

Theorem 7: The Frobenius solution is globally relatively stable iff $\lim_{t\to\infty}\frac{x(t)}{e^{\mu^*(C)t}}=x^*$.

Proof: From eqn [4], we have:

$$x(t)/e^{\mu^*(C)t}=x^*+\sum_{j=2}^{n}\alpha_j e^{(\lambda_j-\mu^*(C))t}p^j(t)$$

The result follows straightforwardly.

From our discussion above, we conclude that the dynamic Leontief model is not necessarily relatively stable. At this juncture, we may refer to §4.1.13, where we examined a system of linear differential equations for non-negative solutions.
From Theorem 19 of Chapter 4, we know that $dx/dt=Cx$ will have a meaningful solution (i.e. the Frobenius solution will be relatively stable) iff there exists $\beta\geqslant 0$ such that $\beta I+C\geqslant[0]$. This condition (in effect, a sign condition on c_{ij}, for all $i\neq j$) for relative stability is much more easily applied than the one in terms of the roots of C, as examples 1 and 2 above show.

Let us now consider the discrete-time model. We have:

$$x(t+1)=(I+C)x(t) \qquad \cdots[5]$$

The roots of $I+C$ are $1+\lambda_i(C)$, $i=1,\ldots,n$. The roots of $I+C$ stand in the same relationship to one another as do the corresponding roots of C. By an argument similar to that used above (in the differential equations case), we conclude that $1+\mu^*(C)=1+\lambda^*(C^{-1})^{-1}$ is not necessarily that root of $I+C$ with largest absolute value; hence, the associated Frobenius solution will not, in general, dominate

$$x(t)=\sum_{j=1}^{k}\alpha_j(1+\lambda_j)^t p^j(t) \qquad \cdots[6]$$

which is the solution of eqn [5].

The relative stability definition for difference equations is

Definition 2: The Frobenius solution, $(1+\mu^*(C))^t x^*$, is globally relatively stable iff, for every $\varepsilon > 0$, there exists $T > 0$ such that, for all $t > T$:

$$\left| \frac{x_i(t)}{(1+\mu^*(C))^t x_i^*} - \frac{x_1(t)}{(1+\mu^*(C))^t x_1^*} \right| < \varepsilon$$

Corresponding to Theorem 7, we have:

Theorem 8: The Frobenius solution is globally relatively stable iff $\lim\limits_{t\to\infty} \frac{x(t)}{(1+\mu^*(C))^t} = x^*$.
The proof follows from eqn [6] in the same way as Theorem 7 follows from eqn [4].

§4.2.9 provides us with necessary and sufficient conditions for meaningful solution (i.e. relative stability) of eqn [5], viz. $(I+C)^i \geqslant \mathbf{0}$, for all i; as in the differential equations case, the condition involving the signs of the elements of the matrix is much more easily applied than the roots condition.

§5.3.3. *The open model*

We shall concentrate on one particular version of the open physical model, where each component of the final demand vector grows at a constant rate. We have:

$$x(t) = Ax(t) + B[x(t+1) - x(t)] + f(t) \qquad \cdots [2]$$

where:

$$f(t+1) = (I+R)f(t) \qquad \cdots [7]$$

$$R = [r_i \delta_{ij}] \quad r_i \geqslant 0 \quad \text{for all } i. \qquad \cdots [8]$$

The homogeneous equation associated with eqn [2] is:

$$x(t+1) = (I+C)x(t) \qquad \cdots [5]$$

which has solution:

$$x(t) = (I+C)^t \tilde{x}$$

where $\tilde{x}$ is determined by the initial conditions.

Let $\bar{x}(t)$ be a particular solution of eqn [2]. Then the general solution of eqn [2] is:

$$x(t) = (I+C)^t \tilde{x} + \bar{x}(t) \qquad \cdots [9]$$

If $x(0) = \bar{x}(0)$, we have $\tilde{x} = \mathbf{0}$ from eqn [9]. This is the assumption implicit in the paper by Stone and Brown.
In general, we must expect $x(0) \neq \bar{x}(0)$. From eqn [9]:

$$\tilde{x} = x(0) - \bar{x}(0) \qquad \cdots [10]$$

which implies:

$$x(t) = (I+C)^t [x(0) - \bar{x}(0)] + \bar{x}(t) \qquad \cdots [11]$$

There is a variety of particular solutions. From §4.2.6, we have:

$$x(t) = (I+C)^t x(0) - \sum_{\tau=0}^{t-1} (I+C)^{\tau} B^{-1} f(t-1-\tau) \qquad \cdots [12]$$

Other solutions have been derived by Stone and Brown, Mathur and Mukerji, with considerable space being devoted to demonstrations of equivalence of solutions.

We shall consider two solutions, one based on Stone and Brown's "simple method", the other due to Mathur.

First, the Stone–Brown solution. We start with a provisional estimate of the investment demands vector, v; say $v^1 = \mathbf{0}$.
Then from eqn [2]:

$$x^1 = (I-A)^{-1} f \qquad \cdots [13]$$

Applying the operator $\mathscr{E}$, we have:

$$\mathscr{E}x^1 = (I-A)^{-1}\mathscr{E}f = (I-A)^{-1}(I+R)f \qquad \cdots [14]$$

from eqn [9].
Subtracting eqn [13] from eqn [14]:

$$\mathscr{E}x^1 - x^1 = \Delta x^1 = (I-A)^{-1} Rf \qquad \cdots [15]$$

Let $v^2 = B(\mathscr{E}x^1 - x^1)$ or

$$v^2 = B(I-A)^{-1} Rf \qquad \cdots [16]$$

from eqn [15].
Then

$$x^2 = Ax^2 + v^2 + f$$

or

$$x^2 = (I-A)^{-1}(v^2 + f)$$
$$= (I-A)^{-1}[B(I-A)^{-1}Rf + f]$$

i.e.

$$x^2 = (I-A)^{-1}[I + B(I-A)^{-1}R]f \qquad \cdots [17]$$

We now apply the operator $\mathscr{E}$ to eqn [17] so that:
$\mathscr{E}x^2 = (I-A)^{-1}[I + B(I-A)^{-1}R]\mathscr{E}f$

i.e.

$$\xi x^2 = (I-A)^{-1}(I + B(I-A)^{-1}R)(I+R)f \qquad \cdots [18]$$

Subtracting eqn [17] from eqn [18] yields:

$$\mathscr{E}x^2 - x^2 = (I-A)^{-1}(I + B(I-A)^{-1}R)Rf \qquad \cdots [19]$$

Let

$$v^3 = B(\mathscr{E}x^2 - x^2) \qquad \cdots [20]$$

and

$$x^3 = Ax^3 + v^3 + f \qquad \cdots [21]$$

Substituting from eqns [19] and [20] into [21] yields:

$$x^3 = (I-A)^{-1}[I + B(I-A)^{-1}R + (B(I-A)^{-1})^2R^2]f \qquad \cdots [22]$$

Continuing indefinitely, we obtain:

$$v = \sum_{\tau=1}^{\infty} (B(I-A)^{-1})^{\tau}R^{\tau}f \qquad \cdots [23]$$

and

$$x = Ax + v + f$$

or

$$x = (I-A)^{-1}\left[I + \sum_{\tau-1}^{\infty} (B(I-A)^{-1})^{\tau}R^{\tau}\right]f$$

or

$$x = (I-A)^{-1}\left[\sum_{\tau=0}^{\infty} (B(I-A)^{-1})^{\tau}R^{\tau}\right]f \qquad \cdots [24]$$

The usefulness of this expansion lies in the interpretation that can be placed on the vectors in the series. To supply the final demand vector f, a current output of $(I-A)^{-1}f$ is required. In the next (and all subsequent) periods, there will be increased final demand equal to Rf. This will require an increase in output of $(I-A)^{-1}Rf$ next period, which implies an increase in investment of $B(I-A)^{-1}Rf$ this period; in turn, the increased investment this period implies an increase in gross output this period of $(I-A)^{-1}B(I-A)^{-1}Rf$. In the second (and all subsequent) periods hence, there will be a further increase in final demand of R^2f to be met. This requires an increased gross output in that period of $(I-A)^{-1}R^2f$; this implies an increase in investment in the next period of $B(I-A)^{-1}R^2f$; this requires an increase in gross output next period of $(I-A)^{-1}B(I-A)^{-1}Rf$, which implies an increase in investment in the current period of $B(I-A)^{-1}B(I-A)^{-1}R^2f$; to meet this investment, there must be an increase in gross output in the current period of $(I-A)^{-1}(B(I-A)^{-1})^2R^2f$.
The terms in the current output series, [24], so far examined are:

$(I-A)^{-1}f$; $(I-A)^{-1}B(I-A)^{-1}Rf$; $(I-A)^{-1}(B(I-A)^{-1})^2R^2f$; the first three terms of the series [24].

Continuing in the way outlined above, we derive current output requirements so that consumption grows proportionally.

Eqn [24] is a generalisation of the matrix multiplier outlined in Exercises §2.3 and discussed further in §5.1.

Let us now derive an alternative particular solution due to Mathur which will provide us with another insight into the model. Let:

$$f^i(t) = (f_i(t)\delta_{ij}) \quad j = 1, \ldots, n \qquad \cdots [25]$$

Then

$$f(t) = \sum_{i=1}^{n} f^i(t) \qquad \cdots [26]$$

Let $\mathbf{x}^i(t)$ and $v^i(t)$ denote the gross output and investment demand vectors corresponding to $f^i(t)$, i.e.

$$\mathbf{x}^i(t) = A\mathbf{x}^i(t) + v^i(t) + f^i(t) \quad i = 1, \ldots, n \qquad \cdots [27]$$

Evidently:

$$\mathbf{x}(t) = \sum_{i=1}^{n} \mathbf{x}^i(t); \quad v(t) = \sum_{i=1}^{n} v^i(t) \qquad \cdots [28]$$

Applying the operator $\mathscr{E}$ to eqn [27] yields:

$$\mathscr{E}\mathbf{x}^i(t) = A\mathscr{E}\mathbf{x}^i(t) + \mathscr{E}v^i(t) + (1 + r_i)f^i(t)$$

or

$$(I - A)\mathscr{E}\mathbf{x}^i(t) - \mathscr{E}v^i(t) = (1 + r_i)f^i(t) \qquad \cdots [29]$$

Substituting for $f^i(t)$ from eqn [27] yields:

$$(I - A)\mathscr{E}\mathbf{x}^i(t) - \mathscr{E}v^i(t) = (1 + r_i)(I - A)\mathbf{x}^i(t) - (1 + r_i)v^i(t) \qquad \cdots [30]$$

which implies:

$$\mathscr{E}\mathbf{x}^i(t) = (1 + r_i)\mathbf{x}^i(t); \; \mathscr{E}v^i(t) = (1 + r_i)v^i(t) \qquad \cdots [31]$$

$$\mathscr{E}\mathbf{x}^i(t) = (1 + r_i)\mathbf{x}^i(t) + \bar{\mathbf{x}}^i \quad \text{and} \quad \mathscr{E}v^i(t) = (1 + r_i)v^i(t) + \bar{v}^i$$

also satisfy eqn [30], where $\bar{\mathbf{x}}^i$ and $\bar{v}^i$ satisfy:

$$(I - A)\mathscr{E}\mathbf{x}(t) - \mathscr{E}v(t) = \mathbf{0} \qquad \cdots [32]$$

i.e. a consumptionless system. So, for our purposes, $\bar{\mathbf{x}}^i$ and v^i can be assigned zero values.

$$v^i(t) = B(\mathscr{E}\mathbf{x}^i(t) - \mathbf{x}^i(t)) = r_i B\mathbf{x}^i(t) \qquad \cdots [33]$$

from eqn [31]

Substituting in eqn [27], we have:

$$\mathbf{x}^i(t) = A\mathbf{x}^i(t) + r_i B\mathbf{x}^i(t) + f^i(t)$$

or

$$(I - A - r_i B)\mathbf{x}^i(t) = f^i(t)$$

or

$$x^i(t)=(I-A-r_iB)^{-1}f^i(t) \qquad \cdots[34]$$

and

$$x(t)=\sum_{i=1}^{n}(I-A-r_iB)^{-1}f^i(t) \qquad \cdots[35]$$

In eqn [34]:

$$(I-A-r_iB)^{-1}=[(I-r_iB(I-A)^{-1})(I-A)]^{-1}$$
$$=(I-A)^{-1}[\rho_iI-B(I-A)^{-1}]^{-1}$$

where $\rho_i=1/r_i$.

$$(I-A)^{-1}\geqslant[0];\ (\rho_iI-B(I-A)^{-1})^{-1}\geqslant[0]$$

iff

$$\rho_i>\lambda^*(B(I-A)^{-1}) \quad \text{or iff} \quad 1/\lambda^*(B(I-A)^{-1})>r_i.$$

These necessary and sufficient conditions play a crucial role in the process of obtaining non-negative solutions to eqn [35]. We may conclude that each consumption growth rate must be less than the reciprocal of the Frobenius root of $B(I-A)^{-1}$. This result is similar to the one derived in §5.2.2.

§5.3.4. *The dual stability theorem*

In this section, we aim to introduce price-determining equations and examine the mutual consistency of the price and output systems. In Chapter 2, we derived necessary and sufficient conditions for the existence of meaningful solutions to the static input–output model–in particular, in Theorem 4, we proved that the output system has a meaningful iff the price system has. We shall see that this result does not carry over to the closed dynamic input–output model; it is possible to derive simultaneously meaningful solutions to the two systems in the case of the open model.

Dual to eqn [1] of §5.3.1, we have the following:

$$p'=p'A+rp'B-\frac{\mathrm{d}p'}{\mathrm{d}t}B+v' \qquad \cdots[1]$$

where r is the rate of intersect.
Equation [1] is explained as follows: the price of each good is set equal to its unit cost of production; $p'A$ is the vector of costs of current inputs; $rp'B$ refers to interest charges; $\frac{\mathrm{d}p'}{\mathrm{d}t}B$ is the vector of capital gains/losses.

The discrete-time version of eqn [1] is:

$$p(t+1)'=p(t+1)'A+rp(t)'B-(p(t+1)-p(t))'B+v(t)' \qquad \cdots[2]$$

(We explain eqn [2], and hence [1], more fully as follows:
Suppose an individual possesses at the beginning of period t a sum of money $\sum_{i=1}^{n} p_i(t)b_{ij}$. If he lends at the rate of interest r, he will have, at the end of the period, $(1+r)\sum_{i=1}^{n} p_i(t)b_{ij}$.
On the other hand, suppose that he can become an entrepreneur, producing one unit of commodity l. His current costs will be $\sum_{i=1}^{n} p_i(t+1)a_{ij} + v_j(t)$, assuming costs are incurred simultaneously with the sale of output. His sales revenue is $p_j(t+1)$ and the value of his capital equipment (ignoring depreciation) will be $\sum_{i=1}^{n} p_i(t+1)b_{ij}$.
In equilibrium, the two options are equally attractive.
Hence:

$$(1+r)\sum_{i=1}^{n} p_i(t)b_{ij} = p_j(t+1) - \sum_{i=1}^{n} p_i(t+1)a_{ij} - v_j(t) + \sum_{i=1}^{n} p_i(t+1)b_{ij}$$

or

$$(1+r)p(t)'B = p(t+1)'(I-A+B) - v(t)'$$

or

$$p(t+1)'(I-A+B) = (1+r)p(t)'B + v(t)'$$

which is eqn [2].)

The price equation for the closed model is:

$$p' = p'A + rp'B - \frac{\mathrm{d}p'}{\mathrm{d}t}B \qquad \cdots [3]$$

where the A and B have been modified to take account of the household sector.

Implicit in eqns [1]–[3] is the assumption of perfect foresight. The entrepreneur takes prices, $p(t)$, at the beginning of the period as given but decides on a course of action on the basis of knowing the end of period prices, $p(t+1)$. This assumption is dual to that implicit in eqn [1] of §5.3.1, namely that the gross outputs of the following period are known.

What we do now is to examine the mutual consistency of these assumptions about the price and output systems.
The quantity and price equations for the closed model are:

$$\frac{\mathrm{d}x}{\mathrm{d}t} = B^{-1}(I-A)x = Cx \qquad \cdots [4]$$

$$\frac{\mathrm{d}p'}{\mathrm{d}t} = p'rI - (I-A)B^{-1} = p'(rI-H) \qquad \cdots [5]$$

It is well known that C and H have the same roots.
Suppose that A is indecomposable. Then $C^{-1}>[0]$ and $C^{-1}x^*=\lambda^*(C^{-1})x^*$, $p^{*\prime}C^{-1}=\lambda^*(C^{-1})p^{*\prime}$, where $x^*>\mathbf{0}$ and $p^*>\mathbf{0}$ are the only possible non-negative right and left characteristic vectors respectively of C^{-1}.

Suppose that eqn [4] is relatively stable. Then $\mu^*(C)=\lambda^*(C^{-1})^{-1}$ is that root of C with largest real part. The roots of $rI-H$ are given by $r-\mu_j(C)$. Hence, $r-\mu^*(C)$ is not that root of $rI-H$ with largest real part. As the characteristic solution associated with $r-\mu^*(C)$ (and the vector $p^*>\mathbf{0}$) is the only possible non-negative characteristic solution, it follows that relative stability does not hold for the price system.

Now suppose that eqn [5] is relatively stable, i.e. that root of $rI-H$ with largest real part is $r-\mu^*(C)$. It then follows straightforwardly that $\mu^*(C)$ cannot be that root of C with largest part. Hence eqn [5] is not relatively stable.

Summarising our discussion, we have:

Theorem 9: The price and output systems of the dynamic Leontief model are not simultaneously relatively stable.

Let us now turn our attention to the open model.
The equations are:

$$x=A_x+B\frac{dx}{dt}+f \qquad \cdots [6]$$

$$p'=p'A+rp'B-\frac{dp'}{dt}B+v' \qquad \cdots [7]$$

or

$$\frac{dx}{dt}=B^{-1}(I-A)x-B^{-1}f \qquad \cdots [8]$$

$$\frac{dp'}{dt}=p'[rI-(I-A)B^{-1}]-v'B^{-1} \qquad \cdots [9]$$

Let $\alpha+i\beta$ represent any root of $C=B^{-1}(I-A)$ except $\mu^*(C)$.
Suppose $0\leqslant r<\alpha<\mu^*(C)$.
Immediately, we see that eqn [8] is relatively stable.
Now consider eqn [9]. From the hypothesis $0\leqslant r<\alpha<\mu^*(C)$, we deduce that each root of $rI-(I-A)B^{-1}$ has a negative real part. The solution of the homogeneous equation:

$$\frac{dp'}{dt}=p'[rI-(I-A)B^{-1}]$$

tends to the zero vector as $t\to\infty$.
A particular solution to eqn [9] is obtained by putting $p=\bar{p}$, a constant

vector. Then we have:

$$\bar{p}'(I-A-rB)=v'$$

or

$$\bar{p}'=v'(I-A-rB)^{-1} \qquad \cdots[10]$$

For relative stability of eqn [9], we require $(I-A-rB)^{-1}>[0]$.
As in §5.3.3, we have:

$$\begin{aligned}(I-A-rB)^{-1}&=(I-A)(I-r(I-A)^{-1}B)^{-1}\\&=[(I-r(I-A)^{-1}B]^{-1}(I-A)^{-1}\\&=[(1/r)I-(I-A)^{-1}B]^{-1}r^{-1}(I-A)^{-1}\end{aligned}$$

$(I-A)^{-1}>[0]$. So $(I-A-rB)^{-1}>[0]$ iff $[(1/r)I-(I-A)^{-1}B]^{-1}>[0]$ i.e. iff $1/r>\lambda^*[(I-A)^{-1}B]=\lambda^*(C^{-1})=1/\mu^*(C)$, i.e. $\mu^*(C)>r$. This is certainly implied by $0\leqslant r<\alpha<\mu^*(C)$.
So, $\bar{p}>\mathbf{0}$ in eqn [10] and hence eqn [9] is relatively stable.

On the other hand, suppose that eqns [8] and [9] are relatively stable. By eqn [8], $\mu^*(C)>\alpha$; from eqn [9], $\alpha>r$. Combining these, we have: $\mu^*(C)>\alpha>r\geqslant 0$.

So, we have derived the following:

Theorem 10: The dynamic open Leontief model and its associated price system are relatively stable iff

$$\mu^*(C)>\alpha>r\geqslant 0$$

where $\mu^*(C)=\lambda^*(C^{-1})^{-1}$ and α is the real part of any root of C.

§5.4. Long-run multiplier models

§5.4.1. *A simple model involving super-multipliers*

The model to be discussed here is similar in structure to those of §5.1. We consider a multi-sector model where the sectoral expenditure functions are linear and where there is a one-period expenditure lag. If all investment is autonomous, we have as our income-determining equation:

$$y(t)=Cy(t-1)+f(t) \quad f(t)\geqq\mathbf{0},\ y(0)\geqslant\mathbf{0} \qquad \cdots[1]$$

where $C=[c_{ij}]$, $c_{ij}=j$'s propensity to spend on i's goods.
We now suppose that autonomous expenditures grow at a constant rate. Then: $f(t)=\psi^t f$. Eqn [1] becomes:

$$y(t)=Cy(t-1)+\psi^t f \qquad \cdots[2]$$

The associated homogeneous equation is:

$$y(t)=Cy(t-1) \qquad \cdots[3]$$

If $\sum_{i=1}^{n} c_{ij} < 1$, for all j (with the usual modification in the indecomposable case), we know that the Frobenius root of C is less than 1. Hence, the solution of eqn [3], $\tilde{y}(t)$, tends to $\mathbf{0}$ over time. We now need a particular solution of eqn [2]. Suppose $\psi \neq \lambda^*(C)$. Then putting $y(t) = \bar{y}(t) = \psi^t \bar{y}$ in eqn [2], we obtain:

$$\psi^t \bar{y} = C\psi^{t-1}\bar{y} + \psi^t f$$

or

$$\bar{y} = (\psi I - C)^{-1}\psi f \qquad \cdots [4]$$

If $\psi > \lambda^*(C)$, $(\psi I - C)^{-1} \geqslant [0]$. A sufficient condition for $\psi > \lambda^*(C)$ is that autonomous expenditures are not decreasing, while each sector has a (total) propensity to spend of less than 1 (with appropriate modification in the indecomposable case).

The general solution of eqn [2] is:

$$y(t) = \tilde{y}(t) + \psi^{t+1}(\psi I - C)^{-1} f = \tilde{y}(t) + \psi^t \bar{y} \qquad \cdots [5]$$

Under the conditions outlined above, $\psi^t \bar{y}$ is a meaningful solution (i.e. it is non-negative). It then makes sense to think of the particular solution as a moving equilibrium solution.

It is evident from eqn [5] that under the conditions stated

$$y(t)/\psi^t \rightarrow \bar{y} = \psi(\psi I - C)^{-1} f$$

i.e. the moving equilibrium is relatively stable.

$(\psi I - C)^{-1}$ is a generalisation of the matrix multiplier concept encountered in Chapter 2 and §5.1 and is called a matrix super-multiplier.

§ 5.4.2. *An integration of input-output and matrix multiplier*

We now introduce production relations into the model outlined in §5.4.1. We maintain the assumption (to begin with) of a one-period expenditure lag, but we revert to the assumption of Chapter 2 that there is no production lag.

Let $y(t)$ = vector of sectoral incomes at t

$x(t)$ = vector of sectoral gross outputs at t

Total final expenditures in $(t+1)$ consists of two parts: autonomous expenditures, denoted by $a(t+1)$; endogenous expenditures denoted by $Cy(t)$, as in §5.4.1. Let

$$e(t+1) = Cy(t) + a(t+1) \qquad \cdots [1]$$

Let $\hat{p} = [p_i \delta_{ij}]$, $p_i > 0$; $i, j = 1, \ldots, n$; p being a price vector

Then the final demand vector in $(t+1)$ is:

$$f(t+1) = \hat{p}^{-1} e(t+1) = \hat{p}^{-1}(Cy(t) + a(t+1)) \qquad \cdots [2]$$

The gross output vector in $(t+1)$ solves:

$$x(t+1) = Ax(t+1) + f(t+1) \qquad \cdots [3]$$

Using eqn [2], we have:

$$x(t+1) = (I-A)^{-1}\hat{p}^{-1}(Cy(t) + a(t+1)) \qquad \cdots [4]$$

Let $\hat{v} = [v_i\delta_{ij}]$, $v_i > 0$; $i, j = 1, \ldots, n$

$$y(t+1) = \hat{v}x(t+1) \qquad \cdots [5]$$

assuming v_i constant over time.
Substituting from eqn [4] into eqn [5], we obtain:

$$y(t+1) = \hat{v}(I-A)^{-1}\hat{p}^{-1}Cy(t) + \hat{v}(I-A)^{-1}\hat{p}^{-1}a(t+1) \qquad \cdots [6]$$

or

$$y(t+1) = By(t) + \mathrm{d}(t) \qquad \cdots [7]$$

where

$$B = \hat{v}(I-A)^{-1}\hat{p}^{-1}C \qquad \cdots [8]$$

$$d(t) = \hat{v}(I-A)^{-1}\hat{p}^{-1}a(t+1) \qquad \cdots [9]$$

$B \geqslant [0]$, if the economy is "workable".
This model is now similar to the one discussed in §5.4.1.
Suppose that $d(t) = \psi^t d$, $\psi > \lambda^*(B)$. A particular solution of eqn [7] is obtained by putting $\bar{y}(t) = \psi^t \bar{y}$. Then, we have:

$$\bar{y} = (\psi I - B)^{-1}d \qquad \cdots [10]$$

$y(t)$ represents a moving equilibrium, with $(\psi I - B)^{-1}$ the matrix super-multiplier.

We now modify our model by generalising the lag structure of the expenditure functions. Hence, properties of the model just outlined may be derived as special cases of the more general model below.
First, a little more notation:
$c_{ij}(t-\tau)$ is sector j's propensity to spend in the t-th period (out of its income in period $t-\tau$) on the output of the i-th sector; $i, j = 1, \ldots, n$; $\tau = 1, \ldots, s$.
$c_{ij}(t-\tau)y_j(t-\tau)$ is the amount spent in the t-th period on the output of the i-th sector by the j-th sector out of its income in period $t-\tau$.
Let:

$$c_j(t-\tau) = \sum_{i=1}^{n} c_{ij}(t-\tau) \qquad \cdots [11]$$

which is the total propensity to spend of the j-th sector in the t-th period out of its income in period $t-\tau$.
Let:

$$c_j(t) = \sum_{\tau=1}^{s} c_j(t-\tau) \qquad \cdots [12]$$

which is the total propensity to spend of the j-th sector in period t.
We make the following assumptions:

$c_{ij}(t-\tau) \geqslant 0$, for all i, j, τ; $c_j(t-\tau) > 0$, for all j, τ.
Let:

$$C(t-\tau) = [c_{ij}(t-\tau)]', \quad i,j = 1, \ldots, n; \quad \tau = 1, \ldots, s \qquad \cdots [13]$$

Stacking the $C(t-\tau)$ matrices, we have:

$$C = [C(t-1) \quad C(t-2) \quad \ldots \quad C(t-s)] \qquad \cdots [14]$$

which is of dimension $n \times ns$.
The value of total final expenditures in period t is given by:

$$e(t) = CY(t) + a(t) \qquad \cdots [15]$$

where C is defined in eqn [14] and

$$Y(t) = (y(t-1) \quad y(t-2) \quad \ldots \quad y(t-s))' \qquad \cdots [16]$$

The final demand vector is given by:

$$f(t) = \hat{p}^{-1}e(t) = \hat{p}^{-1}CY(t) + \hat{p}^{-1}a(t) \qquad \cdots [17]$$

Substituting in eqn [3], we have:

$$x(t) = (I-A)^{-1}\hat{p}^{-1}CY(t) + (I-A)^{-1}\hat{p}^{-1}a(t) \qquad \cdots [18]$$

Substituting from eqn [18] into

$$y(t) = \hat{v}x(t)$$

we obtain:

$$y(t) = \hat{v}(I-A)^{-1}\hat{p}^{-1}CY(t) + \hat{v}(I-A)^{-1}\hat{p}^{-1}a(t) \qquad \cdots [19]$$

Define:

$$\begin{aligned} M &= \hat{v}(I-A)^{-1}\hat{p}^{-1}C > [0] \\ N &= \hat{v}(I-A)^{-1}\hat{p}^{-1} > [0] \end{aligned} \qquad \cdots [20]$$

Then eqn [19] can be written as:

$$y(t) = MY(t) + Na(t) \qquad \cdots [21]$$

We introduce the following transformation of variables:

$$\begin{aligned} &w_{(\tau-1)n+j}(t-1) = y_j(t-\tau) \quad j = 1, \ldots, n; \quad \tau = 1, \ldots, s \\ &f(t) = (Na(t+1) \quad \mathbf{0}_n \quad \mathbf{0}_n \quad \ldots \quad \mathbf{0}_n)' \end{aligned} \qquad \cdots [23]$$

where $f(t)$ is of dimension ns.
This enables us to rewrite eqn [21] as:

$$w(t) = Bw(t-1) + f(t-1) \quad t = s, s+1, \ldots \qquad \cdots [24]$$

where

$$B = \begin{bmatrix} & M & \\ I_{n(s-1)} & & [0]_{n(s-1)\times n} \end{bmatrix} \qquad \cdots [25]$$

is a square matrix of order ns and

$$w(t-1) = (y(t-1) \quad y(t-2) \quad \ldots y(t-s))' \qquad \cdots [26]$$

As $M > [0]_{n\times ns}$, note that B is indecomposable.

We now examine the model of eqn [24] for balanced growth and relative stability. Suppose that autonomous expenditures obey the following scheme:

$$a(t+1) = \alpha a(t) \quad \text{or} \quad f(t+1) = \alpha f(t) \qquad \cdots [27]$$

Our first result provides us with necessary and sufficient conditions for the existence of a relatively stable balanced growth solution of eqn [24] consistent with eqn [27].

Theorem 11: The balanced growth solution of eqn [24] exists and is relatively stable iff $\alpha > \lambda^*(B)$.

Proof: We shall deal separately with existence and relative stability.
Existence:
Sufficiency: Assume $\alpha > \lambda^*(B)$. Then $(\alpha I - B)^{-1} > [0]_{ns\times ns}$.
We shall prove existence by induction.
Suppose $f(s-1) \geqslant \mathbf{0}_{ns}$. Then $w(s) = \alpha w(s-1)$ is feasible because using eqn [24], we have:

$$\alpha w(s-1) = Bw(s-1) + f(s-1)$$

or

$$w(s-1) = (\alpha I - B)^{-1} f(s-1) > \mathbf{0}_{ns} \qquad \cdots [28]$$

Now assume that:

$$w(s+\sigma-1) = \alpha^{\sigma} w(s-1) \qquad \cdots [29]$$

Then

$$w(s+\sigma) = Bw(s+\sigma-1) + f(s+\sigma-1)$$
$$= \alpha^{\sigma} Bw(s-1) + \alpha^{\sigma} f(s-1)$$

using eqns [27] and [29]

$$= \alpha^{\sigma}(Bw(s-1) + f(s-1))$$
$$= \alpha^{\sigma} w(s)$$

from eqn [24]

$$= \alpha^{\sigma}(\alpha w(s-1))$$

from above, i.e.

$$w(s+\sigma)=\alpha^{\sigma+1}w(s-1) \qquad \cdots[30]$$

as required.

Necessity: Suppose that the balanced growth path exists, i.e.

$$w(t)=\alpha w(t-1)=Bw(t-1)+f(t-1),\ t=s,\ s+1,\ldots \qquad \cdots[31]$$

with $w(t)\geqslant \mathbf{0}_{ns}$. Hence:

$$\alpha w(s-1)=Bw(s-1)+f(s-1)\geqslant \mathbf{0}_{ns}$$

or

$$(\alpha I-B)w(s-1)=f(s-1)\geqslant \mathbf{0}_{ns}$$

has a non-negative solution $w(s-1)$.

By Theorem 1 of Chapter 2, this implies that $(\alpha I-B)$ is a P-matrix. Hence, $\alpha>\lambda^*(B)$.

Relative stability:

Denote the balanced solution of eqn [24] by $w^*(t)$, $t=s,\ s+1,\ldots,$ with $w^*=w^*(s-1)$ the vector of initial conditions generating it. Let $w(t)$ denote any solution of eqn [24] originating from the vector $w(s-1)$.

The balanced growth solution is relatively stable iff

$$\lim_{\sigma\to\infty}\frac{w(s+\sigma)}{\alpha^{\sigma+1}}=w^* \qquad \cdots[32]$$

From eqn [24], we have:

$$w(s+\sigma)=Bw(s+\sigma-1)+f(s+\sigma-1) \qquad \sigma=0,1,\ldots \qquad \cdots[33]$$

Using eqn [27], we have on dividing eqn [33] by α^σ:

$$\alpha\frac{w(s+\sigma)}{\alpha^{\sigma+1}}=\frac{Bw(s+\sigma-1)}{\alpha^\sigma}+f(s-1) \qquad \cdots[34]$$

On the balanced path, we have:

$$\alpha w^*=Bw^*+f(s-1) \qquad \cdots[35]$$

Subtracting eqn [35] from eqn [34], we obtain:

$$\alpha\left[\frac{w(s+\sigma)}{\alpha^{\sigma+1}}-w^*\right]=B\left[\frac{w(s+\sigma-1)}{\alpha^\sigma}-w^*\right] \qquad \cdots[36]$$

Dividing by α and iterating, we have:

$$\frac{w(s+\sigma)}{\alpha^{\sigma+1}}-w^*=\frac{B^{\sigma+1}}{\alpha^{\sigma+1}}[w(s-1)-w^*] \qquad \cdots[37]$$

Sufficiency: If $\alpha>\lambda^*(B)$, then $(\alpha I-B)^{-1}>[0]_{ns\times ns}$.

Hence $\lim_{\sigma\to\infty}\frac{B^\sigma}{\alpha^\sigma}=[0]_{ns\times ns}$ (using Exercises §2.3, Q9).

Relative stability follows immediately from eqn [37].
Necessity: Suppose that the balanced path is relatively stable. From eqns [32] and [37], we conclude that:

$$\lim_{\sigma\to\infty}\frac{B^{\sigma+1}}{\alpha^{\sigma+1}}=[0]_{ns\times ns}$$

If B has distinct roots, there exists T such that $T^{-1}BT=D$, the diagonal matrix of characteristic roots. Otherwise, T may be interpreted as that unitary matrix which reduces B to a triangular form, i.e. $T^{-1}BT=J_B$, which has the roots of B along the main diagonal (see Exercises §2.4, questions 6, 8).
It is evident that:

$$\lim_{\sigma\to\infty}\frac{B^{\sigma+1}}{\alpha^{\sigma+1}}=[0]_{ns\times ns}\quad\text{iff}\quad\lim_{\sigma\to\infty}\frac{J_B^{\sigma+1}}{\alpha^{\sigma+1}}=[0]_{ns\times ns}$$

As the elements of $J_B^{\sigma+1}$ will be polynomial functions of the roots of B, it follows from relative stability that each root of B is less than α in absolute value. In particular, $\lambda^*(B)<\alpha$.

§5.4.3. *The effect of the lag structure on stability*

In this section, we compare the stability of our model [24] of §5.4.2 with that of another model employing the same consumption and production coefficients, but with a much simpler lag structure.

Given the $C(t-\tau)$ matrices of §5.4.2, let us define:

$$\bar{C}=\sum_{\tau=1}^{s}C(t-\tau) \qquad \cdots[1]$$

Let

$$M(t-\tau)=\hat{v}(I-A)^{-1}\hat{p}^{-1}C(t-\tau) \qquad \cdots[2]$$

$$\bar{B}=\sum_{\tau=1}^{s}M(t-\tau)=\hat{v}(I-A)^{-1}\hat{p}^{-1}\bar{C} \qquad \cdots[3]$$

Then

$$y(t)=\bar{B}y(t-1)+Na(t) \qquad \cdots[4]$$

is the first-order system corresponding to:

$$w(t)=Bw(t-1)+f(t-1) \qquad \cdots[5]$$

In eqn [5], expenditures are spread over s periods, whereas in eqn [4] they are bunched into that period following receipt of income. Note that the total propensity to consume is the same in both eqns [5] and [4]. The "potential" of the models is thus the same. In the context of a model with constant autonomous expenditures, we have proved in §4.2.10 that stability is invariant with respect to changes in the lag structure; so, if the autonomous terms were replaced by constant vectors, eqn [5] would be stable iff eqn [4] were stable. However, if autonomous expenditures are not constant but obey eqn [27] of §5.4.2, a change in the lag structure generally affects stability properties.

We now summarise our main results in this section: in the case of non-increasing autonomous expenditures, eqn [4] has a relatively stable balanced growth solution if eqn [5] has; in the case of non-decreasing autonomous expenditures, eqn [5] has a relatively stable balanced growth solution if eqn [4] has.

We shall make considerable use of the diagonal dominance concept to derive these results. First, we have:

Lemma 2: Let $S \geqslant [0]$. Each root of S is less than α in absolute value iff $(\alpha I - S)$ has a positive D.D.
The proof, which is left as an exercise, follows straightforwardly from Theorem 35 of Chapter 4.

Theorem 12: If $(\alpha I - B)$ has a positive D.D. and $\alpha \leqslant 1$, then $(\alpha I - \bar{B})$ also has a positive D.D.
The proof involves a slight modification of the "Necessity" proof of Theorem 37 of Chapter 4 and is left as an exercise.

Immediately, we can derive:

Theorem 13: Given $\alpha \leqslant 1$, if eqn [5] has a relatively stable balanced growth solution, then eqn [4] also has a relatively stable balanced growth solution.

Proof: By Theorem 11, eqn [5] has a relatively stable balanced growth solution iff $\alpha > \lambda^*(B)$. By Theorem 35 of Chapter 4, $\alpha > \lambda^*(B)$ iff $(\alpha I - B)$ has a positive D.D. By Theorem 12, if $\alpha \leqslant 1$, $(\alpha I - B)$ has a positive D.D. implies $(\alpha I - \bar{B})$ has a positive D.D. Again by Theorem 35 of Chapter 4, $\alpha > \lambda^*(B)$, which by Theorem 11 implies that eqn [4] is relatively stable.

We now provide an example to demonstrate that the converse of Theorem 13 is not true.
Let $n = s = 2$.

$$\text{Let } M(t-1) = \begin{bmatrix} \frac{1}{3} & 0 \\ 0 & \frac{1}{3} \end{bmatrix}, \qquad M(t-2) = \begin{bmatrix} 0 & \frac{1}{3} \\ \frac{1}{3} & 0 \end{bmatrix}$$

$\bar{B}$ has roots 0 and 2/3. The largest root of B is approximately 0.85. So, if we choose α in the interval 0.67 to 0.84, eqn [4] will be relatively stable while eqn [5] is not.

Let us now turn our attention to the case where autonomous expenditures are not decreasing.

Analogous to Theorem 12, we have:

Theorem 14: If $(\alpha I-\bar{B})$ has a positive D.D. and $\alpha \geqslant 1$, then $(\alpha I-B)$ also has a positive D.D.
The proof involves a slight modification of the "Sufficiency" proof of Theorem 37 and is left as an exercise.

Immediately, we can derive:

Theorem 15: Given $\alpha \geqslant 1$, eqn [5] has a relatively stable balanced growth solution if eqn [4] has.
The proof is almost identical with that of Theorem 13.

We now provide an example to show that the converse of Theorem 15 is not valid.
Again, let $n=s=2$.

Let $M(t-1)=\begin{bmatrix}1 & 0\\ 0 & 1\end{bmatrix}$, $M(t-2)=\begin{bmatrix}0 & 1\\ 1 & 0\end{bmatrix}$

$\bar{B}$ has roots 0 and 2. The largest root of B is approximately 1.70. So, if we choose α in the interval 1.71 to 2.00, then eqn [5] is relatively stable while eqn [4] is not.

So, from Theorem 15 we can conclude that, with non-decreasing autonomous expenditures, the introduction of lags cannot destabilise a stable system. From Theorem 13, we conclude that, with non-increasing autonomous expenditures, the removal of lags (by bunching expenditures into that period following receipt of income) cannot destabilise a stable lagged system.

§5.4.4. *A sufficient condition for stability*

In this section, we provide a sufficient condition for the relative stability of eqns [4] and [5] of §5.4.3 in terms of the sectoral total propensities to spend. Under our assumptions on technology and the consumption coefficients, $\bar{B}>[0]$. Let

$$\bar{B}z=\lambda^*(\bar{B})z \qquad \lambda^*(\bar{B})>0, \qquad z>\mathbf{0} \qquad \cdots[1]$$

Let $\mathbf{1}=(1,\ldots,1)'$ be a vector of order n.
Then

$$\mathbf{1}'\bar{B}=\mathbf{1}'\hat{v}(I-A)^{-1}\hat{p}^{-1}\bar{C} \quad \text{from eqn [3] of §5.4.3}$$
$$=v'(I-A)^{-1}\hat{p}^{-1}\bar{C}$$

or

$$\mathbf{1}'\bar{B}=\mathbf{1}'\bar{C} \qquad \cdots[2]$$

using $v'=p'(I-A)$.
Pre-multiplying eqn [1] by $\mathbf{1}'$ and using eqn [2], we have:

$$\mathbf{1}'\bar{B}z=\mathbf{1}'\bar{C}z=\lambda^*(\bar{B})\mathbf{1}'z \qquad \cdots[3]$$

Now

$$\bar{C}=\sum_{\tau=1}^{s} C(t-\tau)=\left[\sum_{\tau=1}^{s} c_{ij}(t-\tau)\right] \qquad i, j=1,\ldots,n \qquad \cdots[4]$$

So

$$\mathbf{1}'\bar{C}=\left[\sum_{i=1}^{n}\sum_{\tau=1}^{s} c_{ij}(t-\tau)\right]' \qquad j=1,\ldots,n$$

$$=\left[\sum_{\tau=1}^{s}\left(\sum_{i=1}^{n} c_{ij}(t-\tau)\right)\right]'$$

$$=\left[\sum_{\tau=1}^{s} c_j(t-\tau)\right]'$$

$$=[c_j(t)]' \quad \text{using eqn [11] of §5.4.2.}$$

That is, $\mathbf{1}'\bar{C}$ is the row vector with the j-th sector's total propensity to spend as its j-th component.

Let $\beta=\max_j c_j(t)$. Then $\mathbf{1}'\bar{C}\leqslant\beta\mathbf{1}'$. If $\beta<\alpha$, we have:

$$\mathbf{1}'\bar{C}\leqslant\beta\mathbf{1}'<\alpha\mathbf{1}' \qquad \cdots[5]$$

Using this in eqn [3], we have:

$$\lambda^*(\bar{B})\mathbf{1}'z=\mathbf{1}'\bar{C}x<\alpha\mathbf{1}'z \qquad \cdots[6]$$

As $z>\mathbf{0}_n$, $\mathbf{1}'z>0$. Hence, from eqn [6], we have: $\lambda^*(\bar{B})<\alpha$.

By Theorem 11, we have relative stability of eqn [4] of §5.4.3.

If $\alpha\geqslant 1$, relative stability of eqn [5] of §5.4.3 follows by Theorem 15.

Summarising our discussion, we have:

Theorem 16: If $\alpha\geqslant 1$, a sufficient condition for relative stability of eqns [4] and [5] of §5.4.3 is that each sector's total propensity to spend be less than α.

Let us consider the case of $\alpha>1$. It follows from Theorem 16 that each sector might have a total propensity to spend which is greater than unity and yet the models possess relative stability. This compares with the familiar sufficient condition for relative stability of the static multiplier models of §5.1.3 that the total propensity to spend of each sector be less than unity (with the usual modification in the indecomposable case).

The phenomenon of total propensities to spend being greater than unity yet implying relative stability might seem counter-intuitive; for, at first glance, it might appear that consumption is greater than output. However, it should be remembered that income is growing and consumption is based on past income levels. With no production lags, future income accommodates current demand.

It is perhaps worth emphasising that the condition derived in Theorem 16 is only a sufficient condition. Consequently, some sector might have a total propensity to spend which is greater than α. Such a sector might be called a destabilising sector; given $\alpha > \lambda^*(\bar{B})$, it follows that such a sector would have to be linked to at least one stabilising sector (i.e. one which has a total propensity to spend of less than α). This would be achieved in our model by the indecomposability of technology and our assumptions about consumption coefficients.

§5.4.5. *A generalised Metzler model*

In §§5.4.1–5.4.4, we have re-examined the expenditure models of §§5.1.1 and 5.1.2, extending them to the long run and attempting an integration with production models. We now devote out attention to such an extension of the Metzler models of §§5.1.3 and 5.1.4.

For each country in the trading system, we have:

$$Y_j = C_j + X_j - M_j + I_j \qquad j = 1, \ldots, n \qquad \cdots [1]$$

as in §5.1.3.

In §5.1.3, we postulated an expenditure function:

$$U_j(Y_j) = C_j(Y_j) + I_j(Y_j) \quad \text{for all } j \qquad \cdots [2]$$

Once we specify:

$$M_j = M_j(Y_j) = \sum_{i \neq j} M_{ij}(Y_j) \quad \text{for all } j \qquad \cdots [3]$$

we have also specified X_j, for all j:

$$X_j = \sum_{i \neq j} M_{ji}(Y_i) \qquad \cdots [4]$$

In §5.1.3, we took a Taylor series around an equilibrium and examined the conditions for stability. Here, we shall specify the consumption and import functions more closely in order to examine long-run behaviour. Instead of eqn [3], we write:

$$M_{rs}(t) = m_{rs} Y_s(t) + l_{rs}(Y_s(t) - Y_s(t-1)) + k_{rs} \quad \text{for all } r \neq s \qquad \cdots [5]$$

Then

$$\begin{aligned} M_j(t) &= \sum_{i \neq j} M_{ij}(t) \\ &= \sum_{i \neq j} m_{ij} Y_j(t) + \sum_{i \neq j} l_{ij}(Y_j(t) - Y_j(t-1)) + \sum_{i \neq j} k_{ij} \end{aligned} \qquad \cdots [6]$$

Let:

$$m_j = \sum_{i \neq j} m_{ij}; \qquad l_j = \sum_{i \neq j} l_{ij} \qquad \cdots [7]$$

So eqn [6] becomes:

$$M_j(t) = m_j Y_j(t) + l_j(Y_j(t) - Y_j(t-1)) + \sum_{i \neq j} k_{ij} \qquad \cdots [8]$$

$$X_j(t) = \sum_{i \neq j} M_{ji}(t)$$

$$= \sum_{i \neq j} m_{ji} Y_i(t) + \sum_{i \neq j} l_{ji}(Y_i(t) - Y_i(t-1)) + \sum_{i \neq j} k_{ji} \qquad \cdots [9]$$

Then:

$$X_j(t) - M_j(t) = \sum_{i \neq j} m_{ji} Y_i(t) - m_j Y_j(t) + \sum_{i \neq j} l_{ji}(Y_i(t) - Y_i(t-1)) -$$

$$- l_j(Y_j(t) - Y_j(t-1)) + \sum_{i \neq j} k_{ij} - \sum_{i \neq j} k_{ji} \qquad \cdots [10]$$

We must now specify a consumption function:

$$C_j(t) = a_j Y_j(t) + b_j C_j(t-1) + c_j \qquad \cdots [11]$$

The interpretations of eqns [8] and [11] are straightforward. Rewriting eqns [1], [10] and [11] in matrix–vector form, we have:

$$Y(t) = C(t) + X(t) - M(t) + I(t) \qquad \cdots [12]$$

$$X(t) - M(t) = MY(t) + L(Y(t) - Y(t-1)) + k \qquad \cdots [13]$$

$$C(t) = \hat{a} Y(t) + \hat{b} C(t-1) + c \qquad \cdots [14]$$

$$\text{where } M = \begin{bmatrix} -m_1 & m_{12} & \cdots & m_{1n} \\ m_{21} & -m_2 & \cdots & m_{2n} \\ \cdot & \cdot & \cdot & \cdot \\ \cdot & \cdot & \cdot & \cdot \\ \cdot & \cdot & \cdot & \cdot \\ m_{n1} & m_{n2} & \cdots & -m_n \end{bmatrix}, \quad L = \begin{bmatrix} -l_1 & l_{12} & \cdots & l_{1n} \\ l_{21} & -l_2 & \cdots & l_{2n} \\ \cdot & \cdot & \cdot & \cdot \\ \cdot & \cdot & \cdot & \cdot \\ \cdot & \cdot & \cdot & \cdot \\ l_{n1} & l_{n2} & \cdots & -l_n \end{bmatrix},$$

$\hat{a} = [a_i \delta_{ij}]$, $\hat{b} = [b_i \delta_{ij}]$, k and c are vectors with typical components given by the last terms on the right-hand sides of eqns [10] and [11] respectively. Elementary manipulations of eqns [12]–[14] yield:

$$(I - \hat{a} - M - L) Y(t) = [\hat{b}(I - M - L] Y(t-1) + \hat{b} Y(t-2) +$$

$$+ I(t) - \hat{b} I(t-1) + (I - \hat{b}) k \qquad \cdots [15]$$

or

$$E_1 Y(t) + E_2 Y(t-1) + E_3 Y(t-2) = g(t) + h \qquad \cdots [16]$$

where

$$E_1 = I - \hat{a} - M - L \qquad \cdots [17]$$

$$E_2 = -\hat{b}(I - M - L) + L \qquad \cdots [18]$$

$$E_3 = -\hat{b} L \qquad \cdots [19]$$

$$g(t) = I(t) - \hat{b} I(t-1) \qquad \cdots [20]$$

$$h = (I - \hat{b}) k \qquad \cdots [21]$$

There are three different types of multiplier to be derived from eqn [16].

First, we have the "impact" or short-term multipliers, measured by E_1^{-1} (the generalisation of the multiplier $(I-U-M)^{-1}$ of §5.1.3). These multipliers measure the immediate effects on the incomes of all countries of an increase in autonomous expenditures, when all repercussions through the trading system have been permitted, as well as the direct effects through consumption.

Second, we have the long-run multipliers, measured by $(E_1+E_2+E_3)^{-1}$. These measure the long-term effects of an increase in the vector h.

Finally, we have the "super-multipliers."

First, we consider the "impact" multipliers. We wish to derive the result corresponding to Theorem 3. We assume:

$$1 > a_j > m_j + l_j \quad \text{for all } j \qquad \cdots [22]$$

Hence, $\hat{a}+M+L \geqslant [0]$. Also:

$$\begin{aligned}\mathbf{1}'(I-\hat{a}-M-L) &= \mathbf{1}'-\mathbf{1}'\hat{a}-\mathbf{1}'M-\mathbf{1}'L\\ &= \mathbf{1}'-a'-\mathbf{0}'-\mathbf{0}' \quad \text{using eqn [7]}\\ &= (1-a_j) \quad j=1,\ldots,n \qquad \cdots [23]\\ &> \mathbf{0} \quad \text{given eqn [22]}\end{aligned}$$

The matrix $I-\hat{a}-M-L$ thus has a dominant diagonal (in the original sense). From §2.3.3, we know that:

$$(I-a-M-L)^{-1} \geqslant [0] \qquad \cdots [24]$$

If we assume that $a+M+L$ is indecomposable, this result becomes:

$$(I-\hat{a}-M-L)^{-1} > [0] \qquad \cdots [25]$$

From eqn [23], we have:

$$\mathbf{1}' = (\mathbf{1}-a)'(I-\hat{a}-M-L)^{-1} \qquad \cdots [26]$$

Using inequality [24], we conclude from eqn [26] that:

$$1 \geqslant (1-a_j)(I-\hat{a}-M-L)^{-1}[ij]$$

or

$$1/(1-a_j) \geqslant (I-\hat{a}-M-L)^{-1}[ij] \qquad \cdots [27]$$

(Under inequality [25], strict inequality holds in [27].)

$1/(1-a_j)$ is the j-th country's closed economy multiplier. Following the method used in the proof of Theorem 3, we can derive:

$$(I-\hat{a}-M-L)^{-1}[ij] \geqslant 1/(1-a_j+m_j+l_j) \qquad \cdots [28]$$

where the right-hand side measures the (one-way) foreign-trade multiplier which does not permit all repercussions through the trading system (again, the inequality is strict if [25] holds).

Summarising our discussion, we have:

Theorem 17: The diagonal impact multiplier (i.e. a diagonal element of $(I-\hat{a}-M-L)^{-1}$) lies between the closed-economy multiplier and the (one-way) foreign-trade multiplier.

The proof of the next theorem follows from the properties of *M*-matrices derived in Chapter 2 (especially Theorem 51).

Theorem 18: The diagonal impact multiplier is not less than any off-diagonal impact multiplier in the same row.

This completes our discussion of impact multipliers. We now turn our attention to long-run multipliers.

The general solution of eqn [16] may be written as the solution of

$$E_1Y(t)+E_2Y(t-1)+E_3Y(t-2)=\mathbf{0} \qquad \cdots [29]$$

plus a particular solution of:

$$E_1Y(t)+E_2Y(t-1)+E_3Y(t-2)=g(t) \qquad \cdots [30]$$

plus a particular solution of:

$$E_1Y(t)+E_2Y(t-1)+E_3Y(t-2)=h \qquad \cdots [31]$$

We now obtain a particular solution of eqn [31].
Putting $Y(t)=Y(t-1)=Y(t-2)=Y$ (a constant), we obtain:

$$(E_1+E_2+E_3)Y=h$$

or

$$Y=(E_1+E_2+E_3)^{-1}h \qquad \cdots [32]$$

From eqns [17]–[19]:

$$E_1+E_2+E_3=I-\hat{a}-\hat{b}-(I-\hat{b})M \qquad \cdots [33]$$

We now assume that:

$$a_j+b_j<1 \quad \text{for all } j \qquad \cdots [34]$$

It can be easily verified that inequality [34] implies:

(i) $1-a_j-b_j+m_j-b_jm_j>0$ for all j
(ii) $\mathbf{1}'[I-\hat{a}-\hat{b}-(I-\hat{b})M]>\mathbf{0}'$

So $[I-\hat{a}-\hat{b}-(I-\hat{b})M]$ has positive diagonal elements and positive column sums, which imply that it has a positive dominant diagonal. Hence:

$$E^{-1}=(E_1+E_2+E_3)^{-1}=[I-\hat{a}-\hat{b}-(I-\hat{b})M]^{-1}\geqslant[0] \qquad \cdots [35]$$

with strict inequality under appropriate indecomposability assumptions.

We now seek to establish for the long-run multipliers propositions similar to those established for the impact multipliers.

The (one-way) long-run foreign trade multiplier is given by

$$1/(1-a_j-b_j+(1-b_j)m_j) \qquad j=1,\ldots,n \qquad \cdots[36]$$

Let $\hat{m}=[m_i\delta_{ij}]$. Then

$$[I-\hat{a}-\hat{b}+(I-\hat{b})\hat{m}]\geqq[I-\hat{a}-\hat{b}-(I-\hat{b})M]=E$$

Hence, from $EE^{-1}=I$, we derive:

$$[I-\hat{a}-\hat{b}+(I-\hat{b})\hat{m}]E^{-1}\geqq I \qquad \cdots[37]$$

whence

$$E^{-1}\geqq(I-\hat{a}-\hat{b}+(I-\hat{b})\hat{m})^{-1} \qquad \cdots[38]$$

So

$$(E^{-1})_{jj}\geqslant 1/(1-a_j-b_j+(1-b_j)m_j) \quad \text{for all } j \qquad \cdots[39]$$

$(E^{-1})_{jj}$ measures the j-th country's long-run multiplier when all repercussions are allowed.

The long-run closed economy multiplier is given by:

$$1/(1-a_j-b_j) \quad \text{for all } j \qquad \cdots[40]$$

which provides obvious justification for inequality [34].
Consider:

$$(I-\hat{b})^{-1}[I-\hat{a}-\hat{b}-(I-\hat{b})M]=(I-\hat{b})^{-1}(I-\hat{a}-\hat{b})-M \qquad \cdots[41]$$

Pre-multiplying by $\mathbf{1}'$:

$$\begin{aligned}\mathbf{1}'(I-\hat{b})^{-1}E&=\mathbf{1}'(I-\hat{b})^{-1}(I-\hat{a}-\hat{b})-\mathbf{1}'M\\&=\mathbf{1}'(I-\hat{b})^{-1}(I-\hat{a}-\hat{b})\end{aligned} \qquad \cdots[42]$$

Hence:

$$\mathbf{1}'(I-\hat{b})^{-1}=\mathbf{1}'(I-\hat{b})^{-1}(I-\hat{a}-\hat{b})E^{-1} \qquad \cdots[43]$$

$$\begin{aligned}\mathbf{1}'(I-\hat{b})^{-1}(I-\hat{a}-\hat{b})=[&(1-a_1-b_1)/(1-b_1),\\&(1-a_2-b_2)/(1-b_2),\ldots,(1-a_n-b_n)/(1-b_n)]\end{aligned} \qquad \cdots[44]$$

Under inequality [34], eqn [35] holds. This implies that:

$$1/(1-b_j)\geqslant(1-a_j-b_j)/(1-b_j)\,.\,(E^{-1})_{jj} \quad \text{for all } j \qquad \cdots[45]$$

Hence:

$$1/(1-a_j-b_j)\geqslant(E^{-1})_{jj} \qquad \cdots[46]$$

Summarising our discussion, we have:

Theorem 19: The diagonal long-run multiplier lies between the (long-run) closed economy multiplier and the (one-way) long-run foreign trade multiplier.

We also have the result corresponding to Theorem 18 on the relation between diagonal and off-diagonal multipliers.

We now turn our attention to deriving a particular solution where the non-homogeneous term is not constant. We have:

$$E_1Y(t)+E_2Y(t-1)+E_3Y(t-2)=g(t) \qquad \cdots [47]$$

where

$$g(t)=\hat{\psi}^t g(0) \qquad \hat{\psi}=[\psi_i\delta_{ij}] \qquad \cdots [48]$$

We follow the method of Brown and Jones to solve eqn [47].
First of all, define the vector:

$$g^j(t)=[\psi_j^t g_j(0)\delta_{ij}] \qquad j=1,\ldots,n \qquad \cdots [49]$$

Then, suppose that eqn [47] has solution:

$$Y(t)=Kg(t) \qquad \cdots [50]$$

where K is the matrix of "super-multipliers", Substituting in eqn [47], we have:

$$E_1Kg(t)+E_2Kg(t-1)+E_3Kg(t-2)=g(t) \qquad \cdots [51]$$

As $g(t)=\sum_{j=1}^{n} g^j(t)$, eqn [51] may be replaced by the following n equations:

$$E_1Kg^j(t)+E_2Kg^j(t-1)+E_3Kg^j(t-2)=g^j(t) \qquad j=1,\ldots,n \qquad \cdots [52]$$

It is evident from the form of the vectors $g^j(t)$ that the j-th equation of [52] will determine the j-th column of K, $j=1,\ldots,n$.
Eliminating $\psi_j^t g_j(0)$ from eqn [52], we obtain:

$$E_1Ke^j+E_2Ke^j\,.\,\psi_j^{-1}+E_3Ke^j\,.\,\psi_j^{-2}=e^j \qquad \cdots [53]$$

or

$$E_1K^j+E_2K^j\,.\,\psi_j^{-1}+E_3K^j\,.\,\psi_j^{-2}=e^j \qquad \cdots [54]$$

or

$$(E_1+\psi_j^{-1}E_2+\psi_j^{-2}E_3)K^j=e^j \qquad \cdots [55]$$

or

$$F_jK^j=e^j \qquad \cdots [56]$$

which implies:

$$K^j=F_j^{-1}e^j \qquad \cdots [57]$$

Then:

$$K = [K^1 \quad K^2 \quad \cdots \quad K^n] \qquad \cdots [58]$$

where

$$K^j = ([E_1 + \psi_j^{-1} E_2 + \psi_j^{-2} E_3]^{-1})^j, \qquad j = 1, \ldots, n \qquad \cdots [59]$$

Using eqns [17]–[19], and after elementary manipulations, we obtain:

$$F_j = (I - \hat{a} - \psi_j^{-1}\hat{b}) - (I - \psi_j^{-1}\hat{b})[M + (1 - \psi_j^{-1})L] \qquad \cdots [60]$$

We now introduce the assumption:

$$\psi_j > 1 \quad \text{for all } j \qquad \cdots [61]$$

We aim to show that the matrix of super-multipliers satisfies the same conditions as the other matrix multipliers, under inequalities [34] and [61]. From eqn [60], we see that under [61]: the diagonal elements of F_j are positive, the off-diagonal elements of F_j are non-positive.
Now consider:

$$\begin{aligned} \mathbf{1}'(I - \psi_j^{-1}\hat{b})^{-1}F_j &= \mathbf{1}'(I - \psi_j^{-1}\hat{b})^{-1}(I - \hat{a} - \psi_j^{-1}\hat{b}) - \\ &\quad - \mathbf{1}'(I - \psi_j^{-1}\hat{b})^{-1}(I - \psi_j^{-1}\hat{b})(M + (1 - \psi_j^{-1})L) \\ &= \mathbf{1}'(I - \psi_j^{-1}\hat{b})^{-1}(I - \hat{a} - \psi_j^{-1}\hat{b}) - \\ &\quad - \mathbf{1}'(M + (1 - \psi_j^{-1})L) \end{aligned} \qquad \cdots [62]$$

Now $\mathbf{1}'M = \mathbf{1}'L = \mathbf{0}'$. Hence:

$$\mathbf{1}'(I - \psi_j^{-1}\hat{b})^{-1}F_j = \mathbf{1}'(I - \psi_j^{-1}\hat{b})^{-1}(I - \hat{a} - \psi_j^{-1}\hat{b}) \qquad \cdots [63]$$

Under inequalities [34] and [61]:

$$\mathbf{1}'(I - \psi_j^{-1}\hat{b})^{-1}(I - \hat{a} - \psi_j^{-1}\hat{b}) > \mathbf{0}' \qquad \cdots [64]$$

Hence, F_j has a positive D.D. So, we have:

$$F_j^{-1} \geqslant [0] \quad \text{for all } j \qquad \cdots [65]$$

As in the previous cases, we relate our super-multiplier to other—closed economy and foreign trade—super-multipliers. The one-way foreign trade super-multiplier is given by:

$$1/[1 - a_j - b_j - (1 - b_j)(m_j - (1 - \psi_j^{-1})l_j)] \qquad \cdots [66]$$

i.e. the inverse of the j-th diagonal element of F_j.
From the equation $F_j^{-1}F_j = I$, we conclude that:

$$(F_j^{-1})_{jj} \geqslant 1/(F_j)_{jj} \qquad \cdots [67]$$

given the sign conditions on F_j.
The closed economy super-multiplier is:

$$1/(1 - a_j - b_j) \qquad \cdots [68]$$

From eqn [63], we have:

$$\mathbf{1}'(I-\psi_j^{-1}\hat{b})^{-1}=\mathbf{1}'(I-\psi_j^{-1}\hat{b})^{-1}(I-a-\psi_j^{-1}\hat{b})F_j^{-1} \qquad \cdots[69]$$

whence:

$$1\geqslant(1-a_j-\psi_j^{-1}b_j)(F_j^{-1})_{jj}.$$

So:

$$1/(1-a_j-b_j)\geqslant(F_j^{-1})_{jj} \qquad \cdots[70]$$

Summarising, we have:

Theorem 20: Under our hypotheses, the diagonal super-multiplier lies between the closed economy super-multiplier and the one-way foreign trade super-multiplier.

To conclude this section, we must now examine the homogeneous eqn [29], which may be rewritten as:

$$\begin{bmatrix} Y(t) \\ Y(t-1) \end{bmatrix}=\begin{bmatrix} -E_1^{-1}E_2 & -E_1^{-1}E_3 \\ I & 0 \end{bmatrix}\begin{bmatrix} Y(t-1) \\ Y(t-2) \end{bmatrix} \qquad \cdots[71]$$

Unfortunately, sufficient conditions for stability are difficult, not to say impossible, to find.

While we can state sufficient conditions for the existence of meaningful multipliers (i.e. the particular solutions are non-negative), we are unable to obtain a meaningful solution of the homogeneous equation. Brown and Jones experienced similar difficulties with their (simpler) model, though, to their credit, they did derive a sufficient condition for instability of their homogeneous equation (see the exercises).

§5.4.6. *A side glance at reality: speed of adjustment*

Suppose an economy is initially in equilibrium when it experiences a change in autonomous expenditures. A new equilibrium is not, in general, achieved in finite time. We aim to find the time taken to cover a given proportion of the distance to the new equilibrium.

Suppose that units of measurement are chosen so that $p=\mathbf{1}$. National income is given by $\omega(t)=p'(I-A)x(t)=\mathbf{1}'(I-A)x(t)$.

Let $c(t)$ and $a(t)$ denote the vectors of consumption and investment (respectively) at t.

Suppose that there is a one-period consumption lag and:

$$c(t)=h\omega(t-1) \qquad \cdots[1]$$

h being a vector of average propensities to consume.

Abstracting from production lags, the balance equation is:

$$x(t)=Ax(t)+c(t)+a(t) \qquad \cdots[2]$$

$$=Ax(t)+h\mathbf{1}'(I-A)x(t-1)+a(t)$$

$$=Ax(t)+Bx(t-1)+a(t) \qquad \cdots[3]$$

where:

$$B = h\mathbf{1}'(I - A) \qquad \cdots [4]$$

Implicit is the assumption that the model is workable, i.e. $(I-A)^{-1} \geqslant [0]$. We introduce the following assumption (which implies workability):

$$\sum_{i=1}^{n} a_{ij} < 1 \quad \text{for all } j \qquad \cdots [5]$$

Under this assumption, $B \geqslant [0]$.

Further, suppose $h_i > 0$, for all i, and $\gamma = \sum_{i=1}^{n} h_i < 1$. If we then make the additional assumption that A is indecomposable, we have $(I-A)^{-1} > [0]$, $B > [0]$.

We assume that the economy is initially in equilibrium, when it experiences a change in autonomous expenditures in the first period which is sustained in subsequent periods.

The static multiplier effects are given by the equation:

$$\Delta x = (I - A - B)^{-1} \Delta a \qquad \cdots [6]$$

in the sense that the equilibrium level of outputs corresponding to a level of autonomous expenditures of $a + \Delta a$ is given by $x + \Delta x$, x being known initially and Δx being known from eqn [6].

The time path of outputs on the "traverse" between the equilibria is given by:

$$\Delta x(t) = [I - \{(I-A)^{-1}B\}^{t}](I - A - B)^{-1} \Delta a \qquad \cdots [7]$$

We wish to find t such that:

$$\Delta x(t) \geqq \rho \Delta x \qquad \rho \in (0, 1) \qquad \cdots [8]$$

by which time (at least) $\rho \times 100$ per cent of the "distance" between the equilibria has been covered.

From eqns [6] and [7], we have in eqn [8]:

$$\rho(I - A - B)^{-1} \Delta a \leqq [I - \{(I-A)^{-1}B\}^{t}](I - A - B)^{-1} \Delta a$$

or

$$\delta(I - A - B)^{-1} \Delta a \geqq ((I-A)^{-1}B)'(I - A - B)^{-1} \Delta a \qquad \delta = 1 - \rho \qquad \cdots [9]$$

We now make use of the following results (see the exercises):

$$(I - A - B)^{-1} = \left[I + \sum_{r=1}^{\infty} ((I-A)^{-1}B)^{r} \right] (I - A)^{-1} \qquad \cdots [10]$$

$$((I-A)^{-1}B)^{r} = \gamma'(I-A)^{-1}B \qquad \cdots [11]$$

Substituting from eqns [10] and [11] into eqn [9], we have:

$$\delta\left[I+\frac{1}{1-\gamma}(I-A)^{-1}B\right](I-A)^{-1}\Delta a \geqslant \gamma^{t-1}(I-A)^{-1}B\left[I+\frac{1}{1-\gamma}(I-A)^{-1}B\right](I-A)^{-1}\Delta a$$

The right-hand side of this inequality may be simplified so that we obtain:

$$\left[I+\frac{1}{1-\gamma}(I-A)^{-1}B\right](I-A)^{-1}\Delta a \geqslant \frac{\gamma^{t-1}}{1-\gamma}(I-A)^{-1}B(I-A)^{-1}\Delta a \qquad \cdots [12]$$

To find the time required for x_j to cover the given distance (assuming a change in a_j only), we have from eqn [12]:

$$\delta\alpha_{jj}+\frac{\delta}{1-\gamma}\beta_{jj} \geqslant \frac{\gamma^{t-1}}{1-\gamma}\beta_{jj} \qquad \cdots [13]$$

where

$$\alpha_{jj}=((I-A)^{-1})_{jj}, \qquad \beta_{jj}=[(I-A)^{-1}B(I-A)^{-1}]_{jj}$$

or

$$\delta\left[\frac{\alpha_{jj}}{\beta_{jj}}(1-\gamma)+1\right] \geqslant \gamma^{t-1}$$

or

$$t \geqslant 1+\frac{(\log_e\delta+\log_e(\alpha_{jj}(1-\gamma)+\beta_{jj})-\log_e\beta_{jj})}{\log_e\gamma} \qquad \cdots [14]$$

To measure the "cross" effect (i.e. the time required for x_i to cover the given distance consequent on a change in a_j, $j \neq i$), we have from eqn [12] simply:

$$\delta \geqslant \gamma^{t-1}$$

or

$$t \geqslant 1+\frac{\log_e\delta}{\log_e\gamma} \qquad \cdots [15]$$

Equation [15] gives the time for *any* $i \neq j$.

It may be easily seen that the time to achieve the "straight" effect (i.e. t in eqn [14]) is less than the time to achieve the "cross" effect (i.e. t in eqn [15]).

The case of constantly growing autonomous expenditures can be handled by the model outlined above (see the exercises).

§5.5. Review

The multiplier is one of the basic concepts in income analysis. In elementary macroeconomics, we are introduced to at least two multiplier concepts—the simple closed economy multiplier, given by $1/(1-u_i)$, u_i being the i-th country's marginal propensity to consume; and the foreign trade multiplier which takes account of leakages in the form of imports and is given by $1/(1-u_i+m_i)$, m_i being the i-th country's marginal propensity to import. The question of income determination in a system of n mutually dependent economies (countries) must be a general equilibrium question. However, the multiplier concepts mentioned so far are relevant only to partial equilibrium models. The general equilibrium analyst would wish to take account of such "second-round" effects as country i's increased exports to all countries whose income had increased as a result of their increased exports to country i in the "first-round." Doubtless, the analyst would wish to take account of "third-", "fourth-", . . . , "n-th-round" effects as well. The matrix multiplier is the concept we require for the n-country model for it describes the effects on income after *all* repercussions have been allowed.

Though published in 1950, Metzler's paper on a multi-country theory of income and trade was completed some years earlier; thus it contains one of the earliest (and clearest) expositions of this matrix multiplier concept. We mention this detail by way of explanation; Metzler's work was done before the advances made in the 1950s on existence theory. So, in Metzler's work, as in Hicks's and Samuelson's, an equilibrium is assumed to exist. Local stability of equilibrium is examined (by use of a Taylor's series to linearise the economic relationships so that a matrix differential equation is obtained; see eqn [14] of §5.1.3). Having established local stability of the multi-country model, Metzler then then went onto the "local" comparative statics of the model. This is impeccable general equilibrium methodology for the comparative statics results, which are essentially statements about changes in the equilibrium values of economic variables when the equilibrium is disturbed, can be described as almost meaningless if the equilibrium is unstable. The main tool of comparative statics analysis pioneered by Metzler was the matrix multiplier.

Exercises

§5.1

1. Consider the following two-country model where only consumption goods are traded:

$$Y_i = C_i + X_i \qquad i = 1,2$$

$$C_i = C_{ii}(Y_i) + M_{ji}(Y_i)$$

$$X_i = X_{ii}(Y_i) + M_{ij}(Y_j) - M_{ji}(Y_i) \qquad i = 1, 2; j \neq i.$$

Total consumption, C_i, is given by the sum of consumption of domestic goods, $C_{ii}(Y_i)$, and consumption of foreign goods, $M_{ji}(Y_i)$. Net investment, X_i, is the sum of domestic investment, $X_{ii}(Y_i)$, and the trade balance, $M_{ij}(Y_j)-M_{ji}(Y_i)$.
Assume a one-period expenditure lag so that:

$$C_i(t)=C_{ii}[Y_i(t-1)]+M_{ji}[Y_i(t-1)]$$
$$X_i(t)=X_{ii}[Y_i(t-1)]+M_{ij}[Y_j(t-1)]-M_{ji}[Y_i(t-1)] \qquad i=1,2;\ j\neq i.$$

Substitute now in the first equation to obtain expressions for $Y_i(t)$, $i=1, 2$.
Take a Taylor series around the equilibrium to obtain:

$$Y_i(t)-Y_i^0=c_{ii}\,.\,(Y_i(t-1)-Y_i^0)+x_{ii}\,.\,(Y_i(t-1)-Y_i^0)+ \\ +m_{ij}\,.\,(Y_j(t-1)-Y_j^0) \qquad i=1,2;\ j\neq i,$$

where

$$c_{ii}=\mathrm{d}C_{ii}/\mathrm{d}Y_i; \qquad x_{ii}=\mathrm{d}X_{ii}/\mathrm{d}Y_i; \qquad m_{ij}=\mathrm{d}M_{ij}/\mathrm{d}Y_j,$$

or

$$y(t)=\begin{bmatrix} c_{11}+x_{11} & m_{12} \\ m_{21} & c_{22}+x_{22}\end{bmatrix}y(t-1); \qquad y_i(t)=Y_i(t)-Y_i(0)$$

(i) Prove that this model is stable iff:

$$c_{11}+x_{11}+c_{22}+x_{22}<1+(c_{11}+x_{11})(c_{22}+x_{22})-m_{12}m_{21}<2$$

(ii) What is the stability condition for a single economy in isolation? What is the stability condition for a single economy when world (i.e. the other country's) reactions can be neglected?
(iii) Hence show that the condition derived in (i) implies that at least one country is stable in isolation.
(iv) Prove that if both countries are stable (unstable) in isolation, the system is stable (unstable). (Metzler, 1942a)

2. Consider the following modification of the model outlined in Q1.

$$C_1=C_{11}(Y_1)+M_{21}(Y_1)+\beta+\delta$$
$$X_1=X_{11}(Y_1)+M_{12}(Y_2)-M_{21}(Y_1)+\alpha-\gamma-\delta$$
$$C_2=C_{22}(Y_2)+M_{12}(Y_2)$$
$$X_2=X_{22}(Y_2)+M_{21}(Y_1)-M_{12}(Y_2)+\gamma+\delta$$

where the shift parameters may be interpreted thus:
α measures a change in public expenditure (say)
β measures a change in the average propensity to consume domestic goods
γ measures a change in consumption from domestic to foreign goods
δ measures a change in the average propensity to consume foreign goods.

Evaluate the effects of changes in these parameters on: Y_1, Y_2, C_1, C_2, X_1, X_2 (using the stability conditions of the previous question). (Metzler 1942a)

3. Consider the following representation of an income transfer from country 1 to country 2:

$$Y_1 = C_{11}(Y_1) + X_{11}(Y_1) + M_{12}(Y_2) - \theta - \tau$$
$$Y_2 = C_{22}(Y_2) + X_{22}(Y_2) + M_{21}(Y_1) + \sigma + \tau$$
$$b = M_{12}(Y_2) - M_{21}(Y_1)$$

where:
θ represents a transfer which directly affects income only in the paying country (country 1)
σ represents a transfer which directly affects income only in the receiving country (country 2)
τ represents a transfer which directly affects income in both countries.
Evaluate the effects of the various types of transfers on Y_1, Y_2 and b, making use of the stability conditions of Q1.
In particular, try to find conditions under which the balance of trade moves in country 1's favour by *more* than the amount of the transfer. (Metzler, 1942b)

§5.2

1. Prove that $\lim_{t\to\infty} \lambda' y(t) = \mathbf{0}$. Interpret this result.

2. Prove that if $x(0) > \sum_{v=0}^{\infty} A^v f(v+1)$, then $\lim_{t\to\infty} \frac{x_i(t)}{u_i(t)} = 1$.

§5.3

1. Consider the continuous-time version of the closed dynamic Leontief model. Prove that the (unique) Frobenius solution is globally relatively stable iff:

$$\mu^*(C) = 1/\lambda^*(C^{-1}) > \alpha_j/(\alpha_j^2 + \beta_j^2)$$

where

$$\lambda_j(C^{-1}) = \alpha_j + i\beta_j.$$

Hence, prove that a characteristic solution associated with any real root of C (and hence C^{-1}) will dominate the Frobenius characteristic solution iff the root is positive.

2. Introduce a "gestation period", T, into the discrete-time version of the model, $T \geqslant 1$.
Show that this leads to the equation:

$$x(t) = Ax(t) + \frac{1}{T} B(x(t+T) - x(t))$$

or

$$x(t+T)=(I+TC)x(t).$$

Rewrite this as a first-order equation:

$$y(t+1)=Ey(t)$$

i.e. specify the vector $y(t)$ and the matrix E.
What is the relation between the roots of E and those of $I+TC$?

3. Consider the original discrete-time version of the model. Prove that the (unique) Frobenius solution is globally relatively stable iff:

$$1+\mu^*(C)>\left|1+\frac{1}{\lambda_j(C^{-1})}\right|=\left|1+\frac{1}{(\alpha_j^2+\beta_j^2)^{\frac{1}{2}}}\right|$$

4. Consider the model outlined in Q2.
Let the roots of $E=I+TC$ be denoted by ν_j.
From Q3, we have relative stability iff:

$$\nu^*>|\nu_j| \quad j\neq 1$$

where

$$\nu^*=1+\frac{T}{\lambda^*(C^{-1})}=1+\frac{T}{\lambda^*}$$

Show that this implies:

$$T\left[\frac{1}{|\lambda_j|^2}-\frac{1}{\lambda^{*2}}\right]<2\left[\frac{1}{\lambda^*}-\frac{\alpha_j}{|\lambda_j|^2}\right]$$

Hence, derive:

$$T<2\left[\frac{1}{\lambda^*}-\frac{\alpha_j}{|\lambda_j|^2}\right]\Big/\left[\frac{1}{|\lambda_j|^2}-\frac{1}{\lambda^{*2}}\right]$$

Using the result in Q1, prove that:

(i) if the differential equation model is relatively stable, there exists a value of T such that the difference equation model is relatively stable;

(ii) if the differential equation model is relatively unstable, so is the difference equation model;

(iii) if T is sufficiently large, relative stability becomes impossible.

5. Consider the equation:

$$x(t+1)=Hx(t)$$

where

$H=I+F$ and $F^{-1}>[0]$.

Prove that there exists a positive integer m such that $H^m > [0]$ iff there exists a root of H, $\lambda_1(H)$, such that:

$$\lambda_1(H) > |\lambda_i(H)| \quad i = 2, \ldots, n$$

(Hint to the sufficiency part:
Let ν_1 be the Frobenius root of F^{-1}, with x^1 and u^1 satisfying: $F^{-1}x^1 = \nu_1 x^1$; $u^{1\prime}F^{-1} = \nu_1 u^{1\prime}$.
From Lemma 8 of Chapter 2, we know that $u^{1\prime}x^i = 0$, where x^i is a characteristic vector associated with any root of F^{-1} other than ν_1.
Suppose that H has n distinct roots. Then from §4.2, we know that the solution of:

$$x(t + t1) = Hx(t)$$

may be written as:

$$x(t) = \sum_{i=1}^{n} \alpha_i \lambda_i^t x^i \quad x(t) = H^t x(0)$$

where the α_i are determined by the initial conditions.
Let $x(0) = e^i$. Then:

$$x(0) = e^i = \sum_i \alpha_i x^i$$

Then $H^t e^i = H^t x(0) = (x(t) =) \sum_i \alpha_i \lambda_i^t x^i$

$u^{1\prime}e^i = \sum_i \alpha_i u^{1\prime}x^i = \alpha_1 u^{1\prime}x^1$ from the result derived above. $\alpha_1 > 0$ can now be derived easily.
Then from the equation above for $H^t e^i$, we see that as $\lambda_1 > |\lambda_i|$, there exists T_i such that $H^t e^i > \mathbf{0}$ for all $t > T_i$. Let $m = \max_i T_i$. Then $H^m e^i > \mathbf{0}$ for all i, or $H^m > [0]$.)

6. Using the result in Q5, prove the following:
   (i) If there exists a positive integer m such that $H^m > [0]$, $F^{-1} > [0]$, then $x^*(t) = \lambda_1^t x^1$ is relatively stable.
   (ii) If $x^*(t)$ is relatively stable and $F^{-1} > [0]$, there exists a positive integer m such that $H^m > [0]$.

   Assume also that $H = I + F \geqslant [0]$ is indecomposable. Then prove that:
   (iii) If H is primitive, $x^*(t)$ is relatively stable.
   (iv) If $x^*(t)$ is relatively stable and $F^{-1} > [0]$, H is primitive.

7. (i) Prove that if $H = I + F$, $F^{-1} > [0]$, and $\lambda_1 < |\lambda_i|$, there exists a positive integer m such that $H^{-m} > [0]$, where $H^{-m} = (H^m)^{-1}$.
   (ii) Hence, derive a sufficient condition for relative instability of the model: $x(t+1) = Hx(t)$.

8. Prove that:

$x=(I-A+B)^{-1}\sum_{\tau=0}^{\infty}[B(I-A+B)^{-1}]^{\tau}(I+R)^{\tau}f$ is a particular solution of the open dynamic Leontief model, given by eqns [2], [7] and [8] of §5.3.3.
(Stone and Brown)

9. Examine the particular solutions of the open dynamic Leontief model in the case where $R=rI$, r a scalar.

10. Prove that a necessary condition for the convergence of eqn [24] of §5.3.3 is that $[B(I-A)^{-1}]^{\tau}R^{\tau}\rightarrow[0]$ as $\tau\rightarrow\infty$. Therefore, the largest root of R must be less than the smallest root of $(I-A)B^{-1}$.

11. How does the existence of a non-diagonal R affect the particular solutions derived for the open dynamic Leontief model?

12. Consider a closed Leontief-type dynamic model. The first h commodities are consumption goods only, the next $m-h$ are capital goods, the n-th commodity is labour. Given a one-period production lag, the basic balance equation is:

$$x(t)=Ax(t+1)+B(x(t+1)-x(t))$$

Suppose that A is indecomposable.
(i) Find the unique, positive balanced rate of growth.
(ii) Show that in equilibrium growth at rate γ, the following equation is satisfied:

$$p(t)'[A+rB-I/(1+\eta)]=\mathbf{0}'$$

where r is the rate of interest.
(iii) Prove that in equilibrium growth, there exists a positive price vector (unique up to scalar multiplication) iff $r=\gamma/(1+\gamma)$.
(iv) The assumption of a common rate of profit, ρ, implies:

$$p(t+1)'=(1+\rho)p(t)'(A+rB)$$

Using the result in (ii), derive:

$$p(t+1)=p(t).(1+\rho)/(1+\gamma).$$

§5.4

1. Consider the model of §§5.4.2–5.4.4. Aggregation over time is performed in §§5.4.3 and 5.4.4.

Now aggregate over sectors to reduce the multi-sectoral model to a one-sector model.

Let $\omega(t) = \sum_{i=1}^{n} w_i(t) = \sum_{i=1}^{n} y_i(t)$ be the national income at t

$\delta(t) = \sum_{i=1}^{n} d_i(t)$ be the value of autonomous expenditures at t

Write down the first n equations of [24] of §5.4.2.
Pre-multiplying by $\mathbf{1}'$. obtain:

$$\omega(t) = \sum_{\tau=1}^{s} \left[\sum_{j=1}^{n} c_j(t-\tau) y_j(t-\tau) \right] + \delta(t)$$

Now suppose that $c_j(t-\tau) = \gamma(t-\tau)$ for all j. Then, we obtain:

$$\omega(t) = \sum_{\tau=1}^{s} \gamma(t-\tau)\omega(t-\tau) + \delta(t)$$

Interpret and solve this equation.

2. Consider the following (multiplier–accelerator) model:

$$x(t) = c(t) + i(t) + f(t)$$
$$c(t) = \alpha x(t-1)$$
$$i(t) = \beta(x(t-1) - x(t-2))$$

Rewrite the model as a second-order difference equation in x, and then as a first-order matrix equation.
Using the theory of §4.2.9, examine the solution of the model or non-negativity over time.

3. (Continuation of Q2.) Suppose:

$$c(t) = \alpha_1 x(t-1) + \alpha_2 x(t-2)$$

the other equations remaining the same. Test the solution of this model for non-negativity over time.

4. Find conditions for non-negativity of the solution of the following model:

$$c(t) = \sum_{\tau=1}^{T} \alpha_\tau x(t-\tau)$$

$$i(t) = \sum_{\tau=1}^{T-1} \beta_\tau (x(t-\tau) - x(t-\tau-1))$$

$$x(t) = c(t) + i(t)$$

5. Consider the following model based on the capital stock adjustment principle:

$$c(t) = \alpha x(t-1) + \beta k(t-1)$$

$$i(t) = \gamma x(t-1) - \delta k(t-1)$$

$$k(t) = k(t-1) + i(t-1) - d(t)$$

$$d(t) = \varepsilon k(t-1)$$

where all the parameters are non-negative.
Derive:
(i) an equation for $k(t)$ in terms of $k(t-1)$ and $x(t-1)$;
(ii) an equation for $x(t)$ in terms of $k(t-1)$ and $x(t-1)$.
Find conditions for this model to exhibit non-negativity over time.

6. Consider the model of §5.4.6.
Suppose $a(t) = (1+g)^t a$. Find the particular solution of the model (investigate the conditions on g for relative stability).
Suppose that the economy is initially in dynamic equilibrium when there is a change in autonomous expenditures $(1+g)^t \Delta a$. What is the effect on the equilibrium path?
Find the equation expressing outputs on the "traverse" between equilibria?

7. (Continuation of Q6.) Show that the time required to achieve the "cross-effect" is given by:

$$t \geqslant 1 + (\log_e \delta)/(\log_e \gamma - \log_e (1+g))$$

and for the "straight-effect":

$$t \geqslant 1 + [\log_e \delta + \log_e \{\alpha_{jj}(1+g-\gamma+\beta_{jj} - \log_e \beta_{jj}\}]/[\log_e \gamma - \log_e (1+g)]$$

(Morishima-Kaneko)

8. Derive eqns [10] and [11] of §5.5.6 (by use of induction).

9. Interpret the following model of multi-country income propagation:

$$Y(t+1) = AY(t) + B(Y(t+1) - Y(t)) + (I+\hat{g})^t a$$

where $\hat{g} = [g_i \delta_{ij}]$ (cf. the model outlined in §5.4.5). Find a particular solution of this model (i.e. the super-multipliers), by rewriting the above equation as:

$$(I-B)Y(t+1) + [(I-A)-(I-B)]Y(t) = (I+g)^t a.$$

Derive the equation:

$$(I-F)K^j = [(1+g_j)\delta_{ij}] = (1+g_j)e^j,$$

where

$$F = A - g_j(I-B)$$

Consider the case where:

$b_{ii} > 1 - a_{ii}/g_i$, for all i

and

$\sum_i b_{ik} \leq 1 + (1 - \sum_i a_{ik})/g_i$, for all k.

Show that, under these conditions, F is a P-matrix. Derive the solution in this case.

10. Consider the homogeneous equation:

$$Y(t+1) = AY(t) + B(Y(t+1) - Y(t))$$

Prove that if $b_{ii} > 1$, for all i, the model is unstable. Relate this result to the instability results derived in §5.1 for Metzler models.

11. Examine the effects of changes in the structural parameters (i.e. the a_{ij} and b_{ij}) and in autonomous expenditures on the income vector Y.

12. Experiment with different lag structures in the model outlined in Q9. (A reference for questions 9–12 is the paper by Brown and Jones)

References

§5.1

Metzler, L. A.: "Underemployment equilibrium in international trade", *Econometrica*, **10** (1942). (This is referred to in the exercises as Metzler, 1942a.).

Metzler, L. A.: "The transfer problem reconsidered", *Journal of Political Economy*, **50** (1942). (This is referred to in the Exercises as Metzler, 1942b.)

Metzler, L. A.: "A multiple-region theory of income and trade", *Econometrica*, **18** (1950).

Metzler, L. A.: "A multiple-country theory of income transfers", *Journal of Political Economy*, **59** (1951).

These and Metzler's other papers are available in: The Collected Papers of Lloyd A. Metzler (Harvard U.P., 1973; volume 140 in the Harvard Economic Studies).

§5.2

Nikaido, H.: "Some dynamic phenomena in the Leontief model of reversely-lagged type", *Review of Economic Studies*, **29** (1962).

§5.3
§(5.3.1) & §(5.3.2)

Leontief, W. W.: "Dynamic analysis" in *Studies in the Structure of the American Economy* by W. W. Leontief et al., New York, Oxford U.P., 1953.

§(5.3.3)

Mathur, P. N.: "Output and investment for exponential growth in consumption – an alternative formulation and derivation of their technological upper limits", *Review of Economic Studies*, **31** (1964).

Mukerji, V.: "Output and investment for exponential growth in consumption – general solution and some comments", *Review of Economic Studies*, **31** (1964).

An empirical application of this theory is contained in: Barker, T. S.: "A maximum sustainable growth rate for British industrial outputs", *Review of Economic Studies*, **38** (1971).

Stone, R. & J. A. C. Brown: "Output and investment for exponential growth in consumption", *Review of Economic Studies*, **29** (1962).

§(5.3.4)

Jorgenson, D. W.: "A dual stability theorem", *Econometrica*, **28** (1960).

Solow, R. M.: "Competitive valuation in a dynamic input–output system", *Econometrica*, **27** (1959).

Other work that might be consulted includes:

Jorgenson, D. W.: "The stability of a dynamic input–output system", *Review of Economic Studies*, **28** (1961).

Leontief, W. W.: "The dynamic inverse" in *Contributions to Input-Output Analysis* (A. P. Carter & A. Brody, eds.), North-Holland, London, 1970.

McManus, M.: "Notes on Jorgenson's model", *Review of Economic Studies*, **30** (1963).

Sargan, J. D.: "The instability of the Leontief dynamic model", *Econometrica*, **26** (1958).

§5.4

Brown, M. & R. Jones: "Economic growth and the theory of international income flows", *Econometrica*, **30** (1962).

Morishima, M. & Y. Kaneko: "On the speed of establishing multi-sectoral equilibrium", *Econometrica*, **30** (1962).

§5.5

Hicks, J. R.: *Value and Capital*, Clarendon Press, 1946.

Samuelson, P. A.: *Foundations of Economic Analysis*, Harvard U.P., 1947.

6

Non-linear statics and dynamics

In Chapter 2, we were concerned with deriving, *inter alia*, the Hawkins–Simon theorem and the Perron–Frobenius theorem in our study of (linear) input–output models. In this chapter, we shall try to extend the theory to the non-linear case. In the search for meaningful solutions to a non-linear input–output model, we shall derive a generalised Hawkins–Simon theorem. The study of balanced growth under constant returns to scale seems to require a generalised Perron–Frobenius theorem.

In §6.1.1, we derive some results on linear inequalities. The inclusion of this material is justified on (at least) two grounds: first, it helps us to solve von Neumann's model in an elementary way (see Chapter 7); but, more immediately, it enables us to derive the Gale–Nikaido theorem (of §6.1.2), which in turn is basic to the generalised Hawkins–Simon theorem of §6.2.1. The factor price equalisation theorem (of §6.2.2) is, in some ways, similar to the generalised Hawkins–Simon theorem, as it is concerned with obtaining a unique non-negative solution to an equation such as $f(x)=c$; of course, the interpretation of the symbols differs between the two theorems.

In §6.3, we shall be concerned with non-linear generalisations of two types of problems discussed in Chapter 2: (i) characteristic root problems of non-negative matrices, $Ax=\lambda x$; (ii) postive resolvents, that is, the solution of $\alpha x = Ax + c$, $c \geqslant \mathbf{0}$, $A \geqslant [0]$. Using Brouwer's fixed point theorem, we derive a generalised Perron–Frobenius theorem, which we then apply to solve a closed production model. Armed with this generalised Perron–Frobenius theorem, we can then solve the non-linear resolvent equation; this is applied to the solution of an open model.

§6.1. Some theory on linear inequalities and the Gale-Nikaido theorem

§6.1.1. *Linear inequalities*

Let A be an arbitrary $m \times n$ real matrix.

Theorem 1: The pair of inequalities:

$$w'A \geqslant \mathbf{0}'$$
$$Ax = \mathbf{0}, \quad x \geqslant \mathbf{0} \qquad \cdots [1]$$

possess solutions w, x such that:

$$w'A^1 + x_1 > 0 \qquad \cdots [2]$$

(A^1 being the first column of A, x_1 the first component of x).

Proof: By induction.
Let $n = 1$. Then $A = A^1$. There are two cases to consider:
(i) $A = \mathbf{0}$. w is arbitrary. Put $x_1 > 0$.
(ii) $A \neq \mathbf{0}$. Put $w = A$, $x_1 = 0$.
Now suppose that the result holds for a matrix A with n columns. Let $\bar{A} = [A \quad A^{n+1}]$ be a matrix with $n+1$ columns. By the induction hypothesis:

$$w'A \geqslant \mathbf{0}'$$
$$Ax = \mathbf{0}$$

have solutions w, x such that $w'A^1 + x_1 > 0$.
We must now consider $w'A^{n+1}$. Again there are two cases to consider:
(i) If $w'A^{n+1} \geqslant 0$, then $w'\bar{A} \geqslant \mathbf{0}'$.
Define $\bar{x} = (x \quad 0)'$. Then we can easily see that:

$$\bar{A}\bar{x} = Ax + A^{n+1} \,.\, 0 = Ax = \mathbf{0}$$
$$\bar{x} = (x \quad 0)' \geqslant \mathbf{0}$$

As $\bar{x}$ and x have the same first component and $w'A^1 + x_1 > 0$ by hypothesis, it follows that we have:

$$w'\bar{A} \geqslant \mathbf{0}'$$
$$\bar{A}\bar{x} = \mathbf{0}, \quad \bar{x} \geqslant \mathbf{0}$$

have solutions w, $\bar{x}$ such that:

$$w'\bar{A}^1 + \bar{x}_1 > 0.$$

So the induction proof is complete for this case.
We now consider:
(ii) $w'A^{n+1} < 0$.
Define

$$\alpha_j = -w'A^j / w'A^{n+1}, \quad j = 1, \ldots, n \qquad \cdots [3]$$

As $w'A \geqslant \mathbf{0}'$, it follows that $\alpha_j \geqslant 0$.
Consider the matrix:

$$B = [A^1 + \alpha_1 A^{n+1} \ldots A^n + \alpha_n A^{n-1}] \qquad \cdots [4]$$

Then:

$$w'B^j = w'[A^j + \alpha_j A^{n+1}] = w'A^j - w'A^j \,.\, w'A^{n+1}/w'A^{n+1} = 0.$$

Hence

$$w'B = \mathbf{0}' \qquad \cdots [5]$$

So apply the result to the matrix B. Then the inequalities:

$$\begin{aligned} &y'B \geqslant \mathbf{0}' \\ &Bz = \mathbf{0}, \quad z \geqslant \mathbf{0} \end{aligned} \qquad \cdots [6]$$

have solutions y, z such that:

$$y'B^1 + z_1 > 0 \qquad \cdots [7]$$

Define

$$\bar{z} = \left(z \quad \sum_{j=1}^{n} \alpha_j z_j \right) \qquad \cdots [8]$$

Then

$$\bar{A}\bar{z} = [A \quad A^{n+1}]\bar{z} = [A \quad A^{n+1}] \begin{bmatrix} z \\ \sum_{j=1}^{n} \alpha_j z_j \end{bmatrix}$$

$$= Az + \sum_{j=1}^{n} \alpha_j A^{n+1} z_j$$

$$= Bz = \mathbf{0} \text{ from eqn [6].}$$

Also $\bar{z} \geqslant \mathbf{0}$ as $z \geqslant \mathbf{0}$ and $\alpha_j \geqslant 0$ for all j.
Now define:

$$u = y + \beta w \qquad \cdots [9]$$

where

$$\beta = -y'A^{n+1}/w'A^{n+1} \qquad \cdots [10]$$

Then

$$\begin{aligned} u'A^{n+1} &= (y + \beta w)'A^{n+1} \\ &= y'A^{n+1} - y'A^{n+1} \,.\, w'A^{n+1}/w'A^{n+1} = 0 \end{aligned} \qquad \cdots [11]$$

Hence:

$$u'A = u'B \qquad \cdots [12]$$

using eqn [11]

Now

$$u'\bar{A} = u'[A \quad A^{n+1}] = u'A \text{ again using eqn [11]}$$
$$= u'B \text{ using eqn [12]}$$
$$= y'B + w'B = y'B \text{ using eqn [5]}$$
$$\geqslant \mathbf{0} \text{ using eqn [6].}$$

Also

$$u'\bar{A}^1 = u'A^1 = u'B^1 = y'B^1.$$

Hence

$$u'\bar{A}^1 + z_1 = y'B^1 + z_1 > 0 \text{ from eqn [7].}$$

So the inequalities:

$$u'\bar{A} \geqslant \mathbf{0}'$$
$$\bar{A}z = \mathbf{0}, \quad z \geqslant \mathbf{0}$$

have solutions u, z such that:

$$u'\bar{A}^1 + z_1 > 0.$$

This completes the induction proof for the second case. The theorem is now proved.

We may strengthen the result of Theorem 1 to:

Theorem 2: The pair of inequalities:

$$w'A \geqslant \mathbf{0}' \qquad \cdots [13]$$
$$Ax = \mathbf{0}, \quad x \geqslant \mathbf{0}$$

have solutions w, x such that:

$$w'A + x' > \mathbf{0}' \qquad \cdots [14]$$

Proof: By renumbering, any column of A can perform the role of A^1 in Theorem 1. So there exist pairs w^j, x^j such that:

$$w^{j\prime}A \geqslant \mathbf{0}' \qquad \cdots [15]$$
$$Ax^j = \mathbf{0}, \quad x^j \geqslant \mathbf{0}$$

imply:

$$w^{j\prime}A^j + x_j^j > 0 \quad (x_j^j \text{ being the } j\text{-th component of } x^j) \qquad \cdots [16]$$

Define:

$$w = \sum_{j=1}^{n} w^j, \quad x = \sum_{j=1}^{n} x^j \qquad \cdots [17]$$

Then

$$w'A = \sum_{j=1}^{n} w^{j\prime}A \geqslant \mathbf{0}'$$

$$Ax = \sum_{j=1}^{n} Ax^j = \mathbf{0} \qquad \cdots [18]$$

$$x \geqslant \mathbf{0}$$

using [15] and [16].

$$w'A^j + x_j = \sum_{i=1}^{n} (w^{i\prime}A^j + x_j^i)$$

$$\geq w^{j\prime}A^j + x_j^j \text{ using [15]}$$

$$> 0 \text{ using [16].}$$

Hence $w'A + x' > \mathbf{0}'$ as required.

Corollary (Stiemke): $Ax = \mathbf{0}$ has solution:

(i) $x > \mathbf{0}$ if there does not exist w such that $w'A \geq \mathbf{0}'$;
(ii) $x \geq \mathbf{0}$ if there does not exist w such that $w'A > \mathbf{0}'$.

Proof: From Theorem 2, there exist w, x such that:

$$w'A \geqslant \mathbf{0}', \quad Ax = \mathbf{0}, \quad x \geqslant \mathbf{0}$$

imply $\cdots$ [19]

$$w'A + x' > \mathbf{0}'$$

If there does not exist w such that $w'A \geq \mathbf{0}'$ (i.e. if $w'A = \mathbf{0}'$), then $x > \mathbf{0}$. Hence (i).
If $w'A \geq \mathbf{0}'$ (i.e. $w'A \not> \mathbf{0}'$), then from [19], it is evident that $x \geq \mathbf{0}$. Hence (ii).

This corollary will be used later in this section. Our next theorem is the one to be used in Chapter 7 when we consider von Neumann's model.

Theorem 3: The inequalities:

$$y'C \geqslant \mathbf{0}', \quad y \geqslant \mathbf{0}$$
$$-Cz \geqslant \mathbf{0}, \quad z \geqslant \mathbf{0} \qquad \cdots [20]$$

have solutions y, z such that:

$$y - Cz > \mathbf{0}, \quad y'C + z' > \mathbf{0}'. \qquad \cdots [21]$$

Proof: Let $[I \quad C]$ be the matrix A in Theorem 2.

From the theorem, we know that:

$$w'[I \quad C] \geqslant \mathbf{0}'$$

$$[I \quad C]\begin{bmatrix} u \\ v \end{bmatrix} = \mathbf{0}, \quad \begin{bmatrix} u \\ v \end{bmatrix} \geqslant \mathbf{0} \qquad \cdots [22]$$

have solutions w, u, v such that:

$$w'[I \quad C] + (u' \quad v') > \mathbf{0}' \qquad \cdots [23]$$

From eqns [22]:

$$\begin{aligned} &w \geqslant \mathbf{0}, \quad w'C \geqslant \mathbf{0}' \\ &-Cv = u \geqslant \mathbf{0} \end{aligned} \qquad \cdots [24]$$

From eqns [23]:

$$\begin{aligned} &w - Cv > \mathbf{0} \\ &w'C + v > \mathbf{0} \end{aligned} \qquad \cdots [25]$$

substituting for u from eqns [24].

Put $w = y$ and $v = z$ and we have eqns [21].

We now specialise to inequalities involving P-matrices. The remaining results in this section serve as lemmata to the Gale–Nikaido theorem to be derived in §6.1.2.

Theorem 4: If A is a P-matrix, the inequalities:

$$Ax \leqq \mathbf{0}, \quad x \geqslant \mathbf{0} \qquad \cdots [26]$$

imply $x = \mathbf{0}$.

Proof: By induction.
The result is evident for $n = 1$.
Suppose that the result is true for $n - 1$.
If A is a P-matrix, $A^{-1} = B = [b_{ij}]$ exists. $b_{11} > 0$, as it is the ratio of two principal minors of A, which we know are all positive. So B^1 has some positive components (where B^1 is the first column of B).
Let $\alpha = \min_i x_i/b_{i1}$, where we consider only those ratios for which $b_{i1} > 0$.
Suppose $\alpha = x_k/b_{k1}$. As $x \geqslant \mathbf{0}$, it follows that $\alpha \geqslant 0$. Let $y - \alpha B^1$. Then $y \geqslant \mathbf{0}$ with $y_k = 0$.

$$Ay = Ax - \alpha AB^1 = Ax - \alpha e^1 \leqslant \mathbf{0} \qquad \cdots [27]$$

Let $\bar{A}$ be the principal sub-matrix of A obtained by deleting the k-th row and column of A, $\bar{y}$ be the vector obtained from y by deleting the k-th component. Using eqn [27], we have:

$$\bar{A}\bar{y} \leqslant \mathbf{0}, \quad \bar{y} \geqslant \mathbf{0}.$$

By the induction hypothesis, $\bar{y} = \mathbf{0}$. As $y_k = 0$, we have $y = \mathbf{0}$. Then from eqn

[27], we have:

$$\mathbf{0} = Ax - \alpha e^1$$

or

$$Ax = \alpha e^1 \geqslant \mathbf{0} \qquad \cdots [28]$$

From eqn [28] and the first inequality of [26], we have $Ax = \mathbf{0}$. As A is non-singular, we have $x = \mathbf{0}$.

Theorem 5: Let A be a P-matrix. There exists a scalar $\gamma > 0$ such that for all $x \geqslant \mathbf{0}$, $\|x\| = 1$, some component of Ax is greater than or equal to γ.

Proof: Let $y = Ax$. Let $\gamma(x) = \max_i |y_i|$. $\gamma(x)$ is continuous. The set $S = \{x \geqslant \mathbf{0} : \|x\| = 1\}$ is compact. Hence $\gamma(x)$ attains its minimum, γ, on S. If $Ax \leqslant \mathbf{0}$, Theorem 4 implies $x = \mathbf{0}$. But $x \neq \mathbf{0}$. Hence $Ax \geqslant \mathbf{0}$ and $\gamma > 0$.

Finally, we have:

Theorem 6: If A is a P-matrix, the inequalities:

$$Ax > \mathbf{0}, \quad x > \mathbf{0} \qquad \cdots [29]$$

have a solution.

Proof: As A is a P-matrix, so is A'. Then, by Theorem 4, the inequalities:

$$A'p \leqslant \mathbf{0}, \quad p \geqslant \mathbf{0} \qquad \cdots [30]$$

imply $p = \mathbf{0}$.
The inequalities in [30] may be combined so that we have:

$$p'[I \quad -A] \geqslant \mathbf{0}' \text{ implies } p = \mathbf{0}, -p'A = \mathbf{0}'.$$

The matrix $[I \quad -A]$ plays the role of A in the Corollary (i).
Then by the Corollary (i), there exist $u > \mathbf{0}$, $x > \mathbf{0}$ such that:

$$[I \quad -A]\begin{bmatrix} u \\ x \end{bmatrix} = \mathbf{0}$$

i.e. $Ax = u > \mathbf{0}$, $x > \mathbf{0}$, as required.

§6.1.2. *The Gale–Nikaido theorem*

We shall assume that the proof of the following local univalence theorem is known.

Theorem 7: Let $f : R^n \to R^n$. Suppose that each component of f has continuous first order partial derivatives on the open set $S \subseteq R^n$, i.e. $f \in C^1$ on S. Let $T = f(S)$. Denote the Jacobian of f at x by $J_f(x)$. Suppose that $\det J_f(x^0) \neq 0$, for some $x^0 \in S$. Then there exists a uniquely determined function g and two open sets $X \subset S$, $Y \subset T$ such that:

(i) $x^0 \in X, f(x^0) \in Y$;
(ii) $Y = f(x)$;
(iii) f is 1–1 on X;
(iv) g is defined on Y, $g(Y) = X$, $g(f(x)) = x$, for all $x \in X$;
(v) $g \in C^1$ on Y.

For a proof consult Apostol (Theorem 7.5).

This theorem provides us with a sufficient condition for local univalence (or one-to-one-ness) of mappings. To find sufficient conditions for global univalence is a legitimate topic for enquiry.

Let $f(x) = c$ represent a non-linear input–output model. We are interested in deriving unique meaningful solutions, i.e. $x = f^{-1}(c) \geqslant \mathbf{0}$. The factor price equalisation theorem in international trade (to be discussed below) is concerned with obtaining a meaningful solution to a similar equation; however, the interpretation of the symbols is different, f being a cost function, c a vector of commodity prices, x a vector of factor prices.

We shall discuss these applications after we have derived the Gale–Nikaido theorem. First, a preliminary, the non-linear analogue of Theorem 4:

Theorem 8: Let $f : X \to R^n$, where $X = \{x : p \leqslant x \leqslant q\} \subset R^n$. Let $f \in C^1$. If $J_f(x)$ is a P-matrix for all $x \in X$, then for any $a, x \in X$, the inequalities:

$$f(x) \leqslant f(a), \quad x \geqslant a \qquad \cdots [1]$$

imply $x = a$.

Proof: Without loss of generality, we may suppose that $f(a) = \mathbf{0}$. Let Y denote the solution set of eqn [1]. By continuous differentiability, we have:

$$f_i(x) = f_i(a) + \sum_{j=1}^{n} f_{ij}(a) \,.\, (x_j - a_j) + \varepsilon_i(x - a) \qquad \cdots [2]$$

where

$$f_{ij}(a) = \partial f_i(a)/\partial x_j, \text{ for all } i, j = 1, \ldots, n$$

and

$$\varepsilon_i(x - a) \to 0 \quad \text{as} \quad x \to a.$$

Noting $f_i(a) = 0$, for all i, we have from eqn [2]:

$$\lim_{x \to a} \left[\frac{f(x)}{\|x - a\|} - J_f(a) \frac{(x - a)}{\|x - a\|} \right] = \mathbf{0} \qquad \cdots [3]$$

The vector $(x - a)/\|x - a\|$ has norm 1. As $J_f(a)$ is a P-matrix, we have from Theorem 5 that $J_f(a)(x - a)/\|x - a\|$ has a component greater than some positive constant for all $x \geqslant a$. Equation [3] implies that, in a neighbourhood

of a where $x \geqslant a$, $f(x)$ must have at least one positive component. Combining this with eqn [1], we see that $f(a)=\mathbf{0}$ is satisfied only by a in this neighbourhood.
Delete a from Y. Let the new set be $\bar{Y}$. $\bar{Y}$ is compact.
Suppose $\bar{Y} \neq \emptyset$. Then there exists a minimal element of $\bar{Y}$, say $\bar{x}$ such that $x \geqq \bar{x}$, for all $x \in \bar{Y}$. We consider two cases:
(i) $\bar{x} > a$. As $J_f(\bar{x})$ is a P-matrix, by Theorem 6 there exists $u < \mathbf{0}$ such that $J_f(\bar{x})u < \mathbf{0}$. As $\bar{x} > a$, we can choose $\gamma > 0$ but sufficiently small so that:

$$x(\gamma) = \bar{x} + \gamma u > a. \qquad \cdots [4]$$

Then $a < x(\gamma) < \bar{x}$. So, $x(\gamma) \in X$. Then by continuous differentiability:

$$\begin{aligned} f(x(\gamma)) &= f(\bar{x}) + J_f(\bar{x})(x(\gamma) - \gamma u) + \varepsilon(x(\gamma) - \gamma u) \\ &= f(\bar{x}) + \gamma J_f(\bar{x})u + \varepsilon(\gamma u) \end{aligned}$$

Dividing by $\gamma\|u\|$, we have:

$$\frac{f(x(\gamma)) - f(\bar{x})}{\gamma\|u\|} - J_f(\bar{x})\frac{u}{\|u\|}$$

can be made as small as we like by choosing sufficiently small positive values of γ. This implies that:

$$f(x(\gamma)) < f(\bar{x}) \leqslant f(a).$$

So, $x(\gamma) \in X$ which contradicts the definition of $\bar{x}$.
Therefore, $\bar{Y} = \emptyset$.
(ii) $\bar{x} \geqq a$, but $\bar{x} \not> a$.
Suppose $\bar{x}_1 = a_1$, renumbering if necessary. Define a new mapping

$$\phi : \bar{X} \to R^{n-1}$$

by

$$\phi_i(x_2, \ldots, x_n) = f_i(a_1, x_2, \ldots, x_n) \quad i = 2, \ldots, n \qquad \cdots [5]$$

where

$$\bar{X} = \{(x_2, \ldots, x_n) : p_i \leqslant x_i \leqslant q_i,\ i = 2, \ldots, n\}$$

J_ϕ is a P-matrix.

$$\begin{aligned} \phi_i(a_2, \ldots, a_n) &= 0 \text{ (as } f_i(a) = 0 \text{ by construction)} \\ &\geqslant \phi_i(x_2, \ldots, x_n) \text{ using eqn [1].} \end{aligned}$$

Then using induction, we have $a_i = x_i$, $i = 2, \ldots, n$. Hence $\bar{x} = a$. But $a \notin \bar{Y}$. So $\bar{Y} = \emptyset$.
The proof is now complete.

We can now derive the global univalence theorem.

Theorem 9: Let $f: X \to R^n$. Let $f \in C^1$. If $J_f(x)$ is a P-matrix for all $x \in X$, then f is univalent in X.

Proof: Let $a, b \in X$ such that $f(a) = f(b)$. Suppose:

$$a_i \leqslant b_i \text{ for } i \leqslant k; \qquad a_i \geqslant b_i \text{ for } i > k, \qquad \cdots [6]$$

renumbering if necessary. If $k = n$, we have $a \leqslant b$ and $f(a) = f(b)$ which implies by Theorem 8 that $a = b$. Likewise $k = 0$.
So, suppose $0 < k < n$. Define the new mapping $F: R^n \to R^n$ by

$$F(x_1, \ldots, x_n) = (x_1, \ldots, x_k, -x_{k+1}, \ldots, -x_n) \qquad \cdots [7]$$

Evidently, F is 1–1 and $F^{-1} = F$. $F(X)$ is a closed rectangular region. Let:

$$F(a) = \bar{a}, \quad F(b) = \bar{b}. \qquad \cdots [8]$$

Let $g: F(X) \to R^n$ be defined by $g = F^{-1}fF$.

$$g(\bar{a}) = F^{-1}fF(\bar{a}) = F^{-1}f(a)$$
$$g(\bar{b}) = F^{-1}fF(\bar{b}) = F^{-1}f(b)$$

As $f(a) = f(b)$, we have $g(\bar{a}) = g(\bar{b})$. Using eqns [7] and [8], $\bar{a} \leqslant \bar{b}$. Also, J_g is a P-matrix as it is obtained from J_f by multiplying the last $n-k$ rows and columns by -1; this operation does not affect the signs of principal minors.
Applying Theorem 8:

$$g(\bar{a}) = g(\bar{b}), \ \bar{b} \geqslant \bar{a} \text{ implies } \bar{b} = \bar{a}.$$

Hence $b = a$ and we have global univalence.

Of interest is the sub-class of functions yielding Jacobians with non-positive off-diagonal elements. For here, not only global univalence but also monotonicity obtains.

Theorem 10: Under the same hypotheses as Theorem 9, if in addition we have $f_{ij}(x) \leqslant 0$ for all $x \in X$, then $f(a) \leqslant f(b)$ implies $a \leqslant b$, $a, b \in X$.

Proof: By induction.
The result is evident for $n = 1$.
If $f(a) \leqslant f(b)$, then $a_k \leqslant b_k$, for some k, by Theorem 8. Let $k = 1$, renumbering if necessary. As $f_{i1} \leqslant 0$ for $i \neq 1$, we have:

$$f_i(b_1, a_2, \ldots, a_n) \leqslant f_i(a_1, a_2, \ldots, a_n) \leqslant f_i(b_1, b_2, \ldots, b_n) \qquad \cdots [9]$$

Define $\theta: \bar{X} \to R^{n-1}$ by

$$\theta_i(x_2, \ldots, x_n) = f_i(b_1, x_2, \ldots, x_n) \qquad i = 2, \ldots, n \qquad \cdots [10]$$

where $\bar{X}$ is as defined in Theorem 8.
Using eqn [9], $\theta(a_2, \ldots, a_n) \leqslant \theta(b_2, \ldots, b_n)$.
As J_θ is a P-matrix, we have by the induction hypothesis $a_i \leqslant b_i$, $i = 2, \ldots, n$. As $a_1 \leqslant b_1$, we have $a \leqslant b$, as required.

§6.2. Non-linear statics

In §6.2.1, we shall consider a non-linear generalisation of the input–output model of Chapter 2. In §6.2.2, we branch into international trade theory to discuss the factor price equalisation theorem.

§6.2.1. *Non-linear input-output*

In this section, we generalise the static input–output model of Chapter 2, the basic balance equation of which is:

$$x_i = \sum_{j=1}^{n} X_{ij} + c_i \quad i = 1, \ldots, n \qquad \cdots [1]$$

Assuming:

$$X_{ij} = a_{ij} x_j \qquad \cdots [2]$$

for all i, j, where a_{ij} are constants, we obtain:

$$x_i = \sum_{j=1}^{n} a_{ij} x_j + c_i \quad i = 1, \ldots, n \qquad \cdots [3]$$

Now suppose that we generalise eqn [2] thus:

$$X_{ij} = X_{ij}(x_j) \text{ for all } i, j \qquad \cdots [4]$$

i.e. the inter-sectoral flow, X_{ij}, depends in general, in a non-linear way on x_j. So eqn [3] becomes:

$$x_i = \sum_{j=1}^{n} X_{ij}(x_j) + c_i \qquad \cdots [5]$$

Let:

$$X_i(x) = \sum_{j=1}^{n} X_{ij}(x_j), \qquad X(x) = [X_1(x)] \qquad i = 1, \ldots, n \qquad \cdots [6]$$

So eqn [5] is: $x - X(x) = c$

or

$$f(x) = c \quad \text{where} \quad f(x) = x - X(x) \qquad \cdots [7]$$

We shall impose the following conditions on $X_{ij}(x_j)$:

$$X_{ij}(0) = 0 \qquad \cdots [8]$$

$$X_{ij}(x_j) \in C^1 \quad \text{on} \quad R(0, +) \qquad \cdots [9]$$

$$X'_{ij}(0) \geqslant X'_{ij}(x_j) \geqslant 0 \quad \text{for all} \quad x_j \in R(0, +)$$

where

$$X'_{ij}(x_j) = \frac{dX_{ij}}{dx_j}. \qquad \cdots [10]$$

Concave functions satisfy eqn [10], including the linear input–output model of Chapter 2.

We now enquire into the conditions for a meaningful solution of eqn [7]. The basic result is the following generalised Hawkins–Simon theorem due to Sandberg.

Theorem 11: Under conditions [8]–[10]:
(i) $f(x) = c$ has a unique meaningful solution;
(ii) $f^{-1}(c) = Ac + \delta(c), \dfrac{\|\delta(c)\|}{\|c\|} \to 0$ as $\|c\| \to 0$

iff $J_f(\mathbf{0})$ is a P-matrix.

Proof: *Sufficiency:* From eqn [7],

$$J_f(x) = [\delta_{ij} - X'_{ij}(x_j)] \qquad \cdots [11]$$

From eqn [10],

$$-X'_{ij}(x_j) \geqslant -X'_{ij}(0) \text{ for all } i, j \qquad \cdots [12]$$

$J_f(\mathbf{0})$ is a P-matrix. From eqn [12], $J_f(x) \geqq J_f(\mathbf{0})$. So from §2.4.2 (in particular, Exercises §2.4, Q2 (i)), it follows that $J_f(x)$ is also a P-matrix for all $x \in R^n(0, +)$ (in fact, $J_f(x)$ is an M-matrix).
Using Theorems 8 and 10, we may derive $f(x) \geqslant \mathbf{0}$, for all $x \geqslant \mathbf{0}$.
There are two cases to consider:
(i) $f(x) \leqq \mathbf{0}$, $x \geqq \mathbf{0}$.
Theorem 8 immediately implies $x = \mathbf{0}$.
(ii) $f_i(x) \geqslant 0$, for $i = 1, \ldots, k$; $f_i(x) < -\kappa < 0$ for $i = k+1, \ldots, n$. $x \geqslant \mathbf{0}$. Let $\{x(\nu)\}$ be a decreasing sequence of vectors such that $\lim_{\nu \to \infty} x(\nu) = \mathbf{0}$.
Theorem 10 implies that $f(x(\nu+1)) \leqslant f(x(\nu))$ for $x(\nu+1) \leqslant x(\nu)$. By continuity, $f(x(\nu)) \to \mathbf{0}$. However, $f_i(x(\nu)) < -\kappa$, for all ν and for $i = k+1, \ldots, n$.
So, $f(x)$ cannot have negative components.
It remains to establish that $f(x) = c$ has a unique meaningful solution for any $c \geqslant \mathbf{0}$. To this end, let us extend the mapping f to the domain $S = \{x \in R^n : x > -\alpha\mathbf{1}, \alpha > 0 \text{ and arbitrary}\}$. Denote the extended mapping by h, where:

$$h_i(x) = \left\{x_i - \sum_{j=1}^{n} Y_{ij}(x_j)\right\} \qquad i = 1, \ldots, n \qquad \cdots [13]$$

where:

$$\begin{aligned} Y_{ij}(x_j) &= X_{ij}(x_j) \text{ for all } x_j \geqslant 0 \\ Y'_{ij}(x_j) &= X'_{ij}(0) \text{ for all } x_j \in (-\alpha, 0) \end{aligned} \qquad \cdots [14]$$

$J_h(x)$ is a P-matrix, in fact an M-matrix, for all $x \in S$; so, we have global univalence.

Let $c > \mathbf{0}$. By continuous differentiability, we have:

$$h(x) = c = h(\mathbf{0}) + J_h(\mathbf{0})x + \varepsilon(\|x\|) \quad \cdots [15]$$

Choosing c sufficiently small, we have:

$$\mathbf{0} < c - \varepsilon(\|x\|) = J_h(\mathbf{0})x \quad \cdots [16]$$

As $J_h(\mathbf{0})$ is an M-matrix, its inverse is semi-positive.
Hence $x > \mathbf{0}$, i.e. $f(x) = c > \mathbf{0}$ has a unique solution $x > \mathbf{0}$.
By Theorem 10, $f(x) = c$, $f(\bar{x}) = \bar{c}$, $\bar{c} \geqslant c$ imply $\bar{x} \geqslant x > \mathbf{0}$.
The semi-positive case (i.e. $c \geqslant \mathbf{0}$, but not $c > \mathbf{0}$) has already been dealt with above.
So f is a continuous 1–1 mapping from $R^n(0, +)$ to itself, with $\det J_f(\mathbf{0}) \neq 0$.
So f^{-1} exists.
$h \in C^1$ at $\mathbf{0} \in S$ with $\det J_h(\mathbf{0}) \neq 0$. The hypotheses of Theorem 7 are satisfied.
So there exist open sets U, V in neighbourhoods of $\mathbf{0}$ on the domain and range spaces of h respectively and a unique function g such that:

(a) $\mathbf{0} \in U$, $h(\mathbf{0}) = \mathbf{0} \in V$;
(b) $V = h(U)$;
(c) h is 1–1 on U;
(d) g is defined on V, $g(V) = U$, $g(h(x)) = x$, for all $x \in U$;
(e) $g \in C^1$ on V.

The Jacobian of g is $(J_h)^{-1}$.
$h(u) = v$ is satisfied by:

$$u = (J_h(\mathbf{0}))^{-1}v + \delta(v), \qquad u \in U, \qquad v \in V \quad \cdots [17]$$

and

$$\|\delta(v)\|/\|v\| \to 0 \quad \text{as} \quad \|v\| \to 0.$$

As J_h is a P-matrix, $u \in S$ and $h(u) - h(\mathbf{0}) \geqslant \mathbf{0}$ imply $u \geqslant \mathbf{0}$, from Theorem 10.
So, for all $c \in U \cap R^n(0, +)$, we have:

$$f^{-1}(c) = (J_f(\mathbf{0}))^{-1}c + \delta(c) \quad \cdots [18]$$

Put $(J_f(\mathbf{0}))^{-1} = A$, and we have the required result.
Necessity: Suppose $f^{-1} : R^n(0, +) \to R^n(0, +)$ exists and

$$f^{-1}(c) = Ac + \delta(c), \text{ where } \|\delta(c)\|/\|c\| \to 0 \text{ as } \|c\| \to 0. \quad \cdots [19]$$

As $h \in C^1$ at $\mathbf{0}$, there exists a neighbourhood of $\mathbf{0}$, denoted by $U \subset S$ such that for all $u \in U$:

$$h(u) = J_h(\mathbf{0})u + \eta(u), \|\eta(u)\|/\|u\| \to 0 \quad \text{as} \quad u \to 0 \quad \cdots [20]$$

Choose $\omega > 0$ such that $c \in R^n(0, +)$ and $\|c\| < \omega$ imply

$$f^{-1}(c) \in U \cap R^n(0, +) \quad \cdots [21]$$

Then for all $c \in R^n(0, +)$ such that $0 < \|c\| < \omega$, we have:

$$c = h(f^{-1}(c))$$
$$= J_h(\mathbf{0})[Ac + \delta(c)] + \eta(Ac + \delta(c)) \text{ using eqns [19] and [20]}$$

or

$$(I - J_h(\mathbf{0})A)c = J_h(\mathbf{0})\delta(c) + \eta(Ac + \delta(c))$$

or

$$(I - J_h(\mathbf{0})A)\frac{c}{\|c\|} = J_h(\mathbf{0})\frac{\delta(c)}{\|c\|} + \frac{\eta(Ac + \delta(c))}{\|c\|} \qquad \cdots [22]$$

The right-hand side of eqn [22] tends to $\mathbf{0}$ as $\|c\|$ tends to 0. Hence:

$$I - J_h(\mathbf{0})A = [0]$$

or

$$I - J_f(\mathbf{0})A = [0] \quad \text{as} \quad J_h(\mathbf{0}) = J_f(\mathbf{0})$$

So $I = J_f(\mathbf{0})A$, which implies $(J_f(\mathbf{0}))^{-1} = A$.
Suppose $(J_f(\mathbf{0}))^{-1}$ has a negative component, say in the j-th column. Then, putting $c = \alpha e^i$, $\alpha < \omega$, we have:
$f^{-1}(c) \geqslant \mathbf{0}$ by hypothesis, but $Ac + \delta(c) \leqslant \mathbf{0}$ from eqn [19].
The resulting contradiction implies that $(J_f(\mathbf{0}))^{-1} \geqslant [0]$.
Given the sign conditions on the elements of $J_f(x)$, it follows that $J_f(\mathbf{0})$ is a P-matrix.
This completes the proof of the theorem.

The result just derived is the non-linear analogue of Theorem 1 of Chapter 2. If we are prepared to introduce indecomposability assumptions, we have the non-linear analogue of Theorem 2 of Chapter 2.

Theorem 12: Let $f(x) = c$, $f(y) = d$, $d \geqslant c$. If $J_f(\mathbf{0})$ is a P-matrix and $J_f(x)$ is indecomposable, then $y > x$.

Proof: We have by continuous differentiability:

$$f^{-1}(c + z) = f^{-1}(c) + (J_f(x))^{-1}z + \varepsilon(z)$$

where $\|\varepsilon(z)\|/\|z\| \to 0$ as $\|z\| \to 0$, for all $z \in R^n(0, +)$.
As $J_f(x)$ is indecomposable, it follows from Exercises §2.3, Q1 (iii) that $(J_f(x))^{-1} > [0]$.
Let $z = \alpha(d - c)$, where $\alpha \in (0, 1)$.
Then $f^{-1}(c + \alpha(d - c)) > f^{-1}(c)$.
As $d \geqslant c + \alpha(d - c)$, we have, using Theorem 10:

$$f^{-1}(d) \geqslant f^{-1}(c + \alpha(d - c)) > f^{-1}(c)$$

Substituting $f^{-1}(c) = x$, $f^{-1}(d) = y$, we have $y > x$, as required.

We can also derive the non-linear analogues of the comparative statics results in Theorems 79 and 80 of Chapter 2. We begin with:

Theorem 13: Let $f(x)=c\geqslant\mathbf{0}$, $f(y)=c+\gamma e^k$, $\gamma>0$. Let $J_f(x)$ be indecomposable. Then:
(i) $x>\mathbf{0}$; (ii) if $X_{ij}(\alpha x_j)\geqslant\alpha X_{ij}(x_j)$, for all $\alpha\in(0,1)$, for all $x_j\geqslant 0$, for all i, j, we have:

$y_k/x_k \geqslant y_i/x_i > 1$, for all i.

Proof:
(i) follows from Theorem 12.
(ii) From Theorem 12, $y>x$ or

$$x_i=\beta_i y_i\ \beta_i\in(0,1) \text{ for all } i \quad\cdots[23]$$

Let

$$\beta_0=\min\beta_i; \qquad I=\{i:\beta_i=\beta_0\} \quad\cdots[24]$$

$\beta_0<\beta_k$ from eqn [24]. $\quad\cdots$[25]

Let $i\in I$. Then we have:

$$x_i=\sum_{j=1}^{n} X_{ij}(x_j)+c_i \quad\cdots[26]$$

$$y_i=\sum_{j=1}^{n} X_{ij}(y_j)+c_i \quad\cdots[27]$$

Using eqn [23] in eqn [26], we have:

$$\beta_i y_i=\sum_{j=1}^{n} X_{ij}(\beta_j y_j)+c_i \quad\cdots[28]$$

Multiplying eqn [27] by β_i:

$$\beta_i y_i=\sum_{j=1}^{n} \beta_i X_{ij}(y_j)+\beta_i c_i \quad\cdots[29]$$

From the right-hand sides of eqns [28] and [29], we have:

$$\sum_{j\in I} X_{ij}(\beta_0 y_j)+\sum_{j\notin I} X_{ij}(\beta_j y_j)+c_i=\sum_{j\in I}\beta_0 X_{ij}(y_j)+\sum_{j\notin I}\beta_0 X_{ij}(y_j)+\beta_0 c_i \quad\cdots[30]$$

as $\beta_i=\beta_0$, $i\in I$.
From the hypothesis $X_{ij}(\alpha x_j)\geqslant\alpha X_{ij}(x_j)$:

$$\sum_{j\in I} X_{ij}(\beta_0 y_j)\geqslant\sum_{j\in I}\beta_0 X_{ij}(y_j) \quad\cdots[31]$$

Using eqn [31] in eqn [30], we obtain:

$$\sum_{j\notin I}[X_{ij}(\beta_j y_j)-\beta_0 X_{ij}(y_j)]+c_i(1-\beta_0)\leqslant 0 \quad\cdots[32]$$

Again using the hypothesis, this time in eqn [32], we obtain:

$$\sum_{j \notin I} (\beta_j - \beta_0) X_{ij}(y_j) + c_i(1 - \beta_0) \leq 0 \qquad \cdots [33]$$

For $j \notin I$, $\beta_j > \beta_0$. As $\beta_0 < 1$, $c_i \geq 0$, $X_{ij}(y_j) \geq 0$, for all i, j, we have in fact from eqn [33]:

$X_{ij}(y_j) = 0 \quad$ for all $\quad i \in I, j \in I.$

Hence

$X'_{ij}(0) = 0 \quad$ for all $\quad i \in I, j \in I.$

From eqn [10],

$X'_{ij}(x_j) = 0 \quad$ for all $\quad i \in I, j \in I.$

Therefore $J_f(x)$ is decomposable for all x. This contradicts the hypothesis of the theorem. Therefore:
$y_k/x_k \geq y_i/x_i > 1$, for all i, as required.

Our final result in this section is:

Theorem 14: Under the same hypotheses as the previous theorem, we have:

$$e_{ik} = (c_k/\gamma) \,.\, (y_i - x_i)/x_i \leq 1 \text{ for all } i \qquad \cdots [34]$$

Proof: From Theorem 13, $\beta_i \geq \beta_k$, for all i.

$$x_k = \sum_j X_{kj}(x_j) + c_k \qquad \cdots [35]$$

$$y_k = \sum_j X_{kj}(y_j) + c_k + \gamma \qquad \cdots [36]$$

Using eqn [23] in eqn [35], we obtain:

$$\beta_k y_k = \sum_j X_{kj}(\beta_j y_j) + c_k \qquad \cdots [37]$$

Multiplying eqn [36] by β_k:

$$\beta_k y_k = \sum_j \beta_k X_{kj}(y_j) + \beta_k(c_k + \gamma) \qquad \cdots [38]$$

Suppose $c_k > \beta_k(c_k + \gamma)$. From eqn [38], we have, using $\beta_j \geq \beta_k$, for all j,

$$\beta_k y_k < \sum_j \beta_j X_{kj}(y_j) + c_k \qquad \cdots [39]$$

Now using the hypothesis $X_{ij}(\alpha x_j) \geq \alpha X_{ij}(x_j)$, we have from eqn [39]:

$$\beta_k y_k < \sum_j X_{kj}(\beta_j y_j) + c_k \qquad \cdots [40]$$

Eqn [40] plainly contradicts eqn [37]. So we have:

$$c_k \leqslant \beta_k(c_k + \gamma) \qquad \cdots [41]$$

whence

$$(c_k/\gamma) \cdot (1-\beta_k)/\beta_k \leqslant 1 \qquad \cdots [42]$$

Using eqn [23], [42] may be written as:

$$(c_k/\gamma) \cdot (y_k - x_k)/x_k \leqslant 1 \qquad \cdots [43]$$

From Theorem 13, $\beta_i \geqslant \beta_k$, for all i. So

$$1 > \beta_i \geqslant \beta_k > 0 \qquad \cdots [44]$$

$$\begin{aligned} e_{ik} &= (c_k/\gamma) \cdot (y_i - x_i)/x_i \\ &= (c_k/\gamma) \cdot (1-\beta_i)/\beta_i \\ &\leqslant \beta_k/(1-\beta_k) \cdot (1-\beta_i)/\beta_i \quad \text{using eqn [42],} \end{aligned}$$

i.e.

$e_{ik} \leqslant 1$, for all i, using eqn [44], as required.

§6.2.2. *Factor price equalisation*

1. Free trade equalises commodity prices, but does it also equalise factor prices without international factor movements? Consider a world in which there are n commodities and also n factors; joint production and externalities are assumed away; there are no international differences in technology and all commodities are produced.
Let p denote a vector of commodity prices, w a vector of factor prices.
Let $a_{ij}(w)$ denote the input of factor i per unit of output of commodity j.

If we hypothesise in addition that each country has a strictly convex, compact production set, then, given $w > \mathbf{0}$, there exists a unique, continuous, cost-minimising input vector:

$A^j(w) = (a_{1j}(w), \ldots, a_{nj}(w))'$ (see §8.1.2 below)

We may write:

$$c_j(w) = \sum_{i=1}^{n} w_i a_{ij}(w) \qquad \cdots [1]$$

The a_{ij} satisfy:

$$\sum_{i=1}^{n} w_i \partial a_{ij}(w)/\partial w_k = 0 \qquad \cdots [2]$$

In a competitive equilibrium with all goods produced, we have:

$$p_j = c_j(w)$$

or

$$p = c(w) \qquad \cdots [3]$$

Given the assumption of no international differences in technology, the question of factor price equalisation resolves itself into one of uniqueness of solution of eqn [3], i.e. given p, does eqn [3] have a unique solution, w?

Samuelson (1953) asserted that, if the upper left-hand principal minors of the Jacobian matrix, $J_c(w)$, did not vanish in a region, global univalence obtained in that region. Gale and Nikaido (1965) cast doubt on this conjecture—indeed, the Samuelson assertion stimulated the derivation of the Gale–Nikaido theorem (Theorem 9 above), which is sufficient for global univalence (in our case under discussion here, for factor price equalisation). Before we go further, let us examine the Jacobian matrix, $J_c(w)$:

$$\partial p_j/\partial w_k = c_{jk} = a_{kj} + \sum_{i=1}^{n} w_i \partial a_{ij}/\partial w_k = a_{kj}, \quad \text{for all } k, j, \text{ using eqn [2].} \qquad \cdots [4]$$

McKenzie (1960) has suggested for discussion the case in which $J_c(w) = A'$ has a dominant diagonal. As the elements of A' are non-negative (in particular, the diagonal elements are positive), this is certainly sufficient to ensure that A' is a P-matrix. Diagonal dominance of A' can be interpreted as meaning that with each commodity there can be associated one factor that is uniquely important (or intensive) in the production of that commodity.

Let us pursue this in the 2×2 case. If the elements of the Jacobian matrix satisfy:

$$a_{11}(w)/a_{21}(w) > a_{12}(w)/a_{22}(w) \quad \text{for all } w \qquad \cdots [5]$$

we may say that the first (second) factor is intensive in the production of the first (second) commodity. (A renumbering of either factors or goods would yield the reverse inequality in [5]; without loss of generality, we consider only [5].) It follows immediately from [5] that $\det J_c(w) > 0$ and hence that $J_c(w)$ is a P-matrix. So, under the assumption of no factor reversals, i.e. inequality [5], we have factor price equalisation in the 2×2 case.

2. Maintaining this assumption of no factor reversals, we have:

$$(J_c(w))^{-1} = 1/\det J_c(w) \begin{bmatrix} a_{22}(w) & -a_{21}(w) \\ -a_{12}(w) & a_{22}(w) \end{bmatrix} \qquad \cdots [6]$$

We may now derive the Stolper–Samuelson theorem, which states that a rise in the price of a good implies a rise in the price of its associated factor (i.e. that factor intensive in the production of the good), a fall in the price of the other factor. This result follows immediately from eqns [3] and [6].

3. We shall now discuss extensions of the Stolper–Samuelson theorem to the $n\times n$ case and its relation to the factor price equalisation theorem. We shall find it convenient to conduct the analysis in terms of:

$s_{ij} = w_i a_{ij}/p_j$ for all i, j $\cdots$ [7]

rather than in terms of the a_{ij}. s_{ij} is evidently the share of the i-th factor in the cost of production of the j-th commodity. Let:

$S = [s_{ij}], \quad i, j = 1, \ldots, n; \quad S = \hat{p}^{-1} A \hat{w}$ $\cdots$ [8]

Note that:

$$\sum_{i=1}^{n} s_{ij} = 1/p_j \sum_{i=1}^{n} w_i a_{ij} = p_j/p_j = 1$$

i.e. S' is a stochastic matrix.

Ex: 1. Show that the transformation of variables, ([7] in para. 3. §6.2.2), arises naturally if we decide to work in terms of $\log_e p = (\log_e p_i)$ and $\log_e w = (\log_e w_i)$.

2. Prove that S^{-1} has the sign pattern $\begin{bmatrix} + & - \\ - & + \end{bmatrix}$ iff $s_{11}/s_{21} > s_{12}/s_{22}$.

4.

4.1. In attempting to generalise the 2×2 case, we shall seek conditions on the matrix S (defined in para 3, §6.2.2) which imply that $s_{11}/s_{21} > s_{12}/s_{22}$ if $n = 2$, and that S^{-1} has positive diagonal elements, negative off-diagonal elements; then, we shall be able to state that an increase in the price of commodity j implies an increase in the price of its associated factor, a fall in all other factor prices.

4.2. We can derive the following result due to Chipman.

Suppose S^{-1} has positive diagonal elements, negative off-diagonal elements (call these sign conditions the SS-conditions). Then S is a P-matrix.

Proof: The proof is similar to that of the Hawkins–Simon theorem of Chapter 2.

Let $B = S^{-1}$ to simplify the notation. Then:

$BS = I$ $\cdots$ [9]

Let $c > \mathbf{0}$. Then:

$Bd = c > \mathbf{0}, \quad d = Sc > \mathbf{0}$ $\cdots$ [10]

By the Hawkins–Simon theorem, B is a P-matrix. From eqn [9], we have: $\det B \cdot \det S = 1$, which implies $\det S > 0$.

To derive the result, we have to demonstrate that each principal sub-matrix of S of order $n-1$ is a P-matrix. Consider, without loss of generality, that sub-matrix obtained by deleting the first row and column of S; denote this sub-matrix by $\bar{S}$. Following the proof of the Hawkins–Simon theorem, pre-multiply $BS = I$ by

$$C = \begin{bmatrix} 1 & 0 & \cdots & 0 \\ -b_{21}/b_{11} & 1 & \cdots & 0 \\ \cdot & & \cdot & \cdot \\ \cdot & & \cdot & \cdot \\ \cdot & & \cdot & \cdot \\ -b_{n1}/b_{11} & 0 & \cdots & 1 \end{bmatrix} \qquad \cdots [11]$$

Note that $b_{11} > 0$, as B is a P-matrix. We obtain:

$$\begin{bmatrix} b_{11} & b_{12} & \cdots & b_{1n} \\ 0 & & & \\ \cdot & & \bar{B} & \\ \cdot & & & \\ \cdot & & & \\ 0 & & & \end{bmatrix} \begin{bmatrix} s_{11} & s_{12} & \cdots & s_{1n} \\ s_{21} & & & \\ \cdot & & \bar{S} & \\ \cdot & & & \\ \cdot & & & \\ s_{n1} & & & \end{bmatrix} = C \qquad \cdots [12]$$

From eqns [11] and [12], we have:

$$\bar{B}\bar{S} = I_{n-1} \quad \text{where} \quad \bar{B} = [\bar{b}_{ij}], \qquad i, j = 2, \ldots, n \qquad \cdots [13]$$

and

$$\bar{b}_{ij} = b_{ij} - b_{i1}b_{1j}/b_{11} \qquad \cdots [14]$$

Given the sign conditions, $\bar{b}_{ij} < 0$, for all $i \neq j$, $\bar{b}_{ii} > 0$, for all $i, j = 2, \ldots, n$. The result now follows immediately by induction, as in the Hawkins–Simon theorem.

Ex: 3. Prove that if S^{-1} has the sign pattern indicated in **4.2** (i.e. S satisfies the SS-conditions), then each diagonal element of S^{-1} is greater than 1. (The following is required: If S has unit column sums and S^{-1} exists, then S^{-1} also has unit column sums. $\mathbf{1}'S = \mathbf{1}'$ implies $\mathbf{1}' = \mathbf{1}'S^{-1}$).

4. Consider the matrix $S = \begin{bmatrix} 0{\cdot}55 & 0{\cdot}05 & 0{\cdot}25 \\ 0{\cdot}40 & 0{\cdot}50 & 0{\cdot}35 \\ 0{\cdot}05 & 0{\cdot}45 & 0{\cdot}40 \end{bmatrix}$

Show that S is a P-matrix, yet does not satisfy the SS-conditions.

4.3. First of all, note from the result in **4.2** that the SS-conditions imply factor price equalisation. Secondly, using Ex. 1 of §**4.2** we see that S^{-1} has a dominant diagonal.

5. We now generalise the factor intensity concept and derive a relation with the SS-conditions.

5.1. We shall define factor i as being intensive in the production of commodity i iff:

$$\max_j s_{ij}/s_{kj} = s_{ii}/s_{ki} \qquad \cdots [15]$$

Suppose that eqn [15] holds for all i:

$$s_{ii}/s_{ki} > s_{ij}/s_{kj} \qquad i \neq k,\ i \neq j. \qquad \cdots [16]$$

5.2. We now prove that if the SS-conditions hold, eqn [16] is satisfied.

Proof: As in **4.2**, let $B = S^{-1}$. Given Ex. 3 in §4.2, it follows that not only B but each principal sub-matrix of B has a dominant diagonal and is thus a P-matrix; given the sign conditions on B, this implies that each principal sub-matrix of B is an M-matrix and thus has a positive inverse. By Jacobi's theorem (Exercises §2.4, Q12):

$$B_{ii}B_{jk} - B_{ji}B_{ik} = \det B \,.\, B_{ii;jk} \qquad \cdots [17]$$

or

$$(B_{ii}/\det B)\,.\,(-1)^{j+k}(B_{jk}/\det B) - (-1)^{j+i}(B_{ji}/\det B)\,.\,(-1)^{i+k}(B_{ik}/\det B) =$$
$$= (-1)^{j+k}(B_{ii;jk}/B_{ii})\,.\,(B_{ii}/\det B) \qquad \cdots [18]$$

By the argument above:

$$(-1)^{j+k}(B_{ii;jk}/B_{ii}) > 0 \qquad \cdots [19]$$

as it is an element of the inverse of a principal sub-matrix of B.
Now $B_{ii}/\det B = s_{ii}$; $(-1)^{i+j}B_{ji}/\det B = s_{ij}$. So, from eqns [18] and [19]:

$$s_{ii}s_{kj} > s_{ij}s_{ki}$$

or

$$s_{ii}/s_{ki} > s_{ij}/s_{kj}$$

as required.

5.3. Finally, we prove that, if the SS-conditions are satisfied, $s_{ii} > s_{ij}$, for all $i \neq j$.

Proof: Using **5.2**, we know that eqn [16] is satisfied:

$$s_{ii}s_{kj} - s_{ij}s_{ki} > 0$$

Summing over $k \neq i$:

$$s_{ii}\sum_{k\neq i} s_{kj} - s_{ij}\sum_{k\neq i} s_{ki} > 0$$

or

$$s_{ii}(1 - s_{ij}) - s_{ij}(1 - s_{ii}) > 0$$

as each column sum of S is unity. Obviously, $s_{ii} > s_{ij}$.

§6.3. The generalised Perron-Frobenius theorem and relative stability

§6.3.1. *The generalised Perron-Frobenius theorem and a closed production model*

We have seen the usefulness of Perron–Frobenius theorems in deriving meaningful solutions to dynamic linear models. We begin by extending the Perron–Frobenius theorem to the non-linear case and conclude with an application of this theory to a closed production model.

Definition 1: $F(x)=(F_1(x),\ldots,F_n(x))'$ is a point-to-point mapping (or function) from R^n to R^n.

We now state the conditions to be imposed on F:

(i) $F(x)\geqq \mathbf{0}$ for all $x\geqq \mathbf{0}$.
(ii) F is continuous.
(iii) F is homogeneous of degree 1, i.e. $F(\alpha x)=\alpha F(x)$, $\alpha>0$, $x\geqslant \mathbf{0}$.
(iv) F is monotonic, i.e. $F(x)\geqq F(y)$, for all $x\geqq y$.
(v) F is indecomposable, defined as follows. Let $x\geqq y\geqq \mathbf{0}$. Let $N(x,y)=\{j:x_j=y_j\}\subset N$. F is indecomposable if $F_i(x)\neq F_i(y)$ for some $i\in N(x,y)$.

Lemma 1: Under conditions (i)–(v), $F(x)\geqslant \mathbf{0}$ for all $x\geqslant \mathbf{0}$.

Proof: Suppose $F(x)=\mathbf{0}$ for some $x\geqslant \mathbf{0}$. Without loss of generality, let $x=(x^1\quad x^2)'$, $x^1>\mathbf{0}$, $x^2\geqq \mathbf{0}$, x^1 having $m<n$ components.
Let $y=(x^1\quad \mathbf{0})'$. Then by (iv) and (v), $F_i(x)>F_i(y)$ for some $i=1,\ldots,m$. That is, $0>F_i(y)$ for $y\geqslant \mathbf{0}$, which plainly contradicts (i). The result follows.

We are now in a position to derive a non-linear Perron–Frobenius theorem:

Theorem 15: Under conditions (i)–(v), $F(x)=\lambda x$ has a solution $\lambda^*(F)>0$, $x^*>\mathbf{0}$.

Proof: By (iii), we can restrict ourselves, without loss of generality, to the set $S=\left\{x\geqslant \mathbf{0}:\sum_{i=1}^{n} x_i=1\right\}$.

Consider the function $f:S\rightarrow R^n$ defined by:

$$f_i(x)=F_i(x)\Big/\sum_{j=1}^{n} F_j(x)\quad \text{for all } i.$$

$\sum_{i=1}^{n} f_i(x)=1$. Note that the denominator of each $f_i(x)$ is non-zero by Lemma 1. Given this, f is continuous if F is. As f is a continuous function from S to itself, it follows by Brouwer's fixed point theorem that there exists $x^*\in S$ such that $f(x^*)=x^*$; i.e. $F(x^*)=\left[\sum_{j=1}^{n} F_j(x^*)\right]x^*$. Let $\lambda^*(F)=\sum_{j=1}^{n} F_j(x^*)>0$, by Lemma 1. Suppose $x^* \not> \mathbf{0}$. Let $x^* = (x^{*1} \quad x^{*2})'$, $x^{*1} > \mathbf{0}$, $x^{*2} \geqq \mathbf{0}$, as in Lemma 1. Let $y = (x^{*1} \quad \mathbf{0})'$. Then, as in Lemma 1, $0 > F_i(y)$ for some $i = 1, \ldots, m$. This contradicts condition (i). So $x^* > \mathbf{0}$.

This theorem is the non-linear analogue of Theorem 24 in Chapter 2. We now derive the properties of the Frobenius root ($\lambda^*(F)$) and vector (x^*).

Theorem 16: $\lambda^*(F)$ has only one (positive) characteristic vector. $\lambda^*(F) \geq |\lambda_i(F)|$, where $\lambda_i(F)$ is any other root of F.

Proof: Suppose $F(x) = \lambda^*(F)x$, $x \neq x^*$, $x \geq \mathbf{0}$. By Theorem 15, $x > \mathbf{0}$. Let $\theta = \max_i x_i/x_i^* = x_r/x_r^* > 0$. Then $\theta x^* \geq x$. Consider:

$$\begin{aligned}\lambda^*(F)\theta x_r^* &= \lambda^*(F)x_r = F_r(x) \\ &< F_r(\theta x^*) \quad \text{by (iv) and (v)} \\ &= \theta F_r(x^*) \quad \text{by (iii)} \\ &= \lambda^*(F)\theta x_r^*.\end{aligned}$$

From this contradiction, we conclude that $\lambda^*(F)$ cannot have another semi-positive characteristic vector.
Now suppose $F(x) = \lambda^*(F)x$, $x \not\geqq \mathbf{0}$. Let $y_i = |x_i|$, $y = (y_i)$.
Then $F(y) \geqq |F(x)|$ by (iv), where $|F(x)| = (|F_i(x)|)$
$= |\lambda^*(F)x| = \lambda^*(F)y$.
Let $I = \{i : x_i \neq 0\}$. Let $\beta = \min_{i \in I} x_i^*/|x_i| = x_r^*/y_r > 0$.

Let $z = x^* - \beta y \geqq \mathbf{0}$.

$$\begin{aligned}F(z + \beta y) = F(x^*) &= \lambda^*(F)x^* = \lambda^*(F)[z + \beta y] \\ &= \lambda^*(F)z + \beta\lambda^*(F)y \\ &\leqq \lambda^*(F)z + \beta F(y) \text{ from above} \\ &= \lambda^*(F)z + F(\beta y) \text{ by (iii).}\end{aligned}$$

So,

$$F(z + \beta y) - F(\beta y) \leqq \lambda^*(F)z.$$

Now

$$z_r = 0; \qquad z_r + \beta y_r = \beta y_r.$$

Using (iv) and (v), we have: $F_r(z + \beta y) > F_r(\beta y)$. The last two inequalities yield a contradiction. So $\lambda^*(F)$ has only one characteristic vector, as required. This completes the first half of the theorem.
To prove the second half, let us suppose that there exists a root, $\lambda_i(F) = \lambda$, such that $|\lambda| > \lambda^*(F)$. Write $F(x) = \lambda x$, $x \neq \mathbf{0}$.
Define the vectors y and z, the set I and the scalar β as above.
By (iv) again, $F(y) \geqq |F(x)| = |\lambda x| = |\lambda|\, y > \lambda^*(F)y$.

Also:

$$F(z+\beta y)=F(x^*)=\lambda^*(F)x^*=\lambda^*(F)[z+\beta y]$$
$$<\lambda^*(F)z+\beta\,|\lambda|\,y \quad \text{from above}$$
$$\leqslant\lambda^*(F)z+F(\beta y) \quad \text{from above and (iii)}$$

So:

$$F(z+\beta y)-F(\beta y)<\lambda^*(F)z. \qquad z_r=0.$$

Again by (iv) and (v), $F_r(z+\beta y)>F_r(\beta y)$. Again, the last two inequalities yield a contradiction. Hence, $\lambda^*(F)\geqslant|\lambda_i(F)|$.

The results that we have just derived might be compared with those in Theorems 20 and 27 of Chapter 2. Our next result, on the Frobenius vector, is the analogue of Theorem 28 of Chapter 2.

Theorem 17: x^* is the only semi-positive characteristic vector of F.

Proof: Suppose that there exist $\lambda_i(F)=\lambda$, $x\geqslant\mathbf{0}$ such that $F(x)=\lambda x$. By Lemma 1, $\lambda>0$. Suppose $x\not>\mathbf{0}$. Then, by the same argument as in Theorem 15, we have $x>\mathbf{0}$. Define θ as in Theorem 16.
Then:

$$\lambda\theta x_r^*=\lambda x_r=F_r(x)<F_r(\theta x^*) \quad \text{by (iv) and (v)}$$
$$=\theta F_r(x^*)=\lambda^*(F)\theta x_r^*.$$

Hence, $\lambda<\lambda^*(F)$.
Now define $\rho=\max x_i^*/x_i=x_j^*/x_j>0$. $\rho x\geqslant x^*$. We can now derive $\lambda^*(F)\rho x_j<\lambda\rho x_j$, which implies that $\lambda^*(F)<\lambda$.
From the resulting contradiction, we infer the result.

This theorem completes the non-linear Perron–Frobenius theory that we shall require to analyse the closed production model

$$x(t+1)=F(x(t)) \qquad \cdots[1]$$

where $x(t)$ is the vector of outputs in period t; as the model is closed, these outputs become the inputs of period $t+1$. Not too many questions are asked about F, the "economic sausage grinder; we simply observe that inputs flow into the economy and outputs appear." (1) Within F we subsume optimisation and allocation rules. It is a veritable "black box."

We know from Theorem 15 that, under conditions (i)–(v), eqn [1] has a positive balanced solution:

$$x(t)=\lambda^*(F)^t x^* \qquad x^*>\mathbf{0}, \qquad \lambda^*(F)>0 \qquad \cdots[2]$$

We wish to examine the relative stability of this Frobenius solution, eqn [2].

At this juncture, let us consider the linear analogue of eqn [1], with the same conditions as those under which eqn [2] is derived, i.e.

$$x(t+1) = Ax(t) \qquad \cdots [3]$$

where $A \geqslant [0]$ is indecomposable.
We know from our work in Chapters 2 and 4 that eqn [3] has a unique, Frobenius characteristic solution, which forms the basis of a meaningful solution. Yet, we know from Chapter 4 (exercises) that our assumptions on A are insufficient for the relative stability of the Frobenius solution. Consideration of the example $A = \begin{bmatrix} 0 & 1 \\ 1 & 0 \end{bmatrix}$ should make this point clear.

By analogy with the linear case, the derivation of relative stability of the Frobenius solution of the non-linear model might require some sort of primitivity assumption. From Theorem 41 of Chapter 2, we know that the semi-positive indecomposable matrix A is primitive iff A^t is a positive matrix, for some positive integer t. We may rewrite this condition as follows: if $y \geqslant x \gneqq \mathbf{0}$, $A^t y > A^t x$ for some positive integer t. A special case of primitivity occurs if A is positive; then $t = 1$ in the condition stated. Let us now generalise to the non-linear case. We have the condition:

(vi): F is primitive, i.e. given $x \gneqq \mathbf{0}$, there exists a positive integer t such that $F^t(y) > F^t(x)$, for $y \geqslant x$.

Corresponding to the positivity assumption on A, we have the following condition on F:

(viii): F is strictly monotonic, i.e. $F(y) > F(x)$ for $y \geqslant x \geqslant \mathbf{0}$.

Condition (vii) is clearly a restriction of (iv) above.

It is now time to examine the implications of the primitivity and monotonicity conditions for our "production function," F. The monotonicity condition, (iv), implies that each input has a non-negative marginal product in the production of each output. Strict monotonicity, (vii), implies positive marginal productivity of each input in each use. So, if we possess a stock of bananas this period and apply them to the production of each output, we shall derive a positive quantity of each output next period. To interpret primitivity, (vi), let us retain this example. From bananas this period, we may derive bananas and steel next period, from which we may derive in the following period bananas, steel and tractors; and so on, until after t periods, we have a positive quantity of each good.

Having clarified these conditions, we may now derive our relative stability result:

Theorem 18: Under conditions (i)–(vi), the Frobenius solution of eqn [1] is relatively stable, i.e.

$$\lim_{t\to\infty} x_i(t)/\lambda^*(F)^t x_i^* = \gamma \quad \text{for all } i$$

where $x(t)$ is the solution of eqn [1].

Proof: Let

$$z_i(t)=x_i(t)/\lambda^*(F)^t x_i^* \quad \cdots [4]$$

Substituting in eqn [1], we obtain:

$$\lambda^*(F)^{t+1}x_i^* z_i(t+1)=F_i[\lambda^*(F)^t x_1^* z_1(t),\ldots,\lambda^*(F)^t x_n^* z_n(t)]$$

Dividing through by $\lambda^*(F)^t$ and employing homogeneity of F, we have:

$$\lambda^*(F)x_i^* z_i(t+1)=F_i[x_1^* z_1(t),\ldots,x_n^* z_n(t)] \quad \cdots [5]$$

Now define the following sequences:

$$\{M(t)\}=\left\{\max_i z_i(t)\right\}$$

$$\{m(t)\}=\left\{\min_i z_i(t)\right\} \quad \cdots [6]$$

Now

$$F_i[x_1^* z_1(t),\ldots,x_n^* z_n(t)]\leqslant F_i[x_1^* M(t),\ldots,x_n^* M(t)]$$

by monotonicity

$$=M(t)F_i[x_1^*,\ldots,x_n^*]$$

by homogeneity

$$=M(t)\lambda^*(F)x_i^* \quad \cdots [7]$$

using

$F_i(x^*)=\lambda^*(F)x_i^*$.

Combining eqns [5] and [7], we have:

$$z_i(t+1)\leqslant M(t). \quad \cdots [8]$$

Likewise, we derive:

$$z_i(t+1)\geqslant m(t). \quad \cdots [9]$$

It is evident from eqns [6], [8] and [9] that:

$$M(0)\geqslant M(1)\geqslant\cdots\geqslant m(1)\geqslant m(0) \quad \cdots [10]$$

Hence the following limits exist:

$$\lim_{t\to\infty} M(t)=M \quad \cdots [11]$$

$$\lim_{t\to\infty} m(t)=m \quad \cdots [12]$$

where $M\geqslant m$.
Suppose $M>m$.

Given any small positive number ε, we have $m-\varepsilon \leqslant z_i(t)$, for all i, for sufficiently large t.
As $M(t) \geqslant M$, we have $z_j(t) \geqslant M$, for $j=1, \ldots, r$, say. Suppose $x_j(t_\nu) \geqslant M$ for some increasing sequence $\{t_\nu\}$, where $\lim_{\nu \to \infty} t_\nu = \infty$.
Then, we have:

$$x_i^* \lambda^*(F) z_i(t+1) = F_i[x_1^* z_1(t), \ldots, x_r^* z_r(t), x_{r+1}^* z_{r+1}(t), \ldots, x_n^* z_n(t)]$$
$$\geqslant F_i[x_1^* M, \ldots, x_r^* M, x_{r+1}^* \cdot (m-\varepsilon), \ldots, x_n^* \cdot (m-\varepsilon)] \quad \cdots [13]$$

by monotonicity.
Define two sequences of vectors:

$$\{y^{(\varepsilon)}(t+1)\} = \{F[y^{(\varepsilon)}(t)]\}$$
$$\{y^{(0)}(t+1)\} = \{F[y^{(0)}(t)]\} \quad \cdots [14]$$

where:

$$y^{(\varepsilon)}(0) = (x_1^* M, \ldots, x_r^* M, x_{r+1}^* \cdot (m-\varepsilon), \ldots, x_n^* \cdot (m-\varepsilon))$$
$$y^{(0)}(0) = (x_1^* M, \ldots, x_r^* M, x_{r+1}^* m, \ldots, x_n^* m) \quad \cdots [15]$$

From the definitions, we see that the right-hand side of eqn [13] is $F_i[y^{(\varepsilon)}(0)]$, which using [14] is $y_i^{(\varepsilon)}(1)$. So, we have from eqn [13]:

$$x_i^* \lambda^*(F) z_i(t+1) \geqslant y_i^{(\varepsilon)}(1) \quad \cdots [16]$$

By monotonicity, it follows that:

$$x_i^* \lambda^*(F)^{s+1} z_i(t_\nu + s + 1) \geqslant y_i^{(\varepsilon)}(s+1) = F_i[y^{(\varepsilon)}(s)] \quad \text{for all } s \quad \cdots [17]$$

By primitivity:

$$F^s[y^{(0)}(0)] = F[y^{(0)}(s)] \quad \cdots [18]$$
$$y^{(0)}(0) \geqslant mx^* \quad \text{as} \quad M > m.$$

So:

$$F^s[y^{(0)}(0)] > F^s[mx^*] = \lambda^*(F)^s F(mx^*) = \lambda^*(F)^{s+1} mx^*$$

i.e.

$$F[y^{(0)}(s)] > \lambda^*(F)^{s+1} mx^* \quad \cdots [19]$$

Letting $\varepsilon \to 0$, $t_\nu \to \infty$, we have:

$$\lim_{t_\nu \to \infty} x_i^* \lambda^*(F)^{s+1} z_i(t+s+1) \geqslant \lim_{\varepsilon \to 0} F_i[y^{(\varepsilon)}(s)]$$

$$= F_i[y^{(0)}(s)]$$

by continuity

$$> \lambda^*(F)^{s+1} m x_i^* \quad \cdots [20]$$

Now

$$\lim_{t_\nu\to\infty} x_i^* \lambda^*(F)^{s+1} z_i(t+s+1) = x_i^* \lambda^*(F)^{s+1} \lim_{t_\nu\to\infty} z_i(t+s+1)$$

$$\geqslant x_i^* \lambda^*(F)^{s+1} m \qquad \cdots [21]$$

The inequalities [20] and [21] yield the required contradiction, from which we conclude that $M = m$.

So, using eqn [4], we have:

$$\lim_{t\to\infty} x_i(t)/\lambda^*(F)^t x_i^* = M = m = \gamma, \quad \text{for all } i$$

i.e. the Frobenius solution is relatively stable.

§6.3.2. *Positive resolvents and an open model*

From Chapter 2, we recall the close connection between the problems:

(a) the characteristic root problem: find $\lambda \geqslant 0$, $x \geqslant \mathbf{0}$ such that $Ax = \lambda x$, where $A \geqslant [0]$;

(b) the resolvent equation problem: find $\alpha \geqslant 0$, $x \geqslant \mathbf{0}$ such that $\alpha x = Ax + c$, where $c \geqslant \mathbf{0}$, $A \geqslant [0]$.

Having attended in §6.3.1 to the generalisation of (a) to the non-linear case and its application to a closed production model, we now concentrate on the generalisation of (b) to the non-linear case with application to an open model. Our basic equation is:

$$\alpha x = F(x) + c \qquad c \geqslant \mathbf{0} \qquad \cdots [1]$$

where F satisfies conditions (i)–(v) of §6.3.1. (Primitivity is not required to solve either linear or non-linear resolvent equations.)

Theorem 19: Under conditions (i)–(v), $x > \mathbf{0}$ in eqn [1] iff $\alpha > \lambda^*(F)$.

Proof:

Sufficiency: Suppose $\alpha > \lambda^*(F)$, $c \geqslant \mathbf{0}$. Consider the function $f: S \to R^n$ defined by:

$$f_i(x) = [F_i(x) + r(x)c_i] \Big/ \left[\sum_j F_j(x) + \max\left(\alpha - \sum_j F_j(x), 0\right)\right] \qquad \cdots [2]$$

where

$$r(x) = \max\left(\alpha - \sum_j F_j(x), 0\right) \Big/ \sum_j c_j \qquad \cdots [3]$$

The denominator of eqn [2] is always greater than or equal to α, which is positive by hypothesis. $r(x)$ and $f(x)$ are continuous. It can easily be shown that $f(x) \geqslant \mathbf{0}$ and $\sum_i f_i(x) = 1$. So, $f: S \to S$. Then, by Brouwer's fixed point theorem, there exists $x^* \in S$ such that $f(x^*) = x^*$. Suppose that $r(x^*) = 0$; from eqn [3], we have:

$$\alpha = \sum_j F_j(x^*) \qquad \cdots [4]$$

From eqn [2]:

$$x_i^* = f_i(x^*) = F_i(x^*) \Big/ \sum_j F_j(x^*)$$

or

$$F(x^*) = \left[\sum_j F_j(x^*)\right] x^* \qquad \cdots [5]$$

So, $\sum_j F_j(x^*)$ is a root of F; from eqn [4], α is also a root of F. This plainly contradicts the hypothesis $\alpha > \lambda^*(F)$. As $r(x) \geqslant 0$, for all x, it follows that $r(x^*) > 0$. From eqn [3], we have $\alpha > \sum_j F_j(x^*)$.

Hence eqn [2] becomes:

$$f_i(x^*) = [F_i(x^*) + r(x^*)c_i]/\alpha$$

or

$$\alpha f(x^*) = F(x^*) + r(x^*)c \qquad \cdots [6]$$

But $x^* = f(x^*)$. So eqn [6] becomes:

$$\alpha x^* = F(x^*) + r(x^*)c$$

Dividing by $r(x^*) > 0$, we have:

$$\alpha(x^*/r(x^*)) = F(x^*/r(x^*)) + c$$

by condition (iii), or

$$\alpha x = F(x) + c \qquad x = x^*/r(x^*) \geqslant \mathbf{0} \qquad \cdots [7]$$

To prove that $x > \mathbf{0}$ in eqn [7], suppose that $x_j = 0$. Then from eqn [1], $F_j(x) = 0$, $c_j = 0$, by condition (i). Let $x \geqslant y \geqslant \mathbf{0}$, where $y_j = 0$. Then by conditions (iv) and (v), we have: $0 = F_j(x) > F_j(y)$. This contradicts condition (i). So $x > \mathbf{0}$. This completes the sufficiency part of the theorem.

Necessity: Let

$$F(x^*) = \lambda^*(F)x^*, \qquad \lambda^*(F) > 0, \qquad x^* > \mathbf{0}$$

by Theorem 15. Let

$$\eta = \min x_i/x_i^* = x_k/x_k^* > 0. \qquad x \geqslant \eta x^*.$$

Then:

$$\begin{aligned}\alpha\eta x_k^* = \alpha x_k &= F_k(x) + c_k > F_k(\eta x^*) + c_k \quad \text{by (iv) and (v)}\\ &= \eta F_k(x^*) + c_k \quad \text{by (i)}\\ &= \eta\lambda^*(F)x_k^* + c_k\\ &\geqslant \eta\lambda^*(F)x_k^*\end{aligned}$$

As $\eta > 0$, $x^* > \mathbf{0}$, it follows that $\alpha > \lambda^*(F)$, as required.

We now examine the effect of a change in c on x. This is of interest in its own right, but it also serves as a lemma to our uniqueness result below.

Theorem 20: Under conditions (i)–(v), if $c^2 \geqslant c^1 \geqslant \mathbf{0}$, then $x^2 > x^1$.

Proof: Let

$$\alpha x^i = F(x^i) + c^i \qquad i = 1, 2.$$

As in the proof of the sufficiency part of Theorem 19, $x^i > \mathbf{0}$, $i = 1, 2$. Let

$$\theta = \max x_i^1 / x_i^2 = x_k^1 / x_k^2 > 0. \qquad \theta x^2 \geqslant x^1.$$

Then:

$$\alpha \theta x_k^2 = \alpha x_k^1 = F_k(x^1) + c_k^1 < F_k(\theta x^2) + c_k^2 \quad \text{by (iv) and (v)}$$
$$= \theta F_k(x^2) + c_k^2 \quad \text{by (iii)}$$

So $c_k^2 > \theta(\alpha x_k^2 - F_k(x^2)) = \theta c_k^2$. Hence $\theta < 1$, which implies $x^2 > x^1$.

We are now in a position to derive uniqueness in:

Theorem 21: Under conditions (i)–(v), the solution of the resolvent equation is unique.

Proof: Suppose that there are two solutions, x^1 and x^2, to the resolvent equation. $x^i > \mathbf{0}$, from Theorem 19. Defining θ as in Theorem 20, we obtain $\theta < 1$ so that $x^2 > x^1$.
Define $\rho = \max x_i^2 / x_i^1$. By exactly the same argument, we obtain $\rho < 1$ so that $x^1 > x^2$. From this contradiction, we conclude that the solution is unique.

The basic equation to describe our open model is:

$$x(t+1) = F(x(t)) + a(t) \qquad \cdots [8]$$

We may think of eqn [8] as a straightforward non-linear generalisation of the expenditure model of §5.4.1; $x(t)$ is then interpreted as the vector of sectoral incomes at t. Alternatively, we may generalise the model of §5.4.2. by the introduction of non-linear expenditure models into an input–output model. Employing the same notation as in §5.4.2, we have as the basic balance equation:

$$x_i(t+1) = \sum_j a_{ij} x_j(t+1) + c_i(y(t)) + d_i(t)$$

$x_i(t+1)$ being the gross output of good i at $t+1$, $c_i(y(t))$ being the total consumption demand for good i at $t+1$, assumed dependent on incomes at t:

$$c_i(y(t)) = \sum_j c_{ij}(y(t)) \quad \text{where} \quad c_{ij}(y(t))$$

is the j-th sector's demand for the i-th good for consumption purposes.

Then:

$$x(t+1)=(I-A)^{-1}[c(y(t))+d(t)],$$

where

$$c(y(t))=[c_i y(t))]$$

Using the relation $y(t+1)=\hat{v}x(t+1)$ from eqn [5] of §5.4.2, we have:

$$y(t+1)=\hat{v}(I-A)^{-1}c(y(t))+\hat{v}(I-A)^{-1}d(t)$$

or

$$y(t+1)=F(y(t))+a(t) \qquad \cdots[9]$$

Assume that F satisfies conditions (i)–(v). Suppose that the autonomous component exhibits balanced growth:

$$a(t)=\rho^t a \geqslant \mathbf{0} \qquad \cdots[10]$$

From Theorem 19, we know that eqn [9] has a meaningful balanced growth solution $\rho^t y > \mathbf{0}$ iff $\rho > \lambda^*(F)$. We are naturally interested in examining this balanced solution for relative stability.

Theorem 22: Under conditions (i)–(v), we have relative stability of the balanced path $\rho^t y$, i.e.

$$\lim_{t\to\infty} y_i(t)/\rho^t y_i = 1 \quad \text{for all } i \qquad \cdots[11]$$

Proof: The proof is similar to that of Theorem 18. Define:

$$\alpha(t)=\min_i y_i(t)/\rho^t y_i: \qquad \beta(t)=\max_i y_i(t)/\rho^t y_i \qquad \cdots[12]$$

Now:

$$\begin{aligned} y_i(t+1) &= F_i(y(t))+a_i(t) \geqslant F_i(\alpha(t)\rho^t y)+a_i(t) \quad \text{by condition (iv)} \\ &= \alpha(t)F_i(\rho^t y)+a_i(t) \quad \text{by condition (iii)} \\ &= \alpha(t)[\rho^{t+1}y_i - a_i(t)]+a_i(t) \end{aligned} \qquad \cdots[13]$$

using eqn [9]. Hence:

$$\frac{y_i(t+1)}{\rho^{t+1}y_i} \geqslant \alpha(t)\left[1-\frac{a_i(t)}{\rho^{t+1}y_i}\right]+\frac{a_i(t)}{\rho^{t+1}y_i} \qquad \cdots[14]$$

Using eqn [10], this becomes:

$$\frac{y_i(t+1)}{\rho^{t+1}y_i} \geqslant \alpha(t)\left[1-\frac{a_i}{\rho y_i}\right]+\frac{a_i}{\rho y_i} \qquad \cdots[15]$$

So we have:

$$\alpha(t+1) \geqslant \min_i \left\{\alpha(t)\left[1-\frac{a_i}{\rho y_i}\right]+\frac{a_i}{\rho y_i}\right\} \qquad \cdots[16]$$

and likewise:

$$\beta(t+1) \leqslant \max_i \left\{ \alpha(t)\left[1-\frac{a_i}{\rho y_i}\right]+\frac{a_i}{\rho y_i} \right\} \quad \cdots [17]$$

Under conditions (i)–(v), $y > \mathbf{0}$ given $a \geqslant \mathbf{0}$. Then from the resolvent equation:

$$\rho y - F(y) = a$$

we see that:

$$1 \geqslant 1 - a_i/\rho y_i > 0 \quad \cdots [18]$$

Now define:

$$\sigma(t+1) = \min_i \left\{ \sigma(t)\left[1-\frac{a_i}{\rho y_i}\right]+\frac{a_i}{\rho y_i} \right\}$$
$$\eta(t+1) = \max_i \left\{ \eta(t)\left[1-\frac{a_i}{y_i}\right]+\frac{a_i}{\rho y_i} \right\} \quad \cdots [19]$$

with

$$\sigma(0) = \min(\alpha(0), 1); \qquad \eta(0) = \max(\beta(0), 1) \quad \cdots [20]$$

By induction, we have:

$$\sigma(t) \leqslant \alpha(t) \leqslant \beta(t) \leqslant \eta(t) \quad \cdots [21]$$

Let:

$$\phi = \max_i (1 - a_i/\rho y_i) \qquad 0 \leqslant \phi < 1 \quad \cdots [22]$$

From eqns [19]–[22], we have:

$$0 \geqslant \sigma(t+1) - 1 \geqslant \phi(\sigma(t) - 1)$$
$$0 \leqslant \eta(t+1) - 1 \leqslant \phi(\eta(t) - 1) \quad \cdots [23]$$

Hence:

$$\lim_{t\to\infty} \sigma(t) = \lim_{t\to\infty} \eta(t) = 1 \quad \cdots [24]$$

Using eqns [19], we have:

$$\lim_{t\to\infty} \alpha(t) = \lim_{t\to\infty} \beta(t) = 1 \quad \cdots [25]$$

Relative stability follows.

§6.4. Review

The extent to which the results of Chapters 2 and 5 depend on linearity assumptions is a legitimate topic for enquiry—it would, after all, be regarded as an unsatisfactory state of affairs if the linear results could not be extended to non-linear cases, given that non-constant returns to scale are commonly supposed to exist. Success in this endeavour must depend to some extent on the way in which the linearity assumptions are relaxed; in our context, this refers to the mathematical statement of the assumptions (in so far as this is possible). We may illustrate this point by reference to the non-linear input–output model of §6.2.1. The crucial assumption is:

$$X'_{ij}(0) \geqslant X'_{ij}(x_j) \geqslant 0 \quad \text{for all} \quad x_j \in R(0, +) \qquad \cdots [1]$$

for it is this which enables us to infer that $J_f(x)$ is a P-matrix, for all x, if $J_f(\mathbf{0})$ is a P-matrix; and as we have seen in §6.1.2, a sufficient condition for uniqueness is that $J_f(x)$ is a P-matrix for all $x \in R^N(0, +)$. Equation [1] is certainly a convenient mathematical assumption. In Figure 1, we provide illustrations of a couple of functions, X_{ij}, satisfying eqn [1]:

Fig. 1. Examples of relations between X_{ij} and x_j which satisfy eqn [1]

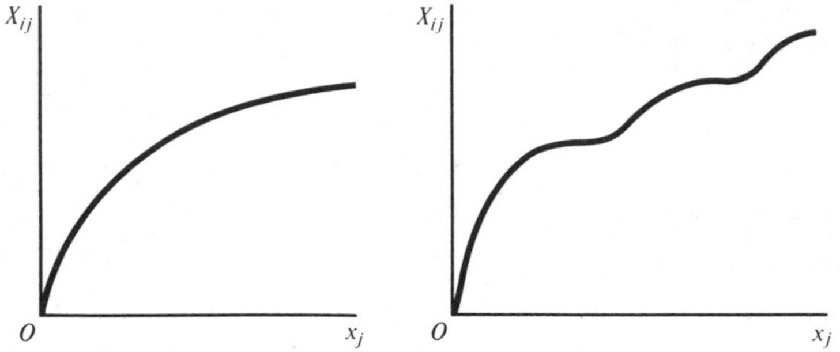

As mentioned above, we may derive existence and uniqueness by use of eqn [1]. If we impose the further condition:

$$X_{ij}(\alpha x_j) \geqslant \alpha X_{ij}(x_j) \quad \text{for all} \quad \alpha \in (0, 1) \qquad \cdots [2]$$

then we may derive the same comparative statics results as those for the linear model (the three Hicksian laws of comparative statics) and establish an iterative procedure, using matrix multipliers, for locating the unique equilibrium.(2) A function X_{ij}, such as in Figure (1), satisfying eqns [1] and [2], has the interpretation that successive equal increases in x_j require successively smaller increases in X_{ij}.

Some economic justification may thus be provided for this non-linear input–output model. This may be contrasted with the non-linear dynamic models of §6.3, in particular the closed production model. As the "economic sausage grinder," F, is poorly specified, it is difficult to provide economic justification for the homogeneity, monotonicity and primitivity assumptions—why should F be homogeneous (of any degree) if we do not know what it is? However, we may provide some mathematical justification; the conditions imposed on F suffice to yield a generalised Perron–Frobenius theorem, which enables us to define a balanced growth solution.

Exercises

§6.1

1. Prove that either $Ax=b$ has a solution or $y'A=\mathbf{0}'$, $y'b=1$ have a solution (but not both).

2. Prove that either $Ax=b$ has a non-negative solution or $y'A\geqslant\mathbf{0}'$, $y'b<0$ have a solution (but not both).

3. Using Q2, prove:
(a) that either $y'A\geqslant c'$ has a solution or $Ax=\mathbf{0}$, $c'x=1$ have a solution (but not both);
(b) that either $Ax\leqslant b$ has a non-negative solution or $y'A\geqslant\mathbf{0}'$, $y'b<0$ have a non-negative solution (but not both);
(c) that either $Ax=\mathbf{0}$ has a semi-positive solution or $y'A>\mathbf{0}'$ has a solution (but not both).

4. Prove that either $Ax=\mathbf{0}$ has a positive solution or $y'A\geq\mathbf{0}'$ has a solution (but not both).

5. Using Q3(b), prove that either $Ax\leqslant\mathbf{0}$ has a semi-positive solution or $y'A>\mathbf{0}'$ has a non-negative solution (but not both).
(In questions 1–5, A is an arbitrary $m\times n$ matrix. A reference for these questions is Gale, Chapter 2.)

6. Let $D=[d_i\delta_{ij}]$, where each d_i takes the value $+1$ or -1. Prove that A is a P-matrix iff $DADx\leqslant\mathbf{0}$, $x\geqslant\mathbf{0}$ imply $x=\mathbf{0}$.
(This is a compact way of writing Theorem 2 of Gale and Nikaido: i.e. A is a P-matrix iff A reverses the sign of no vector except zero. Let $y=Ax$. Then A reverses the sign of x if $x_iy_i\leqslant 0$, for all i.)

7. The global univalence result (Theorem 8) obtains also if $J_f(x)$ is an $(N-P)$-matrix, i.e. each odd-ordered (even-ordered) principal minor of $J_f(x)$ is negative (positive). This follows straightforwardly from Theorem 8 as $-J_f(x)$ would be a P-matrix. However, no such simple transformation permits extension of the global univalence result to the following cases:
(a) each principal minor of $J_f(x)$ is negative;
(b) each odd-ordered (even-ordered) principal minor of $J_f(x)$ is positive (negative).
Inada has extended the global univalence result to these cases. (Note that once global univalence has been derived under one of (a) or (b), the simple transformation referred to above permits derivation of global univalence under the other.)

8. Using the same hypotheses as Theorem 8, prove that if $J_f(x)$ is a P-matrix:

$$(x_i-a_i)(f_i(x)-f_i(a))\leqslant 0 \qquad i=1,\ldots,n$$

imply $x=a$.

§6.2

Q1–4 are incorporated in text.

5. Suppose $X'_{ij}(x_j) \geqslant X'_{ij}(\bar{x}_j)$ for all i, j, for all $x_j \geqslant \bar{x}_j \geqslant 0$.
For each $c \in R^n(0, +)$, there exists a unique $x \in R^n(0, +)$ such that $f(x) = c$, if $J_f(\mathbf{0})$ is a P-matrix.
For any $y(0) \in R^n(0, +)$, the iterates $y(\tau)$, $\tau = 1, 2, \ldots$, defined by:

$$y(\tau+1) = y(\tau) - J_f^{-1}(y(\tau))[f(y(\tau)) - c] \qquad \tau > 0$$

satisfy $y(\tau) \geqslant y(\tau+1) \geqslant x$, and converge to x.
$J_f^{-1}(y(\tau))$ is the value of the inverse at $y(\tau)$.
Interpret this matrix in terms of matrix multipliers.
(Sandberg)

6. Consider the following condition I on $A \geqslant [0]$:
Given any non-empty subset $J \subset N = \{1, \ldots, n\}$, there exists $x > \mathbf{0}$, where x depends of J, such that:

$$\sum_{j \in J} a_{ij} x_j > \sum_{j \notin J} a_{ij} x_j \quad \text{for any} \quad i \in J$$

$$\sum_{j \in J} a_{ij} x_j < \sum_{j \in J} a_{ij} x_j \quad \text{for any} \quad i \notin J$$

Prove that A is a P-matrix iff A satisfies condition I.
(Hint: *Necessity:* Use Exercises §6.1, Q3(b) and Q6;
Sufficiency: Exercises §6.1, Q6.)
(The condition has the following interpretation:
Let industries be aggregated into two conglomerates, denoted by J and $\bar{J}$. Then there exists a set of outputs, denoted by x, such that more (less) of the i-th factor is used in J than in $\bar{J}$, $i \in J$ ($i \in \bar{J}$).)

7. Consider the following condition II on the matrix $A \geqslant [0]$:
For any non-empty subset $J \subset N$, there exists $\bar{x} = (\bar{x}_i) > \mathbf{0}$, $i \in J$, such that:

$$\sum_{i \in J} \bar{x}_i a_{ij} > \sum_{i \in J} \bar{x}_i a_{ik} \quad \text{for} \quad j \in J, k \notin J.$$

Prove that if A satisfies condition II, then A is a P-matrix.
(Interpretation: From $\log_e p_j = \log_e g_j(w)$, we obtain:

$$\mathrm{d}p_j / p_j = \sum_{i=1}^{n} (\mathrm{d}w_i / w_i) \cdot s_{ij}$$

Then for any J, we have $\mathrm{d}w_i / w_i > 0$, $i \in J$; $\mathrm{d}w_i / w_i = 0$, $i \notin J$.
With $\mathrm{d}w_i / w_i$ as $\bar{x}_i$, s_{ij} as a_{ij} in condition II above, we have:

$$\mathrm{d}p_r / p_r > \mathrm{d}p_s / p_s \qquad r \in J, s \notin J.)$$

8. Prove that if S satisfies condition II, then the SS conditions hold; in fact, each diagonal element of the inverse matrix is greater than one and greater than each of the other elements in the same row.
(A reference for questions 6–8 is Uekawa)

9. A positive matrix the inverse of which has positive diagonal and negative off-diagonal elements (negative diagonal and positive off-diagonal elements) satisfies the SSS-I (SSS-II) condition.
   Prove that if a positive matrix satisfies SSS-I (SSS-II), then any principal sub-matrix satisfies SSS-I (SSS-II).

10. Prove that if a positive matrix satisfies SSS-II, then $a_{ii}/a_{ki} < a_{ij}/a_{kj}$. (See **5.1** and **5.2** above.)

11. Suppose that the positive matrix A satisfies SSS-II. Prove that the inverse of any proper principal sub-matrix of A^{-1} (i.e. except A^{-1} itself) is negative.

12. Using Exercises §6.1, Q7, prove that if the Jacobian matrix satisfies SSS-II, it is a $(P-N)$-matrix (i.e. it satisfies (b) of Q7, Exercises §6.1) and so univalence holds.

13. Prove that if a stochastic matrix satisfies SSS-II, then

    $s_{ii} < s_{ij}$, for all $j \neq i$.

    (A reference for questions 9–13 is Inada.)

14. Consider the following alternative generalisation of the non-linear input–output model:

    $$x_i = \sum_{j=1}^{n} a_{ij}(x)x_j + c_i \qquad a_{ij}(x) = X_{ij}(x)/x_j$$

    or

    $$x = A(x)x + c \qquad \cdots [1]$$

    Suppose that the $a_{ij}(x)$ are bounded and that for all

    $$x^2 \geqslant x^1 \geqslant \mathbf{0}, \qquad A(x^2)x^2 \geqslant A(x^1)x^1 \geqslant \mathbf{0}.$$

    Consider the following iterative scheme (see Exercises §2.4, Q31):

    $$\left.\begin{aligned} x^0 &= c \\ x &= A(x^{\tau-1})x^{\tau-1} + c \end{aligned}\right\} \qquad \cdots [2]$$

    Evidently, $x^{\tau+1} \geqslant x^{\tau} \geqslant \mathbf{0}$, for all $\tau = 0, 1, 2, \ldots$ (by induction).
    But does the scheme yield convergence to a solution of

    $$x = A(x)x + c \qquad \cdots [3]$$

    and when is the solution unique?

    Prove that x^{τ} in eqn [2] converges iff eqn [3] has a solution,

    $$x = \lim_{\tau \to \infty} x^{\tau}.$$

15. Generalise the condition outlined in Exercises §2.4, Q32, as follows:
    Let ν be a vector norm. Prove that if there exists $\alpha \in (0, 1)$ such that

    $$\nu[A(x^1)x^1 - A(x^2)x^2] < \alpha\nu(x^1 - x^2) \quad \text{for all} \quad x^1, x^2,$$

    then eqn [3] has a unique solution.

16. In the light of §3.2, discuss the effect of introducing heterogeneous capital goods in to the trade model outlined in §6.2.2. (Metcalfe and Steedman)

§6.3

Unless otherwise stated, assume that any function satisfies conditions (i)–(v).

1. If $F(x) \geqslant (\leqslant) \mu x$, for some $x \in S$, prove that $\lambda^*(F) > (<) \mu$.

2. If $F(x) \geqslant G(x)$ for all $x \in S$, prove that $\lambda^*(F) > \lambda^*(G)$.

3. Prove that:
   (i) if $x \geqslant y \geqq \mathbf{0}$, then $F(x) \geqslant F(y)$;
   (ii) if $x > y \geqq \mathbf{0}$, then $F(x) > F(y)$.

4. Prove that $\lambda^*(F) > (<)\ 1$ iff there exists $x \geqslant \mathbf{0}$ such that $F(x) \geqslant (\leqslant) x$.

5. Derive eqn [21] of §6.3.2.

6. Solve the closed production model (i.e. eqn [1] of §6.3.1) under conditions (i)–(iii) and (vii). (Solow and Samuelson)

7. Prove that, under conditions (i) and (ii), $F(x) = \lambda x$ has a solution $\lambda \geqslant 0$, $x \geqslant \mathbf{0}$.

8. Prove that under conditions (i)–(iv), there is a finite number of roots λ_j such that $F(x^j) = \lambda_j x^j$, $x^j \in S$. (Morishima)

9. Compare the relative stability of the following closed production models:
   (i) $x(t+1) = F(x(t))$
   (ii) $x(t+1) = B^{-1}(I - A)x(t)$ (i.e. the closed dynamic Leontief model)

Notes

1. Solow, R. M. & P. A. Samuelson: "Balanced growth under constant returns to scale", *Econometrica*, **21** (1953). p. 412.

2. It is to be expected that more conditions will be required to establish convergence to equilibrium (i.e. a dynamic problem) than to establish existence of equilibrium (i.e. a static problem).

References

§6.1

§6.1.1

Gale, D. & H. Nikaido: "The Jacobian matrix and global univalence of mappings", *Mathematische Annalen*, **159** (1965), reprinted in *Readings in Mathematical Economics*, vol. 1, (P. Newman, ed.), Johns Hopkins U.P., 1968.

Tucker, A. W.: "Dual systems of homogeneous relations" in *Linear Inequalities and Related Systems*, (H. W. Kuhn & A. W. Tucker, eds.), Princeton U.P., 1956.

§6.1.2

Apostol. T.: *Mathematical Analysis*, Addison-Wesley, 1957.

Gale, D. & H. Nikaido: op. cit.

§*Exercises*

Gale, D.: *The Theory of Linear Economic Models*, McGraw-Hill, 1960.

Inada, K-I.: "The production coefficient matrix and the Stolper–Samuelson condition", *Econometrica*, **39** (1971).

§6.2

§6.2.1

Sandberg, I. W.: "A non-linear input–output model of a multi-sectored economy", *Econometrica*, **41** (1973).

§6.2.2

Chipman, J. S.: "Factor-price equalisation and the Stolper–Samuelson theorem", *International Economic Review*, **10** (1969).

Gale, D. & H. Nikaido: "The Jacobian matrix and the global univalence of mappings", *Mathematische Annalen*, **159** (1965).

McKenzie, L. W.: "Matrices with dominant diagonals and economic theory", in *Mathematical Methods in the Social Sciences* (K. J. Arrow et al, eds.), Stanford U.P., 1960.

Samuelson, P. A.: "Prices of factors and goods in general equilibrium", *Review of Economic Studies*, **21** (1953).

§*Exercises*

Inada, K-I.: "The production coefficient matrix and the Stolper–Samuelson condition", *Econometrica*, **39** (1971).

Metcalfe, J. S. & I. Steedman: "Heterogeneous capital and the Heckscher–Ohlin–Samuelson theory of trade" in *Essays in Modern Economics*, (M. Parkin & A. R. Nobay, eds.), Longman, 1973.

Uekawa, Y.: "Generalisation of the Stolper–Samuelson theorem", *Econometrica*, **39** (1971).

§6.3

Morishima, M.: "Generalisations of the Frobenius–Wielandt theorems for non-negative square matrices", *Journal of the London Mathematical Society*, **36** (1961).

Nikaido, H.: "Balanced growth in multi-sectoral income propagation under autonomous expenditure schemes", *Review of Economic Studies*, **31** (1964).

Solow, R. M. & P. A. Samuelson: "Balanced growth under constant returns to scale", Econometrica, **21** (1953).

A more advanced paper is:

Morishima, M.: "On the two theorems of growth economics: a mathematical exercise", *Econometrica,* **33** (1965).

7

Closed production models

In this chapter, we shall discuss a model which does *not* rely on assumptions (i)–(iv) of §2.1. We have at various stages through the book relaxed these assumptions individually. In §2.7, we considered a generalised Leontief model, in which (ii) was relaxed; somewhat paradoxically, the main result of that section—the non-substitution theorem—justifies the use of the original Leontief model (i.e. that input–output model outlined in §2.1) in situations where the generalised Leontief model is a more faithful representation of technology. Production lags were introduced in §5.2, capital goods in §5.3 though the treatment of them could hardly be called satisfactory. A generous interpretation of the closed model of §6.3.1 would be that it permitted joint production; however, as the function F was inadequately specified, such an interpretation would seem generous indeed. Accordingly, a model which permits simultaneous relaxation of (i)–(iv) demands consideration.

Section 7.1 is devoted to the von Neumann model. We specialise in §7.2 to consider the so-called von Neumann–Leontief model, but generalise in §7.4 to examine a general balanced growth model. Section 7.3 is devoted to separation theorems on convex sets, mathematical theory for §7.4 and Chapter 8.

§7.1. Von Neumann's model of an expanding economy

§7.1.1. *Introduction*

Let us immediately drop assumption (i) of no joint production. We may continue to talk of industries but we must develop a notation to describe their technical possibilities, i.e. techniques of production. We may describe the economy by the set of all available techniques, i.e. the book of blueprints. Following the ideas developed in §2.7, we may describe a technique of production by a pair of vectors—an input vector $(a^j, l_j) = (a_{1j}, a_{2j}, \ldots, a_{mj}, l_j)$ and an output vector $b^j = (b_{1j}, b_{2j}, \ldots, b_{mj})$

where:

a_{ij} = quantity of good i required per unit intensity of technique j;
b_{ij} = quantity of good i produced per unit intensity of technique j;
l_j = number of workers employed per unit intensity of technique j;
$i = 1, \ldots, m; j = 1, \ldots, n.$

No relation is specified between the number of goods (m) and the number of techniques (n). We now drop assumption (ii) that each industry has only one technique of production. We may drop assumption (iii) of no production lag by stating that each technique requires one period to produce its output. So really we should write $(a^j(t), l_j(t))$ as the input vector, and $(b^j(t+1))$ as the output vector. We shall demonstrate below how to handle a technique requiring more than one period to produce its output. More important than this is to relax (iv), the assumption of no capital goods. This we do now.

It is one thing to assume the existence of capital goods; it is another to develop a satisfactory treatment of them. We may refer at this stage to our discussion of the dynamic Leontief model in §5.3. The treatment of depreciation—by evaporation—is unsatisfactory for it supposes that a capital good produced years ago and subject to wear and tear is physically equivalent to a smaller quantity of a new capital good of the same type. This point may be illustrated by the following (fairly trivial) example: an entrepreneur may have a certain quantity of a capital good that is in its last year of "life," that is, he will have no capital next year; on the other hand, he may own an equivalent quantity of a new capital good of the same type (equivalent, that is, according to our concept of depreciation), which will be extant next year. As this example illustrates, it is in general impossible to derive equivalence between new and old capital goods of the same type. In other words, we should treat the same type of capital goods at different stages of wear and tear as different goods. The joint production assumption allows us to make this concept operational. Suppose that a given type of capital good (say k), t years old, is used in the j-th technique. Then one of the input coefficients, say a_{ij}, will refer to this capital input. If this capital good survives the production process, it will appear as a capital good of type k, $t+1$ years old, in the output vector of the technique, to be represented by say $b_{i+1,j}$.

To recapitulate briefly: we distinguish not only between different types of capital goods, but also between the same type of capital good of different ages. We may refine this distinction even further for we may differentiate between the same type of capital good of the same age used in different techniques—this enables us to dispense with the perfect transferability of capital assumption implicit in §5.3, for a machine of a given type and age that has been used in a given technique will not in general be transferred to use in another technique.

A further problem to be considered is that of determination of the economic lifetime of a capital good. This problem was by-passed in §5.3

where the current and capital input–output coefficients were taken as technical data. There is a simple relation between the coefficients—$b_{ij} = \tau_{ij}a_{ij}$, τ_{ij} being the length of life of capital good i when used in the production of good j. To take the coefficients as technical data is equivalent to taking τ_{ij} as technical data. However, the τ_{ij} are economic, not technical nor physical, variables, for the economic life of a capital good (while not greater than its physical life) is dependent on its profitability and hence must be determined within the economic system. We shall be able to solve this problem within the context of von Neumann's model, to which we now turn.

§7.1.2. *Outline and solution of the model*

In §7.1.1, we discussed the criteria to be applied in defining commodities, in particular, capital goods. We know how to represent a technique of production by a pair of vectors. However, we are still operating under the assumption that each technique has a unit period of production. It is now convenient to demonstrate how we can accommodate different techniques having different periods of production.

We have to begin with a definition of a unit period of production, which may be three calendar months, say. Obviously, all techniques must require positive integral multiples of three months to produce their outputs, or else we redefine our unit. Let us suppose that the technique j requires $t+$ periods to transform the input vector $(a_{ij}, \ldots a_{mj}, \ l_j)$ into the output vector $(b_{1j}, \ldots, b_{mj})$. Note that the very statement of the input and output vectors implies that we have already defined commodities (and techniques) satisfactorily.

What we do now is to introduce t "dummy" of fictitious commodities and techniques as follows:

In the first unit production period, we have the following "technique":

$(0, \ldots, 0, \bar{a}_{t+1,j}, \ldots, \bar{a}_{t+m,j}, \bar{l}_j)$ is the input vector;
$(\bar{b}_{1j}, 0, \ldots, 0, \bar{b}_{t+1,j}, \ldots, \bar{b}_{t+m,j})$ is the output vector.

In the second unit production period, we have as the "technique":

$(\bar{a}_{1,j+1}, 0, \ldots, 0, \bar{a}_{t+1,j+1}, \ldots, \bar{a}_{t+m,j+1}, 0)$ is the input vector;
$(0, \bar{b}_{2,j+1}, 0, \ldots, 0, \bar{b}_{t+1,j+1}, \ldots, \bar{b}_{t+m,j+1})$ is the output vector.

In the third unit production period, we have as the "technique":

$(0, \bar{a}_{2,j+2}, 0, \ldots, 0, \bar{a}_{t+1,j+2}, \ldots, \bar{a}_{t+m,j+2}, 0)$ is the input vector;
$0, 0, \bar{b}_{3,j+2}, 0, \ldots, 0, b_{t+1,j+2}, \ldots, \bar{b}_{t+m,j+2})$ is the output vector.

And so on, until we have in the $(t+1)$-th production period:

$(0, \ldots, 0, \bar{a}_{t,j+t}, \bar{a}_{t+1,j+t}, \ldots, \bar{a}_{t+m,j+t}, 0)$ is the input vector;
$(0, \ldots, 0, 0, \bar{b}_{t+1,j+t}, \ldots, \bar{b}_{t+m,j+t})$ is the output vector,

where

$$a_{ij} = \bar{a}_{t+i,j}, \qquad l_j = \bar{l}_j, \qquad b_{ij} = \bar{b}_{t+i,j+t}, \qquad i = 1, \ldots, m.$$

The "dummy" commodities have been numbered $1, \ldots t$, being the first t components of the input and output vectors. The "dummy" techniques have been numbered $j, j+1, \ldots, j+t$.

Having completed this demonstration, we may now assume without loss of generality that each technique has a unit period of production or has been converted into such a technique. Let M be the number of commodities, fictitious and real, N the number of techniques, fictitious and real. Let

$$A = [a_{ij}], \qquad B = [b_{ij}], \qquad l = [l_j], \qquad i = 1, \ldots, M; \qquad j = 1, \ldots, N.$$

$l \geqslant \mathbf{0}$, as fictitious techniques may not employ labour.
The j-th column of $A(B)$ contains the input (output) coefficients of the j-th technique.

We shall make the following assumptions:

(i) constant returns to scale;
(ii) for each technique j, there exists $a_{ij} > 0$, i.e. each technique uses at least one input;
(iii) for each good i, there exists j such that $b_{ij} > 0$, i.e. each good can be produced;
(iv) the labour supply "can be expanded in unlimited quantities" (1);
(v) "consumption of goods takes place only through the processes of production which include necessities of life consumed by workers" (2);
(vi) "all income in excess of necessities of life will be reinvested." (3)

With regard to (v), let us define:

q_i = quantity of good i as subsistence per man.

Then

$q_i l_j$ = quantity of good i required as subsistence for workers operating technique j at unit intensity,
$i = 1, \ldots, M; j = 1, \ldots, N.$

Let us redefine the input coefficients so as to incorporate this notion of subsistence. Then define:

$$c_{ij} = a_{ij} + q_i l_j \qquad i = 1, \ldots, M; \qquad j = 1, \ldots, N.$$

to be the quantity of good i required per unit intensity of technique j.
The subsistence wage, w, is then given by:

$$w = \sum_{i=1}^{M} q_i p_i$$

where $p = (p_1, \ldots, p_M)$ is the price vector.
Let $x = (x_1, \ldots, x_N)$ denote the vector of intensities at which techniques are operated.

"We are interested in those states where the economy expands without change of structure, i.e. where the ratios $x_1 : x_2 : \cdots : x_N$ remain unchanged although $x_1, \ldots, x_N$ themselves may change. In such a case, they are multiplied by a common factor α per unit of time. This factor is the coefficient of expansion of the whole economy." (4)

Such states have been described by Champernowne as "quasi-stationary states." The unknowns of the problem are: the intensity vector, x; the coefficient of expansion, α; the price vector, p; the interest factor, β.

As each technique has unit production period:

$\sum_{j=1}^{N} b_{ij}x_j =$ quantity of good i produced at the end of the current period;

$\sum_{j=1}^{N} c_{ij}x_j =$ quantity of good i used up in production (including workers' consumption) at the beginning of the current period.

As the model is closed, the inputs for next period are met from this period's outputs. In a quasi-stationary state:

$$\sum_{j=1}^{N} b_{ij}x_j \geqslant \alpha \sum_{j=1}^{N} c_{ij}x_j \qquad i=1,\ldots,M \qquad \cdots [1']$$

In equilibrium, those goods in excess supply become free goods. So, we have the following rule of free goods:

If

$$\sum_j b_{ij}x_j > \alpha \sum_j c_{ij}x_j, \quad \text{then} \quad p_i = 0 \qquad \cdots [2']$$

The cost of operating technique j at unit intensity is:

$$\beta\left(\sum_{i=1}^{M} p_i a_{ij} + wl_j\right) = \beta\left(\sum_i p_i a_{ij} + \sum_i p_i q_i l_j\right)$$

$$= \beta \sum_i p_i(a_{ij} + q_i l_j)$$

$$= \beta \sum_i p_i c_{ij}$$

β being the interest factor, equal to one plus the rate of interest.

$\sum_{i=1}^{M} p_i b_{ij} =$ receipts from operating technique j at unit intensity.

In equilibrium, given constant returns to scale, we have zero profits. Hence:

$$\beta \sum_i p_i c_{ij} \geqslant \sum_i p_i b_{ij} \qquad j=1,\ldots,N \qquad \cdots [3']$$

Given the price vector p, the costs of operating technique j at unit intensity (or any non-zero intensity) may be greater than the receipts; they could certainly not be less, under our hypotheses.

If the costs are greater than the receipts, technique j will evidently not be operated at all (i.e. zero intensity). So, we have the following rule of profitability:
If

$$\beta \sum_i p_i c_{ij} > \sum_i p_i b_{ij}, \quad \text{then} \quad x_j = 0 \qquad \cdots [4']$$

Equations [1′]–[4′] may be rewritten in more compact, matrix notation thus:

$$(B - \alpha C)x \geqslant \mathbf{0} \qquad \cdots [1]$$

$$p'(B - \alpha C)x = 0 \qquad \cdots [2]$$

$$p'(B - \beta C) \leqslant \mathbf{0}' \qquad \cdots [3]$$

$$p'(B - \beta C)x = 0 \qquad \cdots [4]$$

Von Neumann also imposed the condition:

$$B + C > [0] \qquad \cdots [5]$$

However, we shall follow Kemeny, Morgenstern and Thompson by imposing instead of condition [5]:

$$p'Bx > 0 \qquad \cdots [6]$$

from which we infer that something of value must be produced by the economy.

The problem is to find $x \geqslant \mathbf{0}_N$, $p \geqslant \mathbf{0}_M$, $\alpha \geqslant 0$, $\beta \geqslant 0$ such that conditions [1]–[4] and [6] are satisfied. We have immediately:

Lemma 1: If there is a solution of eqns [1]–[4] and [6], then $\alpha = \beta$.

Proof: Using eqns [2] and [4], $p'Bx = \alpha p'Cx = \beta p'Cx$. Then eqn [6] implies $\alpha = \beta$.

This lemma permits us to reduce the five conditions expressed in [1]–[4] and [6] to the following three conditions:

$$(B - \alpha C)x \geqslant \mathbf{0} \qquad \cdots [7]$$

$$p'(B - \alpha C) \leqslant \mathbf{0}' \qquad \cdots [8]$$

$$p'Bx > 0 \qquad \cdots [9]$$

Condition [2], or [4], follows straightforwardly from [7] and [8] given $p \geqslant \mathbf{0}$, $x \geqslant \mathbf{0}$.

Let us call the model outlined in this section a modified von Neumann model. Our main result is:

Theorem 1: The modified von Neumann model has a meaningful solution.

Proof: The proof begins with derivation of properties of the set $S=\left\{\alpha: \text{there exists } x\geqslant \mathbf{0},\ \sum_i x_i=1 \text{ such that } (B-\alpha C)x\geqq\mathbf{0}\right\}$.

In particular, we prove that S is a non-empty, closed set which is bounded from above. Then S will have a greatest element, say α^*.

By Tucker's theorem (Theorem 3 of Chapter 6), we can immediately show that eqns [7] and [8] are satisfied with $\alpha=\alpha^*$. It remains then to demonstrate that eqn [9] is satisfied.

First, we derive the properties of S.

That S is non-empty follows by putting $\alpha=0$, $x=\mathbf{1}/N$. By assumption (iii), $(B-\alpha C)x=B\mathbf{1}>\mathbf{0}$.

To demonstrate boundedness from above, consider the i-th component of $(B-\alpha C)x\geqq\mathbf{0}$, where $\alpha\in S$, i.e.

$$\sum_{j=1}^{N} b_{ij}x_j-\alpha\sum_{j=1}^{N} c_{ij}x_j\geqslant 0$$

Summing over i, we have:

$$\sum_{i=1}^{M}\sum_{j=1}^{N} b_{ij}x_j-\alpha\sum_{i=1}^{M}\sum_{j=1}^{N} c_{ij}x_j=\sum_{j=1}^{N} x_j\sum_{i=1}^{M} b_{ij}-\alpha\sum_{i=1}^{N} x_j\sum_{i=1}^{M} c_{ij}\geqslant 0$$

By assumption (ii), $\sum_{i=1}^{M} c_{ij}>0$, for some j.

Therefore,

$$\alpha\leqslant\left(\sum_j x_j\sum_i b_{ij}\right)\Big/\left(\sum_j x_j\sum_i c_{ij}\right)$$

$$\leqslant\max_j\left[\sum_i b_{ij}\Big/\sum_i c_{ij}\right]$$

Therefore, S is bounded from above.

Finally, we have to demonstrate closedness. Let $\{\alpha_\nu\}$ be a sequence in S. As S is bounded, $\alpha_\nu\to\alpha_0$.

Let $\{x(\alpha_\nu)\}$ be the corresponding sequence of x vectors in

$$X=\left\{x\geqslant\mathbf{0}: \sum_i x_i=1\right\}.$$

Let $\{\bar{x}^\nu\}$ be a subsequence of $\{x(\alpha_\nu)\}$ which converges to $x\in X$. Let $\{\bar{\alpha}_\nu\}$ be the corresponding sequence of α's.

Then $\bar{\alpha}_\nu\to\alpha_0$.

So $\lim_{\nu\to\infty}(B-\bar{\alpha}_\nu C)\bar{x}=(B-\alpha_0 C)\bar{x}\geqq\mathbf{0}$, as it is the limit of a sequence of non-negative vectors. So $\alpha_0\in S$ and S is closed. As S is closed and bounded, there exists a greatest α such that $(B-\alpha C)x\geqq\mathbf{0}$, $x\geqslant\mathbf{0}$. Let this value of α be α^*.

Consider the matrix $B-\alpha^* C$. By Tucker's theorem (Theorem 3 of Chapter

6), the inequalities:

$$\begin{aligned} &x'(B-\alpha^*C)' \geqq \mathbf{0}'_M \\ &-(B-\alpha^*C)'p \geqq \mathbf{0}_N \end{aligned} \qquad \cdots [10]$$

have solutions $p^* \geqq \mathbf{0}_M$, $x^* \geqq \mathbf{0}_N$ such that:

$$\begin{aligned} &x^* - (B-\alpha^*C)'p^* > \mathbf{0} \\ &x^{*\prime}(B-\alpha^*C)' + p^{*\prime} > \mathbf{0}' \end{aligned} \qquad \cdots [11]$$

(We associate $(B-\alpha^*C)'$ with the matrix C of Tucker's theorem, x with y and p with z.)
From eqn [10], we have:

$$(B-\alpha^*C)x^* \geqq \mathbf{0} \quad \text{i.e. eqn [7]}$$

$$p^{*\prime}(B-\alpha^*C) \leqq \mathbf{0}' \quad \text{i.e. eqn [8]}$$

We have to demonstrate that eqn [9] is satisfied. To this end, we demonstrate first that $x^* \geqslant \mathbf{0}$, $p^* \geqslant \mathbf{0}$.
Suppose $p^* = \mathbf{0}$. Then from the second inequality of eqn [11]:

$$x^{*\prime}(B-\alpha^*C)' > \mathbf{0}' \quad \text{or} \quad (B-\alpha^*C)x^* > \mathbf{0}.$$

Hence there exists $\bar{\alpha} > \alpha^*$ such that $(B-\bar{\alpha}C)x^* \geqq \mathbf{0}$. But this contradicts the definition of α^*. So $p^* \geqslant \mathbf{0}$.
Now suppose $x^* = \mathbf{0}$. Then, from the first inequality of [11]:

$$(B-\alpha^*C)'p^* < \mathbf{0} \quad \text{or} \quad p^{*\prime}(B-\alpha^*C) < \mathbf{0}' \qquad \cdots [12]$$

From the definition of α^*, there exists $\tilde{x} \geqslant \mathbf{0}$ such that:

$$(B-\alpha^*C)\tilde{x} \geqq \mathbf{0} \qquad \cdots [13]$$

Post-multiplying eqn [12] by $\tilde{x}$, and pre-multiplying eqn [13] by $p^*(>\mathbf{0}$, from the second inequality of [11]), we obtain:

$$p^{*\prime}(B-\alpha^*C)\tilde{x} < 0 \qquad \cdots [14]$$

$$p^{*\prime}(B-\alpha^*C)\tilde{x} \geqslant 0 \qquad \cdots [15]$$

The contradiction implies that $x^* \neq \mathbf{0}$. So, we have $x^* \geqslant \mathbf{0}$, $p^* \geqslant \mathbf{0}$. $\alpha^* \neq \mathbf{0}$, for we have shown that $(B-\alpha^*C)x = B\mathbf{1}/M > \mathbf{0}$, when $\alpha^* = 0$, $x = \mathbf{1}/M$. Hence there exists $\alpha > 0$ such that $(B-\alpha C)\mathbf{1}/M \geqq \mathbf{0}$.
We are now in a position to demonstrate that eqn [9] is satisfied. From eqn [10],

$$p^{*\prime}(B-\alpha^*C)x^* = p^{*\prime}Fx^* = 0, \quad F = B - \alpha^*C \qquad \cdots [16]$$

Apply permutations, represented by square matrices P and Q, so that

$$p^{*\prime}PP^{-1}FQ^{-1}Qx^* = (p^{*1} \quad \mathbf{0})' \begin{bmatrix} F_{11} & F_{12} \\ F_{21} & F_{22} \end{bmatrix} \begin{bmatrix} x^{*1} \\ \mathbf{0} \end{bmatrix} \qquad \cdots [17]$$

$p^{*1} > \mathbf{0}$, $x^{*1} > \mathbf{0}$.

From eqns [16] and [17], we have:

$$p^{*1\prime}F_{11}x^{*1}=0 \qquad \cdots [18]$$

Let

$$F_{ij}=B_{ij}-\alpha^{*}C_{ij} \quad i,j=1,2 \qquad \cdots [19]$$

So we have:

$$p^{*1\prime}(B_{11}-\alpha^{*}C_{11})x^{*1}=0 \qquad \cdots [20]$$

Now suppose that $p^{*\prime}Bx^{*}=0$. This implies that $p^{*1\prime}B_{11}x^{*1}=0$ or $B_{11}=[0]$. From eqn [20], we see that $C_{11}=[0]$. So:

$$B_{11}-\alpha^{*}C_{11}=[0]. \qquad \cdots [21]$$

From the second inequality of [11]:

$$p_i^{*}=0 \text{ implies } {}^{i}(B-\alpha^{*}C)'x^{*}>0, \qquad \cdots [22]$$

where ${}^{i}(\ )$ denotes the i-th row of the matrix ( ), the prime denoting the inner product operation.
Considering eqn [22] for all i such that $p_i^{*}=0$, we obtain:

$F_{21}x^{*1}+F_{22}\mathbf{0}>\mathbf{0}$ using eqn [17], or

$$(B_{21}-\alpha^{*}C)x^{*1}>\mathbf{0} \qquad \cdots [23]$$

Taking eqn [23] in conjunction with eqn [21], we obtain:

$$\begin{bmatrix} [0] & B_{12}-\alpha^{*}C_{12} \\ B_{21}-\alpha^{*}C_{21} & B_{22}-\alpha^{*}C_{22} \end{bmatrix}\begin{bmatrix} x^{*1} \\ \mathbf{0} \end{bmatrix} \geqslant \mathbf{0} \qquad \cdots [24]$$

From eqns [23] and [24], there exists $\tilde{\alpha}>\alpha^{*}$ such that:

$$(B_{21}-\tilde{\alpha}C_{21})x^{*1}\geqslant\mathbf{0} \qquad \cdots [25]$$

or

$$Fx^{*}\geqslant\mathbf{0} \qquad \cdots [26]$$

using eqn [19].
This contradicts the definition of α^{*}. So $p^{*\prime}Bx^{*}>0$, as required.
This completes the proof of the theorem.

We now consider the question of uniqueness. We have derived $\alpha=\beta$, but not uniqueness of the solution. Consider the following, very simple example:

$$A=\begin{bmatrix} 1 & 0 \\ 0 & 1 \end{bmatrix}, \qquad B-\begin{bmatrix} 1 & 0 \\ 0 & 2 \end{bmatrix}$$

(i) $\alpha=\beta=1$; $p=(1 \quad 0)'$; $x=(1 \quad 0)'$ and

(ii) $\alpha=\beta=2$; $p=(0 \quad 1)'$; $x=(0 \quad 1)'$

satisfy eqns [7]–[9].

These solutions are not unique for x_2 in (i) and p_1 in (ii) may be assigned arbitrary positive values.

As mentioned above, von Neumann's original model consisted of eqns [1]–[5]. Von Neumann rationalised eqn [5] thus: "Since the c_{ij}, b_{ij} may be arbitrarily small, this restriction is not very far reaching, although it must be imposed to assure uniqueness of α, β as otherwise the economy might break up into disconnected parts."(5)
This is exactly what happens in our numerical example above, for the economy can be completely decomposed into two separate sub-economies.

Theorem 2: The solution of the original von Neumann model, eqns [1]–[5], is unique.

Proof: Let (α, β, x, p) solve eqns [1]–[5].
From eqn [2]: $p'Bx = \alpha p'Cx$
From eqn [4]: $p'Bx = \beta p'Cx$
Adding $p'Cx$ to these equations, we obtain:

$$(1+\alpha)p'Cx = p'(B+C)x = (1+\beta)p'Cx.$$

By eqn [5], $p'(B+C)x > 0$ so that $p'Cx > 0$. Hence, $\alpha = \beta$.
So the solution is (α, α, x, p).
Assume there exists another solution $(\bar{\alpha}, \bar{\alpha}, \bar{x}, \bar{p})$.
From eqn [1]:

$$(B-\alpha C)x \geqslant \mathbf{0} \qquad \cdots [27]$$

Then

$$\bar{p}'(B-\alpha C)x \geqslant 0$$

or

$$\bar{p}'Bx \geqslant \alpha \bar{p}'Cx \qquad \cdots [28]$$

From eqn [3]:

$$\bar{p}'(B-\bar{\alpha}C) \leqslant \mathbf{0}' \qquad \cdots [29]$$

Then

$$\bar{p}'(B-\bar{\alpha}C)x \leqslant 0$$

or

$$\bar{p}'Bx \leqslant \bar{\alpha}\bar{p}'Cx \qquad \cdots [30]$$

Adding $\bar{p}'Cx$ to eqns [28] and [30], we obtain using eqn [5]:

$$\bar{\alpha} \geqslant \alpha \qquad \cdots [31]$$

From eqn [1]:

$$(B-\bar{\alpha}C)\bar{x} \geqslant \mathbf{0} \qquad \cdots [32]$$

From eqn [3]:

$$p'(B-\alpha C) \leqslant \mathbf{0} \qquad \cdots [33]$$

Manipulating eqns [32] and [33] in the same way as we manipulated eqns [27] and [29], we obtain:

$$\alpha \geqslant \bar{\alpha} \qquad \cdots [34]$$

From eqns [31] and [34], we have $\alpha = \bar{\alpha}$
i.e. uniqueness.

Further work on uniqueness is relegated to the exercises.

§7.2. Von Neumann–Leontief model

The analysis of the von Neumann model is much simplified if we abstract from joint production. Familiar mathematical theorems proved in Chapter 2 become applicable and the evaluation of growth rates, outputs and prices becomes more apparent. Accordingly, there may be pedagogical advantages in considering the von Neumann model under the assumption of no joint production—the model thus resembles the generalised Leontief model of §2.7. The difference between the von Neumann–Leontief and the generalised Leontief models lies in the assumption regarding production periods. Time was excluded from the generalised Leontief model, whereas here we maintain the (von Neumann) assumption of unit production period. As was made clear in the discussion in §7.1.1, the assumption of no joint production rules out a satisfactory treatment of capital goods.

We now proceed to describe the technology.

The j-th sector (which produces the j-th commodity) has available n_j techniques, each described by an input and an output vector. The output vector for the j-th sector is of a very simple form, for it is just e^j, the j-th unit vector.

Let us write the input vectors of the n_j techniques available to the j-th sector as:

$$c^{1_j}, c^{2_j}, \ldots, c^{n_j}.$$

Let I_j denote the ordered set $\{1_j, 2_j, \ldots, n_j\}$, $j = 1, \ldots, m$.

The input matrix for the economy is obtained by stacking the input vectors thus:

$$C = [c^{1_1} \quad \cdots \quad c^{n_1};\ c^{1_2} \quad \cdots \quad c^{n_2}; \quad \cdots;\ c^{1_j} \quad \cdots \quad c^{n_j}; \quad \cdots;\ c^{1_m} \quad \cdots \quad c^{n_m}] \qquad \cdots [1]$$

the input vectors for the first sector being written first, followed by those for the second sector, and so on, until we have those for the m-th sector.

The output matrix for the economy is:

$$B = [e^1 \quad \cdots \quad e^1;\ e^2 \quad \cdots \quad e^2; \cdots;\ e^j \quad \cdots \quad e^j; \cdots \quad e^m \quad \cdots \quad e^m] \qquad \cdots [2]$$

where e^j occurs n_j times, $j = 1, \ldots, m$.

Let $\sum_{j=1}^{m} n_j = n$. So C and B are $m \times n$ matrices. Let p be the m-dimensional price vector, x the n-dimensional vector of activity levels, as in §7.1.

We seek a solution of the same problem as in §7.1, viz. eqns [7]–[9] of §7.1.2, which we rewrite here as:

$$(B-\alpha C)x \geqslant \mathbf{0} \qquad \cdots [3]$$

$$p'(B-\alpha C) \leqslant \mathbf{0}' \qquad \cdots [4]$$

$$p'Bx > 0 \qquad \cdots [5]$$

We specify that each sector chooses one of its available techniques. The input vectors of the techniques chosen can be stacked to form the $m \times m$ matrix

$$C_h = [c^{h_1} \quad c^{h_2} \quad \cdots \quad c^{h_m}] \qquad h_j \in I_j, \qquad j=1,\ldots,m \qquad \cdots [6]$$

The output vectors of the techniques chosen can be stacked to yield obviously:

$$B_h = I_m, \quad \text{the identity matrix of order } m \qquad \cdots [7]$$

There are obviously $\prod_{j=1}^{m} n_j$ possible technique matrices of the form C_h.

We now discuss the choice of the matrix C_h.
From the Perron–Frobenius theorem of Chapter 2, we have:

$$C_h y^h = \lambda^*(C_h)y^h, \qquad p^{h\prime}C_h = \lambda^*(C_h)p^{h\prime} \qquad \cdots [8]$$

where

$$\lambda^*(C_h) \geqslant 0, \qquad p^h \geqslant \mathbf{0}, \qquad y \geqslant \mathbf{0}.$$

We choose the matrix C_h which has the smallest Frobenius root.
Let this matrix be:

$$C_g = [c^{g_1} \quad c^{g_2} \quad \cdots \quad c^{g_m}] \qquad g_j \in I_j, \qquad j=1,\ldots,m.$$

We assume that the matrix C_g is indecomposable and that $\lambda^*(C_g) < \lambda^*(C_h)$ for all $h \neq g$. The indecomposability assumption is the main assumption here, for once we assume indecomposability, $C_g \neq C_h$ implies $\lambda^*(C_g) \neq \lambda^*(C_h)$ by Theorem 25 of Chapter 2; $C_g \neq C_h$ is a trivial condition. We then have:

$$C_g y^g = \lambda^*(C_g)y^g, \qquad p^{g\prime}C_g = \lambda^*(C_g)p^{g\prime} \qquad \cdots [9]$$

where

$$\lambda^*(C_g) > 0, \qquad y^g > \mathbf{0}, \qquad p^g > \mathbf{0}.$$

Lemma 2: Let $C_k = [c^{k_1} \quad c^{k_2} \quad \cdots \quad c^{k_m}]$ be such that

$$c^{k_j} \neq c^{g_j} \qquad \text{for all } j=1,\ldots,m.$$

Then

$$p^{g\prime}C_k > \lambda^*(C_g)p^{g\prime} \qquad \cdots [10]$$

Proof: Suppose that each of the first i components of $\lambda^*(C_g)p^{g'}$ is greater than the corresponding component of $p^{g'}C_k$, i.e.

$$\lambda^*(C_g)p_r^g > \sum_{s=1}^{m} p_s^g c_s^{k_r} \qquad r=1,\ldots,i \qquad \cdots[11]$$

where subscripts refer to components of vectors.
Let C_p be that matrix consisting of the first i columns of C_k, the last $(m-i)$ columns of C_g, i.e.

$$C_p = [c^{k_1} \quad \cdots \quad c^{k_i} \quad c^{g_{i+1}} \quad \cdots \quad c^{g_m}] \qquad \cdots[12]$$

Then:

$$\lambda^*(C_g)p^{g'} \geqslant p^{g'}C_p \qquad \cdots[13]$$

using eqns [9], [11] and [12].
Now:

$$C_p y^p = \lambda^*(C_p)y^p, \qquad \lambda^*(C_p) \geqslant 0, \quad y^p \geqslant \mathbf{0} \qquad \cdots[14]$$

as in eqn [8].
Post-multiplying eqn [13] by y^p, we obtain:

$$\lambda^*(C_g)p^{g'}y^p \geqslant p^{g'}C_p y^p = p^{g'}\lambda^*(C_p)y^p \qquad \cdots[15]$$

from eqn [14].
$p^g > \mathbf{0}$ and $y^p \geqslant \mathbf{0}$ imply $p^{g'}y^p > 0$. Hence, $\lambda^*(C_g) > \lambda^*(C_p)$, from eqn [15]. This contradicts the definition of C_g as that matrix with smallest Frobenius root. So, we have eqn [10], as required.

We can now derive our main result on the existence of unique solutions to the von Neumann–Leontief model.
First, let us define an n-dimensional vector x^g using the components of the Frobenius vector y^g. Let:

$$y^g = (y_{g_1}, y_{g_2}, \ldots, y_{g_m})' \qquad g_j \in I_j, \qquad j=1,\ldots,m$$

g_j refers to the technique chosen by the j-th sector.

Consider the ordered set $I = \bigcup_{j=1}^{m} I_j$ which may be written in extensive form as:

$$I = \{1_1, \ldots, n_1;\ 1_2, \ldots, n_2;\ \ldots;\ 1_j, \ldots, n_j;\ \ldots;\ 1_m, \ldots, n_m\}.$$

Define:

$$x^g = (0, \ldots, y_{g_1}, 0, \ldots, 0;\ 0, \ldots, 0, y_{g_2}, 0, \ldots, 0;\ \ldots;\ 0, \ldots, 0, y_{g_j}, 0, \ldots, 0;\ \ldots;\ 0, \ldots, 0, y_{g_m}, 0, \ldots, 0)' \qquad \cdots[16]$$

y_{g_j} occurring in the place corresponding to g_j in the set I. From eqns [1], [2] and [16]:

$$Cx^g = C_g y^g, \qquad Bx^g = y^g \qquad \cdots[17]$$

We have:

Theorem 3: (i) Equations [3]–[5] have solution $x = x^g$, $p = p^g$, $\alpha = 1/\lambda^*(C_g)$. (ii) if x, p, α solve eqns [3]–[5], then $x = \beta x^g$, $p = \gamma p^g$,

$\alpha = 1/\lambda^*(C_g)$.

Proof: From eqns [3] and [17]:

$$(B - \alpha C)x^g = y^g - C_g y^g/\lambda^*(C_g) = \mathbf{0} \qquad \cdots [18]$$

from eqn [9].
Now consider

$$p^{g\prime}(B - \alpha C) = p^{g\prime}B - p^{g\prime}C/\lambda^*(C_g) \qquad \cdots [19]$$

Extract from C those columns which constitute the matrix C_g and from B the corresponding columns. We will then have:

$$p^{g\prime}I_m - p^{g\prime}C_g/\lambda^*(C_g) = \mathbf{0} \qquad \cdots [20]$$

from eqn [9].
Consider the remaining columns of C, denoted by C^s say. From Lemma 2:

$$p^g_s < p^{g\prime}C^s/\lambda^*(C_g) \quad \text{for all} \quad s \neq g_1, g_2, \ldots, g_m \qquad \cdots [21]$$

Combining eqns [20] and [21], we have:

$$p^{g\prime}B - p^{g\prime}C/\lambda^*(C_g) \leqslant \mathbf{0} \qquad \cdots [22]$$

Hence: $p^{g\prime}(B - \alpha C) \leqslant \mathbf{0}$ with $\alpha = 1/\lambda^*(C_g)$, as required.
It remains to establish eqn [5].

$p^{g\prime}Bx^g = p^{g\prime}y^g > 0$ as $p^g > \mathbf{0}$, $y^g > \mathbf{0}$, using eqns [9] and [17].

This completes the proof of (i).
We now consider (ii).
Suppose that x, p and α solve eqns [3]–[5].
From eqn [3]:

$$Bx \geqslant \alpha Cx$$

or

$$\alpha^{-1}p^{g\prime}Bx \geq p^{g\prime}Cx \qquad \cdots [23]$$

as $p^g > \mathbf{0}$
By Lemma 2: $\lambda^*(C_g)p^{g\prime}B \leq p^{g\prime}C$. Hence as $x \geq \mathbf{0}$, we have:

$$\lambda^*(C_g)p^{g\prime}Bx \leq p^{g\prime}Cx \qquad \cdots [24]$$

From eqns [23] and [24]:

$$\alpha^{-1}p^{g\prime}Bx \geq p^{g\prime}Cx \geq \lambda^*(C_g)p^{g\prime}Bx \qquad \cdots [25]$$

$Bx \geq \mathbf{0}$, as eqn [5] is satisfied. Then as $p^g > \mathbf{0}$, we have $p^{g\prime}Bx > 0$. So, from eqn [25], we have:

$$\alpha^{-1} \geqslant \lambda^*(C_g) \qquad \cdots [26]$$

From eqns [9] and [17]:

$$\lambda^*(C_g)Bx^g = Cx^g \qquad \cdots [27]$$

As $Bx^g > \mathbf{0}$, we have on pre-multiplying by $p' \geqslant \mathbf{0}'$:

$$0 < \lambda^*(C_g)p'Bx^g = p'Cx^g \qquad \cdots [28]$$

From eqn [4]: $p'(B - \alpha C) \leqslant \mathbf{0}$. Post-multiplying by $x^g \geqslant \mathbf{0}$, we obtain:

$$\alpha^{-1}p'Bx^g \leqslant p'Cx^g \qquad \cdots [29]$$

So, from eqns [28] and [29]:

$$\alpha^{-1}p'Bx^g \leqslant p'Cx^g = \lambda^*(C_g)p'Bx^g \qquad \cdots [30]$$

This implies:

$$\alpha^{-1} \leqslant \lambda^*(C_g) \qquad \cdots [31]$$

From eqns [26] and [31], $\alpha = 1/\lambda^*(C_g)$
We must now relate x and p to x^g and p^g respectively.
Consider

$$\lambda^*(C_g)p'Bx^g = p'Cx^g$$

from eqn [30], or

$$\lambda^*(C_g)p'y^g = p'C_g y^g \qquad \cdots [32]$$

Suppose

$$\lambda^*(C_g)p' \neq p'C_g \qquad \cdots [33]$$

Then post-multiplying by $y^g > \mathbf{0}$, we have:

$$\lambda^*(C_g)p'y^g \neq p'C_g y^g$$

which plainly contradicts eqn [32]. So:

$$\lambda^*(C_g)p' = p'C_g \qquad \cdots [34]$$

As C_g is indecomposable, eqn [34] clearly implies that $p = \gamma p^g$.
Now consider:

$$p^{g\prime}Cx = \lambda^*(C_g)p^{g\prime}Bx \qquad \cdots [35]$$

from eqn [25].
Suppose $Bx = y \neq \beta y^g \geqslant \mathbf{0}$. Then:

$$Cx = C_k y \geqslant \mathbf{0} \qquad \cdots [36]$$

Substituting in eqn [35], we obtain:

$$p^{g\prime}C_k y = \lambda^*(C_g)p^{g\prime}y \qquad \cdots [37]$$

From Lemma 2:

$$p^{g\prime}C_k > \lambda^*(C_g)p^{g\prime} \qquad \cdots [38]$$

As $y \geqslant \mathbf{0}$, we obtain from eqn [38]:

$$p^{g\prime}C_k y > \lambda^*(C_g)p^{g\prime}y \qquad \cdots [39]$$

Equations [37] and [39] plainly contradict each other.
So $Bx = \beta y^g$, which implies $x = \beta x^g$ as required. The theorem is now proved.

§7.3. Separation theorems

In this section, we digress to derive separation theorems for convex sets. This material will be applied later in §7.4 and also in Chapter 8.

The notions of convexity and closedness were introduced in §2.7. We restate them here for convenience.

Definition 1: The set X is *convex* if, for any x^1, $x^2 \in X$, α_1, $\alpha_2 \geqslant 0$, $\alpha_1 + \alpha_2 = 1$, $\alpha_1 x^1 + \alpha_2 x^2 \in X$.

Definition 2: The element $x \in X$ is a *limit point* of X if each neighbourhood of x contains at least one element of X different from x. Then X is a closed set if it contains all its limit points.

Definition 3: Given a set X and $\bar{X}$, the set of limit points of X, we define the *closure of* X, $\mathcal{A}(X)$, by: $\mathcal{A}(X) = X \cup \bar{X}$.

Examples of closed and convex sets are provided in the exercises. Let us restrict ourselves to R^n and its subsets.
We begin by introducing the concept of a hyperplane in:

Definition 4: A *hyperplane* in R^n is defined by:

$$H(a, \alpha) = \{x : a'x = \alpha\}.$$

To determine the hyperplane, it is necessary to specify the vector a and the scalar α, a total of $n+1$ parameters. However, $H(a, \alpha) = H(\beta a, \beta\alpha)$ for any scalar β. So, we have one degree of freedom, that is, only n parameters to determine. We must know two distinct vectors in R^n to be able to determine a line; it might be thought that knowledge of n vectors in R^n suffices to determine a hyperplane. However, to obtain a unique hyperplane, we must specify further conditions.

Theorem 4: Let $\{x^1, \ldots, x^n\}$ be a set of vectors in R^n such that $\{x^1 - x^n, \ldots, x^{n-1} - x^n\}$ is a linearly independent set. Then the set determines a unique hyperplane.

Proof: Consider

$$a'x^i = \alpha \qquad i = 1, \ldots, n \qquad \cdots [1]$$

Subtracting the n-th equation from the previous $n-1$, we obtain:

$$a'(x^i - x^n) = 0 \qquad i = 1, \ldots, n-1 \qquad \cdots [2]$$

or

$$a'B' = \mathbf{0}' \qquad \cdots [3]$$

B' being the $n \times n-1$ matrix with $x^i - x^n$ as its i-th column, $i = 1, \ldots, n-1$. Transposing eqn [3], we obtain:

$$Ba = \mathbf{0} \qquad \cdots [4]$$

We now appeal to the following standard theorem: column rank of B + column nullity of B = dimension of domain of $B = n$.
Column rank of B = rank of $B = n-1$. Therefore, column nullity of $B = 1$. So there exists only one vector, unique up to scalar multiplication, which solves eqn [4]. α may then be derived from $a'x^n = \alpha$.
If the rank of B is less than $n-1$, the column nullity of B is greater than one. This implies that a unique hyperplane does not exist.

The hyperplane $H(a, \alpha)$ can be used to define subsets of R^n thus:

Definition 5: $H(a, \alpha)$ determines the following subsets of R^n: $H_1(a, \alpha) = \{x : a'x \geq \alpha\}$, $H_2(a, \alpha) = \{x : a'x \leq \alpha\}$ are called *closed half-spaces*: $H_3(a, \alpha) = \{x : a'x > \alpha\}$, $H_4(a, \alpha) = \{x : a'x < \alpha\}$ are called *open half-spaces.* H_1 and H_2 are the closures of H_3 and H_4 respectively.

We are interested in particular in the sub-classes of hyperplanes described in the next three definitions.

Definition 6: $H(a, \alpha)$ is a *bounding hyperplane* for X if X is contained in either $H_1(a, \alpha)$ or $H_2(a, \alpha)$.

We may distinguish two cases, according as $X \cap H(a, \alpha) = \emptyset$ or $X \cap H(a, \alpha) \neq \emptyset$.

Definition 7: The bounding hyperplane $H(a, \alpha)$ is a *supporting hyperplane* for X if X lies in one of the closed half-spaces of $H(a, \alpha)$ and $X \cap H(a, \alpha) \neq \emptyset$.

In the following definition, let X and Y be subsets of R^n.

Definition 8: The bounding hyperplane $H(a, \alpha)$ is a *separating hyperplane* for X and Y if X is contained in one of the closed half-spaces of $H(a, \alpha)$, Y is contained in the other.

In the theorems, we shall be concerned with convex and closed convex sets. We begin with:

Theorem 5: Let X be a closed convex set, $y \notin X$. Then there exists a hyperplane $H(a, \alpha)$ such that $y \in H(a, \alpha)$ and X is contained in one of the open half-spaces of $H(a, \alpha)$.

Proof: We may write the theorem more compactly as:

$$\min_{x \in X} a'x > a'y \quad \left(\text{or} \quad \min_{x \in X} a'x < a'y\right)$$

By closedness, there exists a unique $x^0 \in X$ such that:

$$|y-x^0| = [(y-x^0)'(y-x^0)]^{\frac{1}{2}} = \min_{x \in X} |y-x| \qquad \cdots [5]$$

For, if x^1 also satisfies eqn [5], we have by the triangle inequality:

$$\begin{aligned} |y-\tfrac{1}{2}(x^0+x^1)| &= \tfrac{1}{2}|(y-x^0)+(y-x^1)| \\ &\leq \tfrac{1}{2}[|y-x^0|+|y-x^1|] \end{aligned} \qquad \cdots [6]$$

Strict inequality holds iff $y-x^1=\rho(y-x^0)$. As this equation does not hold, we have strict inequality in [5], i.e. $\frac{1}{2}(x^0+x^1)$ is closer to y. So, we have uniqueness.

For $x \in X$, consider $x(\gamma)=\gamma x+(1-\gamma)x^0 = x^0+\gamma(x-x^0)$, $0 \leq \gamma \leq 1$. $x(\gamma) \in X$ by convexity.

By choice of x^0, we must have:

$$|x(\gamma)-y|^2 \geq |x^0-y|^2 \qquad \cdots [7]$$

or

$$2\gamma(x-x^0)'(x^0-y)+\gamma^2(x-x^0)'(x-x^0) \geq 0 \qquad \cdots [8]$$

Dividing by $\gamma > 0$ and taking the limit as $\gamma \to 0$, we have:

$$(x-x^0)'(x^0-y) \geq 0$$

or

$$x'(x^0-y) \geq x^{0\prime}(x^0-y) \qquad \cdots [9]$$

Also $(x^0-y)'(x^0-y)>0$, which implies

$$x^{0\prime}(x^0-y) > y'(x^0-y) \qquad \cdots [10]$$

Combining eqns [9] and [10], we obtain:

$$x'(x^0-y) \geq x^{0\prime}(x^0-y) > y'(x^0-y) \qquad \cdots [11]$$

Let $x^0-y=a$; $a \neq \mathbf{0}$. Then eqn [11] is:

$$x'a \geq x^{0\prime}a > y'a \qquad \cdots [12]$$

As eqn [12] is true for any $x \in X$, we have:

$$\min_{x \in X} a'x > a'y$$

as required.

By a similar method, we may derive:

Theorem 6: Let X be a convex set, $y \notin \mathrm{Cl}(X)$. Then there exists a separating hyperplane for X and $Y=\{y\}$.

Theorem 7: If y is a boundary point of the closed convex set X, there exists a supporting hyperplane for X through y.

Proof: Consider the sequence of vectors $\{y^\nu\}$, $y^\nu \in X$, such that $\lim_{\nu\to\infty} y^\nu = y$. By Theorem 5, there exists a^ν, with $a^{\nu\prime}a^\nu = 1$, such that

$$\min_{x\in X} x'a^\nu > y^{\nu\prime}a^\nu$$

Taking the limit, a, of $\{a^\nu\}$, we have for any $x \in X$:

$$a'x = \lim_{\nu\to\infty} x'a^\nu \geqslant \lim y^{\nu\prime}a^\nu = a'y$$

So $\min_{x\in X} a'x = a'y$, i.e. X has a supporting hyperplane through y.

Just as Theorem 5 was weakened to Theorem 6, so Theorem 7 may be weakened to:

Theorem 8: If y is a boundary point of the convex set X, there is a supporting hyperplane through y.

Theorem 9: If X and Y are convex sets with no interior points in common, there exists a separating hyperplane for X and Y.

Proof: Consider the set $Z = \{z = x - y : x \in X,\ y \in Y\}$. Z is a convex set. $\mathbf{0} \notin$ interior of Z, though $\mathbf{0}$ may be a boundary point of Z. Then by Theorems 6 and 8, there exists $a \neq \mathbf{0}$ such that $a'z \geqslant a'\mathbf{0}$ for all $z \in Z$, i.e. $a'(x-y) \geqslant 0$ or $a'x \geqslant a'y$ for all $x \in X$, $y \in Y$.
So there exists a pair (a, α) such that:

$$a'x \geqslant \alpha \quad \text{for all} \quad x \in X$$

$$a'y \leqslant \alpha \quad \text{for all} \quad y \in Y$$

This pair (a, α) defines the hyperplane $H(a, \alpha)$, which is the required separating hyperplane for X and Y.

Finally, we have the following theorem to be used in §7.4:

Theorem 10: Let X be a convex set such that $X \cap R^n\,(0,+) = \emptyset$. Then there exists $a \geqslant \mathbf{0}$ such that $a'x \leqslant 0$ for all $x \in X$.

Proof: By the previous theorem, there exists $a \neq \mathbf{0}$ such that:

$$a'x \leqslant 0 \quad \text{for all} \quad x \in X$$

$$a'y \geqslant 0 \quad \text{for all} \quad y \in Y = R^n(0, +)$$

Putting $y = e^i$, $i = 1, \ldots, n$, yields $a \geqq \mathbf{0}$. As $a \neq \mathbf{0}$, it follows that $a \geqslant \mathbf{0}$, as required.

§7.4. Balanced growth in a closed model

In this final section, we shall outline a closed production model permitting balanced growth, of which the von Neumann model is a special case. Our work is thus a generalisation of §§7.1 and 7.2. Assume that there are n commodities. Let y be the output vector, w the input vector. The technology set, T, is the set of all ordered pairs (w, y) such that output y can be produced from input w. We impose the following conditions on T:

(A1): T is convex.
(A2): T is a cone.
(A3): If $(\mathbf{0}, y) \in T$, then $y = \mathbf{0}$ ("the impossibility of the land of Cockaigne").
(A4): For each $i = 1, \ldots, n$, there exists $(w^i, y^i) \in T$ such that $y^i_i > 0$ (i.e. every commodity can be produced).
(A5): T is closed.
(A6): If $(w, y) \in T$, $\bar{w} \geqq w$, $\mathbf{0} \leqq \bar{y} \leqq y$, then $(\bar{w}, \bar{y}) \in T$ (i.e. free disposal).

The list here corresponds to that given in §2.7.
Note that (A1), (A2), (A4) and (A5) imply that there exists $(w, y) \in T$ such that $y > \mathbf{0}$.
We now introduce:

Definition 9: For a feasible pair $(w, y) \in T$, the *growth factor*, $\mu(w, y)$, is defined by:

$$\mu(w, y) = \max\{\mu : y \geqq \mu w\} \qquad \cdots [1]$$

From (A1)–(A3), we have:

$$0 \leqslant \mu(w, y) < \infty \qquad \cdots [2]$$

Our main result is:

Theorem 11: (i) There exists $(w^*, y^*) \in T$ such that:

$$y^* = \mu^* w^*, \qquad \mu^* = \mu(w^*, y^*), \qquad w^* \geqslant \mathbf{0} \qquad \cdots [3]$$

$$\mu^* \geqslant \mu(w, y) \qquad \cdots [4]$$

(ii) There exists $p^* \geqslant \mathbf{0}$ such that $p^{*\prime} y \leqslant \mu^* p^{*\prime} w$ for all $(w, y) \in T$.

Proof: (i) Define $\mu^* = \sup\{\mu(w, y) : (w, y) \in T, w \geqslant \mathbf{0}\}$ $\cdots$ [5]

We show that μ^* is positive and finite.
As noted above, (A1), (A2), (A4), (A5) imply that there exists a pair $(w, y) \in T$ such that $y > \mathbf{0}$. For this pair, it is obvious that $\mu(w, y) > 0$. Then $\mu^* \geqslant \mu(w, y) > 0$.
Now suppose that μ^* is not finite. Then there exists a sequence $(w^\nu, y^\nu) \in T$ such that $y^\nu \geqslant \mathbf{0}$, $y^\nu \geqq \mu(w^\nu, y^\nu) w^\nu$, $\lim_{\nu \to \infty} \mu(w^\nu, y^\nu) = \infty$.

Without loss of generality, we may normalise so that $\sum_{i=1}^{n} y_i = 1$.

Then

$$y^\nu / \mu(w^\nu, y^\nu) \geqq w^\nu.$$

Taking the limit as $\nu \to \infty$, we have:

$$(\mathbf{0}, \tilde{y}) \in T, \qquad \tilde{y} = \lim_{\nu \to \infty} y^\nu \neq \mathbf{0}.$$

This contradicts (A3). So μ^* is finite. By (A1) and (A3), there exists a pair $(\bar{w}, \bar{y}) \in T$ such that $\mu^* = \mu(\bar{w}, \bar{y})$, i.e. $\bar{y} \geqslant \mu^* \bar{w}$. Then by using free disposability, (A6), there exists a pair $(w^*, y^*) \in T$ such that

$$y^* = \mu^* w^*, \qquad \mu^*(w^*, y^*) = \mu^*(\bar{w}, \bar{y}).$$

This completes the proof of (i)

(ii) Define $X = \left\{ y - \mu^* w : (w, y) \in T, \ \sum_{i=1}^{n} (w_i + y_i) \leqslant 1 \right\}$.

X is a closed convex set. Also $X \cap R^n(0, +) = \emptyset$. By Theorem 10, there exists $p^* \geqslant \mathbf{0}$ such that $p^{*\prime}(y - \mu^* w) \leqslant 0$ or

$p^{*\prime} y \leqslant \mu^* p^{*\prime} w$ as required.

This completes the proof of the theorem.

§7.5. Review

In this chapter, we continued the demonstration, begun in Chapter 5, of the importance of the Perron–Frobenius theorem in dynamic economic analysis. In open models, both linear and non-linear, the Frobenius root provides a limit to the rate of balanced growth of the economy, while in closed models, together with its associated vector, it defines a balanced solution. In the context of the von Neumann–Leontief model, we applied the Perron–Frobenius theorems to evaluate outputs, prices and the growth rate.

However, the main purpose of the chapter was to develop an adequate treatment of fixed capital, an issue evaded so far. As far as the incorporation of fixed capital goes, the appropriate generalisation of the input–output model was the von Neumann model.

The concluding section of the chapter introduced us to a set theoretic approach to general equilibrium analysis, an approach that will be pursued in the next chapter (the basis for this approach is the theory of convex sets). The closed production model outlined in this section includes the von Neumann and input–output models as special cases.

Exercises

§§7.1 *and* 7.2

1. How can consumer demand be introduced into the von Neumann model? What is its effect on the growth rate?
(See Kemeny, Morgenstern & Thompson.)

2. Consider the effect of small changes in the coefficients on prices and intensities.
(a) Compare the solution of

$$C = \begin{bmatrix} 1 & \varepsilon \\ \varepsilon & 1 \end{bmatrix}, \ B = \begin{bmatrix} 1 & 2\varepsilon \\ \varepsilon & 1+\varepsilon \end{bmatrix}$$

with the solution of

$$C=\begin{bmatrix}1 & \varepsilon\\ \varepsilon & 1\end{bmatrix},\ B=\begin{bmatrix}1+\varepsilon & \varepsilon\\ 2\varepsilon & 1\end{bmatrix}$$

(b) Compare the solution of

$$C=\begin{bmatrix}1 & 2\varepsilon\\ 2\varepsilon & 1\end{bmatrix},\ B=\begin{bmatrix}1-\varepsilon & \varepsilon\\ 2\varepsilon & 1\end{bmatrix}$$

with that of

$$C=\begin{bmatrix}1 & 2\varepsilon\\ 2\varepsilon & 1\end{bmatrix},\ B=\begin{bmatrix}1 & 2\varepsilon\\ \varepsilon & 1-\varepsilon\end{bmatrix}$$

(Kemeny, Morgenstern & Thompson)

3. Generalise the indecomposability concept of Chapter 2 to the case of rectangular matrices, i.e. derive a concept that will be applicable to the von Neumann model. (Weil)

4. In the text, it was proved that the growth and interest factors, not the growth and interest rates, were positive. Prove that α and β are greater than one if there exists $x > 0$ such that $(B-A)x > \mathbf{0}$.

5. Discuss the relation between the von Neumann model with $B = I$ and the backward difference equation models of §4.2.13 and §5.2, in particular with reference to the existence of meaningful solutions.

6. (a) Prove that if the von Neumann economy is indecomposable, the growth rate is unique.
(b) Solve the following example to show that the converse in (a) is not true:

$$C=\begin{bmatrix}1 & 1\\ 0 & 1\end{bmatrix},\ B=\begin{bmatrix}2 & 3\\ 0 & 3\end{bmatrix}$$

(c) Prove that, if there is more than one growth rate, the von Neumann economy must be decomposable.
(d) Decomposability is necessary but not sufficient for multiple growth rates, as the example in (b) illustrates.
(e) Find all (three) solutions of the following model:

$$C=\begin{bmatrix}1 & 2 & 1\\ 0 & 1 & 4\\ 0 & 0 & 1\end{bmatrix},\ B=\begin{bmatrix}4 & 3 & 2\\ 0 & 3 & 2\\ 0 & 0 & 2\end{bmatrix}$$

(Weil)

§§7.3 *and* 7.4

1. Are the following sets closed and/or convex?
   (i) $H(a, \alpha)$; $H_1(a, \alpha)$; $H_2(a, \alpha)$; $H_3(a, \alpha)$; $H_4(a, \alpha)$.
   (ii) $X \cap Y$; $X \cup Y$, if X and Y are closed and convex.
   (iii) $\cap X_i$; $\cup X_i$, if X_i is closed and convex for all i.
   (iv) $H(a^1, \alpha_1) \cap H(a^2, \alpha_2)$.
   (v) The solution set of $Ax = b$.
   (vi) The solution set of $Ax = b$, $b \geqslant \mathbf{0}$.
   (vii) The solution set of $Ax \geqslant b$, $b \geqslant \mathbf{0}$.
   (viii) Given $x^1, \ldots, x^m$, the set $\left\{x = \sum_{i=1}^{m} \mu_i x^i : \mu_i \geqslant 0, \text{ for all } i, \sum_{i=1}^{m} \mu_i = 1\right\}$
   (ix) $X + Y = \{x + y : x \in X, y \in Y\}$; $X - Y = \{x - y : x \in X, y \in Y\}$ if X and Y are closed convex sets.

2. Prove that the hyperplane $a'x = 0$ in R^n is a subspace of dimension $n-1$. Conversely, prove that any subspace in R^n of dimension $n-1$ is a hyperplane through the origin.

3. Let $T: R^n \to R^m$ be a linear mapping. Let $X \subseteq R^n$ be a convex set. Prove that $Y = f(X) = \{y = f(x) : x \in X\}$ is also a convex set.

4. Prove that if $\{a^1, \ldots, a^k\}$ is a linearly independent set, the intersection of the k hyperplanes $a^{i\prime}x = 0$ in R^n is a subspace of dimension $n-k$.

5. Let X and Y be closed convex sets.
   (a) If $X \cap Y = \emptyset$, prove that there exists a separating hyperplane $H(a, \alpha)$ for X and Y such that X is contained in one open half-space of $H(a, \alpha)$, Y is contained in the other.
   (b) If X and Y intersect at only one point, prove that there exists a separating hyperplane $H(a, \alpha)$ which is also a supporting hyperplane for X and Y.

Notes

1. Von Neumann, J.: "A model of general economic equilibrium", *Review of Economic Studies*, **13** (1945–46). p. 2.

2. ibid.

3. ibid.

4. ibid.

5. op. cit. p. 3.

References

§7.1

The original references are:

Champernowne, D. G.: "A note on J. von Neumann's article on 'A model of economic equilibrium' ", *Review of Economic Studies*, **13** (1945).

von Neumann, J.: "A model of general economic equilibrium", *Review of Economic Studies,* **13** (1945).

These two papers are reprinted in:
Hahn, F. H. (ed.): *Readings in the Theory of Growth,* Macmillan, 1971.

Newman, P. (ed.): *Readings in Mathematical Economics,* vol. 2, Johns Hopkins U.P., 1968.

Other papers to be consulted include:
Howe, C. W.: "An alternative proof of the existence of general equilibrium in a von Neumann model", *Econometrica,* **28** (1960).

Kemeny, J. G., O. Morgenstern & G. L. Thompson: "A generalisation of the von Neumann model of an expanding economy", *Econometrica,* **24** 1956.

Weil, R. L.: "Solutions to the decomposable von Neumann model", *Econometrica,* **38** (1970).

§7.2
Morishima, M.: "Proof of a turnpike theorem: the 'no joint production' case", *Review of Economic Studies,* **28** (1961).

§7.3
Karlin, S.: *Mathematical Methods and Theory in Games, Programming and Economics,* Pergamon Press, 1959.

§7.4
Karlin, S.: op. cit.

8

General equilibrium

§8.1. Introduction

§8.1.1. *Preview*

1. In previous chapters, the emphasis has been on the analysis of interactions between producers. There have been one or two exceptions to this—for example, in §2.5, we examined a model of exchange equilibrium; there was no production and attention was concentrated on consumers' behaviour with particular regard to the question of existence of equilibrium: and in Chapters 5 and 6, we considered dynamic expenditure and production-expenditure models; the expenditure models were basically macroeconomic in nature, as exemplified by Metzler's multi-country trade model for the analysis of income determination. By contrast, this chapter will be basically microeconomic in nature; we seek to analyse the behaviour of an economy in terms of its individual constituents, which we assume to be consumers (or households) and firms. We must specify the mode of interaction for these individual constituents, or agents. We shall assume the existence of a market organisation—goods and the services of factors of production can be exchanged freely; we make the further assumption that the prices at which the exchanges occur are beyond the control of each agent. Finally, we assume, *pro tempore*, that time does not enter into the analysis in any essential way—the behaviour of each agent in any given time period is independent of his behaviour in any other time period, past or future; for example, we do not permit the storing of commodities which would allow the transfer of wealth from one time period to the next. So the economy is assumed to be timeless, or atemporal.

We shall examine first of all the question of consistency of actions of all agents, i.e. can firms supply the goods to satisfy consumers' demands, at the ruling prices. This statement of the problem resembles that in Chapter 2 in our analysis of the static input–output model—there, the final demand vector was considered exogenous with no restrictions placed on it except non-negativity.

Now if we are to examine the interactions between consumers and producers, some hypotheses must be advanced to explain the behaviour of consumers and firms. We shall suppose that an individual's consumption pattern is determined only by the prices of commodities and his income; the individual's income is determined by the amount of his resources (primarily labour) that he can sell and by his share of profits distributed by firms; as the individual's income is determined by the ruling price vector, so will be his demand for commodities. We suppose that a firm's supply function is determined only by the ruling price vector. So, in examining the question of consistency (or, more formally, the existence of equilibrium), we are searching for a price vector that will clear the market for each commodity simultaneously.(1) By market clearance, we understand that no demand will be left unsatisfied; or that the total demand for a commodity is equal to the total supply of that commodity; or that the excess demand for a commodity, that is total demand minus total supply, is zero. Even though we stated that our analysis would be based on the individual agents, we find that such aggregate concepts as excess demand arise naturally in our discussion of the existence of equilibrium.

They also arise in stability analysis: "If a commodity is in excess demand (supply), its price rises (falls)" is an assumption commonly made. It is appropriate at this juncture to consider the following remarks, due to Koopmans: "If, for instance, the net rate of increase in price is assumed to be proportional to the excess of demand over supply, whose behaviour is thereby expressed? And how is it motivated?"(2)

This issue does not arise only when we try to answer such dynamic questions as: how do prices change? For to make the prior assumption of the existence of prices (which are treated by all agents as given and outside their control) is equivalent to making a specific assumption about the organisation of markets; no explanation is offered of why quotes prices and why.

Explanations in terms of a fictitious auctioneer, embodying the competitive spirit, or a "Secretary of Market" are unconvincing.

2. The foundations of equilibrium theory are provided by the microeconomic theories of the consumer and the firm, which are reviewed in §8.1.1. To describe an equilibrium, we must know how each agent will react when a price vector is called. The theory that we outline below is by no means the most general one available, for we restrict each agent to a unique response (in the form of a supply or demand vector) to a given price vector. This restriction is achieved by two types of assumption: we assume that each agent is a "maximiser" (a household maximises its utility function, a firm its profits); we make appropriate strict convexity assumptions to ensure continuity of "action" by each agent.(3)

With regard to a consumer, an appropriate strict convexity assumption is that his utility function (or his preference relation) is strictly quasi-concave; to illustrate this, consider the case of an individual who is indifferent between red and green apples but prefers all of his apples to be the same colour, rather than some red and some green; his preferences are obviously not strictly quasi-concave; if red apples are originally cheaper, the individual will consume only red apples and continue to do so until the prices of red and green apples are the same, in which event his action is not uniquely determined for he may consume either red or green; once red apples are more expensive, the individual will consume only green apples. So we have a discontinuity in the individual's demand. Likewise, if the firm does not have a strictly convex production set, there is a possibility of discontinuity in supply.

3. We have so far supposed our economy to be atemporal. By a redefinition of the concept of a commodity, we can establish a similarity between an atemporal economy and an intertemporal economy (i.e. where time does enter in an essential way). The criteria to be used in the definition of a "commodity" are the physical characteristics (which enable us to distinguish apples from bananas), the location at which a good will be supplied (which enables us to distinguish apples in Paris from apples in Rome), and the date at which a good will be supplied (which enables us to distinguish apples in Paris this year from apples in Paris next year). Suppose that there are ν invariant physical commodities, (apples, bananas, . . .), l locations (Paris, Rome, . . .) and a time horizon, T periods hence, after which no consideration is given by any agent. So we may distinguish $\nu lT = n$ commodities in our intertemporal economy. If we introduce the idea of futures markets, one for each of the $\nu l(T-1)$ commodities to be traded in future periods, we can permit all transactions over the time horizon to take place in the present period. It is clear what is meant by the prices of the νl commodities actually traded in the present period. But what of the prices for the remaining $\nu l(T-1)$ commodities? The price of such a commodity is the price quoted now for future delivery. Suppose commodity 1 is an apple in Paris in this period; commodity $\nu l+1$ is an apple in Paris next period; commodity $\nu\tau l+1$ is an apple in Paris τ periods hence. So, by extending the concept of a commodity (and hence of a market), we have established a formal similarity between the atemporal economy with ν commodities traded and the intertemporal economy with $\nu lT = n$ commodities traded.

The definition of a commodity can be refined even further to take account of uncertainty; the consumption of lemonade in Paris may depend on the state of the weather (either good or bad); so we introduce the contingent commodities: lemonade in Paris in good weather and lemonade in Paris in bad weather. It is not surprising that objections should be raised against this fabulous construction.

Consumers, constructing intertemporal consumption plans, are still supposed to have strictly quasi-concave preferences over the set of νlT commodities. Firms still operate in the context of strictly convex production sets, though with the introduction of time a treatment of fixed capital is possible.

As in the atemporal case, each agent is supposed to have complete knowledge of the price system—this applies equally to consumers and firms.

The extension to the intertemporal economy has important implications for the interpretation of the consumer's budget constraint, which now states that discounted income over the T period horizon must be greater than or equal to discounted expenditure over the horizon. As each agent is now involved in transactions over T periods, credit transactions must now be allowed (there was no place for them in the atemporal economy, by definition); equally a means of enforcing credit contracts must be available, unless each agent is deemed perfectly creditworthy.

Existence of equilibrium for the atemporal/intertemporal economy is proved in §8.2.

4. In §8.3, we examine the optimality properties of a competitive equilibrium. This involves the use of the Pareto efficiency concept—a state of the economy is Pareto efficient if it is impossible to find, using the same resources, another state in which at least one person is better off without any other person being worse off. We derive two results—first of all, that a competitive economy is Pareto efficient and, secondly, that, under certain circumstances, a Pareto efficient state can be realised as a competitive equilibrium. The first result is the more general, being derived without use of convexity assumptions, which are required for the second.

There is *some* comfort to be derived from these results, but it must be realised that the Pareto efficiency concept does not yield a complete relation on the set of all possible states of the economy. There are many states that cannot be compared by the Pareto efficiency criterion, e.g. two distinct Pareto efficient states.

A state might be Pareto efficient even though it yields a considerable disparity in income distribution between individuals; a state with a more equal distribution of income might be preferred (by all but the richest), even though it is not Pareto efficient.

To compare Pareto efficient and non-Pareto efficient states (in fact, all states), we need such a grand concept as a Bergson social welfare function.[(4)]

5. In §8.1.2, our assumptions are chosen so that each agent has a unique response to any price vector. It might be thought that, once the existence of equilibrium had been derived, uniqueness of equilibrium would require few additional assumptions, if any. Such a supposition would be wrong, as we shall see in §8.4. We require such assumptions as gross substitutability, or that the excess supply of each commodity is more sensitive to a change in its own price than to changes in all other prices combined (which yields a q.d.d. condition). Each of these (and most of the others mentioned) imply that the Jacobian of excess supply functions is a P-matrix.

Given our work in §6.1, we should not be surprised to encounter P-matrices (and economic hypotheses yielding them) in the analysis of uniqueness.

The analysis of uniqueness of equilibrium is closely connected with comparative statics analysis (which deals with the comparisons of different equilibria, the result of changes in parameters). If the equilibrium is not unique, the procedure of comparing equilibria before and after the change in parameter(s) may not be well defined.

So, we should not be surprised to learn that gross substitutability, which is a sufficient condition for uniqueness, also plays an important role in §8.8 in obtaining comparative statics results.

6. Such optimality propositions as can be derived about competitive equilibria would seem to be of minimal value if stability of equilibria cannot be derived. Similarly, there would seem to be little point in going through the motions of comparative statics analysis for an unstable economy.

In §§8.5–8.8, we discuss aspects of stability theory, mainly of the local, tatonnement variety. This involves the study of an equation such as: $\mathrm{d}p/\mathrm{d}t = Ap$.

Given the difficulty in deriving stability (except under gross substitutability) in an economy which does not permit trading out of equilibrium, it might seem that by permitting dis-equilibrium trading we make the derivation of stability even less likely.

However, Hahn and Negishi have derived stability of such a non-tatonnement exchange economy (see Exercises §8.8). Tatonnement stability may also be derived, as Hahn showed (see Theorem 41), by placing restrictions on the adjustment process rather than on the excess demand functions (in the form of, say, gross substitution).

However, Hahn's lead does not seem to have been followed.

7. An early idea proposed in the theory of decentralised economic planning was that a socialist economy should try to mimic a (capitalist) competitive economy. The planning procedure, outlined in §8.10, is based on the existence and stability theory developed in this chapter.

8. Finally, we should reiterate that ours is not the most general analysis available. In particular, we have imposed strict convexity conditions to ensure that each agent has a unique, continuous response to any price vector; we are able to use Brouwer's fixed point theorem in §8.2 to derive existence of equilibrium. Now the weakening of the strict convexity conditions introduces the possibility of non-uniqueness of an agent's response; corresponding to a given price vector, an agent may have a *set* of responses (e.g. if we allow for constant returns to scale in production, an individual firm's scale of operation may not be uniquely determined). So, instead of dealing with a point-to-point mapping, as in the strict convexity case, we would have to deal with a point-to-set mapping. Continuity concepts and fixed point theorems are available to handle this case; existence of equilibrium can be derived, though stability analysis is difficult, to say the least. The advantage of our approach is that we can treat all the topics existence, uniqueness, efficiency, stability, comparative statics and even the application to decentralised planning—within the same analytical framework, The pedagogical advantages of this outweigh any loss of generality.

§8.1.2. *Preliminaries*

We begin by outlining the main features of the economic system to be discussed below. There are n commodities, indexed by i; in this context, we may call R^n commodity space.

Commodities are distinguished by their physical properties, by their location (in time and in space) and by the state of the world. Each good has a price (which may be zero); p is the non-negative price vector.

There are two kinds of decision-makers in the economy—households (of which there are M, indexed by j) and firms (of which there are r, indexed by k). Given p, each household maximises its utility function subject to its budget constraint. Likewise, given p, each firm maximises profit subject to the constraint that its course of action, represented by the vector y^k, is technically feasible.

We may now write down the vector of choices of the agents in the economy as: $(x^1, \ldots, x^M; y^1, \ldots, y^r)$. Note that each component of this vector is itself a vector (an n-tuple).

Let $x = \sum_{j=1}^{M} x^j$, $y = \sum_{k=1}^{r} y^k$. The vector of choices is a balancing vector if $x = y$.

We may then define an equilibrium as a balancing vector and a price vector p. A more general concept of equilibrium would permit excess supply. Then the equilibrium is a price vector p and a vector of choices such that $y \geqslant x$.

Having sketched a brief outline, we now proceed to discuss consumer and producer theory in more detail so as to provide a basis for equilibrium analysis.

First, we deal with the theory of the firm:

y^k represents the k-th firm's vector of net outputs.

(P1): Each firm is constrained by technical possibilities represented by a production set Y_k, i.e. a production plan is feasible iff $y^k \in Y_k$.

(P2): Y_k is a strictly convex, compact set.

Compactness rules out constant returns to scale globally; for if constant returns to scale were postulated, $y^k \in Y_k$ implies $\alpha y^k \in Y_k$ for any $\alpha > 0$; hence, Y_k would be unbounded.

Strict convexity rules out constant returns locally.

The purpose of this assumption is to ensure that supply functions are single-valued, for if constant returns were permitted at all, the scale of the firm's operations might not be uniquely determined.

(P3): $\mathbf{0} \in Y_k$.

(P4): y^k is the unique solution to the firm's profit maximisation problem:

maximise $p'y^k$ subject to $y^k \in Y_k$.

To establish this, let us first note that the compactness assumption implies that there exists at least one y^k that acheives profit maximisation. Define the k-th firm's profit function: $\pi_k(p) = \max_{y^k \in Y_k} p'y^k$

Under the hypotheses outlined in (P1)–(P3), we can prove that $\pi_k(p)$ is a strictly convex, continuous function and that the profit maximisation problem has a unique solution, i.e. $Y_k(p)$ contains only one element for each p,

where

$Y_K(p) = \{y^k : p'y^k = \pi_k(p), y^k \in Y_k\}$.

Suppose that y^k, $\bar{y}^k \in Y_k(p)$. Then for $\alpha \in (0, 1)$,

$y^k(\alpha) = \alpha y^k + (1-\alpha)\bar{y}^k$

is contained in the interior of Y_k. Hence, there exists $\bar{\bar{y}}^k > y^k(\alpha)$, $\bar{\bar{y}}^k \in Y_k$. $p \geqslant \mathbf{0}$ implies that:

$p'\bar{\bar{y}}^k > p'y^k(\alpha) = \pi_k(p)$.

This is a contradiction; hence $Y_k(p)$ has the desired property given (P3).

(P5): $y^k(p)$ is continuous, where $y^k(p)$ is the unique solution to the firm's profit maximisation problem.
Let $p(\nu) \to \bar{p}$. As Y_k is compact, $y^k(\nu) \to \bar{y}^k \in Y_k$, where $y^k(\nu) = y^k(p(\nu))$. By definition, $p(\nu)'[y^k(\nu) - y^k(\bar{p})] \geqslant 0$, for all ν. Taking limits, $\bar{p}'[\bar{y}^k - y^k(\bar{p})] \geqslant 0$. As $\bar{y}^k = y^k(\bar{p})$ by the uniqueness result in (P4), we have continuity.

We now turn our attention to consumer theory.

(C1): Each household has a set, S_j, of non-negative pre-trade allocations, w^j (this includes the case where household j supplies labour and possesses some commodities prior to trade).
S_j is assumed to be compact and convex.
As a result of trade, each household has a post-trade allocation, d^j. The j-th household's excess demand vector, x^j, is given by $x^j = d^j - w^j$.

(C2): Each household has a utility function,

$u_j = u_j(x^j) = \max u_j(w^j; d^j)$

$u_j(w^j; d^j)$ is defined for all $w^j \in S_j$, for all $d^j \geqq \mathbf{0}$. Hence $u_j(x^j)$ is defined for all x^j such that there exists $w^j \in S_j$ for which $x^j + w^j \geqq \mathbf{0}$.

(C3): u_j is continuous.

(C4): For any x^j and for any $\varepsilon > 0$, there exists $\bar{x}^j$ such that $|\bar{x}^j - x^j| < \varepsilon$ and $u_j(\bar{x}^j) > u_j(x^j)$.
This rules out satiation.

A function f is *strictly quasi-concave* if, given $f(x^1) \geqslant f(x^2)$, $x^1 \neq x^2$, $f(x) > f(x^2)$, where $x = \alpha x^1 + (1-\alpha)x^2$, $\alpha \in (0, 1)$.

(C5): u_j is strictly quasi-concave for all j.
A consequence of this is that the set $\{x^j \in R^n : u_j(x^j) \geqslant \beta\}$ is strictly convex, for any fixed β.

Let α_{kj} be the j-th household's share of the profits of the k-th firm. $\sum_j \alpha_{kj} = 1$, for all k.

(C6): The consumer's maximisation problem is:

maximise $u_j(x^j)$ subject to $p'x^j \leqslant \sum_{k=1}^{r} \alpha_{kj}\pi_k = \rho_j$.

Our hypotheses are sufficient to ensure that, given $p > \mathbf{0}$, the set of x^j satisfying the constraint is compact. Hence, u_j is maximised for at least one x^j, say $\bar{x}^j$. If u_j is maximised by $\bar{\bar{x}}^j$, then it follows from strict quasi-concavity that:

$$u_j(\tilde{x}^j) > u_j(\bar{x}^j) = u_j(\bar{\bar{x}}^j)$$

where

$$\tilde{x}^j = \alpha\bar{x}^j + (1-\alpha)\bar{\bar{x}}^j \qquad \alpha \in (0, 1)$$

This contradicts the choice of $\bar{x}^j$. Hence in the case where $p > \mathbf{0}$, we have a unique solution. If $p \geqslant \mathbf{0}$, there is at most one x^j which solves the consumer's maximisation problem.

We now derive properties of the household excess demand functions, x^j.

(C7): x^j are bounded from below.
This follows from the fact that $x^j \geqq -w^j$, where w^j is an element of the compact set S_j.

(C8): Walras' law holds, i.e. $p'x^j(p; \rho_j) = \rho_j$.
Suppose $p'x^j(p; \rho_j) < \rho_j$. Then there exists $\varepsilon > 0$ such that for all $\bar{x}^j$ satisfying $|\bar{x}^j - x^j| < \varepsilon$, $p'\bar{x}^j < \rho_j$.
By (C5), there exists an $\bar{x}^j$ say $\bar{\bar{x}}^j$, such that $p'\bar{\bar{x}}^j < \rho_j$ and $u_j(\bar{\bar{x}}^j) > u_j(x^j)$. This contradicts the fact that x^j solves the consumer's maximisation problem.

(C9): Homogeneity, i.e. $x^j(\lambda p; \lambda\rho_j) = x^j(p; \rho_j)$, for all p, for all $\lambda > 0$.
Suppose $x^j(\lambda p; \lambda\rho_j) \neq x^j(p; \rho_j)$. The problem of maximising u_j subject to $p'x^j \leqslant \rho_j$ is equivalent to maximising u_j subject to $\lambda p'x^j \leqslant \lambda\rho_j$. Hence:

$$u_j(x^j(\lambda p; \lambda\rho_j)) = u_j(x^j(p; \rho_j)).$$

Then by strict quasi-concavity:

$$u_j(\alpha x^j(\lambda p; \lambda\rho_j) + (1-\alpha)x^j(p; \rho_j)) > \alpha u_j(x^j(\lambda p; \lambda\rho_j)) + (1-\alpha)u_j(x^j(p; \rho_j)) \qquad \alpha \in (0, 1)$$

$$p'[\alpha x^j(\lambda p; \lambda\rho_j) + (1-\alpha)x^j(p; \rho_j)] = \rho_j + (1-\alpha)\rho_j,$$

using (C8), i.e. $\alpha x^j(\lambda p; \lambda\rho_j) + (1-\alpha)x^j(p; \rho_j)$ maximises u^j subject to the budget constraint.
Therefore, $x^j(p; \rho_j)$ is not the solution of the consumer's maximisation problem. This contradiction yields the result.

(C10): $x^j(p; \rho_j)$ is continuous for all $p > \mathbf{0}$.
To simplify the notation, we adopt the following conventions:
we drop subscripts and superscripts "j";
we write $x(p(\nu); \rho(\nu)) = x(\nu)$.

Let $p(\nu)\to\bar{p}$, $\rho(\nu)\to\bar{\rho}$ as $\nu\to\infty$, but $x(\nu)\nrightarrow\bar{x}=x(\bar{p};\bar{\rho})$. $u(x(\nu))$ is such that $\liminf_{\nu\to\infty} u(x(\nu))\geqslant u(\bar{x})$.

Let $Q=\{x:\bar{p}'x=\bar{\rho}\}$. As $\nu\to\infty$, $x(\nu)\to x\in Q$ by Walras' law.
By hypothesis, there exists $\varepsilon>0$ such that:

$$|x(\nu)-\bar{x}|>\varepsilon \text{ for arbitrary large } \nu \qquad \cdots[1]$$

There exists a subsequence of $\{p(\nu);\rho(\nu)\}\to(\bar{p};\bar{\rho})$ such that eqn [1] is satisfied. Denote the corresponding subsequence of excess demand vectors by $\{x(\tau)\}$.
If $\bar{p}>\mathbf{0}$, $\{x(\tau)\}$ is bounded above when $\{\rho(\nu)\}$ is bounded above. As $\{x(\tau)\}$ is bounded below, it is in fact bounded and therefore has a convergent subsequence $\{x(\tau)^*\}$ such that $x(\tau)^*\to x^*\neq\bar{x}$. But $u(x^*)\geqslant u(\bar{x})$. Then by application of strict quasi-concavity, we see that $\bar{x}$ cannot solve the consumer's maximisation problem.

We can now synthesise the analysis above to derive properties of the aggregate excess demand function:

$$z(p)=\sum_{j=1}^{M} x^j(p;\rho_j)-\sum_{k=1}^{r} y^k(p)$$

(E1): $z(p)$ is bounded below.
(E2): $p'z(p)=0$ for all p (Walras' law).

$$p'z(p)=\sum_j p'x^j(p;\rho_j)-\sum_k p'y^k(p)=\sum_j \rho_j-\sum_k \pi_k=0$$

(E3): $z(\alpha p)=z(p)$ for all $\alpha>0$ (homogeneity).
(E4): $z(p)$ is continuous for all $p>\mathbf{0}$.

§8.2. Existence of Equilibrium

§8.2.1. *Existence under strong continuity*

Using the work of §8.1.2, we begin by stating the assumptions under which we shall derive existence:

(A1) $z(p)$ is unique for any $p\geqslant\mathbf{0}$.
(A2): (H): $z(p)=z(\alpha p)$ for all $p\geqslant\mathbf{0}$, for all $\alpha>0$.

On the basis of (H), we may restrict p to the set $S=\left\{p\geqslant\mathbf{0}:\sum_{i=1}^{n} p_i=1\right\}$ without loss of generality.

(A3): (W): $p'z(p)=0$ for all $p\in S_n$.
(A4): (B): $z(p)$ is bounded from below for all $p\in S_n$.
(A5): Free disposal—this rules out negative prices.
(A6): (C): $z(p)$ is continuous over S_n.

In §8.1.2, we derived continuity of $z(p)$ for all $p>\mathbf{0}$. The extension of the domain of z to all of S_n is a non-trivial assumption. This may be seen as follows: S_n is a closed and bounded set; as z is (assumed) continuous on S_n, it follows that z is bounded on S_n which contains vectors with zero components; hence the demand for a free good is bounded; now this implies that each individual is satiated with respect to each free good, for otherwise we would have unbounded demand; Walras' law requires non-satiation. So, (A6) may not be compatible with (A3). However, we retain (A3) throughout this section, as it simplifies the existence proof; in §8.2.2, we offer a weaker continuity condition; existence of equilibrium is derived by modifying the proof derived here under the strong continuity condition.

We may describe a state of the economy as an equilibrium if there is a balance between the supply and demand of each commodity (i.e. $z = \mathbf{0}$). Given utility functions (or consumption sets) and production sets, both demand and supply may be considered as functions of prices alone. So, p^* is an equilibrium price vector if $z(p^*) = \mathbf{0}$. This rigid condition may be relaxed to $z(p^*) \leqslant \mathbf{0}$; this allows all demands to be fulfilled and generalises the equilibrium notion to permit excess supply of a commodity with zero price. So, we have:

Definition 1: p^* is an *equilibrium price vector* if $z(p^*) \leqslant \mathbf{0}$.

We must now specify the rules of price formation (if it helps at all, suppose that the rules have been made and are enforced by an auctioneer, or a Secretary of Market):

(i) an arbitrary price vector $p \in S_n$ is "called";

(ii) each agent decides on his response to p; each consumer evaluates his demand vector by utility maximisation, each firm its supply vector by profit maximisation; the aggregate excess demand vector is calculated;

(iii) prices respond to excess demands in the following way:

(a) if there is (positive) excess demand for a commodity, the price of that commodity is raised;

(b) if there is (positive) excess supply of a commodity, the price of that commodity is lowered, subject to the restriction that the price cannot fall below zero;

(c) if demand for a commodity is equal to the supply of that commodity, the price of the commodity is unchanged;

(iv) let $\delta(p)$ denote the vector of price adjustments, defined by (iii) (a)–(c); after (iii) (a)–(c) have been followed, we obtain a price vector $p + \delta(p)$; $p + \delta(p)$ is then divided by $\mathbf{1}'(p + \delta(p))$ so that the resulting price vector $(p + \delta(p))/\mathbf{1}'(p + \delta(p)))$ is an element of S_n;

(v) this vector $(p + \delta(p))/(\mathbf{1}'(p + \delta(p)))$ is "called" and the procedure is repeated until an equilibrium is reached.

These rules incorporate the "law of supply and demand." In our first theorem, we establish that these rules yield an equilibrium.

Theorem 1: An equilibrium exists under assumptions (A1)–(A6).

Proof: Given $p \in S_n$, the vector $\delta(p)$ is determined in accordance with the rules stated above, i.e.

$\delta_i(p)>0$ iff $z_i(p)>0$ $\cdots$[1]

$\delta_i(p)=0$ if $z_i(p)=0$ $\cdots$[2]

$p_i+\delta_i(p)\geqslant 0$ for all i $\cdots$[3]

$p+\delta(p)\geqq\mathbf{0}$, from eqn [3]. Hence $\mathbf{1}'(p+\delta(p))\geqslant 0$. As we wish to prove that $\mathbf{1}'(p+\delta(p))>0$, suppose that $\mathbf{1}'(p+\delta(p))=0$, which implies:

$p+\delta(p)=\mathbf{0}$ $\cdots$[4]

Forming the inner product with $z(p)$, we have:

$(p+\delta(p))'z(p)=\delta(p)'z(p)=0$ $\cdots$[5]

using (W)
From eqns [1] and [2], it is evident that $\delta_i(p)z_i(p)\geqslant 0$, for all i. Using this in eqn [5], we conclude that:

$\delta_i(p)z_i(p)=0$ for all i $\cdots$[6]

As $p\in S_n$, $p_j>0$ for some j. Then from eqn [4]:

$\delta_j(p)=-p_j<0$ $\cdots$[7]

Then $z_j(p)=0$ from [6]. Hence $\delta_j(p)=0$ from eqn [2]. This contradicts eqn [7]. So $\mathbf{1}'(p+\delta(p))>0$.
Evidently, $(p+\delta(p))/[\mathbf{1}'(p+\delta(p))]\in S_n$. The mapping $f:S_n\rightarrow S_n$ defined by:

$f(p)=(p+\delta(p))/[\mathbf{1}'(p+\delta(p))]$ $\cdots$[8]

is continuous if $\delta(p)$ is continuous. Then by Brouwer's fixed point theorem, f has a fixed point, $p^*\in S_n$, i.e.

$f(p^*)=p^*=(p^*+\delta(p^*))/[\mathbf{1}'(p^*+\delta(p^*))]$ $\cdots$[9]

(i.e. if the vector p^* were "called" in accordance with rule (i), it would emerge in rule (v) as the vector to be "called" at the next round of the procedure.)
To complete the proof, we have to establish that p^* is in fact an equilibrium, i.e. $z(p^*)\leqq\mathbf{0}$. From eqn [9]:

$p^*+\delta(p^*)=[1]\mathbf{1}'(p^*+\delta(p^*))p^*$ $\cdots$[10]

Using the fact that $p^*\in S_n$, i.e. $\mathbf{1}'p^*=1$, we have:

$\delta(p^*)=\mathbf{1}'\delta(p^*)p^*$ $\cdots$[11]

Forming the inner product with $z(p^*)$, we obtain:

$\delta(p^*)'z(p^*)=\mathbf{1}'\delta(p^*)p^{*\prime}z(p^*)=0$ by (W) $\cdots$[12]

Again from eqns [1] and [2], $\delta_i(p^*)z_i(p^*)\geqslant 0$ for all i. So, from eqn [12]:

$\delta_i(p^*)z_i(p^*)=0$ for all i $\cdots$[13]

Suppose $z_i(p^*)>0$. Then $\delta_i(p^*)>$ from eqn [1]. Hence $\delta_i(p^*)z_i(p^*)>0$. This contradicts eqn [13]. So $z(p^*)\leqslant\mathbf{0}$, as required.

§8.2.2. *Existence under a weaker continuity condition*

1. We now modify the proof of Theorem 1 to take account of the following weaker continuity condition:

($\bar{C}$): $z(p)$ is defined for all $p>\mathbf{0}$. It may be defined for other $p\in S_n$. $z(p)$ is continuous wherever defined. If $z(p)$ is undefined at $p=\bar{p}$, we have: $\lim_{p\to\bar{p}}\sum_i z_i(p)=+\infty$

We are taking account of those remarks immediately following the list of assumptions in §8.2.1.

2. The proof of existence under assumptions (A1)–(A5) and ($\bar{C}$) rests, in the main, on the construction of a continuous function, related to $\delta(p)$, which will permit an appeal to the fixed point theorem. To this end, define a continuous function, $h(p)$, by:

$$h(p)=0 \text{ if } \mathbf{1}'z(p)\leqslant 0$$
$$h(p)=1 \text{ if } \mathbf{1}'z(p)\geqslant\eta>0 \qquad \cdots[1]$$
$$h(p)\in(0,1) \text{ if } \mathbf{1}'z(p)\in(0,\eta)$$

e.g. $h(p)=\mathbf{1}'z(p)/\eta$ if $\mathbf{1}'z(p)\in(0,\eta)$.
Then define:

$$\varepsilon(p)=\begin{cases}(1-h(p))\delta(p)+h(p)\mathbf{1}, \text{ if } z(p) \text{ is defined}\\ \mathbf{1}, \text{ if } z(p) \text{ is undefined}\end{cases} \qquad \cdots[2]$$

In the range of possible equilibria ($z(p)\leqslant\mathbf{0}$), $h(p)=0$ so that $\varepsilon(p)=\delta(p)$. If $z(p)$ is undefined, $\varepsilon(p)>\mathbf{0}$. By ($\bar{C}$), $\varepsilon(p)>\mathbf{0}$ in any neighbourhood of a point where $z(p)$ is undefined.

To apply the fixed point theorem, we wish to establish, first of all, that $\varepsilon(p)$ is a continuous function.

If $z(p)$ is defined, $\varepsilon(p)$ is continuous.

Let $z(p)$ be undefined at $p=\bar{p}$. By ($\bar{C}$), $\mathbf{1}'z(p)\geqslant\eta$ for all p in a neighbourhood of $\bar{p}$ such that $z(p)$ is defined. For such p, $h(p)=1$, so that $\varepsilon(p)=\mathbf{1}$. For all p in a neighbourhood of $\bar{p}$ such that $z(p)$ is not defined, $\varepsilon(p)=\mathbf{1}$. So for all p in a neighbourhood of $\bar{p}$, $\varepsilon(p)=\mathbf{1}$ and is trivially a continuous function. Analogous to the mapping f of §8.2.1 (eqn [8]), define $F:S_n\to R^n$ by:

$$F(p)=(p+\varepsilon(p))/[\mathbf{1}'(p+\varepsilon(p))] \qquad \cdots[3]$$

We have just derived continuity of $\varepsilon(p)$; so continuity of F follows if $\mathbf{1}'(p+\varepsilon(p))\neq 0$ for all $p\in S_n$. In fact we wish to show that F is a continuous mapping from S_n to itself, so that we require $\mathbf{1}'(p+\varepsilon(p))>\mathbf{0}$ for all $p\in S_n$.

Exercise 1. Suppose that p is such that $z(p)$ is underfined. Prove that $\mathbf{1}'(p+\varepsilon(p))>0$.

Exercise 2. Suppose p is such that $z(p)$ is defined. Prove that $\mathbf{1}'(p+\varepsilon(p))>0$. Then by Brouwer's fixed point theorem, there exists $p^*\in S_n$ such that

$$F(p^*)=p^*=(p^*+\varepsilon(p^*))/[\mathbf{1}'(p^*+\varepsilon(p^*))]$$

or

$$\varepsilon(p^*)=\mathbf{1}'\varepsilon(p^*)p^* \qquad \cdots [4]$$

(compare this with eqn [11] of §8.2.1).
It remains to prove that p^* is an equilibrium, i.e. $z(p^*)\leqslant\mathbf{0}$.
Exercise 3. Prove that $z(p^*)$ cannot be undefined.
Exercise 4. Then form the inner product of eqn [4] with $z(p^*)$. Use (W) to obtain:

$$\varepsilon(p^*)'z(p^*)=0 \qquad \cdots [5]$$

or

$$[(1-h(p^*))\delta(p^*)+h(p^*)\mathbf{1}]'z(p^*)=0 \qquad \cdots [6]$$

from eqn [2]
Suppose $h(p^*)>0$. Then as $\delta(p^*)'z(p^*)\geqslant 0$ from eqns [1] and [2] of §8.2.1, we have:

$$(1-h(p^*))\delta(p^*)'z(p^*)\geqslant 0 \qquad \cdots [7]$$

Using eqn [7] in eqn [6] yields:

$$h(p^*)\mathbf{1}'z(p^*)\leqslant 0 \qquad \cdots [8]$$

or

$$\mathbf{1}'z(p^*)\leqslant 0 \text{ as } h(p^*)>0 \qquad \cdots [9]$$

But from eqn [1], if $h(p^*)>0$, $\mathbf{1}'z(p^*)>0$. From this contradiction, we conclude that $h(p^*)=0$.
Exercise 5. Substitute for $h(p^*)$ in eqn [6] and prove that $z(p^*)\leqslant\mathbf{0}$, as required.
Exercise 6. Consider the following as candidates for use as $\delta(p)$ in §§8.2.1 and 8.2.2:

$\delta_i(p)=\max(-p_i, \alpha_i z_i(p))$, $\alpha_i>0$; $\delta_i(p)=\max(0, z_i(p))$.

§8.3. Competitive equilibrium and Pareto efficiency

In §§8.1 and 8.2, we have examined the hypothesis that an individual consumer's behaviour is determined by utility maximisation subject to his budget constraint. To analyse the individual consumer's behaviour, we need to know his utility function, u_j, (or his preferences) and his sources of income (his initial endowment of resources, w^i, and his shares of profits $\alpha_{1j},\ldots,\alpha_{rj}$). So to analyse consumption behaviour, we need to know each utility function, u_j, (or each preference ordering $\underset{i}{\succsim}$) each endowment vector w^i and the share matrix $\mathscr{A}=[\alpha_{kl}]$, $k=1,\ldots,r$; $j=1,\ldots,M$.

The corresponding hypothesis for firms is profit maximisation. To analyse the k-th firm's behaviour, we need to know Y_k, the k-th firm's production set. Hence to analyse production behaviour, we need to know each Y_k. The economy is thus completely described by the quadruple $(U, W, \mathscr{A}, Y)$,

$$U=\{u_1, \ldots, u_M\}, \qquad W=\{w^1, \ldots, w^M\}$$

$$\text{and} \quad Y=\left\{y=\sum_{k=1}^{r} y^k : y^k \in Y_k \quad \text{for all} \quad k\right\}.$$

A state of the economy is then defined by the set of choices $(d^1, \ldots, d^M; y^1, \ldots, y^r)$ with respect to the quadruple $(U, W, \mathscr{A}, Y)$. In this section, our interest is in examining the optimality properties of a competitive equilibrium. We now introduce the following concept of social optimality:

Definition 2: The state of the economy defined by the set of choices $(d^1, \ldots, d^M; y^1, \ldots, y^r)$ with respect to the quadruple $(U, W, \mathscr{A}, Y)$ is *Pareto efficient* if there does not exist another vector of choices $(\bar{d}^1, \ldots, d^M; \bar{y}^1, \ldots, \bar{y}^r)$ such that:

(i) $u_j(\bar{d}^j; w^j) \geqslant u_j(d^j; w^j)$ for all j with at least one strict inequality; and

(ii) $\bar{y}+w \geqq \bar{d}$ where $w=\sum_{j=1}^{M} w^j$, $\bar{d}=\sum_{j=1}^{M} \bar{d}^j$

As mentioned in §8.1.1, the Pareto efficiency concept does not yield a complete relation on the set of all states of the economy; nor does it take account of distributional considerations. However, we have:

Theorem 2: A competitive equilibrium is Pareto efficient.

Proof: Let a competitive equilibrium be described by $(d^1, \ldots, d^M; y^1, \ldots, y^r)$ and a price vector $p \geqslant \mathbf{0}$. From the definition of a competitive equilibrium, we have:
For consumers:

$$p'(\bar{d}^j - w^j) > p'(d^j - w^j) \text{ for all } \bar{d}^j \text{ such that}$$

$$u_j(\bar{d}^j; w^j) > u_j(d^j; w^j)$$

or

$$p'\bar{d}^j > p'd^j \qquad \cdots [1]$$

We assert:

$$p'\bar{d}^j \geqslant p'd^j \text{ for all } \bar{d}^j \text{ such that } u_j(\bar{d}^j; w^j) = u_j(d^j; w^j) \qquad \cdots [2]$$

for if not, we obtain a straightforward contradiction to eqn [1] by (C4). Hence:

$$p'\bar{d}^j \geqslant p'd^j \text{ for all } \bar{d}^j \text{ such that } u_j(\bar{d}^j; w^j) \geqslant u_j(d^j; w^j) \qquad \cdots [3]$$

For firms:

$$p'y^k \geqslant p'\bar{y}^k \text{ for all } \bar{y}^k \in Y_k, \text{ for all } k \qquad \cdots [4]$$

Hence:

$$p'y \geqslant p'\bar{y} \text{ for all } y \in Y \qquad \cdots [5]$$

Now suppose that the competitive equilibrium is not Pareto efficient. Then there exists a set of choices $(\bar{d}^1, \ldots, \bar{d}^M; \bar{y}^1, \ldots, \bar{y}^r)$ with respect to the quadruple $(U, W, \mathscr{A}, Y)$ such that:

$$u_j(\bar{d}^j; w^j) \geqslant u_j(d^j; w^j) \text{ for all } j \qquad \cdots [6]$$

with at least one strict inequality.
Then from eqn [3]:

$$p'\bar{d}^j \geqslant p'd^j \text{ for all } j \qquad \cdots [7]$$

with at least one strict inequality, or

$$p'\bar{d} > p'd \qquad \cdots [8]$$

But from eqn [5]:

$$p'y \geqslant p'\bar{y}.$$

Hence:

$$p'(y+w) \geqslant p'(\bar{y}+w).$$

From eqn [8]:

$$p'\bar{d} > p'd = p'(y+w) \geqslant p'(\bar{y}+w)$$

i.e. $p'\bar{d} > p'(\bar{y}+w)$. This implies $\bar{d} \geqslant \bar{y}+w$, which contradicts the definition of the Pareto efficient state. Hence a competitive equilibrium in which each consumer is not satiated, is Pareto efficient.

This theorem is quite general as it does not depend on convexity assumptions, in marked contrast to its converse:

Theorem 3: Let the state of the economy defined by the set of choices $(d^1, \ldots, d^M; y^1, \ldots, y^r)$ be Pareto efficient with respect to the quadruple $(U, W, \mathscr{A}, Y)$. If (P2), (C4) and (C5) are satisfied, there exists a price vector such that this state may be obtained as a competitive equilibrium.

Proof: Consider the set:

$$Z = \{\bar{z} = \bar{d} - \bar{y} - w \colon u_j(d^j; w^j) \geqslant u_j(d^j; w^j) \text{ for all } j, \text{ with at least one strict inequality}\} \qquad \cdots [9]$$

Under the hypotheses, Z is a convex set. Suppose there exists $\bar{z} \in Z$ such that $\bar{z} \leqslant \mathbf{0}$. Then there exist $\bar{d}$, $\bar{y}$ such that $\bar{d} \leqslant \bar{y} + w$.

Evidently there exists $\tilde{d}$ such that $\bar{d} \leqslant \tilde{d} \lneqq \bar{y} + w$, i.e. the state defined by the set of choices $(\tilde{d}^1, \ldots, \tilde{d}^M; \bar{y}^1, \ldots, \bar{y}^r)$ is preferred to the original state defined by $(d^1, \ldots, d^M; y^1, \ldots, y^r)$. However, this original state was assumed to be Pareto efficient. Plainly, we have a contradiction. So there does not exist $\bar{z} \in Z$ such that $\bar{z} \leqslant \mathbf{0}$. Hence $Z \cap R^n(0, -) = \emptyset$. By Theorem 10 of Chapter 7, there exists $p \geqslant \mathbf{0}$ such that $p'\bar{z} \geqslant 0$ for all $\bar{z} \in Z$.
Let $z = d - w - y$ be the excess demand vector resulting from the Pareto efficient state. Then $p'z \leqslant 0$. As there are points in Z arbitrarily close to z, we must have $p'z = 0$. As $z_i \leqslant 0$, $p_i \geqslant 0$, for all i, we must have $p_i z_i = 0$, for all i. (In particular, if $z_i < 0$, $p_i = 0$—which suggests the result.)
So, for all $\bar{z} \in Z$, we have:

$$p'(\bar{z} - z) \geqslant 0 \qquad \cdots [10]$$

where $z = d - w - y$, $\bar{z} = \bar{d} - w - \bar{y}$.

Then from eqn [10], we have:

$$p'(\bar{d} - \bar{y} - d + y) \geqslant 0$$

or

$$p'(y - \bar{y}) + p'(\bar{d} - d) \geqslant 0 \qquad \cdots [11]$$

or

$$\sum_{k=1}^{r} p'(y^k - \bar{y}^k) + \sum_{j=1}^{M} p'(\bar{d}^j - d^j) \geqslant 0 \qquad \cdots [12]$$

Now the vectors $\bar{y}^k$, $\bar{d}^j$ are independent of each other. So eqn [12] holds only if:

$$p'(y^k - \bar{y}^k) \geqslant 0 \text{ for all } k \qquad \cdots [13]$$

and

$$p'(\bar{d}^j - d^j) \geqslant 0 \text{ for all } j \qquad \cdots [14]$$

From eqn [13], we see that each firm is maximising its profits.
From eqn [14], we have $p'\bar{d}^j \geqslant p'd^j$ for all $\bar{d}^j$ such that $u_j(\bar{d}^j; w^j) \geqslant u_j(d^j; w^j)$. Hence, d^j minimises cost subject to attaining the given utility $u_j(d^j; w^j)$.
If $p'\bar{d}^j \leqslant p'd^j$, then $p'\alpha\bar{d}^j < p'd^j$ for $\alpha \in (0, 1)$. As d^j minimises cost, $u_j(d^j; w^j) > u_j(\alpha\bar{d}^j; w^j)$. Let $\alpha \to 1$. In the limit:

$$u_j(d^j; w^j) \geqslant u_j(\bar{d}^j; w^j)$$

so that d^j maximises utility subject to the budget constraint.
So each consumer is maximising his utility subject to his budget constraint.
Hence, all agents in the economy are in equilibrium. Hence the set of choices $(d^1, \ldots, d^M; y^1, \ldots, y^r)$ and the price vector $p \geqslant \mathbf{0}$ constitute an equilibrium, as required.

§8.4. Uniqueness of equilibrium

§8.4.1. *Basic uniqueness result*

In this section, we shall discuss sufficient conditions for uniqueness of equilibrium. We retain the assumptions under which existence was derived. Our first result is an extension of the Gale–Nikaido theory of §6.1.2.

Lemma 1: Let $f: X \to R^n$. If $J_f(x)$ is a P-matrix and X is rectangular, then:

$$(x_i - a_i)(f_i(x) - f_i(a)) \leqslant 0 \qquad i = 1, \ldots, n \qquad \cdots [1]$$

implies $x = a$.

Proof: Suppose eqn [1] has a solution $x \neq a$. As in Theorem 9 of Chapter 6, let:

$$a_i \leqslant x_i \quad \text{for} \quad i \leqslant k; \; a_i \geqslant x_i \quad \text{for} \quad i > k \qquad \cdots [2]$$

Define $F: R^n \to R^n$ thus:

$$F(z_1, \ldots, z_n) = (z_1, \ldots, z_k, -z_{k+1}, \ldots -z_n) \qquad \cdots [3]$$

Evidently, $F = F^{-1}$. Let

$$F(z) = \bar{z} \qquad \cdots [4]$$

From eqns [2] and [3], we have:

$$\bar{x} \geqslant \bar{a}. \qquad \cdots [5]$$

Again as in Theorem 9 of Chapter 6, define $g: F(X) \to R^n$ by

$$g(x) = F^{-1} f F(x) \qquad \cdots [6]$$

Then:

$$f(x) = FgF^{-1}(x) = Fg(\bar{x}) = F(g(\bar{x})) = [F_i(g(\bar{x}))] \qquad \cdots [7]$$

Now consider eqn [1]: we have, using eqn [7]:

$$(x_i - a_i)(f_i(x) - f_i(a)) = (x_i - a_i)(F_i(g(\bar{x})) - F_i(g(\bar{a})))$$

For $i \leqslant k$, we have using eqn [3]:

$$(x_i - a_i)(F_i(g(\bar{x})) - F_i(g(\bar{a}))) = (x_i - a_i)(g_i(\bar{x}) - g_i(\bar{a})) \leqslant 0 \qquad \cdots [8]$$

For $i > k$:

$$(x_i - a_i)(F_i(g(\bar{x})) - F_i(g(\bar{a}))) = (x_i - a_i)(-g_i(\bar{x}) + g_i(\bar{a})) \leqslant 0$$

using eqn [3], or

$$(-x_i + a_i)(g_i(\bar{x}) - g_i(\bar{a})) \leqslant 0$$

or using eqn [4]:

$$(\bar{x}_i - \bar{a}_i)(g_i(\bar{x}) - g_i(\bar{a})) \leqslant 0 \qquad \cdots [9]$$

Combining eqns [8] and [9], we have:

$$(\bar{x}_i - \bar{a}_i)(g_i(\bar{x}) - g_i(\bar{a})) \leqslant 0 \text{ for all } i \qquad \cdots [10]$$

Also:

$$\bar{x} \geqslant \bar{a} \qquad \cdots [11]$$

Now let.

$$S = \{j : \bar{x}_j > \bar{a}_j\} = \{1, \ldots, s\} \qquad \cdots [12]$$

Define the function $\theta : Y \to R^s$ by:

$$\theta_i(y) = g_i(y_1, \ldots, y_s, \bar{a}_{s+1}, \ldots, \bar{a}_n) \qquad i = 1, \ldots, s \qquad \cdots [13]$$

where

$$Y = \{y : y = (y_1, \ldots, y_s, \bar{a}_{s+1}, \ldots, a_n) \in F(X)\} \qquad \cdots [14]$$

$J_\theta(y)$ is a principal sub-matrix of $J_g(y)$, $y \in Y$, formed from its first s rows and columns. If J_f is a P-matrix, then so is J_g. Hence, J_θ is also a P-matrix. Now:

$$\begin{aligned}\theta_i(\bar{x}_1, \ldots, \bar{x}_s) &= g_i(\bar{x}_1, \ldots, \bar{x}_s, \bar{a}_{s+1}, \ldots, \bar{a}_n)\\ &\leqslant g_i(\bar{a}_1, \ldots, \bar{a}_s, \bar{a}_{s+1}, \ldots, \bar{a}_n)\\ &= \theta_1(\bar{a}_1, \ldots, \bar{a}_s) \qquad i = 1, \ldots, s \end{aligned} \qquad \cdots [15]$$

Remember also that:

$$\bar{x}_i > \bar{a}_i \qquad \text{for } i = 1, \ldots, s \qquad \cdots [16]$$

As stated above, J_θ is a P-matrix. Then eqns [15] and [16] imply $\bar{x}_i = \bar{a}_i$, by Theorem 8 of Chapter 6, $i = 1, \ldots, s$.
Hence $\bar{x} = \bar{a}$ or $x = a$, as required.

It will be convenient in this section to talk of excess supply rather than excess demand functions. Let $s_i(p)$ denote the excess supply function for good i; $s_i(p) = -z_i(p)$; $s(p) = [s_i(p)]$.
p^* is an equilibrium price vector iff $s(p^*) \geqq \mathbf{0}$.
To make use of Lemma 1, we must strengthen the continuity assumption used in §8.2. Here, we assume:

(A7) : (D) : $s_i(p)$ is differentiable for all p in S_n, for all i.

(A8) : (N) : There is a good, indexed by n, which always has a positive price. The n-th good is the numeraire.

We may now derive:

Theorem 4: Under assumptions (A1)–(A5), (A7) and (A8), there is a unique equilibrium if $J_s(p) = [s_{ij}(p)]$, $i, j = 1, \ldots, n-1$, is a P-matrix.

Proof: Let p^* and q^* be equilibrium price vectors ($p_n^* = q_n^*$, without loss of generality). Then we have:

$$\begin{aligned} s_i(p^*) &\geqslant 0\\ p_i^* s_i(p^*) &= 0 \qquad i = 1, \ldots, n-1\\ p_i^* &\geqslant 0 \end{aligned} \qquad \cdots [17]$$

and

$$s_i(q^*) \geqslant 0$$
$$q_i^* s_i(q^*) = 0 \qquad i = 1, \ldots, n-1 \qquad \cdots [18]$$
$$q_i^* \geqslant 0$$

From eqns [17] and [18]:

$$(p_i^* - q_i^*)(s_i(p^*) - s_i(q^*)) = p_i^* s_i(p^*) + q_i s_i(q^*) - p_i^* s_i(q^*) - q_i^* s_i(p^*)$$
$$= -p_i^* s_i(q^*) - q_i^* s_i(p^*) \leqslant 0 \qquad \cdots [19]$$

$p^* = q^*$ follows directly from Lemma 1, if $J_s(p)$ is a P-matrix.

We discuss below various restrictions on the excess supply functions which permit us to derive uniqueness. Pre-eminence is given to the gross substitute case, to which we now turn.

§8.4.2. *Uniqueness: strong gross substitutes*

Definition 3: Two goods, i and j, are *strong gross substitutes* if $s_{ij}(p) = \partial s_i / \partial p_j < 0$.
The economy has the *strong gross substitutes property* (SGS) at p if $s_{ij}(p) < 0$ for all $i \neq j$, for all $p \in S_n$.
The non-differential form of (SGS) is as follows:
Let $\bar{p} \geqslant p$, $\bar{p}_i = p_i$. Then $s_i(p) > s_i(\bar{p})$.

Theorem 5: Let (SGS) hold for all p. If p^* is an equilibrium, $p^* > \mathbf{0}$.

Proof: Suppose p^* is an equilibrium with $p_i^* = 0$. Then with $\alpha > 1$, we have, using the non-differential form of (SGS):

$$s_i(p^*) > s_i(\alpha p^*).$$

This obviously contradicts (H). So $p^* > \mathbf{0}$.

It may be worth remarking that the hypothesis of the last theorem may be weakened to (SGS) holding only at an equilibrium price vector and not for all possible price vectors.
We can prove, by a method similar to the one used in Theorem 5, that, if (SGS) holds at a price vector p with $p_i = 0$, then $s(p)$ is not defined and by convention $\sum_i s_j(p) = -\infty$. Then if we impose (SGS) at p^*, an equilibrium price vector, it follows straightforwardly that $p^* > \mathbf{0}$.

Theorem 6: If (SGS) holds for all p, equilibrium is unique.

Proof: By (H) and Euler's theorem:

$$\sum_{j \neq n} s_{ij}(p) p_j + s_{in}(p) = 0 \qquad i = 1, \ldots, n-1$$

or

$$\sum_{j \neq n} s_{ij}(p)p_j = -s_{in}(p) \qquad \cdots [1]$$

or

$$J_s(p)\tilde{p} = c \qquad \cdots [2]$$

where $\tilde{p} = (p_1, \ldots, p_{n-1})' > \mathbf{0}$; $c = [-s_{in}(p)]$ $i = 1, \ldots, n-1$. $c > \mathbf{0}$. $s_{ii}(p) > 0$; $s_{ij}(p) < 0$, for all $i \neq j$. Hence, by Theorem 1 of Chapter 2, $J_s(p)$ is a P-matrix. Uniqueness follows from Theorem 1 above.

§8.4.3. *Uniqueness: weak gross substitutes*

Definition 4: Two goods, i and j, are *weak gross substitutes* at p if $s_{ij}(p) \leq 0$.
The economy has the *weak gross substitutes property* (WGS) at p if $s_{ij}(p) \leq 0$, for all $i \neq j$.

Definition 5: The economy is *indecomposable* at p if there does not exist a set I such that $s_{ij}(p) = 0$, for all $i \in I$, $j \notin I$.

Armed with these definitions, we can derive the analogue of Theorem 6 in the (WGS) case:

Theorem 7: If (WGS) and indecomposability hold for all p, there is a unique positive equilibrium vector, p^*.

Proof: Suppose $p^* \ngtr \mathbf{0}$, say $p_i^* = 0$. $s_{ij}(p^*) < 0$, for some $j \neq i$, otherwise indecomposability is contradicted.
Suppose that only $s_{ih}(p^*) < 0$; $s_{ij}(p^*) = 0$, for all $j \neq i, h$.
By (H) and Euler's theorem:

$$\sum_{j=1}^{n} s_{ij}(p^*)p_j^* = 0$$

or $s_{ih}(p^*)p_h^* = 0$, using $p_j^* = 0$, $s_{ij}(p^*) = 0$ for all $j \neq i, h$.
Hence, $p_h^* = 0$. So, p^* has two zero components p_i^* and p_h^*.
Now repeat the argument above with respect to $s_h(p^*)$. First of all, we know by indecomposability that $s_{hj}(p^*) < 0$, some $j \neq i, h$.
Suppose that only $s_{hk}(p^*) < 0$; $s_{hj}(p^*) = 0$, for all $j \neq i, h, k$.
Then again by (H) and Euler's theorem, we see that $p_k^* = 0$.
The drift of the argument is by now clear, so that we end up with $p^* = \mathbf{0}$ or $s_j(p^*) = -\infty$, for some j. Either contradicts the assumption that p^* is an equilibrium.
Hence, $p^* > \mathbf{0}$.
We now establish uniqueness.
As in Theorem 6, we have:

$$J_s(p)\tilde{p} = c.$$

By indecomposability, $s_{in}(p) \neq 0$, for some i. Hence $c \geq \mathbf{0}$. $\tilde{p} > \mathbf{0}$.

Hence, again by Theorem 1 of Chapter 2, $J_s(p)$ is a P-matrix, so that uniqueness follows from Theorem 1 above.

§8.4.4. *Uniqueness: other conditions*

We know from Exercises §2.2 that, if the matrix A has a positive q.d.d., then A is a P-matrix. It follows from Theorem 1 that, if we can interpret the q.d.d. condition, we have a sufficient condition for uniqueness. Consider the notion that the excess demand (or supply) of a commodity is more responsive to a change in its own price than to a change in all other prices combined. Formalising this, we have:

Definition 6: If, to a given vector p, there corresponds a vector $d(p) > \mathbf{0}$ such that:

(i) $s_{ii}(p)d_i(p) \geqslant \sum_{\substack{j \neq i \\ j=1}}^{m} |s_{ij}(p)|d_j(p)$ for all $i = 1, \ldots, m$ with at least one strict inequality when $J_s(p)$ is indecomposable; with at least one strict inequality for $i \in I$ when $J_s(p)$ is indecomposable (i.e. $s_{ij}(p) = 0$ for $i \in I, j \notin I$);

(ii) $s_{ii}(p) > 0$ for all $i = 1, \ldots, m$;

then the economy possesses (QDD) at p.

By (H), it follows that (QDD) is not possible if all commodities are included (see Exercises §2.2, Q12).

Theorem 8: If the economy has (QDD) for all p, then the equilibrium is unique.

Proof: If the economy has (QDD), then $J_s(p)$ has a q.d.d.; let $D(p) = [d_i(p)\delta_{ij}]$. Then $J_s(p)D(p)$ satisfies the hypothesis of Theorem 8 of Chapter 2; so $J_s(p)D(p)$ is non-singular. From Gersgorin's theorem, it follows that $\det(J_s(p)D(p)) > 0$. As $\det D(p) > 0$, it follows that $\det J_s(p) > 0$. As this argument may be applied to each principal sub-matrix of $J_s(p)$, we conclude that $J_s(p)$ is a P-matrix.
Uniqueness follows from Theorem 1.

We now recall two concepts first outlined in Exercises §2.4:

Definition 7: The symmetric matrix A is *positive definite* if $x'Ax > 0$ for all $x \neq \mathbf{0}$.
The arbitrary real matrix A is *quasi-positive definite* if $x'Ax > 0$ for all $x \neq \mathbf{0}$.

A sufficient condition for $J_s(p)$ to be positive definite is that income effects vanish in the aggregate (see Exercises §8.5, Q4).

Theorem 9: If $J_s(p)$ is positive definite or quasi-positive definite for all p, then equilibrium is unique.

Proof: Either positive definiteness or quasi-positive definiteness suffices to ensure that $J_s(p)$ is a P-matrix (see Exercises §2.4).

§8.5. Stability of equilibrium

§8.5.1. *Hicksian stability*[5]

"What do we mean by stability in multiple exchange? Clearly, . . . that a fall in the price of (good i) in terms of the (numeraire) will make the demand for (i) greater than the supply. But are we to suppose that it must have this effect (a) when the prices of other commodities are given, or (b) when other prices are adjusted so as to preserve equilibrium in the other markets? Strictly we should distinguish a series of conditions: that a rise in the price of i will make the supply greater than demand, (i) all other prices given, (ii) allowing for the price of j to maintain equilibrium in the j-th market, (iii) allowing for the prices of j and k being adjusted, and so on, until all prices have been adjusted."[6]

On the basis of this discussion, Hicks proposed two stability concepts, summarised in:

Definition 8: Let I be an arbitrary subset of $M=\{1,\ldots,m\}$. An equilibrium is: (a) *perfectly stable* if the excess demand for commodity i is negative (positive) when its price is above (below) equilibrium, given that an arbitrary set of prices, indexed by $j\in I$, may be adjusted to clear all the markets in I, all other prices being held constant;
(b) *imperfectly stable* if excess demand for commodity i is negative (positive) when its price is above (below) equilibrium, given that all other prices are adjusted to clear all markets except that for commodity i.

Hicks derived the following theorem (for a proof, see Quirk & Saposnik)

Theorem 10: An equilbrium is perfectly stable iff the Jacobian matrix of excess demand functions is an $(N\text{–}P)$-matrix.

Hicks's work was criticised on the grounds that his "stability conditions are not deduced from a dynamic model except implicitly."[7] While "In the mathematical formulation of the theory of stability of economic equilibrium, the basic assumption of that theory, namely that excess demand for a good makes its price rise and excess supply makes it fall, does not appear explicitly ··· (it) is tacitly implied in the choice of condition that excess demand should occur when the price is below equilibrium and excess supply should occur when it is above equilibrium. . . . To clarify all the implications of stability analysis, the basic assumption mentioned above must be explicitly introduced into the mathematical formulation."[8]

The basic assumption can be formulated thus:

$$\text{sign}\ \mathrm{d}P_i/\mathrm{d}t=\text{sign}\ z_i \qquad i=1,\ldots,m \qquad \cdots[1]$$

or

$$\mathrm{d}P_i/\mathrm{d}t=F_i(z_i(P)) \qquad i=1,\ldots,m \qquad \cdots[2]$$

where $F(0)=0$ and $F(\ )$ is a monotonic increasing function. Expanding eqn [2] in a Taylor series around the equilibrium, P^*, we have:

$$\mathrm{d}P_i/\mathrm{d}t = F_i(z_i(P^*)) + F_i' \sum_{j=1}^{m} (\partial z_i/\partial P_j) \, . \, (P_j - P_j^*) \qquad \cdots [3]$$

As $z_i(P^*)=0$, and $\mathrm{d}P_i/\mathrm{d}t = \mathrm{d}(P_i - P_i^*)/\mathrm{d}t$, we have:

$$\mathrm{d}p_i/\mathrm{d}t = F_i' \sum_{j=1}^{m} a_{ij}p_j \qquad p_i = P_i - P_i^* \qquad \cdots [4]$$

or

$$\mathrm{d}p/\mathrm{d}t = DAp \qquad D = [F_i'\delta_{ij}], \qquad \mathrm{d}p/\mathrm{d}t = [\mathrm{d}p_i/\mathrm{d}t] \qquad \cdots [5]$$

$i, j = 1, \ldots, m$

From Theorem 16 of Chapter 4, we know that eqn [5] is stable, i.e. $p \to \mathbf{0}$ or $P \to P^*$, iff $\mathrm{Re}\lambda_i(DA) < 0$, for all i.

F_i' may be interpreted as the speed of adjustment in the i-th market. Given any system such as eqn [2], with its linear approximation [3], we can always redefine units of measurement so that $F_i' = 1$, for all i. Then $D = I$ and eqn [5] reduces to the slightly simpler:

$$\mathrm{d}p/\mathrm{d}t = Ap \qquad \cdots [6]$$

Stability obtains iff $\mathrm{Re}\lambda_i(A) < 0$. (This redefinition of units may mask an interesting problem to which we return later—that of investigating conditions under which eqn [5] is stable for any positive diagonal matrix D.)

Samuelson has proved conclusively that neither Hicksian perfect nor imperfect stability is either necessary or sufficient for true dynamic stability (see the exercises). We may see this directly from our work above in §2.4.1 on P-matrices.

By Theorem 43, each real root of an $(N\text{–}P)$-matrix is negative; however, complex roots may have positive real parts. These roots, with their associated oscillatory motions, are undetected by the Hicksian stability conditions.

We may at this stage, consider the following:

Theorem 11 (Fisher–Fuller): If A is a real $n \times n$ matrix with all its upper left-hand principal minors non-zero, there exists a real diagonal matrix D such that the roots of DA are real, negative and simple.

A non-trivial corollary of the Fisher–Fuller theorem is the following:

Theorem 12: If A is an $(N\text{–}P)$-matrix, there exists a positive diagonal matrix D such that all the roots of DA are real, negative and simple.

Proof: The proof follows directly from Theorem 45 of Chapter 2.

Hence any matrix which satisfies the Hicksian perfect stability conditions can be "stabilised" by appropriate choice of speeds of adjustment,

d_i, $i = 1, \ldots, m$. We can interpret this result in the following way: there is a ranking of markets in terms of decreasing speeds of adjustment—without loss of generality, this ranking can be taken as $1, 2, \ldots, m$. Consider the market for good i; the prices in markets $i+1, \ldots, m$ are fixed, while those in $1, \ldots, i-1$ are adjusted to achieve equilibrium in these markets. By the Hicksian perfect stability conditions, there is a unique partial equilibrium price for the i-th market such that when price is less (greater) than this partial equilibrium, there is excess demand (supply).

§8.5.2. *D-stability*

It was Metzler who achieved some rehabilitation of Hicks's work. "From the Samuelson examples, one might infer that Hicksian stability is only remotely connected with true dynamic stability. For some problems this is correct. But for others the Hicks conditions are highly useful despite their lack of generality. They provide a set of stability conditions which are independent of the speed of response of individual prices to discrepancies between supply and demand .... It will be shown that the Hicks conditions of perfect stability are necessary if stability is to be independent of such price responsiveness."[(9)] (Metzler also proved the equivalence of the Hicksian perfect stability conditions and the true dynamic stability conditions in the gross substitutes case.)

We now introduce the following:

Definition 9: The matrix A is D-stable if DA is stable for every positive diagonal matrix D.

Then the system: $\mathrm{d}p/\mathrm{d}t = DAp$ is D-stable if the solution $p \to \mathbf{0}$ for any positive diagonal matrix D. We are obviously considering a situation in which the speed of adjustment is finite in each market.

Lange and Metzler implicitly introduced the following generalisation of D-stability:

Definition 10: The matrix A is *totally stable* if each principal sub-matrix of A is D-stable.

Trivially, total stability implies D-stability.
The total stability concept is relevant in a system in which some prices are inflexible; for example, $F_i' = 0$, $i = k+1, \ldots, m$.
Then eqn [5] of §8.5.1 becomes a system of order k, say:

$$\mathrm{d}\bar{p}/\mathrm{d}t = \bar{D}\bar{A}p \qquad \bar{p} = (p_1, \ldots, p_k)'; \qquad \bar{D} = [d_i\delta_{ij}]; \qquad \bar{A} = [a_{ij}]; \quad i, j = 1, \ldots, k.$$

Evidently, $\bar{A}$ is a principal sub-matrix of A.
The following theorem is useful in stability analysis:

Theorem 13 (Routh–Hurwitz): Let $k_i = (-1)^i$ times the sum of all i-rowed principal minors of the matrix C. C is stable iff:

(i) $k_i > 0$ for all $i = 1, \ldots, m$;

(ii) $\det\begin{bmatrix} k_1 & k_3 \\ 1 & k_2 \end{bmatrix} > 0; \qquad \det\begin{bmatrix} k_1 & k_3 & k_5 \\ 1 & k_2 & k_4 \\ 0 & k_1 & k_3 \end{bmatrix} > 0; \ldots;$

$$\det\begin{bmatrix} k_1 & k_3 & \cdots & 0 \\ 1 & k_2 & \cdots & 0 \\ \cdot & \cdot & \cdot & \cdot \\ \cdot & \cdot & \cdot & \cdot \\ \cdot & \cdot & \cdot & \cdot \\ 0 & 0 & \cdots & k_m \end{bmatrix} > 0$$

For a proof consult Lancaster.

Theorem 14: If A is D-stable, then A is an $(N\text{–}P)_0$-matrix.

Proof: Suppose that A is not an $(N\text{–}P)_0$-matrix. Then there is a principal minor of order k, say $\det\tilde{A}$, that has sign $(-1)^{k+1}$. $\tilde{A}$ will be premultiplied by the positive diagonal matrix $\tilde{D}$ of order k. The diagonal elements of $\tilde{D}$ can be chosen so that $\det\tilde{D}\tilde{A}$ is greater in absolute value than the sum of all the other principal minors of DA of order k. This clearly implies that the sum of all k-th order principal minors of DA has sign $(-1)^{k+1}$. This contradicts the Routh–Hurwitz theorem. Hence A is an $(N\text{–}P)_0$-matrix.

Related to this we have the following result due to Metzler:

Theorem 15: If A is totally stable, A is an $(N\text{–}P)$-matrix.

Proof: Suppose that A is not an $(N\text{–}P)$-matrix. Then there is a principal minor of order k, say $\det\tilde{A}$, that has sign 0 or $(-1)^{k+1}$. If $\det\tilde{A} = 0$, $\det\tilde{D}\tilde{A} = 0$ which implies that $\tilde{D}\tilde{A}$ is not stable. If sign $\det\tilde{A} = (-1)^{k+1}$, sign $\det\tilde{D}\tilde{A} = (-1)^{k+1}$. This again implies that $\tilde{D}\tilde{A}$ is not stable.
The contradiction in both cases yields the result.

We now present some sufficient conditions for D-stability and total stability.

Theorem 16: If there is a positive diagonal matrix E such that $EA + A'E$ is negative definite, then A is D-stable.

Proof: Consider DA. To demonstrate stability of DA, it suffices to find a positive definite matrix V such that $V(DA) + (DA)'V = -W$, where W is positive definite (by Theorem 17 of Chapter 4). Put $V = ED^{-1} = V'$. Then $VDA + A'DV = ED^{-1}DA + A'DD^{-1}E = EA + A'E$ which is negative definite by hypothesis.

Theorem 17: (i) If A is quasi-negative definite, or (ii) if A has a negative q.d.d., then A is totally stable.

Proof: (i) We may use Theorem 16. Quasi-negative definiteness of A implies $x'(A+A')x<0$, for all $x\neq \mathbf{0}$, or $A+A'$ is negative definite. Then any principal sub-matrix of $A+A'$, say $\bar{A}+\bar{A}'$, is also negative definite. Using Theorem 16, with $E=I$, we see that $\bar{A}$ is D-stable. Hence A is totally stable.
(ii) If A has a negative q.d.d., there exist $c_j>0, j=1,\ldots,m$, such that:

$$c_j|a_{ij}|\geq \sum_{i\neq j} c_i|a_{ij}| \qquad \cdots[1]$$

for all $i=1,\ldots,m$, with at least one strict inequality.
Putting $c_i=b_id_i$, we have:

$$b_j|d_ja_{ij}|\geq \sum_{i\neq j} b_i|d_ia_{ij}|$$

for all i, with at least one strict inequality. Hence DA has a negative q.d.d. and therefore is stable.
As eqn [1] is true for any principal sub-matrix of A, it follows that each principal sub-matrix of A is D-stable, i.e. A is totally stable.

To conclude this section, we have the following result on stability in an exchange economy:

Theorem 18: In an exchange economy, if there is no trade at equilibrium, the equilibrium is D-stable.

Proof: We have:

$$a_{ik}=\partial z_i/\partial p_k=\sum_{j=1}^{M} s^j_{ik}-\sum_{j=1}^{M}(x^j_k-w^i_k)\partial x^i_k/\partial \rho_j$$

where s^j_{ik} is the substitution term for the j-th consumer. If there is no trade at equilibrium, $x^j_k-w^j_k=0$ for all j. Then $A=A'$ and is negative definite. The result follows.

§8.6. Stability, substitutability and complementarity

§8.6.1. *Gross substitutes*

As mentioned in §8.5.1, Metzler proved that, in the (SGS) case, the Hicksian perfect stability conditions and the true dynamic stability conditions were equivalent. Metzler's ingenious proof is rather lengthy and, in any event, is superseded by the result, due to Arrow and Hurwicz, Negishi, and Hahn, that the (SGS) case is stable.

Theorem 19: The (SGS) case is D-stable.

Proof: By (W):

$$\sum_{i=1}^{n} p_iz_i=0 \qquad \cdots[1]$$

Differentiating with respect to p_j, we obtain:

$$\sum_{i=1}^{n} p_i a_{ij} + z_j = 0 \qquad j = 1, \ldots, m \qquad \cdots [2]$$

Evaluating at equilibrium and employing (SGS), we have:

$$\sum_{i=1}^{m} p_i^* a_{ij} = -p_n^* a_{nj} < 0 \qquad j = 1, \ldots, m \qquad \cdots [3]$$

Then

$$-p_j^* a_{jj} > \sum_{\substack{i=1 \\ i \neq j}}^{m} p_i^* a_{ij} \qquad j = 1, \ldots, m$$

or

$$p_j^* |a_{jj}| > \sum_{i \neq j} p_i^* |a_{ij}| \qquad j = 1, \ldots, m \qquad \cdots [4]$$

So A has a negative q.d.d. and is D-stable by Theorem 17.

As an alternative proof we have the following:
From eqn [3]:

$$-\sum_{i=1}^{m} p_i^* a_{ij} = p_n^* a_{nj} > 0 \qquad j = 1, \ldots, m$$

or

$$p^{*\prime} B = c > \mathbf{0} \qquad B = -A; \qquad c = [p_n^* a_{nj}], \qquad j = 1, \ldots, m \qquad \cdots [5]$$

B has negative off-diagonal elements and positive diagonal elements. Then, using the Hawkins–Simon theorem, we conclude from eqn [5] that B is a P-matrix. In fact, given the sign restrictions, it is an M-matrix. By Theorem 57 of Chapter 2, $\mathrm{Re}(\lambda_i(B)) > 0$, for all i. Given the relation between the roots of A and the roots of B, we have $\mathrm{Re}(\lambda_i(A)) < 0$, for all i. So, A is a stable matrix.

Our aim is to derive D-stability. Note that, if B is an M-matrix, so is DB, where D is the positive diagonal matrix of speeds of adjustment; for B and DB have the same sign pattern and if B is a P-matrix, so is DB.

So DB is an M-matrix. Then $\mathrm{Re}(\lambda_i(DB)) > 0$, for all i. Hence, $\mathrm{Re}(\lambda_i(DA)) < 0$, for all i. Hence A is D-stable.

We have proved D-stability under (W) by using the theory of M-matrices and q.d.d. matrices. D-stability may be derived alternatively under (H) using the same mathematical theory (see the exercises).

§8.6.2. *Complementarity: the Morishima case*

In §§8.6.2–8.6.4, we shall discuss various ways of incorporating complementarity into stability analysis. Our basic equation is:

$$\mathrm{d}p/\mathrm{d}t = DAp \qquad \cdots [1]$$

Morishima, following Hicks, imposed the following sign conditions on the elements of A:

$$\text{sign } a_{ij} = \text{sign } a_{ji}$$

$$\text{sign } a_{ij} = \text{sign } a_{ik}a_{kj} \qquad i \neq j \neq k \neq i \qquad \cdots [2]$$

These rules apply to the non-numeraire commodities.
A is a sign-symmetric matrix. We have the following result, originally due to Morishima:

Theorem 20: Eqn [1] is stable iff A is an (N–P)-matrix.

Proof: $a_{ii} < 0$, for all i. Choose $\alpha > \max_i |d_i a_{ii}|$. Let λ_i be any root of DA. Then $\lambda_i + \alpha = \mu_i$ is a root of $DA + \alpha I = B$. B satisfies the sign conditions given in Definition 15 of Chapter 2. Then by Theorem 61 of Chapter 2, there exists a root

$$\mu^*(B) > |\mu_i(B)|.$$

Now suppose that A is an $(N-P)$-matrix. Then so is DA. The characteristic equation of DA is given by:

$$f_{DA}(\lambda) = \det(DA - \lambda I) = (-\lambda)^m + c_{m-1}(-\lambda)^{m-1} + \cdots + c_1(-\lambda) + c_0 = 0 \qquad \cdots [3]$$

where c_r is the sum of all (m–r)-rowed principal minors of DA. Using the relation between λ and μ, we may write the characteristic equation as:

$$(\alpha - \mu)^m + c_{m-1}(\alpha - \mu)^{m-1} + \cdots + c_1(\alpha - \mu) + c_0 = 0$$

or

$$(\mu - \alpha)^m + (-1)c_{m-1}(\mu - \alpha)^{m-1} + \cdots + (-1)^{m-1}c_{m-1}(\mu - \alpha) + (-1)^m c_0 = 0 \qquad \cdots [4]$$

after multiplying through by $(-1)^m$.
As DA is an (N–P)-matrix, it follows that:

$$\text{sign } c_{m-r} = (-1)^r. \qquad \cdots [5]$$

Then:

$$\text{sign } (-1)^r c_{m-r} = \text{sign } (-1)^{2r} = +1.$$

Suppose there exists $\mu_i \geqslant \alpha$. Then the left-hand side of eqn [4] is positive—if $\mu_i > \alpha$, each term on the left-hand side of eqn [4] is positive; if $\mu_i = \alpha$, then $c_0 \neq 0$, in fact sign $c_0 = (-1)^m$. This is a contradiction. So $\mu^*(B) < \alpha$. Hence $\text{Re}(\lambda_i) < 0$, for all i, and stability follows.

Now suppose that eqn [1] is stable.
Consider $B = DA + \alpha I$, which is a Morishima matrix. By Theorems 60 and 61 of Chapter 2:

$$C = P^{-1}BP = \alpha I + P^{-1}DAP > [0] \qquad \cdots [6]$$

Then

$$\alpha I - C = -P^{-1}(DA)P \qquad \cdots [7]$$

where P is the matrix used in Theorem 60 of Chapter 2.
As DA is a stable matrix, it follows that each root of B has real part less than α (in particular, $\mu^*(B) < \alpha$, where $\mu^*(B) > |\mu_i(B)|$). As B and C are similar matrices, it follows that α is greater than the real part of each root of C, i.e. the real part of each root of $\alpha I - C$ is positive.
Now consider the signs of the elements of $\alpha I - C$. $\alpha I - C$ has negative off-diagonal elements and positive diagonal elements, from eqns [6] and [7]. Then by Theorem 57 of Chapter 2, $\alpha I - C$ is an M-matrix. In particular, it is a P-matrix. So:

$$-(\alpha I - C) = P^{-1}(DA)P \quad \text{is an } (N\text{–}P)\text{-matrix.}$$

Given the form of $P = \begin{bmatrix} I & 0 \\ 0 & -I \end{bmatrix}$, it is evident that DA is also an (N–P)-matrix. As D is a positive diagonal matrix, it follows that A is an (N–P)-matrix, as required. This completes the proof of the theorem.

As mentioned above, in Morishima's original treatment, the sign rules, given in eqn [2] above, apply to the non-numeraire commodities. We now consider what happens if we extend the sign rules to all commodities. Morishima objected to

"such an inflexionless extension of the condition [2], originally intended to be applied to non-numeraire goods, to the entire economy including the numeraire. In order to preserve stability, it must be carefully extended such that it does not contradict other properties, such as (H) and (W), which should have priority over [2] in characterising the system."(10)

As may be seen from Theorem 59 of Chapter 2, the sign conditions are equivalent to the proposition that the set of commodities, $N = \{1, \ldots, m, n\}$, can be partitioned into two non-empty subsets, say S and T, such that any two commodities in the same subset are gross substitutes, any two commodities in different subsets are gross complements. (H) and/or (W) implies only that there does not exist a commodity which is a gross complement to every other commodity; in other words, (H) and/or (W) restrict each of S and T to contain at least two commodities. Morishima's criticisms may thus be deflected if we make the appropriate assumption about S and T.

(H) and/or (W) imply that the Jacobian matrix (of excess demand functions) of the whole system (i.e. including the numeraire) is necessarily singular and so cannot be an (N–P)-matrix.
We introduce the related condition:

(O): $\det A = 0$ and each principal sub-matrix of A is an (N–P)-matrix.

Theorem 21: If the sign conditions are applied to all commodities including the numeraire, the Jacobian matrix of the whole system does not satisfy condition (O).

Proof: Without loss of generality, aggregate all commodities in T into a composite commodity, say $s+1$. Consider the commodities in $S=\{1,\ldots,s\}$. By (H), we have:

$$\sum_{j=1}^{s} a_{ij}p_j^* + a_{i,s+1}p_{s+1}^* = 0 \qquad i=1,\ldots,s \qquad \cdots[8]$$

or

$$A_{ss}\bar{p}^* = -c \qquad A_{ss}=[a_{ij}], \qquad c=[a_{i,s+1}p_{s+1}^*]; \qquad i,j=1,\ldots,s. \qquad \cdots[9]$$

Without loss of generality, $p_{s+1}^*=1$. Given $a_{i,s+1}<0$ by the gross complementarity condition, $i=1,\ldots,s$, we have:

$$B_{ss}\bar{p}^* = c < \mathbf{0} \qquad B_{ss} = -A_{ss} \qquad \cdots[10]$$

If condition (O) is satisfied, A_{ss} is an (N–P)-matrix and therefore B_{ss} is a P-matrix. Given the sign restrictions, B_{ss} is then an M-matrix. Hence $(B_{ss})^{-1}>[0]$. From eqn [10]:

$$\bar{p}^* = (B_{ss})^{-1}c < 0. \qquad \cdots[11]$$

This is plainly a contradiction. So condition (O) is not satisfied.

Theorem 21 serves as a lemma to the next result:

Theorem 22: If the sign conditions are applied to all commodities including the numeraire, the system is unstable.

Proof: Suppose condition (O) is not satisfied. Let the t-th commodity be assigned to role of numeraire, $t \in T$. Then by Theorem 21, A_{ss} is not an (N–P)-matrix. Consider the dynamic system with t as numeraire:

$$\mathrm{d}p/\mathrm{d}t = \bar{D}\bar{A}p \qquad \bar{A}=[a_{ij}], \qquad i,j \neq t. \qquad \cdots[12]$$

A_{ss} is a principal sub-matrix of $\bar{A}$. But A_{ss} is not an (N–P)-matrix Therefore, $\bar{A}$ is not an (N–P)-matrix. By Theorem 20, stability obtains iff $\bar{A}$ is an (N–P)-matrix. So, we do not have stability in this case.
Now consider the only other possible case—where condition (O) is satisfied. However, this is not consistent with the existence of gross complementarity under the Morishima sign rules, by Theorem 21. So, if the sign conditions are applied to all commodities, there is instability.

We shall try to discuss the problem of complementarity in a more general framework in the next section.

§8.6.3 *Generalised gross substitutes*

Our basic differential equation is:

$$\mathrm{d}p/\mathrm{d}t = Ap \qquad \cdots[1]$$

where $D=I$ after appropriate definition of units of measurement. Now suppose that the units of measurement are changed, with the new prices being given by:

$$\bar{p} = Tp \qquad T \geqslant [0] \quad \text{non-singular} \qquad \cdots [2]$$

Substitution of eqn [2] into eqn [1] yields:

$$d\bar{p}/dt = T^{-1}AT\bar{p} \qquad \cdots [3]$$

Eqns [1] and [3] have the same stability properties—that is, [1] is stable iff [3] is. The brief discussion so far is similar to that of §4.2.11, yet a general equilibrium system imposes further restrictions, in particular (W). For if prices are redefined according to eqn [2], then the excess demand vector is subject to:

$$\bar{z} = (T')^{-1}z \qquad \cdots [4]$$

if (W) is to be satisfied.

If we had begun by redefining excess demands, we then have $T^{-1} \geqslant [0]$. The imposition of (W) requires $\bar{p} = Tp$. So, a symmetrical treatment of redefinition of units seems to suggest that we impose a semi-positivity condition on either T or T^{-1} (only in the diagonal case will both matrices be semi-positive). Immediately, we may observe that this semi-positivity condition is not satisfied by the matrix $P = \begin{bmatrix} I & 0 \\ 0 & -I \end{bmatrix}$ employed in the discussion of the Morishima system.

In §8.6.1, we derived the positive result that the (SGS) case is stable. Our aim here is to discuss systems involving complementary commodities; with reference to eqn [1], this means $a_{ij} < 0$, some $i \neq j$. However, by employing the similarity transformation illustrated in eqn [3], it may be possible to obtain a generalised gross substitutes matrix, G, which has the same sign pattern as the ordinary gross substitutes matrix considered in §8.6.1. We summarise our discussion so far in the following:

Definition 11: The system is a *generalised gross substitute system* (GGS-I) if there exists T such that:

(i) $T^{-1}A^*T = G^* = [g_{ij}]$; $g_{ij} \geqslant 0$, for all $i \neq j$; $i, j = 1, \ldots, m, n$;
(ii) G^* is indecomposable;
(iii) either T or T^{-1} is semi-positive.

Condition (ii) is included on the grounds of mathematical convenience.

We shall be appealing to the Perron–Frobenius theorems, which are stronger in the indecomposable than in the decomposable case. In the (SGS) and Morishima systems, the Jacobian matrix is sign-symmetric. It is worth noting that our formulation permits relaxation of this condition.

Our stability analysis so far has been of systems with a numeraire. In the (SGS) case of §8.6.1, any commodity could be chosen as numeraire. Stability properties of numeraire systems were shown to be more problematical, once complementarity was introduced. This seems a convenient opportunity to consider non-numeraire systems; that is, the differential equation:

$$\mathrm{d}p_i/\mathrm{d}t = z_i(p) = \sum_{j=1}^{n} a_{ij}p_j{}^{(11)} \quad . \qquad \cdots [5]$$

applies to all commodities. Let us define:

$$A^* = [a_{ij}] \qquad i, j = 1, \ldots, n \qquad \cdots [6]$$

By (H) or (W), A^* is singular, as $A^*p = \mathbf{0}$ and $p'A^* = \mathbf{0}'$. So eqn [5], written in matrix form as:

$$\mathrm{d}p/\mathrm{d}t = A^*p \qquad \cdots [7]$$

cannot be stable in the sense of Chapter 4 because it has a zero root. However, stability of eqn [7] should not be defined in terms of convergence to the zero vector; rather, by (H), we expect convergence to the ray defined by the/an equilibrium price vector p^*. Given singularity of A^*, we can write the solution of eqn [7] as:

$$p(t) = \alpha_1 q^1(t) + \sum_{i=2}^{k} \alpha_i e^{\lambda_i t} q^i(t) \qquad \cdots [8]$$

using the theory of Chapter 4. We assume that there are k distinct roots. $q^1(t) = \tilde{q}^1(t) + P^*$.(12)

Stability of eqn [7] occurs iff $p(t) \to P^*$, i.e. iff

(i) 0 is a simple root of A^*;

(ii) each other root of A^* has negative real part.

We summarise this in:

Theorem 23: The non-numeraire system $\mathrm{d}p/\mathrm{d}t = A^*p$, where A^* satisfies $A^*P^* = \mathbf{0}$, $P^{*\prime}A^* = \mathbf{0}'$, is stable iff 0 is a simple root of A^* and each other root of A^* has negative real part.

We may now derive our first stability result for the (GGS-I) system:

Theorem 24: If $P^* > \mathbf{0}$, the (GGS-I) system is stable.

Proof: $T^{-1}A^*T = G^*$.

Suppose $T \geqslant [0]$. By Exercises §2.3, Q3 and Q12, $G^*x = \phi(G)x$, $x > \mathbf{0}$, $\phi(G^*) \geqslant \mathrm{Re}(\lambda_i(G^*))$.
Now $P^{*\prime}A' = \mathbf{0}'$ by (W), or $P^{*\prime}TG^*T^{-1} = \mathbf{0}'$ or $(P^{*\prime}T)G^* = \mathbf{0}'$, post-multiplying by T, i.e. $P^{*\prime}T$ is a characteristic vector of G^* corresponding to the root 0. If $\phi(G^*) > 0$, it follows by Lemma 8 of Chapter 2 that $(P^{*\prime}T)x = 0$. As $x > \mathbf{0}$, $P^{*\prime}T > \mathbf{0}$, this is plainly a contradiction. So $\phi(G^*) = 0$.
Now suppose $T^{-1} \geqslant [0]$. by (H), $A^*P^* = \mathbf{0}$ or $TG^*T^{-1}P^* = \mathbf{0}$ or $G^*(T^{-1}P^*) = \mathbf{0}$, i.e. $T^{-1}P^*$ is a root of G^* corresponding to the root 0. $T^{-1}P^* > \mathbf{0}$.
Again by Exercises §2.3, Q3 and Q12, we have: $q'G^* = \phi(G^*)q'$, $q > \mathbf{0}$. As

above, $q'(T^{-1}P^*)=0$, if $\phi(G^*)>0$. Hence $\phi(G^*)=0$. In both cases, the fact that 0 is a simple root follows from indecomposability of G^*.

We may now reconsider the Morishima case of §8.6.2.

Theorem 25: If $P^*>\mathbf{0}$ and either $P^{*\prime}T$ or $T^{-1}P^*$ has both positive and negative components. A^* is unstable in the sense of Theorem 23.

Proof: Suppose $P^{*\prime}T$ has both positive and negative components. $P^{*\prime}A^*=\mathbf{0}'$ by (W) or $(P^{*\prime}T)G^*=\mathbf{0}'$ as in Theorem 24. As in Theorem 24: $q'G^*=\phi(G^*)q'$, $q>\mathbf{0}$. If stability holds in the sense of Theorem 23, $\phi(G^*)=0$ is a simple root. Then $P^{*\prime}T$ and q must be proportional. They are plainly not proportional; so stability cannot hold.
A similar argument holds when $T^{-1}P^*$ has both positive and negative components—stability requires proportionality of $T^{-1}P^*$ and x (where x is as in Theorem 24).

This theorem suggests the instability of the non-numeraire Morishima system, for the matrix P used in the analysis of the model is $\begin{bmatrix} I & 0 \\ 0 & -I \end{bmatrix}$. This would obviously lead to a mixture of signs as in Theorem 25.

Theorem 26: The non-numeraire Morishima system is unstable.

The proof follows from Theorem 25.

Let us now consider a numeraire system—the numeraire is assumed to be a gross substitute of every other commodity and vice versa. We restrict Definition 11 to non-numeraire commodities, rather as Morishima did. So there exists a matrix S such that $S^{-1}AS-II$, with either S or $S^{-1}\geqslant[0]$.
Under these conditions, we may derive stability.

Theorem 27: Consider a numeraire system. If there exists a matrix S such that $S^{-1}AS=H$, where H has non-negative off-diagonal elements and is indecomposable, and either S or S^{-1} is semipositive, then A is a stable matrix (in the sense of Chapter 4).

Proof: Using the gross substitutes property of the numeraire, we have immediately:

$$\bar{P}^{*\prime}A<\mathbf{0}' \text{ by (W)}; \quad A\bar{P}^*<\mathbf{0} \text{ by (H)}$$

where $\bar{P}^*$ is obtained from P^* by deleting the price of the numeraire. Suppose $S\geqslant[0]$. Using (W), we have:

$$\bar{P}^{*\prime}SHS^{-1}<\mathbf{0}' \quad \text{or} \quad (\bar{P}^{*\prime}S)H<\mathbf{0}', \quad \text{post-multiplying by } S\geqslant[0],$$

or

$$d'H<\mathbf{0}', \qquad d=s\bar{P}^*>\mathbf{0}.$$

So H has a negative q.d.d. and is stable. Now suppose that $S^{-1}\geqslant[0]$. Using (H) and a method similar to that above, we may derive: $Hd<\mathbf{0}$, $d=S^{-1}\bar{P}^*>\mathbf{0}$. Again H has a negative q.d.d. so that stability follows.

We shall conclude here with the following generalisation of Definition 11:

Definition 12: The system is *generalised gross system* (GGS-II) if there exists a matrix T such that:

(i) $T^{-1}(A^*+A^{*\prime})T=G^*$, $g_{ij}\geqslant 0$, for all $i\neq j$;
(ii) G^* is indecomposable;
(iii) either T or T^{-1} is semi-positive.

We now present stability results using this concept, beginning with one for the non-numeraire system; in this case, 0 must be a simple root and be greater than the real part of any other root.

Theorem 28: If $P^*>\mathbf{0}$, (GGS-II) implies that the system is stable.

Proof: $T^{-1}(A^*+A^{*\prime})T=G^*$.
Say $T\geqslant[0]$. Using (H) and (W): $P^{*\prime}(A^*+A^{*\prime})=\mathbf{0}'$. So $P^{*\prime}TG^*T^{-1}=\mathbf{0}'$ or $(P^{*\prime}T)G^*=\mathbf{0}'$ post-multiplying by T; $P^{*\prime}T>\mathbf{0}$.
As in Theorem 24, $G^*x=\phi(G^*)x$, $x>\mathbf{0}$. Then $\phi(G^*)=0$ as in Theorem 24.
Now suppose $T^{-1}\geqslant[0]$. Then $(A^*+A^{*\prime})P^*=\mathbf{0}$ or $TG^*(T^{-1}P^*)=\mathbf{0}$; or $G^*(T^{-1}P^*)=\mathbf{0}$ pre-multiplying by T^{-1}. Again as in Theorem 24, $q'G^*=\phi(G^*)q'$, $q>\mathbf{0}$. $\phi(G^*)=0$ again as in Theorem 24.
That 0 is a simple root follows by indecomposability.
$A^*+A^{*\prime}$ is symmetric and therefore has only real roots. As $\phi(G^*)=0$ is simple, $A^*+A^{*\prime}$ has one zero root, $n-1$ negative roots. So $A^*+A^{*\prime}$ is negative semi-definite, i.e.

$$x'(A^*+A^{*\prime})x\leqslant 0 \quad \text{with equality iff } x=\gamma P^*.$$

Hence:

$$x'A^*x\leqslant 0 \quad \text{with equality iff } x=\gamma P^*.$$

Using a method similar to that employed in Exercises §2.4, Q23, we are able to conclude that A^* has one zero root, each of the other $n-1$ roots having a negative real part. Stability follows.

To derive results for a numeraire system under (GGS-II), we require the following result due to Quirk:

Theorem 29: Consider a matrix B such that $B^*P^*=\mathbf{0}$, $P^{*\prime}B^*=\mathbf{0}'$, $P^*\geqslant\mathbf{0}$. Let B_{ij} denote the cofactor of b_{ij} and $J=\{1:P_i^*>0\}$. Then:

(i) $B_{ij}/P_i^*P_j^*=B_{rs}/P_r^*P_s^*$ for all $i, j, r, s\in J$:
(ii) $B_{ij}=0$ if $i\in J$, $j\notin J$ and if $i\notin J$, $j\in J$.

Proof: Consider $B\,.\,\text{adj}B=\text{adj}B\,.\,B=[0]$.
If $B_{ij}=0$ for all i, j, the result is proved.
Suppose $B_{ij}\neq 0$ for some i, j. Then $r(B)=n-1$. Then the solution sets of $x'B=\mathbf{0}'$, $By=\mathbf{0}$ are vector spaces of dimension 1.

As $P^{*\prime}B = \mathbf{0}'$, $BP^* = \mathbf{0}$, it follows that x and y are both multiples of P^*. Any row (column) of adj$B$ satisfies $x'B = \mathbf{0}'$ ($By = \mathbf{0}$) and hence is a multiple of P^*. Let the i-th row or column of adj$B$ be $\alpha_i P^*$. Then $B_{ij} = \alpha_i P_j^* = \alpha_j P_i^*$. Then for any $i, j, r, s \in J$, we have: $B_{ij}/P_j^* = \alpha_i = B_{is}/P_s^* = \alpha_s P_i^*/P_s^* = B_{rs}P_i^*/P_r^* P_s^*$.
Part (i) follows. Part (ii) is evident.

This result serves as a lemma to:

Theorem 30: (GGS-II) implies that A is totally stable.

Proof: $A^* + A^{*\prime}$ is negative semi-definite with zero a simple root, i.e. $r(A^* + A^{*\prime}) = n - 1$. Suppose $\det(A + A') = 0$.
Let $\det(A + A') = B_{nn}$ in the notation of the previous Theorem. $n \in J$. Hence, for all $i, j \in J$, we have from (i) of Theorem 29 that $B_{ij} = 0$. If one or both of the indices i, j is not in J, it follows from (ii) that $B_{ij} = 0$.
Hence, $B_{ij} = 0$, for all i, j, i.e. all cofactors of $A^* + A^{*\prime}$ (of order $n-1$) are zero. Hence, $r(A^* + A^{*\prime}) < n - 1$. This is a contradiction. So $\det(A + A') \neq 0$. So $A + A'$ is non-singular and, being a principal sub-matrix of $A^* + A^{*\prime}$, is negative semidefinite, i.e. $A + A'$ is negative definite. So A is quasi-negative definite. Then A is totally stable by Theorem 17 (i).

Corresponding to Theorem 27, we have:

Theorem 31: If $T^{-1}(A + A')T = H$, T or T^{-1} is semi-positive, and the numeraire is a gross substitute for every other commodity and vice versa, then the numeraire system is stable.

Proof: By (W) and (H): $\bar{P}^{*\prime}(A + A') < \mathbf{0}'$.
Say $T \geqslant [0]$. Then $\bar{P}^{*\prime}THT^{-1} < \mathbf{0}'$ or $(\bar{P}^{*\prime}T)H < \mathbf{0}'$, post-multiplying by $T \geqslant [0]$, i.e. $d'H < \mathbf{0}'$, $d = T'\bar{P}^* > \mathbf{0}$. So H has a negative q.d.d. and is stable. Then $A + A'$ is negative definite which implies that A is quasi-negative definite.
Now suppose $T^{-1} \geqslant [0]$. By (H) and (W): $(A + A')\bar{P}^* < \mathbf{0}$ or $THT^{-1}\bar{P}^* < \mathbf{0}$ or $H(T^{-1}\bar{P}^*) < \mathbf{0}$, pre-multiplying by $T^{-1} \geqslant [0]$.
So $Hd < \mathbf{0}$, $d = T^{-1}\bar{P}^* > \mathbf{0}$. Again H has a negative q.d.d. Repeating the argument above, we conclude that A is quasi-negative definite. From Theorem 17 (i), we derive total stability.

§8.6.4. *Complementarity: Quirk's result*

The cases discussed in §§8.6.1 and 8.6.2 were characterised by sign-symmetric matrices. The use of similarity transformations permitted us to dispense with sign symmetry in §8.6.3. However, we now revert to the sign symmetry assumption to derive Quirk's result—that the presence of complementarity precludes the proof of stability of equilibrium unless other information is supplied, e.g. that there is no trade at equilibrium. As we are dealing with sign-symmetric matrices, we introduce:

Definition 13: Given the $n \times n$ matrix A, define the matrix sign$A$ to have as its (i, j) component signa_{ij} where:

$$\text{sign}a_{ij} = \begin{cases} +1 & \text{if} \quad a_{ij} > 0 \\ 0 & \text{if} \quad a_{ij} = 0 \\ -1 & \text{if} \quad a_{ij} < 0 \end{cases}$$

$Q_A = \{B : \text{sign}B = \text{sign}A\}$, i.e. Q_A is the set of all matrices having the same sign pattern as A.

The matrix A is typically the Jacobian matrix of excess demand functions. The Jacobian matrix statisfies further conditions if we impose (H) and (W):

$$\sum_{j=1}^{n} a_{ij} = 0, \quad \text{for all } i$$

$$\sum_{i=1}^{n} a_{ij} = 0, \quad \text{for all } j$$

where we have chosen units of measurement so that each price is 1.

Let us consider the subset of Q_A given by:

Definition 14: $S_{A^*} = \{B^* : B^* \in Q_{A^*}$ and B^* satisfies the row and column sum conditions dictated by (H) and (W)$\}$.

Definition 15: A is *qualitatively stable* under (H) and (W) if $B^* \in S_{A^*}$ implies that B is stable.

The gross substitute case of §8.6.1 is an example of qualitative stability. Each matrix with non-negative off-diagonal elements, negative diagonal elements satisfying (H) and (W) is stable; in fact, such a matrix is D-stable.

Theorem 32: Let A^* be sign symmetric. Then if A is qualitatively stable under (H) and (W), $B^* \in S_{A^*}$ implies that B is quasi-negative definite.

Proof: Under sign symmetry, $B^* \in S_{A^*}$ implies $B^* + B^{*\prime} \in S_{A^*}$, as the row and column sum conditions are satisfied for $B^* + B^{*\prime}$. If A is qualitatively stable, then each matrix C such that $C^* \in S_{A^*}$ is stable; in particular, $B + B'$ is stable. As this matrix is symmetric, $B + B'$ is negative definite. Hence, B is quasi-negative definite.

Theorem 33: Assume that B is quasi-negative definite. Then if B^* satisfies (H) and (W), each $m \times m$ principal sub-matrix of B^* is quasi-negative definite.

Proof: Let $x^* = (x_1, \ldots, x_m, x_n)$.

$$x^{*\prime} B^* x^* = \sum_{i,j=1}^{m} x_i b_{ij} x_j + x_n \left(\sum_{j=1}^{m} b_{nj} x_j + \sum_{i=1}^{m} b_{i0} x_i \right) + x_n^2 b_{nn}$$

Using (H) and (W):

$$x^{*\prime}B^*x^* = \sum_{i,j=1}^{m} x_i b_{ij} x_j - x_n\left[\sum_{i,j=1}^{m} b_{ij}x_j + \sum_{i,j=1}^{m} b_{ij}x_i\right] + x_n^2 \sum_{i,j=1}^{m} b_{ij}$$

If $x_n = 0$, then $x^{*\prime}B^*x = x'Bx < 0$ by quasi-negative definiteness of B. Let $x_n \neq 0$, $y_i = x_i/x_n$ for $i = 1, \ldots, m$. Then

$$\begin{aligned}(1/x_n^2)x^{*\prime}B^*x^* &= \sum_{i,j=1}^{m} b_{ij}(y_i y_j - y_i - y_j + 1)\\ &= \sum_{i,j=1}^{m} b_{ij}(y_i - 1)(y_j - 1)\\ &= z'Bz \qquad z = (z_i), \qquad z_i = y_i - 1; \qquad 1, \ldots, m.\end{aligned}$$

As B is quasi-negative definite, it follows that the quadratic form is negative unless $z = \mathbf{0}$, i.e. unless $y_i = 1$ for all i. i.e. unless $x_i = x_j$.
To obtain the quadratic form associated with any principal sub-matrix of B^* (of order m), we merely put $x_i = 0$, for some i. But from above, such a quadratic form would be negative. So, we have the required result.

Theorem 34: Let A^* be sign-symmetric. Then if A is qualitatively stable under (H) and (W), $B^* \in S_{A^*}$ implies that each $m \times m$ principal sub-matrix of B^* is an (N–P)-matrix.

Proof: Given the hypotheses, we have that B is quasi-negative definite, by Theorem 32, and that each $m \times m$ principal sub-matrix of B^* is quasi-negative definite, by Theorem 33. Let $\bar{B}$ denote any principal sub-matrix of B^*. Then by Exercises §2.4, Q23, it follows that $\bar{B}$ is an (N–P)-matrix.

We are now in a position to derive the main result:

Theorem 35: Assume that A^* is sign symmetric. If A^* has negative off-diagonal elements, A is not qualitatively stable under (W) and (H).

Proof: Let $a_{rs} < 0$, $a_{sr} < 0$.
Suppose that A is qualitatively stable under (W) and (H), $B^* \in S_{A^*}$ implies that B is stable from Definition 16.
Consider the 2×2 principal sub-matrix involving rows r and s.
Let α_r and α_s denote the row sums in this case, i.e.

$$b_{rr} + b_{rs} = \alpha_r; \qquad b_{sr} + b_{ss} = \alpha_s.$$

By Theorem 34, $b_{rr} < 0$, $b_{ss} < 0$, $b_{rr}b_{ss} - b_{rs}b_{sr} > 0$.
Also, $b_{rs} < 0$, $b_{sr} < 0$. So $\alpha_r < 0$, $\alpha_s < 0$.
Now consider the matrix $C^* \in Q_{A^*}$, where $c_{ij} = b_{ij}$ for $i, j \neq r, s$ and

$$\begin{aligned}c_{rr} &= \alpha_r^2/(\alpha_r + \alpha_s) + \varepsilon\\ c_{ss} &= \alpha_s^2/(\alpha_r + \alpha_s) + \varepsilon\\ c_{rs} = c_{sr} &= \alpha_r\alpha_s/(\alpha_r + \alpha_s) - \varepsilon\end{aligned}$$

where ε is chosen so that $c_{rr}<0$, $c_{ss}<0$, $c_{rs}=c_{sr}<0$. As $c_{rr}+c_{rs}=\alpha_r$, $c_{sr}+c_{ss}=\alpha_s$, it follows that $C^* \in S_{A^*}$. However, $c_{rr}c_{ss}-c_{rs}c_{sr}=\varepsilon(\alpha_r+\alpha_s)<0$. So, we have a 2×2 principal sub-matrix of C^* which is not an $(N–P)$-matrix. Hence, A is not qualitatively stable under (W) and (H).

As a straightforward corollary, we have:

Theorem 36: Let A^* be sign-symmetric and indecomposable. Then A is qualitatively stable under (W) and (H) iff A^* is (WGS).

§8.7. Expectations and stability

In this section, we discuss the incorporation of expectations into the stability analysis, first by means of an extrapolative mechanism, then by means of an adaptive mechanism.

§8.7.1. *Extrapolative expectations*

Let us suppose that we can write:

$$z_i = z_i(P; P_i^e) \qquad i=1,\dots,m \qquad \cdots [1]$$

where P_i^e is the expected future price of the i-th commodity; or, taking a linear approximation, we have:

$$z_i = \sum_{i=1}^{m} a_{ij}(P_j - P_j^*) + b_j(P_i^e - P_i^*) \qquad \cdots [2]$$

where $b_i = \partial z_i/\partial P_i^e$. Suppose:

$$\mathrm{d}P_i/\mathrm{d}t = k_i z_i \qquad \cdots [3]$$

and

$$P_i^e = P_i + \eta_i \mathrm{d}P_i/\mathrm{d}t \qquad \cdots [4]$$

which defines the generation of expectations. Then by straightforward substitution, we obtain:

$$\mathrm{d}P_i/\mathrm{d}t = k_i \sum_j a_{ij}(P_j - P_j^*) + k_i b_i (P_i - P_i^*) + k_i b_i \eta_i \mathrm{d}P_i/\mathrm{d}t$$

or

$$(I-D)\mathrm{d}P/\mathrm{d}t = KA(P-P^*) + KB(P-P^*)$$

or

$$(I-D)\mathrm{d}p/\mathrm{d}t = K(A+B)p \qquad p = P - P^*; \qquad D = [d_i\delta_{ij}]; \qquad \cdots [5]$$
$$d_i = k_i b_i \eta_i$$

Metzler proved that, in the gross substitutes case (i.e. $a_{ii}<0$, $a_{ij}>0$, for all $i\neq j$, $b_i>0$), if $\eta_i=0$ for all i, stability obtains if $K(A+B)$ is an $(N–P)$-matrix.

Theorem 37: If $K(A+B)$ is an $(N\text{–}P)$-matrix, eqn [5] is stable iff $1>d_i$, for all i.

Proof:
Sufficiency: If $1>d_i$, for all i, then $I-D\geqslant[0]$ and is non-singular. Eqn [5] becomes: $\mathrm{d}p/\mathrm{d}t=(I-D)^{-1}K(A+B)p$.
The matrix $(I-D)^{-1}K(A+B)$ is evidently an $(N\text{–}P)$-matrix if $K(A+B)$ is. Hence, we have stability. This completes the Sufficiency part of the theorem.
Necessity: If eqn [5] is stable, $I-D$ is non-singular. So eqn [5] may be written as:

$$\mathrm{d}p/\mathrm{d}t=FCp \qquad F=(I-D)^{-1}, \qquad C=K(A+B) \qquad \cdots[6]$$

We have to prove that $f_i=1/(1-d_i)>0$, for all i. We require the following lemmata:

Lemma 2: Let C be a stable matrix with non-negative off-diagonal elements, F a non-singular diagonal matrix. Then $\phi(FC)\neq 0$, where $\phi(FC)=\max_i \mathrm{Re}(\lambda_i(FC))$.

Proof: Choose α such that $M=\alpha I+C\geqslant[0]$. Suppose $\phi(FC)=0$. Then, as FC cannot have a zero real root, we have:

$$FCx=\beta x \quad \beta \text{ is purely imaginary}$$

or

$$Cx=\beta F^{-1}x$$

or

$$(\alpha I+C)x=Mx=(\alpha I+\beta F^{-1})x$$

Taking absolute values:

$$\sum_j |m_{ij}x_j|=\sum_j m_{ij}\,|x_j|\geqslant(\alpha+\beta/f_i)\,|x_i|$$

Let $\gamma=\min(\alpha+\beta/f_i)$; $y_i=|x_i|$, $y=(y_i)$. Then we have:

$$My\geqq\gamma y,\ y\geqslant 0 \qquad \cdots[7]$$

From Theorem 16 of Chapter 2:

$$\lambda^*(M)\geqslant\gamma, \quad \lambda^*(M) \text{ is the Frobenius root of } M \qquad \cdots[8]$$

$$\lambda^*(M)=\alpha+\phi(C) \qquad \cdots[9]$$

As β is purely imaginary and f_i is real, we have:

$$|\alpha+\beta/f_i|\geqslant\alpha \quad \text{for all} \quad i.$$

So:

$$\gamma\geqslant\alpha \qquad \cdots[10]$$

From eqns [8]–[10]: $\alpha + \phi(C) \geqslant \alpha$ which implies that $\phi(C) \geqslant 0$. This is a contradiction as C is assumed stable. So, $\phi(FC) \neq 0$.

Lemma 3: If C has negative diagonal elements, non-negative off-diagonal elements, F is diagonal, C and FC are stable, then $f_i > 0$, for all i.

Proof: F must be non-singular for FC to be stable. Consider $C(t)$ defined for $t \in [0, 1]$ by:

$$c_{ij}(t) = c_{ij} \quad \text{for} \quad i \leqslant j; \quad c_{ij}(t) = (1-t)c_{ij} \quad \text{for} \quad i > j.$$

$C(0) = C$ and $c_{ij}(t) \geqslant 0$, for $i \neq j$, $t \in [0, 1)$.

As t increases, some elements of $C(t)$ decrease while none increases. Hence, by Exercises §2.3, Q3, $\phi(C(t))$ is a non-increasing function of t, $t \in [0, 1)$.
So $\phi(C(t)) \leqslant \phi(C(0)) = \phi(C) < 0$. So $C(t)$ is stable for $t \in [0, 1)$.
By Lemma 2, $\phi(FC(t)) \neq 0$ for $t \in [0, 1)$. As $FC(0) = FC$ is stable, we have $\phi(FC(0)) < 0$. By continuity, we have: $\phi(FC(t)) < 0$ for $t \in [0, 1)$, and also $\phi(FC(1)) \leqslant 0$.
$FC(1)$ is a triangular matrix, with roots $f_i c_{ii}$. Hence, $f_i c_{ii} \leqslant 0$, for all i. As $c_{ii} < 0$, for all i, we have $f_i \geqslant 0$. But $f_i \neq 0$, for all i. So, $f_i > 0$, for all i, as required.
Given Lemma 3, the Necessity part of Theorem 37 follows immediately.

Negishi has provided a justification for the approach above in terms of rational expectations. First of all, excess demand functions are estimated on the basis of current prices:

$$z_i = \sum_{j=1}^{m} \alpha_{ij} P_j + \beta_i \mathrm{d}P_i/\mathrm{d}t + \gamma_i \qquad \cdots [11]$$

The expected future price, P_i^e, is calculated by:

$$z_i = 0 = \alpha_{ii} P_i^e + \sum_{j \neq i} \alpha_{ij} P_j + \gamma_i \qquad \cdots [12]$$

where $P_j^e = P_j$, $j \neq i$.
The linear approximation of z_i in the neighbourhood of an equilibrium is given by eqn [2]:

$$z_i = \sum_{j=1}^{m} a_{ij}(P_j - P_j^*) + b_i(P_i^e - P_i^*)$$

Suppose units are chosen so that $k_i = 1$, for all i, in eqn [3]:

$$\mathrm{d}P_i/\mathrm{d}t = z_i$$

From eqns [3] and [11], we have after elementary manipulation:

$$\sum_{j \neq i} \alpha_{ij} P_j = (1 - \beta_i)\mathrm{d}P_i/\mathrm{d}t - \alpha_{ii} P_i - \gamma_i \qquad \cdots [13]$$

Substituting into eqn [12], we obtain:

$$P_i^e = P_i - (1 - \beta_i)/\alpha_{ii} \,.\, \mathrm{d}P_i/\mathrm{d}t \qquad \cdots [14]$$

This compares directly with eqn [4]:

$$\eta_i = -(1-\beta_i)/\alpha_{ii} \qquad \cdots [15]$$

Using eqn [14] in eqn [2]:

$$z_i = \sum_j a_{ij}(P_j - P_j^*) + b_i(P_i - P_i^*) - b_i(1-\beta_i)/\alpha_{ii} \, . \, \mathrm{d}P_i/\mathrm{d}t \qquad \cdots [16]$$

Comparing with eqn [11], we have:

$$\alpha_{ii} = a_{ii} + b_i \qquad \cdots [17]$$

$$\alpha_{ij} = a_{ij} \qquad i \neq j \qquad \cdots [18]$$

$$\beta_i = b_i(\beta_i - 1)/\alpha_{ii} \qquad \cdots [19]$$

$$\gamma_i = \sum_j a_{ij} P_j^* - b_i P_i^* \qquad \cdots [20]$$

From eqns [17] and [19], we obtain:

$$\beta_i = -b_i/a_{ii} \qquad \cdots [21]$$

Substituting into eqn [16] using eqn [3], we have:

$$(1-\beta_i)\mathrm{d}P_i/\mathrm{d}t = \sum_j a_{ij}(P_j - P_j^*) + b_i(P_i - P_i^*)$$

By Theorem 37, the stability condition for this model is $1 > \beta_i$, for all i. By (H) and Euler's theorem:

$$\sum_j a_{ij} P_j^* + b_i P_i^* < 0 \quad \text{for all} \quad i \qquad \cdots [22]$$

Under (SGS), $b_i > 0$. Hence $\beta_i > 0$. Dividing through eqn [22] by $a_{ii} < 0$ and rearranging, we obtain:

$$(1-\beta_i)P_i^* + \sum_{j \neq i} a_{ij}/a_{ii} \, . \, P_j^* > 0 \qquad \cdots [23]$$

using eqn [21].
So $1 > \beta_i$. Hence $1 > \beta_i > 0$, i.e. the stability condition is satisfied.

§8.7.2. *Adaptive expectations*

Let us now suppose that expectations are generated according to:

$$\mathrm{d}P_i^e/\mathrm{d}t = \rho_i(P_i - P_i^e) \qquad \cdots [1]$$

We may use the framework of §8.7.1 to enable us to derive the following equations for the system with expectations:

$$\left.\begin{aligned} \mathrm{d}p/\mathrm{d}t &= K(Ap + Bp^e) \\ \mathrm{d}p^e/\mathrm{d}t &= \hat{\rho}p - \hat{\rho}p^e \qquad p^e = P^e - P^* \end{aligned}\right\} \qquad \cdots [2]$$

or

$$\mathrm{d}q/\mathrm{d}t = Gq \qquad \cdots [3]$$

where $q = (p \quad p^e)'$ and $G = \begin{bmatrix} KA & KB \\ \hat{\rho} & -\hat{\rho} \end{bmatrix}$.
This may be compared with the following expectation-less system:

$$\mathrm{d}p/\mathrm{d}t = K(A+B)p = Cp \qquad \cdots [4]$$

Theorem 38: Under gross substitution, eqn [3] is stable if eqn [4] is.
Proof:
Sufficiency: If eqn [4] is stable, by Exercises §2.3, Q3,

$$Cx = \phi(C)x \qquad \phi(C) < 0, \qquad x \geqslant \mathbf{0}.$$

Define $y = (x \quad x)'$. Then $Gy = \begin{bmatrix} Cx \\ \mathbf{0} \end{bmatrix} = \begin{bmatrix} \phi(C)x \\ \mathbf{0} \end{bmatrix} \leqslant \mathbf{0}$.
Hence, $\phi(G) < 0$, again by Exercises §2.3, Q3.
Necessity: If eqn [3] is stable: $Gw = \phi(G)w \leqslant \mathbf{0}$, $\phi(G) < 0$, $w \geqslant \mathbf{0}$.
or $\begin{bmatrix} KA & KB \\ \hat{\rho} & -\hat{\rho} \end{bmatrix} \begin{bmatrix} w^1 \\ w^2 \end{bmatrix} \leqslant \begin{bmatrix} \mathbf{0} \\ \mathbf{0} \end{bmatrix}$ which implies $w^1 \leqslant w^2$. $w^1 \geqslant \mathbf{0}$, $w^2 \geqslant \mathbf{0}$.
Let $z = w^1$. Then $[KA \quad KB] \begin{bmatrix} w^1 \\ w^2 \end{bmatrix} \geqslant [KA \quad KB] \begin{bmatrix} z \\ z \end{bmatrix} =$

$KAz + KBz = Cz$
So $Cz \leqslant \mathbf{0}$, $z \geqslant \mathbf{0}$. Hence $\phi(C) < 0$, i.e. stability of C.

§8.8. Global stability

In this section, we widen our horizons to consider at last the global stability of the system of equations:

$$\mathrm{d}P_i/\mathrm{d}t = z_i(P) \qquad i = 1, \ldots, n \qquad \cdots [1]$$

under (H) and (W). As a preliminary to our first theorem, we have:

Lemma 2: $P^{*\prime}z(P) > 0$ for all $P \neq P^*$ under (SGS).

Proof: We prove that $P^{*\prime}z(P)$ has a unique minimum at $P = P^*$. i.e. $P^{*\prime}z(P) > P^{*\prime}z(P^*) = 0$ by (W). Restricting P to S_n, which implies that P is bounded, and noting that $z(P)$ is bounded from below, we infer by continuity, that a minimum exists. Suppose it is attained at $\tilde{P}(>\mathbf{0})$.
A necessary condition for a minimum is:

$$\sum_{i=1}^{n} P_i^* z_{ij}(\tilde{P}) = 0 \qquad j = 1, \ldots, n \qquad \cdots [2]$$

Differentiating (W) with respect to P_j and evaluating first at P^* and then at

$\tilde{P}$, we obtain:

$$\sum_{i=1}^{n} P_i^* z_{ij}(P^*) = 0 \qquad j = 1, \ldots, n \qquad \cdots [3]$$

$$\sum_{i=1}^{n} \tilde{P}_i z_{ij}(\tilde{P}) = -z_j(\tilde{P}) \qquad j = 1, \ldots, n \qquad \cdots [4]$$

Let $\alpha = P_k^*/\tilde{P}_k = \max_i P_i^*/\tilde{P}_i$. Then, using [3]:

$$\alpha z_k(\tilde{P}) = -\sum_{i=1}^{n} \alpha \tilde{P}_i z_{ik}(\tilde{P}) < -\sum_{i=1}^{n} P_i^* z_{ik}(\tilde{P}) \qquad \cdots [5]$$

Or:

$$\sum_{i=1}^{n} P_i^* z_{ik}(\tilde{P}) < -\alpha z_k(\tilde{P}) \qquad \cdots [6]$$

By (SGS):

$$z_k(\tilde{P}) > z_k(P^*) = 0 \qquad \cdots [7]$$

Using [7] in [6]:

$$\sum_{i=1}^{n} P_i^* z_{ik}(\tilde{P}) < 0 \qquad \cdots [8]$$

[8] contradicts [2] and so the result follows.

We can now derive:

Theorem 39: If (SGS) holds, eqn [1] is globally stable.

Proof: Consider first $\sum_{i=1}^{n} P_i(t)^2$. Differentiating with respect to t:

$$\frac{d}{dt}\left[\sum_{i=1}^{n} P_i(t)^2\right] = 2\sum_{i=1}^{n} P_i(t)\frac{dP_i(t)}{dt} = 2\sum_{i=1}^{n} P_i(t) z_i(P) = 0 \quad \text{by} \quad (W).$$

Hence $\sum_{i=1}^{n} P_i(t)^2$ is a constant. So $\sum_{i=1}^{n} P_i(t)^2 = \sum_{i=1}^{n} P_i(0)^2$.

Now consider $v(P) = \frac{1}{2}\sum_{i=1}^{n} (P_i(t) - P_i^*)^2$, where P^* satisfies $\sum_{i=1}^{n} P_i^{*2} = \sum_{i=1}^{n} P_i(0)^2$.

Differentiating $v(P)$ with respect to t,

$$dv/dt = \sum_{i=1}^{n} (P_i(t) - P_i^*) dP_i/dt = \sum_{i=1}^{n} (P_i(t) - P_i^*) z_i(P)$$

$$= -\sum_{i=1}^{n} P_i^* z_i(P) < 0 \quad \text{using (W) and Lemma 2.}$$

Hence convergence to P^* is monotonic. Suppose that $P(t)$ does not reach P^*. Let $N(P^*)$ be an δ-neighbourhood (or ball of radius δ) around P^*.

Then $P(t) \in T = \{Q(t): Q(t) \notin N_\delta(P^*)$ and $\sum_{i=1}^{n} Q_i(t)^2 = \sum_{i=1}^{n} P_i(0)^2\}$. dv/dt is continuous in $P(t)$ and T is compact. But $dv/dt < 0$ for $P(t) \in T$. So there exists $\eta > 0$ such that $dv/dt \leqslant -\eta < 0$. Integrating, we obtain: $v(t) - v(0) \leqslant -\eta t$ or $v(t) \leqslant v(0) - \eta t$. For sufficiently large t, $v(t) < 0$. This is a contradiction. So, we have global stability.

The hypothesis of this last theorem can be weakened and stability derived, as the following result, due to McKenzie, demonstrates:

Theorem 40: Global stability obtains under (WGS).

Proof: By (W):

$$\sum_{i=1}^{n} P_i z_i(P) = 0 \qquad \cdots [9]$$

Differentiating with respect to P_j:

$$\sum_{i=1}^{n} P_i a_{ij} = -z_j \qquad \cdots [10]$$

Define

$$J = \{i : z_i(P) > 0\}$$

$$v(P) = \tfrac{1}{2} \sum_{i \in J} (z_i(P))^2 \qquad \cdots [11]$$

Then

$$dv/dt = \sum_{i \in J} \sum_{j=1}^{n} z_i(P) a_{ij} z_j(P) \qquad \cdots [12]$$

Consider $\sum_{i \in J} \sum_{j \notin J} z_i z_{ij} z_j$. In the (WGS) case, $a_{ij} \geqslant 0$; $z_i > 0$, $z_j \leqslant 0$. Hence:

$$\sum_{i \in J} \sum_{j \notin J} z_i a_{ij} z_j \leqslant 0 \qquad \cdots [13]$$

So consider:

$$\sum_{i \in J} \sum_{j \in J} z_i a_{ij} z_j = \bar{z}' \bar{A} \bar{z} \qquad \bar{A} = [a_{ij}], \qquad \bar{z} = (z_i), \qquad i, j \in J \qquad \cdots [14]$$

From eqn [10], for $j \in J$:

$$\sum_{i \in J} P_i a_{ij} \leqslant \sum_{i=1}^{n} P_i a_{ij} = -z_j < 0 \qquad \cdots [15]$$

using (WGS). Hence $\bar{A}$ has a negative D.D.

Now using homogeneity:

$$\sum_{j=1}^{n} a_{ij}P_j = 0 \qquad \cdots [16]$$

By (WGS):

$$\sum_{j\in J} a_{ij}P_j \leqslant \sum_{j=1}^{n} a_{ij}P_j = 0 \qquad \cdots [17]$$

Combining eqns [15] and [17], we see that $\frac{1}{2}(\bar{A}+\bar{A}')$ has a negative D.D. As this matrix is symmetric, all its roots are negative.
So $\bar{z}'\bar{A}\bar{z}<0$ unless $z_i(P)=0$ for all $i\in J$. Combining this with eqn [13], we see that $dv/dt<0$ unless $z_i(P)=0$ for all $i\in J$.
By (W), $z_i(P)=0$ for all $i\in J$ iff $z_i(P)=0$ for all i.
Then using Theorem 27 of Chapter 4, we have global stability.

Most of our work in §§8.5–8.8 has been concerned with the stability analysis of such tatonnement processes as:

$$dP/dt = Kz \quad \text{or} \quad dP/dt = z \qquad \cdots [18]$$

with some restrictions on the excess demand functions (e.g. gross substitution). On the basis of Scarf's work (See Exercises §8.5, Q9), we must be pessimistic about the stability of the familiar tatonnement process, unless restrictions are imposed.
So, to conclude this section, we consider an alternative price-adjustment equation. Instead of eqn [18], consider:

$$(1/P_i)(dP_i/dt) - z_i/x_i \qquad \cdots [19]$$

i.e. the proportional change in the i-th price is equal to the ratio of the excess demand for i to the demand for i. If excess demand is small (large) relative to total demand, the change in price will be correspondingly small (large).

Let us suppose that $x(P)>\mathbf{0}$ for all $P\geqslant\mathbf{0}$. Then, as long as $P(0)>\mathbf{0}$, we can derive $P(t)>\mathbf{0}$ for all t (so that eqn [19] is well defined for all t). As z is bounded from below, it follows from Walras' law—$P'z=P'(x-y)=0$— that x is bounded from above.

Theorem 41: Under eqn [19], the exchange economy is stable (i.e. each limit point of [19] is an equilibrium, if $P(0)>\mathbf{0}$).

Proof: Consider the function:

$$v(t) = P'x(P) \qquad \cdots [20]$$

If $P(0)>\mathbf{0}$, we have $P(t)>\mathbf{0}$ for all t. By hypothesis, $x(P)>\mathbf{0}$ for all $P\geqslant\mathbf{0}$. So $v(t)>\mathbf{0}$ for all t. Consider:

$$dv/dt = (dP/dt)'x(P) + P'dx/dt \qquad \cdots [21]$$

By eqn [19]:

$$(\mathrm{d}P/\mathrm{d}t)'x(P) = \sum_{i=1}^{n} (P_i z_i/x_i)x_i = \sum_{i=1}^{n} P_i z_i \qquad \cdots [22]$$
$$= P'z = 0 \quad \text{by Walras' law}$$

Differentiating Walras' law, we have:

$$(\mathrm{d}P/\mathrm{d}t)'z + P'\mathrm{d}z/\mathrm{d}t = 0 \qquad \cdots [23]$$

$$(\mathrm{d}P/\mathrm{d}t)'z = \sum_{i=1}^{n} P_i z_i^2/x_i > 0 \qquad \cdots [24]$$

unless we have an equilibrium.
Using eqn [24] in eqn [23], we have:

$P'\mathrm{d}z/\mathrm{d}t < 0$ unless we have an equilibrium.

In an exchange economy, $P'\mathrm{d}z/\mathrm{d}t = P'\mathrm{d}x/\mathrm{d}t$. So $P'\mathrm{d}x/\mathrm{d}t < 0$ unless we have an equilibrium.
We have shown that v is a positive, bounded, continuous function of P with $\mathrm{d}v/\mathrm{d}t < 0$ (unless the system is in equilibrium). Then v is a Lyapunov function and the result follows.

§8.9. Comparative statics

The purpose of this section is to analyse the effect of a given parameter change on the equilibrium of the economy. We begin with local analysis, in the gross substitutes case, the Morishima and the generalised gross substitutes cases (of §8.6.2 and §8.6.3 respectively), and conclude with global analysis in the gross substitutes case.

§8.9.1. *Formulation of the "local" problem*

Consider a system in which endogenous variables are denoted by x_i, $i = 1, \ldots, n$, parameters by α_r, $r = 1, \ldots, s$; $\alpha = [\alpha_r]$. Let us hypothesise single-valued functions:

$$F_i = F_i(x; \alpha) \qquad i = 1, \ldots, n. \qquad \cdots [1]$$

Given $\alpha = \alpha^*$, an equilibrium of the system is a vector x^* such that:

$$0 = F_i(x^*; \alpha^*) \qquad i = 1, \ldots, n \qquad \cdots [2]$$

Suppose that there is a change in the vector of parameters (or exogenous variables) from α^* to α^1 which results in a new equilibrium, x^1. We abstract from the (stability) questions of adjustment to the new equilibrium, preferring just to compare equilibria. The comparison of equilibria, x^* and x^1, would seem to be based on the assumption of uniqueness of equilibrium (i.e. unique solution of eqn [2] for x in terms of α), for otherwise the procedure may well break down. So, we should not be surprised to find some of the sufficient conditions for uniqueness of equilibrium being used in the comparison of equilibria. Assuming that the F_i are continuously differentiable, we have from eqn [2]:

$$dF_i = \sum_{j=1}^{n} \partial F_i/\partial x_j \, . \, dx_j^* + \sum_{r=1}^{s} \partial F_i/\partial \alpha_r \, . \, d\alpha_r^* = 0 \qquad \cdots [3]$$

or

$$Aw = b \qquad A = [\partial F_i/\partial x_j], \qquad w = [dx_j^*],$$
$$b = -\left[\sum_{r=1}^{s} \partial F_i/\partial \alpha_r \, . \, d\alpha_r^*\right], \qquad i, j = 1, \ldots, n \qquad \cdots [4]$$

If A is non-singular, we have:

$$w = A^{-1}b \qquad \cdots [5]$$

We now suppose that we have only qualitative information available, i.e. we know the sign pattern of A and b in terms of the three signs +, −, 0.

Definition 16: $Aw = b$ is *qualitatively solvable* (or Q-solvable) if $\text{sign}B = \text{sign}A$, $\text{sign}c = \text{sign}b$ and $By = c$ imply $\text{sign}y = \text{sign}w$.

That is, we are able to determine the sign pattern of w from only the sign patterns of the Jacobian matrix, A, and b.

Definition 17: The $n \times n$ matrix A is *qualitatively invertible* (or Q-invertible) if $\text{sign}B = \text{sign}A$ implies $\text{sign}(B^{-1}) = \text{sign}(A^{-1})$.

In these definitions, we are concerned with the availability of complete information on the vector w and the inverse of the matrix A. For many purposes, the availability of partial information will suffice—for example, a liberal sprinkling of zeros, say $n-1$ of them, in the vector b, implies that we do not need to know the sign of each element of A (assumed to be non-singular) to determine the sign pattern of w. As an immediate example, we have the following result:

Theorem 42: If there is no trade at equilibrium, a shift in tastes from the numeraire to commodity k leads to an increase in the equilibrium price of commodity k.

Proof: Let α be the parameter shifting demand away from the numeraire (the n-th commodity) to commodity k, but not directly affecting the demand for any other commodity. Then, we have instead of eqn [2]:

$$z_i(P_1^*, P_2^*, \ldots, P_m^*, P_n^*; \alpha) = 0 \quad \text{for all} \quad i \qquad \cdots [6]$$

Differentiating, we have:

$$\sum_{j=1}^{m} \partial z_i/\partial P_j^* \, . \, dP_j^* + \delta_{ik} \, . \, \partial F_k/\partial \alpha \, . \, d\alpha = 0 \qquad i = 1, \ldots, m \qquad \cdots [7]$$

after dropping the n-th equation relating to the numeraire.

Eqn [7] may be rewritten as:

$$Aw = b \qquad A = [a_{ij}], \qquad a_{ij} = [\partial z_i/\partial P_j^*]; \qquad w = [dP_j^*]; \qquad b = [-\delta_{ik}\,.\,\partial F_k/\partial\alpha\,.\,d\alpha] \qquad \cdots [8]$$

As in Theorem 20, we see that A is negative definite. From eqn [8]:

$$dP_k^* = -(A_{kk}/\det A)\,.\,\partial F_k/\partial\alpha\,.\,d\alpha \qquad \cdots [9]$$

Given negative definiteness of A, it follows that A_{kk} and $\det A$ are of opposite sign. $\partial F_k/\partial\alpha$ is positive, by hypothesis. So $\text{sign}\, dP_k^* = \text{sign}\, d\alpha$ and the result follows.

§8.9.2. *The three Hicksian laws of comparative statics*

Theorem 43: Suppose (WGS) and indecomposability hold (see definition 5 in §8.4.3). Suppose that there is a shift in tastes from the numeraire to the k-th commodity. Then:
(i) P_k increases; (ii) P_i increases, for all $i \neq k$; (iii) P_k increases by the greatest proportion.

Proof: As in Theorem 42:

$$Aw = b \qquad \cdots [1]$$

or

$$\sum_{j=1}^{m} -(a_{ij}P_j^*)dP_j^*/P_j^*) = \delta_{ik}\,.\,\partial F_k/\partial\alpha\,.\,d\alpha \qquad \cdots [2]$$

or

$$Bq = b \qquad q = [dP_j^*/P_j^*]; \qquad B = [b_{ij}], \qquad b_{ij} = -a_{ij}P_j^* \qquad \cdots [3]$$

By (H):

$$\sum_{j=1}^{m} a_{ij}P_j^* + a_{in} = 0 \quad \text{for all} \quad i,$$

or:

$$\sum_{j} -a_{ij}P_j^* = a_{in} > 0 \quad \text{for all} \quad i,$$

or

$$\sum_{j=1}^{m} b_{ij} > 0 \quad \text{for all} \quad i.$$

Then, using the theorems of §2.4.2, we have:
B is a P-matrix (by Theorem 49), in fact an M-matrix with:

$$B_{kk} > B_{kj} \quad \text{for all} \quad j \neq k \qquad \cdots [4]$$

by Theorem 51. From eqn [3]:

$$q = B^{-1}b \qquad \cdots [5]$$

As $B^{-1} > [0]$, (i) and (ii) follow immediately.
(iii) follows directly from eqn [4].

§8.9.3. *Complementary commodities*

We deal first with the Morishima case, under the additional hypothesis of stability. That is, we have the basic comparative statics equation:

$$Aw = b \qquad \cdots [1]$$

where $A = C - \alpha I$, C being a Morishima matrix and $\alpha > \lambda^*(C)$.
A is then an $(N\text{–}P)$-matrix. Then from:

$$\mathrm{d}P_k^* = -(A_{kk}/\det A) \cdot \partial F_k/\partial\alpha \cdot \mathrm{d}\alpha$$

we conclude that $\mathrm{d}P_k^* > 0$, as A_{kk} and $\det A$ have opposite sign.

$$\mathrm{d}P_i^* = -(A_{ki}/\det A) \cdot \partial F_k/\partial\alpha \cdot \mathrm{d}\alpha.$$

Using Theorem 63 of Chapter 2, we see that

$$\mathrm{sign}(-A_{ki}/\det A) = \mathrm{sign}\, a_{ki}.$$

Summarising, we have:

Theorem 44: In the stable Morishima case:
(i) P_k^* rises; (ii) P_i^* rises (falls) if i and k are substitutes (complements); when there is a shift in tastes from the numeraire to commodity k.

We now use the theory outlined in §8.6.3, in particular the (GGS-II) concept.
From Theorem 30, we know that A is quasi-negative definite (and totally stable), an immediate implication of which is that A is an $(N\text{–}P)$-matrix. Hence, as in Theorem 44, we have $\mathrm{d}P_k^* > 0$. However, it seems that, without further information, we are unable to determine the sign of the off-diagonal cofactors, A_{ki}. So, we cannot determine the sign of $\mathrm{d}P_i^*$, $i \neq k$. Summarising, we have:

Theorem 45: In the (GGS-II) case, P_k^* rises as a result of a shift in tastes from the numeraire to good k.

§8.9.4. *Global results*

We now derive a comparative statics result, under (WGS) and (I), which does not depend on infinitesimal changes.

Theorem 46: Suppose that there is shift in tastes from the numeraire to good k. Then:
(i) P_k^* increases; (ii) P_i^* increases; (iii) P_k^* increases by the greatest proportion.

Proof: From Theorem 7, we know that any equilibrium price vector will be positive and unique.
Define $p^* = (p_1^*, \ldots, p_m^*)$, $p_i^* = P_i^*/P_n^*$, $i = 1, \ldots, m$, as the original equilibrium price vector; $\bar{p}^* = (\bar{p}_1^*, \ldots, \bar{p}_m^*)$ as the new equilibrium vector.
Define $\mu_i = p_i^*/\bar{p}_i^*$. Suppose $\max_i \mu_i > 1$.
Let $\max_i \mu_i = \mu_h$, $h = 1, \ldots, r \leq m$. By (H):

$$\bar{z}_i(\bar{p}^*, 1) = \bar{z}_i(\mu_h \bar{p}^*, \mu_h)$$
$$= \bar{z}_i(p_1^*, \ldots, p_r^*, \mu_h p_{r+1}^*, \ldots, \mu_h p_m^*, \mu_h) \qquad \cdots [1]$$

As $\mu_h > 1$, it follows from (WGS) (the non-differential from) and (I) that there exists at least one $i \in R = \{1, \ldots, r\}$ such that:

$$\bar{z}_i(p_1^*, \ldots, p_r^*, \mu_h p_{r+1}^*, \ldots, \mu_h p_m^*, \mu_h) > \bar{z}_i(p^*, 1) \qquad \cdots [2]$$

Combining eqns [1] and [2]:

$$\bar{z}_i(\bar{p}^*, 1) > \bar{z}_i(p^*, 1) \quad \text{for at least one} \quad i \in R \qquad \cdots [3]$$

But

$$\bar{z}_k(p^*, 1) > z_k(p^*, 1)$$

$$\bar{z}_i(p^*, 1) = z_i(p^*, 1) \quad \text{for} \quad i \neq k$$

and

$$\bar{z}_i(\bar{p}^*, 1) = z_i(p^*, 1) = 0.$$

Hence:

$$z_k(p^*, 1) > \bar{z}_k(\bar{p}^*, 1) = 0 \qquad \cdots [4]$$

$$\bar{z}_i(p^*, 1) = \bar{z}_i(\bar{p}^*, 1) = 0 \qquad i \neq k \qquad \cdots [5]$$

Equation [3] contradicts eqns [4] and [5].
Hence $\max_i \mu_i \leq 1$; so $\bar{p}_i^* \geq p_i^*$ for all i.
Let $\min_i \mu_i = \mu_h$, $h = 1, \ldots, r \leq m$. Suppose $k \notin R$. By (H), eqn [1] holds. As $\mu_k < 1$, (WGS) and (I) implies that there exists $i \in R$ such that:

$$\bar{z}_i(p_1^*, \ldots, p_r^*, \mu_k \bar{p}_{r+1}^*, \ldots, \mu_k \bar{p}_m^*, \mu_k) < \bar{z}_i(p^*, 1)$$

Hence:

$$\bar{z}_i(\bar{p}^*, 1) < \bar{z}_i(p^*, 1) \qquad \cdots [6]$$

Eqn [6] contradicts eqn [5]. So, there are no goods whose prices rise more than k.

§8.10. A price-guided decentralised planning procedure

We shall first summarise the mathematical theory required to enable us to describe a planning procedure.

§8.10.1. *Mathematical preliminaries*

1. Functions

We will make use of the theory of concave and convex functions outlined in Exercises §8.1.

2. Gradient methods

2.1. We now consider the problem of locating a maximum of a strictly concave function, f. In general, an iterative procedure will be required, such as one in which: $\operatorname{sign} \mathrm{d}z_i/\mathrm{d}t = \operatorname{sign} \partial f/\partial z_i$ for all i, i.e. given a value of z, say z^0, z_i^0 is increased/decreased/kept constant according as $\partial f(z^0)/\partial z_i$ is greater than/is less than/equals zero. Without loss of generality, this notion can be formalised in the following gradient method:

$$\mathrm{d}z_i/\mathrm{d}t = \partial f/\partial z_i \quad \text{for all} \quad i \qquad \cdots [1]$$

Exercise 1. More generally than [1], we have: $\mathrm{d}z_i/\mathrm{d}t = k_i\, \partial f/\partial z_i$, $k_i > 0$, for all i. Show that by redefining units, this can be reduced to [1].

2.2. We have the following result:

If f is strictly concave, the gradient method converges to the strong global maximum, z^*.

Proof: Using the function $v(t) = \frac{1}{2}\sum_i (z_i(t) - z_i^*)^2$, it is easy to show that $\mathrm{d}v/\mathrm{d}t < 0$ for all $z \neq z^*$, using strict concavity. The result follows from Theorem 18 of Chapter 4. (See also **5.3** below.)

Exercise 2. Formulate a gradient method for locating a strong global minimum of a strictly convex function; derive convergence.

3. Non-negativity constraints

It is now time to take account of the non-negativity restriction, $z \geq \mathbf{0}$.

3.1. The necessary and sufficient conditions of Exercises §8.1, Q9, in the strictly concave case, are modified to:

$$\partial f(z^*)/\partial z_i \leq 0 \quad \text{for all} \quad i; \quad \text{if} \quad \partial f(z^*)/\partial z_i < 0, \quad \text{then} \quad z_i^* = 0 \qquad \cdots [2]$$

Exercise 3. Write down the conditions for a strong global minimum in the strictly convex case, given the non-negativity constraint.

3.2. The gradient method also requires modification. If $z_i = 0$ and $\partial f/\partial z_i < 0$, then using eqn [1], z_i would be decreased further. As this would contravene the non-negativity restriction, we modify the gradient method to:

$$\mathrm{d}z_i/\mathrm{d}t = \begin{cases} 0 & \text{if} \quad z_i = 0 \quad \text{and} \quad \partial f/\partial z_i < 0 \\ \partial f/\partial z_i & \text{otherwise} \end{cases} \qquad \cdots [3]$$

Conditions [2] are necessary and sufficient for $\mathrm{d}z_i/\mathrm{d}t = 0$ for all i, i.e. z^* is the equilibrium of the system [3].

Exercise 4. Derive convergence of the gradient method [3] to z^*. (See also **5.3** below)

Exercise 5. Formulate a gradient method for a minimum, where f is strictly convex (see Ex. 2 above). Derive convergence.

4. Functional constraints

4.1. Further modifications are required to our framework if we are to have a basis for describing a planning procedure—in particular, we must introduce such constraints as:

$$g_j(z) \geqslant 0 \quad j = 1, \ldots, r \qquad \cdots [4]$$

So our problem becomes one of maximising $f(z)$ subject to the r constraints, [4], and the non-negativity constraints, $z \geqslant \mathbf{0}$. Define:

$$L(z; \boldsymbol{\lambda}) = f(z) + \sum_{j=1}^{r} \lambda_j g_j(z) \qquad \cdots [5]$$

The Lagrangean, $L(z; \boldsymbol{\lambda})$, has a saddle-point at $(z^*; \boldsymbol{\lambda}^*)$ if

$$L(z; \boldsymbol{\lambda}^*) \leqslant L(z^*; \boldsymbol{\lambda}^*) \leqslant L(z^*; \boldsymbol{\lambda}) \qquad \cdots [6]$$

4.2. The importance of the saddle-point concept is illustrated in the following result:
Let $f(z)$ and $g_j(z)$, $j = 1, \ldots, r$, be concave functions. Then z^* maximises $f(z)$ subject to $g_j(z) \geqslant 0$, for all j, $z \geqslant \mathbf{0}$, iff there exists $\boldsymbol{\lambda}^* \geqslant \mathbf{0}$ such that $L(z; \boldsymbol{\lambda})$ has a saddle-point at $(z^*; \boldsymbol{\lambda}^*)$.

5. Gradient Methods and Saddle-Points

5.1. The result just stated is of interest in characterising an optimum (or equilibrium). Our general aim is to find conditions under which an iterative procedure (gradient method) will locate an optimum—in other words, our concern is with a dynamic problem (i.e. convergence to an optimum) rather than solely with a static problem (i.e. existence of an optimum). Arguing by analogy with the simpler case outlined above, we shall expect that the conditions guaranteeing convergence will be stronger than those guaranteeing existence.

5.2. We have mentioned above the use of a gradient method to locate an optimum in the unconstrained case. In the constrained case, we must locate a saddle-point—$L(z; \boldsymbol{\lambda})$ is maximised with respect to z, $\boldsymbol{\lambda}$ being given, and minimised with respect to $\boldsymbol{\lambda}$, z being given. Our gradient method is defined by:

$$\mathrm{d}z_i/\mathrm{d}t = \begin{cases} 0 & \text{if} \quad z_i = 0 \quad \text{and} \quad \partial L/\partial z_i < 0 \\ \partial L/\partial z_i & \text{otherwise} \end{cases} \qquad \cdots [7]$$

$$\mathrm{d}\lambda_j/\mathrm{d}t = \begin{cases} 0 & \text{if} \quad \lambda_j = 0 \quad \text{and} \quad \lambda L/\partial \lambda_j > 0 \\ -\partial L/\partial \lambda_j & \text{otherwise} \end{cases} \qquad \cdots [8]$$

5.3. We have the following result:
If $L(z; \boldsymbol{\lambda})$ is strictly concave in z, given $\boldsymbol{\lambda}$, and convex in $\boldsymbol{\lambda}$, given z, the gradient method, described by eqns [7] and [8], converges to a saddle-point $(z^*; \lambda^*)$ of $L(z; \boldsymbol{\lambda})$.[13]

Proof: Define the sets:

$$I = \{i : z_i = 0, \partial L/\partial z_i < 0\}$$
$$J = \{j : \lambda_j = 0, \partial L/\partial \lambda_j > 0\} \quad \cdots [9]$$

Consider the function:

$$v(z(t); \boldsymbol{\lambda}(t)) = \tfrac{1}{2}\sum_{i=1}^{n}(z_i(t) - z_i^*)^2 + \tfrac{1}{2}\sum_{j=1}^{r}(\lambda_j(t) - \lambda_j^*)^2 \quad \cdots [10]$$

Then

$$\begin{aligned} dv/dt &= \sum_{i=1}^{n}(z_i(t) - z_i^*)dz_i/dt + \sum_{j=1}^{r}(\lambda_j(t) - \lambda_j^*)d\lambda_j/dt \\ &= \sum_{i \notin I}(z_i(t) - z_i^*)\partial L/\partial z_i - \sum_{j \notin J}(\lambda_j(t) - \lambda_j^*)\partial L/\partial \lambda_j \\ &= (z(t) - z^*)'\partial L/\partial z - (\boldsymbol{\lambda}(t) - \boldsymbol{\lambda}^*)'\partial L/\partial \boldsymbol{\lambda} \\ &\quad - \sum_{i \in I}(z_i(t) - z_i^*)\partial L/\partial z_i + \sum_{j \in J}(\lambda_j(t) - \lambda_j^*)\partial L/\partial \lambda_j \end{aligned} \quad \cdots [11]$$

By strict concavity of L in z:

$$L(z^*; \boldsymbol{\lambda}) - L(z; \boldsymbol{\lambda}) < (z^* - z(t))'\partial L/\partial z \quad \cdots [12]$$

By convexity of L in $\boldsymbol{\lambda}$:

$$L(z; \boldsymbol{\lambda}^*) - L(z; \boldsymbol{\lambda}) \geqslant (\boldsymbol{\lambda}^* - \boldsymbol{\lambda}(t))'\partial L/\partial \boldsymbol{\lambda} \quad \cdots [13]$$

From eqns [12] and [13]:

$$(z(t) - z^*)'\partial L/\partial z - (\boldsymbol{\lambda}(t) - \boldsymbol{\lambda}^*)'\partial L/\partial \boldsymbol{\lambda}$$
$$< L(z; \boldsymbol{\lambda}^*) - L(z^*; \boldsymbol{\lambda}) < 0 \quad \text{for} \quad z \neq z^*. \quad \cdots [14]$$

Also, from the definitions of I and J:

$$-\sum_{i \in I}(z_i(t) - z_i^*)\partial L/\partial z_i \leqslant 0; \qquad \sum_{j \in J}(\lambda_j(t) - \lambda_j^*)\partial L/\partial \lambda_j \leqslant 0 \quad \cdots [15]$$

Hence, $dv/dt < 0$ for $z \neq z^*$. $dv/dt = 0$ iff $(z; \boldsymbol{\lambda})$ is a saddle-point of L. Then by Theorem 18 of Chapter 4, the result follows.

§8.10.2. *A planning procedure*

6. The model

6.1. We begin by assuming the existence of a utility (or welfare) function for society as a whole:

$$u(x) = u(x_1, \ldots, x_n) \quad \cdots [16]$$

x being the final demand vector.
To assume the existence of such a function is heroic by any standards. We shall also assume that u is strictly concave.

6.2. There are r firms (or processes) in the economy; y_h denotes the scale of operation of operation of the h-th firm. $g_i^h(y_h)$ denotes the h-th firm's net output of good i when it is operating at a level y_h. $g_i^h(y_h)$ is assumed to be strictly concave. ω_i denotes the amount of commodity i initially available. $i=1,\ldots,nr$; $h=1,\ldots,r$. For x to be feasible:

$$x_i \leq \sum_{h=1}^{r} g_i^h(y_h)+\omega_i \qquad i=1,\ldots,n \qquad \cdots[17]$$

or

$$g_i(x, y)=\sum_{h=1}^{r} g_i^h(y_h)-x_i+\omega_i \geq 0 \quad \text{for all} \quad i \qquad \cdots[18]$$

$g_i(x, y)$ is the excess supply of good i.

7. Maximisation and decentralisation

Associate z with $(x, y)=(x_1,\ldots,x_n, y_1,\ldots,y_r)$.
The constrained maximisation problem is:

$$\max u(x) \quad \text{subject to} \quad g_i(x, y)\geq 0, \quad \text{for all} \quad i, x\geqslant\mathbf{0}, \qquad y\geqslant\mathbf{0} \qquad \cdots[19]$$

Form the Lagrangean:

$$L(x, y; \boldsymbol{\lambda})=u(x)+\sum_{i=1}^{n} \lambda_i g_i(x, y)$$

$$=u(x)+\sum_{i=1}^{n} \lambda_i\left[\sum_{h=1}^{r} g_i^h(y_h)-x_i+\omega_i\right]$$

$$=\left(u(x)-\sum_{i=1}^{n} \lambda_i x_i\right)+\sum_{h=1}^{r}\left[\sum_{i=1}^{n} \lambda_i g_i^h(y_h)\right]+\sum_{i=1}^{n} \lambda_i\omega_i \qquad \cdots[20]$$

From the theorem in **4.2** above, $u(x)$ has a maximum subject to the constraints iff there exists $\boldsymbol{\lambda}^*\geqslant\mathbf{0}$ such that $L(x, y; \boldsymbol{\lambda})$ has a saddle-point at $(x^*, y^*; \boldsymbol{\lambda}^*)$, i.e. when considered as a function of x and y, $L(x, y; \boldsymbol{\lambda}^*)$ has a maximum at $(x, y)=(x^*, y^*)$. Hence, from eqn [20]:

$u(x)-\sum_{i=1}^{n} \lambda_i^* x_i$ attains its maximum with respect to x at $x=x^*$;

$\pi_h(y_h)=\sum_{i=1}^{n} \lambda_i^* g_i^h(y_h)$ attains its maximum with respect to y at $y=y^*$.

λ has the obvious interpretation of a vector of prices.

So, we see that, given the set of equilibrium prices, the choice of final demand vector can be made independently of the choice of scale of operation of each firm. Suppose that each firm is controlled by a manager and that there is a distributor whose task is to decide on the final demand vector. As outlined above, given $\boldsymbol{\lambda}^*$, each manager maximises profits and the distributor maximises the difference between utility and cost. The manager of the h-th firm needs to know only the h-th firm's technology, described by $g^h(y_h)=(g_1^h(y_h),\ldots,g_n^h(y_h))$, and the price vector; the distributor needs to know only the utility function and the price vector.

To complete the description of the essentials of a decentralised price-guided planning procedure, we have only to introduce the central planning board (which may also be the distributor) whose task is to choose prices.

8. The procedure
A constrained maximisation problem is equivalent to a suitable saddle-point problem. Under certain conditions, a saddle-point may be determined by a gradient method (see **5** above).
The central planning board informs each manager and the distributor of a vector of prices.

Each manager acts according to:

$$dy_h/dt = \begin{cases} 0 & \text{if} \quad y_h = 0 \quad \text{and} \quad d\pi_h/dy_h < 0 \\ d\pi_h/dy_h & \text{otherwise} \end{cases} \qquad \cdots [21]$$

i.e. each manager, taking prices as given, changes the scale of operation of his firm (or process) at a rate proportional to its marginal profitability, except that, if the scale is already zero and the marginal profitability negative, the scale remains at zero.

The distributor acts according to:

$$dx_i/dt = \begin{cases} 0 & \text{if} \quad x_i = 0 \quad \text{and} \quad \partial u/\partial x_i - \lambda_1 < 0 \\ \partial u/\partial x_i & \text{otherwise} \end{cases} \qquad \cdots [22]$$

i.e. the distributor, taking prices as given, alters the final demand for the i-th commodity at a rate proportional to the difference between marginal utility and price, subject to the proviso that, if final demand is already zero and marginal utility is less than price, final demand remains at zero.

Each manager reports his net output vector to the central planning board; the distributor reports the final demand vector to the board.

The central planning board then evaluates the excess demand for each commodity and acts according to:

$$d\lambda_i/dt = \begin{cases} 0 & \text{if} \quad \lambda_i = 0 \quad \text{and} \quad g_i > 0 \\ -g_i & \text{otherwise} \end{cases} \qquad \cdots [23]$$

i.e. the central planning board changes prices in proportion to excess demands, except that, if the price of a good is already zero and the good is in excess supply, the price remains at zero.

By the result outlined in **5.3** above, we know that the gradient method will yield convergence to the saddle-point $(x^*, y^*; \boldsymbol{\lambda}^*)$.

Exercise 6. Prove that the hypotheses of **5.3** are satisfied, in particular that $L(x, y; \boldsymbol{\lambda})$ is strictly concave in x and y.

While the process described above is based on restrictive assumptions about technology, it is efficient in respect of the information that has to be transmitted between the agents in the economy.
The central planning board announces a price vector to each agent; each agent then submits a quantity vector to the board; the board has only to add up all these quantity vectors and call a new price vector.

§8.11. Review

In this concluding section of the book, we return to themes discussed in Chapter 3. There, we considered the aggregate versions of neo-classical distribution theory; here, we consider the dis-aggregate version in terms of general equilibrium theory.

All commodities are treated on all equal footing. An equilibrium price vector is determined by demand and supply in each market. Hence, given individuals' initial endowments, distribution is determined by an equilibrium price vector, i.e. the theory of income distribution is a special case of price theory.

The general equilibrium version of income distribution theory, as distinct from the aggregate versions, may emerge intact from the "reswitching" debate;(14) it cannot be criticised on the same grounds of aggregation. The theory may be logically consistent but

"it cannot be denied that there is something scandalous in the spectacle of so many people refining the analyses of economic states which they give no reason to suppose will ever, or have ever, come about. . . . It is an unsatisfactory and slightly dishonest state of affairs."(15)

Can the study of an economy, apparently so abstracted from the world, be justified? Arrow and Hahn discuss the

"proposition that a decentralised economy motivated by self-interest and guided by price signals would be compatible with a coherent disposition of economic resources that would be regarded in a well-defined sense as superior to a large class of possible alternative dispositions. . . . The proposition having been put forward and very seriously entertained, it is important to know not only whether it *is* true, but also whether it *could be* true. . . . In attempting to answer the question 'Could it be true?,' we learn a great deal about why it might not be true."(16)

In other words, general equilibrium is "a set of consistent equilibrium relations and rigorous statements of what *cannot* be said."(17)

Broadly speaking, the general equilibrium model discussed in this chapter is Walrasian in nature, the linear production model of Chapter 3 is Ricardian. The two yield contrasting theories of value. The Walrasian model consists of a large number of individual agents—consumers whose behaviour is determined by utility maximisation subject to budget constraints and firms whose behaviour is determined by profit maximisation. Consumers sell the services of factors and buy goods; firms sell goods and buy the services of factors; goods and services thus move in a circular flow; prices are determined by supply and demand, competitive forces ensuring the absence of excess demand in any market.

By contrast, in a Ricardian model, neither individual agents nor maximising behaviour is mentioned. Prices are determined by technology; competition ensures uniformity of the rate of profits; consumer demand determines the scale of operation of each industry or sector. Whereas in the Walrasian model the flow of commodities in one direction is matched by a corresponding flow in the other, in the Ricardian model, the payment (of profits) to capital is the distribution of (part of) the surplus, with no corresponding exchange.

The choice between these models is essentially an ideological one. For ideology "enters on the very ground floor, into the pre-analytical cognitive act" and into the beginnings of theory "with material provided by our vision of things." "This vision (is) ideological almost by definition" as "it embodies the picture of things as we see them."[(18)]

Exercises

§8.1

1. (Existence of utility functions)
Suppose that a consumer has a preference ordering on his consumption set, X. Define the preference ordering in terms of the binary relation "$\gtrsim$" thus:
$x^1 \gtrsim x^2$ means that the consumer prefers x^1 to x^2 or is indifferent between x^1 and x^2.
$\gtrsim$ is assumed to be:
complete, i.e. $x^1 \gtrsim x^2$ or $x^2 \gtrsim x^1$ or both, for all $x^1, x^2 \in X$;
transitive, i.e. $x^1 \gtrsim x^2$ and $x^2 \gtrsim x^3$ imply $x^1 \gtrsim x^3$.
Hence, $\gtrsim$ is reflexive.
Strict preference ($>$) and indifference ($\sim$) can then be defined in terms of:

$$x^1 > x \quad \text{if} \quad x^1 \gtrsim x^2 \quad \text{and not} \quad x^2 \gtrsim x^1;$$

$$x^1 \sim x^2 \quad \text{if} \quad x^1 \gtrsim x^2 \quad \text{and} \quad x^2 \gtrsim x^1.$$

The set X is *connected* if it *not* the union of two non-empty disjoint subsets closed in R^n. A convex set is connected. A preference ordering on X is *continuous* if, for any $\bar{x} \in X$, the sets $\{x \in X : \bar{x} \gtrsim x\}$ and $\{x \in X : x \gtrsim \bar{x}\}$ are closed in X, i.e. if whenever a sequence of points belonging to one of these sets has a limit point in X, that limit point also belongs to the same set.
A *utility function* for a preference ordering on X is a function $u : X \to R$ such that for all $x^1, x^2 \in X$, $x^1 \gtrsim x^2$ iff $u(x^1) \geq u(x^2)$.
Evidently, $x^1 > / \sim x^2$ iff $u(x^1) > / = u(x^2)$.
Debreu has derived the following theorem:
If $\gtrsim$ is continuous on the connected set, X, there exists a continuous utility function on X for $\gtrsim$.

2. An example of a preference ordering which does not yield a utility function is a lexicographic ordering (denoted here by L): $\tilde{x} L \bar{x}$ iff $\tilde{x}_i > \bar{x}_i$ for the smallest integer i $(1 \leq i \leq n)$ such that $\tilde{x}_i \neq \bar{x}_i$.

3. A preference ordering $\gtrsim$ on X is convex if:
(a) X is convex;
(b) $x^1 > x^2$ implies $\alpha x^1 + (1-\alpha)x^2 > x^2$ $\alpha \in (0, 1)$;
(c) $x^1 \sim x^2$ implies $\alpha x^1 + (1-\alpha)x^2 \gtrsim x^2$ $\alpha \in (0, 1)$.
Prove that if $\gtrsim$ is convex, the sets $\{x \in X : x \gtrsim \bar{x}\}$ and $\{x \in X : x > \bar{x}\}$ are convex. Interpret this convexity assumption in terms of diminishing marginal rates of substitution.

4. The function f defined on a convex set, S, is concave if, given $x^1, x^2 \in S$:

$$f(x) \geqslant \alpha f(x^1) + (1-\alpha) f(x^2) \qquad \alpha \in [0, 1]$$

where

$$x = \alpha x^1 + (1-\alpha) x^2.$$

f is convex if the inequality is reversed.
Show that any linear function is both concave and convex.
f is strictly concave if: $f(x) > \alpha f(x^1) + (1-\alpha) f(x^2)$, $\alpha \in (0, 1)$.
Likewise for strict convexity.

5. Suppose that f is differentiable over S. Prove that f is concave iff;

$$f(x^2) - f(x^1) \leqslant (x^2 - x^1)' \partial f(x^1)/\partial x.$$

For strict concavity, the weak inequality is replaced by strict inequality. The inequalities are reversed for the convex and strictly convex cases.

6. Suppose that f has continuous second-order partial derivatives over S. Prove that f is concave (convex) over S iff $H(x) = [\partial^2 f/\partial x_i \partial x_j]$ is negative (positive) semi-definite for all $x \in S$.
(Hint: Approximating f near $x = \alpha x^1 + (1-\alpha) x^2$, $\alpha \in [0, 1]$, we have:

$$f(\bar{x}) = f(x) + h' \partial f(x)/\partial x + (1/2!) h' H(x + \theta h) h \qquad \cdots [1]$$

where

$$h = x - \bar{x}, \qquad \theta \in [0, 1].$$

Suppose that f is concave over S. From eqn [1]:

$$f(\bar{x}) - f(x) - h' \partial f(x)/\partial x = (1/2!) h' H(x + \theta h) h$$

By Q5, the left-hand side $\leqslant 0$. So $h' H(x + \theta h) h \leqslant 0$, for all $h \neq \mathbf{0}$, and negative semi-definiteness follows by continuity.
Now suppose that H is negative semi-definite.
Put $\alpha = 0$ and 1 in eqn [1] above to obtain expressions for $f(x^2)$ and $f(x^1)$ respectively:

$$f(x^i) = f(x) + h^{i\prime} \partial f(x)/\partial x + (1/2!) h^{i\prime} H(x + \theta_i h^i) h^i$$

$i = 1, 2$; $\theta_i \in [0, 1]$.
Weighting $f(x^1)$ by α and $f(x^2)$ by $(1-\alpha)$ and adding, we obtain, after noting that $\alpha h^1 + (1-\alpha) h^2 = \mathbf{0}$ and H is negative semi-definite, concavity of f.)

7. Prove that if $H(x)$ is negative (positive) definite, f is strictly concave (convex), but not vice versa.

8. Let f be strictly concave (convex) over the closed convex set S. Prove that any local maximum (minimum) of f is a strong global maximum

(minimum) of f over S. (i.e. x^* is a global maximum over S if $f(x^*) \geqslant f(x)$, for all $x \in S$. x^* is a strong global maximum if $f(x^*) > f(x)$. Likewise for a global minimum and strong global minimum.)

9. Suppose that f is strictly concave (convex) over the closed convex set S and differentiable in the interior of S. Prove that f has a strong global maximum (minimum) at x^* iff $\partial f(x^*)/\partial x = \mathbf{0}$.

§8.3

1. Theorem 2 uses the following:

Let $f(z) = \sum_{i=1}^{n} f(z^i)$ be an additive function defined on

$$Z = \sum_{i=1}^{n} Z_i = \left\{ z = \sum_{i=1}^{n} z^i : z^i \in Z_i, \text{ for all } i \right\}.$$

Prove that, if for $\bar{z}^i \in Z_i$, $f(\bar{z}^i) > f(z^i)$, for all $z^i \in Z_i$, then $f(\bar{z}) > f(z)$ for all $z \in Z$, where $\bar{z} = \sum_{i=1}^{n} \bar{z}^i$.

Conversely, prove that if $f(\bar{z}) > f(z)$ for all $z \in Z$, $\bar{z} = \sum_{i=1}^{n} \bar{z}^i$, then $f(\bar{z}^i) > f(z^i)$ for all $z^i \in Z_i$.

§8.4

1. Prove that $u(x) = \sum_{j=1}^{n} \alpha_j \log_e x_j$, $\alpha_j > 0$ for all j, $\sum_j \alpha_j = 1$, yields demand functions exhibiting (SGS).
2. Establish the equivalence of the differential and the non-differential forms of (SGS).
3. Using the non-differential form of (SGS), prove that (under (SGS)):
(a) the equilibrium price set contains only positive vectors;
(b) the equilibrium is unique.
4. Suppose $P \geqslant \mathbf{0}$, $\bar{P} > \mathbf{0}$. Let $\alpha_i = P_i/\bar{P}_i$; $\alpha_k = \max_i \alpha_i$; $\alpha_h = \min_i \alpha_i$. Suppose (SGS) holds for all P. Prove that $s_k(P) > s_k(\bar{P})$, $s_h(P) < s_h(\bar{P})$.
5. Provide a non-differential form of (WGS). Consider the following non-differential form of indecomposability (I):
$p_i = \bar{p}_i$, $i \in J$, and $p_j < \bar{p}_j$, $j \notin J$, imply that there exists at least one $i \in J$ such that $s_i(p) \neq s_i(\bar{p})$.
Derive Theorem 7 under the non-differential (WGS) and (I).
(Hint: Suppose $p_i = 0$, $s_i(p)$ finite for some $i \in J$. By (WGS) and (I), there exists at least one i such that $s_i(p) > s_i(\alpha p)$, $\alpha > 1$. This contradicts (H), from which we have $p > \mathbf{0}$.
Uniqueness: Let p, p^* be equilibrium price vectors.
Let $\alpha = \min p_i^*/p_i$; $\alpha p_k^* < p_k$, for some $k \notin J = \{i : p_i^*/p_i = \alpha\}$.
For $i \in J$, $s_i(p^*) < s_i(\alpha p) = s_i(p) = 0$, by (WGS), (I) and (H).
So p^* is not an equilibrium.)

6. Prove that (SGS) implies (QDD); (WGS) and (I) imply (QDD); (QDD) does not necessarily imply either (SGS) or (WGS).

7. Consider the following argument, due to Rader, that factor inputs are never normally gross substitutes. (So, we must question the wisdom of giving pre-eminence to the (SGS) and (WGS) cases.)
The firm maximises: $\pi = p_0 f(z) - p'z$, where p_0 is the price of output, z is the vector of factor inputs, p is the vector of factor prices ($p > \mathbf{0}$), f is the production function. Assume that $f \in C^2$ and that $\partial f/\partial z > \mathbf{0}$. Also, $F = [f_{ij}]$ is negative definite, implying that f is a strictly concave production function. The necessary and sufficient conditions for profit maximisation are:

$$p_0 \partial f/\partial z = p \qquad \cdots [1]$$

Differentiating eqn [1], with respect to p, we obtain:

$$p_0 F \partial z/\partial p = I$$

where

$$\partial z/\partial p = [\partial z_i/\partial p_j]$$

Hence

$$\partial z/\partial p = (p_0)^{-1} F^{-1}.$$

Normally, $f_{ii} < 0$, for all i; $f_{ij} \geqslant 0$, for all $i \neq j$. Given negative definiteness of F, we see that $-F$ is an M-matrix. Hence,

$$F^{-1} \leqslant [0]. \quad \text{So} \quad \partial z/\partial p \leqslant [0].$$

However, the gross substitutes condition requires $\partial z_i/\partial p_i < 0$, for all i; $\partial z_i/\partial p_j \geqslant 0$, for all $i \neq j$.

§8.5

1. Prove that a system satisfies the Hicksian imperfect stability conditions iff $\det A/\det A^{ii} < 0$, for all i. Also, prove Theorem 10.

2. Use the following matrices to prove that neither Hicksian perfect nor imperfect stability is either necessary or sufficient for true dynamic stability:

$$\begin{bmatrix} -2 & 4 \\ -1 & 1 \end{bmatrix}; \begin{bmatrix} 1 & -1 \\ -2 & 1 \end{bmatrix}; \begin{bmatrix} -\varepsilon & -1 & 0 & 0 \\ 0 & -\varepsilon & -1 & 0 \\ 0 & 0 & -\varepsilon & -1 \\ 1 & -1 & 1 & -1-\varepsilon \end{bmatrix} \quad \text{where } \varepsilon \in (0, \cos 2\pi/5).$$

(Samuelson)

3. The matrix A is S-stable if SA is stable for every positive definite matrix S. Prove that a quasi-negative definite matrix is S-stable. (Arrow & McManus)

4. In Theorem 18, the matrix A is the sum of the individual substitution matrices (for non-numeraire commodities). It is well known that the individual substitution matrix (for all commodities, including the numeraire) is negative semi-definite, of rank $m = n - 1$. Prove that the individual substitution matrix (for non-numeraire commodities) is negative definite and hence that A is negative definite (see Barten, Lempers & Kloek).

5. Prove that any matrix with sign pattern $\begin{bmatrix} - & + \\ - & 0 \end{bmatrix}$ is D-stable but not totally stable.

6. Prove that the Hicksian perfect stability conditions are equivalent to the true dynamic stability conditions when there are price rigidities. (Hint: Partition commodities into three groups: those with infinite speed of adjustment, those with finite, non-zero speed of adjustment, and those with zero speed of adjustment.
Suppose all commodities except the i-th are in the first group, the i-th being in the second group ($\mathrm{d}p_i/\mathrm{d}t = z_i(p)$). Taking a linear approximation and permitting all repercussions, derive

$\mathrm{d}p_i/\mathrm{d}t = \det A / \det A^{ii}$.

Now suppose that the j-th commodity is in the third group, the i-th is in the second group, all other commodities are in the first group. Following the method outlined above, derive

$\mathrm{d}p_i/\mathrm{d}t = \det A^{jj} / \det A^{ii;jj}$, etc.)

7. Give an example of a stable matrix that is not D-stable.

8. Consider the following multiple exchange system:

$$x_i = \sum_{j=1}^{n} x_{ij} P_j + b_i \qquad x_{ii} < 0; \quad x_{ij} \geqslant 0, \quad \text{for all} \quad i \neq j$$

$$y_i = \sum_{j=1}^{n} y_{ij} P_j + c_i \qquad y_{ii} > 0; \quad y_{ij} \leqslant 0, \quad \text{for all} \quad i \neq j.$$

$$z_i = x_i - y_i = \sum_{j=1}^{n} (x_{ij} - y_{ij}) P_j + b_i - c_i$$

or

$$z = AP + d \qquad a_{ij} = x_{ij} - y_{ij}; \qquad d_i = b_i - c_i.$$

Suppose $\mathrm{d}P/\mathrm{d}t = Kz$, $K = [k_i \delta_{ij}]$, $k_i > 0$ for all i. Then:

$\mathrm{d}P/\mathrm{d}t = KAP + Kd.$

Also

$\mathbf{0} = KAP^* + Kd.$

Let $p = P - P^*$, so that we have $\mathrm{d}p/\mathrm{d}t = KAp$. Prove that if $d > \mathbf{0}$, the system is stable. (Hint: Prove that $d > \mathbf{0}$ implies that A has a negative d.d.) What interpretation can be placed on $d > \mathbf{0}$?

9. Is the tatonnement process unconditionally stable (i.e. without such restrictions on the excess demand functions as gross substitution)? (Consider the following exchange economy in which there are three individuals and three commodities. Let x_{ij} denote the i-th individual's demand for good j. Denote initial endowments by w^i; suppose $w_{ii} = 1$, $w_{ij} = 0$ for all $i \neq j$; $i, j = 1, 2, 3$.
Let the utility functions be: $u_1(x) = \min(x_{11}, x_{12})$:

$$u_2(x) = \min(x_{22}, x_{23}); \qquad u_3(x) = \min(x_{31}, x_{33}).$$

(a) Evaluate the excess demand for each commodity, $z_i = x_i - w_i$.
(b) Show that $P_1 = P_2 = P_3$ is the only possible equilibrium.
(c) Consider the price adjustment equation:

$$\mathrm{d}P_i/\mathrm{d}t = x_i - w_i \qquad \cdots [1]$$

Prove that $\|P(t)\|^2 = \sum_{i=1}^{3} P_i(t)^2$ is constant for all t and that $\prod_{i=1}^{3} P_i(t)$ is constant.

(d) Choose initial prices such that $\sum_{i=1}^{3} P_i(0)^2 = 3$ and $\prod_{i=1}^{3} P_i(0) \neq 1$. As the only possible equilibrium is the price vector (1, 1, 1), using the results in (c), prove that the system is not stable (i.e. the solution of eqn [1] does not converge to (1, 1, 1)). (Scarf)

10. An assumption implicit in the text is that each price is always non-negative, i.e. we hope that the price-adjustment equation: $\mathrm{d}p/\mathrm{d}t = z(p)$ will yield non-negativity rather than enforce non-negativity through such a modified price-adjustment equation as:

$$\mathrm{d}p_i/\mathrm{d}t = \begin{cases} 0 & \text{if } p_i = 0 \text{ and } z_i(p) < 0 \\ z_i & \text{otherwise} \end{cases} \qquad \cdots [1]$$

This restriction of the price vector to the set of non-negative vectors implies that the right-hand side of eqn [1] may not be continuous. In general, continuity of F is sufficient for the existence of a solution to: $\mathrm{d}p/\mathrm{d}t = F(p; t)$. The solution of eqn [1] thus requires special methods. Consult the paper by Henry.
An alternative to eqn [1] is the following, due to Nikaido and Uzawa:

$$\mathrm{d}p_i/\mathrm{d}t = \max[z_i(p), -p_i] \qquad \cdots [2]$$

in which the right-hand side is continuous.

§8.6

1. Derive D-stability for the (SGS) case under (H).

2. Consider a system in which $p = \mathbf{1}$, so that:

$$\text{(H)}\ldots \sum_{j=1}^{n} a_{ij} = 0 \text{ for all } i; \qquad \sum_{i=1}^{n} a_{ij} = 0 \text{ for all } j \ldots \text{(W)}$$

Assume that $a_{in} > 0$, for all $i = 1, \ldots, m$; $a_{nj} > 0$, for all $j = 1, \ldots, m$.
Define the system as:
G_1-Metzlerian if there exists an $m \times m$ positive definite stochastic matrix, G, such that GA is a (WGS) matrix;
G_2-Metzlerian if there exists an $m \times m$ positive definite stochastic matrix, G, such that $G(A + A')$ is a (WGS) matrix;
G_3-Metzlerian matrix if there exists an $m \times m$ positive definite stochastic matrix, G, such that GA and $G(A + A')$ are each (WGS) matrices.
(a) Prove that if GA is a (WGS) matrix, GA and $A'G$ each has a d.d.
(b) Prove that if $G(A + A')$ is a (WGS) matrix, $G(A + A')$ and $(A + A')G$ each has a d.d.

3. Prove that, if the system is G_1-Metzlerian, it is locally stable. (Hint: By Q2 (a), GA and $A'G$ each has a d.d., which implies that $GA + A'G$ has a d.d. Each diagonal element of $GA + A'G$ is negative. So the matrix is stable by Theorem 7 of Chapter 2. $GA + A'G$, being symmetric, is thus negative definite and the result follows from Lyapunov's theorem (Theorem 17 of Chapter 4), G being positive definite.)

4. Prove that, if the system is G_2-Metzlerian, it is D-stable. Also, A is an $(N\text{–}P)$-matrix.
(Hint: Use Q2(b) and an argument similar to that in Q3 to derive stability of $A + A'$, i.e. negative definiteness of $A + A'$, or quasi-negative definiteness of A. Then by Exercises §2.4, Q23, A is stable and an $(N\text{–}P)$-matrix.)
(For questions 2–4, consult the paper by Ohyama.)

5. $A = B - \rho I$ is a (power-transformed) gross substitutes matrix of the k-th exponent if there exists a positive integer k such that $C = B^k - \rho^k I$ is a (SGS) matrix, $B^k > [0]$, $\rho > 0$. If we put $k = 1$, we have the (SGS) case; hence stability obtains
$\rho > \lambda^*(B)$.
Using the theory of power-positive matrices (see §2.4.4), prove that, in a system containing complementary commodities:
(i) if the Jacobian matrix of excess demand functions is a (power-transformed) gross substitutes matrix of odd exponent (i.e. k is odd), then stability holds iff $\rho > \lambda^*(B)$, as in the (SGS) case.
(ii) if A is a (power-transformed) gross substitutes matrix of even exponent, and at least one commodity is a weak gross substitute for all

others (or all others are weak gross substitutes for at least one), then stability holds iff $\rho > \lambda^*(B)$. (Sato)

6. It is known that in the (SGS) case, stability holds independently of the choice of numeraire. We now consider other conditions for stability to hold in this case.

   Let $A^* = [\partial z_i(P^*)/\partial P_j]$, $\quad i, j = 1, \ldots, n.$

   $A^*_{kk} = [\partial z_i(P^*)/\partial P_j]$, $\quad i, j = 1, \ldots, n, i, j \neq k.$

   $A_{kk} = [\partial z_i(p^*)/\partial p_j]$, $\quad i, j = 1, \ldots, n, i, j \neq k.$

   Prove that:
   (a) A_{kk} is quasi-negative definite iff A^*_{kk} is quasi-negative definite.
   (b) If $P^*_i \neq 0$, $P^*_k \neq 0$, A^*_{kk} is quasi-negative definite iff A^*_{ii} is quasi-negative definite.
   (Hint: Use Theorem 29.)
   (c) Hence, using (a) and (b), if A_{kk} is quasi-negative definite for any k, the system is locally stable for any choice of numeraire.
   (d) Also, if A is symmetric, the system is stable for any choice of numeraire iff it is stable for all possible choices of numeraire.
   (e) Is the assumption that A_{nn} has a q.d.d. sufficient for stability independent of choice of numeraire?
   (f) Prove that, if income effects are zero when aggregated, stability holds independently of choice of numeraire. (Mukerji)

7. The $m \times m$ matrix A is sign stable iff every matrix in Q_A is stable. The following result is due to Quirk and Ruppert:
   The indecomposable matrix A is sign stable iff:
   (a) $a_{ij}a_{ji} \leq 0$, for all $i \neq j$;
   (b) $i_1 \neq i_2 \neq \cdots \neq i_r$, $a_{i_1 i_2} \neq 0$, $a_{i_2 i_3} \neq 0, \ldots, a_{i_{r-1} i_r} \neq 0$ imply $a_{i_r i_1} = 0$, for any $r > 2$;
   (c) $a_{ii} < 0$, for all i with at least one strict inequality;
   (d) there is a non-zero term in the expansion of $\det A$.

8. Let $\bar{A}$ be a Morishima matrix, $\alpha > \lambda^*(\bar{A})$. Prove that $A = \bar{A} - \alpha I$ is stable iff A has a negative q.d.d.

9. Let $S_A = \{B : B \in Q_A;\ B$ is stable; $b_{ij} \neq 0$, for all i, j; B has a q.d.d.$\}$
   Prove that $B \in S_A$ iff $B = \bar{B} - \beta I$, where $\bar{B}$ is a Morishima matrix, $\beta > \lambda^*(\bar{B})$.

10. Given Q8 above, any result indicating whether or not A has a q.d.d. is useful. So consider the following:
    $A = \bar{A} - \alpha I$, where $\bar{A}$ is a Morishima matrix, $\alpha > \lambda^*(\bar{A})$.
    Consider a sub-matrix A^{kk} of A, with row and column indices $i_1, \ldots, i_k$. If:

$$\sum_{i=i_1}^{i_k} a_{ij} \geq 0 \quad \text{for} \quad j = i_1, \ldots, i_k$$

and

$$\sum_{j=i_1}^{i_k} a_{ij} \geqslant 0 \quad \text{for} \quad i = i_1, \ldots, i_k$$

then A does not have a negative q.d.d.
This result can be applied to derive the following:
$\mathrm{d}p/\mathrm{d}t = Ap$ is unstable under (H) and (W) if:
$a_{nj} \leqslant 0$ for all $j = 1, \ldots, k$ and $a_{in} \leqslant 0$ for all $i = 1, \ldots, k$; or
$a_{nj} \leqslant 0$ for all $j = k+1, \ldots, m$ and $a_{in} \leqslant 0$ for all $i = k+1, \ldots, m$.

11. (a) Using Exercises §2.2, Q12, derive the following:
Suppose the numeraire is a strong gross substitute for every other commodity and vice versa, and $a_{ij} < 0$, for some $i \neq j$. Then there are values of A consistent with (W) and (H) such that the system is unstable.
(b) Relaxing the conditions on a_{nj} and a_{in}, $i, j = 1, \ldots, m$, there are values of A consistent with (W) and (H) such that the system is unstable.
(For questions 9–11, consult the paper by Bassett, Habibagahi & Quirk.)

12. (a) Suppose that: $a_{in} + 2\sum_{j \in S} a_{ij} > 0$, for all $i \in R$, where R and S partition the set of non-numeraire commodities.
Using (H), derive stability of the system by establishing that A has a negative q.d.d.
(b) Likewise if: $a_{nj} + 2\sum_{i \in S} a_{ij} > 0$ for all $i \in R$, prove that the system is stable under (W).

§8.7

1. Consider the example introduced in Exercises §8.5, Q8.
Suppose

$$x_i = \sum_j x_{ij} P_j + b_i + f_i t \qquad f_i \geqslant 0.$$

Then

$$z = AP + ft + d.$$

Differentiate this equation and substitute from $\mathrm{d}P/\mathrm{d}t = Kz$ to obtain: $\mathrm{d}z/\mathrm{d}t = KAz + f$.
(a) Suppose that A is stable. Prove that KA is stable.
(b) Suppose $z(0) = \mathbf{0}$. Prove that z increases from $\mathbf{0}$ to its asymptotic limit, $-K^{-1}A^{-1}f$.
(c) Hence prove that prices rise on all markets and $\lim_{t \to \infty} \dfrac{\mathrm{d}P}{\mathrm{d}t} = -A^{-1}f$.

(d) P^* solves: $\mathbf{0} = AP^* + ft + d$. Using the same method as in Exercises §8.5, Q8, derive:

$$dP/dt = -KAp \quad \text{or} \quad p = -(KA)^{-1}dP/dt.$$

Prove that $p(t) \geqslant \mathbf{0}$ for all t and evaluate $\lim p(t)$.

2. Now introduce expectations into the model so that:

$$z = AP + BP^e + ft + d \qquad B \geqslant [0].$$

(a) Prove that under static expectations ($P^e = P$), the results derived in Q1 remain valid (assuming $(A+B)K$ is stable).

(b) Consider the adaptive expectations mechanism:

$$dP^e/dt = G(P - P^e) \qquad G = [g_i\delta_{ij}], \qquad g_i > 0 \quad \text{for all } i.$$

or

$$dP^e/dt = Gq^e, \qquad q^e = P - P^e.$$

Define:

$$\bar{P} = \begin{bmatrix} P \\ P^e \end{bmatrix}; \quad q = \begin{bmatrix} q \\ q^e \end{bmatrix}; \quad \bar{A} = \begin{bmatrix} A & B \\ I & -I \end{bmatrix};$$

$$\bar{K} = \begin{bmatrix} K & 0 \\ 0 & G \end{bmatrix}; \quad \bar{f} = \begin{bmatrix} f \\ \mathbf{0} \end{bmatrix}; \quad \bar{d} = \begin{bmatrix} d \\ \mathbf{0} \end{bmatrix}.$$

Then, we have the following equations:

$$d\bar{P}/dt = \bar{K}q$$

$$q = \bar{A}\bar{P} + \bar{f}t + \bar{d}$$

With appropriate assumptions, this model can be identified with that of Q1 above. Suppose that $(A+B)K$ is a stable matrix, with negative diagonal, non-negative off-diagonal elements. Then, using Theorem 38, $\bar{K}\bar{A}$ is stable. Derive results corresponding to those in Q1 (b)–(d).

§8.8

1. Generalise Theorem 18 to the global case as follows:
If there is no trade at equilibrium, which is assumed unique, the system is globally stable.
2. Prove that:
(a) A is quasi-negative definite;
(b) A has a negative q.d.d.
are sufficient for a unique, globally stable equilibrium.
3. Consider the derivation of global stability under (SGS) in terms of the following Lyapunov functions:

(a) $v(t) = \max_i[(P_i(t) - P_i^*)/P_i^*]$;

(b) $v(t) = \sum_j |P_j(z_j(P) - z_j(P^*))|$.

(Hint: (a) requires the result in Exercises §8.4, Q4.) (Negishi, 1962)

4. Consider the alternative price-adjustment eqn [13] and Theorem 41.
   (a) Prove that $P(t) > \mathbf{0}$ for all t if $P(0) > \mathbf{0}$.
   (b) Prove Theorem 41 for a production economy.
   (Hint: By profit maximisation, $P'\mathrm{d}y/\mathrm{d}t > 0$. From eqn [19] in Theorem 41, which holds for a production economy, we may derive $P'\mathrm{d}x/\mathrm{d}t < 0$ again, unless we have an equilibrium.) (Hahn)

5. Let us now drop the assumption that recontracting is always possible. Dis-equilibrium exchange is possible, so that individual endowment vectors vary. Thus, a non-tatonnement process is one such as:

$$\begin{aligned} \mathrm{d}P_i/\mathrm{d}t &= z_i(P, w) \qquad z = x - w, w = y \\ \mathrm{d}w_{ij}/\mathrm{d}t &= g_{ij}(P, w) \end{aligned} \qquad \cdots [1]$$

   w_{ij} being the i-th individual's endowment of commodity j. As we are dealing with an exchange economy, we have:

$$\sum_{i=1}^{m} g_{ij}(P, w) = 0 \qquad \cdots [2]$$

   Impose the following (barter) condition:

$$\sum_{j=1}^{n} P_j \mathrm{d}w_{ij}/\mathrm{d}t = 0 \qquad \cdots [3]$$

   (i.e. to obtain something an individual must offer something else of equal value in return.)
   Prove that each limit point of eqn [1] is an equilibrium under eqns [2], [3], (W) and (GS).
   (Hint: Consider the function:

$$v(t) = \sum_{j \in J^+(t)} P_j(t)(z_j - w_j)$$

   where

$$J^+(t) = \{j : z_j(t) - w_j > 0, \quad \text{or} \quad z_j(t) - w_j = 0 \quad \text{and} \quad \mathrm{d}z_j/\mathrm{d}t > 0\}$$

   Consult Negishi (1961) or (1972), Chapter 14.)

6. Consider the following non-tatonnement process for an exchange economy, due to Hahn and Negishi. We retain eqns [1]–[3] of Q5, in addition to which we impose the following condition:

$$\begin{aligned} &\mathrm{sign}\, z_{ij} = \mathrm{sign}\, z_j, \quad \text{if} \quad z_{ij} \neq 0, \quad \text{for all } i, j; \\ &\text{if} \quad z_j = 0, \quad \text{then} \quad z_{ij} = 0, \quad \text{for all } i. \end{aligned} \qquad \cdots [4]$$

   (z_{ij} being the i-th individual's excess demand for the j-th commodity.) The implication of eqn [4] is that each market is sufficiently well organised so that there cannot exist in any market excess demand and excess supply simultaneously. From eqn [4] and the price-adjustment eqn [1], we see that, in a dis-equilibrium, the commodities the i-th consumer wants to buy (and cannot) are becoming more expensive, while the commodities he wishes to sell (and cannot) are becoming cheaper. So the i-th individual is a position in which his planned utility (i.e. expected utility on the basis of completion of all transactions) is decreasing. For this reason, we consider $v(t) = \sum_{i=1}^{m} u_i(x^i)$.

Prove that each limit point of eqn [1] is an equilibrium under eqns [2], [3] and [4].

(Hint: $\mathrm{d}(u_i(x^i))/\mathrm{d}t = \sum_{j=1}^{n} (\partial u_i/\partial x_{ij})\mathrm{d}x_{ij}/\mathrm{d}t = \sum_{j=1}^{n} \lambda_i P_j \mathrm{d}x_{ij}/\mathrm{d}t$, $\lambda_i > 0$ being the i-th individual's marginal utility of income.

Then

$$\mathrm{d}\left(\sum_{i=1}^{m} u_i\right) \Big/ \mathrm{d}t = \sum_{i=1}^{m} \lambda_i \sum_{j=1}^{n} P_j \mathrm{d}x_{ij}/\mathrm{d}t.$$

To obtain an expression for $\sum_{j=1}^{n} P_j \mathrm{d}x_{ij}/\mathrm{d}t$, differentiate the budget constraint $P'x' = P'w^i$, and use eqns [3] and [4] to show that $\sum_{j=1}^{n} P_j \mathrm{d}x_{ij}/\mathrm{d}t < 0$.)

§8.9

1. (a) Suppose that the system is D-stable. Prove that, if there is a shift in tastes from the numeraire to commodity k, the k-th price cannot fall.
   (b) How can this result be strengthened if we assume that the system is totally stable?

2. Consider the generalised gross substitute concepts introduced in Exercises §8.6, Q2.
   (a) Suppose that the system is G_1-Metzlerian. Prove that, if there is a shift in tastes from the numeraire to the k-th commodity, p_k increases and p_i does not decrease, $i \neq k$.
   (Hint: From the basic equation $Aw = b$, we have $w = A^{-1}b$ or $w = (GA)^{-1}Gb$. GA has a negative d.d., with non-negative off-diagonal elements. So $-GA$ is an M-matrix, which implies that $(GA)^{-1} \leqslant [0]$.)
   (b) Prove that, in the G_2-Metzlerian case, a shift in tastes from the numeraire to the k-th commodity results in a rise in p_k; in general, the effect on p_i, $i \neq k$, is indeterminate.

3. As an example of a result yielding complete comparative statics information (i.e. knowledge of the sign pattern of A^{-1}), consider the following due to Bassett, Habibagahi & Quirk:
   Let A be a stable qualitative matrix, $a_{ii} < 0$, for all i, $a_{ij} \neq 0$, for all i, j. Then the sign pattern of A^{-1} can be determined iff:
   (a) A is a 2×2 matrix; or
   (b) $A = \bar{A} - \alpha I$, $\bar{A}$ being a Morishima matrix.

Notes

1. The requirement that each market must clear (i.e. demand equals supply) is rather strong and will subsequently be relaxed.

2. Koopmans, T. C.: *Three Essays on the State of Economic Science*, McGraw-Hill, 1957. p. 179.

3. See (P2) and (C5) in §8.1.2. Convexity assumptions would suffice if more general continuity concepts are employed—see note [8].

4. On this topic, consult: Graaff, J. de V.: *Theoretical Welfare Economics*, Cambridge U.P., 1957.

5. Notation: $\{N = 1, \ldots, m, n\}$ is the set used to index prices. The n-th commodity is the numeraire, so that the non-numeraire commodities are indexed by $1, \ldots, m$ (i.e. we write $m = n - 1$). Up to eqn [17], P_i denotes the relative price of the i-th commodity, $i = 1, \ldots, m$; p_i denotes the displacement from equilibrium. Previously in this chapter, P_i has been used to denote the absolute price of the i-th good, $i \in N$, p_i the relative price, $i = 1, \ldots, m$.

6. Hicks, J. R.: *Value and Capital*, Clarendon Press, 1946. p. 66.

7. Samuelson, P. A.: "Stability of equilibrium: comparative statics and dynamics", *Econometrica*, **9** (1941). p. 109.

8. Lange, O.: *Price Flexibility and Employment*, Bloomington, Indiana, 1945. p. 94.

9. Metzler, L. A.: "Stability of multiple markets: the Hicks conditions", *Econometrica*, **13** (1945). p. 279.

10. Morishima, M.: "A generalisation of the gross substitute system", *Review of Economic Studies*, **37** (1970). p. 177.

11. Note that p is the displacement of P from P^* (i.e. p has n components).

12. We write $q^1(t)$ in this way to allow for the possibility that 0 is a repeated root, in which case the primitive solution associated with this zero root of multiplicity, m_1 say, will be a vector of polynomials of order less than or equal to $m_1 - 1$. See Theorem 14 of Chapter 4 and §4.1.5.

13. In eqns [7] and [8], $\mathrm{d}z_i/\mathrm{d}t$ and $\mathrm{d}\lambda_j/\mathrm{d}t$ are not continuous functions for all values of z and $\boldsymbol{\lambda}$; discontinuities may arise when the non-negativity constraints become binding. So, strictly speaking, Theorem 18 of Chapter 4 is inapplicable. However, Henry has extended Theorem 18 to cover these cases. Consult the paper by Henry mentioned in the references.
The problem encountered here is similar to that in Exercises §8.5, Q10.

14. Garegnani, for one, would dispute this; see his article: "Heterogeneous capital, the production function and the theory of capital," *Review of Economic Studies*, **37** (1970) from which quotations are taken.

"Traditional theory—reduced to its core as the explanation of distribution in terms of demand and supply—rests in fact on a single premise . . . (that) any change of system (of production) brought about by a fall of r must increase the ratio of 'capital' to labour in the production of the commodity; 'capital' being the value of physical capital in terms of some unit of consumption goods, a value which is thought to measure the consumption given up or postponed in order to bring that physical capital into existence." (p. 422).

This premise (or "unobtrusive postulate") and its associate—that a fall in r lowers the relative price of the consumption goods whose production requires a higher capital–labour ratio—are expressions of a single principle, "according to which a fall of r cheapens the more capital-intensive processes of production." (p. 423) Then a fall in r would raise the capital–labour ratio, because consumers would favour the more capital-intensive goods and because of switches in production of consumption goods. If there is full employment of labour, it follows that the quantity of capital employed increases as r falls; the relation between r and the quantity of capital employed then constitutes a demand function for capital; competition in the capital market ensures the absorption of saving through falls in r. Now the validity of the principle is called into question by the results on reswitching and capital-reversing derived in Chapter 3.

Garegnani then discusses the effects of a tendency to net saving which, it is assumed, brings about a fall in r from r^* to $\bar{r}$. Let us ignore questions of the traverse between equilibria by supposing that the transitional process works smoothly; then, can we find a new (long-run equilibrium) situation in which the additional quantity of capital is equal to the intended net savings. From Chapter 3, we know that with a fall in r there may be associated a rise or a fall in K.

"The form of the relation between r and K implies that such a new situation cannot always be found; however high r^* is, and however small ΔK, there may well not exist any lower rate of profits $\bar{r}$ at which $\bar{K} = K^* + \Delta K$. Or, to find a situation with an amount $\bar{K}$ of capital just larger than K^*, we may need a fall of r so drastic as to make it clear that, in this case too, it is impossible to determine r by the demand and supply of 'capital' (saving)." (p. 426)

Garegnani is applying the theory developed by comparison of different states to the analysis of change (just as neo-classical economists might). He concludes that

"the traditional theory of distribution was built, and accepted, in the belief that a fall of r would always raise the proportion of 'capital' to labour in the economy: the theory becomes implausible once it is admitted that this principle is not always valid." (p. 426)

15. Hahn, F. H.: "Some adjustment problems", *Econometrica*, **38** (1970). pp 1–2.

16. Arrow, K. J. & F. H. Hahn: *General Competitive Analysis*, Oliver & Boyd, 1972. pp vi–vii.

17. Harcourt, G. C.: "The Cambridge controversies: the afterglow", in *Contemporary Issues in Economics* (M. Parkin & A. R. Nobay, eds), Manchester U.P., 1975. p. 310.

18. Schumpeter, J. A.: *History of Economic Analysis*, Allen & Unwin, 1954. pp 41–2.

References

§8.1
§8.1.1

Graaff, J. de V.: *Theoretical Welfare Economics*, Cambridge U.P., 1957.

Koopmans, T. C.: *Three Essays on the State of Economic Science*, McGraw-Hill, 1957.

§8.1.2

Arrow, K. J. & F. H. Hahn: *General Competitive Analysis*, Oliver & Boyd, 1972.

Debreu, G.: *Theory of Value*, Yale U.P., 1959.

Malinvaud, E.: *Lectures on Microeconomic Theory*, North-Holland, 1972.

Exercises

Debreu, G: "Representation of a preference ordering by a numerical function" in *Decision Processes* (R. M. Thrall et al, eds.), Wiley, 1954, reprinted in *Readings in Mathematical Economics*, vol 1 (P. Newman, ed.), Johns Hopkins U.P., 1968.

§8.2

Arrow, K. J. & F. H. Hahn: *General Competitive Analysis*, Oliver & Boyd, 1972, Chapter 2.

Uzawa, H.: "Walras' tatonnement in the theory of exchange", *Review of Economic Studies*, **27** (1959).

More general models are outlined in:
Arrow, K. J. & F. H. Hahn: op. cit.

Debreu, G.: *Theory of Value*, Yale U.P., 1959.

Newman, P. (ed.): *Readings in Mathematical Economics*, vol 1, Johns Hopkins U.P., 1968. (This contains papers by Gale, Kuhn, Nikaido, McKenzie and Aumann.)

Quirk, J. & R. Saposnik: *Introduction to General Equilibrium Theory and Welfare Economics*, McGraw-Hill, 1968.

§8.3

Arrow, K. J.: "An extension of the basic theorems of classical welfare economics" in *Second Berkeley Symposium on Mathematical Statistics and Probability* (J. Neyman, ed.), California U.P., 1950, reprinted in *Readings in Mathematical Economics*, vol 1 (P. Newman, ed.), Johns Hopkins U.P., 1968.

Debreu, G.: *Theory of Value*, Yale U.P. 1959, Chapter 6.

§8.4

Arrow, K. J. & F. H. Hahn: *General Competitive Analysis*, Oliver & Boyd, 1972 (Chapter 9).

Rader, T.: "Normally, factor inputs are never gross substitutes", *Journal of Political Economy*, **76** (1968).

§8.5

§8.5.1

Fisher, M. E. & A. T. Fuller: "On the stabilisation of matrices and the convergence of linear iterative processes", *Proceedings of the Cambridge Philosophical Society*, **54** (1958).

Hicks, J. R.: *Value and Capital*, Clarendon Press, 1946.

Lange, O.: *Price Flexibility and Employment*, Cowles Commission Monograph no. 8, Bloomington, Indiana, 1945.

Quirk, J. & R. Saposnik: *Introduction to General Equilibrium Theory and Welfare Economics*, McGraw-Hill, 1968.

Samuelson, P. A.: "Stability of equilibrium: comparative statics and dynamics", *Econometrica*, **9** (1941).

§8.5.2

Carlson, D.: "A new criterion for H-stability of complex matrices", *Linear Algebra and its Applications*, **1** (1968).

Lancaster, P.: *Theory of Matrices*, Academic Press, 1969.

Lange, O.: *Price Flexibility and Employment*, Bloomington, Indiana, 1945.

Metzler, L. A.: "Stability of multiple markets: the Hicks conditions", *Econometrica*, **13** (1945).

Exercises

Arrow, K. J. & M. McManus: "A note on dynamic stability", *Econometrica*, **26** (1958).

Barten, A. P. F. B. Lempers & T. Kloek: "A note on a class of utility and production functions yielding everywhere differentiable demand functions", *Review of Economic Studies*, **36** (1969).

Henry, C.: "An existence theorem for a class of differential equations with multi-valued right-hand side", *Journal of Mathematical Analysis and Applications*, **41** (1973).

Nikaido, H. & H. Uzawa: "Stability and non-negativity in a Walrasian tatonnement process", *International Economic Review*, **1** (1960).

Samuelson, P. A.: "The relation between Hicksian stability and true dynamic stability", *Econometrica*, **12** (1944).

Scarf, H.: "Some examples of global instability of the competitive equilibrium", *International Economic Review*, **1** (1960).

§8.6

§8.6.1

Arrow, K. J. & L. Hurwicz: "On the stability of competitive equilibrium", *Econometrica*, **26** (1958).

Hahn, F. H.: "Gross substitutes and the dynamic stability of general equilibrium", *Econometrica*, **26** (1958).

Metzler, L. A.: "Stability of multiple markets: the Hicks conditions", *Econometrica*, **13** (1945).

Negishi, T.: "A note on the stability of an economy where all goods are gross substitutes", *Econometrica*, **26** (1958).

§8.6.2

Kennedy, C. M.: "The stability of the 'Morishima system", *Review of Economic Studies*, **37** (1970).

Morishima, M.: "On the laws of change of the price-system in an economy which contains complementary commodities", *Osaka Economic Papers*, **1** (1952).

§8.6.3

Mukerji, A.: "On the sensitivity of stability results to the choice of numeraire", *Review of Economic Studies*, **40** (1973).

Quirk, J.: "The competitive equilibrium: a qualitative analysis", in *Economic Models, Estimation and Risk Programming* (K. A. Fox et al, eds.) Springer-Verlag, 1969.

§8.6.4

Quirk, J.: "Complementarity and stability of equilibrium", *American Economic Review*, **60** (1970).

Exercises

Bassett, L., H. Habibagahi & J. Quirk: "Qualitative economics and Morishima matrices", *Econometrica*, **35** (1967).

Mukerji, A.: op. cit.

Ohyama, M.: "On the stability of generalised Metzlerian systems", *Review of Economic Studies*, **39** (1972).

Quirk, J. & R. Ruppert: "Qualitative economics and the stability of equilibrium", *Review of Economic Studies*, **32** (1965).

Sato, R.: "The stability of the competitive system which contains complementary commodities", *Review of Economic Studies*, **39** (1972).

§8.7

§8.7.1

Arrow, K. J. & M. McManus: "A note on dynamic stability", *Econometrica*, **26** (1958).

Enthoven, A. C. & K. J. Arrow: "A theorem on expectations and the stability of equilibrium", *Econometrica*, **24** (1956).

Negishi, T.: "Stability and rationality of extrapolative expectation", *Econometrica*, **32** (1964).

§8.7.2

Arrow, K. J. & M. Nerlove: "A note on expectations and stability", *Econometrica*, **26** (1958).

Exercises

Arrow, K. J.: "Price-quantity adjustments in multiple markets with rising demands", in *Mathematical Methods in the Social Sciences* (K. J. Arrow et al, eds.) Stanford U.P., 1960.

§8.8

Hahn, F. H.: "A stable adjustment process for a competitive economy", *Review of Economic Studies*, **29** (1962).

Hahn, F. H. & T. Negishi: "A theorem on non-tatonnement stability", *Econometrica*, **30** (1962).

McKenzie, L. W.: "Matrices with dominant diagonals and economic theory" in *Mathematical Methods in the Social Sciences* (K. J. Arrow et al., eds.) Stanford U.P., 1960.

Negishi, T.: "On the formation of prices", *International Economic Review*, **2** (1961).

Negishi, T.: "The stability of a competitive equilibrium: a survey article", *Econometrica*, **30** (1962).

Negishi, T.: *General Equilibrium Theory and International Trade*, North-Holland, 1972.

§8.9

Bassett, L., H. Habibagahi & J. Quirk: "Qualitative economics and Morishima matrices", *Econometrica*, **35** (1967).

Morishima, M.: "On the three Hicksian laws of comparative statics", *Review of Economic Studies*, **27** (1960).

The following is a useful survey of qualitative theory

Maybee, J. & J. Quirk: "Qualitative problems in matrix theory", *SIAM Review*, **11** (1969).

§8.10

Arrow, K. J. & L. Hurwicz: "Decentralisation and computation in resource allocation" in *Essays in Economics and Econometrics* (R. W. Pfouts, ed.), University of North Carolina Press, 1960.

Arrow, K. J., L. Hurwicz & H. Uzawa: *Studies in Linear and Non-linear Programming*, Stanford U.P., 1958.

Heal, G. M.: *The Theory of Economic Planning*, North-Holland, 1973.

Henry, C.: "Differential equations with discontinuous right-hand sides in mathematical economics", *Journal of Economic Theory*, **4** (1972).

Malinvaud, E.: *Lectures on Microeconomic Theory*, North-Holland, 1972.

Index

Author index

Subject index